동시토익
RC 신토익 1000제

지은이 신정원
에디터 조서봉
출판사 제이제이북스
2쇄 인쇄 2017년 11월 10일

동시토익 서문

통역사의 길을 접고 토익강의를 시작한지 언 10년이 넘었습니다. 10년. 하루하루가 쌓여 10년이 되다니, 놀라운 일입니다. 강의를 하면서 가장 뿌듯한 순간은, 역시 우리 학생들의 시험후기를 볼 때입니다. 시험성적을 확인하고, 가슴이 벅차 주체할 수 없이 써 내려간 여러분의 후기를 읽을 때, 제가 정말 좋은 직업을 가졌다는 생각을 다시 한번 되새깁니다. 그러나, 이런 가슴 뿌듯한 성취감은 그냥 오는 것은 아닙니다. '왜 나만 점수가 오르지 않나'라는 좌절감을 누구나 한번씩은 맛보게 됩니다. 하고 싶은 세상의 모든 일을 뒤로 한 채 나 혼자만의 싸움, 처절한 시간관리, 'XX는 점수가 얼마 나왔다더라'는 비보를 접했을 때도 평정심을 유지하기 위한 mind control. 이런 고된 과정을 거쳤기 때문에 이 점수가 의미 있고 빛이 납니다. 사회에서 여러분의 토익 점수를 인정해주는 것은, 여러분의 토익점수 자체가 업무수행능력에 직결되기 때문이 아닙니다. 이 점수를 받기 위해 여러분이 겪었을 이 험난한 과정, 그리고 이 과정을 통한 여러분의 성장을 인정해 주는 것입니다. 지금 이 힘든 터널을 걷고 있는 여러분들! 이 시간 자체가 여러분을 성장시켜주고 있다는 것을 잊지 마세요! 여러분의 멋진 도전에 동시토익이 힘을 보태드립니다!

동시토익의 라인업이 기초, 정규에 이어 실전서를 통해 드디어 완성되었습니다. 그간 실전반은 현장강의만이 제공되었기 때문에, 현장강의를 들을 수 없는 친구들에게 대안을 제시해줄 수 없어 안타까웠고, 그래서 시작한 작업이 드디어 마무리되었습니다.

2016년 5월 신토익이 출범되면서, '독해' 비중이 절대적으로 강화되었습니다. 이제 독해력이 없이는 토익 고득점을 받을 수 없습니다. 동시토익 정규과정을 교재나 강의로 접해 본 분들은 동시토익이 처음부터 독해력을 강화하는 커리큘럼을 가지고 있음을 이미 알고 있을 겁니다. 이제 실전서를 통해 독해력을 완성해야 합니다. 그런데 독해력은 파트7 문제를 많이 풀어본다고 쌓이지는 않습니다. 한 문장, 한 문장을 정확하게 '해석'하는 연습이 우선 가장 중요합니다. 실제 동시토익 실전반에서 토익점수가 많이 오른 친구들과 얘기해보면, 파트7 자체를 공부해서 점수가 오르기보다는 실전반에서 내주는 '파트5 문장 해석연습'이 도움이 됐다는 친구들이 많습니다. 교재를 통해 똑 같은 연습을 여러분이 해볼 수 있도록 이 교재는 '워크북'을 수록해두었습니다. 반드시 파트5 문장들을 정확하게 해석해 나가면서 정확한 '해석' 능력을 쌓아가야 합니다. 파트7을 푸는데, 한 문장을 꼬이게 해석했다면, 그 다음부터 나의 독해는 산으로 가게 됩니다. 정말 신기하게도 그 다음 문장들도 내가 '헛짚은' 잘못된 논리에 맞게 해석이 되기 시작합니다. 열심히 읽고 죄다 오답을 골라오게 됩니다. 반드시 한 문장, 한 문장을 정확하게 해석해보고, 정답과 대조해가면서, 나의 잘못된 부분을 '수정'하고 가야 합니다.

그런데 여기서 끝나지는 않습니다. '해석'과 '독해'는 엄연히 다른 개념입니다. '해석'은 '독해'를 위한 기본적인 필수조건일 뿐입니다. '독해'는 지문의 내용을 이해하는 능력입니다. 그러기 위해서는 우선 '해석'이 되어야겠지만, 한 문장, 한 문장을 해석하는데 모든 에너지를 써버린다면, 전체 내용을 놓치게 됩니다. 그러면 파트7에서 정답을 고를 수 없습니다. 실제로 수업시간에 학생들에게 파트7문제를 '우리말'로 해석해주고 문제를 풀어보게 한 적이 있습니다. 결과는 충격적이었습니다. 정답률이 1/3 밖에 되지 않았습니다. 우리의 문제는 '영어'가 아니라 '논리력'인 거죠. 영어는 매우 논리적인 언어입니다. 처음 통역대학원에 들어갔을 때 수업시간에 교수님이 우리말로 된 10분짜리 인터뷰를 들려주고, 다시 복원해보도록 시킨 적이 있습니다. 디테일한 내용까지 모두 살려서 열심히 대답을 했다가 된통 깨진 기억이 있습니다. 통역은 '암기'가 아니라는 거죠. 통역은 그 사람이 한 말의 '논리적 흐름'을 전달하는 게 중요하다는 가르침이었습니다. 통역대학원의 2년은 '논리력'을 쌓는 훈련이었다고도 말할 수 있을 것 같습니다. 우리말은 '논리력'을 그리 강조하지 않습니다. 우리 모두가 '논리력'이 부족한 것이 사실입니다. 파트7에서 정답률을 높이기 위해서는 이 훈련이 굉장히 중요합니다. 다음 페이지에 나오는 '파트7 리뷰 방법'을 반드시 읽어보시고, 이 훈련을 통해 여러분이 쌓은 '해석' 능력이 고스란히 토익점수로 결실을 맺을 수 있도록 논리력과 함께 독해력을 쌓아가시길 바랍니다.

실전서를 통한 연습은 지금까지 쌓아온 여러분의 실력을 다듬는 과정입니다. 마지막 마무리가 가장 중요합니다! 여러분의 얼굴에 환한 미소가 번질 머지 않은 그날을 고대합니다!!

2016년 저자 동시토익 신정원

동시토익 차례

토익 파트별 공략법 ·················· 6

동시토익 실전서 구성 ·············· 10

토익 RC 점수 환산표 ··············· 12

TEST 01 ·················· 14
    Workbook 01 ············ 42

TEST 02 ·················· 46
    Workbook 02 ············ 74

TEST 03 ·················· 78
    Workbook 03 ············ 108

TEST 04 ·················· 112
    Workbook 04 ············ 140

TEST 05 ·················· 144
    Workbook 05 ············ 174

TEST 06 ·········· 178
　Workbook 06 ·········· 208

TEST 07 ·········· 212
　Workbook 07 ·········· 240

TEST 08 ·········· 244
　Workbook 08 ·········· 274

TEST 09 ·········· 278
　Workbook 09 ·········· 308

TEST 10 ·········· 312
　Workbook 10 ·········· 342

해석 TEST 01 ·········· 346

해석 TEST 02 ·········· 356

해석 TEST 03 ·········· 366

해석 TEST 04 ·········· 376

해석 TEST 05 ·········· 386

해석 TEST 06 ·········· 396

해석 TEST 07 ·········· 406

해석 TEST 08 ·········· 416

해석 TEST 09 ·········· 426

해석 TEST 10 ·········· 436

정답 ·········· 446

OMR 답안지 ·········· 452

동시토익 토익 파트별 공략법

Questions 101~ 130
단문 빈칸에 정답 찾기
30문항 시간배정: 11-13분

문제유형 (총 30문항) 문제의 **보기**부터 확인한다! 문제유형에 따라 접근법이 달라져야 한다!			
어형 (11-12개)	(A) happy (B) happily (C) happiness (D) happier	구조 > 해석	어형문제는 해석부터 하면 오히려 더 많이 틀린다. 문장 구조를 이해했는지 묻는 문제! 빈칸의 앞뒤 품사를 확인하고 문장구조부터 이해한다!
어휘 (7-8개)	(A) offer (B) acceptance (C) return (D) admission	해석 > 구조	짝꿍단어가 출제된 게 아니라면, 꼼꼼히 해석을 해야 한다. 동사어휘는 목적어가 제일 중요! 형용사어휘는 수식하는 명사가 제일 중요! 부사어휘는 누구를 수식하는 지를 먼저 파악하는 것이 중요! 명사어휘는 문장 전체에 대한 꼼꼼한 해석이 필요하다!
문법 (10-12개)	(A) After (B) Since (C) Despite (D) Therefore	구조 > 해석	문법문제에서 가장 많이 출제되는 유형은 보기 중에 전치사/접속사/부사가 섞여있는 유형! 무조건 해석으로 접근하다 틀리는 경우가 굉장히 많다. 문장 구조부터 파악한다!

Questions 131 ~ 146
짧은 지문 (4문항 X 4세트 =16문항)
시간배정: 7-9분

Context Question & 신토익 문장찾기 문제

신토익에 새로 도입된 '문장찾기' 문제를 제외하면, 파트6의 문제유형은 파트5와 동일하다. '문법, 어휘, 구조' 문제가 출제된다. 그러나 파트5와 다른 점은 파트6에 '독해' 요소가 첨가되어 있다는 것이다. '어휘' 문제지만, 빈칸이 들어있는 한 문장만을 봐서는 답을 찾을 수 없다. 지문의 전체내용을 이해해야만 답이 보인다. 이런 문제를 'Context Question' 이라고 한다. 그러므로 반드시 내용을 파악하면서 문제에 접근해야 한다. 문장찾기 문제는 빈칸의 앞문장과 뒷문장을 읽고 두 문장과 연결되는 문장을 찾는 문제다. 빈칸을 보자마자 보기문장을 바로 읽게 되면 승산이 없다. 보기 문장들이 다 말이 되는 것처럼 보이기 때문이다. 반드시 앞뒤 문장을 다시 읽어서 머리에 새겨놓고, 그와 연결된 문장, 공통된 내용이 들어간 문장을 보기에서 찾아야 한다. 이 유형에 취약한 사람은 이것만 기억하자. 앞뒤 문장과 '공통된 내용' 이 들어가 있는 문장이 정답이다!

147–175 Single 지문 (10개지문–29문항)
176–200 다중지문 (5문항 X 5세트 = 25문항)
시간배정: 55분

| 문제유형 |

1) 주제문제 (15%)
2) 키워드 문제 (25%)
3) What is suggested (20%)
4) NOT 문제 (10%)
5) 자리찾기 문제 (3%)
6) 동의어문제 (15%)
7) 다중지문 Combined (15%)

여기서 고득점의 Key는 3), 4) 유형!
여기서 점수가 갈린다.

| 지문 먼저? 문제 먼저? |

고득점이 필요하다면, 문제 먼저 읽어서는 승산이 없다! 반드시 지문먼저 읽는다!
다만, 지문을 읽어가면서 단골 단서들은 표시해두자! 표시하면서 머리에 새겨두자!
표시해야 하는 단서 두 가지: 고유명사 / 숫자(날짜)

| 파트 7을 잘하려면 뭘 해야 하나요? |

특별히 따로 준비해야 할 건 없다. 다 잘해야 한다.
파트7은 구조분석, 어휘, 문법, 이 삼박자가 다 맞아야 점수가 터진다. 이 중에 하나라도 낙제점 수준이라면 파트7은 점수를 내기 힘들다. 이 세 가지가 모두 일정 수준에 오르면 그때 점수가 움직인다.

결국 이 세가지는 파트5에서 테스트하는 3가지 문제유형이다. 그런데 나는 파트5는 잘하는데 파트7만 문제가 된다면? 그건 해석연습의 부족이다. 독해는 피아노 연습과 같아서, 많이 해보면 속도와 정확도가 늘고, 연습을 게을리하면 속도가 느려진다. 그렇다고 파트7을 주구장창 풀어보는 건 별 도움이 되지 않는다. 파트5의 문장들로 정밀하게 해석하는 연습을 하는 것이 훨씬 효과적이다! 다음 페이지 워크북 이용방법을 참고하자!

| 직독직해 NO! |

'나는 만났다 / 부서의 부장님을 / 미팅에서 / 프로젝트를 기획하기 위해서 / 다음 달에 시작될'
절대 이런 직독직해로는 점수를 낼 수 없다. 해석은 열심히 공들여 다했는데, 결국 머릿속에 내용이 남지 않는다. 우리말 어순에 맞게 해석하는 습관을 들여야 한다. 많이 하다 보면, 영어 어순으로 읽어가면서, 내용 정리는 우리말 어순에 맞게 머리에 쌓인다. 그래야 점수가 나온다!

| 매번 4지문씩 놓쳐요. 어떻게 해야 빨리 풀 수 있나요? |

모두의 고민은 시간이다. 시간이 부족하다. 그렇다고 빨리 푸는걸 연습하다 보면 대충 풀게 된다. 한 번 대충 읽는 습관이 들면, 이 습관은 나중에 고치기 힘들다. 시간을 억지로 끌어올리려 하지 말자! 앞서 얘기한 삼박자가 어느 수준에 올라오면 속도가 한 순간에 급격히 붙기 시작한다. '독해 하다가 제 속도에 깜짝 놀랐더요!'라는 학생들의 후기를 자주 읽는다. 이 책에 있는 워크북 10세트에 공을 들여보자! 다음 시험에 여러분도 향상된 독해 속도에 깜짝 놀라게 될 것이다!

동시토익 파트7 리뷰 방법 대공개

파트7 문제 10세트를 다 풀어봤다고 실력이 월등히 향상될 거라 믿는다면 착각이다! 파트7은 문제를 푸는 것 보다 풀고 나서 어떻게 리뷰를 하느냐가 중요하다.

수업시간 중에 파트7 문제를 우리말로 해석해서 나눠준 적이 있다. 영어가 아닌 우리말로 파트7을 풀어본 것이다. 결과는 매우 충격적이었다. 실전반에서 우리말 파트7 문제를 다 맞은 친구가 1/3에 그쳤던 것이다. 우리말로 풀어봤는데, 2/3는 오답을 골라온 것이다. 왜 일까! 문제는 영어 자체가 아니었던 것이다.

우리는 시험지만 받아 들면, 마음이 급해진다. 어서 답을 찾아야겠다는 마음만 앞선다. 그러다 보니, 글을 읽는데 수박 겉핥기 식의 리딩을 하게 된다. 읽긴 읽었는데, 그 지문에 나온 상황은 머리 속에 구체적으로 그려지지 않는다. 무슨 의도로 어떤 상황에서 쓴 글인지 이해하려고 하지 않고 문제를 풀어야 한다는 강박증에만 빠져있다. 그러니 유추문제를 풀어낼 수가 없다. 읽긴 읽었는데 헛읽은 것이다.

리뷰가 중요한 이유가 여기에 있다. 내가 틀린 문제뿐만 아니라, 모든 문제들에 대해 꼼꼼히 리뷰를 하다 보면, 문제유형에 대해 감이 잡히기 시작한다. 어떻게 문제가 출제되는지, 문제유형을 익히고 나면, 어느 정도 깊이까지 들어가서 심층적인 해석을 해야 하는지를 체득하게 된다. 리뷰를 많이 해보면 해볼수록 지문을 보는 눈이 깊어진다.

일단, 아래 문제를 풀어보고, 오른쪽 페이지에서 리뷰하는 방법을 확인해보자.

Questions 158-160 refer to the following advertisement.

The Galacite Inn

Thanks for staying at the Galactic Inn. We'd like to make your stay as comfortable as possible. While here, feel free to try our new restaurant, Steak Planet.

The restaurant is open on weekdays from 11 a.m. to 11 p.m. and on weekends from 10 a.m. to 12 a.m.⁵⁸ Guests of the hotel may order room service from the normal menu or the children's menu any time the restaurant is open. If the restaurant is closed, please use the special room-service menu, including exclusive desserts and wines, until 3 a.m.

Guests of the hotel are also welcome to a free buffet dinner,⁶⁰ with food from chef Hurt, from 5 p.m. to 7 p.m. this Sunday. This flyer is required for guests to gain entrance to the buffet area.

---

158. At what time does the restaurant open on Saturdays?
(A) 10:00 a.m.
(B) 11:00 a.m.
(C) 12:00 a.m.
(D) 5:00 p.m.

159. What is NOT indicated about the room service menu?
(A) It includes desserts and wines.
(B) It features choices that are not as expensive as the restaurant.
(C) It has food that is made especially for children.
(D) It is available at Steak Planet.

160. What will the Galactic Inn offer its guests?
(A) A tour of the city
(B) Free wine sampling
(C) A complimentary dinner
(D) A chance to meet a TV personality

정답은 [A/B/C]. 일단 형광펜을 색깔 별로 준비한다. 각 문제 별로 정답이 되는 '지문의 단서'와 '보기 혹은 문제'를 함께 표시해둔다. 만약 내가 159번에서 오답 (D)를 골라서 틀렸다면, 이 부분은 내가 고른 보기 가 왜 오답인지 확인할 수 있는 단서를 표시한다. 이렇게 오답을 표시하는 경우는 색깔을 바꿔서 차별화하자. 지문 중에 모르는 어휘가 있다면 역시 다른 색깔로 모두 표시해두자. 특히 보기 중에 알긴 아는데 확실하게 의미가 와 닿지 않아서 의미파악이 안 되는 경우가 굉장히 많다. 모두 표시해두자.

그러면 어떤 효과가 날까?

58번, 표시해둔 부분을 자꾸 보다 보면 '아, 날짜가 항상 중요한 단서구나'를 자동으로 인지하게 된다. 그러면 앞으로 지문을 볼 때 날짜 관련 정보는 의도하지 않아도 저절로 눈여겨 보게 된다.

59번, 일단 보기 문장의 주어가 'It'과 같이 대명사로 시작할 때 오답률이 무지 높아진다. 보기에 나온 대명사는 항상 문제에 등장한 명사(room service menu)를 받아 온다. 이 문제를 틀렸다면 이 부분을 간과했기 때문이다. 식당이 열려있는 동안은 식당 메뉴를 룸 서비스로 주문할 수 있다고 했다. 그러므로 'It'이 의미하는 '룸서비스 메뉴'는 식당 영업시간 중 '식당 메뉴'와 동일하다. 그러므로 '룸서비스 메뉴'는 식당에서도 구할 수 있는 메뉴. 반복적으로 리뷰를 하다 보면, '아, 대명사 나올 때 주의해야겠구나', '아, 룸 서비스하고 룸서비스 메뉴는 다른 거구나, 앞으로 더 꼼꼼하게 봐야 하는구나' 등, 내가 하는 실수를 반복적으로 보면서 머리에 각인이 된다. 이 작업을 거치지 않으면, 실수는 반복되고 오답률은 줄어들지 않는다.

또 하나! 59번은 유추문제. 가장 오답률이 높은 문제가 유추문제. '식당메뉴를 룸서비스로 주문할 수 있다'는 문장을 보고, 우리는 '룸서비스 메뉴=식당 메뉴'라는 판단이 서야 한다. 이런 판단을 하기 위해서는 한 단계 더 깊이 들어가는 '심층 해석'을 해야 한다. 영어로는 **critical reading**이라고 한다. 어떻게 해야 이게 가능할까. '영어' 문장을 해석하는데 그치지 않고 '글의 내용'을 파악하려는 자세를 가져야 한다. 가령 내가 돈을 모아서 친구들과 해외여행을 왔다고 해보자. 호텔에 갔는데 이 지문에 나온 안내문이 써있다. 그 식당에 정말 맛있는 파스타를 판다는 정보를 우리는 이미 입수한 상태다. 그렇다면 이 안내문을 읽을 때 자세가 달라질 것이다. '아, 파스타를 방에서 룸서비스로 시켜먹을 수도 있구나. 토요일은 주말이니까 10시부터 사먹을 수 있구나'라고 훨씬 **적극적인 리딩**을 하게 될 것이다. 이러한 자세가 파트7을 접하는데 필요한 자세다! 유추문제를 좀 더 살펴보자.

> [본문] 이번 공연은 이 배우의 최고의 공연이었다.
> [정답] 이 배우는 여러 공연에 출연해왔다.

'최고'의 공연이었다는 말은 이 공연과 비교할만한 다른 공연들이 존재했다는 의미다. 그러므로 이 배우가 다른 여타 공연에 이미 출연한 적이 있다는 보기가 정답이 된다.

> [본문] 이번 달 이 회사 매출이 처음으로 반등했다.
> [정답] 이 회사는 실적이 좋지 않았었다.

'반등'했다는 것을 읽는 동시에 '이 회사가 원래 매출이 저조했구나'를 함께 이해해야만 정답보기를 골라올 수 있다.

간혹, 똑같은 글을 읽었는데 옆에서 '딴소리'하는 친구들이 있다. 내가 만약 그런 부류라면 나는 영어가 아닌 다른 이유로 파트7에 취약한 것이다. 꼼꼼한 리뷰작업을 통해 'critical reading'을 연습해가야 한다. 토익 점수뿐만 아니라 이 능력을 키우는 것 자체가 앞으로 나의 커리어를 위해서 훨씬 더 중요하다.

명심해야 할 것은! 형광펜으로 이쁘게 색칠을 하는 것이 리뷰가 아니라는 것! 반복적으로 보는 것이 중요하다! 반복적으로 보면서 문제유형을 체득해야 한다. 그래야 앞으로 글을 접할 때 한 단계 더 깊이 들어가는 'critical reading'이 가능해질 것이다! 문제유형이 익숙해지면 심지어 지문을 읽으면서 어떤 문제가 나올 지를 예측하는 것까지 가능해질 것이다!

동시토익 동시토익 실전서 구성

| 문제만 푸는 건 공부가 아니다! |

시중에 나온 실전서 다~ 풀어봤는데 점수는 여전히 700점대인 친구들이 허다하다. 문제를 푸는 건 나의 취약점을 확인하는 작업! 취약점을 확인했으면 이제 개선해야 한다. 개선작업을 하지 않으면 점수는 움직이지 않는다.

동시토익 실전서가 여타 실전서와 다른 점은 어휘노트와 워크북의 구성이다. 어휘노트와 워크북을 통해 실전서 활용을 극대화 하자!

어휘 note

_10세트만 제대로 소화해도 엄청나게 점수가 오를 수 있다! 내가 특정 어휘를 몰라서, 한 문제를 틀렸는데, 이 어휘를 외우고 가지 않는다면 다음 시험에서 내 실력은 역시 또 제자리일 뿐이다! 특히, 파트7의 경우는 출제되는 주제가 항상 비슷하기 때문에, 출제되는 어휘들도 유사하다. 내가 이번 테스트에서 몰랐던 어휘는, 다음 시험에 출제될 가능성이 매우 높다!

_반드시 모르는 어휘는 표시해두고, 아래 어휘 note에 정리해두자! 더 중요한 것은 자주 보는 것! 표시한 영어 단어를 보고서 뜻을 먼저 연상해보자! 그리고 아래 적어둔 뜻과 비교해보자! 어느 정도 익숙해졌다면, 이번에는 우리말 뜻을 보고 영어단어를 연상해보자! 이때 내가 그 단어를 뱉어낼 수 있다면 이 단어는 완전히 '내 것'이 된 것이다.

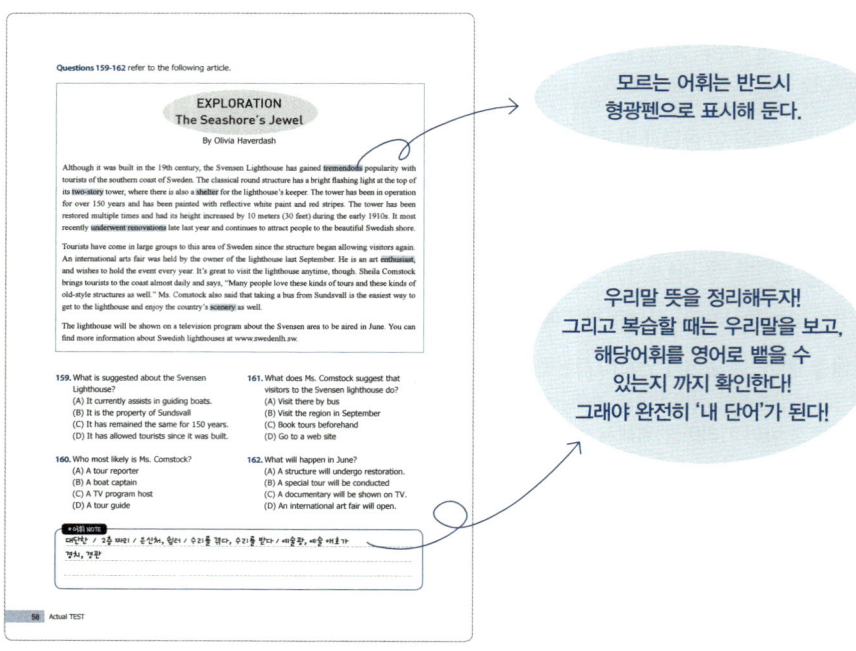

워크북

_ **최근** 토익 RC파트에서 Key는 파트7이 쥐고 있다. 파트7 점수가 오르지 않으면 목표달성은 남의 집 일이 되고 만다. 그런데 파트7 실력을 쌓기 위해 파트7을 무조건 많이 풀어보는 건 사실 도움이 되지 않는다. 정밀한 해석연습이 되지 않기 때문이다. 파트5 문장들로 해석연습을 하는 것이 훨씬 효과적이며, 그 효과는 동시토익 실전반에서 입증되었다.

_ **동시토익 실전반에서는** 파트5 문제를 풀고 나서 이 문제들을 해석해오는 숙제를 내준다. 이 숙제를 처음 도입하면서, 실전반 조교에게 해석을 직접 해서 정답을 동시토익 카페에 올리도록 시켰다. 모든 실전반 학생들이 내 정답을 본다고 생각하니, 긴장이 될 수 밖에 없었을 것이다. 아는 단어도 사전을 찾아보고, 남들은 1시간이면 끝나는 숙제를 우리 조교는 2시간 반을 소요하며 작업을 했다. 이 조교친구는 파트5는 잘하는 친구였다. 파트5는 틀린 개수가 3-4개 정도. 그런데 문제는 파트7이었다. 보통 2지문은 놓치고, 다 푼 문제 중에서도 7-8개는 꼭 틀렸다. 그런데 해석작업을 한지 단 3주만에 본 시험. 끝까지 다 풀고 틀린 개수는 단 4개. 이 친구뿐만 아니라 나 자신도 너무 놀라서 한동안 입이 다물어지지 않았다. 그리고 이런 성과는 많은 학생들에 의해 그 이후로도 계속 반복되고 있다. 내가 어느 정도 어휘, 구조, 문법이 쌓여있다면, 이제 남은 건 연습이다. 이 세가지를 조합해서 정밀하게 해석하는 연습. 워크북을 통해 그 동안 부족했던 나머지 2%를 이제 채우자!

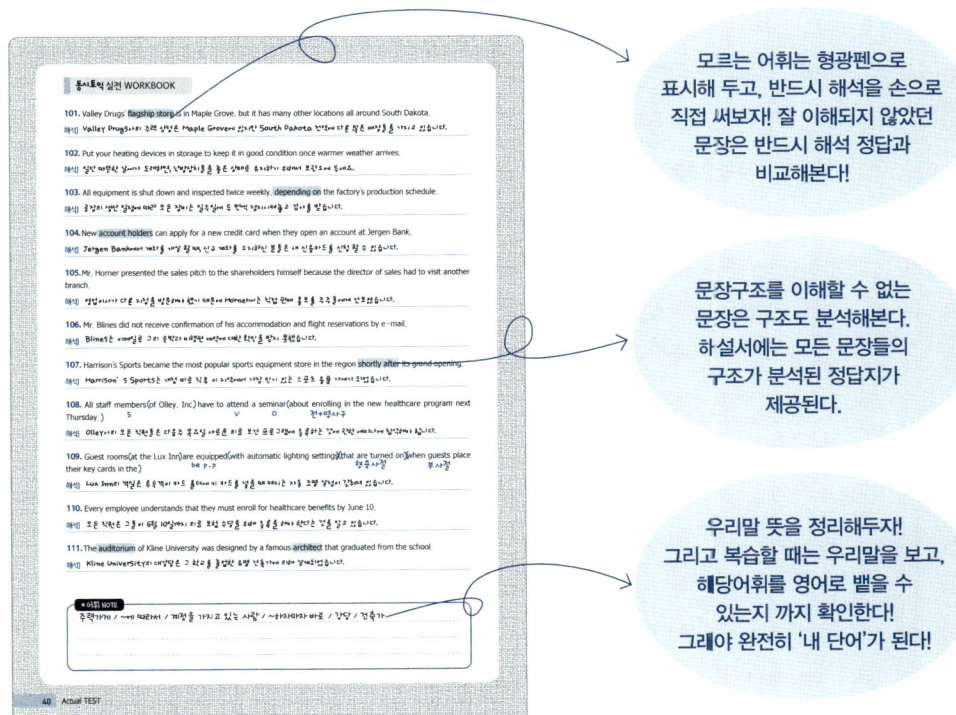

토익 RC 점수환산표

토익 시험 출제기관인 ETS는 정확한 배점방법을 공개하지 않습니다. 배점은 상대평가로 이루어지기 때문에, 해당 월의 시험 난이도에 따라, 틀린 개수가 같더라도 점수가 달라질 수 있습니다. 그러므로 정확한 점수를 산출할 수는 없으며, 아래 도표와 같이 점수대를 예상하는 정도만 가능합니다.

맞은 개수	환산 점수
96–100	465-495
91–95	435-460
86–90	410-430
81–85	380-405
76–80	355-375
71–75	325-350
66–70	295-320
61–65	265-290
56–60	240-260
51–55	215-235
46–50	185-210
41–45	155-180
36–40	130-150
31–35	100-125

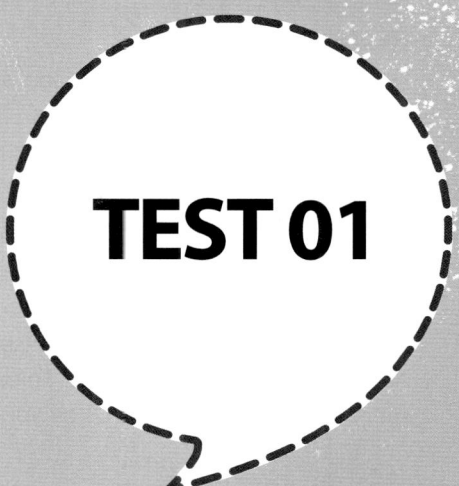

동시토익 CONTEMPORARY **TOEIC**

TEST 01

READING TEST

In the Reading test, you will read a variety of texts and answer several different types of reading comprehension questions. The entire Reading test will last 75 minutes. There are three parts, and directions are given for each part. You are encouraged to answer as many questions as possible within the time allowed.

You must mark your answers on the separate answer sheet. Do not write your answers in your test book.

Part 5

Directions: A word or phrase is missing in each of the sentences below. Four answer choices are given below each sentence. Select the best answer to complete the sentence. Then mark the letter (A), (B), (C), or (D) on your answer sheet.

101. Put your heating devices in storage to keep them in good condition once warmer weather _____.
(A) arrived
(B) arrives
(C) will arrive
(D) arrive

102. New account holders can apply for a new credit card _____ they open an account at Jergen Bank.
(A) when
(B) from
(C) above
(D) even

103. Mr. Horner presented the sales pitch to the shareholders _____ because the director of sales had to visit another branch.
(A) he
(B) his
(C) him
(D) himself

104. Mr. Blines did not receive _____ of his accommodation and flight reservations by e-mail.
(A) confirming
(B) confirm
(C) confirms
(D) confirmation

105. Harrison's Sports became the most popular sports equipment store in the region _____ after its grand opening.
(A) shortly
(B) recently
(C) extremely
(D) presently

106. All staff members of Olley, Inc. have to _____ a seminar about enrolling in the new healthcare program next Thursday.
(A) attended
(B) attends
(C) attend
(D) attending

107. _____ employee understands that they must enroll for healthcare benefits by June 10.
(A) All
(B) Most
(C) Every
(D) Many

108. The auditorium of Kline University was designed by a famous _____ that graduated from the school.
(A) architecture
(B) architectural
(C) architect
(D) architects

109. Carltec's notebook computers were _____ priced upon release, but the company raised the prices after receiving favorable reviews.
(A) moderate
(B) moderately
(C) moderating
(D) moderated

110. Letters to the Editor of the Lawson Daily are _____ by the editor prior to publication.
(A) reviewed
(B) created
(C) staffed
(D) founded

111. Throughout his career, Ian Carter _____ to become the most renowned marketing consultant in the industry.
(A) aspiring
(B) aspire
(C) has aspired
(D) is aspiring

112. Caring Airways provides the most _____ domestic flights in Canada.
(A) afford
(B) affording
(C) affordable
(D) affordably

113. Mantel Pharmaceuticals will not release their new painkiller because of _____ findings in clinical tests.
(A) recent
(B) full
(C) whole
(D) late

114. Mr. Fisher told his staff that he was _____ to work with such a dedicated and passionate team at Lester Automotive.
(A) honor
(B) honors
(C) honored
(D) honorable

115. _____ recent consumer reports, Everton Industries has produced the most highly rated toaster oven this year.
(A) Provided that
(B) According to
(C) Rather than
(D) Even if

116. Overton Party Supplies acknowledged that _____ that was rented for Xenor Technologies award ceremony was returned.
(A) either
(B) anything
(C) everything
(D) those

117. Thanks to our extensive research, our study was able to predict sales rates more _____ than our previous studies.
(A) accuracy
(B) accurate
(C) accurately
(D) accuracies

118. _____ conflicting schedules, next week's visit from the regional manager has been postponed until next month.
(A) In case
(B) Such as
(C) Because
(D) Due to

119. Revel Bohem's new line of living room furniture was a _____ effort between Revel's design department and artist Teresa Gile.
(A) collaborating
(B) collaborates
(C) collaboratively
(D) collaborative

120. On our upgraded Web site, you can find a calendar _____ direct links to major upcoming art and antiques sales in London.
(A) past
(B) with
(C) up
(D) toward

121. New residents of Telville _____ do not update their address information on their identification cards may be subject to fines.
(A) they
(B) who
(C) all
(D) you

122. Following a _____ in its fiscal policy, a more sizable budget has been allocated for the marketing department of Thilsen, Inc.
(A) shortage
(B) loss
(C) shift
(D) prediction

123. The level of customer satisfaction at Lyle's Sandwiches is the _____ of any local restaurant.
(A) high
(B) highest
(C) highly
(D) heightened

124. At the last city council meeting, Congressman Dale Harper announced the council's _____ not to renovate Fairley's community center.
(A) decision
(B) recognition
(C) progress
(D) result

125. Applicants will be notified if they have been selected for the position _____ two weeks of their interviews.
(A) by
(B) within
(C) just
(D) or

126. The research department is currently conducting studies to _____ the effectiveness of Philter's latest heartburn remedy.
(A) gauge
(B) administer
(C) settle
(D) comply

127. Halico has become the largest broadband provider in the country _____ the acquisition of Island Telecom earlier this month.
(A) but
(B) both
(C) with
(D) among

128. All residents of Champlain are welcome to join a complementary painting class _____ by local artist, Beverly Summers.
(A) taught
(B) kept
(C) divided
(D) caused

129. The gas mileage of the new Operton sedan is _____ depending on how often it is driven.
(A) supportive
(B) portable
(C) variable
(D) occasional

130. Only _____ members who have registered by November 30th will be able to attend the national conference in January.
(A) whose
(B) which
(C) each
(D) those

PART 6

Direction: Read the texts that follow. A word, phrase, or sentence is missing in parts of each text. Four answer choices for each question are given below the text. Select the best answer to complete the text. Then mark the letter (A), (B), (C), or (D) on your answer sheet.

Questions 131-134 refer to the following letter.

Dear Mr. Troyer,

This letter is in regards to your -------- of 15 of 200 drinking glasses that we shipped on May 4. We
                                    131.
guarantee the quality of all Valsin Glassware products, so any flaws are always -------- unacceptable
                                                                                 132.
even to us. We have always appreciated your business as one of our most valued customers. --------,
                                                                                            133.
we will give you a refund for the total cost of the damaged glasses. We do ask that you ship the
damaged items back to us so that we can inspect them and improve our crafting process. --------.
                                                                                        134.

131. (A) creation
 (B) rejection
 (C) coordination
 (D) disposal

132. (A) to consider
 (B) considering
 (C) considered
 (D) considers

133. (A) However
 (B) Additionally
 (C) Therefore
 (D) Regardless

134. (A) Please do this at your earliest convenience.
 (B) We offer reduced shipping rates for frequent customers.
 (C) We hope you find our products to your liking.
 (D) Please check our refund policy for the amount you can expect.

Question 135-138 refer to the following advertisement.

Enroll at BTR today to learn how to play piano.

The Bradwell Recreation Center welcomes all citizens to sign up to learn piano from Ms. Rita Masterson. Ms. Masterson studied at the International Arts Academy and ------- and instructing students for twenty-five years.
135.

During her career, she has been a studio musician and played with ------- of the most renowned musicians of our time, including Girgio Amatano, Wesley Kines, and the Decker Brothers Band.
136.

Ms. Masterson will be able to instruct students of any level to play piano in many different musical ------- She is qualified in playing everything from classical sonatas to jazz piano solos.
137.

Classes are available for groups from March 4 and one-on-one lessons will start from March 10.

138.

135. (A) been played
(B) has played
(C) will be playing
(D) has been playing

136. (A) one
(B) much
(C) some
(D) few

137. (A) instruments
(B) performances
(C) styles
(D) notes

138. (A) Learning to play piano has many benefits.
(B) Call 555-8812 for more detailed schedules.
(C) Ms. Masterson's classical concerts have been critically acclaimed.
(D) If you would like to hire Ms. Masterson, please call our office.

Questions 139-142 refer to the following e-mail.

To : Company Staff
From : Rita Kim
Date : September 12
Re : Announcement

Dear Co-workers.

I told the executive committee about my ------- to resign from the position this morning. -------.
                                          139.   **140.**

A hiring panel ------- put together and human resources department anticipates that an appropriate
               141.
successor for my position will be found in the near future. Let your supervisor know by September 20 if you would like to be considered for a position on the panel. Supervisors will choose panel members on that day.

I know some employees may be wondering ------- my plans are after retiring. At this time, I plan
                                       142.
to lecture at Gordon University on a part-time basis so that I can be with my family more often.

Sincerely,
Rita Kim
Staunton, Inc.

---

139. (A) intention
(B) reluctance
(C) attitude
(D) consideration

140. (A) I am very grateful to have been given this promotion.
(B) A schedule of my lectures can be found on the university Web site.
(C) My last day in this position will be on November 20.
(D) The committee will host the shareholder's meeting next week.

141. (A) was
(B) will have
(C) is
(D) is being

142. (A) about
(B) what
(C) if
(D) even

Questions 143-146 refer to the following letter.

April 15
Dr. Sylvia Lucas
888 Fillings Street
Fargo, ND 58122

Dear Dr. Lucas,

------. We have currently arranged for one of our staff to prepare for an ------ of our services.
143.   144.

Serton Custodial ------ in providing medical facilities in the Elm Grove region with janitorial
                  145.
services. We use only the safest, most ecologically sound cleaning chemicals and methods.

As you requested, one of our associates will visit your office on April 18 to determine the requirements for cleaning your facility. Based on this assessment, the final price quote for our services will be provided ------ one business day. We look forward to working with you.
                                                146.

143. (A) I am writing in regards to your question about medical care.
 (B) I have reviewed your application for employment with our company.
 (C) We appreciate you for choosing us as your custodial service provider.
 (D) Thank you again for your inquiry about Serton Custodial services.

144. (A) endorsement
 (B) opportunity
 (C) estimate
 (D) advance

145. (A) specializes
 (B) will specialize
 (C) specialized
 (D) could specialize

146. (A) before
 (B) within
 (C) for
 (D) about

PART 7

Direction: In this part you will read a selection of texts, such as magazine and newspaper articles, letters, e-mails, and instant messages. Each text or set of texts is followed by several questions. Select the best answer for each question and mark the letter (A), (B), (C), or (D) on your answer sheet.

Questions 147-148 refer to the following invitation.

To thank you for your support of the Galestorm Theater, we'd like to invite you to The 12th annual Galestorm Theater Festival.

Friday, March 24
The East Wing of the Lakeside Hotel
6833 Drake Street
Greenton

5:30 p.m. Meal
Hors d'oeuvres, entrees, drinks, and cake

7:00 p.m. Music and Dancing
A performance by The Tangoliers

8:30 p.m. Appreciation Ceremony
A special presentation to thank major donors to the theater

Please let us know how many guests you will participate with by March 2. To do so, please visit www.galestormtheater.com.

147. What is the purpose of the event?
(A) To advertise a company's goods
(B) To welcome participants to a conference
(C) To honor donors to the Galestorm Theater
(D) To congratulate a staff member on his achievements

148. What must guests do before attending the event?
(A) Respond to a questionnaire
(B) Enroll in an arts course
(C) Turn in a donation
(D) Go to a Web site

Questions 149-150 refer to the following notice.

ATTENTION CITIZENS

The Annual Tarburg Reuse – Recycle Fest will be taking place on Sunday, April 24 from 10 a.m. to 6 p.m. at Postman Park. The event is being sponsored by the Tarburg Neighborhood Association. At the festival, members of the community can rid themselves of items they no longer use and pick up others that they will, including electronics, kitchen appliances, computers, and more. Auctions will be held for items and if not sold, they will be recycled. Your donations will help keep both house and our environment clean.

If you have a large item that doesn't fit in your car, we can help. Call Ted Booker at 555-6788 to arrange for a truck to pick up your item. Those who wish to volunteer to arrange recycled items should call Gil Ronson at 555-4338.

149. What are Tarburg citizens asked to do?
(A) Place recycling bins in certain areas
(B) Make donations of unwanted things
(C) Shut down computers when not in use
(D) Register for a festival

150. Why should citizens call Mr. Booker?
(A) To help recycle a truck
(B) To join the Tarburg Neighborhood Association
(C) To reserve a space at Postman Park
(D) To ask for assistance moving an item

Questions 151-152 refer to the following notice.

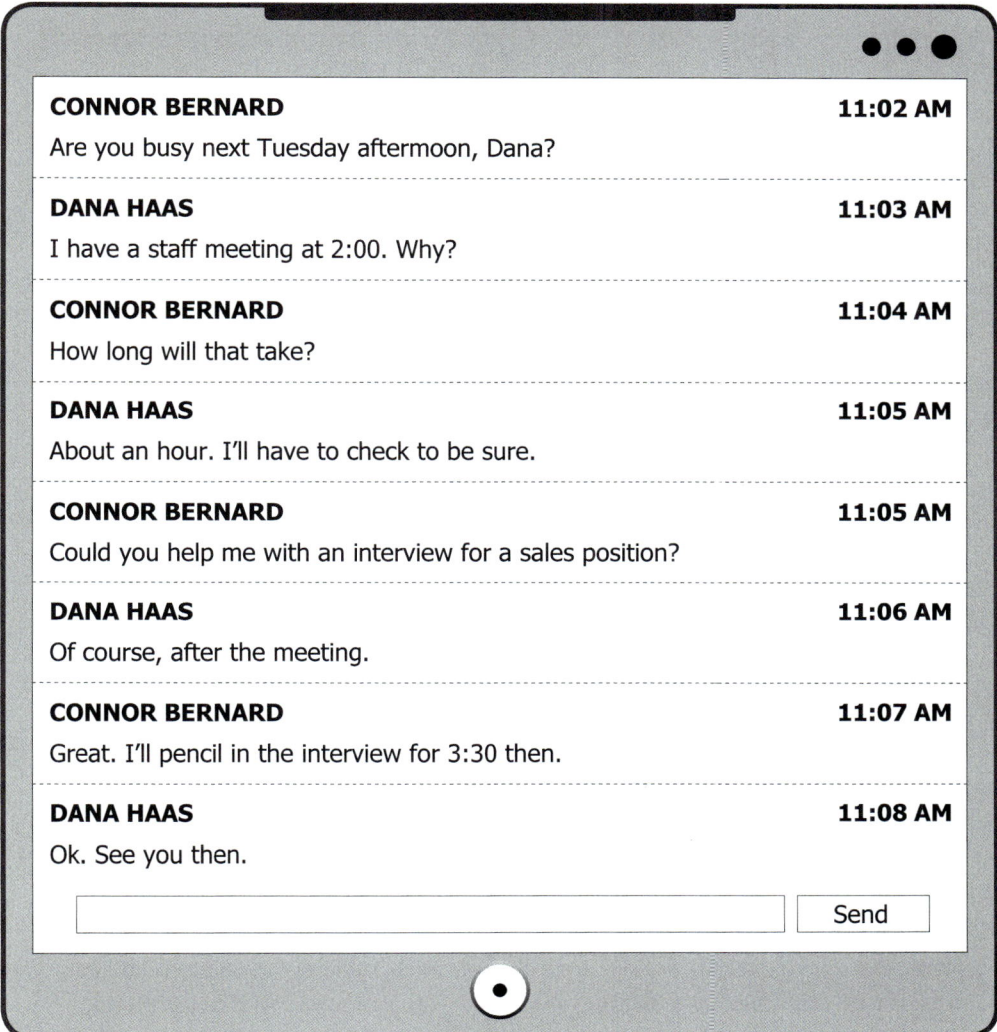

151. What does Mr. Bernard need help with?
(A) Interviewing a candidate
(B) Holding a staff meeting
(C) Organizing a convention
(D) Contacting a colleaguel

152. At 11:06, what does Ms. Haas mean when she writes, "Of course"?
(A) She will check the schedule.
(B) She will take over a sales position.
(C) She will give her assistance to Mr. Bernard.
(D) She will postpone a staff meeting.

Question 153-154 refer to the following e-mail

To :	Wesley Dawkins < wesleyd33@titannet.com >
From :	Shipping department < donotreply@liquistpharmacy.com >
Date :	November 22 3:45 p.m.
Subject :	Your recent purchase

We greatly appreciate your business at Liquist Pharmacy, the easiest place to buy medicine online. This e-mail is to confirm delivery of your most recent order. Prescription orders are sent within one day of being placed. Please check the purchase details below.

Purchase # : 853694
Date and time of order : November 22, 3:42 p.m.
Delivery address : Wesley Dawkins, 2433 Hines Street, Louisville, KY 40223
Items purchased : 1 bottle of Vimitor, prescribed by Dr. Harry Burns
Total charges: $20.42, paid with credit card (the card ending number 3285)

If this prescription includes refills, call our customer service department at 1-800-555-1414 to set up automatic filling and delivery.

You can receive a discount on your next order by registering on our Web site at www.liquistpharmacy.com.

153. What is indicated about Mr. Dawkins' order?
(A) It was discounted by the company.
(B) It will probably be sent by the end of November 23.
(C) It has to be confirmed by a doctor.
(D) It includes non-prescription medication.

154. Why is Mr. Dawkins invited to contact the customer service department?
(A) To make a change to his order
(B) To verify his shipping address
(C) To speak with a pharmacist
(D) To arrange automatic service

Questions 155-157 refer to the following e-mail.

E-mail Message

To : Company staff <employees@partnersdrug.com>
From : Vera Mackey <vmackey@partnersdrug.com>
Subject : Cambert Kids Camp
Date : May 24

Partners Drug is going to be helping prepare for the Cambert Kids Camp this June. This camp is run by a non-profit group and solicits assistance from Partners Drug and other businesses to make their enrollment costs minimal so that more local kids can join the camp. Children ages four to eleven attend the camp, and I know some of our staff send their children to the camp every year.

Our Cambert Kids Camp Donation Campaign will start tomorrow, so there will be some boxes in our reception area of our main building. Art supplies, children's games, swimming accessories and sunscreen will be especially appreciated. Equipment for sports, like footballs and badminton sets would be great as well.

The boxes will be placed in the reception area through June 29. Donating money is also acceptable. Please give financial contribution to Becky Hansen on the third floor in the accounting department.

Bill Carlson
Public Outreach Organizer, Partners Drug

---

155. What is the purpose of the E-mail?
 (A) To arrange a gift exchange
 (B) To offer a discount for a camp
 (C) To solicit support for a local organization
 (D) To suggest vacation destinations for children

156. What would probably NOT be placed in the boxes?
 (A) Crayons
 (B) Checkers sets
 (C) Baseball bats
 (D) Drinking water

157. According to the e-mail, what is Ms. Hansen responsible for?
 (A) Collecting monetary donations
 (B) Transporting enrolled children
 (C) Collecting children's toys
 (D) Encouraging staff participation

Questions 158-160 refer to the following notice.

Summerville Public Transportation Committee
Notice for Blue Line service over the weekend

The construction planned for Blue Line stations will cause some changes in service between Summerville Park and University Street from Friday, June 12 at 6:00 a.m. While construction is ongoing, the Blue Line will operate in two parts. The first part will run from Summerville Park to Carrer Drive and the second will run from Hanter Museum to University Street. The railway will be under construction at Marston Station, between Carrer Drive and Hanter Museum station, so trains will be unable to operate between these stations. Complimentary shuttle busses will be available for passengers who need to travel between these stations. The Blue Line will operate as usual from Sunday, June 14 at 10:00 a.m. and all other lines will run normally during this construction.

158. At what station is construction work scheduled?
(A) Summerville Park Station
(B) Marston Station
(C) Hanter Museum Station
(D) Carrer Station

159. What is indicated about the service changes?
(A) They change routes for all trains.
(B) They will increase train fares.
(C) They are not permanent.
(D) They were not expected.

160. According to the announcement, what is the purpose of the shuttle buses?
(A) To help travel between two stations
(B) To lower the number of people on trains
(C) To provide service to customers outside of the city
(D) To offer transportation to less popular destinations

Questions 161-163 refer to the following e-mail.

To :	hwilton@miltonmfg.com
From :	totoole@orangeplanning.com
Date :	January 12
Subject :	Re: Question about services

Dear Ms. Wilton,

I just received your inquiry about Orange Planning's services and I'm happy to help. Orange Planning is very interested in working with your company, Milton Manufacturing, to raise the output of your production lines for the main products of your company. —[1]—.

Orange Planning has been offering engineering consulting services for the past twenty years for many companies around the world. Some of the companies we have worked with include Babushka Mart in Moscow, Pitchfork Industries in Orlando, and Hord Robotics in Hong Kong. —[2]—.

If you choose Orange Planning, I assure you that you will be satisfied with the results. All companies that we have worked with have had extremely remarkable results, especially as we have a great record of finishing companies' projects within their budgets and before their deadlines. —[3]—.

—[4]—. Call me at 466-555-3755 if you'd like to talk about working together. I'd be happy to address any concerns that you may have. I'll be looking forward to your call.

Regards,

Tom O'Toole
Head of Client Assistance, Orange Planning

161. Why does Mr. O'Toole send the e-mail?
 (A) To verify the time of a meeting at Milton Manufacturing
 (B) To encourage a company to pursue a business relationship
 (C) To give directions to a production facility
 (D) To explain a new procedure for production

162. What is mentioned about Orange Planning?
 (A) It has recently built several facilities.
 (B) Its costs are not as expensive as other consulting companies.
 (C) It deals with companies in multiple countries.
 (D) Its main office is in Moscow.

163. In which of the positions marked [1], [2], [3], and [4] does the following sentence best belong?

"We have helped these companies and others become more efficient and fast in their production facilities."

 (A) [1]
 (B) [2]
 (C) [3]
 (D) [4]

Questions 164-167 refer to the following online chat discussion.

Online Chat

Sienna Reynolds [3:30 p.m.] Does anyone know who I would talk to about getting some business cards? I know I've only been here for about a week, but I was told that I would need business cards to give clients and I haven't received them yet.

Jason Welch [3:35 p.m.] Actually, that's something you have to set un on your own. There are actually three printing companies that our firm goes to for business cards.

Sienna Reynolds [3:33 p.m.] Does that mean I have to pay for the cards on my own? I thought the company covers that sort of thing.

Jason Welch [3:35 p.m.] No, you don't. The company has accounts with each printing company and each one sends the bill to our company.

Sienna Reynolds [3:36 p.m.] Ok. So, what are my options?

Shamarr Murphy [3:37 p.m.] I suggest Highland Document Printing. The cards that I got from it were very high quality and they delivered the order very quickly.

Jason Welch [3:38 p.m.] I got mine from Highland, too. The other options are Ace Print Shop and Coastal Printers. Ace has the best quality, but they take a long time to print and deliver the cards. Highland can't be beaten if you need them quickly.

Sienna Reynolds [3:40 p.m.] Alright. Do you two mind if I take a look at your business cards before I order mine?

Jason Welch [3:41 p.m.] Not a problem. If you want to stop by my office in five minutes, you can see mine.

Shamarr Murphy [3:42 p.m.] I'll go by Jason's office, too, so you don't have to make two stops, Sienna.

164. What is the main topic of the discussion?
 (A) Delivering a shipment to clients
 (B) Obtaining name cards
 (C) Where to send an invoice
 (D) Choosing a benefits package

165. What is indicated about Highland Document Printing?
 (A) It processes orders quickly.
 (B) It is located close to the writer's company.
 (C) It makes the best products available.
 (D) It has many choices for designs.

166. At 3:38, what does Jason Welch mean when he writes, "Highland can't be beaten"?
 (A) Highland has the fastest response to orders.
 (B) Highland has the most favorable reviews.
 (C) Highland is more expensive than other options.
 (D) Highland is what most employees choose.

167. What will Shamarr Murphy most likely do next?
 (A) Make an order for some name cards
 (B) Prepare some documents for a meeting
 (C) Meet colleagues in an office
 (D) Contact clients about an order

Questions 168-171 refer to the following advertisement.

EnviroOffice

243 Victoria Street
Vancouver, British Columbia V5K 1N9
(604) 555-4486

Want to have beautiful plants in your office, but just don't have enough time in the office to care for them? Then consider EnviroOffice's services. We have the best selection of plants in the area for large and small offices. Not only do we sell plants, but we provide care services for a nominal fee for every plant that we sell. We stock common plants as well as more exotic plants, so you're sure to leave our store with something suitable for your office. If you sign up for our services for more than one year, we also provide free floral arrangements made by our specialists. Decorating your office with plants can make your work environment seem more refreshing, so call today to find out more about our products and services and receive a free estimate.

168. What is being advertised?
(A) A home-landscaping company
(B) An event floral arranger
(C) A magazine about gardening
(D) A service that sells and cares for plants

169. What does EnviroOffice NOT advertise in the notice?
(A) Complimentary estimates
(B) Shipment of imported plants
(C) Plant maintenance for offices
(D) A various selection of plants

170. In the advertisement, the word "consider" in paragraph 1, line 2 is closest in meaning to
(A) regard
(B) identify
(C) think about
(D) improve

171. What special offer is mentioned?
(A) Self-maintaining plants
(B) Complimentary flower arrangement
(C) Discounts on exotic plants
(D) Fruit producing plants for half price

Questions 172-175 refer to the following e-mail.

E-mail

From:	Henry Connors <hconnors@prostaffing.com>
To:	Kimberly Stevens <kimstevens@qpost.com>
Subject:	Registering
Date:	June 26

Dear Kimberly,

I have received your resume and transcripts from your university and I will be able to finish putting your information into the Pro Staffing system.

—[1]—. At this time, there are multiple temporary jobs that we are trying to fill that match your education and qualifications. Two of these are telemarketing jobs, one is an administrative assistant at a distribution firm, and the other is a receptionist at a dental clinic. —[2]—. If you perform well during your internship, you would be offered a permanent position as a junior editor at a newspaper. With the degree you have just received in journalism, this would be great for you. —[3]—. The only issue is that the job is in Hastings, which is a long way away from your home in Rochester. Would you be willing to make the commute? The temporary jobs are located near you, but if you're not concerned about commute time, we can also find other jobs for you. —[4]—.

Our agency will need three references and then we can start contacting companies where you can work. The references can be from managers, teachers, and former co-workers. Send me the documents by email or fax and make sure you include their contact information. The next step in the registration process will be for you to have an interview with our employment consultant. Please give me a call so we can set up a time for the interview.

Regards,

Henry Connors
Pro Staffing

172. What is indicated about Ms. Stevens?
(A) She is a qualified reporter.
(B) She has recently graduated.
(C) She is working for Pro Staffing.
(D) She has sent a package to Mr. Connors.

173. What is true about the receptionist position?
(A) It is located around Rochester.
(B) It leads to a permanent career.
(C) It has a flexible schedule.
(D) It is for a distribution company.

174. What has Mr. Connors NOT asked Ms. Stevens to do?
(A) Send references
(B) Set up an appointment
(C) Clarify her willingness to travel
(D) Submit signed paperwork

175. In which of the positions marked [1], [2], [3], and [4] does the following sentence best belong?

"We have a permanent position as well, but you would be working as an intern for three months."

(A) [1]
(B) [2]
(C) [3]
(D) [4]

Questions 176–180 refer to the following Web site and e-mail form.

http://www.valorfootwear.com/businessprogram

Valor Footwear's Business Program

| About | Business Program | Catalog | Contact us |

Want to keep your employees safe at your workplace? Valor Footwear can help make sure your workers have suitable shoes or boots for your business setting.

Valor Footwear offers a variety of styles for many workplaces, such as hospitals, factories, hotels, and restaurants. All footwear is available with slip-resistant soles. We also offer free consultation to help you determine which shoes would fit best for your business environment. A custom shopping Web site for your company can also be made so that your employees can easily check which shoes are acceptable to wear to work.

If you're ready to set up an account, all you need to do is click the button below to fill out a short questionnaire about your business needs. One of our customer account specialists will call you within two days to set up your account with Valor Footwear and answer any questions you may have.

< Register for the Valor Footwear Business Program >

* E-mail *

Name: Gregory Sample	
Business: International Eateries, Inc.	Position : Senior Director of Operations
Contact Number :618-555-1229	E-mail Address : gsample@intleateries.com

Preferred Contact Form (Select One) :
Email ☐   Telephone ☑   in Person ☐   Any form of contact is acceptable ☐

Why are you contacting us today?

I am in charge of operations of multiple restaurants and we've just introduced a policy that requires all employees to wear shoes with slip-resistant soles. I am hoping that your consultant can assist me in putting together a collection of five different styles of restaurant-appropriate shoes. I want to have a custom Web site by April 2 if possible. I'd like to also establish an invoicing system so that each employee at our company choose one pair of shoes and have the bill directly sent to the company instead of the employee.

<submit>

176. To whom is the Web page directed?
(A) Professional chefs
(B) Fashion designers
(C) Clothing manufacturers
(D) Business managers

177. According to the form, what change recently occurred at International Eateries, Inc.?
(A) Management established a new policy.
(B) A marketing campaign was started.
(C) A new branch was opened.
(D) Staff uniforms were changed.

178. What will many International Eateries employees probably be expected to do in April?
(A) Be trained in a safety technique
(B) Operate new equipment
(C) Buy products online
(D) Learn a new order-taking system

179. What service does Mr. Sample request that is NOT mentioned on the Web site?
(A) Recommending suitable shoes
(B) Developing a billing system
(C) Setting up a custom Web site
(D) Changing the style of a shoe

180. How most likely will Valor Footwear respond to Mr. Sample's form?
(A) It will give him a personal catalog of products.
(B) It will calculate how much a manager should be charged.
(C) It will schedule an inspection of several restaurants.
(D) It will have a consultant contact him within 48 hours.

Questions 181-185 refer to the following schedule and memo.

Hindelmintz Industires
Safety Workshop
March 15

10:00–10:50	Keeping your Work Area Organized: The Easiest Way to Stay Safe at Work Lead by Dietrich Packer, Director of Workplace Operations Committee
11:00–11:50	Safety Necessities on the Factory Floor: Review and Practice Lead by Samuel Rochard, Manufacturing Supervisor
12:00-1:00	Lunchtime
1:00 – 1:50	Maintenance and Usage of Factory Machinery Lead by Patricia Long, Senior Technician
2:00-2:50	How to Manage and Dispose of Hazardous Materials Lead by Olivia Mackie, Senior Examiner of the Lampwick Occupational Safety Department
3:00-3:50	Machine Demonstration from Renner Factory Instruments Lead by Emily Slattery, Representative from Renner Factory Instruments

---

Date: March 7
From: Jessica Woodard
To: All employees in the manufacturing facilities
Re: Changes to the Safety Workshop Schedule

This message is to inform you of some changes that have been made to the safety workshop coming up. Renner Factory Instruments' representative has a conflicting appointment later that afternoon, so she will be leading her workshop at an earlier time. Her session will now take place at 1:00 and the other sessions in the afternoon will each take place one time slot later than originally scheduled.

All staff that work on the factory floor and the surrounding offices are required to attend this safety workshop. Also, some staff from the research and development department will be attending as well. If you do not know whether your attendance is expected, please check directly with me. Of course, if you have any questions, comments, or concerns about training in general, you are free to contact me at any time.

Thanks for your cooperation.

-Jessica

181. What is the primary purpose of the workshop?
(A) To assist staff in accurately reporting time worked
(B) To help managers better communicate with their subordinates
(C) To demonstrate a new operating system
(D) To train staff on safe practices and procedures

182. What is most likely one of Mr. Rochard's job duties?
(A) Making handbooks for the company's merchandise
(B) Managing Hindelmintz Industires' merchandise production
(C) Creating advertisements for new products
(D) Handling questions and complaints from customers

183. Why is the schedule for the workshop being changed?
(A) A presenter has another commitment that day.
(B) A presenter had to be replaced because of an illness.
(C) The workshop's location need to be changed.
(D) The sessions conflicted with another event at Hindelmintz Industires.

184. Whose presentation is NOT being changed to a different time?
(A) Ms. Long's
(B) Ms. Mackie's
(C) Ms. Slattery's
(D) Mr. Packer's

185. In the memo, the word "expected" in paragraph 2, line 3, is closest in meaning to
(A) acceptable
(B) upcoming
(C) mandatory
(D) consistent

Questions 186–190 refer to the following e-mails and receipt.

E-mail Message

From : draymond@treetechnology.com
To : nate.amos@webpost.com
Date : November 10
Subject : Purchase #186550

Dear Mr. Amos

Your order of a desktop computer and monitor for $725 has been completed. We greatly appreciate your business and hope you are satisfied with your purchase. Included with your desktop computer are a keyboard and mouse and the monitor comes with a remote control. Since your order was over $700, we have also included a free HDMI cable.

The order will be sent from our distribution center in Carbondale and the scheduled delivery date for your purchase is November 20. However, this order is eligible for expedited shipping for only $5. With this upgrade, your order will arrive 6 days earlier on November 14. To request this service, please notify us of your intent to upgrade your shipping on or before November 12, after which this option will no longer be available. This and other updated information will be reflected on your online account, but not your printed receipt.

Regards,

Diane Raymond
Customer Assistance
Tree Technology
Elk Springs, CO

From : nate.amos@wepost.com
To : draymond@treetechnology.com
Date : November 11
Subject : Re: Purchase #186550

Dear Ms. Raymond,

I'd like to take advantage of the expedited shipping option that you mentioned.

Also, I am in the process of moving to a new residence, so I would like the shipment to be delivered to my office. The address is the one that is specified in the "bill to" section on my order. Please disregard the information in "ship to" section that I entered when I placed my order.

Sincerely,

Nate Amos

Tree Technology
Your Top Choice for the Best Technology
Purchase #186550

Item	Price
Tech+ Desktop Computer	$560
High Performance Mouse	$20
High Performance Keyboard	$45
Ultraview HDMI Monitor	$100
Ultraview HDMI Cable	$0
Subtotal	$725
Shipping and Handling	$3
Total	$728

Billing Address: 634 Ashley St.
Pittsfield, MA

Shipping Address: 880 Prospect Ave
Gloversville, MA

Thanks for shopping with us!

186. What is one reason the first e-mail was sent?
(A) To cancel an order
(B) To change a shipment's contract
(C) To explain why a shipment is late
(D) To present a limited time promotion

187. In the first e-mail, the word "reflected" in paragraph 2, line 5, is closest in meaning to
(A) indicated
(B) considered
(C) replicated
(D) returned

188. When will Mr. Amos most likely receive his purchase?
(A) On November 10
(B) On November 12
(C) On November 14
(D) On November 20

189. What information was not on the printed receipt?
(A) Billing address
(B) Product costs
(C) Expedited shipping costs
(D) Order number

190. Where most likely will the purchase be delivered?
(A) Carbondale
(B) Elk Springs
(C) Pittsfield
(D) Gloversville

Questions 191–195 refer to the following article, e-mail, and Web page.

October 8. How can you get the most out of life? Amanda Thibido, president of the Style Life, Inc., was curious about this question five years ago. "I was speaking with a man on a train and he was enthralled by a biography of Sun Ling, the renowned violinist. Her story made the man think about his own past. It made me think about how we can relate our own stories with the lives of famous and well-known individuals. I thought it could really help people."

After returning from her trip, Ms. Thibido started IntertwinedLives.com, a blog which has won awards, recognition, and millions of visitors from around the world. The blog is updated every week and already features thousands of stories of famous people. "I think the site is successful because people can really relate to the stories," says Ms. Thibido. "People reflect on their own lives as they read the stories of renowned people."

Ms. Thibido's Web site has drawn so many visitors that it will be issuing a print magazine titled Humans Being. The new monthly publication will print inspirational stories about famous figures of past and present, as well as impressive ordinary individuals. It is Ms. Thibido's hope that the readers will realize that their lives are just as fulfilling as those of well-known people. The Web site www.intertwinedlives.com/remarkablepeople has information about subscriptions as well as a suggestion form for future stories.

From: ptorn@stylelife.com
To: athibido@stylelife.com
Subject: Good news
Date: October 20

Hi Ms. Thibido,

I wanted to let you know that the publication of the article in the newspaper seems to have been very beneficial. The number of subscriptions has almost doubled. That's remarkable! The Web site, IntertwinedLives.com, currently has a link to the article, so it seems that some of our frequent readers are pre-ordering subscriptions. We've also had many first-time visitors that are coming to the Web site. One more thing that you should know is that many suggestions are being made for film actors, especially Ivan Sloan. We should write our next story about him.

Peter Torn
Senior editor

InterwinedLives.com

| Home | Archives | Human Beings | Suggestions |

Name: Teri Wilson
How did you hear about IntertwinedLives.com? (Select all that apply)
_____ Web site
___X___ Print publication (Newpaper, magazine, etc.)
_____ Friend or acquaintance
_____ Other

Suggested person:
Owen Rocha

Reason(s) for suggestion:
Mr. Rocha is the mayor of our town of Burns. He came to the country as an immigrant as a teenager and was not well-educated. He overcame many hardships and because of his diligence and friendly personality, he has really risen in society. Everyone that meets him agrees he is a very inspiring character.

---

191. What's a purpose of the article?
(A) To suggest a travel destination
(B) To profile Ms. Thibido's work
(C) To give tips to Internet writers
(D) To detail Ms. Ling's career

192. In the article, the word "renowned" in paragraph 1, line 5, is closest in meaning to
(A) well-known
(B) selected
(C) nominated
(D) recovered

193. In the e-mail, what does Mr. Torn state about the article?
(A) It was recommended by a famous violinist.
(B) It was republished in a magazine.
(C) It seemed to raise the number of subscribers.
(D) It was featured in a talk show.

194. What is suggested about Mr. Sloan?
(A) He gave a suggestion to Mr. Torn.
(B) He works at Style Life, Inc.
(C) He will be written about in Humans Being.
(D) He was the focus of a story on IntertwinedLives.com.

195. What is most likely true about Teri Wilson?
(A) She is a longtime reader of IntertwinedLives.com.
(B) She read the October 8 article.
(C) She is interested in the life of Ivan Sloan.
(D) She subscribes to Human Beings.

Questions 196–200 refer to following article, e-mail, and memo.

Industry Reports

March 18- Hyde and David Marketing will be increasing the number of staff it employs in the near future. Company spokesperson Susie Ellis said the agency will add at least 25 more employees to adapt to changing business practices.

"We are still heavily relying on traditional means to market products and services, but the significance of online marketing is definitely increasing," said Ms. Ellis. "Because of this, we need to find skilled individuals that are creative and qualified in marketing and also have experience with new media."

Hyde and David will participate in job fairs in the area in the hopes of finding qualified applicants. The next fairs in Chicago will be held on April 2 at the Henley Convention Hall and on May 4 at Park Community College.

Hyde and David is based in Columbus, OH and offers marketing services and consulting with 230 employees currently on staff.

---

* E-mail *

To :	<lgaines@hoopmail.com>
From :	<chong@hydeanddavidmarketing.com>
Date :	May 5
Subject:	Follow up

Dear Mr. Gaines,

It was very nice to meet you yesterday at the career fair. I'm happy that you're interested in working with David and Hyde Marketing and your portfolio from the Sundin School of Arts looks great.

I would like you to come in for an interview with our design department director Hillary Kline and some of her staff on May 13. If this is possible, please let me know what time between 8 a.m. and 3 p.m. would work best for you.

I'm looking forward to hearing from you soon.

Cindy Hong
Head of Staff Recruitment

Memo for Marketing Staff

This month's marketing workshop will focus on the usage of new media for our marketing campaigns and will take place on June 14. This workshop will feature presentations from several employees who recently started, so feel free to introduce yourself to them at the workshop if you haven't already done so. The titles of the presentations and presenter names are below.

Social Networking: Avoiding Backlash – Lyle Gaines
Professional Online Media Interaction – Amy Fiore
Blogs and Marketing – Judah Reid

---

196. What does Ms. Ellis suggest about online marketing?
(A) It will be more significant than traditional marketing.
(B) It has been a common interest among university students.
(C) It is cheaper to execute than traditional marketing.
(D) It requires companies to find staff with various skills.

197. According to the article, what is Hyde and David Marketing preparing to do?
(A) Dispatch a representative to events in Chicago
(B) Raise bonus payments for professionals
(C) Make changes to hiring policies
(D) Renovate its headquarters

198. What is the reason for sending the e-mail?
(A) To offer employment
(B) To arrange a meeting
(C) To submit a resume
(D) To request work samples

199. Where did Ms. Hong most likely meet Mr. Gaines?
(A) At Park Community College
(B) At the Henley Convention Hall
(C) At the main office of Hyde and David Marketing
(D) At the Sundin School of Arts

200. What is indicated about Lyle Gaines?
(A) He was hired by Hyde and David Marketing.
(B) He graduated with honors from his university.
(C) He lives in Columbus, OH.
(D) He is friends with Amy Fiore.

Stop! This is the end of the test. If you finish before time is called, you may go back to Parts 5, 6, and 7 and check your work.

동시토익 실전 WORKBOOK

101. Put your heating devices in storage to keep them in good condition once warmer weather arrives.

해석]

102. New account holders can apply for a new credit card when they open an account at Jergen Bank.

해석]

103. Mr. Horner presented the sales pitch to the shareholders himself because the director of sales had to visit another branch.

해석]

104. Mr. Blines did not receive confirmation of his accommodation and flight reservations by e-mail.

해석]

105. Harrison's Sports became the most popular sports equipment store in the region shortly after its grand opening.

해석]

106. All staff members of Olley, Inc. have to attend a seminar about enrolling in the new healthcare program next Thursday.

해석]

107. Every employee understands that they must enroll for healthcare benefits by June 10.

해석]

108. The auditorium of Kline University was designed by a famous architect that graduated from the school.

해석]

109. Carltec's notebook computers were moderately priced upon release, but the company raised the prices after receiving favorable reviews.

해석]

110. Letters to the Editor of the Lawson Daily are reviewed by the editor prior to publication.

해석]

111. Throughout his career, Ian Carter has aspired to become the most renowned marketing consultant in the industry.

해석]

*어휘 NOTE

112. Caring Airways provides the most affordable domestic flights in Canada.

해석]

113. Mantel Pharmaceuticals will not release their new painkiller because of recent findings in clinical tests.

해석]

114. Mr. Fisher told his staff that he was honored to work with such a dedicated and passionate team at Lester Automotive.

해석]

115. According to recent consumer reports, Everton Industries has produced the most highly rated toaster oven this year.

해석]

116. Overton Party Supplies acknowledged that everything that was rented for Xenor Technologies award ceremony was returned.

해석]

117. Thanks to our extensive research, our study was able to predict sales rates more accurately than our previous studies.

해석]

118. Due to conflicting schedules, next week's visit from the regional manager has been postponed until next month.

해석]

119. Revel Bohem's new line of living room furniture was a collaborative effort between Revel's design department and artist Teresa Gile.

해석]

120. On our upgraded Web site, you can find a calendar with direct links to major upcoming art and antiques sales in London.

해석]

121. New residents of Telville who do not update their address information on their identification cards may be subject to fines.

해석]

＊어휘 NOTE

122. Following a shift in its fiscal policy, a more sizable budget has been allocated for the marketing department of Thilsen, Inc.

해석]

123. The level of customer satisfaction at Lyle's Sandwiches is the highest of any local restaurant.

해석]

124. At the last city council meeting, Congressman Dale Harper announced the council's decision not to renovate Fairley's community center.

해석]

125. Applicants will be notified if they have been selected for the position within two weeks of their interviews.

해석]

126. The research department is currently conducting studies to gauge the effectiveness of Philter's latest heartburn remedy.

해석]

127. Halico has become the largest broadband provider in the country with the acquisition of Island Telecom earlier this month.

해석]

128. All residents of Champlain are welcome to join a complementary painting class taught by local artist, Beverly Summers.

해석]

129. The gas mileage of the new Operton sedan is variable depending on how often it is driven.

해석]

130. Only those members who have registered by November 30th will be able to attend the national conference in January.

해석]

* 어휘 NOTE

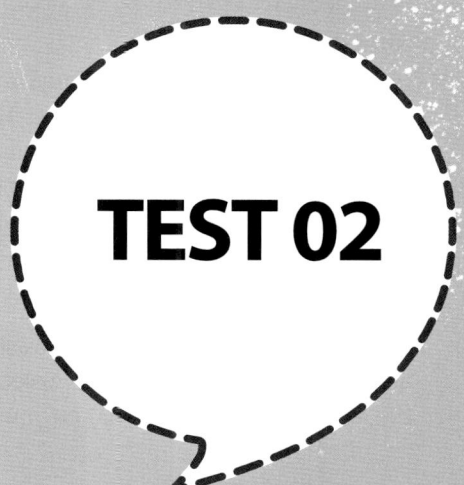

동시토익 CONTEMPORARY **TOEIC**

TEST 02

READING TEST

In the Reading test, you will read a variety of texts and answer several different types of reading comprehension questions. The entire Reading test will last 75 minutes. There are three parts, and directions are given for each part. You are encouraged to answer as many questions as possible within the time allowed.

You must mark your answers on the separate answer sheet. Do not write your answers in your test book.

Part 5

Directions: A word or phrase is missing in each of the sentences below. Four answer choices are given below each sentence. Select the best answer to complete the sentence. Then mark the letter (A), (B), (C), or (D) on your answer sheet.

101. Last month, architect Diane Lewis _____ for her design for the Hilldale Public Library.
(A) was praised
(B) praises
(C) praised
(D) is praising

102. Conditions for returns and exchanges are printed _____ the backs of receipts for all purchased products.
(A) to
(B) on
(C) next
(D) about

103. All _____ applicants are required to provide identification with proof of address when opening a Goals Bank account.
(A) reside
(B) resided
(C) residents
(D) residential

104. Because of the hard work of our volunteers, the goal for funding the Manley Art Museum's restoration has been _____.
(A) meets
(B) meeting
(C) met
(D) meet

105. _____ no other employees are in the office when you leave, please make sure to lock the door.
(A) If
(B) that
(C) only
(D) for

106. New tablet computers will be _____ to all information technology employees on April 6.
(A) distributed
(B) imported
(C) desired
(D) claimed

107. Ms. Harkin will be temporarily in charge of the human resources department during Mr. Vogon's _____ absence.
(A) condensed
(B) concise
(C) straight
(D) brief

108. There are no more Gilly's Fried Chicken restaurants left in the country, _____ the original one in Flagstaff.
(A) than
(B) considering
(C) over
(D) except

46 Actual TEST

109. The _____ of copyrighted materials is forbidden without the publisher's written authorization.
(A) photocopying
(B) photocopies
(C) photocopier
(D) photocopied

110. Passengers must check that their seat belts are _____ fastened before the plane takes off and lands.
(A) securely
(B) secure
(C) secured
(D) security

111. Nelson Lenses boasts such an _____ amount of choices that you're sure to get just what you want.
(A) extend
(B) extends
(C) extensive
(D) extensively

112. All diners at The Round Table _____ the best service regardless of whether they order a three course meal or simply an appetizer.
(A) satisfy
(B) deserve
(C) complete
(D) produce

113. The mayor and his wife were happy with the photographs that Karl Ingram took of _____ for the newspaper.
(A) their
(B) theirs
(C) they
(D) them

114. Johnson Medical Center's mission is to _____ each patient with medical professionals who can personally address their needs.
(A) miss
(B) resemble
(C) match
(D) need

115. The employee manual details packing techniques for shipping products _____ damaging any merchandise.
(A) without
(B) except
(C) unless
(D) though

116. By _____ integrating the latest technology with their products, Polton Computers has increased its market share.
(A) to act
(B) more active
(C) acted
(D) actively

117. Please speak with your manager if you wish to attend the professional _____ seminar on Monday.
(A) develops
(B) developmentally
(C) development
(D) developed

118. Books _____ every section are on sale for up to 70 percent off at Calvin Booksellers this weekend.
(A) over
(B) in
(C) onto
(D) about

119. The interpersonal communication seminar seems to have helped increase _____ in all departments.
(A) produces
(B) producer
(C) productive
(D) productivity

120. Articles from Science Monthly Journal may not be reprinted _____ written consent from the publication's editor.
(A) under
(B) regarding
(C) along
(D) without

GO ON TO THE NEXT PAGE

121. Employees were notified by a memo _____ this week about a position opening in the sales department.
(A) issued
(B) issuing
(C) to issue
(D) was issued

122. If you _____ like to receive a special gift voucher valid at any Livwell store locations, simply complete a short survey placed in the lobby.
(A) had
(B) were
(C) could
(D) would

123. Notices on recent changes to bus routes are _____ displayed at all Belleton Public Transit bus stops.
(A) prominently
(B) critically
(C) intensely
(D) mutually

124. The Menoly Metals' researchers use _____ sound research methods to create an incredibly strong steel to be used for construction.
(A) statistic
(B) statistical
(C) statistics
(D) statistically

125. _____ the increased demand for Polver's new line of winter coats, the company has hired more factory workers to increase production.
(A) Like
(B) Because
(C) Although
(D) Given

126. To improve the comfort of our guests, the Liberty Inn offers _____ access to transportation and shopping.
(A) convenient
(B) initiated
(C) preventive
(D) insistent

127. Bill's Car Repair has a high level of customer satisfaction largely because it repairs cars _____ than its competitors do.
(A) quick
(B) most quickly
(C) quickest
(D) more quickly

128. A majority of workplace injuries are easily _____ with proper safety training and supervision.
(A) preventing
(B) preventable
(C) prevent
(D) prevention

129. Telson Insurance Company has attributed its success _____ to the dedication of its sales and customer service agents.
(A) importantly
(B) primarily
(C) tightly
(D) extremely

130. To ensure records are complete, accounting department employees must take the _____ in asking other departments for their expense reports.
(A) initiative
(B) advice
(C) result
(D) expectation

PART 6

Direction: Read the texts that follow. A word, phrase, or sentence is missing in parts of each text. Four answer choices for each question are given below the text. Select the best answer to complete the text. Then mark the letter (A), (B), (C), or (D) on your answer sheet.

Questions 131-134 refer to the following memo.

You are all aware that ------- your working hours are reported at the end of the week after you
                          131.
have finished. For the first week of September, though, this will change slightly. -------. Due to this,
                                                                                     132.
work-hour reports that include September 5 and 6 will have to be turned in by September 4 at the
latest, meaning that many staff will not have actually worked all of their hours yet. Therefore, you
must ------- your working hours for those dates in advance. If you need to adjust your timesheet to
     133.
reflect your hours actually worked, you can make a request to your immediate supervisors -------.
                                                                                          134.

131. (A) intensely
     (B) considerably
     (C) ordinarily
     (D) especially

132. (A) Our offices will be closed for the first week of September.
     (B) Your work hours are needed to accurately calculate your compensation.
     (C) During that week, our accounting software will undergo an update.
     (D) Supervisors frequently work longer hours than their staff.

133. (A) estimate
     (B) postpone
     (C) extend
     (D) delete

134. (A) latest
     (B) later
     (C) lately
     (D) lateness

Question 135-138 refer to the following letter.

June 10

Harry Burton
9847 Illinois Avenue
Janesville, IA 50647

Dear Mr. Burton:

We are very happy with the article you have contributed to Economics Monthly entited "Careers in Financial Consultation."

The editor wants to ------- **135.** it in our August issue, but in its current state, the article is not in line with our word-count requirements. Technically, the article is too ------- **136.** to be included in our Helpful Advice section. ------- **137.**. We will have you work in ------- **138.** with Cecilia Fine, a junior editor. The article has to be submitted in the proper length by July 15.

Let me know if you have any questions. You can reach me at 555-0086.

Regards,

Tory Hillman, Submissions Editor
Economics Monthly

135. (A) include
(B) promote
(C) reserve
(D) refer

136. (A) formal
(B) lengthy
(C) technical
(D) expected

137. (A) We have forwarded the article to our printing department.
(B) Our publication has a base of 3,000 subscribers.
(C) We'd like you to visit our offices at the end of next week.
(D) It should be cut to 2,500 words if possible.

138. (A) consults
(B) consulting
(C) consultation
(D) consultant

Questions 139-142 refer to the following e-mail.

To: hbolker@emailcity.com
From: renewal@womenstime.com
Subject: Renewing your subscription
Date: February 28

Dear Ms. Bolker,

This is a reminder that your subscription to Feminine Galaxy Magazine ------- on March 31. If you would like to keep having Feminine Galaxy delivered to your mailbox, you'll need to renew your subscription.

Since you are one of our valued subscribers, we are offering you a discounted price of $20.00 for a whole year. -------, renewing early will entitle you to take advantage of this discounted rate for other magazines published by Harley & Company Publications, such as Home Styles and Cars and Motors. -------. Simply visit our Web site at www.wandapublishing.com and complete the renewal form ------- March 20.

Sincerely,
Harley & Company Publications

139. (A) expired
 (B) expiring
 (C) will expire
 (D) having expired

140. (A) However
 (B) Consequently
 (C) Instead
 (D) Additionally

141. (A) We greatly appreciate you starting a new subscription.
 (B) This offer is valid for a limited time only.
 (C) Harley & Company Publications has won multiple awards.
 (D) We hope you have enjoyed your subscription to Feminine Galaxy.

142. (A) by
 (B) at
 (C) with
 (D) above

GO ON TO THE NEXT PAGE

Questions 143-146 refer to the following instructions.

Getting Rid of Stains

All you need to get rid of a ------- spot on your Forrester Furniture is some baking soda, vinegar
                                  143.
and a soft cloth. Just follow these easy instructions to remove even the toughest stains. Prepare
one tablespoon of baking soda, and simply ------- it with one half tablespoon of vinegar and one
                                             144.
tablespoon of water. -------. Next, put this solution onto the cloth and gently rub the stained area.
                     145.
Use a vacuum to remove any baking soda only ------- the area has dried, if there are any white
                                             146.
spots on the fabric. Then, you will find that the stain is nowhere to be seen.

143. (A) defective
(B) capable
(C) faulty
(D) persistent

144. (A) mix
(B) mixed
(C) mixture
(D) mixes

145. (A) Baking soda has many uses for cleaning and deodorizing your home.
(B) Cleaners that use bleach should be avoided when cleaning your furniture.
(C) Stir the solution until the baking soda has completely dissolved in the vinegar.
(D) For especially tough stains, call our customer service center for advice.

146. (A) clearly
(B) before
(C) near
(D) once

PART 7

Direction: In this part you will read a selection of texts, such as magazine and newspaper articles, letters, e-mails, and instant messages. Each text or set of texts is followed by several questions. Select the best answer for each question and mark the letter (A), (B), (C), or (D) on your answer sheet.

Questions 147-148 refer to the following text message.

To: Jamie Shwartz   1:00 p.m.
From: Trent Railway Passenger Assistance

TRAVEL NOTICE: A change has been made to Trent Railways Train 47B. See below for details.

Train 47B
Chicago Station to Chattanooga Station

Delayed
Original departure time 1:35 p.m.
New departure time 1:50. P.m.
Original arrival time 9:20 p.m.
New arrival time 9:35 p.m.
Boarding platform: Platform 8
Disembarking platform: Platform 9

If you are transferring to another train at your destination, please speak to an information clerk.

---

147. Why was the text message sent?
(A) To report a train schedule change
(B) To verify the purchase of a boarding pass
(C) To notify a passenger of a cancellation
(D) To give information about transferring trains

148. What is indicated about Mr. Schwartz?
(A) He didn't make it to a transfer on time.
(B) He will leave from Chicago.
(C) He will meet someone at the platform.
(D) He bought his train ticket in Chattanooga.

Questions 149-150 refer to the following flyer.

Hurley Airways   *Cheaper Fares!*

Groups of 12 or more flying with Hurley Airways can save 20% on economy class air fare. Families with five or more members are able to save 15%. To qualify for the offer, the flight must be taken between September and October.

Please keep in mind that these fares can NOT be obtained at the ticket desk on the day of your travel. In order to purchase a flight ticket at the discounted prices, flights should be booked in advance. To ensure that your group receives the discounts, tickets should be bought on our Web site, www.hurleyairways.com, at least one week prior to the flight. More information about flights, prices, and baggage restrictions can be found on the site.

---

149. What is indicated about Hurley Airways?
(A) It will plan fewer flights in September.
(B) It flies to over 30 cities.
(C) It is discounting fares for families.
(D) It doesn't charge for extra baggage.

150. What are passengers recommended to do?
(A) Pay by credit card
(B) Avoid flying during weekends
(C) Purchase tickets before the day of a flight
(D) Inquire about discounts at the ticket desk

Questions 151-152 refer to the following text message chain.

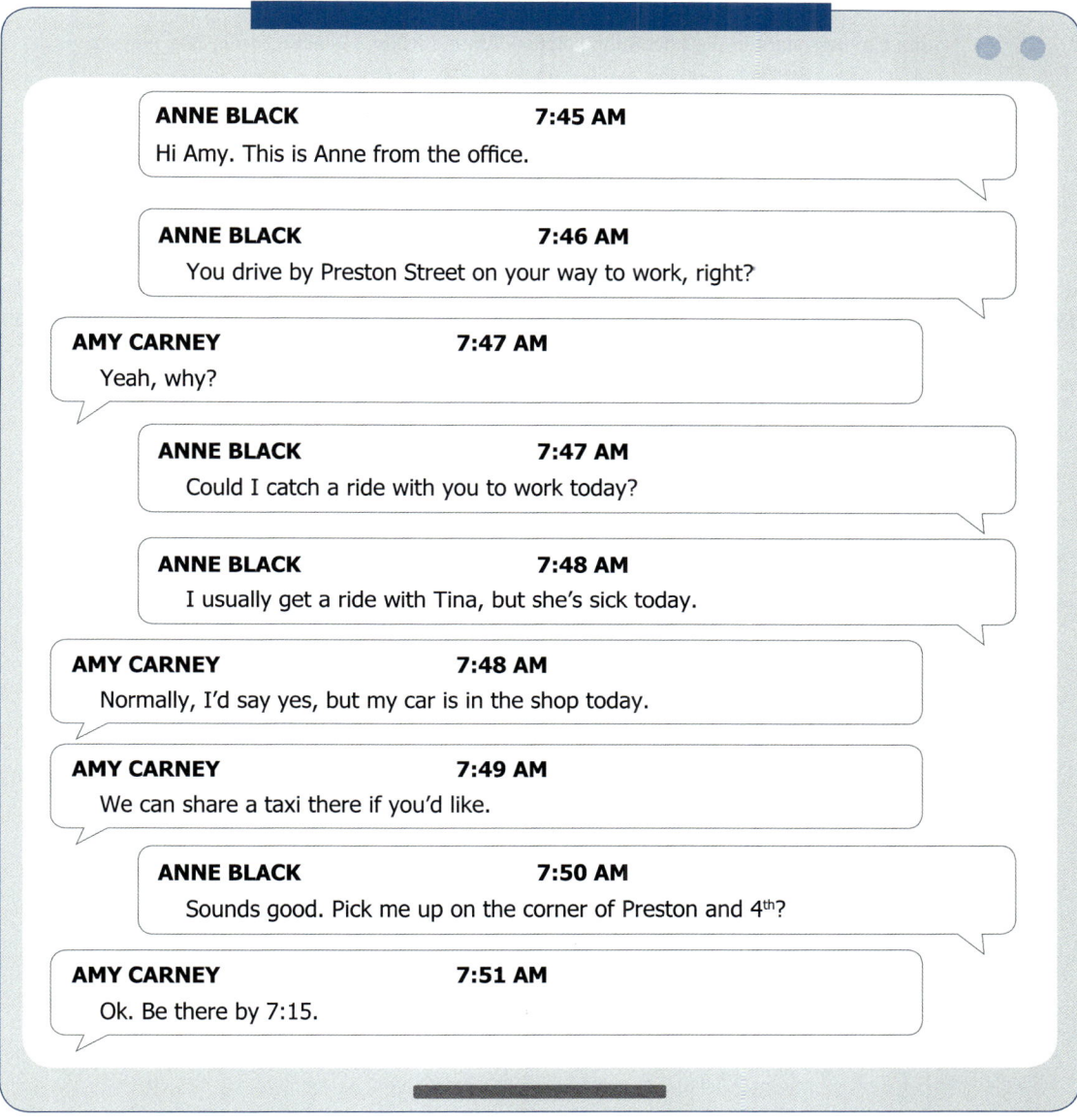

151. What are the writers mainly discussing?
(A) Taking a day off of work
(B) Contacting an ill co-worker
(C) Finding a way to get to work
(D) Where to go for lunch

152. At 7:47 AM, what does Ms. Black mean when she writes, "Could I catch a ride"?
(A) She wants to borrow Ms. Carney's car.
(B) She wants Ms. Carney to pick her up.
(C) She wants to take the bus with Ms. Carney.
(D) She wants to give a ride to Ms. Carney.

Question 153-154 refer to the following article.

> Cidra Cavings stars in the upcoming science fiction thriller, Galactic Strife. She plays the role of Vanna Humphrey, an astronaut whose mission to repair a space station takes an unexpected turn when she finds the crew of the space station behaving strangely. This exciting film, directed by Jeremy Hill, will keep viewers on the edge of their seat. It's coming to theaters on Wednesday, March 13.

153. Who is Cidra Cavings?
(A) A film director
(B) A scientist
(C) An actress
(D) An astronaut

154. According to the article, what will happen on March 13?
(A) A review will be published.
(B) A film will be released.
(C) A shuttle will be launched.
(D) A director will be interviewed.

Questions 155-158 refer to the following article.

EXPLORATION
The Seashore's Jewel

By Olivia Haverdash

Although it was built in the 19th century, the Svensen Lighthouse has gained tremendous popularity with tourists of the southern coast of Sweden. The classical round structure has a bright flashing light at the top of its two-story tower. The tower has been in operation for over 150 years and has been painted with reflective white paint and red stripes. The tower has been restored multiple times and had its height increased by 10 meters (30 feet) during the early 1910s. It most recently underwent renovations late last year and continues to attract people to the beautiful Swedish shore.

Tourists have come in large groups to this area of Sweden since the structure began allowing visitors again. An international arts fair was held by the owner of the lighthouse last September. He is an art enthusiast, and wishes to hold the event every year. It's great to visit the lighthouse anytime, though. Sheila Comstock brings tourists to the coast almost daily and says, "Many people love these kinds of tours and these kinds of old-style structures as well." Ms. Comstock also said that taking a bus from Sundsvall is the easiest way to get to the lighthouse and enjoy the country's scenery as well.

The lighthouse will be shown on a television program about the Svensen area to be aired in June. You can find more information about Swedish lighthouses at www.swedenlh.sw.

155. What is suggested about the Svensen Lighthouse?
(A) It currently assists in guiding boats.
(B) It is the property of Sundsvall.
(C) It has remained the same for 150 years.
(D) It has allowed tourists since it was built.

156. Who most likely is Ms. Comstock?
(A) A tour reporter
(B) A boat captain
(C) A TV program host
(D) A tour guide

157. What does Ms. Comstock suggest that visitors to the Svensen lighthouse do?
(A) Visit there by bus
(B) Visit the region in September
(C) Book tours beforehand
(D) Go to a web site

158. What will happen in June?
(A) A structure will undergo restoration.
(B) A special tour will be conducted.
(C) A documentary will be shown on TV.
(D) An international art fair will open.

Questions 159-161 refer to the following e-mail

---

* E-mail *

To : Harper Manufacturing Employees
From : Alphonse Grave
Subject : Yearly suggestion request
Date : July 14

Harper Manufacturing strives to provide the best employment experience for our staff, but we know that we can still improve in some areas. —[1]—. So, we'd like to have your suggestions in what we can do in areas such as rules, management, items that we manufacture, benefit packages, and marketing on a yearly basis. —[2]—.

We'd like to make sure that working here is satisfying for you, so the employee relations department asks that you fill in and submit a career satisfaction questionnaire by July 30. The form can be accessed on Jacob's Consultation Web site by clicking here. —[3]—.

We remind you that your answers will be kept confidential and that the forms have no information that identifies the respondents. The forms will go straight to consultants at Jacob's Consultation. —[4]—.

Please let me know by e-mail or phone if you have any questions.

Alphonse Grave
Employee Relations Director

---

159. What is suggested about Harper Manufacturing?
(A) It asks employees to complete a survey annually.
(B) It manages databases and information.
(C) It makes questionnaire answers public.
(D) It has great benefit packages for staff.

160. According to the e-mail, what should happen by July 30?
(A) A new product will be manufactured.
(B) Benefit packages will be changed.
(C) Workers will go to a company's home page.
(D) The results of a survey will be released.

161. In which of the positions marked [1], [2], [3], and [4] does the following sentence best belong?

"After they review the results, they will discuss them with the employee relations department."

(A) [1]
(B) [2]
(C) [3]
(D) [4]

Questions 162-165 refer to the following online chat discussion.

Marshall Dennis [1:20 p.m.] Has anyone seen Paula Castillo today? I need an update on her story about the town's new mayor.

Dane Houston [1:21 p.m.] I talked to her this morning. She was heading out for an interview with an old colleague of the mayor. She said she'd be back after lunch.

Marshall Dennis [1:22 p.m.] Do you have any idea what time exactly? The editor-in-chief wants to know when the story will be ready for printing.

Dane Houston [1:23 p.m.] Sorry, no idea, boss. She just told me that she had a packed morning and she would be back in the office after lunch. As far as I know, she has an interview with the new mayor later this afternoon.

Elle Goldberg [1:25 p.m.] I've just confirmed that with the mayor's assistant. Ms. Castillo will meet with Brian Greenwood at 3 at City Hall in his new office. She should be back at the office before 2 if you'd like to talk to her, Mr. Dennis.

Marshall Dennis [1:27 p.m.] Yes, when she gets back in, tell her to come by my office, Elle. I want to make sure that she asks the new mayor about his budget plan for the town.

Elle Goldberg [1:28 p.m.] I believe that she already has some questions about that, but I'll let her know that you want to go over those questions when she gets here.

Marshall Dennis [1:30 p.m.] Thanks. In the meantime, Dane, can you come to my office? I'd like to do some final editing on your piece about the upcoming festival so we can publish it in tomorrow's edition.

Dane Houston [1:31 p.m.] Sure, I'll be right there.

162. What kind of company do the writers most likely work for?
(A) A publishing company
(B) A marketing agency
(C) A newspaper
(D) A consulting firm

163. Who most likely is Brian Greenwood?
(A) A newly elected official
(B) A newspaper reporter
(C) A budget consultant
(D) An assistant

164. At 1:23 p.m., what does Dane Houston mean when he writes, "she had a packed morning"?
(A) Ms. Castillo brought her lunch from home.
(B) Ms. Castillo wouldn't be working in the morning.
(C) Ms. Castillo woke up early today.
(D) Ms. Castillo was very busy until lunch.

165. What is indicated about Marshall Dennis?
(A) He is writing several stories at once.
(B) He works closely with City Hall.
(C) He is in a managerial position.
(D) He is not happy with Mr. Houston's work.

Questions 166-168 refer to the following letter.

Porton Monorail

February 2

Dear passengers,

As operation costs for the monorail continue to rise, we have no option but to raise fares for our passengers starting February 15. Fares for adults, university students, and school-aged children will go up by 7%. Children aged 7 and younger will still not have to pay a fare.

We are sorry for inconveniences our customers may experience because of this. Please remember that this is the first time we have had to raise fares in six years. All earnings from fares go toward paying our employees and regularly maintaining the monorail.

We greatly appreciate you for using Porton Monorail

166. What is indicated about Porton Monorail?
(A) It is changing routes for construction.
(B) It increased its prices six years ago.
(C) It is asking for suggestions from passengers.
(D) It is seeing fewer passengers using the service recently.

167. What is suggested about university students?
(A) They can receive a discount card from their schools.
(B) Their fares will rise by the same percentage as the one for adults.
(C) They must renew identification to receive the student fare.
(D) They will no longer have a special fare provided for them.

168. According to the notice, what is one way that earnings collected from fares are spent?
(A) To compensate staff
(B) To increase the number of routes
(C) To restore train stations
(D) To advertise their service

Questions 169-171 refer to the following notice.

Hector Rodriguez to Speak at Chapala City Hall

Prize-winning writer and CEO of Quatro Perro, Inc., Hector Rodriguez will give a presentation at Chapala City Hall on April 4. The presentation will focus on making an impact in the corporate business world. Following the presentation, Mr. Rodriguez will be available to sign copies of any of his volumes in the South Wing of City Hall. There is no charge for entry, but attendees must register by April 1 since there are limited seats available. Email the organizer Maria Ortega (mortega@chapalacity.go.mx) to register or find out information.

Mr. Rodriguez started his career as a sales representative with Hernandez Industries and was promoted quickly. Following a decade of working at Hernandez, Mr. Rodriguez started his own company and has attained great success. His latest book, Stand Tall and Succeed, will be available at bookstores beginning on April 3.

169. What event is being promoted?
(A) An opening at a company
(B) A celebration of a successful company
(C) A ceremony for a prize recipient
(D) A business talk

170. What is suggested about Hector Rodriguez?
(A) He is preparing to start a new company.
(B) He writes articles for a Web site.
(C) He visits Chapala City Hall often.
(D) He has written several books.

171. What are the attendees asked to do before the event?
(A) Write an email to Hector Rodriguez
(B) Purchase an admission ticket
(C) Contact Maria Ortega
(D) Go to the South Wing

Questions 172-175 refer to the following article.

July 10—The Lorville Association of Developing Culture (LADC) released a statement that it has selected Harold Miller as the winner of its Fifth Biennial Amateur Painting Contest. Mr. Miller's painting, "Letters Upon Letters," and works of those who entered the contest will be exhibited at the LADC Gallery from August 10 to August 28. An opening ceremony will be held on the first day of the exhibition where Mr. Miller will be given a monetary award of $2,000 in recognition of his achievement by LADC's chairwoman, Nancy Mael. —[1]—.

LADC will also have the paintings available for viewing on its Web site, something the organization has never done before. —[2]—. "We hope that the online gallery will allow more people to enjoy the paintings of some of the area's gifted amateur artists," said Ms. Mael. —[3]—.

Residents should remember that the Gallery will not be open during its annual fall break from August 30 to September 28. The gallery's new season begins on September 30 with a presentation by music professor, Dr. James Haver on the history of jazz music. —[4]—.

172. What is NOT a purpose of the article?
(A) To announce a contest's winner
(B) To promote a Web site's update
(C) To profile an organization's director
(D) To publicize an upcoming talk

173. What is indicated about Mr. Miller?
(A) He is a painting instructor.
(B) He will rate paintings for a competition in June.
(C) He will be participating in an event at a gallery on August 10.
(D) He works for a cultural institution.

174. What does the article imply about the gallery?
(A) It provides painting classes to the residents.
(B) Paintings from past contests will be posted on its Web site.
(C) It has recently undergone renovations.
(D) The painting exhibit is the last exhibit for the season.

175. In which of the positions marked [1], [2], [3], and [4] does the following sentence best belong?

"There is no admission fee to the exhibit, but donations are appreciated to help support LADC."

(A) [1]
(B) [2]
(C) [3]
(D) [4]

Questions 176-180 refer to the following guidelines and letter.

Mara & Associates
What to Consider When Making a Cover Letter

Cover letters are required to be the first page of each packet of surveys that is sent out to potential survey respondents. The cover letter gives the researcher an opportunity to solicit participation in a survey by explaining the value and significance of the participants' responses. Cover letters should be easy to understand, so they must be written in simple language and provide respondents the information listed below.

- The reason the research is being done
- Who is doing the research and made the questionnaire
- The importance of responding to the questionnaire
- How long the survey is (for example, two pages)
- How long it will take to finish the survey
- The date by which the completed survey should be submitted
- Whether the responses will be treated confidentially and for what they will be used

---

Mara & Associates
P.O. Box 564388 • Atlanta, GE 30312

August 6

Lupita Rose
2983 Delouise Drive
Monroe, LA 71212

Dear Ms. Rose:

Strong Life Exercise Equipment has employed Mara & Associates to survey customers who bought Strong Life products online. Since you purchased your Strong Life product online on June 18, you have been specially chosen to receive one of these surveys. Your completed survey will help us learn what customers find important when buying exercise equipment online.

Please answer the questions on the two-page survey and return it by the due date of September 30. We have included a pre-paid self-addressed envelope for your convenience. Please do not include any personal information, such as your name or contact details, as all surveys are to be kept confidential. A summary of all responses will be available after November 30. If you wish to receive a copy, please mark the box indicating this on the final page of the questionnaire.

Regards,
Mara & Associates

Enclosure

176. What kind of company is Mara & Associates most likely?
(A) A biological research group
(B) A maker of exercise products
(C) A consumer research agency
(D) A business training consulting firm

177. What do the guidelines imply about cover letters written by Mara & Associates' employees?
(A) They are one page long.
(B) They can be made available in multiple languages.
(C) They usually contain confidential information.
(D) They relate Mara & Associate's mission statement.

178. According to the letter, what did Ms. Rose do recently?
(A) She submitted an application for an opening.
(B) She complained about a faulty product
(C) She purchased goods on the Internet.
(D) She hired a marketing agency.

179. What information mentioned in the guidelines is NOT included in the letter?
(A) The time by which a form should be returned
(B) How many pages are in the survey
(C) The business that made the survey
(D) How long it will take to complete the questionnaire

180. According to the letter, what can Ms. Rose request?
(A) A discount on future purchases
(B) The results of a survey
(C) A copy of her receipt
(D) A product catalog

Questions 181–185 refer to following article and e-mail.

Inglewood University's Department of Architecture on the Road to Success Again
By Marilyn Nedson

Inglewood (January 10) - For five consecutive years, an Inglewood University project has been nominated for one of the prestigious Mitchell-McBrien medals. The new Ballard Building, which was designed by students of the Department of Architecture, was announced as a candidate for the award in the Best Design category.

The medals have been awarded to young architects throughout the world to celebrate their achievements in the field of architecture. The organization that awards the medals was set up primarily to encourage architects who are new to the field. The medals are highly sought-after.

The dean of students at Inglewood University, Ian Neighbors, stated that he thinks the reason that Inglewood students have been nominated so many times is partly because of the university's mentoring program, Inglewood Mentors. The aim of the program is to team up architecture students with architects who are already in the field to assist them with projects over the course of a year. "Working with real professionals in their field helps students get valuable experience and see what the career they strive for is like in real life. The results have been very satisfactory," stated Neighbors.

The Ballard Building, as with the projects that were previously nominated from Inglewood, was made by students who were participating in the program. The mentor for the group of students, Nia Varice, an architect from Polysum Design, has been working with them since the beginning of the project. She has been generous enough to donate her time to the program since its beginning, but this is the first time that her protégées have been considered for the award. "Usually, my reward is just working with young minds," stated Varice. "Having them nominated for this award is even more exciting."

The recipients for the awards will be announced on March 5. Those interested in seeing the completed designs for the Ballard Building are invited to visit the Inglewood University library, where they are on display until the end of February.

To: Nia Varice <nvarice@polysumdesign.com>
From: Jerry Ling <jling@somemail.com>
Subject: Great news
Date: March 6

Dear Nia,

I just read the article about the Ballard Building in the Lancing Herald today and I just wanted to say congratulations. I know that the architectural department at Inglewood is very happy and I'm sure that your company must be thrilled as well. I hope we can get together soon to catch up. I heard that Polysum is working on the new Sonitor Planetarium. It would be great to hear how that's going and to get some advice about mentoring from you whenever you're available.

Regards,
Jerry

181. What is suggested about the Mitchell-McBrien Medals?
(A) They are awarded every three years.
(B) They are currently on display at Inglewood University's library.
(C) They can be given to students from any country.
(D) They are awarded to exceptional mentors.

182. What is mentioned about the Inglewood Mentors program?
(A) It allows students to have professional assistance.
(B) It provides grants for students.
(C) It allows students to act as mentors to other students.
(D) It partners students from multiple universities for joint projects.

183. What is indicated about Ms. Varice?
(A) She got her degree from Inglewood University.
(B) She established her own architectural business.
(C) She was a mentor for all projects that were considered.
(D) She has mentored students in the program since it began.

184. Why did Mr. Ling most likely congratulate Ms. Varice?
(A) She was a highlighted architect in a journal.
(B) She was given a raise.
(C) A prize was given to students with whom she worked.
(D) Her company received a large grant.

185. Who most likely is Mr. Ling?
(A) Ms. Varice's supervisor
(B) Ms. Varice's student
(C) An employee of Polysum Design
(D) A volunteer for an Inglewood Mentors

Questions 186-190 refer to the following announcement, membership form, and article.

The Society for Arts Preservation
invites you to its premiere presentation of
A Night with the Stars

Featuring Bradley Kowalski

On Thursday, June 13 at 8 p.m.
at The Candlelight Theater

Renowned film actor, Bradley Kowalski will talk about his 45 year long career, including traveling to many countries, working with respected directors, and his partnership with musician Sheila Son.

Admission fee - $12.00
Student price - $9.00

Reception following the presentation: 9:30 p.m. – 11 p.m. (Must be reserved in advance)
Reservations can be made by calling The Society for Art Preservation support advisor at 1-800-555-8663

Support The Society for Arts Preservation (TSAP) by becoming a member today!

Supporters enjoy these benefits:
No charge for admission to TSAP events (excluding A Night with the Stars presentations)
No reservations required for receptions following events
Our monthly journal, Arts Preservation Now, delivered directly to your home

Individual memberships are $40 per year and family memberships are $60 per year.
Name _____
Address _____
Phone number _____
Membership choice and payment _____

Send your completed form to the following address:
Barbara Lueck, Support Advisor, The Society for Arts Preservation, 808 Washington Street, Portland, OR 97211

A Wonderful Night with Bradley Kowalski

- By Cooper Cohn, editor-in chief of Arts Preservation Now

This month's "A Night with the Stars" was TSAP's biggest event yet thanks largely to our supporting members. Bradley Kowalski told many wonderful stories during his talk, with a story about director Andrew Geddes drawing a lot of laughs. Mr. Kowalski stated that he really enjoyed the talk and reception and would be happy to do it again sometime in the future. It is thanks to the support of our members that TSAP is able to offer these events. Members should remember to re-register for membership as our members are given preference for events such as receptions for "A Night with the Stars" and many other events.

186. What is this advertisement about?
(A) A film
(B) A theater opening
(C) A talk
(D) A concert

187. What is indicated about the event on June 13?
(A) The Society for Arts Preservation members have to pay $12 for entry.
(B) Reservations can be made on the TSAP Web site.
(C) It will include a question and answer session.
(D) It is only available to TSAP supporters.

188. What should people do if they want to go to the reception after the event on June 13?
(A) Talk to Bradley Kowalski's secretary
(B) Purchase a ticket at the Candlelight Theater
(C) Talk to Sheila Son
(D) Phone Barbara Lueck

189. In the article, the word "largely" in paragraph 1, line 2 is closest in meaning to
(A) spaciously
(B) primarily
(C) sizably
(D) sparsely

190. Where most likely does the article appear?
(A) A national arts newspaper
(B) A theater's Web site
(C) An organization's monthly journal
(D) A pamphlet about an event

어휘 NOTE

Questions 191–195 refer to the following e-mail, information and e-mail.

E-mail Message

From :	Suda Hunsuk <shunsuk@portmobile.com>
To :	Paj Poonpratin <ppoonpratin@tomindustries.com>
Date :	19 November
Subject :	Your Order

Dear Mr. Poonpratin

We at Port Mobile greatly appreciate your choosing us as your mobile service provider. The details of your phone and service purchases are below:

Product Name	Number ordered	Service
Patti	6	National Advantage
Moody	12	Country Light
Phatta	6	Fast Lane
Hoot	2	Top Speed

We will send the phones from our Chiang Rai supply center within five business days. After you have received them, you will need to activate the devices by calling (+66 351) 555-4868 using the phone. Your Tom Industries credit card will be charged for recurring charges as you requested. Phones that have prepaid service will receive a message on the phone when the balance is below 4 USD. More credit can be charged, on our Web site or by phone.

Thank you again for your business and we look forward to serving you.

Regards,

Suda Hunsuk
Port Mobile

The mobile service plans for business accounts are listed below. Customers using plans with unlimited data usage and unlimited national calls are allowed to call abroad free of charge during the weekend.

Service features

Service	Phone Calls		Data	Charges (Monthly)
	National	Abroad		
Top Speed	No limit	600 minutes	No limit	60 USD
National Advantage	No limit	200 minutes	6 GB	40 USD
Country Light	250 min	0 min	12 GB	25 USD
Fast Lane (prepaid)	0 min	0 min	0 GB	0 USD

Extra Charges (charged if the usage exceeds monthly plan time or data)

Additional Abroad Calls	Additional Data	Additional National Calls
0.25 USD per minute	5.00 USD per gigabyte	0.10 USD per minutes

E-mail Message

To : Paj Poonpratin <ppoonpratin@tomindustries.com>
From : Country Light <customerservice@countrylight.com>
Date : January 7
Subject : Re: Service change

Dear Mr. Poonpratin,

Thank you for contacting us about upgrading the service on your phone. From January 10, your service will be upgraded to National Advantage. To show our appreciation for your business, 10.00 USD for the extra gigabytes used on your plan last month will be waived. This will be reflected on your next invoice. Thank you again for your patronage.

Sincerely,
Leonard Magnotta
Country Light Customer Service Associate

---

191. How is Mr. Poonpratin instructed to activate the devices?
(A) By bringing them to a shop
(B) By dialing a number on the phone
(C) By submitting a message by text
(D) By going to an online store

192. What is provided in the information?
(A) Charges for service
(B) Device specifications
(C) Delivery options
(D) Company information

193. What plan allows customers to make free international calls on weekends?
(A) Top Speed
(B) National Advantage
(C) Country Light
(D) Fast Lane

194. Who will automatically receive text messages with account information?
(A) Patti phone owners
(B) Moody phone owners
(C) Phatta phone owners
(D) Hoot phone owners

195. What is indicated about Mr. Poonpratin's service usage last month?
(A) He used Fast Lane service before.
(B) He used 2 GB of extra data.
(C) He was not charged for service.
(D) He made additional national calls.

Questions 196-200 refer to the following guidelines, form and e-mail.

Gorland Business Innovation Convention – Presenter Guideline

Submitting a proposal:
Submit a proposal using the submission form on our Web site
The proposal should have:
— a summary of a presentation or talk
— a profile of the presenter
— how to contact the presenter

Keep in mind:
— Convention proposals will be accepted from April 4 and the deadline for submission is April 23. There is no exception to this.
— No marketing presentations for certain products will be accepted.
— You will be contacted within three weeks if your proposal is accepted.

Presenters must:
— Give an expert-level presentation concerning the topic described in your proposal.
— Speak with a convention organizer to arrange audio or visual equipment that you need for your presentation at least three weeks before the presentation.

Submission Form for Presentation Proposal

Presenter Name: Frank Conning   Occupation: Senior Marketing Director
Company: Electron Corp.   Date: April 29
E-mail: fconning@electroncorp.com   Telephone: 683-555-8863
Profile: See attached file
Proposed Title for Presentation: Success in the Digital Generation

Abstract: Many consumers visit company Web sites and this makes an initial impression of companies. Many firms, however, lack the knowledge of how to make the best use of their Web sites to promote their goods and services. This presentation will show how companies can use the Internet to attract customers successfully.

Session Type: ___ Discussion Panel   ___ Pre-Convention Seminar
              _X_ Convention Presentation   _X_ I have reviewed the presenter's guide.

* E-mail *

To: Frank Conning <fconning@electroncorp.com>
From: Jill Avery <javery@gbi.org>
Date: May 2
Subject: Your proposal

Dear Mr. Conning,

While we are unable to accept your presentation proposal request for this year's convention, the Gorland Business Innovation Association still finds its subject matter prescient and interesting. If possible, we would like to include you in an upcoming panel discussion that will be held at an expo that the GBIA is organizing in August, one month after the convention. One advantage to the panel discussion at the expo is that you will be able to freely promote your company during the discussion if you so wish. If you would be interested in this, please respond back to me at this email.

Regards,

Jill Avery
Coordinator
Gorland Business Innovation Association

196. What is the purpose of the guideline?
(A) To list what companies need to do to sell goods at a convention
(B) To offer recommendations for making presentations better
(C) To provide an explanation for convention registration
(D) To instruct possible presenters on convention requirements

197. What are convention presenters required to do?
(A) Have a talk with a convention organizer
(B) Go to an orientation
(C) Send a signed copy of the guideline
(D) Submit a list of recommendations

198. Who is Mr. Conning?
(A) A staff at the Gorland Business Innovation Convention
(B) A director at a corporation
(C) A seminar participant
(D) An Electron Corp client

199. Why will Mr. Conning's proposal probably be rejected?
(A) It advertises his company's products.
(B) It does not have some required information.
(C) It was submitted past the deadline.
(D) It was presented at last year's convention.

200. What will be the topic of a panel discussion in August?
(A) Improving the usage of Internet marketing
(B) Improving presentations to potential clients
(C) Presenting a business in an expo setting
(D) Employing environmentally safe business practices

Stop! This is the end of the test. If you finish before time is called, you may go back to Parts 5, 6, and 7 and check your work.

동시토익 실전 WORKBOOK

101. Last month, architect Diane Lewis was praised for her design for the Hilldale Public Library.
해석]

102. Conditions for returns and exchanges are printed on the backs of receipts for all purchased products.
해석]

103. All residential applicants are required to provide identification with proof of address when opening a Goals Bank account.
해석]

104. Because of the hard work of our volunteers, the goal for funding the Manley Art Museum's restoration has been met.
해석]

105. If no other employees are in the office when you leave, please make sure to lock the door.
해석]

106. New tablet computers will be distributed to all information technology employees on April 6.
해석]

107. Ms. Harkin will be temporarily in charge of the human resources department during Mr. Vogon's brief absence.
해석]

108. There are no more Gilly's Fried Chicken restaurants left in the country, except the original one in Flagstaff.
해석]

109. The photocopying of copyrighted materials is forbidden without the publisher's written authorization.
해석]

110. Passengers must check that their seat belts are securely fastened before the plane takes off and lands.
해석]

★어휘 NOTE

111. Nelson Lenses boasts such an extensive amount of choices that you're sure to get just what you want.
해석]

112. All diners at The Round Table deserve the best service regardless of whether they order a three course meal or simply an appetizer.
해석]

113. The mayor and his wife were happy with the photographs that Karl Ingram took of them for the newspaper.
해석]

114. Johnson Medical Center's mission is to match each patient with medical professionals who can personally address their needs.
해석]

115. The employee manual details packing techniques for shipping products without damaging any merchandise.
해석]

116. By actively integrating the latest technology with their products, Polton Computers has increased its market share.
해석]

117. Please speak with your manager if you wish to attend the professional development seminar on Monday.
해석]

118. Books in every section are on sale for up to 70 percent off at Calvin Booksellers this weekend.
해석]

119. The interpersonal communication seminar seems to have helped increase productivity in all departments.
해석]

120. Articles from Science Monthly Journal may not be reprinted without written consent from the publication's editor.
해석]

121. Employees were notified by a memo issued this week about a position opening in the sales department.
해석]

★ 어휘 NOTE

122. If you would like to receive a special gift voucher valid at any Livwell store locations, simply complete a short survey placed in the lobby.

해석]

123. Notices on recent changes to bus routes are prominently displayed at all Belleton Public Transit bus stops.

해석]

124. The Menoly Metals' researchers use statistically sound research methods to create an incredibly strong steel to be used for construction.

해석]

125. Given the increased demand for Polver's new line of winter coats, the company has hired more factory workers to increase production.

해석]

126. To improve the comfort of our guests, the Liberty Inn offers convenient access to transportation and shopping.

해석]

127. Bill's Car Repair has a high level of customer satisfaction largely because it repairs cars more quickly than its competitors do.

해석]

128. A majority of workplace injuries are easily preventable with proper safety training and supervision.

해석]

129. Telson Insurance Company has attributed its success primarily to the dedication of its sales and customer service agents.

해석]

130. To ensure records are complete, accounting department employees must take the initiative in asking other departments for their expense reports.

해석]

*어휘 NOTE

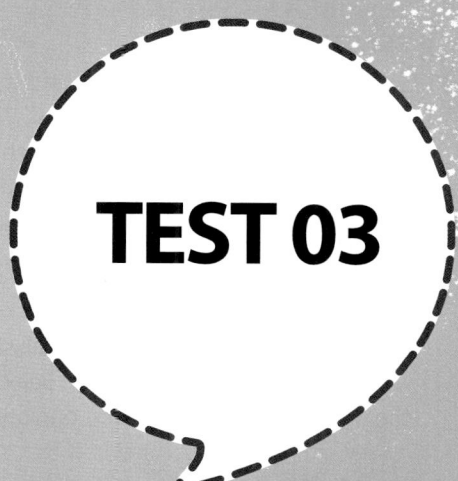

동시토익 CONTEMPORARY **TOEIC**

TEST 03

READING TEST

In the Reading test, you will read a variety of texts and answer several different types of reading comprehension questions. The entire Reading test will last 75 minutes. There are three parts, and directions are given for each part. You are encouraged to answer as many questions as possible within the time allowed.

You must mark your answers on the separate answer sheet. Do not write your answers in your test book.

Part 5

Directions: A word or phrase is missing in each of the sentences below. Four answer choices are given below each sentence. Select the best answer to complete the sentence. Then mark the letter (A), (B), (C), or (D) on your answer sheet.

101. Elling Web Radio is _____ to offer its new online music service to music lovers on the Internet.
(A) excite
(B) excites
(C) excitedly
(D) excited

102. Sherley Banking Services provides Internet banking _____ lets customers receive a variety of support services online.
(A) either
(B) for
(C) and
(D) after

103. Cold Rock's latest line of winter jackets were all purchased almost _____ after being released in stores.
(A) slightly
(B) briefly
(C) truly
(D) immediately

104. The paperwork for the construction grant was _____ submitted before all of the items had been completed.
(A) mistake
(B) mistakenly
(C) mistook
(D) mistaken

105. Holbrook Books Online became one of the most popular online booksellers after only a _____ time.
(A) short
(B) popular
(C) long
(D) low

106. Many employees at Isen Industries began _____ careers as interns before being offered full-time positions.
(A) them
(B) theirs
(C) their
(D) they

107. _____ two to three weeks for processing of your application for the Headley Credit Card.
(A) Allows
(B) To allow
(C) Allowing
(D) Allow

108. You have until the end of next week to turn in your _____ project proposal to the head of marketing.
(A) revise
(B) revised
(C) revising
(D) revision

109. The Kitchen Appliance Expo has been postponed as many presenters' schedules conflicted _____ the Expo's timetable.
(A) down
(B) against
(C) with
(D) inside

110. According to the recent study, _____ one million deaths every year in China are caused by tobacco.
(A) approximately
(B) approximate
(C) approximated
(D) approximation

111. Mrs. Nelson will take a train to ensure she arrives in time _____ the shareholders' meeting.
(A) for
(B) there
(C) soon
(D) while

112. When you want to run your business efficiently, you need _____ with your accountant.
(A) consult
(B) consultant
(C) to consult
(D) consultative

113. _____ who wishes to apply for the supervisor position should speak to his or her direct supervisor to find out if they can be considered.
(A) Whichever
(B) Anyone
(C) Other
(D) Themselves

114. Dolton Tech's new line of laptop computers has seen increased _____ due to their eye-catching ad campaign.
(A) popularize
(B) popular
(C) popularly
(D) popularity

115. As of January 1, _____ managers will be required to attend at least three professional development seminars.
(A) every
(B) all
(C) as
(D) next

116. The marketing department's latest _____ to increase consumer's interest in the new digital camera has been partially successful.
(A) conclusion
(B) container
(C) industry
(D) attempt

117. Children two years and younger are free and are not required to show a membership card or a guest pass _____ admittance to aquatic facilities.
(A) near
(B) from
(C) between
(D) for

118. All reservations _____ through the TravelSmart Web site are eligible for a discount at the Landing Hotel's restaurant.
(A) book
(B) are booked
(C) booked
(D) will book

119. The table shows expenses for business trips made by executives _____ the last year.
(A) about
(B) between
(C) over
(D) toward

GO ON TO THE NEXT PAGE

120. _____ making a time-off request, make sure that your employee ID number is printed clearly on the form.
(A) In order to
(B) When
(C) So that
(D) As

121. The new _____ regarding overtime pay will be put into effect in the new fiscal year.
(A) likelihood
(B) procedure
(C) instruction
(D) capacity

122. The _____ of Main Street to include a bicycle lane will be completed in April.
(A) widest
(B) wider
(C) widely
(D) widening

123. To fund its continuing research in solar energy, Upton Laboratories was _____ with a grant from the Earth First Association.
(A) presented
(B) committed
(C) related
(D) attracted

124. _____ being a beautiful modern hotel, it has tremendous staff that provide very pleasant service.
(A) Consisting of
(B) In view of
(C) Besides
(D) Seeing that

125. _____ figures for this fiscal year the financial department has compiled may be found in the annual report released on March 1st.
(A) Vacant
(B) Detailed
(C) Experienced
(D) Responsive

126. _____ the ceremony for its re-opening, the Jarling Community Center underwent inspection by state and federal safety commissions.
(A) As long as
(B) While
(C) As opposed to
(D) In advance of

127. More than one-third of respondents indicated that HIV research had contributed _____ to advances in diagnostics and drug and vaccine development.
(A) substantial
(B) substantially
(C) substantive
(D) substantiate

128. _____ other employees in the marketing department, director Sylvia Gorn has attended every marketing conference held in the region.
(A) Similarly
(B) For example
(C) Like
(D) Altogether

129. All restaurant staff should make sure to inspect their work area closely in _____ for the examination from the Health Department.
(A) prediction
(B) operation
(C) preparation
(D) exception

130. After your payment is received, the total amount due on your online invoice will be adjusted _____.
(A) accordingly
(B) typically
(C) immeasurably
(D) implicitly

PART 6

Direction: Read the texts that follow. A word, phrase, or sentence is missing in parts of each text. Four answer choices for each question are given below the text. Select the best answer to complete the text. Then mark the letter (A), (B), (C), or (D) on your answer sheet.

Questions 131-134 refer to the following e-mail.

Dear Mr. Eisen,

The Sacramento Small Business Society (SSBS) has ------- your application to join our organization.
131.

We have approved your membership because your shop's reputation for customer service, commercial performance, and current member's recommendations were excellent. To finalize your membership, please ------- register your account on our Web site at www.ssbs.org.
132.

Your account ID is Sacramento Attire and your password is SA9865 until you change it. Your benefits as a member will be activated immediately after registering. -------.
133.

SSBS is sure that you'll find your membership to our organization quite -------.
134.

131. (A) submitted
   (B) started
   (C) accepted
   (D) revised

132. (A) nevertheless
   (B) immediately
   (C) elsewhere
   (D) further

133. (A) You will find details about services we provide to our members on the Web site.
   (B) Please return the attached application form at your earliest convenience.
   (C) We will let you know our decision after contacting your references.
   (D) We ask that you closely review the terms and conditions of the agreement.

134. (A) reward
   (B) rewardingly
   (C) rewards
   (D) rewarding

Question 135-138 refer to the following brochure excerpt.

Visit scenic Shireton and take one of our five walking tours to see the sights of our beautiful city. Provided by the Shireton Tourism Commission, ------- tour is conducted by an experienced guide and shows attendees remarkable parts of the city.
                                                            135.

Our most popular tour goes through Selby Plaza, part of the city's art -------. Selby Plaza has three
                                                                        136.
independent galleries as well as the city's municipal art museum and several hotels known for their striking architecture. Overall, the tour takes about three hours and ------- with dinner at one of the
                                                                                              137.
spectacular restaurants in the plaza. -------. Make sure to ask your tour guide which restaurants
                                       138.
participate in this discount program.

Sign up for a tour today by visiting the Shireton Tourism Commission office or by calling 555-3756.

135. (A) either
(B) each
(C) whose
(D) this

136. (A) actors
(B) programs
(C) district
(D) school

137. (A) exits
(B) orders
(C) reserves
(D) concludes

138. (A) Some restaurants offer discounts for tour participants.
(B) The plaza is one of the most popular tourist destinations.
(C) The Shireton Tourism Commission plans tours all year long.
(D) Taking pictures in the museum is strictly prohibited.

Questions 139-142 refer to the following e-mail.

From: customercare@webshop.com
To: hcollins@kld.com
Date: April 24
Subject: Purchase #684633

Dear Mr. Collins,

Your purchase (#684633) has been -------. We have shipped two items of your purchase to the address listed on your account and they should arrive within seven business days. -------, we were unable to ship the third item of your purchase.

139. **140.**

The Lansing Bluetooth Headset in silver color will not be ------- for shipping until May 14. We are sorry for any inconvenience you may experience because of this. If you would like to cancel this part of your order before it is available, please contact our customer service department at service@jollystore.com. -------.

141. **142.**

We greatly appreciate your patronage.

Regards,

Georgia Smith
Customer Care Associate, Web Shop

139. (A) delivered
(B) processed
(C) canceled
(D) repaired

140. (A) Whereas
(B) Consequently
(C) Rather
(D) Unfortunately

141. (A) availability
(B) availabilities
(C) available
(D) availably

142. (A) Otherwise, we will send out the last part of your order as soon as it is in stock.
(B) We will ship your entire order after the last part has arrived.
(C) Lansing Bluetooth Headsets have consistently received favorable reviews.
(D) Our customer service department will be closed over the weekend.

GO ON TO THE NEXT PAGE

Questions 143-146 refer to the following announcement.

The Bradford Gallery will hold an exhibition of Belinda Hartness' latest collection titled 'Humans of Brasilia'. The exhibition shows vivid images of ------- life and the people who live it and will be on
143.
display at the gallery from February 12 to March 1.

Large cities are a major focus of Ms. Harness' -------, due largely to her youth spent in New York,
144.
Paris, and Bangkok.

Ms. Hartness works as a curator at the Score Museum in Chicago. Ms. Hartness has had her work, ------- for her unique camera angles, displayed in museums all around the world. -------.
145. 146.

143. (A) traditional
(B) urban
(C) marine
(D) agricultural

144. (A) poems
(B) performances
(C) sculptures
(D) photographs

145. (A) knowing
(B) know
(C) known
(D) knew

146. (A) Her last exhibition held in Paris, France garnered critical acclaim.
(B) Humans of Brasilia has received many positive reviews.
(C) Ms. Hartness prefers to open her exhibitions in large cities.
(D) Ms. Hartness has decided to move into the field of sculpture.

PART 7

Direction: In this part you will read a selection of texts, such as magazine and newspaper articles, letters, e-mails, and instant messages. Each text or set of texts is followed by several questions. Select the best answer for each question and mark the letter (A), (B), (C), or (D) on your answer sheet.

Questions 147~148 refer to the following advertisement.

Gardening Company

Our company in Acorn Valley is looking for a skilled and competent receptionist. This person will have a variety of duties including greeting customers, receiving and forwarding phone calls, and taking messages. Excellent file organization skills are required, as are some skills in dealing with copy and fax machines and other office machinery.

It is necessary for the candidate to have a background in graphic design. The hourly wage for this position is $14 – 16 per hour.

147. What position is available?
(A) Service associate
(B) Landscaper
(C) Receptionist
(D) Secretary

148. What kind of experience is NOT required for the job?
(A) Document filing
(B) Gardening skills
(C) Phone operation
(D) Graphic design

Questions 149-150 refer to the following advertisement.

Nightingale

Messages by Song

Nightingale Singing Telegram Artists have been helping people to celebrate their special days or send congratulations in a fun manner. Our Nightingales have been a great way to send messages with songs to a wide range of occasions such as birthday parties, anniversary celebrations, graduation parties, and more. We also provide service of surprise appearances by our entertainers.

Think that you could be a Nightingale?

Applicants that can play instruments like guitar or accordion are very likely to succeed. Just send us a short video showing your abilities. Videos should be sent with contact information to Gerald Silver, p.o. box 43, Rockford, IL 61101

149. What is the purpose of the advertisement?
(A) To advertise a special event
(B) To profile an acting troupe
(C) To solicit more staff
(D) To promote a new company

150. What is indicated about the artists who work at Nightingale?
(A) They travel to work at various work sites.
(B) They have to buy work outfits.
(C) They will graduate from university soon.
(D) They record videos at parties.

Questions 151-152 refer to the following memo.

NOTICE

To: Staff members
From: Accounting
Date: August 8
Subject: Reporting hours

In order to make salary payments more efficient and timely, the accounting department will implement a new system for reporting hours online. From September 3, employees will have to report the hours they have worked every week on a Web site managed by our company. The human resources department will train all staff on how to enter the information in the system on August 23 in Conference Room 24. Please choose a session from the list posted outside near the door of Conference Room 24.

151. What is the purpose of the notice?
(A) To confirm that a payment has been received
(B) To inform members of a postponed delivery
(C) To tell staff about a new procedure
(D) To ask staff to register on a Web site

152. Why should employees go to the conference room on August 23?
(A) To have a conference with the accounting department
(B) To take a class about a new system
(C) To enroll in a direct deposit program for paychecks
(D) To learn about a new process for promotions

Questions 153-155 refer to the following advertisement.

Donna's Donuts
89 Main Street in Havelin
635-555-4684

After your first bite of a donut from Donna's Donuts, you won't want to get a donut anywhere else. Our shop is right in the middle of Main Street, and offers treats and beverages for people of all ages. We also have private study rooms for students from local schools.

At Donna's Donuts, you can find:
- Over 50 different kinds of donuts made in our store with ingredients from local businesses.
- A flavorful selection of coffee and tea.
- Healthy breakfast items like whole grain muffins and cereal bars
- Free access to wireless Internet for our customers.

Open from Monday to Saturday from 8 a.m. to 8 p.m.
Open until 9:30 p.m. during the summer, from June to September.
On Thursdays, children under 5 can get a free small juice at 50% off the normal price.

153. What is mentioned about Donna's Donuts?
(A) Its donuts are produced in the shop.
(B) Its food is available in local grocery stores.
(C) It is operated by a family.
(D) It has opened a new branch.

154. According to the advertisement, what happens in June?
(A) The hours of operation change.
(B) The study rooms are not available.
(C) The store employs university students.
(D) The beverage choices change.

155. What is indicated about the discount?
(A) It applies to breakfast items.
(B) It is good for any kind of donut.
(C) It is only for returning customers.
(D) It is available just for one day every week.

Questions 156-157 refer to the following text message chain.

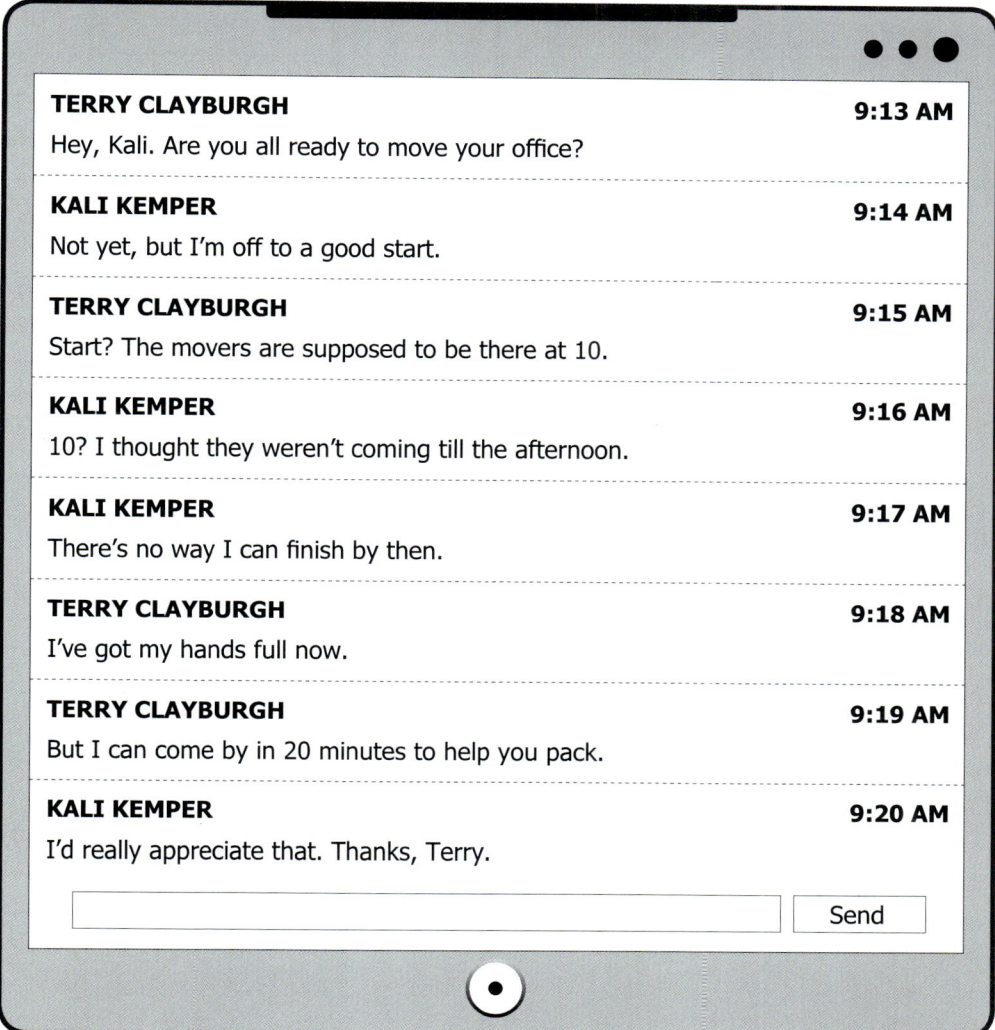

156. What is indicated about Kali Kemper?
(A) She is changing her workspace location.
(B) She is a subordinate of Mr. Clayburgh.
(C) She is currently working on a presentation.
(D) She lost her schedule book.

157. At 9:18 AM, what does Terry Clayburgh mean when he writes, "I've got my hands full now"?
(A) He is carrying a moving box.
(B) He is talking on the phone.
(C) He is very busy at the moment.
(D) He is on his way to Ms. Kemper's office.

Questions 158-160 refer to the following e-mail.

From :	fredad@fredassandwiches.com
To :	aaronlee@webpost.com
Date :	April 15
Subject :	This week

Dear Mr. Lee.

Since you're a frequent visitor to our restaurant, you'll be happy to hear that next week, Freda's Sandwiches will have the "$5 Hero Special" return. This means you can get a large hero sandwich, which is normally $9, from our shop for only $5.

This special includes all of the sandwiches below:

Chicken	Beef	Vegetarian
Five Alarm Chicken Indian Chicken Curry Chinese Chicken	Blue Cow Classic Cheesesteak The Bullhorn Cow Over the Moon	Mondo Avacado. Artichoke Avalanche Cheesy Cheese and Such.

To make a reservation during our busy lunch time, you can visit our Web site at www.fredassandwiches.com. This deal is only available from April 20 to April 26.

See you next week!

Freda Dee
Owner & Head Cook

Freda's Sandwiches

158. Why was the email sent?
(A) To advertise a newly released cookbook
(B) To publicize a new sandwich
(C) To give directions to a restaurant
(D) To provide details about a promotion

159. What is suggested about Mr. lee?
(A) He used to work at Freda's Sandwiches.
(B) He recommended Freda's Sandwiches to his friend.
(C) He is a regular customer of Freda's Sandwiches.
(D) He made a reservation for lunch at Freda's Sandwiches.

160. What is indicated about Freda's Sandwiches?
(A) It is not open in the morning.
(B) It has extensive seating.
(C) It can accept reservations on its Web site.
(D) It is famous for its quality.

Questions 161-163 refers to the following letter.

Sharpton Commercial Consultation

May 19
Lawrence Sturdevant
8655 Heights Avenue
Atlanta, GE 30003

Dear Mr. Sturdevant,

This letter is to confirm the presentation that you will be giving at the conference hosted by Sharpton Commercial Consultation from September 10 to September 12 in Tulsa, Oklahoma. Your presentation will be on September 11.

I wish to also extend an invitation to a dinner and reception following the conclusion of the conference at the Hollings Grace Convention Hall at 7 p.m., on the second floor of where the conference will be held. —[1]—.

My secretary, Gloria Bingham, has made an arrangement for your accommodations during the visit to Tulsa. —[2]—. The Plaza Hotel is a convenient and comfortable lodging. It is within walking distance from the conference hall.

Please remember that our legal and our public relations departments will have to authorize the content of your presentation before the conference. —[3]—.

Our company has heard many good things about your work in online marketing techniques, so I am looking forward to getting to meet you and find out more about your work. —[4]—.

Sincerely,

Harriet Manning
Harriet Manning
Senior Director, Employee Advancement Techniques.

161. Where will Mr. Sturdevant be giving a presentation?
    (A) At a hotel
    (B) At a convention center
    (C) At the main office of a company
    (D) At a law firm

162. What is NOT mentioned in the letter?
    (A) A conference timetable
    (B) A social gathering
    (C) a place to stay
    (D) A date of the presentation

163. In which of the positions marked [1], [2], [3], and [4] does the following sentence best belong?

    "Please send a complete copy of what you plan to present to our office as soon as you can."

    (A) [1]
    (B) [2]
    (C) [3]
    (D) [4]

Questions 164-167 refer to the following advertisement.

Borland Career Development Center

If you'd like to get valuable experience and training for your career, the Borland Career Development Center offers seminars and courses from February 2 for those on a tight schedule.

- Newly added: Two-day seminars on weekends.
- Newly added: Online classes that can be accessed any time.
- Additional evening classes available all week

Borland is the best place for career advancement for jobs in the finance, management, and marketing fields. We offer courses taught by experienced, qualified instructors for beginner, intermediate, and advanced individuals at competitive prices.

Borland has won several awards for its classes, including this year's Most Inventive Course from the Committee for Post-Secondary Education.

You can find more details about class offerings, tuition, and costs by visiting www.borlandcenter.edu. Or simply register by calling (684)555-0686.

164. What is the purpose of the advertisement?
    (A) To advertise an updated schedule
    (B) To announce lower tuition costs
    (C) To search for new instructors
    (D) To explain recent managerial changes

165. How has Borland been changed?
    (A) By changing all class schedules to the evening
    (B) By offering Web-based classes
    (C) By concentrating only on managerial programs
    (D) By arranging seminars at various companies

166. What is NOT indicated about Borland?
    (A) It offers classes related to business.
    (B) It helps students of multiple levels.
    (C) It employs professional instructors.
    (D) It assists students in finding jobs.

167. What reason for visiting the Web site is mentioned in the advertisement?
    (A) To enroll in seminars during the weekend
    (B) To find fees for classes
    (C) To receive the center's awards
    (D) To review teachers' qualifications

Questions 168-171 refer to the following letter.

Salkin Publications
896 Harroldson Road
Portland, OR 97220

September 15

Dear Investors:

Salkin Publications' executive committee has decided to accept the merger deal offered by the Cole Publishing Company. In order for the merger to happen, a majority of our investors as well as the Federal Communications Agency, which makes regulations for publishers and communications companies, have to also approve the merger. —[1]—.

The executive committee is sure that the merger would be beneficial for our company. Even though our company has not been as profitable as planned over the last two years, we think it is possible to turn this around with this merger. —[2]—. Cole Publishing Company is a successful non-fiction publishing company and has had its multiple titles on best-seller lists alongside our own. They have also started endeavors in electronic publishing, as we have, which have been successful. Salkin Publications will hold a meeting for our investors on November 14 at our main office to decide whether to approve the merger. —[3]—.

We have enclosed a copy of the agreement with Cole Publishing Company and the results of an financial and marketing examination of Cole Publishing conducted by an outside consulting firm with this letter. —[4]—. We ask that you look these over prior to making your decision.

On behalf of the entire board of directors, thank you for your actions in this matter.

Regards,

Bill Carlin
Executive Committee Director

Enclosure

168. What does the letter recommend?
(A) Challenging a new competitor
(B) Approving a merger with a company
(C) Discussing online voting
(D) Increasing a division's work

169. What is true of both companies?
(A) They have their products in electronic versions.
(B) They have their main offices in Minneapolis.
(C) They have not been successful with their recent publication.
(D) They print fiction novels.

170. What is included with the letter?
(A) Details about Cole Publishing Company's consulting firm
(B) A study of Cole Publishing Company's financial situation
(C) Instructions on how to get to Salkin Publications' main office
(D) A copy of Salkin Publications' latest release

171. In which of the positions marked [1], [2], [3], and [4] does the following sentence best belong?

"A similar decision will be made by Cole Publishing Company investors at its main office in Minneapolis on November 20."

(A) [1]
(B) [2]
(C) [3]
(D) [4]

Questions 172-175 refer to the following online chat discussion.

Online Chat

Clay Hutchman [4:07 p.m.] How's the work going on updating the computers in the sales department? We're supposed to get started on computers in accounting tomorrow.

Donna Caviezel [4:08 p.m.] We had a bit of a problem when we found that one of the computers had a virus on it. It also sent the virus to three other computers before we were able to clear it. We still have to update about 10 more computers.

Clay Hutchman [4:09 p.m.] 10 more? That's going to take at least five hours. Where did the virus come from?

Donna Caviezel [4:10 p.m.] It looks like Kate Surjik got it sent to her email and opened the message without scanning it first. We made sure to update her anti-virus programs. It's good that we were able to catch it, though. We almost had to go back to square one.

Clay Hutchman [4:12 p.m.] Still, I'm going to need a few people to stay late to make sure that the sales computers are all updated. Is anyone able to?

Donna Caviezel [4:14 p.m.] You know I can't. I already had plans to go to a concert with my sister. I have to get out of here right at 5 to get ready.

Omar Hooks [4:16 p.m.] I don't mind staying, Clay. I can stick it out until at least 10 o'clock tonight. If I'm not able to get all the computers updated by then, I'll get in early tomorrow to finish up.

Clay Hutchman [4:17 p.m.] Thanks, Omar. I appreciate it. I'll order some pizza. Anything special you want on it?

Omar Hooks [4:18 p.m.] Pepperoni and sausage is fine with me. Thanks

172. Which department do the writers most likely work in?
(A) Sales
(B) Accounting
(C) Information technology
(D) Distribution

173. What is indicated about the computers in accounting?
(A) They downloaded a virus.
(B) They were recently purchased.
(C) They have yet to be updated.
(D) They are faster than the computers in sales.

174. At 4:16 p.m., what does Omar Hooks mean when he writes, "I can stick it out"?
(A) He will fix a problem with a damaged computer.
(B) He is able to keep working into the evening.
(C) He can start working on the accounting computers now.
(D) He is able to remove a stuck computer component.

175. What is most likely true about Kate Surjik?
(A) She works in the sales department.
(B) She recently began working at the company.
(C) She receives many email messages.
(D) She doesn't have an anti-virus program on her computer.

Questions 176-180 refer to the following letter and information.

Singer Publications
883 Alameda Street
Norman, OK 73070

June 19
Diana Ballard
144 Switzer Canyon Drive
Flagstaff, AZ 86001

Dear Ms. Ballard,

We are very pleased to work with you as a new contributor to our Singer Tour Guide Series. Based on the contract that you signed, you will need to send an invoice detailing work that has already been approved by the tour guide's senior editor. Please include your contact information, the series and edition of the guide you're working on, and your direct editor's name in the invoice. Please send the invoice to me and I'll forward it to our accounting department. You'll have to talk to Mr. Lafferty about how to submit an invoice for your photographs since our imaging department has a different invoice form that they use. I suspect they will send this to you soon if they haven't already.

Regards,
Amanda Neeson

Singer Publications

Teams for Ongoing Projects

Series Titles	Travel & Tales Picture Diaries	Singer Tour Guide Series	** Around the Globe Series
Senior Editor	Kelly Daniels	Eva Gideon	Roy Becker
Image Editor	Melissa Franco	Damon Lafferty	Melissa Franco
Office Coordinator	Harriet Barry	Amanda Neeson	Samuel Coogan

** Please remember that we will be hiring a new employee to work with Mr. Becker and Mr. Coogan so that Ms. Franco will have more time to focus on the other publication, Travel & Tales Picture Diaries, which involves the release of another issue soon.

176. What does the letter explain?
(A) How to receive compensation
(B) How to turn in tour pictures
(C) How to publish assigned articles
(D) How to apply for project positions

177. What is NOT mentioned in the letter?
(A) Ms. Neeson receives invoices from contracted writers.
(B) Ms. Neeson supervises projects for travel pictures.
(C) Ms. Ballard recently completed a writing project.
(D) Ms. Ballard took pictures for her written work.

178. In the letter, the word "suspect" in paragraph 1, line 7 is closest in meaning to
(A) believe
(B) hope
(C) distrust
(D) accuse

179. What is most likely true about Ms. Gideon?
(A) She recently began working at Singer Publications.
(B) She cooperates with Ms. Franco on many projects.
(C) She has already approved an agreement with Ms. Ballard.
(D) She trained the office coordinators.

180. According to the information provided with the table, how are project assignments going to be changed?
(A) The Travel & Tales Picture Diary team will work on a new project.
(B) The senior editors for each team will rotate to new projects.
(C) A fourth project team is being created.
(D) One of the teams will have a new image editor.

Questions 181-185 refer to the following information and letter.

Policy and Procedure for Borrowing Materials

Materials housed in the Bolivian Institute of Arts (BIA) can be loaned for the purposes of exhibitions or research exclusively to other museums, universities, and institutions. To request loans of materials, a written request must be sent to the senior curator of BIA. Additionally, any organization borrowing materials must properly cite BIA as the lending institution for the materials. Loans are made for a maximum of twelve months.

The institute's collections committee thoroughly reviews all requests for borrowing materials before making recommendations to the general director, who then make a final decision. Loan applications can take up to four weeks to process. As BIA receives the significant amount of requests and there are a lot of preparatory work generally required to transfer items, applicants should submit their requests at least six months before the materials are needed.

The Portuguese Museum of Fine Arts

948 R. da Liberdade
Lisbon, Portugal

23 March

Ms. Camila Amparo
P.O. Box 67336
Cochabamba, Bolivia

Dear Ms. Amparo,

The Portuguese Museum of Fine Arts plans to hold an exhibition entitled South American Modern Art and we are hoping that your organization will grant approval to our museum for borrowing some pieces of fine art that are housed in the Bolivian Institute of Arts so that we can display them along with other pieces of fine art we already hold in our collection. Some local businesses are providing funding for the exhibition. We'd also like to make some poster-sized prints of the pieces that we borrow so that we may sell them in our gift shop.

Below are the pieces we wish to borrow as we believe they are wonderful examples of Bolivian artistic endeavors.

1. Ascension, photograph by Veronica Baros
2. Rios Blanco Y Negro, watercolor painting by Jose Ochoa
3. Chiquitos, Sculpture by Arturo Francisco

According to the requirements on your Web site, we have included information regarding physical attributes of our facility, including building dimensions, temperatures and humidity levels of each wing, security protocols and equipment, storage, and lighting. Please contact me if you have any questions or need more information.

Regards,

Adriana Mendes, Senior Director
Adriana Mendes, Senior DirectorHillary Edgars

181. According to the information, what is true about the Bolivian Institute of Arts?
(A) It receives very few requests for borrowing materials.
(B) It makes loans of a maximum of three pieces.
(C) It does not lend materials to individuals.
(D) It makes loans for up to six months only.

182. What is NOT indicated about the loan decisions?
(A) They involve multiple people.
(B) They take less than a month to make.
(C) Information about the borrowing organization is taken into account.
(D) Priority is given to exhibits focusing on Bolivia.

183. Who is Ms. Amparo?
(A) The senior curator
(B) The institute's committee member
(C) The general director
(D) An official of the business funding the exhibition

184. What is mentioned about the special exhibition?
(A) It will include only borrowed pieces.
(B) It will include various types of art.
(C) It will feature artists' profiles.
(D) It will be open for twelve months.

185. What will mostly likely be printed on the posters?
(A) Pictures of Portugal
(B) Instructions on taking care of pieces of art
(C) Recognition of the lending museum
(D) A map of South America

Questions 186–190 refer to the following letter, information, and e-mail.

August 10

Dear Mr. Arkson,

Since you are a senior member of the Serene Astronomy Society (SAS), we request your participation in making choices that may alter the way our society is managed. Later next week, we will send a voting form to you to decide whether funds that we now use for the publication can be used to buy a new telescope. Clayton Planetarium is no longer able to offer us time on the Mount Aster Telescope. Therefore, unless our proposal is approved, the Mount Aster Discussions will consist solely of guided discussions.

A new telescope will greatly benefit our group, even though we would need to temporarily cease printing our magazine, Galaxy Visions, for six months to allocate funds for the purchase. We appreciate your help in the matter which concerns how our organization will run.

Haley Franz
Director, Serene Astronomy Society

Serene Astronomy Society

Services for Members

* The Astronomer's Friend – Our email newsletter features news about SAS, a monthly schedule, and current events about the field of astronomy.

* Galaxy Visions – Our magazine delivered to you every month, featuring advice about star gazing, stories relating to astronomical science, and reviews of books about astronomy.

* Mount Aster Discussions – Gladys McDonald, a researcher at the Clayton Planetarium, hosts weekly discussions at the Mount Aster Telescope at the planetarium for talking about and looking at astronomical objects.

To: SAS Members <members@sereneastronomysociety.org>
From: Steve Azzara <sazzara@sereneastronomysociety.org>
Date: September 2
Subject: New host

Dear Members,

We regret to inform you that Gladys McDonald has informed us that she will no longer be a member of our organization. The reason for her departure is because she is moving across the country and will no longer be able to fulfill her duties in our association.

However, we are happy to say that Taylor Vasquez, a co-worker of Ms. McDonald, has volunteered his services and will be taking on Ms. McDonald's duties at the SAS Research Center from September 5.

Sincerely,

Steve Azzara
Associate Director, Galactic Study Association

186. What is the purpose of the letter?
(A) To report a change in leadership
(B) To detail a change to a process
(C) To encourage members to subscribe to a publication
(D) To call attention to a vote

187. What is Mr. Arkson asked to do?
(A) Support an equipment purchase
(B) Look over a group calendar
(C) Change the date of a meeting
(D) Recommend a new venue for gathering

188. In the letter, the word "concerns" in paragraph 2, line 3 is closest in meaning to
(A) complicates
(B) worries
(C) involves
(D) intrigues

189. What might be unavailable through SAS for six months?
(A) Decreased equipment costs
(B) Reviews of astronomy publications
(C) Details about astronomy researchers
(D) Chances to get together with other members

190. What will Taylor Vasquez manage from September 5?
(A) The Astronomer's Friend
(B) Galaxy Visions
(C) Mount Aster Discussions
(D) Budget of SAS

Questions 191-195 refer to the following contract, customer survey, and e-mail.

Victorin Rentals

Equipment Rental Agreement   Date: May 10

This contract between Victorin Rentals and The Cornwell Company is for event furniture to be rented on May 29. The furniture will be delivered directly to the location of the event: The Cornwell Company, 668 Heston Avenue, Lawrence, KS 66046. The delivery will be made at 3 p.m. on May 29 and should be ready for return and pick-up by 9 a.m. on May 30. Claire Dinsley, coordinator hired by the company for the event has stated she will be at the location for both delivery and pick up.

Chairs and tables will be set up by employees of Victorin Rentals by 3:30 p.m. at the latest on the day of delivery. The Cornwall Company has agreed to prepare the furniture for pick-up by 9 a.m. at the latest. Extra charges will be incurred if the rented equipment are not cleaned, folded, and stacked on time.

Victorin Rentals

Thank you for choosing us for your service.

Rental Item	Quantity	Cost/unit	Subtotal
Folding chairs	49	$2.00	$98.00
Type LS9 tables	7	$9.00	$63.00
Charge for delivery			$40.00
TOTAL:			$201.00
Shipping Address:		520 Heston Ave Gloversville, MA	
Renter : Claire Dinsley		Sales Representative : Steven Finworth	

Victorin Rentals

To our patron:

Victorin Rentals greatly appreciates your business. Please take a moment to fill out this questionnaire so we can further improve our services.

	Great	Good	Fair	Poor
Rental items quality		×		
Notes:	The furnishings that were delivered were clean and of good quality			
Delivery and preparation of items				×
Notes:	The delivery staff first went to our office on Vine Street instead of the Heston Avenue location. They came to the event location after realizing their mistake, but were 30 minutes late. The delivery supervisor, Nancy Lester, helped everything get prepared quickly, so this was not a big problem. Ms. Lester also said that the charge for that service would be refunded because of the lateness.			
General satisfaction with Victorin Rentals		×		
Notes:	I'll certainly use Victorin Rentals again in July for another event. The service was mostly good and they have the lowest rental prices in the area.			
Patron:	*Claire Dinsley*			

191. What is Claire Dinsley's job?
(A) Professional event planner
(B) Furniture mover
(C) Delivery manager
(D) Agent for a rental company

192. What is suggested about The Cornwell Company?
(A) It has rented from Victorin before.
(B) It plans to buy new furniture.
(C) It has multiple offices.
(D) It is relocating its main office.

193. In the contract, the word "pick up" in paragraph 1, line 4, is closest in meaning to
(A) break down
(B) follow up
(C) take back
(D) catch up

194. What is the amount of the expected refund?
(A) $9
(B) $40
(C) $63
(D) $98

195. What is suggested in the questionnaire about Victorin Rentals?
(A) It sent Steven Finworth to manage the Cornwell gathering.
(B) Its supply rental prices are not as expensive as other companies.
(C) Its delivery team was not on time to retrieve the supplies.
(D) It provided supplies that were of low quality.

Questions 196-200 refer to the following e-mail, survey, and letter.

* E-mail *

From: Michael Higgins
To: Development Division Employees
Date: March 27
Subject: Business Innovation Convention

I'm writing this to remind the staff from our development division who are working at our exhibit at the Business Innovation Convention in Maldives next month that the block of rooms for our staff at the Blue Clam Hotel must be reserved by the end of next week. The final deadline for making reservations is Tuesday, April 4. Employees who have access to a company credit card should make their reservations as soon as possible.

If we don't complete all of our reservations by April 4, then the nightly rate for the hotel rooms will increase greatly, from $110.00 to $220.00

Michael Higgins, Operations Director

Atlas Laboratories

Thank you for staying at Blue Clam Hotel. If there's anything we can do to make any future stays better, please let us know.

Guest name: Robert Paulson
Date of stay: April 21 – April 23

How was the cleanliness of your room?

_____ Very Satisfied __X__ Satisfied _____ Dissatisfied _____ Very dissatisfied

How were the hotel's facilities?

_____ Very Satisfied _____ Satisfied __X__ Dissatisfied _____ Very dissatisfied

How was the service of our hotel staff?

_____ Very Satisfied _____ Satisfied _____ Dissatisfied __X__ Very dissatisfied

Additional comments:

I stayed here during a convention and was pleased with my room. However, during my stay, the business center was being renovated and there were no options for printing documents. I had to use a print shop down the street. The worst part is that I was charged the wrong rate for my room and the check-in staff didn't know how to change this. The manager was not available, so I asked to be contacted later to resolve the problem. I don't think I'll be staying here again.

Blue Clam Hotel

April 29

Robert Paulson
Development Division
Atlas Laboratories
289 DeLuca Drive
Sacramento, CA 94246

Dear Mr. Paulson,

I am very sorry for the mistake we made in processing your invoice. You are right that your room rate should have been the Business Innovation Convention room rate and we charged the normal rate to your company credit card. Some of our new front desk staff were not familiar with the process for checking in a guest with the Convention room rate.

I have included a corrected copy of your invoice, as you requested, so that you may file it with your expense report at your company's accounting division. Please contact me if you need anything else. Thank you again for staying at the Blue Clam Hotel

Regards,

Fatima Benzi
Manager
Blue Clam Hotel

---

196. Why did Mr. Higgins ask that hotel reservations be made quickly?
(A) To receive a discount on nightly room rates
(B) To fulfill a contract with Ms. Banes
(C) Because the expiration date on the company credit card will pass
(D) Because the hotel did not have many rooms left

197. In the e-mail, the word "block" in paragraph 1, line 2 is closest in meaning to
(A) barrier
(B) group
(C) design
(D) structure

198. What is suggested about Mr. Paulson?
(A) He goes to the Business Innovation Convention yearly.
(B) He works with the Atlas Laboratories accounting division.
(C) He made his payment for the hotel room with his own credit card.
(D) He made a reservation by April 4.

199. What did Mr. Paulson ask Ms. Benzi to send to him?
(A) Directions for reserving a room on a Web site
(B) A coupon for a free night at the hotel
(C) Details about the hotel's reservation procedure
(D) A summary of his expenses at the hotel

200. What is indicated about Ms. Benzi?
(A) She also attended the convention.
(B) She was not at the hotel when Mr. Paulson checked in.
(C) She manages multiple hotels in the area.
(D) She responds to all guests' complaints personally.

Stop! This is the end of the test. If you finish before time is called, you may go back to Parts 5, 6, and 7 and check your work.

동시토익 실전 WORKBOOK

101. Elling Web Radio is excited to offer its new online music service to music lovers on the Internet.
해석]

102. Sherley Banking Services provides Internet banking and lets customers receive a variety of support services online.
해석]

103. Cold Rock's latest line of winter jackets were all purchased almost immediately after being released in stores.
해석]

104. The paperwork for the construction grant was mistakenly submitted before all of the items had been completed.
해석]

105. Holbrook Books Online became one of the most popular online booksellers after only a short time.
해석]

106. Many employees at Isen Industries began their careers as interns before being offered full-time positions.
해석]

107. Allow two to three weeks for processing of your application for the Headley Credit Card.
해석]

108. You have until the end of next week to turn in your revised project proposal to the head of marketing.
해석]

109. The Kitchen Appliance Expo has been postponed as many presenters' schedules conflicted with the Expo's timetable.
해석]

110. According to the recent study, approximately one million deaths every year in China are caused by tobacco.
해석]

111. Mrs. Nelson will take a train to ensure she arrives in time for the shareholders' meeting.
해석]

*어휘 NOTE

112. When you want to run your business efficiently, you need to consult with your accountant.

해석]

113. Anyone who wishes to apply for the supervisor position should speak to his or her direct supervisor to find out if they can be considered.

해석]

114. Dolton Tech's new line of laptop computers has seen increased popularity due to their eye-catching ad campaign.

해석]

115. As of January 1, all managers will be required to attend at least three professional development seminars.

해석]

116. The marketing department's latest attempt to increase consumer's interest in the new digital camera has been partially successful.

해석]

117. Children two years and younger are free and are not required to show a membership card or a guest pass for admittance to aquatic facilities.

해석]

118. All reservations booked through the TravelSmart Web site are eligible for a discount at the Landing Hotel's restaurant.

해석]

119. The table shows expenses for business trips made by executives over the last year.

해석]

120. When making a time-off request, make sure that your employee ID number is printed clearly on the form.

해석]

121. The new procedure regarding overtime pay will be put into effect in the new fiscal year.

해석]

★ 어휘 NOTE

122. The widening of Main Street to include a bicycle lane will be completed in April.

해석]

123. To fund its continuing research in solar energy, Upton Laboratories was presented with a grant from the Earth First Association.

해석]

124. Besides being a beautiful modern hotel, it has tremendous staff that provide very pleasant service.

해석]

125. Detailed figures for this fiscal year the financial department has compiled may be found in the annual report released on March 1st.

해석]

126. In advance of the ceremony for its re-opening, the Jarling Community Center underwent inspection by state and federal safety commissions.

해석]

127. More than one-third of respondents indicated that HIV research had contributed substantially to advances in diagnostics and drug and vaccine development.

해석]

128. Like other employees in the marketing department, director Sylvia Gorn has attended every marketing conference held in the region.

해석]

129. All restaurant staff should make sure to inspect their work area closely in preparation for the examination from the Health Department.

해석]

130. After your payment is received, the total amount due on your online invoice will be adjusted accordingly.

해석]

*어휘 NOTE

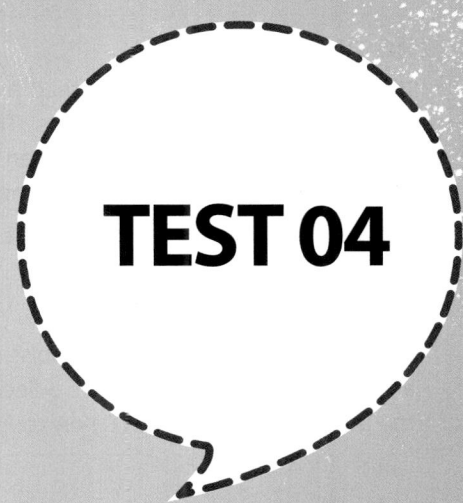

TEST 04

동시토익 CONTEMPORARY **TOEIC**

TEST 04

READING TEST

In the Reading test, you will read a variety of texts and answer several different types of reading comprehension questions. The entire Reading test will last 75 minutes. There are three parts, and directions are given for each part. You are encouraged to answer as many questions as possible within the time allowed.

You must mark your answers on the separate answer sheet. Do not write your answers in your test book.

Part 5

Directions: A word or phrase is missing in each of the sentences below. Four answer choices are given below each sentence. Select the best answer to complete the sentence. Then mark the letter (A), (B), (C), or (D) on your answer sheet.

101. The director of the new film, Halfway Down, stated that the movie is quite _____ from the book on which it is based.
(A) differs
(B) differ
(C) difference
(D) different

102. Ms. Mayner _____ secured the contract with Windhill Distribution and Supply.
(A) ease
(B) easy
(C) easiest
(D) easily

103. Television chef Carol Brinn will _____ how to make a vegetarian dinner that will satisfy your entire family on Thursday.
(A) write
(B) provide
(C) show
(D) prohibit

104. Provided that the manager's request for the purchase of new equipment receives _____, the warehouse will increase its efficiency by up to fifty percent.
(A) approval
(B) approved
(C) approve
(D) approves

105. All staff at Fulton Enterprises have the option to donate all or part of their tax refund _____ the charity of their choice.
(A) of
(B) on
(C) by
(D) to

106. Dr. Hovink was given the Bellvue _____ for his work in quantum physics.
(A) award
(B) question
(C) science
(D) participant

107. We ask that any inquiries _____ the processing of applications be directed to the human resources department.
(A) regard
(B) regards
(C) regarding
(D) regarded

108. The CEO of Tale Industries, Hillary Long, will be finalizing the candidate list for the executive position _____.
(A) herself
(B) she
(C) hers
(D) her

109. Hotshop.com will send an email _____ your purchase following the completion of your order.
(A) verification
(B) verifying
(C) verifiably
(D) verifies

110. Any expenses from meeting with clients at restaurants and other dining establishments can be _____ when filing for a tax refund.
(A) deduct
(B) deducted
(C) deductive
(D) deducting

111. Overtime payment forms need to be submitted to Mr. Argyle _____ the end of the month.
(A) since
(B) within
(C) over
(D) before

112. Stalkin Foods has hired more factory workers to meet the _____ demand for its new line of instant dinners.
(A) growing
(B) growth
(C) grow
(D) grew

113. According to our files, Dillon Electronics business license in Spain will _____ on January 2.
(A) cover
(B) expire
(C) combine
(D) install

114. Linus Construction is currently building a tower _____ will become a high-rise apartment complex.
(A) that
(B) nor
(C) yet
(D) unless

115. Mr. Potter's _____ for education was a key factor when citizens elected him as mayor of Portville.
(A) enthused
(B) enthusiastic
(C) enthusiastically
(D) enthusiasm

116. Port Industries has been _____ waste processing products for residential application for nearly a decade.
(A) instructing
(B) manufacturing
(C) practicing
(D) functioning

117. Longview Bank has provided mortgages to over 100,000 customers since its _____ a decade ago.
(A) establish
(B) established
(C) establishment
(D) establishments

118. The success of the new Helo Ultra sedan has been attributed to the unusual _____ campaign created by The Lobed Ad Agency.
(A) will market
(B) marketed
(C) marketing
(D) markets

119. The payments for the business loan have _____ been received and processed.
(A) more
(B) some
(C) all
(D) any

120. Senti Electric Company seems to have attained its goals this year, but _____ all the data have been finalized, they should be considered only projections.
(A) until
(B) yet
(C) despite
(D) still

GO ON TO THE NEXT PAGE

121. Most readers of Steven Bilk's latest novel will find it to be a very _____ story.
(A) expert
(B) observant
(C) accessible
(D) ultimate

122. Employees at the Stockton News can now refer to the updated staff directory _____ they are unsure which personnel to contact.
(A) by contrast
(B) in summary
(C) whenever
(D) rather than

123. Many diners visit Buena Cabeza for its _____ wide selection of food items.
(A) remarks
(B) remarkably
(C) remark
(D) remarked

124. Employees of Skyhigh Industries offered helpful suggestions _____ interviewed by a consultant from Baker Business Solutions.
(A) when
(B) are
(C) this
(D) from

125. Travelers on a tight budget should be aware that domestic train travel is much less _____ than traveling by plane.
(A) expensive
(B) expensively
(C) expense
(D) expenses

126. Many young people are used to posting content online but should be aware that posting personal information leaves them _____ to identity fraud.
(A) concealed
(B) alarming
(C) obtainable
(D) vulnerable

127. Manderly Enterprises has been looking for a consultant to assist with the company's _____ into the European market.
(A) expansion
(B) qualification
(C) compensation
(D) assets

128. The Hillbrook and Lakeside football clubs faced _____ during the playoffs last year, and will again in this year's championship match.
(A) one another
(B) each
(C) its own
(D) other

129. Guitarist Frank Lenster is credited with _____ the line of electric guitars produced by Excel Instruments.
(A) popularized
(B) popularizing
(C) popularize
(D) popularization

130. Master Audio's latest MP3 player is sold _____ at Portal Electronics store locations.
(A) exclusively
(B) honorably
(C) physically
(D) keenly

PART 6

Direction: Read the texts that follow. A word, phrase, or sentence is missing in parts of each text. Four answer choices for each question are given below the text. Select the best answer to complete the text. Then mark the letter (A), (B), (C), or (D) on your answer sheet.

Questions 131-134 refer to the following advertisement.

If you want to find the best deal on home appliances and electronics, make your way to the Galactic Home Super Store. For a limited time, free delivery and set-up ------- with the purchase of
131.
many home appliances or large electronic devices, such as HDTVs and projectors.

In order to qualify for this -------, the item that you buy has to have a total price of at least $200.
132.
Customers may receive free delivery only once per week.

If you have any questions about this offer or about any of the fine products we have available for you, please visit our homepage at www.galactichome.com or visit ------- local Galactic Home
133.
Super Store. -------.
134.

131. (A) providing
    (B) to provide
    (C) are being provided
    (D) has been provided

132. (A) claim
    (B) offer
    (C) trade
    (D) repair

133. (A) his
    (B) her
    (C) your
    (D) their

134. (A) This sale will start from the beginning of the summer season.
    (B) Delivery and installation can take up to three weeks to be completed.
    (C) We are currently looking to fill positions at many of our retail store branches.
    (D) Our highly qualified customer service specialists will be able to answer any questions you have.

Question 135-138 refer to the following letter.

January 10

Mr. Kevin Nordic
9784 lake Street
Duluth, MN 55808

Dear Mr. Nordic

Below is the price for the purchase and ------- of our Hydrolife Water Filtration System, which we talked about on Monday, January 6.
            135.

Overall, the cost would be $1,590 to buy the unit including labor for installing it. Please remember that this is just an -------. The actual price may be higher or lower depending on actual labor and time spent on the work. -------.
                    136.   137.

If you want to ------- with the purchase, feel free to contact me, so that we can set up an appointment. Thank you.
                138.

Pat Gilley
Hydrolife Water Filtration System

---

135. (A) installs
(B) installed
(C) installer
(D) installation

136. (A) estimate
(B) investment
(C) update
(D) attitude

137. (A) We will visit your home between the hours of 10 a.m. and 12 p.m. on Thursday.
(B) Your own water filtration system means having the purest water available at home.
(C) However, the price difference will be within $50 below or above the estimate.
(D) Our technicians are highly skilled in the field of installation.

138. (A) resign
(B) proceed
(C) work
(D) visit

Questions 139-142 refer to the following article.

JAKARTA (19 October) – From November, Indonesian Architecture Monthly will release a mobile version of their publication. It will include all print edition content, ------- features only available to mobile device subscribers.
139.

The print version of the monthly publication looks at the structure, building, innovation, and other ------- of architecture in Indonesia.
140.

-------. It ------- readers to virtually walk around Indonesia's most beautiful and intriguing Architectural structures.
141.   142.

The mobile version of Indonesia Architecture Monthly is $4.00. Please visit www.indonesiaarchitecture.com for more information.

139. (A) except for
(B) as well as
(C) even if
(D) as soon as

140. (A) elements
(B) statements
(C) measurements
(D) treatments

141. (A) Print subscriptions will not be available from the beginning of next year.
(B) Indonesian Architecture Monthly has won many awards for its print edition.
(C) Indonesia has long been known for its striking architecture.
(D) The mobile version makes this content even better.

142. (A) could have allowed
(B) will allow
(C) has been allowing
(D) is allowed

GO ON TO THE NEXT PAGE

Questions 143-146 refer to the following article.

Barton – May 28 (OH Associated News) – The manager of the Barton branch of Burke Sports Equipment, Steve Lopez has been named one of the best employees of the year by the parent company for his outstanding performance in sales.

To congratulate him on his ------- (143.), the Barton branch held a celebration on May 24 at the store. ------- (144.), he will go to the company's national convention to be held in Seattle in recognition of award receipents from all around the country.

Lopez has worked at the Barton location since the store opened last year. ------- (145.). He is sure that he ------- (146.) the trip to Seattle.

143. (A) studies
(B) promotions
(C) retirements
(D) achievements

144. (A) Provided that
(B) In addition
(C) Alternatively
(D) Consequently

145. (A) The store has been successful thanks largely to his efforts.
(B) New Burke branches will be opened in the northwest region later this year.
(C) He will be unable to take time off during the national convention.
(D) Barton is known for its enthusiastic sports community.

146. (A) enjoy
(B) will enjoy
(C) have enjoyed
(D) had been enjoying

PART 7

Direction: In this part you will read a selection of texts, such as magazine and newspaper articles, letters, e-mails, and instant messages. Each text or set of texts is followed by several questions. Select the best answer for each question and mark the letter (A), (B), (C), or (D) on your answer sheet.

Questions 147-148 refers to the following invoice.

Speed-Up Industries
289 Hadlock Avenue, Trenton, NJ 08650
(609) 555-0852

Invoice # : 984163
Date : April 23
Customer :
Daniel McCormick
55 Paulson Stree
Buffalo, NY 14220
(716) 555-3568

Product	Product No.	Quantity	Cost
Desktop PC	35796	1	$599.99
Laser printer	98633	1	$49.99
Monitor	76598	1	$329.99
	Subtotal	$979.97	
	Sales tax	$63.70	
	Shipping	$20.00	
	Down payment	$450.00	
	Total due	$613.67	

---

147. What does Speed-Up Industries sell?
(A) Security supplies
(B) Computer equipment
(C) Audio systems
(D) Home furnishings

148. What is indicated about Mr. McCormick?
(A) He will have his items delivered on April 23.
(B) He bought an extended warranty from Speed-Up Industries.
(C) He was given a discount on his purchase.
(D) He paid a portion of the total cost.

Questions 149-150 refer to the following notice.

Barton Municipal Library
298 12th Avenue, Barton VT 05822
(802) 555-2986

Member name: Mr. Felix Grimes   Library ID: 3574668

July 25

Dear Mr. Grimes,

According to our records, you have one overdue book listed below:
Summer Back East by Charles Thorn   Borrowed: April 30   Return date: June 30

We have sent two notices about this book. We ask that you return the book to any municipal libraries in the Barton area. We would also like to remind you that there is a late charge of $0.30 for every day that the book is overdue. Your total overdue charges are $7.20 as of July 25. We'd appreciate it if you take care of this matter quickly.

---

149. What is the main purpose of the notice?
(A) To promote community events
(B) To announce differences in borrowing procedures
(C) To advertise the opening of a new library
(D) To request that a member resolve an issue

150. What is indicated about the library?
(A) It received funding from Mr. Grimes.
(B) It has tried to contact Mr. Grimes before.
(C) It is considering hiring Mr. Grimes.
(D) It exchanged a purchased item with Mr. Grimes.

Questions 151-153 refer to the following advertisement.

Morton Grocery
86 Bailey Drive, Boise, ID 83719
(208) 555-6433
www.mortongrocery.com

Morton Grocery is a great choice for finding food and platters for your special event or party. Our platters are perfect for all kinds of events including corporate gatherings, birthday parties, holiday celebrations and many others

Below is a selection of our best-selling platters:

Veggie Party (for 8 – 10 people) A special mix of freshly-cut vegetables with a variety of delicious dips that are sure to please your guests. $15.00

Crazy Cookies (for 12 – 15 people) A tasty selection of cookies fresh from our bakery. Just let us know what kind of cookies you'd like and we'll arrange them. $12.00

Luxurious Lunch (For 10 – 13 people) Includes a selection of fresh meat, cheese, and gourmet bread. Chips and soft drinks are also included. $35.00

Main Dish Mania (for 7 – 9 people) Features full meals with many choices of beef, chicken, pork, and vegetarian entrees. Dishes can be customized upon request. $38 - $55

Orders of 5 or more platters can receive 10% off their order. Orders must be placed two days in advance.

---

151. What is the purpose of the advertisement?
(A) To announce a grocery store's grand opening
(B) To explain menu selections for event catering
(C) To promote new entrées at a restaurant
(D) To promote a line of individually packaged meals

152. What platter includes a beverage?
(A) Veggie Party
(B) Crazy Cookies
(C) Luxurious Lunch
(D) Main Dish Mania

153. How can customers receive a discount at Morton Grocery?
(A) By ordering platters online
(B) By ordering platters before an event
(C) By ordering at least five platters
(D) By ordering one of the main dishes

Questions 154-155 refer to the following information.

Moving and Maintenance

It is important to exercise caution when moving plants to new location so that the plants get to their destination safely and flourish in their new place. Plants should only be carried by their containers as carrying the plants by their tops can damage the plants or their roots. Different plants will require different watering techniques. Brochures detailing how to water plants you purchased properly are available for free at the store entrance.

154. For whom is the information primarily intended?
(A) Customers buying plants
(B) Container salespeople
(C) Shop employees
(D) Maintenance staff

155. What is available at no charge?
(A) Packaging
(B) Transportation
(C) Seedlings
(D) Instructional pamphlets

Questions 156-158 refer to the following e-mail.

To :	<list@corpco.com>
From :	Anna Nanders
Subject :	Computer Assistance Request #35124
Date :	May 24 2:40 p.m.

Hello, everybody.

The manager of the computer assistance department, Greg Kinderman, has told me that multiple employees have had problems with being able to connect to the Internet and e-mail accounts. Many employees have contacted the department about this and technicians have been working on the problem since this morning and it should be fixed by 4:00 p.m. We at the main office have not experienced this issue, but we understand that it has been causing problems for accounting and the marketing department in Porville. Please contact any staff in these departments via telephone if you need to. When I hear that the problem has been fixed from Mr. Kinderman, I'll send a message to everyone again.

Sincerely,

Anna Nanders
Head secretary

156. Who most likely received the e-mail?
(A) Staff at a main office
(B) Marketing employees in Porville
(C) Managers in computer assistance
(D) Accounting department staff

157. According to the e-mail, what are Mr. Kinderman's staff trying to do?
(A) Contact the main office
(B) Reconnect employees to the Internet
(C) Warn employees about an e-mail virus
(D) Send a package to Porville

158. What are recipients of the e-mail advised to do?
(A) Tell Mr. Kinderman about computer problems
(B) Report to accounting to submit documents
(C) Share computers with co-workers
(D) Use alternative ways to communicate

Questions 159-160 refer to the following text message chain.

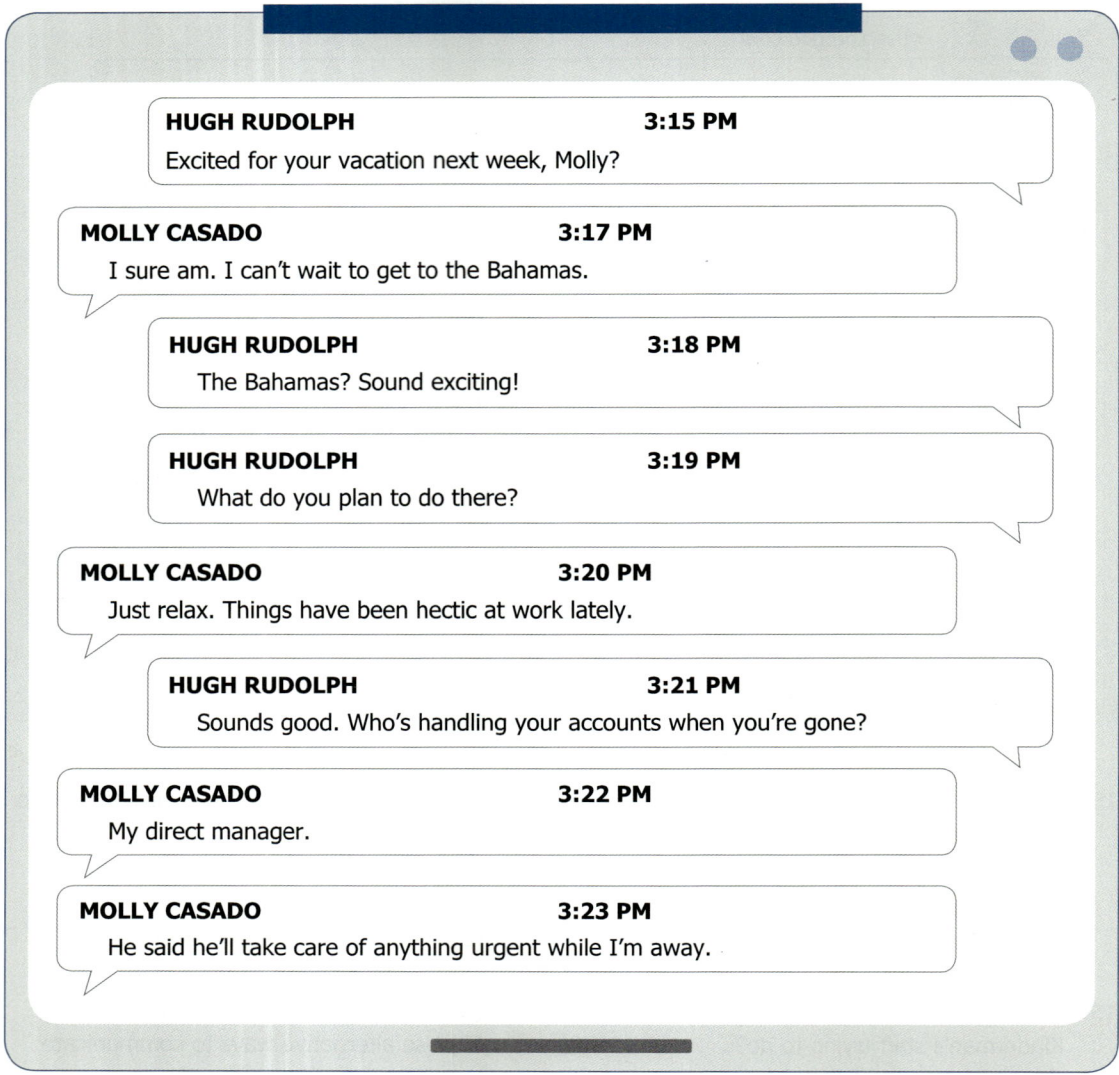

159. What is indicated about Ms. Cadado's accounts?
(A) They will be suspended for a short time.
(B) They are important for the business.
(C) They take a lot of time to manage.
(D) They will be managed by her supervisor.

160. At 3:17 p.m., what does Ms. Casado mean when she writes, "I can't wait to get to the Bahamas"?
(A) She will be leaving immediately.
(B) Her vacation has been postponed.
(C) She is unable to find accommodations now.
(D) She is excited about her travel plans.

Questions 161-163 refer to the following article.

Area Supermarket Introduces New Web Site

PHILADELPHIA (May 10) — Bangles Groceries has created a new Web site for shopping online. The new service is called iMart and will be in service from June.

—[1]—. "iMart is very simple and so convenient to use," said Bangles spokesperson Jake Reiss. "Shoppers can make grocery lists online, look through our weekly specials in our online ad and download coupons from our site." When an order is completed and paid for, shoppers just have to visit the supermarket to receive their items. —[2]—.

—[3]—. Laura Kline, who lives in New Hope, says she is really looking forward to it. "This will save me so much time," she said, "It usually takes me over an hour to shop after work. If I use iMart, I can just choose my groceries online and pick them up as I'm heading home." Ms. Kline also would be happy if iMart creates an app for smartphones so she can order with her phone. —[4]—. However, Reiss says Bangles has no plans for a smartphone app yet.

"At this point, we just want to guarantee that our service is running properly before we do anything else," Reiss stated. For now, the company plans to add home delivery to iMart in September.

161. What is NOT indicated as a feature of iMart?
(A) Receiving discounts on items
(B) Making lists for grocery shopping
(C) Selecting groceries on the phone
(D) Paying for items over the Internet

162. When will Bangles Supermarkets begin offering a delivery service?
(A) In May
(B) In June
(C) In August
(D) In September

163. In which of the positions marked [1], [2], [3], and [4] does the following sentence best belong?

"Bangles will have designated parking places that iMart shoppers can use when picking up their orders."

(A) [1]
(B) [2]
(C) [3]
(D) [4]

Questions 164–167 refer to the following e-mail.

E-mail Message

To :	Gregory Tomlin <gtomlin@hertzairways.com>
From :	Hillary Kwon <hkwon@ausmail.com>
Subject :	My flight in May
Date :	January 3

Dear Mr. Tomlin,

I'd like to first say that I have had many pleasant experiences with Hertz Airways, which is why the situation I'm writing to you about is so surprising. During my flight from Los Angeles to Seattle (HA242) on May 27, there were some problems which delayed the landing of the plane. When my plane finally landed in Seattle, my connecting flight to Minneapolis had already departed. —[1]—. After speaking with a Hertz Airway representative, I was given a voucher for the Piscine Hotel and transportation was provided.

Even though I stayed for one night at the Piscine Hotel, it was a very annoying and unsatisfactory experience. —[2]—. The voucher given to me was rejected by the restaurant at the hotel because the expiration date had passed. I had to pay $23.97 for the meal. —[3]—. When I went back to my room, it was freezing and I found that the thermostat was out of order.

I have made sure that I used Hertz Airways because of the great service I have received in the past. However, this experience with the Piscine Hotel has soured my experience and I suggest you terminate any business relations with the hotel. —[4]—.

I would appreciate being reimbursed for my dinner at the Piscine Hotel since I could not pay with the voucher that your representative gave me (#6513873). Next time I choose Hertz Airways, I expect that the service will be as it has been with my previous experience.

Sincerely,

Hillary Kwon
2877 Hillside Street
Milwaukee, WI 53051

164. What does Ms. Kwon imply in her e-mail?
(A) She usually books her tickets through a travel agency.
(B) She is preparing to reserve a hotel room.
(C) She often flies on Hertz Airways.
(D) She is currently working in a hotel industry.

165. Where is the Piscine Hotel located?
(A) In Los Angeles
(B) In Seattle
(C) In Minneapolis
(D) In Milwaukee

166. What did Ms. Kwon request from Mr. Tomlin?
(A) An invoice
(B) Transfer information
(C) A suggestion for a restaurant
(D) Compensation for costs at a restaurant

167. In which of the positions marked [1], [2], [3], and [4] does the following sentence best belong?

"After this, I tried to use the hotel's fitness center, but it was undergoing restorations."

(A) [1]
(B) [2]
(C) [3]
(D) [4]

Questions 168-171 refer to the following Web page.

---

http://www.onstopsportshop.com/info

One Stop Sport Shop

| Information | Main | Stores | Products | Repairs and maintenance |

One Stop Sport Shop Information

The first One Stop Sport Shop (OSSS) was established ten years ago at 746 David Avenue by Parker Kenny and Steve Stern after playing basketball together for years. The sporting goods stores around them were largely focused on adventure sports goods such as camping gear and rafting equipment, as these were popular among Levart residents. Those with other interests had few options. After the first store's opening, Another OSSS opened at 298 Cork Street. OSSS then found success outside of Levart and has now become the best shop in the nation for people looking for basketball, baseball, and jogging equipment.

Now, OSSS is proud to introduce a new line of clothing designed by Olympian baseball player William Shaugnessy, One Stop Sports Wear. It will be sold at all locations and can be ordered on our Web site.

Please note that our original location exclusively offers repair and maintenance services which are not available at other stores. These services include shoe repair, treadmill maintenance, baseball glove conditioning, and more. Click <u>Repairs and maintenance</u> for more information or to schedule a service.

---

168. What is suggested about the owners of OSSS?
(A) They design athletic attire.
(B) They participated in sporting activities together.
(C) They are avid joggers.
(D) They are planning to sell the OSSS chain.

169. The word "established" paragraph 1, line 1, is closest in meaning to
(A) indicated
(B) competed
(C) introduced
(D) restored

170. What is suggested about OSSS?
(A) It does not carry adventure sports equipment.
(B) It does not own any stores outside of Levart.
(C) It does not sell its products from its Website anymore.
(D) It has closed the store on Cork Street.

171. What is available to OSSS patrons only at the David Avenue Store?
(A) Sports clothing
(B) Athletic footwear
(C) Jogging supplies
(D) Gear repair

Questions 172-175 refer to the following online chat discussion.

Elias Reily	[10:05 a.m.]	Hey everybody. We have an important client coming into town from Tokyo and he's going to be in town for about a week. I was hoping to set up something special for him to do for at least one evening while he's here. Any ideas?
Penelope Dean	[10:07 a.m.]	There's a lot going on next week. Do you know what he's interested in at all? I think there's a few sports matches next week and there's a jazz festival happening in Uptown.
Elias Reily	[10:09 a.m.]	You know, he does talk about baseball a lot. I know he's a big fan of the pitcher on the Burton Cobras, Tyler Boone. Are there any baseball games going on next week?
Penelope Dean	[10:10 a.m.]	Actually, yes there are, and you're in luck. It looks like there's a game on Thursday where you can see him. I bet you can still get tickets for that if you hurry.
Travis Doran	[10:13 a.m.]	Speaking of that jazz festival, my friend is actually one of the organizers. I could get a few free tickets for it just in case.
Elias Reily	[10:14 a.m.]	Thanks, Penelope and that would be great, Travis. Do you know what day the jazz festival is on?
Travis Doran	[10:16 a.m.]	If I recall correctly, it's a weekend event starting Friday evening and ending Sunday afternoon. I'm pretty sure I can get a few weekend passes.
Elias Reily	[10:17 a.m.]	Well, he's leaving Saturday afternoon, so I don't think we need weekend passes. If it's not a problem, can you get a few tickets for just Friday night?
Travis Doran	[10:18 a.m.]	Sure. You can count on me.

172. What is the main topic of the discussion?
(A) Scheduling a company gathering
(B) Organizing a music festival
(C) Making plans for the weekend
(D) Entertaining an important customer

173. What is suggested about Tyler Boone?
(A) He will be in an athletic match next week.
(B) He is the best pitcher in his league.
(C) He may transfer to Tokyo.
(D) He will be attending a jazz festival.

174. At 10:18 a.m., what does Travis Doran mean when he writes, "You can count on me"?
(A) He will attend a jazz festival.
(B) He will report statistics correctly.
(C) He will procure tickets for an event.
(D) He will meet a client Friday evening.

175. What is indicated about the jazz festival?
(A) It takes place over three days.
(B) It attracts many people around the region.
(C) Its tickets are hard to get.
(D) It is the same day as a baseball match.

Questions 176-180 refer to the following comment card and e-mail.

guest survey
The Oak Grove Hotel

We would greatly appreciate it if you fill out the short questionnaire below so that we can maintain and improve the quality of our service here.

	superb	above average	fair	unacceptable
1. Hotel appearance		x		
2. Room condition	x			
3. Food		x		
4. Employee service		x		
5. Fitness center and sauna			x	

Notes :
On my previous stays at the Oak Grove Hotel while visiting Maine, my experiences have always been very pleasant. This time, though, was not as great. The refrigerator in my room did not have a working freezer. In addition, the clerk took an exceptionally long time to check us out of the hotel, which was frustrating since we had a taxi waiting for us at the entrance.

Guest: Carol Weatherbee
Home address: 755 Steel Street
Pittsburgh, PA 15215
E-mail address: carolw@treemail.com

To :	Carol Weatherbee <carolw@treemail.com>
From :	Theodore Crimmel <tcrimmel@oakgrovehotel.com>
Date :	October 3
Subject :	Re: Your recent visit

Dear Ms. Weatherbee,

I appreciate you completing our survey and I am sorry to hear about the inconveniences that you experienced. To make up for the problems you experienced, I am sending you a coupon good for staying at our hotel for a night free of charge. The coupon will expire after one year. I also talked with our reception staff about the check-out procedures to make sure they can check guests out properly in the future.

Regards,

Theodore Crimmel
Manager, The Oak Grove Hotel

176. What is the purpose of the questionnaire?
(A) To gather applications for a job opening
(B) To discover which employees deserve a raise
(C) To give managers details about guest activities
(D) To find out customers' opinions of a lodging

177. What feature of the hotel did Ms. Weatherbee rate highest?
(A) The state of her room
(B) The condition of the fitness facilities
(C) The restaurant staff
(D) The appearance of the hotel

178. What is indicated about Ms. Weatherbee?
(A) She is employed at another hotel.
(B) She travels every month.
(C) She has been a guest of The Oak Grove Hotel before.
(D) She lives in Maine.

179. What did Mr. Crimmel offer Ms. Weatherbee in her e-mail?
(A) A gift certificate for a restaurant
(B) A voucher for a complimentary stay
(C) A paid tour of a Maine state park
(D) A free ticket to the sauna

180. What compliant did Theodore Crimmel talk about with the staff?
(A) The refrigerator was not working.
(B) The key for the room didn't work.
(C) The quality of television pictures was poor.
(D) The check-out took too long to complete

Questions 181–185 refer to the following flyer and webpage.

Aurora Center for Nutrition and Medical Care
605 N Horsecreek Road, Dubois, WY 82513
307-555-2277

Information for New Clients

Thanks for visiting the Aurora Center for Nutrition and Medical Care (ACNMC). For the last three decades, we've been helping Dubois and surrounding areas to be healthier by providing advice on diet and lifestyle to our patients and clients. We also offer culinary classes, which are taught by the former chef at Twilight Garden, Jennifer Church, to help clients improve their eating habits with delicious, healthy food.

You can schedule appointments or register for a class by visiting our Web site at www.acnmc.com. For information about events happening in the area, or for resources about living a healthier life, make sure to visit the online bulletin board. You can also sign up for the ACNMC Healthy Living Card, which you can also use to get discounts of up to 15% at participating restaurants and retailers in Dubois and the surrounding areas.

If you have any questions, feel free to contact ACNMC's senior manager, Zoe Philips.

---

http://www.acnmc.org/bulletinboard

Aurora Center for Nutrition and Medical Care Online Bulletin Board

| Home | Bulletin Board | Physicians | Dietitians |

Culinary Class: Spicing Up Your Healthy Diet, April 14 at 4 p.m.

Has reducing your salt intake taken the flavor out of your meals? We can help you get it back with herbs and spices that'll put the kick back in your food.

[Please be aware that this class will be held at Apollo's Dining at 394 Meckern Street since the center's kitchen class room is undergoing renovations.]

New Takeout Salads now available at Wiseworth Shopping Center

Brett Mars, the owner of Brett's Better Groceries, will begin offering ready-to-eat salads from the beginning of May, giving you a healthy, quick alternative while shopping at the mall.

Marciana Nursery Center Giving Away Garden Plots

Growing your own vegetables and flowers is a great way to get healthy food and get mild exercise. Marciana Nursery Center can help you get started with your own gardening plot. Hurry to call Barry Magnuson to reserve yours since these free gardening plots are going fast!

181. According to the flyer, what is available at Aurora Center for Nutrition and Medical Care?
(A) Tips on making better diet choices
(B) Free community exercise classes
(C) A wide variety of herbs and spices for purchase
(D) Daily vitamin supplements at discounted prices

182. How can ACNMC customers get a discount at certain restaurants?
(A) By shopping frequently at Bret's Better Groceries
(B) By showing a card issued by ACNMC
(C) By visiting a restaurant's grand opening
(D) By receiving a free consultation

183. Who will lead a session at Apollo's Dining?
(A) Zoe Philips
(B) Brett Mars
(C) Jennifer Church
(D) Barry Magnuson

184. Where will an ACNMC event take place in April?
(A) At a Twilight Garden restaurant
(B) At Wiseworth Street
(C) At a 394 Meckern Street
(D) At 605 N Horsecreek Road

185. What is suggested about the Marciana Nursery Center's garden plots?
(A) They are popular with Dubois citizens.
(B) They are used to grow vegetables for local businesses.
(C) They can be leased for a nominal charge.
(D) They can be used exclusively for growing flowers.

Questions 186-190 refer to the following advertisement and e-mails.

Rolfson Family Photo

Make your special event memorable with Rolfson Family Photo!

Your next celebratory events can be made even better with photographer, Dean Rolfson, winner of multiple photography awards. Our prices are reasonable at $500 for five hours or $700 for nine hours, with travel costs included for locations within 20 miles of our studio in Charleston. You'll get thirty printed photographs and all digital copies. Additional editing, enlargements, extra prints, and travel to locations farther than 20 miles are available for additional fees.

For more information, you can visit our Web site. The Web site has examples of our photography and a timetable showing when we are available. You can also find out more about postings from our previous clients about our services and our free monthly photography classes for children.

E-mail Message

To :	Henry Lovett <hlovett@lovettaccounting.com>
From :	Dean Rolfson <dean@rolfsonfamilyphoto.com>
Date :	July 19
Subject :	RE: Lovett Accounting Dinner

Dear Mr. Lovett,

Thank you for sending your payment of $500 for your company dinner on July 2.

The photographs from the event are very good. You can choose which thirty pictures you would like printed at our www.rolfsonfamilyphoto.com/pictureselection.

Also, I remember you said you wanted a large print of the group photo to hang in your company lobby. Below are the rates for our large-scale prints.

Dimensions	40 x 30 cm	65 x 50 cm	80 x 60 cm	100 x 85 cm
Price per print	$12.50	$20.00	$30.00	$45.00

Regards,

Dean Rolfson
Owner, Rolfson Family Photo

E-mail Message

To : All staff <staff@lovettaccounting.com>
From : Henry Lovett <hlovett@lovettaccounting.com>
Date : August 3
Subject : Company pictures

Hi everyone.

I'm happy to let you know that we've scanned all of the pictures from our company dinner held at the Beverly Hotel last month and we've uploaded them to our Web site, so you can show them to your friends and family anytime. We've also received our group portrait, which is hanging in the lobby. We opted for the largest size available so you can see everyone clearly in the picture. Some smaller pictures from the dinner are also hanging around the building.

Sincerely,
Henry Lovett

---

186. According to the advertisement, what service does Mr. Rolfson offer for an extra cost?
(A) Photograph enlargement
(B) Picture-taking classes
(C) Consultation on photography
(D) Digital photographs

187. What is NOT mentioned in the advertisement as being available on the Rolfson Web site?
(A) A list of awards Mr. Rolfson has won
(B) Reviews from former customers
(C) A gallery of Mr. Rolfson's pictures
(D) Mr. Rolfson's available schedule

188. What is indicated about the July 2 party?
(A) It occurred at Lovett Accounting's main office.
(B) It happened within 20 miles of Charleston.
(C) It was coordinated by Mr. Lovett.
(D) It included a video presentation.

189. In the second e-mail, the word "opted for" in paragraph 1, line 3, is closest in meaning to
(A) qualified
(B) looked for
(C) chose
(D) considered

190. What will most likely be the amount of extra payment made by Mr. Lovett?
(A) $12.50
(B) $20.00
(C) $30.00
(D) $45.00

Questions 191-195 refer to the following article, letter, and survey.

STARK GROVE NEWS
July 20

Lodging Review: The Mallister Hotel
Reviewer: Patrick Stuckey

Having undergone restoration in June, the Mallister Hotel has a great location on Central Avenue between 10th Street and 9th Street. The hotel is near a great shopping area and only five minutes on foot from the conference center, making it convenient for guests traveling on business and for pleasure alike. Guests who visit with children will surely value the hotel's swimming pool and playground.

The hotel provides ample parking space in their underground garage and its lobby is beautiful and comfortable. Despite being uncommonly compact, the rooms are moderately priced and pleasantly decorated, with warm color schemes and attractive furniture.

Business travelers may be frustrated as there is currently no wireless Internet connection in the guest rooms. However, the owner of the hotel talked with me during my stay this month and told me that this will be changing. For now, the business center provides the only Internet connection in the hotel.

Even with this small drawback, the Mallister Hotel is a fine hotel that many guests will find more than satisfactory.

STARK GROVE NEWS
Letters from Readers

August 2

Dear Editor:

Concerning your recent review in your July 20 edition, I'm very happy that your reviewer seemed overall pleased with our hotel. I'm especially pleased that he enjoyed our designer decorations that are in our rooms and lobby.

Your reviewer wrote that the guest rooms had no wireless Internet connection and that business travelers may find this frustrating. This issue is being taken care of and I'm glad to report that all guest rooms will be connected to the Internet via a wireless router from September 1.

Regards,

Simon Greyson
Owner, Mallister Inn

Thank you for staying at Mallister Hotel. If there's anything we can do to make your stay better, please tell us in the comments section.

Guest name: Nichelle Faris
Room number: 238

1. How satisfied were you with your room?
_____ Very Satisfied __X__ Satisfied _____ Dissastisfied _____ Very Dissatisfied

2. How satisfied were you with the hotel's facilities?
_____ Very Satisfied _____ Satisfied __X__ Dissastisfied _____ Very Dissatisfied

3. How satisfied were you with the hotel's breakfast?
__X__ Very Satisfied _____ Satisfied _____ Dissastisfied _____ Very Dissatisfied

4. Comments
My room was very comfortable and clean. However, the signal for the wireless Internet was very weak and rather slow. Also, I was disappointed to find that the indoor playground closes at 7 p.m. I think that this is too early and that it should be open later.

---

191. What does the article mention about the location of the Mallister Hotel?
(A) It is close to a commercial district.
(B) It is close to a university.
(C) It is easy to walk to a bus stop from there.
(D) It is next to a conference center.

192. In the article, the work "value" in paragraph 1, line 7, is closest in meaning to
(A) approximate
(B) appreciate
(C) pay for
(D) participate in

193. What characteristic of the guest rooms does the reviewer consider to be uncommon?
(A) Their designs
(B) Their furniture
(C) Their cost
(D) Their size

194. What is a purpose of the letter?
(A) To submit a review
(B) To complain about something
(C) To update information
(D) To recruit new employees

195. What is suggested about Ms. Faris?
(A) She was probably staying with children.
(B) She will not stay at Mallister Hotel again.
(C) She used the wi-fi to download movies.
(D) She spoke to the hotel's owner before checking out.

Questions 196–200 refer to the following article, e-mail, and article.

June 16 – The Mulberry Mall in uptown Clarkton will feature a gallery by photographer Kim Taggert in its lobby from the beginning of July to the end of September. Mall owner, Sharon Bittle has supported artists in the area for many years and the lobby has often been a great place to view art.

"The lobby in the mall is a great place for people to gather, so I thought it would be a great place to display the works of gifted artists from Clarkton," said Ms. Bittle. She said everyone is welcome to come and look at the artwork. "We've also added some new restaurants to our dining area, including a great Thai restaurant called Prai, that I think everyone should try to have diverse cultural experience."

To :	Sandra Luce <scluce@mullmail.com>
From :	Sharon Bittle <sbittle@mulberrymall.com>
Date :	September 20
Subject :	Your exhibition

Dear Ms. Luce,

I'm so happy to be displaying your paintings in the Mulberry Mall's lobby from October. I thought your works at the community center exhibit were wonderful and I think that even more people will be able to see your work at the mall.

I need to know the dimensions of each piece so that we can plan on arranging them in the lobby. If you let me know before the end of September, I would appreciate it.

Regards,
Sharon Bittle
Owner, Mulberry Mall

Try Thai at Prai
By Ed Bennett

One of the latest restaurants to open at the Mulberry Mall, Prai, gives visitors a taste and cultural experience that are hard to find in any other dining establishments in the area. I am not as experienced with Thai cuisine as I could be and the staff at Prai were very helpful in helping me decide what to try.

I highly suggest the Panaeng curry and some sticky rice and mango for dessert. The restaurant is delightfully decorated and from its front window, you can also see some of the paintings on display from local artists. Even if you've never had Thai food before, don't be afraid. Try Thai at Prai!

196. What does the first article explain?
(A) How a mall's lobby is used
(B) A new store in a mall
(C) The exhibit of one photographer
(D) A renovated gallery

197. What is mentioned about Ms. Bittle?
(A) She is a painter.
(B) She is taking photography classes.
(C) She has commissioned a mural.
(D) She supports the promotion of local artists.

198. What does Ms. Bittle invite visitors to do at the mall?
(A) Enjoy free snacks at the lobby
(B) Dine at a restaurant in the mall
(C) Come to a reception for Ms. Taggert
(D) Visit the mall's new art supply store

199. What is implied about Ms. Luce?
(A) She has had exhibits at many galleries.
(B) She is a resident of Clarkton.
(C) She is a portrait painter.
(D) She is an acquaintance of Mr. Mills.

200. What is suggested about Prai?
(A) It has become very popular.
(B) It gives discounts to new customers.
(C) It has won awards for its curry.
(D) It has a view of the lobby from its window.

Stop! This is the end of the test. If you finish before time is called, you may go back to Parts 5, 6, and 7 and check your work.

동시토익 실전 WORKBOOK

101. The director of the new film, Halfway Down, stated that the movie is quite different from the book on which it is based.

해석]

102. Ms. Mayner easily secured the contract with Windhill Distribution and Supply.

해석]

103. Television chef Carol Brinn will show how to make a vegetarian dinner that will satisfy your entire family on Thursday.

해석]

104. Provided that the manager's request for the purchase of new equipment receives approval, the warehouse will increase its efficiency by up to fifty percent.

해석]

105. All staff at Fulton Enterprises have the option to donate all or part of their tax refund to the charity of their choice.

해석]

106. Dr. Hovink was given the Bellvue award for his work in quantum physics.

해석]

107. We ask that any inquiries regarding the processing of applications be directed to the human resources department.

해석]

108. The CEO of Tale Industries, Hillary Long, will be finalizing the candidate list for the executive position herself.

해석]

109. Hotshop.com will send an email verifying your purchase following the completion of your order.

해석]

110. Any expenses from meeting with clients at restaurants and other dining establishments can be deducted when filing for a tax refund.

해석]

*어휘 NOTE

111. Overtime payment forms need to be submitted to Mr. Argyle before the end of the month.

해석]

112. Stalkin Foods has hired more factory workers to meet the growing demand for its new line of instant dinners.

해석]

113. According to our files, Dillon Electronics business license in Spain will expire or January 2.

해석]

114. Linus Construction is currently building a tower that will become a high-rise apartment complex.

해석]

115. Mr. Potter's enthusiasm for education was a key factor when citizens elected him as mayor of Portville.

해석]

116. Port Industries has been manufacturing waste processing products for residential application for nearly a decade.

해석]

117. Longview Bank has provided mortgages to over 100,000 customers since its establishment a decade ago.

해석]

118. The success of the new Helo Ultra sedan has been attributed to the unusual marketing campaign created by The Lobed Ad Agency.

해석]

119. The payments for the business loan have all been received and processed.

해석]

120. Senti Electric Company seems to have attained its goals this year, but until all the data have been finalized, they should be considered only projections.

해석]

121. Most readers of Steven Bilk's latest novel will find it to be a very accessible story.

해석]

*어휘 NOTE

122. Employees at the Stockton News can now refer to the updated staff directory whenever they are unsure which personnel to contact.

해석]

123. Many diners visit Buena Cabeza for its remarkably wide selection of food items.

해석]

124. Employees of Skyhigh Industries offered helpful suggestions when interviewed by a consultant from Baker Business Solutions.

해석]

125. Travelers on a tight budget should be aware that domestic train travel is much less expensive than traveling by plane.

해석]

126. Many young people are used to posting content online but should be aware that posting personal information leaves them vulnerable to identity fraud.

해석]

127. Manderly Enterprises has been looking for a consultant to assist with the company's expansion into the European market.

해석]

128. The Hillbrook and Lakeside football clubs faced one another during the playoffs last year, and will again in this year's championship match.

해석]

129. Guitarist Frank Lenster is credited with popularizing the line of electric guitars produced by Excel Instruments.

해석]

130. Master Audio's latest MP3 player is sold exclusively at Portal Electronics store locations.

해석]

*어휘 NOTE

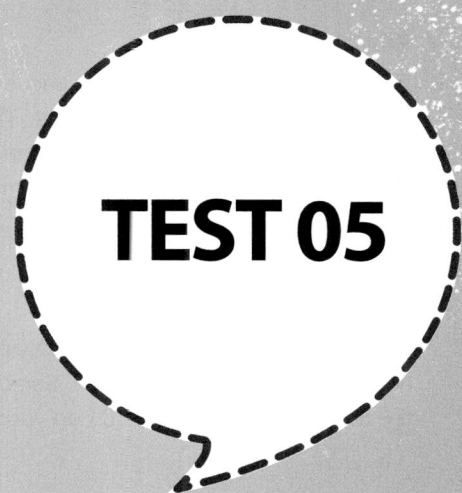

동시토익 CONTEMPORARY **TOEIC**

TEST 05

READING TEST

In the Reading test, you will read a variety of texts and answer several different types of reading comprehension questions. The entire Reading test will last 75 minutes. There are three parts, and directions are given for each part. You are encouraged to answer as many questions as possible within the time allowed.

You must mark your answers on the separate answer sheet. Do not write your answers in your test book.

Part 5

Directions: A word or phrase is missing in each of the sentences below. Four answer choices are given below each sentence. Select the best answer to complete the sentence. Then mark the letter (A), (B), (C), or (D) on your answer sheet.

101. You will find _____ schedule for the workshops included with this letter.
(A) you
(B) your
(C) yours
(D) yourself

102. Michael Balik's new novel was released last week, _____ critics have given it very favorable reviews.
(A) or
(B) if
(C) than
(D) and

103. The Shift Supervisor position requires excellent _____ skills as well as great interpersonal communication abilities.
(A) organizational
(B) organizes
(C) organizations
(D) organize

104. Gilby Hotel provides the _____ nightly rates, while still giving guests the best customer service.
(A) cheapness
(B) cheapen
(C) cheaply
(D) cheapest

105. _____ of Kindet Technology will receive at least twenty vacation days next year.
(A) Employs
(B) Employed
(C) Employment
(D) Employees

106. The bridge, which connects Prince George and Charles City counties, will remain closed _____ further notice due to possible structural damage.
(A) until
(B) during
(C) instead
(D) within

107. The new X90 racing car was produced _____ by Horser Motors and Tolvir Automotive.
(A) joined
(B) joining
(C) jointly
(D) joins

108. The articles in November issue of all investor magazines contain numerous quotations from Mr. Held, _____ of which were especially interesting.
(A) several
(B) another
(C) nothing
(D) who

109. With the release of their new microwave, Dalk Electronics has increased its market share over its _____ in the region.
(A) competitive
(B) competitively
(C) competed
(D) competitors

110. The Metropolitan Symphony Orchestra is _____ primarily through donations from the public.
(A) funds
(B) funding
(C) funded
(D) fund

111. Michelle Kim and Daniel Heely interviewed all candidates by _____ at the Boise Career Fair that was held last month.
(A) itself
(B) himself
(C) ourselves
(D) themselves

112. Halicart is known for having large number of Mexican restaurants in the downtown _____ of the city.
(A) amount
(B) distance
(C) area
(D) plan

113. Library members must pay any fines _____ for any overdue or missing books before being able to borrow any books.
(A) revolved
(B) incited
(C) comprehended
(D) incurred

114. _____ your free gift, you must first activate your Discover Titanium card by making a purchase, transferring a balance, or making a cash advance.
(A) Receiving of
(B) Upon receipt
(C) To be received
(D) To receive

115. Most of the students _____ visited the financial aid office last week needed assistance in completing their applications.
(A) which
(B) they
(C) who
(D) when

116. Much _____ the disappointment of his colleagues and family, Mr. Jackson applied for early retirement.
(A) to
(B) on
(C) at
(D) in

117. The _____ of the agreement state that subscribers must pay a cancelation fee for early termination.
(A) files
(B) terms
(C) signs
(D) views

118. _____ the sun will be shining all week does not mean that the temperature will become warmer during this cold winter.
(A) The fact that
(B) In keeping with
(C) Under the condition that
(D) In regard to

119. Because of _____ operating costs, Reddon, Inc. will begin limiting the amount of overtime that employees are allowed to work.
(A) above
(B) longer
(C) profitable
(D) rising

120. CEO Paul Settler _____ discussed the decision to issue a recall on the defective televisions at the shareholder's meeting.
(A) calmer
(B) calmly
(C) calming
(D) calms

GO ON TO THE NEXT PAGE

121. The Victory Coffee Shop has become the _____ popular venue among youngsters since introducing a new line of fruit smoothies.
(A) increasingly
(B) increase
(C) increases
(D) increasing

122. The recent developments of the productivity improvement program are _____ unprecedented by many experts.
(A) considered to be
(B) considerably
(C) considering
(D) to consider

123. Cybob has been one of the most _____ used operating systems for smartphones for the last five years.
(A) eligibly
(B) commonly
(C) exactly
(D) neutrally

124. With Lightspeed News' new online service, subscribers receive text messages _____ a subject of interest to them is published.
(A) whenever
(B) therefore
(C) however
(D) furthermore

125. Latent Software's file transfer software is _____ with Latent smart phones produced after March of this year.
(A) reportable
(B) reflective
(C) compatible
(D) conclusive

126. Online game distribution company, Joinus, _____ holds huge sales to arouse consumer interest.
(A) recently
(B) occasionally
(C) lately
(D) previously

127. The temporary waiting area is located slightly _____ the airport entrance on the right side of the roadway.
(A) into
(B) over
(C) among
(D) past

128. Invoices are mailed on a monthly _____ to all Grove Cable Services customers.
(A) base
(B) basis
(C) based
(D) basing

129. Sales of Morton Refrigerators have improved since it _____ innovative advertising campaign in May.
(A) educated
(B) participated
(C) launched
(D) appeared

130. _____ the issues many users reported when it was first launched, Norse Playbox has been rated the best video game console of all time.
(A) On the other hand
(B) As a matter of fact
(C) Despite
(D) Eventually

PART 6

Direction: Read the texts that follow. A word, phrase, or sentence is missing in parts of each text. Four answer choices for each question are given below the text. Select the best answer to complete the text. Then mark the letter (A), (B), (C), or (D) on your answer sheet.

Questions 131-134 refer to the following advertisement.

Paulina's Hair Salon and Manicure is holding a community get-together to celebrate our ------- on
                                                                                        131.
Saturday, April 16. All members of the community are welcome to come by our shop from 12 p.m. to 5 p.m. for games (with prizes!), food, drinks, and style advice from our experienced stylists. You'll also be able to ------- a voucher good for 25% off any hair styling service, such as cuts,
                              132.
perms, and coloring. We will only be able to give out one voucher ------- visitor. -------. For more
                                                                    133.   **134.**
details, call us at 555-6833.

131. (A) appointment
(B) nomination
(C) completion
(D) anniversary

132. (A) pick up
(B) find out
(C) pay back
(D) keep on

133. (A) by
(B) per
(C) each
(D) for

134. (A) Food and drinks will not be available during later visits.
(B) Our usual hours of operation are from 9 a.m. to 8 p.m. Monday to Saturday.
(C) It will be valid for one month after the get-together.
(D) Winners of the games will be announced at the end of the get-together.

Question 135-138 refer to the following memo.

To: Factory Staff
From: Paul Carning, Director of Operations
Date: December 15
Subject: Machine malfunction

The other day, one of our workers on the packing floor noticed that the ------- control knob for the machine that we use to seal the bags of cereal doesn't seem to be working properly.
135.

The display shows that the machine is much hotter than it actually is. Even with this problem, the machine itself seems to be -------.
136.

We have scheduled a machine technician to come and take a look at the machine and fix the problem with the knob. -------. Until the repairs are complete, please ------- every bag closely so that we can be sure they are being sealed properly.
137.   138.

If you find any bags that have not been properly sealed, please set them aside so the cereal can be repackaged later.

135. (A) speed
(B) temperature
(C) timing
(D) pressure

136. (A) outdated
(B) familiar
(C) functional
(D) replaceable

137. (A) He will arrive on site around 3 p.m. this afternoon.
(B) The machine has be taken to the repair center and will come back next week.
(C) The packing floor will close until the repairs have been carried out.
(D) We will be offering any resealed bags of cereal to customers at a discount.

138. (A) are inspecting
(B) inspect
(C) to inspect
(D) inspected

Questions 139-142 refer to the following memo.

To: Employees
From: Haley Griggs
Re: Workshops
Date: March 4

The system used by the human resources department is currently being updated. Since it is essential that all affected managers using the system understand the changes, ------- in charge of reporting staff members' working hours will have to attend one of our training sessions.
139.

These ------- for March 9, 8, and 10 from 2 p.m. to 3 p.m. Let the information technology department
140.
supervisor know which date would be best for you via e-mail at inftech@preeton.com.

Should you be ------- during these dates, please e-mail me at hgriggs@preeton.com. -------.
141. **142.**

139. (A) that
(B) this
(C) those
(D) them

140. (A) schedule
(B) are scheduling
(C) were to be scheduled
(D) have been scheduled

141. (A) unavailable
(B) interested
(C) inattentive
(D) concerned

142. (A) Working hours should be reported to your supervisor at the end of the week.
(B) The human resources department will notify us when the update has been completed.
(C) I will train those who cannot participate in a group session myself individually.
(D) Training sessions have been considered quite successful by many participants.

GO ON TO THE NEXT PAGE

Questions 143-146 refer to the following article.

Red Hot Barbecue Increases the Heat in Omaha

The best barbecue restaurant in Alabama, Red Hot Barbecue ------- a huge selection of their spicy dishes to Omaha.
                                                    143.

-------. For the new design, the owners took inspiration from the street vendors in the uptown region. The new Omaha Red Hot Barbecue branch opened two weeks ago at 89 Wimbley Drive and is ------- small that all food is served for takeout only.
144.   145.

The delicious barbecue sandwiches and meat platters are sure to please any barbecue fanatics and spice-lovers. -------, the restaurant has a variety of specialty salads, side dishes, and more.
                         146.

143. (A) will bring
     (B) was bringing
     (C) to bring
     (D) has brought

144. (A) Residents of Omaha have never experienced such spicy barbecue.
     (B) The original layout of the restaurant had to be changed.
     (C) Some food critics gave rave reviews for the food.
     (D) Making a reservation is recommended as seating is limited.

145. (A) truly
     (B) very
     (C) such
     (D) so

146. (A) In addition
     (B) On the contrary
     (C) Therefore
     (D) instead

PART 7

Direction: In this part you will read a selection of texts, such as magazine and newspaper articles, letters, e-mails, and instant messages. Each text or set of texts is followed by several questions. Select the best answer for each question and mark the letter (A), (B), (C), or (D) on your answer sheet.

Questions 147-148 refer to the following notice.

NOTICE

TO: Staff of Hill County Hospital
FROM: Sylvester Trent, Building Superintendent
TIME: March 7
SUBJECT: Construction in the near future

The East Side parking garage will undergo construction from April 2 to April 7 and will not be available for use. Staff who usually park on the East Side parking garage are asked to use the public parking lot on Vern Avenue. Complimentary parking vouchers will be given to all staff from Hill County Hospital. A shuttle bus will also run from the parking lot to the South Wing of the hospital. To obtain the vouchers, please bring your employee registration cards and your car's registration cards to the accounting office in the Haverson Building tomorrow between 8 a.m. and 4 p.m.

147. What is being announced?
(A) The shutdown of a street in an area
(B) The ending of a complimentary shuttle bus
(C) An enrollment procedure for employee registration cards
(D) A temporary change in parking areas

148. When will parking vouchers be given out?
(A) On March 7
(B) On March 8
(C) On April 2
(D) On April 7

Questions 149-150 refer to the following letter.

Riverton Library
September 2
Kim Burns
982 Valley Drive
Reno, NV 89503

Dear Ms. Burns:

According to our records, as of October 3, your membership will no longer be valid. If you would like to continue borrowing books from our library for one more year, please renew your membership by bringing your library card and an identification card with your present address to the information desk. You will have to change your 5-digit personal identification number, but your membership number will not be changed. If you have any outstanding overdue charges for books or other items, they must be paid upon renewal.

Regards,

Steven Kimball, Riverton Library Membership Services

149. Why was this letter written?
(A) To promote a new library program
(B) To verify a new identification number
(C) To explain procedures for starting a membership
(D) To explain how to renew membership

150. What is Ms. Burns instructed to bring to the information desk?
(A) Evidence of her current residence
(B) A recent picture of herself
(C) Any overdue library items
(D) Her new membership number

Questions 151-152 refer to the following text message chain.

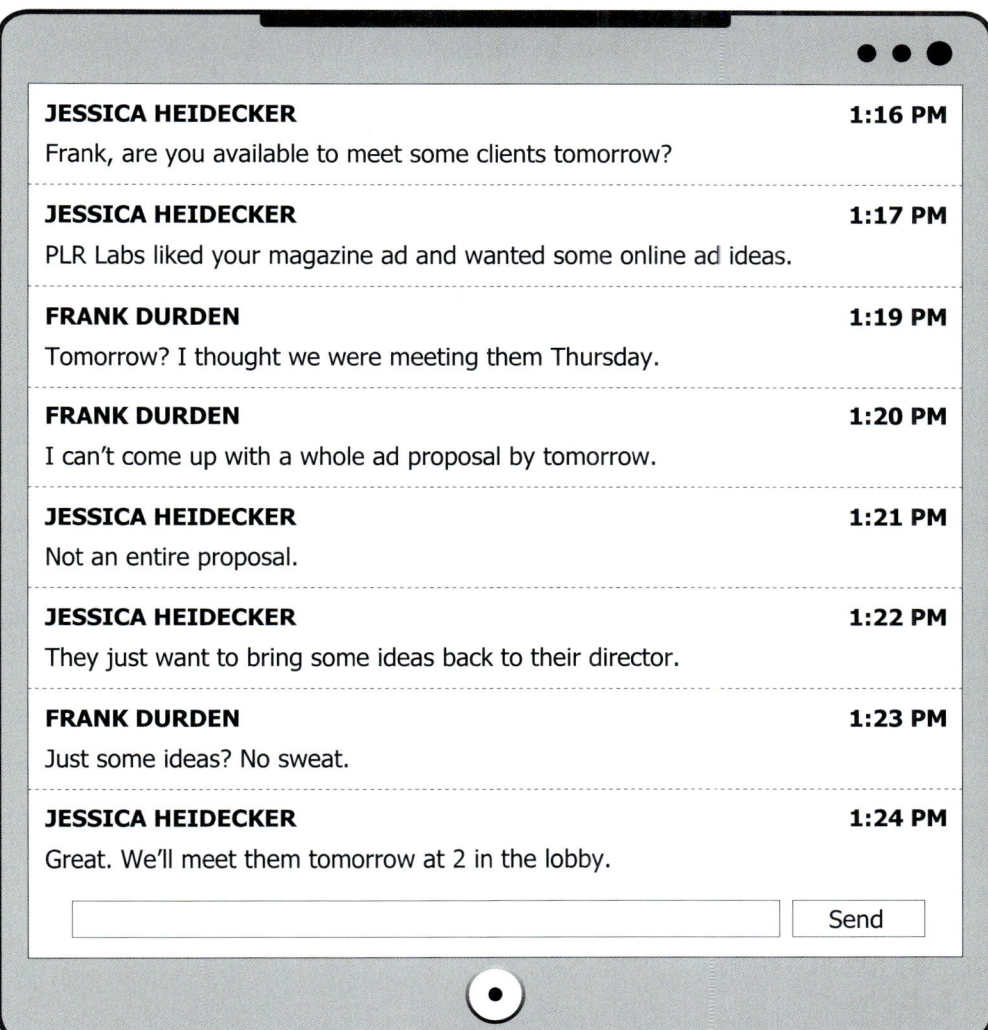

151. What is indicated about Frank Durden's magazine ad?
(A) It took up the whole page.
(B) It won an award.
(C) A client found it pleasing.
(D) It can be completed by Thursday.

152. At 1:23 PM, what does Mr. Durden mean when he writes, "No sweat"?
(A) The temperature is very cool.
(B) He hasn't been working hard today.
(C) He doesn't have any new ideas.
(D) He will have no problems with the request.

Questions 153-155 refer to the following flyer.

Join in on the fun!

Event: The world premiere of Hawk's Ascent, the new movie from director Hans Mixler

Location: Gaverton Theater, Portland, OR

Time: Sunday, August 14. A bus leaves employee parking lot at 4:00 p.m.

Tentative time of return: 11:30 P.M.

Price: $30.00 per guest includes transportation, dinner, and admission to the 7:00 showing. Guests must pay when boarding the bus before departure. Guests will enjoy dinner at Chez Rouge. Snacks and beverages can be purchased at the concession stand before the movie begins.

Notice: If you'd like to join, please sign up using the sheet placed in the east break room. The sheet will be posted until 4:30 p.m. on August 8.

153. What type of event is being publicized?
(A) A sightseeing tour
(B) A camping excursion
(C) A movie viewing
(D) A hiking trip

154. Where should participants submit payment for the event?
(A) At the Gaverton Theater
(B) In the east break area
(C) At the reception desk
(D) On the bus

155. What is included in the price of the outing?
(A) Lunch
(B) Dinner
(C) Beverages
(D) Snacks

Questions 156-158 refer to the following webpage.

Zimmerman Furniture

The best supplier of high quality home and office furniture for 30 years

To register for a Zimmerman Furniture online account, click here.

There are many advantages of registering, such as:
- Updates on sales sent via e-mail

- Discount codes sent only to registered members

- Faster order processing on our Web site

Entering your registration information is easy and takes only a few minutes. Just enter your contact information and your credit card information. Please be assured that we protect our customers' information securely by using the latest encryption technology.

156. What is the reason for the Web page?
(A) To encourage customers to register
(B) To announce the opening of a new store
(C) To confirm the date of a delivery
(D) To request information about a purchase

157. What is NOT mentioned as a benefit of membership?
(A) A quick process for ordering
(B) Special codes for discounted prices
(C) Notices about sales
(D) Discounted delivery charges

158. What is suggested about Zimmerman Furniture?
(A) It is a family-owned company.
(B) It uses current security measures.
(C) It ships items around the world.
(D) It has high reputation for quality.

Questions 159-160 refer to the following e-mail.

To :	Chris Barrett, Marketing Director.
From :	Tricia Wallace, Chief Financial Officer
Subject :	Aaron Copsy
Date :	August 27

Dear Chris,

I heard that your division has secured multiple new contracts over the last month and that your team is short-handed.

I want to recommend Aaron Copsy for a position as a campaign designer on your marketing team. He is very diligent and intelligent, and I know it because I have had him as an intern in my office for the last six months. He is very creative and works well with groups, as well as individually.

Mr. Copsy recently graduated from university with a degree in marketing and is hoping to start his career in that field with us at Carnet, Inc. I'm sure he would be a great asset to your team. If you have any questions, please contact me at any time.

Regards,

Tricia Wallace
Chief Financial Officer
Carnet, Inc.

159. What is reason for sending the e-mail?
(A) To explain a new recruitment procedure
(B) To make a recommendation
(C) To ask for details about new contracts
(D) To recommend a meeting place

160. What does the e-mail suggest about Ms. Wallace?
(A) She will work on a project with the marketing division.
(B) She works for Mr. Barrett.
(C) She is planning to change her career.
(D) She has worked with Mr. Copsy for six months.

* 어휘 NOTE

Questions 161-164 refer to the following advertisement.

DISCOVER THE AUSTRALIAN OUTBACK

With
Steve Shores

If you're interested in seeing the wild beauty of the Australian outback and learning about the lives of the natives, sign up for one of Koala Tours Outback Discovery Tours today. Our agency offers year-round tours of Mungo National Park, Ayers Rock, and other attractions throughout Australia. Every tour is conducted by a professional, experienced guide. We also provide meals from our professional chefs. Below are some of our tour options.

Walking Expedition:	Accommodations at the base camp lodge
	5 days, 4 nights – from AU$800
	8 days, 7 nights – from AU$1150
Outback Experience:	Nightly accommodations in tents across the savannah
	5 days, 4 nights – from AU$600
	8 days, 7 nights – from AU$800

It is also possible to book your entire trip with us with a safari package, where you will be flown from your location to Australia. Advance registration for popular expeditions is recommended. More details and pictures can be found on our Web site at www.koalatours.co.au.

161. What is suggested about the Mungo National Park?
(A) It is near Ayers Rock.
(B) The tour guides live there.
(C) The base camp lodge is located there.
(D) It is open to guests all year.

162. According to the advertisement, what does Koala Tours offer?
(A) Selection of lodging
(B) Training for tour guides
(C) One day expeditions
(D) Outback cooking classes

163. What is NOT indicated about Koala Tours?
(A) It recommends registering in advance.
(B) It provides flights with tour packages.
(C) It hires professional chefs.
(D) It is looking for a new manager.

164. In the advertisement, the word "attractions" in paragraph 1, line 3 is closest in meaning to
(A) fascination
(B) tourist sites
(C) luring power
(D) treatment

Questions 165-167 refer to the following article.

One of Bayden's wonderful historic landmarks, The Sphere Theater, has become severely deteriorated and is in need of restoration. The performing arts center has been in the city of Bayden for nearly 100 years and is a part of the town's history with many remarkable old theater features. —[1]—. The beautifully designed lobby features artistic stonework reminiscent of the time when the theater was first built. Beautiful murals also adorn the walls, as well as photographs of the famous performers who have performed in The Sphere over the years, such as Deidre Mallister and Mark Hintz. —[2]—.

The number of tourists used to be much higher, as did the number of productions in the theater, but these have fallen dramatically. The theater needs a lot of restoration to make sure that it can continue to be used. To accomplish this restoration, The Sphere Theater Revival Society, made up of Bayden citizens, business owners, and community leaders, came together to develop a plan. —[3]—. This preservation project will be carried out over the next six months and the society is trying to raise enough money to restore The Sphere Theater to the state of its former glory.

The Sphere Theater Revival Society will hold special information sessions for citizens of Bayden and the surrounding areas who are interested in the restoration. —[4]—. Information about restoration plans, making a donation, and more can be found at www.sphere theaterrevival.com.

165. What is the article mainly about?
(A) The tour of a city's unique buildings
(B) The outcome of a recently held election
(C) The description of an upcoming city project
(D) The schedule for a play at a theater

166. What is implied about The Sphere Theater?
(A) It is the most famous building in Bayden.
(B) It provides complimentary tickets to supporters.
(C) It is not used for performances anymore.
(D) It featured several well-known performers before.

167. In which of the positions marked [1], [2], [3], and [4] does the following sentence best belong?

"These meetings will take place monthly on the first Thursday of the month at the Bayden Community Center."

(A) [1]
(B) [2]
(C) [3]
(D) [4]

Questions 168-171 refer to the following online chat discussion.

Online Chat

Celia Ashforth [9:32 a.m.] Does anyone happen to have a copy of last month's sales numbers on hand for the line of children's clothing that we recently released? I have a presentation this afternoon and I need to include them.

Marisa Dawkins [9:33 a.m.] I'm pretty sure that the sales reports are all available on the company's shared online hard drive. You just need a log-in ID and password. Do you have those?

Celia Ashforth [9:35 a.m.] I do, but I keep getting a message that my ID and password don't match. I don't know why it happens. I've used the same ID and password since I started.

Kevin McClure [9:37 a.m.] That explains it. Didn't you get the email about the new security protocols? Everyone has to change their password every three months. If you don't change it, your ID only gets limited access, meaning you can't use the online hard drive.

Celia Ashforth [9:38 a.m.] Oh, I do remember that. I just kept putting it off and then it completely slipped my mind. So, how can I change my password now?

Kevin McClure [9:40 a.m.] You'll have to file a password reset request with the IT department. They'll process it and send you an email with a temporary password in about a day.

Celia Ashforth [9:42 a.m.] That's annoying. And I still need a copy of last month's sales report this afternoon. Is anyone able to help me get a copy?

Marisa Dawkins [9:43 a.m.] I'll come by your cubicle and log into the online hard drive with my account and then you can download the reports that way. You may want to download any other documents you might need over the next couple of days.

Celia Ashforth [9:45 a.m.] Thanks, Marisa. Can you come by in about 15 minutes? I'm going to head to IT to take care of my password first.

168. What is indicated about Celia Ashforth?
(A) She is attending a conference in the afternoon.
(B) She is presenting later today.
(C) She works in the IT department.
(D) She can't access her email.

169. What protocols changed in the last three months?
(A) Employees must wear ID badges at all time.
(B) Staff have to update passwords regularly.
(C) Workers may not log in for other workers.
(D) Visitors must be accompanied by employees.

170. At 9:38 a.m., what does Celia Ashforth mean when she writes, "it completely slipped my mind"?
(A) She cannot remember her password.
(B) She doesn't know where the IT department is.
(C) She forgot to follow a new procedure.
(D) She didn't write down an appointment.

171. What will Marisa Dawkins most likely do at 10:00 a.m.?
(A) Speak with an IT employee
(B) Download files from a shared hard drive
(C) Assist a colleague by accessing files
(D) Update her company password

Questions 172-175 refer to the following article.

What does music in bookstores do for sales?
Sander Magrue
Jamestown School of Business

Ever wondered if the music played in a bookstore changes how you shop? Does the music somehow cause customers to look around the store more or even buy more books? Research done by students at the Jamestown School of Business studied the actions of customers in 12 bookstores using different music playlists, one with fast music, one with mid-range tempos, and one with slower music, over a span of a month. —[1]—.

The bookstores were all franchises that had stores in every province. —[2]—. In an effort to make the results consistent, each of the stores selected for the study were located near colleges where the areas were highly populated with people in their twenties.

The study looked at how much time customers spent in each of the stores with the different playlists. After their shopping was done, the customers were surveyed to find out how many books they bought. —[3]—. The study was supervised by faculty of the Jamestown School of business, including myself, to make sure the data was collected accurately and the statistics were analyzed properly.

—[4]—. The findings of the study showed that patrons of the stores that played music with fast tempos spent a shorter amount of time shopping, while stores playing mid-range and slow tempo music exhibited no remarkable difference in the time customers do shopping. Additionally, patrons of the stores playing high-tempo music bought more books on average. Sophomore Jenny Baek has made a hypothesis that the high-tempo music makes customers shop for books more quickly and therefore spend less time deliberating individual purchases. This results in less shopping time and more purchases.

172. What information is stated in the article?
(A) How many customers were questioned
(B) How much time was spent collecting data
(C) How many items each customer bought
(D) How loud the music was played in the store

173. What role did the author play in the research?
(A) He surveyed customers.
(B) He managed students.
(C) He shopped at the stores.
(D) He came up with a hypothesis.

174. According to the article, what is affected by the tempo of music in the shop?
(A) The amount of time customers stay in a shop
(B) The sections most frequented by customers
(C) The interactions between customers and staff
(D) The degree of customer satisfaction

175. In which of the positions marked [1], [2], [3], and [4] does the following sentence best belong?

"All stores comprised a shopping area of 5000 to 7000 square meters."

(A) [1]
(B) [2]
(C) [3]
(D) [4]

Questions 176–180 refer to following letter and e-mail.

* E-mail *

Dear Mr. Smithson,

We are very happy that you have contracted Eco Consulting to assist with your auditing process. We guarantee that your company will be up to date with environmental protection protocols by the end of the audit.

As we discussed, we will audit the procedures of your company to ensure that they comply with current government standards which regulate air quality, water conservation, and disposal of waste. We will be inspecting four sections: general practices, exhaust output, water filtration, and garbage disposal and recycling procedures. We will rate your company's performance in these sections, as well as grade the overall management of your company.

When you requested our services, you asked that the audit be conducted over the first three weeks of August. This timetable works for us. Unless we are notified otherwise, we will proceed with the audit process based on this schedule.

Regards,
Ms. Hines
Eco Consulting

TO:	Dean_Smithson@coltautoparts.com
FROM:	Alan_Shore@coltautoparts.com
SUBJECT:	Third quarter timetable
DATE:	July 18
ATTACHMENT:	tentativetimetable.pdf

Dear Mr. Smithson:

The draft for the company schedule for the months of August, September and October is attached to this e-mail. It looks like the transportation division employees will need to do some overtime work over these months depending on the orders from MTK Automotive. We expect the orders to come in by Friday, at which time we should be able to confirm the timetable.

During our last talk, you said that we may have to change the timetable to add time for the September safety seminars. I have entered it on the schedule already, but is there anything else you'd like to put in? I'd like to have the completed timetable ready to send to the district managers at the start of next week.

Alan Shore

176. Why did Ms. Hines write the letter?
(A) To draw a possible customer
(B) To respond to an information request
(C) To verify a tentative schedule
(D) To report changes to a procedure

177. What service does Eco Consulting provide?
(A) Recruiting transportation and shipping employees
(B) Planning financial practices for businesses
(C) Disposing of harmful chemicals and waste
(D) Grading companies' compliance with government regulations

178. According to the e-mail, what will likely happen next month in the transportation division?
(A) Some staff will work more hours than usual.
(B) Some vehicles will undergo maintenance.
(C) Employees will undergo training for disposal procedures.
(D) The company timetable will be distributed to staff.

179. What does Mr. Shore hope to do before the week ends?
(A) Look over Eco Consulting's contract
(B) Finish the official company timetable
(C) Start an audit of environmental procedures
(D) Order supplies from MTK Automotive

180. What will Mr. Smithson probably say in his response to the e-mail?
(A) Production plants should get ready for increased operation.
(B) The company audit needs to be put in the timetable.
(C) Safety seminars need to be scheduled for September.
(D) The procedure for changing the timetable should be improved.

Questions 181-185 refer to following e-mail and survey.

E-mail Message

TO	Danielle McCourt <dmccourt @ femail.com>
FROM	Service Representative <customerservice @ malachibusinessservices.com>
DATE	August 17
SUBJECT	Recent order

Dear Ms. McCourt,

At Malachi Business Services, our aim is to give the best selection of office products and services to our customers. To the end, we routinely ask our customers about their experience in dealing with us. According to our records, you purchased a product from us on August 3. The survey only takes about five minutes to complete. If you complete the survey by August 31, we will also be happy to give you a voucher good for 20% off your next purchase with us.

To complete the survey, please click the link below:
www.malachibusinessservices.com/questionnair

Thank you very much.

---

www.malachibusinessservices.com/questionnaire

We greatly appreciate you taking the time to complete this questionnaire.

1. Date of submission : **August 20**

2. How satisfied were you with the navigation on the Web site?
☐ Very Satisfied ☑ Satisfied ☐ Dissastisfied ☐ Very Dissatisfied

3. How frequently do you shop on malachibusinessservices.com?
☐ Once a day ☐ Once a week ☐ Once a month ☑ Once every three months ☐ Once a year

4. What was your last purchase?
☑ Printers ☐ Stationery ☐ Shipping supplies
☐ Computers ☐ Computer accessories ☐ Desk organization

Comments :

I was extremely satisfied with the purchase I recently made with malachibusinessservices.com. Normally, I just use the site to buy pens and paper for our office a few times a year. However, we had a problem with our printer and we needed to get a new one quickly. I consulted with one of your online representatives and he suggested a printer based on the information I gave about our office activities. The printer she suggested is working much better than our previous one. The next day delivery was also great since we were able to get back to work quickly.

181. What is stated about Malachi Business Services?
(A) It has recently updated its Web site.
(B) It has multiple branches in the region.
(C) It asks for customer feedback on a regular basis.
(D) It has the lowest prices among its competitors.

182. According to e-mail, the word "aim" in paragraph1, line 1 is closest to in meaning to,
(A) set
(B) direction
(C) requirement
(D) intention

183. What is most likely true about Ms. McCourt?
(A) She updated her account information.
(B) She will get a discount on her next order.
(C) She hadn't shopped at Malachi Business Services before August 3.
(D) She received her order later than expected.

184. What does Ms. McCourt suggest about her latest order?
(A) It took too long to receive it.
(B) She was appreciative of the recommendation.
(C) It was delivered to the wrong location.
(D) She was pleased with the free delivery.

185. What does Ms. McCourt regularly purchase?
(A) Stationery products
(B) Printers
(C) Desk organization
(D) Computers

Questions 186-190 refer to the following announcement, notice, and e-mail.

THIS MONTH

New Releases for Young Adults from Alley Cat Books

To the Lighthouse, My Friend by Patrick Fox
The first in this mysterious thriller series about a group of friends is set in a coastal town with unexpected plot twists.

Giant Heads and More Below by Martin Glint
With his wonderfully readable prose, Glint recounts travels to Easter Island and his experience with the island's inhabitants. Includes a guide for classroom discussion.

Not My Crown by Sally Alex
After the king of Alimar disappears, his only son has to take over the kingdom with hilarious results. Readers will find themselves incapable of holding their laughing.

Oceanside Blues by Leila Moody
A thought-provoking book shows how the past affects us in a story about acquaintances and friends by the winner of the Layton Award for Fiction.

Friday, July 10

Marshall Cartman, senior editor at Writers Monthly Magazine will moderate a panel discussion to be held at Darland Booksellers (229 Forest Drive) with authors Patrick Fox, Martin Glint, and Sally Alex. All authors recently had their first books released by Alley Cat Books earlier this year and will talk about their experiences being published. The three writers will have a question and answer session with the audience and sign books afterwards.

* E-mail *

To: Marshall Cartman <mcartman@writersmagazine.net>
From: Daniella Quinterot <dquintero@alleycatbooks.com>
Date: Tuesday, July 2
Subject: Schedule issues

Dear Mr. Cartman,

I apologize for informing you about this so close to the event, but one of our authors, Martin Glint, will be unable to attend your upcoming panel discussion next Friday. He informed us that he had previously scheduled a reading at a university at that time and that he is contractually-bound to that appointment. However, we are happy to offer a substitute author, Victor Smallwood, who recently published his book entitled, Loathsome Balance. This is also Mr. Smallwood's first publication, so he should be able to contribute to the topic of the panel discussion. If I can assist you with anything else regarding the event, please feel free to contact me.

Sincerely,

Daniella Quintero
Public Relations Director, Alley Cat Books

---

186. What do all of the books in the announcement have in common?
(A) They are works of fiction.
(B) They are from a publisher on Easter Island.
(C) They are written for young adults.
(D) They are each author's first published work.

187. What is the topic of the July 10 event?
(A) How bookshops can increase sales
(B) How writers can have their work published
(C) How to get a job of editing a magazine
(D) How to create lesson plans for classes

188. What will Mr. Cartman do at the event?
(A) Sign books for readers
(B) Provide tips for classroom management
(C) Conduct a discussion with a group
(D) Manage security

189. What is NOT suggested about the author, Leila Moody?
(A) She is an award-winning author.
(B) She will sign the books in the event.
(C) She had her book published by Alley Cat Books.
(D) She has recently written a book for young people.

190. What book will NOT have its author present at the event?
(A) To the Lighthouse, My Friend
(B) Giant Heads and More Below
(C) Not My Crown
(D) Loathsome Balance

Questions 191–195 refer to the following e-mail, schedule, and e-mail.

E-mail Message

To :	William Harvest <wharvest@zeamail.co.nz>
From :	Katie Simm <ksimm@nzaw.org>
Re :	Auckland Convention
Date :	June 2
Attachment :	Seminar timetable

Dear Mr. Harvest

Your registration for the 5th Annual Writer's Convention brought to you by the New Zealand Author's Association has been completed. However, there have been some changes made to the schedule and we need you to respond to this e-mail with the requested information by June 20.

Unfortunately, one of the seminars that you registered for, "Relatable Character Creation" presented by Belinda Corrs was canceled. This has been replaced with "Making Characters Readers Like" presented by Victor Hines. If you would like to attend this seminar, please confirm what you want via e-mail.

There is also a scheduling conflict between two of your seminars. Dylan Burgers' seminar has now been moved to Saturday afternoon instead of Saturday Morning. This means it is at the same time as Evelyn Praymore's presentation, which you also registered for. Please decide which seminar you would prefer to attend and let us know.

Regards,
Katie Simm, Convention organizer

New Zealand Author's Association (NZAA)
5th Annual Convention – 15 – 16 July
Auckland, New Zealand

Saturday Seminars		
Time	Seminar Name	Hosted by
11:15 – 12:10	Setting the tone of New Zealand	Odette Lafleur, author
	Self-publishing and how to start	Alvin Bright, publisher
	12:30 – 1:30 Lunch Break	
1:50 -3:00	New Zealand in the Literary Universe	Evelyn Praymore, novelist
	Writing for a Broad Audience	Dylan Burgers, television writer

Sunday Seminars		
Time	Seminar Name	Hosted by
10:00 – 1:00	Stories that Sell	Mallory Stonch, literary sales analyst
	Lightening Lexicons Lessens Likeability	Liz Trill, poet
	1:15 – 2:15 Lunch Break	
2:40 – 5:00	Making Characters Readers Like	Victor Hines, English professor
	Gaining an Audience Online	Sally Gosh, journalist

E-mail Message

To: Berta West <bwest@jawharppublications.com>
From: William Harvest <wharvest@zeamail.co.nz>
Date: July 18
Subject: Thanks again

Hi Berta.

I wanted to thank you and Jaw Harp Publications for paying for me to attend the author's convention. I really learned a lot there that I think I can use in writing my novel. In addition to my novel, I've decided to start using some of what I learned at the convention to spark some interest in my writing using the Internet. I plan to start a blog as well as contribute some of my short stories to online literary Web sites. If you have any ideas, please let me know.

Regards,
William Harvest

---

191. What is the purpose of the e-mail?
(A) To verify attendance at an association event
(B) To advertise an upcoming convention
(C) To invite people to join a committee
(D) To announce changes made to a convention timetable

192. In the first e-mail, the word "via" in paragraph 2, line 3, is closest in meaning to
(A) for
(B) through
(C) toward
(D) regarding

193. What workshop was originally scheduled for Sunday?
(A) Relatable Character Creation
(B) New Zealand in the Literary Universe
(C) Historical characters in fiction
(D) A Nation of Narratives

194. What is indicated about Mr. Harvest in his email?
(A) He was unable to attend all the presentations he wanted to.
(B) He is currently sending his book out to publishers.
(C) He didn't pay the fee for the convention himself.
(D) He was disappointed by some presentations.

195. Whose presentation did Mr. Harvest most likely attend at the convention?
(A) Alvin Bright
(B) Thomas Gaines
(C) Liz Trill
(D) Sally Gosh

Questions 196-200 refer to the following information, e-mail, and memo.

Chrosin
MEDICAL MACHINERY

Places of Operation
Pittsburgh, Philadelphia
Pittsburgh is where Chrosin started and is still the home of the company's main office. Over 600 staff are employed in the product testing, development, public relations, sales, and management departments at this location.

Portsmith, Maine
Our newly renovated production plant is located in Portsmith with over 250 employees who manufacture our products and ship them all over the globe.

Paris, France
The office in Paris is the hub for our business in Europe. Over 400 people work outside of North America for Chrosin and most of these employees are in Paris.

Hong Kong, Hong Kong
Hong Kong is our latest place of operations for our business in the Pacific for Asian markets. The Hong Kong office will become more important as we expand our markets in the region.

E-mail Message

To : Becca Neilsen
From : Pierre Dumont
Date : August 2
Subject : Transfer

Dear Becca,

I'm happy that you'll begin working with us here in Europe. I'm sure that you'll be a great asset to our office. On August 4, we'll have a staff meeting at 3:00 p.m., or 9:00 a.m. at your location. I want to call you during this meeting so that we can talk about the marketing plans for our new products. Please tell me if you're available for this.

If there's anything we can do to make your transfer from the main office easier, feel free to let me know and we'll be happy to help.

Pierre

Memo to all branch employees:

The farewell get-together for Becca Nielsen will be held this Friday, September 2, two days before she leaves for Europe. The Paris office has been very appreciative of the assistance she has already given them and are looking forward to her joining their team. We will certainly miss her enthusiasm and commitment. We know she is excited to lead her own team directly rather than assisting in management. We wish her the best of luck in her new position. Make sure to come to the farewell party and say goodbye to Ms. Nielsen.

196. In the information, the word "hub" in paragraph 3, line 1, is closest in meaning to
(A) distribution
(B) remedy
(C) plant
(D) center

197. What is implied about the company's Asia-Pacific business?
(A) It is more successful than European operations.
(B) It is managed by Mr. Dumont.
(C) It is expected to increase.
(D) It is not very successful.

198. Where is Ms. Neilsen currently working?
(A) In Pittsburgh
(B) In Portsmith
(C) In Paris
(D) In Hong Kong

199. What does the memo indicate about Ms. Nielsen?
(A) She is dissatisfied with her new position.
(B) Her transfer includes a promotion.
(C) Her travel expenses will be reimbursed.
(D) She is changing departments.

200. How long has Ms. Nielsen been assisting the Paris office?
(A) 1 week
(B) 2 weeks
(C) 3 weeks
(D) 4 week

Stop! This is the end of the test. If you finish before time is called, you may go back to Parts 5, 6, and 7 and check your work.

동시토익 실전 WORKBOOK

101. You will find your schedule for the workshops included with this letter.
해석]

102. Michael Balik's new novel was released last week, and critics have given it very favorable reviews.
해석]

103. The Shift Supervisor position requires excellent organizational skills as well as great interpersonal communication abilities.
해석]

104. Gilby Hotel provides the cheapest nightly rates, while still giving guests the best customer service.
해석]

105. Employees of Kindet Technology will receive at least twenty vacation days next year.
해석]

106. The bridge, which connects Prince George and Charles City counties, will remain closed until further notice due to possible structural damage.
해석]

107. The new X90 racing car was produced jointly by Horser Motors and Tolvir Automotive.
해석]

108. The articles in November issue of all investor magazines contain numerous quotations from Mr. Held, several of which were especially interesting.
해석]

109. With the release of their new microwave, Dalk Electronics has increased its market share over its competitors in the region.
해석]

110. The Metropolitan Symphony Orchestra is funded primarily through donations from the public.
해석]

*어휘 NOTE

111. Michelle Kim and Daniel Heely interviewed all candidates by themselves at the Boise Career Fair that was held last month.
해석]

112. Halicart is known for having large number of Mexican restaurants in the downtown area of the city.
해석]

113. Library members must pay any fines incurred for any overdue or missing books before being able to borrow any books.
해석]

114. To receive your free gift, you must first activate your Discover Titanium card by making a purchase, transferring a balance, or making a cash advance.
해석]

115. Most of the students who visited the financial aid office last week needed assistance in completing their applications.
해석]

116. Much to the disappointment of his colleagues and family, Mr. Jackson applied for early retirement.
해석]

117. The terms of the agreement state that subscribers must pay a cancelation fee for early termination.
해석]

118. The fact that the sun will be shining all week does not mean that the temperature will become warmer during this cold winter.
해석]

119. Because of rising operating costs, Reddon, Inc. will begin limiting the amount of overtime that employees are allowed to work.
해석]

120. CEO Paul Settler calmly discussed the decision to issue a recall on the defective televisions at the shareholder's meeting.
해석]

* 어휘 NOTE

121. The Victory Coffee Shop has become the increasingly popular venue among youngsters since introducing a new line of fruit smoothies.

해석]

122. The recent developments of the productivity improvement program are considered to be unprecedented by many experts.

해석]

123. Cybob has been one of the most commonly used operating systems for smartphones for the last five years.

해석]

124. With Lightspeed News' new online service, subscribers receive text messages whenever a subject of interest to them is published.

해석]

125. Latent Software's file transfer software is compatible with Latent smart phones produced after March of this year.

해석]

126. Online game distribution company, Joinus, occasionally holds huge sales to arouse consumer interest.

해석]

127. The temporary waiting area is located slightly _____ the airport entrance on the right side of the roadway.

해석]

128. Invoices are mailed on a monthly basis to all Grove Cable Services customers.

해석]

129. Sales of Morton Refrigerators have improved since it launched innovative advertising campaign in May.

해석]

130. Despite the issues many users reported when it was first launched, Norse Playbox has been rated the best video game console of all time.

해석]

★ 어휘 NOTE

동시토익 CONTEMPORARY **TOEIC**

TEST 06

READING TEST

In the Reading test, you will read a variety of texts and answer several different types of reading comprehension questions. The entire Reading test will last 75 minutes. There are three parts, and directions are given for each part. You are encouraged to answer as many questions as possible within the time allowed.

You must mark your answers on the separate answer sheet. Do not write your answers in your test book.

Part 5

Directions: A word or phrase is missing in each of the sentences below. Four answer choices are given below each sentence. Select the best answer to complete the sentence. Then mark the letter (A), (B), (C), or (D) on your answer sheet.

101. Mr. DeLay has finished his law school, but Ms. Dylan has not yet finished _____.
(A) her
(B) herself
(C) she
(D) hers

102. You will enhance your simple woodwork by implementing several _____ finishes we offer.
(A) differs
(B) difference
(C) differently
(D) different

103. Formerly a renowned surgeon, Dr. Capuano _____ divides his time between caring for patients and teaching future doctors.
(A) forward
(B) soon
(C) far
(D) now

104. The Lim & Kim Group is committed to helping people make _____ that can earn the rate of return they need for retirement.
(A) invests
(B) invested
(C) investments
(D) investing

105. Seven other specialists will be available _____ consultation at an hourly rate.
(A) for
(B) while
(C) than
(D) as

106. The efficiency of solar energy utilization needs to be _____ verified by a suitable method.
(A) regularity
(B) regular
(C) regularize
(D) regularly

107. Even though the number of disasters has more than _____ since the 1970's, the reported death toll has decreased to less than half.
(A) the third
(B) tripled
(C) a third
(D) three times

108. _____ about the explosion which seemed to cause a great deal of damage to the factory have just been released.
(A) Reports
(B) Report
(C) To report
(D) Reporter

109. Our firm continues to _____ you in maintaining the accounting system.
(A) assist
(B) tell
(C) lend
(D) explain

110. To be considered for a nurse position at Ralf Reed Memorial Hospital, applicants must be _____ to work any shift.
(A) necessary
(B) available
(C) obvious
(D) common

111. Listed cement firms saw an _____ in profits in the first half of this year, compared to the same period last year.
(A) array
(B) effort
(C) increase
(D) insert

112. We asked that guests _____ a half hour prior to commencement of the ceremony.
(A) seat
(B) to sit
(C) seated
(D) be seated

113. Professor Withrow advised students to check if the plan is concise and realistic _____ submitting the business plan.
(A) just as
(B) except for
(C) before
(D) regarding

114. Funn Sports will be _____ its sporting goods business into emerging markets next year.
(A) expanding
(B) cooperating
(C) reserving
(D) selecting

115. The $500 security deposit you gave us will be returned to you only _____ the apartment passes inspection.
(A) when
(B) there
(C) whether
(D) though

116. In order to better serve our customers, we plan _____ our inventory by 20 percent, which means that we need more space.
(A) to increase
(B) increasing
(C) increases
(D) increase

117. Most high income earners are likely to say they intend to boost their property investment portfolios _____ the next few months.
(A) upon
(B) against
(C) over
(D) between

118. Scandi Household is currently offering a _____ to new customers that gives them 25% off their purchase.
(A) realization
(B) destination
(C) contribution
(D) promotion

119. To help your business succeed, we also provide the training course that will help you provide _____ customer service.
(A) distinctly
(B) distinctively
(C) distinction
(D) distinctive

120. While Mr. Karst is away from work, please have every letter and package _____ him delivered to his assistant.
(A) upon
(B) of
(C) on
(D) for

121. Ronald Charities, _____ purpose is to create and support programs for children in need, is an independent nonprofit organization.
(A) what
(B) whose
(C) which
(D) who

122. _____, it is Mr. Goodwill who has to make a final decision on who will be laid off in the next three months.
(A) Ultimately
(B) Timely
(C) Permanently
(D) Widely

123. By the time Jerry Hairston was promoted to CEO, the company _____ reorganizing its capital structure.
(A) begins
(B) will begin
(C) had begun
(D) having begun

124. Many entrepreneurs from all areas of business will join the seminar this year, and _____ are today's top business leaders.
(A) another
(B) anyone
(C) other
(D) some

125. In her new book, a leading _____, Ms. Blanchett writes about the instability of global capitalism.
(A) finances
(B) financier
(C) financial
(D) finance

126. Ms. Sienna decided to start _____ business last month and has since been preparing for it.
(A) hers
(B) her own
(C) she
(D) herself

127. Health boards must take strong security measures so that digital patient records may remain _____.
(A) confidence
(B) confidentially
(C) confidentiality
(D) confidential

128. Togo Food Company guarantees that _____ the highest quality ingredients are used for their products.
(A) when
(B) only
(C) ever
(D) once

129. Please affix an annual parking permit with your name _____ to the lower left hand corner of the windshield at the time of purchase.
(A) direction
(B) directing
(C) directly
(D) directs

130. Due to the time constraints in evaluating workshops conducted this year, we need to receive _____ feedback on December workshop from the attendees.
(A) mutual
(B) determined
(C) probable
(D) immediate

PART 6

Direction: Read the texts that follow. A word, phrase, or sentence is missing in parts of each text. Four answer choices for each question are given below the text. Select the best answer to complete the text. Then mark the letter (A), (B), (C), or (D) on your answer sheet.

Questions 131-134 refer to the following article.

Gerald Art Gallery to Display Works of Graduating Seniors

June 4 - The Gerald Art Gallery at the College of the Holy Cross ------- its annual "Senior Artwork" display.
131.

Student artists participating in this annual event attended the course taught by Michael Beatty, associate professor of visual arts. -------.
132.

Advance tickets to the ------- may be purchased online at www.geraldag.com. Online ticketing
133.
closes four hours before the event. If not sold out, tickets will be available at the box office. For information pertaining to ------- admission fee for groups of ten or more, please call 714-555-2401.
134.

131. (A) will be hosting
 (B) would host
 (C) had been hosting
 (D) is hosted

132. (A) The Gerald Art Gallery is closed every Monday and on holidays.
 (B) Students are encouraged to send their submissions to the art committee.
 (C) He is well-known as a recipient of the Visual Art Award last year.
 (D) Admission to the event is free for all residents.

133. (A) banquet
 (B) concert
 (C) tournament
 (D) exhibit

134. (A) reduce
 (B) reduced
 (C) reduction
 (D) reduces

Question 135-138 refer to the following e-mail.

From: Elizabeth Warren
To: All staff
Date: August 16
Subject: Larry Page

-------. As most of you know, he has ------- an offer from Community Health Charities of Iowa
135.   136.
(CHCI) for the position of Corporate Relations Manager.

It has been his long-cherished dream to contribute to the community in a meaningful way. -------,
                                                                                          137.
we all know we will miss him when he is gone.

A lovely farewell banquet will be held Friday, 30 August in the main conference room ------- his 23
                                                                                      138.
years of hard work and dedication at Kaufmann, Inc. We are looking for speakers for the event
who would like to congratulate Mr. Page as well as share personal stories about their experiences
with him. If you are interested in this, please contact your supervisor.

We wish Mr. Page all the best with his future career.

Regards,

Elizabeth Warren

135. (A) Our organization will be holding its annual charity later this month.
(B) Larry Page announced last week that he will step down from his role as CEO.
(C) Congratulations to Larry Page on his latest promotion in our organization.
(D) Thank you all for contributing your time to the farewell banquet for Larry Page.

136. (A) advertised
(B) supported
(C) accepted
(D) indicated

137. (A) Even so
(B) Besides
(C) Similarly
(D) After that

138. (A) has recognized
(B) is recognizing
(C) would recognize
(D) to recognize

Questions 139-142 refer to the following advertisement.

The Best Services for Your Business at Terwilliger Financial

If you want the best service possible for your business from your financial services company, look no further than Terwilliger Financial. ------- employee of our company does his or her utmost to provide exactly the kind of service our clients desire to help build their business and ------- their company's stability.
139.   140.

Among the client services we offer are financial consultation, efficiency consulting, and filing taxes. -------. Our online services offer greater flexibility and convenience to our clients.
141.

Contact ------- to learn how to strategically manage capital and transactions in a changing world.
142.

139. (A) Every
(B) All
(C) Whole
(D) Multiple

140. (A) enhance
(B) enhancement
(C) enhances
(D) enhancing

141. (A) More details can be found on our company Web site.
(B) Our office is conveniently located in the business district.
(C) A complete list of our services can be obtained by visiting any of our branches.
(D) We have recently upgraded our Web site to improve our service further.

142. (A) theirs
(B) us
(C) me
(D) it

Questions 143-146 refer to the following announcement.

Beginning on April 1, the University of Victoria will host a poster design competition sponsored annually by GOMA Art Gallery. The competition is open only to college students currently attending schools. All entries must be the ------- work of the entrant. Any entries which are determined to be
143.
copies or not the work of the applicant will be disqualified.

The ------- will be won by the students whose posters depict the theme of "Naturally digital".
144.

Students interested in participating should register by sending an email to the competition organizers by April 20. -------. Entries ------- at the upcoming International Digital Forum in Hong
145.   146.
Kong on May 20.

143. (A) commercial
(B) original
(C) collaborative
(D) partial

144. (A) picture
(B) argument
(C) race
(D) contest

145. (A) Tickets for the event may be purchased online next week.
(B) The deadline for submission of entries is May 10.
(C) The schedule of the competition will be finalized soon.
(D) The contest is open to all Hong Kong residents.

146. (A) will be judged
(B) have been judging
(C) will have judged
(D) had been judging

PART 7

Direction: In this part you will read a selection of texts, such as magazine and newspaper articles, letters, e-mails, and instant messages. Each text or set of texts is followed by several questions. Select the best answer for each question and mark the letter (A), (B), (C), or (D) on your answer sheet.

Questions 147-148 refer to the following text message.

From: Ellen Ting
14:10 p.m. January 21

My train just got to the station, but the driver isn't at the station. Do me a favor and contact him to see if he will be here to pick me up soon. I'd like to know if I have to wait long. Thank you and I'll see you at work.

---

147. What is the purpose of the text message?
(A) To find out transportation arrangements
(B) To inquire about a building's location
(C) To postpone a meeting with a client
(D) To report a travel itinerary

148. From where did Ms. Ting send the message?
(A) An airport bus
(B) Her house
(C) A train station
(D) Her workplace

Questions 149-151 refer to the following announcement.

BUSINESS FOR SALE

Brenda's Bakery and Cakery is being sold by the owner at a price of $500,000 or best offer. The successful eatery is visited daily by many customers as it is located in the highly-populated area of uptown Headerton. It is in very close proximity to the Martin Shopping Center, as well as many other restaurants and parks. All supplies, furniture, and equipment are included with the business.

The store's profitability can increase further, by making a larger seating area for customers and adding more area for retail sales. Adding a patio for customers is also an option.

You can get more information and pictures from the real estate agency by contacting Peter Lydon at Atlas Business Realty (plydon@atlasbr.ca).

149. What kind of store is for sale?
 (A) A grocery store
 (B) A coffee shop
 (C) A baked goods shops
 (D) A cooking supplies store

150. What is NOT stated about Brenda's?
 (A) It opens early in the morning.
 (B) It has a lot of customers.
 (C) It is near parks.
 (D) It is a profitable store.

151. What possible change for the store is suggested in the announcement?
 (A) The ingredients could be improved.
 (B) The advertising could be spread wider.
 (C) The sales area could be made larger.
 (D) The goods could be changed.

Questions 152-153 refer to the following table of contents of a magazine.

Table of Contents
Volume 24, March

9	In-Grow-Diets	Bob Treston gives ideas for growing your own herbs.
13	Treats from Trees	Guest contributors provide advice on which kind of fruit tree is best for you.
21	Tips and Hints	Helen Nguyen shows how to get the most out of compost.
24	Essentials	Nick Rogerson details the way to make your yard the greenest.
28	Chef Glenda Anore	Southside Kitchen's gourmet chef shows you how to make a delicious pasta dish with vegetables you can grow at home.
32	Coming Up	A look at what will be in our April issue

152. What is the topic of the magazine?
(A) Cooking
(B) Gardening
(C) Fitness
(D) Cameras

153. On what page would a reader most likely find a recipe?
(A) On page 13
(B) On page 21
(C) On page 28
(D) On page 32

Questions 154-155 refer to the following text message chain.

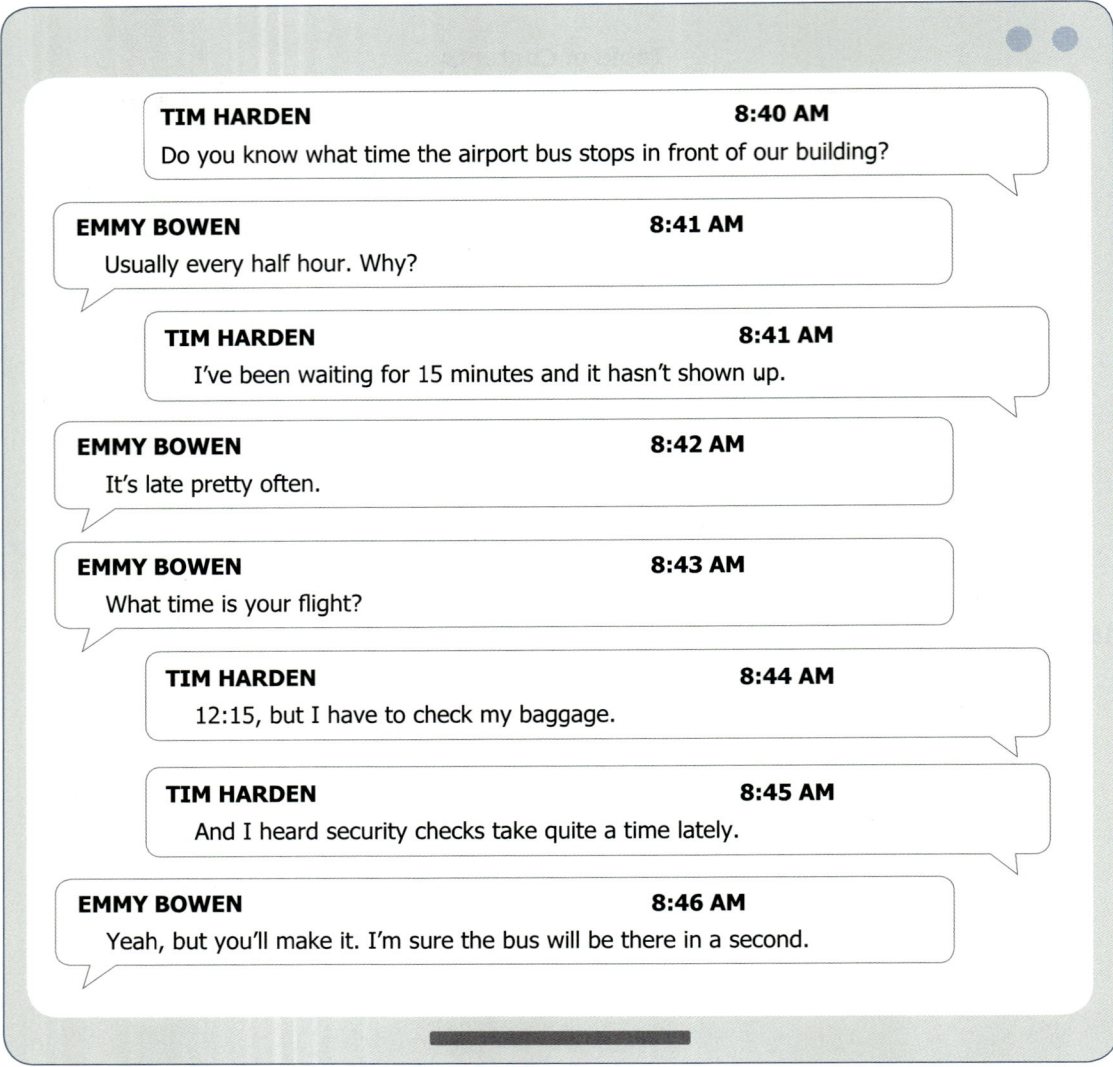

154. What is suggested about Mr. Harden?
(A) He is taking time off.
(B) He will call for a taxi.
(C) He is carrying luggage.
(D) He will meet Ms. Bowen at the airport.

155. At 8:46 AM, what does Ms. Bowen mean when she writes, "the bus will be there in a second"?
(A) The bus requires reservations.
(B) The bus will arrive shortly.
(C) The bus drives very fast.
(D) Mr. Harden needs to flag down the bus.

Questions 156-157 refer to the following letter.

LandWorks Yard Services
14 Philip Road
Perth, Austrlia

15 February

Nelson Foley
New Sun Networks
768 Kings Street
Perth, Australia

Dear Mr. Foley,

We appreciate your continued patronage with LandWorks Yard Services. With the season changing, please remember that we offer services all year round, even during winter. LandWorks Yard Services provides various services during winter, including:

• Removal of snow and ice from lawns and paved areas
• Sheltering outside plants and shrubberies from cold temperatures
• Collection and storage of plants susceptible to low temperatures in our indoor nursery

For more details on prices and other information, feel free to contact us.

Regards,

Larry Green
LandWorks Yard Services

156. Why was the letter written?
(A) To ask about a yard care service
(B) To detail new equipment for removing snow
(C) To encourage continued patronage from a customer
(D) To offer an estimate for a purchase of yard care supplies

157. What is indicated about LandWorks Yard Services?
(A) It is preparing to expand its business.
(B) It maintains a storage facility.
(C) It has three locations in Australia.
(D) Its building is undergoing restoration.

Questions 158-160 refer to the following schedule.

JUNE

Monday	Tuesday	Wednesday	Thursday	Friday	Saturday
2 Monday Night Movie 7:00 p.m. The 70s in Pictures	**3**	**4** Kids' Time 4 p.m. "Exciting Earth"	**5**	**6**	**7**
9 Monday Night Movie 7:00 p.m. Art in the Dark Ages	**10** Presentation 2 p.m. Tien Trahn Postmodern Gallery Curator	**11**	**12** Staff Gathering (Every exhibit will be closed)	**13**	**14**
16 Monday Night Movie 7:00 p.m. The Battle of Modern Photography	**17** 18 Kids' Time 4 p.m. "Freaky Fossils"	**18**	**19**	**20** Presentation, 5 p.m. Praja Khan Fresco Restoration Expert	**21**
23 Monday Night Movie 7:00 p.m. The Masters of the Renaissance	**24**	**25** Sculpting Seminar, 6 p.m. (Beginners welcome)	**26** Workshop 11 a.m. "Impressionist Painting Techniques" (Seats must be reserved)	**27**	**28** Donors' Luncheon 11:30 a.m.

158. What organization most likely released the calendar?
(A) A graduate school
(B) A conference center
(C) A museum
(D) A library

159. For what occasion must attendees register in advance?
(A) A painting workshop
(B) A scientific activity for kids
(C) A lecture about postmodern art
(D) A sculpting seminar

160. What happens once a week?
(A) A presentation
(B) A staff gathering
(C) A showing of a film
(D) An educational time for kids

Questions 161-164 refer to the following online chat discussion.

Frank Noonan	[10:13 a.m.]	Hey everyone. Dennis Bonifant was recently assigned to lead a project for creating a marketing campaign for our new line of beverages. I was hoping to find some volunteers to work on his team.
Angela Viracola	[10:14 a.m.]	How many people are you looking for? I'd do it, but I'm up to my neck in other projects right now. I think that Larry Carrol worked with Dennis on a project before, though.
Larry Carrol	[10:16 a.m.]	Yeah, I did. Dennis and I made a presentation together at the National Soft Drink Convention last year. I'd be happy to work with him on another project.
Frank Noonan	[10:18 a.m.]	Alright, that's great news. Denis actually asked about working with you again on this. I was hoping to get at least two more people to work with him on the campaign.
Larry Carrol	[10:19 a.m.]	I think that Linda McAvoy and Rose Condor might be good choices to help on the campaign. I haven't seen Rose in the office today, though.
Linda McAvoy	[10:21 a.m.]	I'd be happy to help with the marketing campaign, although I really haven't had much experience with that kind of project. If Larry thinks I'd be able to help, I'll trust him. Also, Rose is at a meeting with a client this morning, but she'll be back in the afternoon.
Frank Noonan	[10:23 a.m.]	Actually, I just got a call from Rose and her client had to postpone the meeting to this afternoon, so she's going to stay on site and see them this afternoon. She'll be back at the office tomorrow. Larry, would you want to talk to her about the marketing campaign then?
Larry Carrol	[10:25 a.m.]	Yeah, alright. I'll talk to her first thing in the morning.

161. What industry do the chat participants most likely work in?
(A) Advertising
(B) Soft drink production
(C) Hospitality
(D) Social networking

162. What does Frank Noonan want to find?
(A) A convention schedule
(B) Assistance for a campaign
(C) A client's phone number
(D) An office location

163. At 10:14 a.m., what does Angela Viracola mean when she writes "I'm up to my neck in other projects"?
(A) She is deeply involved in other work.
(B) She may lose her job.
(C) She would like to work on additional projects.
(D) She won't be able to meet a deadline.

164. What is suggested about Rose Condor?
(A) She has worked with Denis Bonifant before.
(B) She has worked on other marketing campaigns.
(C) She will be out of the office all week.
(D) She had a meeting rescheduled.

Questions 165-167 refer to the following memo.

From :	Simon Locklear, head administrative assistant
To :	Company staff
Subject :	Yearly conference
Date :	September 15

Alternative Automotive's annual conference will be held this coming Monday, September 22. There are many people who want to come to this conference considering the growth that our company has seen over the last 12 months. —[1]—. With the increase in people coming, the company has decided to move this year's conference from the Alternative Automative headquarters to the Oak Grove Convention Hall. —[2]—.

An event that should not be missed by any employee is the post-conference socialization that will start around 7:00 p.m. Company chairperson Amanda Fealy will be mingling with guests, and snacks and beverages will be freely available. —[3]—. Staff will need to show their identification cards at the reception desk, so make sure you bring them along. —[4]—. Please contact me if you need more information.

165. Why was the notice sent?
(A) To change the order of a conference timetable
(B) To request the presence of company shareholders
(C) To advise staff about a change in location of an event
(D) To give directions to a company event

166. What are conference attendees asked to do?
(A) To elect candidates for the management committee
(B) To specify how many people will be in their party
(C) To contact Ms. Fealy for more information
(D) To present identification at a reception desk

167. In which of the positions marked [1], [2], [3], and [4] does the following sentence best belong?

"The rest of the conference arrangements will stay the same, including the timetable that I sent to everyone on August 30."

(A) [1]
(B) [2]
(C) [3]
(D) [4]

Questions 168-171 refer to the following article.

PEM AT THE HEAD OF THE INDUSTRY

By Gerald Shall, Economics Report

SHEFFIELD (June 10) - The statistics from industry reports compiled by the research division of Progressive Electronics Multinational (PEM) indicate that the company will become the leader of the MP3 player field for the first time. As a result, the corporation, originally founded in Sheffield, will take the place of its primary rival, Technological Marvels, LLC (TML), which was established fifteen years ago and has unarguably been at the top of the MP3 player market for the last two years. —[1]—.

—[2]—. PEM's profits have increased over the last 5 years by 15 percent on average. With the designation of Jillian Carter as the chairwoman of the board three years ago, the corporation's sales increased even more.

—[3]—. The corporation has only released three completely new players over the previous year. The corporation actually had an advantage when its rivals cut back on advertising costs. —[4]—. By finding ways to lower production costs with the use of advanced equipment, PEM was able to maintain their advertising budget at the same rate as previous years.

168. What is the reason for the article?
(A) To predict managerial changes at an organization
(B) To advertise a new MP3 player
(C) To declare the accomplishments of a corporation
(D) To explain how an electronic device functions

169. What is indicated about PEM's profits?
(A) They were declared by Ms. Carter.
(B) They have been low over the last five years.
(C) They are expected to be the highest in the industry this year.
(D) They will be published later than usual this year.

170. According to the article, how long has TML been in business?
(A) Two years
(B) Three years
(C) Five years
(D) Fifteen years

171. In which of the positions marked [1], [2], [3], and [4] does the following sentence best belong?

"The increase in profits is not related to PEM's release of any brand-new products."

(A) [1]
(B) [2]
(C) [3]
(D) [4]

Questions 172-175 refer to the following advertisement.

The Daesung Z22 Automatic Assembly Apparatus: Components

The Daesung Z22 Automatic Assembly Apparatus can lift and accurately install parts as part of an assembly line in a manufacturing facility. The automatic assembly apparatus is similar to a human appendage with two joints; one at its base and one in the middle. Both joints are able to move left and right. At the end of the arm is a rod that is able to move up and down (i.e. the vertical axis), as well as rotate (i.e. the rotary axis) to make sure parts are put in place accurately. The ends of the rod can have many assorted tools attached, such as grips or suction cups to ensure proper assembly in any factory setting.

The Z22 is able to lift up to five kilograms and move at a speed of 50 centimeters per second. The total reachable diameter is 200 centimeters. The Z22 also includes a cover which can be fitted to the robot to keep any materials safe from contamination, fulfilling requirements of the safety guidelines.

The Daesung Z22 Automatic Assembly Apparatus: Specifications

Joints	Rotation
Base	180 degrees
Middle	180 degrees

Axis	Limits
Vertical	50 centimeters per second
Rotary	360 degrees

172. Where would a Daesung Z22 most likely be used?
(A) In a vocational school
(B) In a sewage treatment plant
(C) In a manufacturing facility
(D) In a power plant

173. How many joints does the automatic assembly apparatus have?
(A) One
(B) Two
(C) Three
(D) Four

174. The word "assorted" in paragraph 1, line 5 is closest in meaning to?
(A) Classified
(B) Advanced
(C) Secure
(D) Various

175. What is stated about the cover?
(A) It helps follow safety guidelines.
(B) It is 200 centimeters in diameter.
(C) It can be used to store additional tools.
(D) It closes with a zipper.

Questions 176-180 refer to the following e-mail and form.

---

* E-mail *

To :	Department Supervisors
From :	Oliver Martin
Subject :	August 2
Date :	Advancement Seminars

Advancement Seminars that can help employees who were hired in the last six months find out more about SecuriPath Logistics have been set up by the personnel department. We would like all supervisors to make sure your staff know the benefits of attending a seminar that is led by employees outside of their own department.

We'd also be thankful if those employees who attend a seminar hand in a completed evaluation sheet after attending their last session. These forms will be near the exit of each of the seminar rooms after the seminar has been concluded.

Below is the timetable for the seminars, which will all be held in the second floor conference room in the Beek Building. There will be a complimentary lunch served for all attending employees.

Department	Presenter	Date	Time
Accounting	Michelle Patton	August 18	12:00 p.m. – 12:45 p.m.
Advertising	Nigel Kent	August 25	11:30 a.m – 12: 15 p.m.
Research & Development	Nam Sudara	September 5	12:00 p.m. – 12:45 p.m.
Sales	Betty Sebastian	September 11	11:30 a.m – 12: 15 p.m.

Sincerely,

Oliver Martin
Personnel Director

Advancement Seminar Evaluation Sheet

Staff name: __Anita Berkin__

To which seminars did you go?
  __v__ Accounting   __v__ Advertising   __v__ Research & Development   _____ Sales

Which seminar did you find the most interesting? Please explain.
  The conductor of the research and development handed out examples of new products that we could try out. It made the seminar much more engaging and made it easy to understand how that department works.

Is there any way the seminars could be improved?
  A few of my co-workers and I weren't able to get to the August 25 seminar on time since our department has a meeting until 11:30 on the last Wednesday of the month. Personnel should try to make sure that employees of all departments don't have conflicting schedules when setting up the next sessions.

176. Why was the e-mail sent?
    (A) To request supervisors to participate in an evaluation
    (B) To report the relocation of a conference room
    (C) To ask supervisors to encourage staff to attend an event
    (D) To announce new listings for open positions

177. What is true about all of the seminars?
    (A) Supervisors must go to all seminars.
    (B) Staff have to sign up before attending.
    (C) They all start at 11:30 a.m.
    (D) Attending staff will be treated to a meal.

178. What is implied about Anita Berkin?
    (A) He has worked at SecuriPath Logistics for less than a year.
    (B) Her supervisor is Oliver Martin.
    (C) She is part of the accounting department.
    (D) She works in the Beek Building.

179. Who handed out examples during a seminar?
    (A) Michelle Patton
    (B) Nigel Kent
    (C) Nam Sudara
    (D) Betty Sebastian

180. To what seminar did Anita Berkin arrive late?
    (A) The accounting seminar
    (B) The advertising seminar
    (C) The research & development seminar
    (D) The sales seminar

Questions 181-185 refer to the following webpage and e-mail.

---

http://www.fittonflavor.com/ads

Valor Footwear's Business Program

| Home | Contact | Order | Testimonials |

Promote your business on FittonFlavor.com!

FittonFlavor.com is one of the most popular Web sites for residents and visitors to Fitton and the surrounding areas, providing information and tips about grocery shopping and restaurants in Fitton.

We offer four designs to advertise your business on our site:

Design 1	Design 2
This design features a banner advertisement at the top of a page, so readers see your business' name before anything else (No image or sound can be included).	Your advertisement appears in a small size in the center of a featured article with one sound and one image possibly included along with text.

Design 3	Design 4
This design is a banner advertisement promoting your business placed vertically alongside a featured article (No image or sound can be included).	This is the largest design, giving your business half a page for promoting your business with text and several image and sound options.

E-mail Message

From : Priya Latesh <priyalatesh@bombayeatery.com>
To : Troy Bauer <tbauer@fittonflavor.com>
Subject : Promotion of Bombay Restaurant
Date : March 14

Dear Mr. Bauer,

I would like to ask about using your promotional services on FittonFlavor.com again. I want to post a half-page design once more. I will send two new photographs showing the recent remodeling of our restaurant, but please include the same text and sound as on our previous ad. Please tell me how big the pictures should be before I submit them.

Regards,

Priya Latesh
Proprietor
Bombay Eatery

181. Where does Mr. Bauer work?
(A) At a restaurant supplies distributor
(B) At an advertising consulting company
(C) At a bakery
(D) At online site related to food

182. What is indicated about Design 1?
(A) It is cheap.
(B) It is promininetly placed.
(C) It can contain the most text.
(D) It can be downloaded by visitors.

183. In what ad design is Ms. Latesh most likely interested?
(A) Design 1
(B) Design 2
(C) Design 3
(D) Design 4

184. What is indicated about Bombay Eatery?
(A) It is being moved to a new location.
(B) It currently has a discounted menu.
(C) It has been promoted previously by FittonFlavor.com.
(D) It will be open during a construction project.

185. What does Ms. Latesh inquire about concerning the images?
(A) How they should be sized
(B) Who will photograph them
(C) How many she should send
(D) What should be in the pictures

Questions 186-190 refer to the following article, e-mail, and advertisement.

DETROIT (September 4)-Marlon Automotive will stop making its long-popular Skylark coupe next month, according to a press release from the company.

The car, released ten years ago, has unique design and cherished safety features, which made it one of the highest selling automobiles in the country.

However, the vehicle has not been selling as well in recent years and Marlon also decided to cut two other automobiles from its lineup this year. Marlon CEO, Lars Storch, stated that more consumers are looking for larger cars that are more comfortable with more storage space, so smaller models are not selling as well. "Car buyers are demanding more space in general and we need to provide customers with what they want," Mr. Storch said recently.

Marlon's dealerships are expected to mark down prices in the near future to clear out existing inventory and make room for the new models for next year, including the Halo.

From:	Evelyn Carson, Regional Director <ecarson@marlon.com>
To:	Marlon Automotive Sales Directors <saleslist@marlon.com>
Date:	October 15
Subject:	Clearance sale

Dear Sales Directors and Supervisors:

I trust that you are all having no problems getting ready for the year-end clearance sale. The sale will be starting on the first of next month. Please remember that prices for the Skylark, Crimson, and Laker models will be discounted by 25 percent. Some branches will also have test models of next year's vehicles. Make sure to review the TV and radio commercials to be aired around the country. They are currently on the Marlon Automotive Web site.

Please remember to put next year's models in the middle of your showrooms.

Thanks,

Evelyn

Marlon's End of the Year Clearance Sale

The Janesville Marlon Dealership will be holding its end of the year clearance sale from November.
Come on down and see the great deals we have on this year's models.

Skylark	25% off
Crimson	25% off
Laker	25% off

We are also the only dealership in the region that has next year's models available for a test drive. Our location can also be seen in Marlon's national TV commercials. For the best selection of new Marlon vehicles, visit the Janesville Marlon Dealership today!

---

186. Why was the article written?
(A) To announce a car maker's product line changes
(B) To give a profile of a company executive
(C) To report a company's cutbacks
(D) To release the outcome of a survey

187. According to the article, why have sales for the Skylark sedan declined?
(A) Because consumers have different desires for designs
(B) Because the vehicles cost too much
(C) Because competitors have more dealerships in the area
(D) Because the cars are not as safe as they could be

188. In the article, the word "mark down" in paragraph 4, line 1 is closest in meaning to
(A) scratch
(B) identify
(C) cut
(D) evaluate

189. What is indicated about the 25 percent discount?
(A) It will be advertised around the country.
(B) It will be increased in following months.
(C) It is being given for every vehicle model.
(D) It will be given at the end of each year.

190. What is indicated about the Janesville Marlon Dealership?
(A) It sells both new and used Marlon vehicles.
(B) Buyers receive a discount on insurance.
(C) It is the largest dealership in the region.
(D) Shoppers can test drive a Halo there.

Questions 191-195 refer to the following website and e-mails.

---

http://www.joycewei.ma

| Book Information | Author Information | **Appearances and Presentations** | Praise for Ms. Wei's Work |

Canada Schedule

- **October 2 - 3: Wendtz Theater – Halifax**
  Both lectures will commence at 8:00 p.m. Visit www.wendtztheater.com to purchase tickets and find more information.

- **October 5: Upton College – Ottawa**
  The lecture will commence at 6:00 p.m. and Ms. Wei will sign books at 7:30 p.m.

- **October 7: Onyx Auditorium – Calgary**
  Information for this appearance can be obtained by calling the box office at (403) 555-7716.

- **October 16: Porthal Hotel and Convention Hall – Victoria**
  Guests of PHCH who reserve a room by September 24 will receive a 20% discount on their room if they purchase a ticket for attending Ms. Wei's lecture. Call Darryl Nern at (250) 555-1164 to receive the discount.

If you are interested in scheduling an appearance by Ms. Wei, please write to Stephanie Pool at spool@joycewei.ma.

---

* E-mail *

From:	tnguyen@traverse.edu
To:	spool@joycewei.ma
Date:	October 10
Subject:	Conference in January

Dear Ms. Pool,

I was able to meet Ms. Wei at her latest appearance at the Onyx Auditorium. When we met, I asked if she could possibly lecture at a conference that I am organizing. She was very interested, but said that I need to talk to you to make sure she is available.

This year's Science and Technology Conference is going to be held from January 14 to 17 at the Wendel Hotel in Montreal, Quebec and its sponsors are Audacious Industrial. Would it be possible for Ms. Wei to give a presentation on the afternoon of January 15, as the focus for that day is the future of robotics in business.

Audacious Industrial would be able to pay for any travel and accommodation costs for Ms. Wei. as well as pay her a small gratuity for her participation. Please let me know if it is possible for Ms. Wei to present by November 10 at the latest and feel free to ask any questions you may have.

Sincerely,

Tien Nguyen

To :	Harold Kim <hkim@mail4you.com>
From :	Porthal Hotel <service@porthalhotel.com>
Date :	September 20
Subject :	Your reservation

Dear Mr. Kim,

We are pleased to confirm your reservation at the Porthal Hotel for October 14 to October 17. We have applied a 20% discount to your nightly rate according to the voucher number you entered when making your reservation. Your ticket for the event in our convention hall has also been reserved. If there is anything we can do to make your stay more comfortable, please don't hesitate to let us know.

Sincerely,
Hayden Burrell
Manager, Porthal Hotel and Convention Hall

191. Who most likely is Ms. Wei?
(A) A writer
(B) A scientist
(C) An advertiser
(D) A convention organizer

192. In the website, the word "appearance" in paragraph 5, line 1, is closest in meaning to
(A) presentation
(B) look
(C) impression
(D) figure

193. Where did Ms. Nguyen meet Ms. Wei?
(A) In Halifax
(B) In Ottawa
(C) In Calgary
(D) In Victoria

194. What is the purpose of Ms. Nguyen's e-mail?
(A) To request a presentation at an event
(B) To arrange payment for members of a committee
(C) To ask for a hotel reservation to be changed
(D) To pay for admission to a forthcoming event

195. What is suggested about Harold Kim?
(A) He spoke with Darryl Nern.
(B) He emailed Stephanie Pool.
(C) He is a colleague of Tien Nguyen.
(D) He will attend a conference in January.

Questions 196-200 refer to the following information and e-mails.

Essense
Warranty concerning repairing and / or replacing your MP3 player

Every Essense MP3 player includes a warranty valid for 12 months from the initial date of purchase. Should you experience any defects or damage during this time, it is possible for you to repair or replace your item.

Customers who wish to extend their warranty for an additional year may purchase the Essense Premium Guarantee Package within one year of purchasing your MP3 player. Prices for the Essence Premium Guarantee Package vary from model to model.

More information can be found at www.essenseaudio.com/premium or by calling 1-800-555-1122.

＊ E-mail ＊

To : maintenance@essenseaudio.com
From: gbeakman@speedcom.net
Date: May 18
Subject: Claim #1865BU651

I'd like to know what is going on with the replacement of my MP3 player (claim #1865BU651).

I filed the claim at an Essense store on May 15 and the clerk told me that my device would be replaced at no cost because of my Premium Guarantee Package. He also mentioned that someone would send me an e-mail to let me know that my claim is being processed the next day. It has now been four days since my player was sent from the store, and I haven't gotten an e-mail about it being processed. Please let me know what is happening with my MP3 player and give me an estimate for when the phone will be delivered to my house.

Thanks,

Gloria Beakman

```
* E-mail *
```

To: gbeakman@speedcom.net
From: maintenance@essenseaudio.com
Date: May 18
Subject: Re: Claim #1865BU651

Dear Ms. Beakman,

I apologize for the inconvenience of having to email us. The reason you did not receive an email notifying you of your repair status is that the email address on the repair request form was listed as gbeakman@speedcom.com. We apologize if this was done by our technician.

Your MP3 player has been repaired and is currently ready for delivery. The problem was with a connection to the headphone jack. The repairs made are guaranteed for 90 days after completion, so if you have any issues with your Essence device again, please let us know.

Sincerely,
Paul Astin
Essence Audio Customer Service Representative

---

196. Whom is the information most likely intended for?
(A) People who recently bought Essense MP3 players
(B) Essense Audio technicians
(C) Customers who wish to buy Essense MP3 players
(D) Essense Audio store clerks

197. In the information, the word "vary" in paragraph 2, line 3, is closest in meaning to
(A) excel
(B) differ
(C) spread
(D) reflect

198. What is most likely true about Ms. Beakman?
(A) She was employed by Essense Audio.
(B) She bought her MP3 player less than a year ago.
(C) The initial warranty for her device is no longer valid.
(D) Her device was replaced over a month ago.

199. What is indicated about Ms. Beakman's repair request form?
(A) It was lost by the technician.
(B) It will be returned to Ms. Beakman.
(C) It had some incorrect information.
(D) It was sent to the wrong department.

200. What requested information was NOT given to Ms. Beakman?
(A) The status of her repairs
(B) The name of the technician
(C) The store she should visit
(D) The arrival date of a delivery

Stop! This is the end of the test. If you finish before time is called, you may go back to Parts 5, 6, and 7 and check your work.

동시토익 실전 WORKBOOK

101. Mr. DeLay has finished his law school, but Ms. Dylan has not yet finished hers.

해석]

102. You will enhance your simple woodwork by implementing several different finishes we offer.

해석]

103. Formerly a renowned surgeon, Dr. Capuano now divides his time between caring for patients and teaching future doctors.

해석]

104. The Lim & Kim Group is committed to helping people make investments that can earn the rate of return they need for retirement.

해석]

105. Seven other specialists will be available for consultation at an hourly rate.

해석]

106. The efficiency of solar energy utilization needs to be regularly verified by a suitable method.

해석]

107. Even though the number of disasters has more than tripled since the 1970s, the reported death toll has decreased to less than half.

해석]

108. Reports about the explosion which seemed to cause a great deal of damage to the factory have just been released.

해석]

109. Our firm continues to assist you in maintaining the accounting system.

해석]

110. To be considered for a nurse position at Ralf Reed Memorial Hospital, applicants must be available to work any shift.

해석]

*어휘 NOTE

111. Listed cement firms saw an increase in profits in the first half of this year, compared to the same period last year.
해석]

112. We asked that guests be seated a half hour prior to commencement of the ceremony.
해석]

113. Professor Withrow advised students to check if the plan is concise and realistic before submitting the business plan.
해석]

114. Funn Sports will be expanding its sporting goods business into emerging markets next year.
해석]

115. The $500 security deposit you gave us will be returned to you only when the apartment passes inspection.
해석]

116. In order to better serve our customers, we plan to increase our inventory by 20 percent, which means that we need more space.
해석]

117. Most high income earners are likely to say they intend to boost their property investment portfolios over the next few months.
해석]

118. Scandi Household is currently offering a promotion to new customers that gives them 25% off their purchase.
해석]

119. To help your business succeed, we also provide the training course that will help you provide distinctive customer service.
해석]

120. While Mr. Karst is away from work, please have every letter and package for him delivered to his assistant.
해석]

*어휘 NOTE

121. Ronald Charities, whose purpose is to create and support programs for children in need, is an independent nonprofit organization.

해석]

123. By the time Jerry Hairston was promoted to CEO, the company had begun reorganizing its capital structure.

해석]

124. Many entrepreneurs from all areas of business will join the seminar this year, and some are today's top business leaders.

해석]

125. In her new book, a leading financier, Ms. Blanchett writes about the instability of global capitalism.

해석]

126. Ms. Sienna decided to start her own business last month and has since been preparing for it.

해석]

127. Health boards must take strong security measures so that digital patient records may remain confidential.

해석]

128. Togo Food Company guarantees that only the highest quality ingredients are used for their products.

해석]

129. Please affix an annual parking permit with your name directly to the lower left hand corner of the windshield at the time of purchase.

해석]

130. Due to the time constraints in evaluating workshops conducted this year, we need to receive immediate feedback on December workshop from the attendees.

해석]

*어휘 NOTE

TEST 07

동시토익 CONTEMPORARY **TOEIC**

TEST 07

READING TEST

In the Reading test, you will read a variety of texts and answer several different types of reading comprehension questions. The entire Reading test will last 75 minutes. There are three parts, and directions are given for each part. You are encouraged to answer as many questions as possible within the time allowed.

You must mark your answers on the separate answer sheet. Do not write your answers in your test book.

Part 5

Directions: A word or phrase is missing in each of the sentences below. Four answer choices are given below each sentence. Select the best answer to complete the sentence. Then mark the letter (A), (B), (C), or (D) on your answer sheet.

101. Please take a moment to let us know what you thought about our services and to leave _____ for improvements.
(A) suggest
(B) suggestions
(C) suggests
(D) suggesting

102. If any refreshments at the snack bar are _____ gone, please let one of our kitchen staff know.
(A) nearest
(B) neared
(C) nearly
(D) nears

103. Workers who _____ forklifts may be injured by the machine, so they must be extremely cautious all the time.
(A) operate
(B) operates
(C) to operate
(D) are operated

104. Personnel staff review the applications in a very thorough manner, which _____ takes two weeks.
(A) totally
(B) quickly
(C) generally
(D) lightly

105. The hotel kindly requests _____ all guests check in after 2 p.m. and check out before 11:00 a.m.
(A) or
(B) that
(C) if
(D) which

106. Marketers in a complex and unpredictable market must be able to both plan ahead and react _____ to changes in its surroundings.
(A) prompt
(B) promptness
(C) prompting
(D) promptly

107. Tomorrow's job interview starts at 10:00 am sharp, so interviewees should be _____.
(A) punctual
(B) advanced
(C) instant
(D) sudden

108. I did not have a chance to look closely at my hotel bill when I received it _____ a hectic schedule that day.
(A) since
(B) due to
(C) as for
(D) among

109. Our grocery store will offer baked beans _____ from the UK for only six dollars a can.
(A) import
(B) imported
(C) importer
(D) importing

110. In a study to explore how meditation enhances concentration, a _____ of quantitative and qualitative methods was used.
(A) combine
(B) combination
(C) combines
(D) combined

111. _____ who complete a customer-focused training program may be considered for management positions afterward.
(A) Ours
(B) Them
(C) Those
(D) Anyone

112. By _____ butter or margarine with other ingredients, you can eliminate saturated fat from your baked goods.
(A) replace
(B) replacing
(C) replacement
(D) replaced

113. _____ team members worked on the budget summary all the weekend, it is not good enough to meet our standards.
(A) Why
(B) Whether
(C) Although
(D) Unless

114. Sales of our new mobile phone have grown at the _____ rate of 5 percent a month over the past five months.
(A) steady
(B) steadily
(C) steadies
(D) steadiness

115. Fresh Scent's soap lasts for quite some time, making them less expensive than other _____ brands.
(A) to lead
(B) had led
(C) leading
(D) was leading

116. Northampton Community college is inviting local residents to a free course designed to help individuals who enjoy helping _____ with mental health issues.
(A) ones
(B) others
(C) any
(D) that

117. As an emergency light, the energy efficient LED bulb is activated _____ when power goes out, so you don't need to turn it on.
(A) potentially
(B) ultimately
(C) automatically
(D) simultaneously

118. Small-business owners _____ advice about tax law can consult one of our accountants.
(A) seeking
(B) attempting
(C) resolving
(D) intending

119. If customers experience any product faults or flaws and ask us to get the money refunded, we offer a full refund _____ 30 days of purchase.
(A) every
(B) within
(C) whenever
(D) notwithstanding

GO ON TO THE NEXT PAGE

120. The Project Secretary will provide support related to _____ of events, ensuring high quality of work and accuracy.
    (A) organizes
    (B) organizer
    (C) organized
    (D) organization

121. _____ gas prices continuing to rise, analysts predict that consumers will cut back on spending in other areas.
    (A) With
    (B) To
    (C) For
    (D) By

122. All luggage must be checked in for your flight at least 60 minutes prior to your scheduled _____.
    (A) exception
    (B) efficiency
    (C) progression
    (D) departure

123. This recent study suggests that there is no longer a _____ market for Mr. Kang's proposed business.
    (A) size
    (B) sized
    (C) sizing
    (D) sizable

124. Before beginning construction, make sure that all architectural designs you are working on _____ with the building codes.
    (A) compliance
    (B) comply
    (C) compliant
    (D) compliantly

125. Starting on Wednesday, May 12, _____ Sculptor, Robert Maki exhibits at Bellevue City Art Gallery at City Hall.
    (A) estimated
    (B) founded
    (C) renowned
    (D) allocated

126. The operating system we use is not compatible with the new software and _____ needs to be updated.
    (A) therefore
    (B) however
    (C) since
    (D) rather

127. Our DIY furniture comes with detailed instruction manual _____ any buyer can assemble all of the furniture on their own.
    (A) in addition
    (B) so that
    (C) just as
    (D) in case

128. Extremely high _____ for the Model T prompted Chalm Corporation to move its operations to a larger plant in Detroit.
    (A) occurrence
    (B) percentage
    (C) demand
    (D) population

129. You should address constant stress with the help of professionals, _____ unless properly handled, can bring about a prolonged depression.
    (A) who
    (B) what
    (C) which
    (D) whom

130. The opening of five more stores on the east coast will also further _____ Mega Office's position as the leader in office supplies.
    (A) accomplish
    (B) incline
    (C) solidify
    (D) administer

PART 6

Direction: Read the texts that follow. A word, phrase, or sentence is missing in parts of each text. Four answer choices for each question are given below the text. Select the best answer to complete the text. Then mark the letter (A), (B), (C), or (D) on your answer sheet.

Questions 131-134 refer to the following letter.

November 2

Dear ticket holders,

We are sorry to inform you that we are forced to change the August ------- series in Central Park.
131.

The weather forecast says that a strong storm is coming next week. We will ------- be postponing
132.
next week's outdoor performances in the park until a later day for better weather.

Ticket holders have ------- options: You can get a full refund or use your tickets for the later
133.
performance. -------. Please contact one of our customer service representatives at (213) 555-
134.
1234 for a full refund.

Sincerely,

David Drummond
Manager

131. (A) cinema
(B) lecture
(C) concert
(D) theater

132. (A) therefore
(B) otherwise
(C) since
(D) likewise

133. (A) either
(B) twice
(C) doubled
(D) two

134. (A) We look forward to seeing you all at next week's concert.
(B) We will let you know the exact performance date as soon as we reschedule it.
(C) The relocated venue for the concert will be announced later this week.
(D) Our most sincere thanks go to Central Park for hosting the concert.

Question 135-138 refer to the following e-mail.

To: dunger@maplegladmc.org
From: gcandell@biolectric.com
Date: December 2

Dear Ms. Unger,

I appreciate your ------- me this morning. Speaking with you was extremely informative and helpful to me.
                    135.

I believe that the venture that we discussed will have very wide-reaching ------- for not only the medical industry in the region, but other fields as well. I firmly believe working together with us ------- beneficial for Maple Glade Medical Center. I've already spoke with several directors from both companies and they also believe we can work together in a positive way. -------. Please let me know if there is anything that you'd like me to add to the proposal.
                                                                                                            138.

Best regards,

George Candell
R&D Director
Biolectric, Inc.

135. (A) assigning
(B) recommending
(C) paying
(D) calling

136. (A) implicate
(B) implicating
(C) implications
(D) implicated

137. (A) will be
(B) being
(C) has been
(D) would have been

138. (A) I look forward to visiting you at your office later this week.
(B) I will be sending you a draft of the official proposal.
(C) There are many benefits to working closely with Bioelectric.
(D) I am also discussing our collaboration with professionals in other fields.

Questions 139-142 refer to the following letter.

16 February

Zack Greinke
NZ Enterprise
PO Box 2376
Wakatipu 9349, New Zealand

Dear Mr. Greinke,

I am writing this letter as a token of appreciation for the outstanding customer service provided by one of your employees, Mary Smith. She was so ------- to work with that I was able to complete the transaction within seconds.
139.

She provided timely and helpful advice regarding the brand of the machine I was purchasing. -------. She ------- ensured that I received all the information regarding the mode of payment to the company and the time by which I would expect the machine to be shipped to Australia.
140. **141.**

I would like to commend Mary for her exceptional -------.
142.

Best regards,

Clayton Kershaw

---

139. (A) challenging
(B) pleasant
(C) familiar
(D) sensitive

140. (A) She sent a catalog with suitable products to my place of work.
(B) I hope that we can resolve the issue with my transaction quickly.
(C) I understand that international shipping can be very expensive.
(D) She let me know all the important information regarding the product.

141. (A) again
(B) then
(C) almost
(D) instead

142. (A) efforts
(B) effortful
(C) effortless
(D) effortlessly

GO ON TO THE NEXT PAGE

Questions 143-146 refer to the following article.

Long Beach, June 15 - Doris Florist has just opened their new store at 233 Long Beach Road, which is down the road from her old store and is in a new and more spacious building.

Doris Kresky, the owner of the store said that she didn't want to ------- the opportunity to lease
143.
the conveniently located store and expand her business.

While the Long Beach Road store is already -------, the grand opening ceremony will be held on
144.
Saturday, July 1, at 11:00 a.m. with a big discount. -------. New items ------- fruit and gift Baskets,
145.   146.
balloon bouquets and other gifts are on display at the new shop.

143. (A) go after
(B) look into
(C) sort out
(D) pass up

144. (A) operationally
(B) operational
(C) operation
(D) operated

145. (A) Doris Florist recently won the award for its floral display.
(B) The closing of the store will be sad news to many in the community.
(C) A wide array of plants are available for same-day delivery.
(D) Doris Florist will open its doors for the first time later this week.

146. (A) includes
(B) inclusion
(C) inclusive
(D) including

PART 7

Direction: In this part you will read a selection of texts, such as magazine and newspaper articles, letters, e-mails, and instant messages. Each text or set of texts is followed by several questions. Select the best answer for each question and mark the letter (A), (B), (C), or (D) on your answer sheet.

Questions 147-148 refer to the following calendar.

	Monday June 14	Tuesday June 15	Wednesday June 16	Thursday June 17	Friday June 18
9:00 a.m.		Kids' Reading Together Time	Children's Storybook Making Activity	Kids' Reading Together Time	
10:00 a.m.	Presentation by Head Librarian Susan Pakowski				Fantasy Book Club Gathering
11:00 a.m.			Library Fundraising Book Sale	Summer Reading Program Party	
12:00 p.m.		Kids' Reading Together Time			Young Poets Get-Together
1:00 p.m.				Staff conference	
2:00 p.m.		Free Career Counseling Workshop			

Timetable for Room C, June 14 – 18

147. Where is Room C probably located?
(A) In career counseling office
(B) In a theater
(C) In a community library
(D) In a children's care center

148. What event is scheduled on the same day as the book-making activity?
(A) Library Fundraising Book Sale
(B) Kids' Reading Together Time
(C) Young Poets Get-Together
(D) Fantasy Book Club Gathering

*어휘 NOTE

Questions 149-151 refer to the following e-mail.

From :	Ellen Funt <ellenf@currentcooking.com>
To :	<subscribers@currentcooking.com>
Subject :	New Features for Our Members!
Date :	November 2

Hello, CurrentCooking.com subscribers!

I'm happy to tell you that we at Current Cooking online magazine have made our website even more helpful to our subscribers. Starting from today, subscribers can watch online instructional videos for exciting cooking recipes by well-known chefs. You can also see demonstrations and reviews of state-of-the-art kitchen equipment. Interviews of famous cooks and gourmets are also featured. And of course, you'll still be able to access news and information in articles on our site as well.

Check out CurrentCooking.com for all your cooking and kitchen needs today!

Sincerely,

Ellen Funt
Editor-In-Chief

149. What is the purpose of the e-mail?
(A) To announce upgraded services
(B) To advertise a new website
(C) To recruit applicants for a job
(D) To ask for members' opinions

150. To whom is the email most likely directed?
(A) Webmasters
(B) chefs
(C) photographers
(D) Magazine writers

151. What is NOT mentioned as a feature of the Current Cooking website?
(A) Interviews
(B) Advertisements
(C) Product reviews
(D) Recipe instruction

Questions 152-153 refer to the following receipt.

Eagle's Place
242 Front Street
Orlando, FL 32789
689-555-0558

March 10	10:05 a.m.
Science Fiction - paperback	
Galactic Zombie Hunter, Sylvester Stanks	7.99
Non-fiction - hardcover	
Recycling and Home Decoration, Freda Biltz	15.99
Subtotal	23.98
Tax-6.5%	1.55
Total	25.53
Cash received	26.00
Change	0.47

Returns and Exchanges Policy

Refunds and exchanges are only available for new purchases that are brought back to the store within two weeks of the original purchase date. Any damaged items or items without a receipt will not be accepted for return. We do not accept any returns of purchases from the used section, but we will exchange used items with an original receipt brought back within four weeks.

---

152. What type of shop is Eagle's Place?
(A) A laboratory supply store
(B) A home decoration shop
(C) A bookseller
(D) A hunting equipment outlet

153. What is true about the store's policy?
(A) All items may be returned within two weeks of purchase.
(B) All purchases being returned incur a 6.5% restocking fee.
(C) All exchanged items must be in brand-new condition.
(D) All exchanged items must be accompanied by a receipt.

Questions 154-156 refer to the following information.

We appreciate your purchase of an Illuminate T-24A desktop printer, so we have included three sample sizes of ink cartridges with your printer. Buying full-size ink cartridges is recommended soon after the sample-sized cartridges are installed, as they are not designed for long term use. New cartridges are available for direct purchase on the Illuminate Web site at www.illuminateprinters.com. Any orders are guaranteed to be received by the customer within one week of ordering, or the payment will be refunded. When ordering, use the code 28874 during checkout in order to receive a preferred customer discount of 30 percent off your total order charges. Customers are also able to buy replacement ink cartridges at most office supplies stores, but the preferred customer discount will be unavailable.

Please call our support center technicians, open at all hours, at 1-800-555-0152 with any questions or concerns regarding your new printer. Our sales center can be reached on weekdays from 8 a.m. to 8 p.m. at 1-800-555-4845.

154. For whom was the notice written?
(A) Printing technicians
(B) Web site designers
(C) Owners of recently purchased printer
(D) Sales representatives

155. What promise is made about placing orders for ink?
(A) Customers' charges are waived if deliveries are late.
(B) Sales associates are always available.
(C) Ink cartridges supply ink for an entire year.
(D) Technicians calls customers back promptly.

156. How can shoppers receive a discount?
(A) By phoning a support center
(B) By using a code in an online store
(C) By going to a local office supplies shop
(D) By sending a voucher

Questions 157-158 refer to the following text message chain.

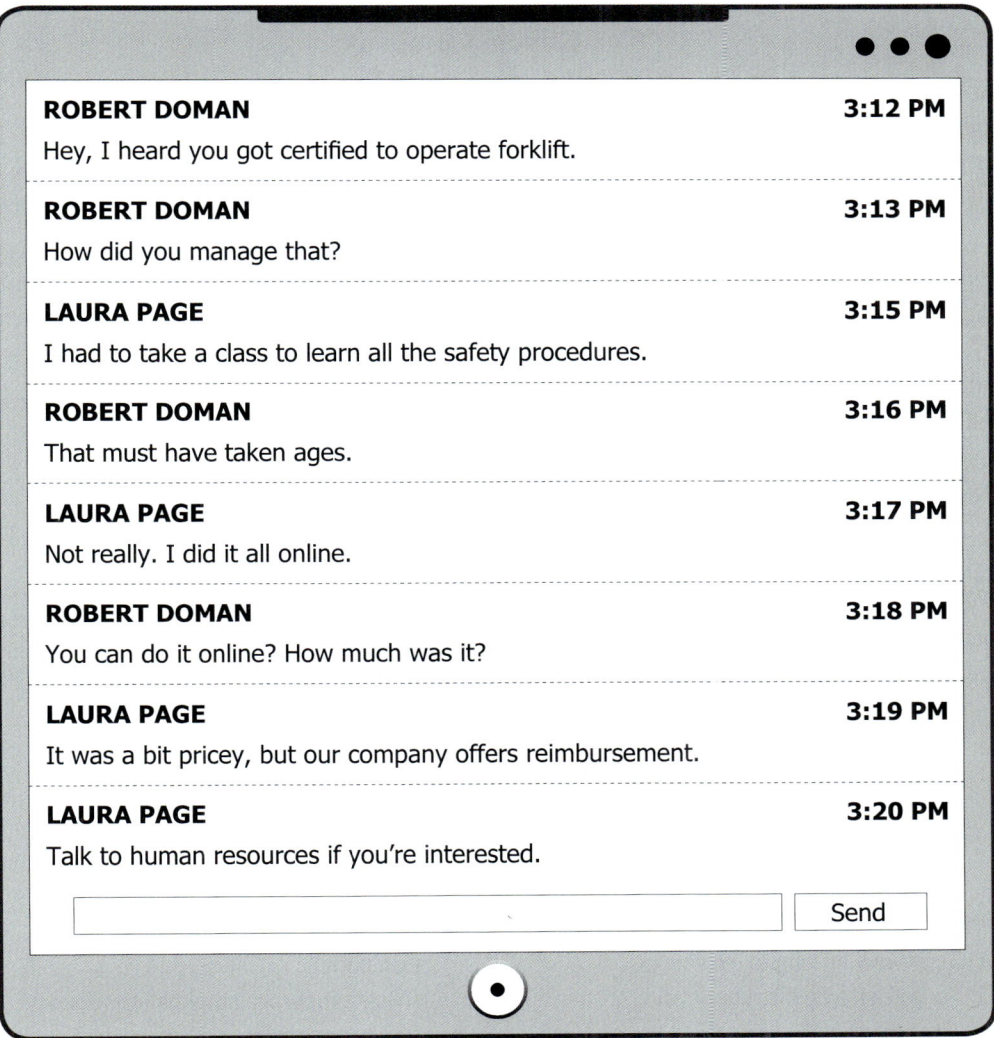

157. What is indicated about Laura Page?
(A) She is taking an online class.
(B) She recently started a new job.
(C) She is a colleague of Mr. Doman.
(D) She works in human resources.

158. At 15:16 PM, what does Mr. Doman mean when he writes, "That must have taken ages"?
(A) A class took a long time to complete.
(B) Participants have to be a certain age.
(C) He is interested in certification.
(D) He is concerned about costs.

Questions 159-160 refer to the following Web page.

The Gildem Company

Your name   : Dalek Prapesh
Item number   : KT55
Item purchased on : May 13

We appreciate your reviewing our products. Your opinion means a lot to us at The Gildem Company and we strive to please our customers with high quality merchandise. After filling out all of the form below, please click the SEND FORM to submit the survey to our customer satisfaction team.

Number of the Gildem items you have bought	☐ 0	☒ 1-3	☐ More than 3
Satisfaction level with the Gildem items you have	☐ High	☒ Adequate	☐ Low
Chances of purchasing other Gildem items in the future	☐ High	☐ Non-existent	☒ Possible
Other comments including details on The Gildem items you have purchased	The Gildem speaker that I bought 6 years ago has worked great. My Gildem MP3 player (KT55) that I purchased a few days ago has poor sound quality with the supplied headphones, which I replaced.		

SEND FORM

159. What is the reason for the questionnaire?
(A) To review an employee's work
(B) To gather opinions about an advertisement
(C) To enhance a business' merchandise
(D) To rate a website's feature

160. What kind of business is The Gildem Company?
(A) A temporary employment agency
(B) A renovation company
(C) A manufacturer of electronics
(D) A design consulting firm

* 어휘 NOTE

Questions 161-163 refer to the following article.

City to Implement New Parking Fees
October 22
By Graham Postman

As the increase in visitors to the downtown area of Peach Valley has resulted in parking shortages, the transportation board is considering implementing new parking fees. "Every evening, it's becoming more and more difficult to find available parking spots," said board member Travis Heinz. —[1]—. Residents are having trouble finding parking spots as many visitors avoid parking lots which charge by the hour for parking. Visitors looking for free street parking also increase traffic jams as they drive around downtown. —[2]—.

—[3]—. At this time, payment on city streets is only required from 8 a.m. to 5:00 p.m., with no payment needed after these times. "This system makes parking a nightmare in the evenings," Mr. Heinz said. "Adopting a system of payment being required around the clock like other cities can help."

This change in parking regulations would be the second time since last month, when the board upgraded the city's parking meters. —[4]—. The meters now allow motorists to pay with either coins or credit cards.

161. What is implied about Peach Valley?
(A) Its streets are in poor condition.
(B) It has to raise taxes to fund public transportation.
(C) It has issues with traffic congestion.
(D) Its parking garages are free for city-dwellers.

162. What is the transportation board considering?
(A) Increasing the number of parking spaces
(B) Installing upgraded traffic signals
(C) Hiring more parking attendants
(D) Implementing charges for parking in the evening

163. In which of the positions marked [1], [2], [3], and [4] does the following sentence best belong?

"Downtown Peach Valley has become more popular with the opening of many new restaurants, cinemas, and shops."

(A) [1]
(B) [2]
(C) [3]
(D) [4]

Questions 164-167 refer to the following online chat discussion.

Online Chat

Alexandra Peters [2:44 p.m.] Hello everyone. The research and development team is going to be revealing their progress on the features of next year's car models at the staff meeting this afternoon. Is anyone interested in going?

Fraser Isaac [2:46 p.m.] I'd like to see what they've been working on. Also, it'd probably be a good idea if Monique Hardy attended since it's her first week here.

Monique Hardy [2:47 p.m.] Yeah, I'd love to go. I've already met some of the people in R & D, so it'd be a great chance to see what they're working on. Does anyone know anything about the features they're going to reveal?

Alexandra Peters [2:48 p.m.] Beats me, Monique, but I'm sure that the presentation will help you with your work in the design department. The meeting will be held in Conference Room D at 4:30 p.m.

Monique Hardy [2:49 p.m.] Ok, great, but I'm not really sure where the conference rooms are.

Fraser Isaac [2:50 p.m.] That's alright, Monique. I can show you where it is. I'm going to be busy right before the meeting, though. Is it alright if I come by now and show you how to get there?

Monique Hardy [2:52 p.m.] Yes, I'd really appreciate that.

Manuel Hoult [2:54 p.m.] I'd like to go too, but I have a dinner meeting with a client that I have to prepare for. Is it possible for anyone to take some notes or even record the presentation for me?

Alexandra Peters [2:55 p.m.] My assistant will be attending the meeting with me and taking notes. I'll make sure to forward a copy of his notes to you after the meeting, Manuel.

164. What is the topic of the research and development's presentation this afternoon?
(A) New conference room designs
(B) A recent marketing campaign
(C) A review of yearly sales figures
(D) Characteristics of new automobiles

165. What is indicated about Monique Hardy?
(A) She will move to the R & D department.
(B) She worked with Fraser Isaac in the past.
(C) She recently began to work for the company.
(D) She will meet clients later in the day.

166. At 2:48 p.m., what does Alexandra Peters mean when she says, "Beats me"?
(A) She will ask the R & D department.
(B) She doesn't know the answer.
(C) She was injured at the workplace.
(D) She has worked on the presentation.

167. What does Fraser Isaac offer to do for Monique Hardy?
(A) Record a presentation for her
(B) Reschedule a client meeting
(C) Take notes at a meeting
(D) Show her a location

Questions 168-171 refer to the following review.

Stewton Gazette Entertainment Section

No Strings Attached
by Annie Newfam, reviewer

On Friday night, No Strings Attached, the new musical by Yann Curset, began its run by the Wheaton Theater Company for its annual spring program series. The musical is based on the life of a cellist who overcame multiple obstacles throughout her life to become a world-famous musician.

Hera Constant, who gained worldwide recognition for her performance in the film, Keep Your Chin Up, is very believable as the famous cellist, Aria Nordak. A Wheaton Theater Company regular, Marcus Galiston, also gives an amazing performance as Mrs. Nordak's supportive husband, Jacob Edmond.

No Strings Attached is much more dramatic and suspenseful than the light-hearted comedies that Wheaton Theater Company frequently showcased. Even with a running time of two and a half hours, the performers draw the audience into the world of the play. The sparse decorations and low-key wardrobe help the audience get lost in the play as well.

Moira Yarco, the Continent Theatrical Award-winner that grew up in Stewton, is the director of No Strings Attached.

The theater box office may be reached at 814-555-1157 for ticket sales and show time information.

168. Who wrote the play?
(A) Hera Constant
(B) Moira Yarco
(C) Yann Curset
(D) Marcus Galiston

169. How does No Strings Attached differ from the Wheaton Theater Company's usual entertainment?
(A) It is about a world-famous person's life.
(B) It features a full orchestra.
(C) It is more dramatic and serious.
(D) It has an entirely local cast.

170. How can the information about the show times be obtained?
(A) By visiting an online site
(B) By sending an e-mail
(C) By phoning the box office
(D) By picking up a pamphlet

171. What is implied about No Strings Attached?
(A) The musical is performed by trained musicians.
(B) The musical recently won an award.
(C) The actors are vividly dressed.
(D) It is only showing during the spring.

Questions 172-175 refer to the following article.

August 18 – Glass Tiger Studios, which helped with the advertisements for the Live 4 Health commercials, has been nominated for the esteemed Calenbach Award. The award has been given over the last 25 years to animation companies and art publishing companies for showing innovation. Glass Tiger Studios was the first and only animation company from Bangkok chosen from nearly 1,500 other eligible companies. —[1]—. The award ceremony where all this year's winners will be announced is to be held in Berlin, Germany on September 20.

—[2]—. "We feel very honored to have been nominated, as it shows how talented, creative and skillful our staff members are," said May Pranathat, senior director of Glass Tiger Studios. "We've done work for children's books, fashion magazines, and product packages among others," said Ms. Pranathat, "and we communicate with our customers carefully to ensure our work goes beyond what they expected."

—[3]—. After the list of nominated candidates was made public, Glass Tiger Studios has been sought out for its work. "With all of the new business we're seeing, it's not likely that we'll be able to fulfill the demand without hiring more animators and directors, so we have begun processes for hiring people." —[4]—.

Glass Tiger Studio's website has more details about their company. More information concerning the Calenbach Award can be found at www.calenbachaward.org.

172. What is the reason for the article?
(A) To explain a nomination process
(B) To announce an prestigious award ceremony
(C) To advertise an opening for a product packing position
(D) To detail the achievements of a company

173. What is indicated about Calenbach Award?
(A) It was funded by a magazine publisher.
(B) It has been previously given to a Bangkok company.
(C) It is presented to several companies annually.
(D) It was awarded for the first time 20 years ago.

174. According to the article, what is Ms. Pranathat planning to do?
(A) To employ more staff
(B) To redesign a commercial
(C) To update a company website
(D) To go to a ceremony in Bangkok

175. In which of the positions marked [1], [2], [3], and [4] does the following sentence best belong?

"Glass Tiger Studios has received increased attention from a number of clients."

(A) [1]
(B) [2]
(C) [3]
(D) [4]

Questions 176-180 refer to the following job posting and letter.

Fresh Delivery's Cape Town office is currently accepting applications for a warehouse manager position. Fresh Delivery has been the leader in the delivery and handling of high-quality produce in South Africa for over three decades. Our customers include grocery stores, restaurants, and other businesses all around the nation.

The warehouse manager has a variety of duties including training new employees, making a timetable, and ensuring quality work from warehouse staff. Successful candidates should have at least five years of experience in the field, including one year of supervisory experience.

On occasion, the warehouse manager will be required to work evenings and weekends in the case of important deliveries. Applicants also need to have extensive experience using the NPL inventory control system.

Interested candidates who meet these requirements can apply by sending a cover letter, resume, and at least two reference letters to Ms. Lydia Herron, Fresh Delivery, 15 Empire Avenue, Cape Town 8001, South Africa.

---

15 June

Ms. Lydia Herron
Fresh Delivery
15 Empire Avenue
Cape Town 8001

Dear Ms. Herron,

It is my pleasure to write in recommendation of Shelley Moon, who is applying to be the warehouse manager of your facility. Ms. Moon has been under my supervision for six years of her ten years at Fernley, Inc., and she moved from a part-time position to a full-time position seven years ago.

Ms. Moon is extremely qualified for this position, especially regarding knowledge of warehouse procedures and handling delicate cargo. The NPL system has been in use at our company for years and Ms. Moon is very proficient in its use and has helped new employees learn to use it as well. She is also studying to earn her bachelor's degree in administration from Thurston University, with extra classes focusing on technical knowledge.

It is my opinion that Ms. Moon would be an asset to your company, as she has all of the requirements needed for the position and is an excellent worker. Please contact me if you would like to ask any questions about Ms. Moon.

Regards,

Charles Robbins
Charles Robbins
Dock manager
Fernley, Inc.

176. What is suggested about Fresh Delivery?
(A) It recently began operating in South Africa.
(B) It provides an extensive variety of computer programs.
(C) It manages a grocery store chain.
(D) It deals primarily with food products.

177. According to the job posting, what must the warehouse manager be willing to do?
(A) To attend a safety seminar
(B) To occasionally work on weekends
(C) To carry heavy objects
(D) To agree to work for one year

178. Why does Mr. Robbins write the letter?
(A) To express a positive opinion of an employee
(B) To postpone a job interview
(C) To ask a question about a job applicant
(D) To introduce a new company system

179. What is indicated about Ms. Moon?
(A) She has worked previously at Fresh Delivery.
(B) She is a professor at Thurston University.
(C) She is knowledgeable about a inventory control system.
(D) She has applied for part-time employment with Fresh Delivery.

180. For how long has Ms. Moon worked for Fernley, Inc.?
(A) One year
(B) Five years
(C) Six years
(D) Ten years

Questions 181-185 refer to the following e-mails.

E-mail Message

To :	Henry Ritter
From :	Marcia Jones
Cc :	Patrick Collins, Roberta Botlin
Date :	November 13
Subject:	Conference calls

You might be aware that I started working with Baron Textiles at the Southeast office four days ago. Part of my duties is to be part of a group telephone meeting about our sales every week. However, this afternoon, I had trouble hearing most of the discussion since the phone kept breaking up. My supervisor told me that Patrick Collins and Roberta Botlin have had the same problems at the North office. It's possible that this is a problem at other offices as well.

Is there any way that we can get better equipment for the telephone meetings so that staff in branch offices are able to better participate in meetings with staff at the main office?

Regards,

Marcia Jones
Southeast office, Sales
Baron Textiles

To :	Marcia Jones, Patrick Collins, Roberta Botlin
From :	Henry Ritter
Date :	November 18
Subject:	Update on phones

Dear Marcia, Patrick, and Roberta,

I ordered three new phones yesterday and they should be at your respective offices by November 24. We will test them and collect your feedback. We have allocated additional funds for as many phones as we need if you find them satisfactory. I'm going to visit Marcia's branch on November 30 to train her on how to use the phone before her sales meeting. After the meeting, I'll get her opinion. On December 7, I'll go to Patrick and Roberta's office to do the same. Other reviews say the Cleartone telephone is very receptive, meaning noises in your office may also be amplified. After checking the phones, if this issue causes problems, we'll look at other options for telecommunications equipment.

Thanks for being patient while we're trying to fix this problem.

Sincerely,

Henry Ritter
Information Technology Consultant
Baron Textiles

181. What is the purpose of the first e-mail?
(A) To report a difficulty
(B) To ask for relocation
(C) To resolve a dispute
(D) To market a communication device

182. What is indicated about Ms. Jones?
(A) She is working in Information Technology.
(B) She has had a discussion with Mr. Ritter's supervisor.
(C) She attempted to take part in his first Baron Testiles meeting on November 13.
(D) She took part in a conference call on November 18.

183. What does Mr. Ritter imply that he will do if the Cleartone telephones are satisfactory?
(A) To check their performance with other phone models
(B) To ask for a price reduction from the manufacturer
(C) To discuss changing suppliers with his manager
(D) To purchase more phones for other branches

184. In the second e-mail, what is stated about the Cleartone telephones?
(A) They are the most popular phone model in the industry.
(B) They are the only phone supplied by a vendor.
(C) They might make background sounds louder.
(D) They might not be available for immediate order.

185. Where will Mr. Henry most likely be on December 7?
(A) At the Southeast office
(B) At the North office
(C) At the main office
(D) At the sales workshop

Questions 186-190 refer to the following newsletter article, e-mail, and schedule.

Wentford Industries Newsletter

August 22

We at Wentford Industries are pleased to report that Janet Flanders was named the Manager of the Year and honored at this year's managerial conference in Ottawa. Ms. Flanders rose to a management position quickly from her start as an intern at our Vancouver branch nine years ago due to her diligence and commitment to her work. After receiving her degree from university, Ms. Flanders accepted a full-time position at our headquarters in Toronto, where she has remained.

Not only has Ms. Flanders proven to be a competent and amiable manager of customer relations, but she also has helped improve the satisfaction of Wentford Industries customers by revising our methods of dealing with customer complaints. Because of her efforts, Wentford's reputation with customers has become overwhelmingly positive. She will receive her award with the other recipients on August 25 at the conference, where several developmental presentations will also be given, as well as a speech about our past given by Wentford's CEO. Congratulations to Ms. Flanders on her accomplishments!

---

* E-mail *

From:	Laura Myers <lmyers@wentfordind.com>
To:	Janet Flanders <jflanders@wentfordind.com>
Subject:	Hi!
Date:	August 26

Dear Janet,

I apologize for not being able to come to the conference this year, but I'm sure you'll understand that my transfer to Minneapolis made attendance impossible. Congratulations on your prize! Do you think you could send me any photos from the conference? I heard that Taylor Cobbin gave a great presentation there. I wish I could have seen it.

My position here is working out, but sales are definitely a difficult department. However, it's wonderful that I finally rose to the position of supervising a whole department.

I'm going to be in your region in September, so why don't you let me buy you lunch to congratulate you on the award.

Sincerely,

Laura

Wentford Industries Managerial Conference

August 25

Schedule (Subject to Change):

3:00 p.m. – 3:40 p.m.: A History of Wentford presented by Gregory Burns

4:00 p.m. – 4:40 p.m.: Communicating Effectively with your Staff presented by Taylor Cobbin

5:00 p.m. – 5:40 p.m.: Increasing Productivity through Delegation presented by Sam Warner

5:40 p.m. – 7:00 p.m.: Intermission and Dinner (Catering provided by Sally's Catering)

7:00 p.m. – 8:00 p.m.: Awards Presentation presented by Arthur Sorensen

186. According to the article, what process did Ms. Flanders improve?
(A) Dealing with unsatisfied customers
(B) Customer satisfaction surveys
(C) Conference enrollment
(D) Ensuring proper communication between departments

187. What is indicated about Ms. Myers?
(A) She likes taking pictures.
(B) She is moving to another company.
(C) She is in charge of many interns.
(D) She manages a sales department.

188. To what city will Ms. Myers most likely travel in September?
(A) Minneapolis
(B) Toronto
(C) Vancouver
(D) Ottawa

189. Which presentation did Ms. Myers want to see?
(A) A history of Wentford
(B) Communicating Effectively with Your Staff
(C) Increasing Productivity through Delegation
(D) Awards Presentation

190. Who most likely is Gregory Burns?
(A) A conference organizer
(B) An award recipient
(C) A caterer
(D) A company executive

Questions 191-195 refer to the following e-mail, list, and receipt.

E-mail Message

To :	Raymond Grace <raygrace@heat.com>
From :	Angelo Martinez <amartinez@amazebooks.com>
Date :	October 14
Subject :	Recommendations
Attachment:	Four Titles

Dear Mr. Grace,

We believe that you will like the four titles that are described in the attached file. These selections are recommended based on your past history of purchases.

Keep in mind that we ship books on the same day they are ordered if they are in stock, and they should arrive at your desired address within four business days. Books which have not yet been released can be pre-ordered at a 10% discount and will be sent to your desired address when they are released.

Keep reading!

Angelo Martinez
Amaze Books

Click here to browse our books.

New Books

Vegetable Party By Rachel Griggs Publisher: Symphonic Publications Price: $15.60 (plus delivery fees) Dozens of recipes for fresh and healthy vegetable dishes the whole family will love. Status: In stock	**The Trees of National Parks** By Robin Pride Publisher: Natural Birth Publications Price: $32.50 (plus delivery fees) An extensive book featuring identification guides for trees in state and national parks across the country. This guide is fully illustrated to help you identify trees. Status: In stock
The Home Guide to Furniture Restoration By Walter Verus Publisher: Symphonic Publications Price: $23.40 (plus delivery fees) The author writes in an easily understandable fashion, making furniture restoration at home easy for even those with no experience restoring furniture. Status: To be released in November. Preorder now.	**Antiquing and You** By Francis O'Gladdery Publisher: P. Newton Publishing Price: $18.40 (plus delivery fees) Antiquing and You gives you easy-to-follow instructions for finding and purchasing real antiques. Status: In stock

Online Purchase Receipt

Date of order: Monday, December 10
Customer's name: Raymond Grace

Item	Price
Vegetable Party	$15.60
The Sailor and the Element	$16.80
The Home Guide to Furniture Restoration	$23.40
Shipping and handling	$5.60
Total charges	$63.70

Thanks for shopping with Amaze Books!

191. Why was this e-mail written?
(A) To confirm an order
(B) To notify a customer of a store's relocation
(C) To request a review of a previous order
(D) To promote suggested items

192. What is suggested about Mr. Grace?
(A) He is a publishing company employee.
(B) He asked for book recommendations.
(C) He has bought books from Amaze Books before.
(D) He is currently waiting for an order to be delivered.

193. What is indicated about The Trees of National Parks?
(A) It includes many pictures.
(B) It is signed by the author.
(C) It includes free delivery.
(D) It is part of a series.

194. When will Mr. Grace most likely receive his order?
(A) October 18
(B) October 22
(C) December 10
(D) December 14

195. What is most likely true about Mr. Grace's order?
(A) Its shipping and handling was upgraded.
(B) It wasn't eligible for a pre-ordering discount.
(C) It was made separately from another order.
(D) It will be delivered to his office.

Questions 196-200 refer to the following web page information and emails.

Elevate Financial

| News | Accounts | Financing | Jobs |

The Dream Savings Plan is the newest way for you to save money.

Elevate Financial's newest savings account, the Dream Savings Plan, has more advantages for our customers than our Select Savings Plan. Among its benefits are higher interest rates and more options to transfer money.

During this promotional period, we are offering all customers the chance to change their Select Savings Plan to Dream Savings without our usual account conversion fees. Also, this plan will be available to customers for the annual service charge of $3 for the first year. After the first year, the annual charge will be raised to $5 a year for the Dream Savings Plan. This special offer is valid until the end of June.

E-mail Message

To : accountcare@elevatefinancial.com
From : ktrump@mercurybroadband.com
Subject : Savings account issue
Date : June 17

When I opened my Dream Savings Plan a week ago, I was told that the balance I had in my Select Savings Plan would be moved to the new account after the plan was opened. I just logged in to my account, though, and there are no available funds for the Dream Savings Plan. I'd like to know when the money from my Select Savings Plan will be moved to the Dream Savings Plan.

Please let me know what's going on as soon as possible.

Karen Trump

To : ktrump@mercurybroadband.com accountcare@elevatefinancial.com
From : accountcare@elevatefinancial.com
Subject : Re: Savings account issue
Date : June 18

Thank you for contacting us about your issue, Ms. Trump. According to my records, you recently changed your account to Dream Savings Plan. It normally takes ten days for the funds to be transferred after opening a new account. This is because of account verification and security measures that are taken to help keep our customers' finances safe. If you need to withdraw money, please use the old account for the time being. If you have any other issues, please feel free to contact me.

Sincerely,
Sharon House
Customer Account Specialist
Elevate Financial

196. What is the purpose of the Web site information?
(A) To explain rises in service charges
(B) To publicize a new savings plan
(C) To explain online banking processes
(D) To announce the opening of a new branch

197. What is stated about the service charge?
(A) Customers must pay it when opening an account.
(B) It will initially be lower than usual.
(C) It is not as high as what other banks charge.
(D) Customers only pay it for two years.

198. What is most likely true about Ms. Trump?
(A) She is looking for a new bank.
(B) Her service charge has risen.
(C) She was not charged for changing accounts.
(D) She cannot currently withdraw money from the Select Savings Plan.

199. In the first email, the word "balance" in paragraph 1, line 1 is closest in meaning to?
(A) amount
(B) harmony
(C) mean
(D) stability

200. When most likely will Ms. Trump's Dream Savings Plan account have funds in it?
(A) June 10
(B) June 20
(C) June 27
(D) June 28

Stop! This is the end of the test. If you finish before time is called, you may go back to Parts 5, 6, and 7 and check your work.

동시토익 실전 WORKBOOK

101. Please take a moment to let us know what you thought about our services and to leave suggestions for improvements.

해석]

102. If any refreshments at the snack bar are nearly gone, please let one of our kitchen staff know.

해석]

103. Workers who operate forklifts may be injured by the machine, so they must be extremely cautious all the time.

해석]

104. Personnel staff review the applications in a very thorough manner, which generally takes two weeks.

해석]

105. The hotel kindly requests that all guests check in after 2 p.m. and check out before 11:00 a.m.

해석]

106. Marketers in a complex and unpredictable market must be able to both plan ahead and react promptly to changes in its surroundings.

해석]

107. Tomorrow's job interview starts at 10:00 am sharp, so interviewees should be punctual.

해석]

108. I did not have a chance to look closely at my hotel bill when I received it due to a hectic schedule that day.

해석]

109. Our grocery store will offer baked beans imported from the UK for only six dollars a can.

해석]

110. In a study to explore how meditation enhances concentration, a combination of quantitative and qualitative methods was used.

해석]

*어휘 NOTE

111. Those who complete a customer-focused training program may be considered for management positions afterward.

해석]

112. By replacing butter or margarine with other ingredients, you can eliminate saturated fat from your baked goods.

해석]

113. Although team members worked on the budget summary all the weekend, it is not good enough to meet our standards.

해석]

114. Sales of our new mobile phone have grown at the steady rate of 5 percent a month over the past five months.

해석]

115. Fresh Scent's soap lasts for quite some time, making them less expensive than other leading brands.

해석]

116. Northampton Community college is inviting local residents to a free course designed to help individuals who enjoy helping others with mental health issues.

해석]

117. As an emergency light, the energy efficient LED bulb is activated automatically when power goes out, so you don't need to turn it on.

해석]

118. Small-business owners seeking advice about tax law can consult one of our accountants.

해석]

119. If customers experience any product faults or flaws and ask us to get the money refunded, we offer a full refund within 30 days of purchase.

해석]

120. The Project Secretary will provide support related to organization of events, ensuring high quality of work and accuracy.

해석]

＊어휘 NOTE

121. With gas prices continuing to rise, analysts predict that consumers will cut back on spending in other areas.

해석]

122. All luggage must be checked in for your flight at least 60 minutes prior to your scheduled departure.

해석]

123. This recent study suggests that there is no longer a sizable market for Mr. Kang's proposed business.

해석]

124. Before beginning construction, make sure that all architectural designs you are working on comply with the building codes.

해석]

125. Starting on Wednesday, May 12, renowned Sculptor, Robert Maki exhibits at Bellevue City Art Gallery at City Hall.

해석]

126. The operating system we use is not compatible with the new software and therefore needs to be updated.

해석]

127. Our DIY furniture comes with detailed instruction manual so that any buyer can assemble all of the furniture on their own.

해석]

128. Extremely high demand for the Model T prompted Chalm Corporation to move its operations to a larger plant in Detroit.

해석]

129. You should address constant stress with the help of professionals, which, unless properly handled, can bring about a prolonged depression.

해석]

130. The opening of five more stores on the east coast will also further solidify Mega Office's position as the leader in office supplies.

해석]

*어휘 NOTE

TEST 08

동시토익 CONTEMPORARY **TOEIC**

TEST 08

READING TEST

In the Reading test, you will read a variety of texts and answer several different types of reading comprehension questions. The entire Reading test will last 75 minutes. There are three parts, and directions are given for each part. You are encouraged to answer as many questions as possible within the time allowed.

You must mark your answers on the separate answer sheet. Do not write your answers in your test book.

Part 5

Directions: A word or phrase is missing in each of the sentences below. Four answer choices are given below each sentence. Select the best answer to complete the sentence. Then mark the letter (A), (B), (C), or (D) on your answer sheet.

101. Because classes are limited only to 12 students, we need a _____ response for you to take this course.
 (A) close
 (B) sharp
 (C) quick
 (D) busy

102. Please allow at least six business days for _____ of your order.
 (A) quantity
 (B) delivery
 (C) method
 (D) model

103. Ms. Taylor asked that her people attend _____ the team building workshop this week and the training session next month.
 (A) so
 (B) both
 (C) either
 (D) neither

104. All the supplies you ordered online will be _____ from our Hong Kong distribution center within 24 hours.
 (A) replied
 (B) stored
 (C) shipped
 (D) arrived

105. Tiffy Bath announced that _____ products have been removed from duty-free shelves in Japan and China.
 (A) themselves
 (B) its
 (C) itself
 (D) they

106. Interviewers agreed that Ronald Belisario is the most _____ of all the applicants for the supervisory position.
 (A) qualify
 (B) qualifier
 (C) qualified
 (D) qualifies

107. The intended market for the book is people who already have experience and want to develop _____ cooking skills further.
 (A) theirs
 (B) they
 (C) them
 (D) their

108. All the facilities in the factory must be inspected _____ to detect signs of excessive wear or damage.
 (A) frequent
 (B) frequents
 (C) frequently
 (D) frequency

109. Various community events have been planned by cities all over the county _____ the week of May 11 to May 18.
(A) among
(B) during
(C) under
(D) above

110. The spokesman _____ that the chairman will appoint a director this week and wait for approval from the board.
(A) specify
(B) to specify
(C) has specified
(D) is specified

111. The best security advice would be to avoid details _____ personal information such as names, birth of date and the like.
(A) about
(B) along
(C) until
(D) into

112. Cardmax will expand _____ opening a new branch in Boston to defend its market share in the east.
(A) region
(B) regional
(C) regionally
(D) regionalize

113. Whenever customers apply for a mobile phone contract, they will be subject to a credit check _____ their application is approved.
(A) until
(B) once
(C) since
(D) before

114. Mr. Crawford's exhibition called Boat Stories has attracted many first-time visitors and he made this his _____ exhibition to date.
(A) popularizes
(B) popularity
(C) must popularize
(D) most popular

115. The city will offer more _____ twice as many jobs to young people this year as it had offered a year ago.
(A) than
(B) as
(C) over
(D) during

116. North Ridge College announced this morning that Ms. Rosa Parks, former dean of St. John's College, _____ the new dean.
(A) named
(B) is named
(C) was named
(D) has named

117. Make your product readily available to the general public to strengthen the company's _____ in the market.
(A) recognize
(B) recognizing
(C) recognition
(D) recognized

118. Please be assured that every employee has _____ October 5 to decide whether to attend next month's training session.
(A) along
(B) as
(C) until
(D) so

119. Unexpected glitches in the system have become _____ due to adequate and regular maintenance.
(A) superb
(B) uninterested
(C) rare
(D) jealous

120. Polynet Corp. announced today that it will expand its international business _____ by setting up subsidiaries in Korea and Japan.
(A) closely
(B) over
(C) further
(D) jointly

GO ON TO THE NEXT PAGE

121. Additional materials _____ to the discussions at the last staff meeting will be posted on the intranet no later than tomorrow morning.
    (A) relevances
    (B) relevantly
    (C) relevance
    (D) relevant

122. This quarter Mega Tele's exports exceeded 40 billion dollars for the first time, thanks to a _____ increase in demand for semiconductors.
    (A) sharpness
    (B) sharply
    (C) sharp
    (D) sharpen

123. Starting next month, Nokicell Inc., _____ affordable smart phones that will improve the quality and ease of Internet access.
    (A) will have provided
    (B) has provided
    (C) will be providing
    (D) has been providing

124. Laptops, tablets, or smart phones provided to you by your employer should be used for work-related _____ only.
    (A) tasking
    (B) tasks
    (C) tasked
    (D) task

125. Last month, the recreation magazine's _____ topped 1 million for the first time.
    (A) improvement
    (B) article
    (C) editor
    (D) readership

126. Competitive salaries _____ generous bonuses will be awarded to sales representatives for big sales.
    (A) so that
    (B) even though
    (C) by the time
    (D) as well as

127. Hatter Footwear predicted a 20 percent rise in the total volume produced, _____ the expansion of the manufacturing facility.
    (A) owing to
    (B) instead of
    (C) even if
    (D) provided that

128. A person or an organization that sells something _____ to as the vendor.
    (A) is referred
    (B) referring
    (C) has referred
    (D) to refer

129. Biowill Chemicals makes plastics, chemicals and energy derived from renewable crops _____ petroleum.
    (A) in case of
    (B) only if
    (C) rather than
    (D) as though

130. The amount of work we do may _____ slightly from week to week.
    (A) vary
    (B) spread
    (C) reflect
    (D) allow

PART 6

Direction: Read the texts that follow. A word, phrase, or sentence is missing in parts of each text. Four answer choices for each question are given below the text. Select the best answer to complete the text. Then mark the letter (A), (B), (C), or (D) on your answer sheet.

Questions 131-134 refer to the following e-mail.

To: MichelleDupont@alphamail.com
From: Groberts@stellaraudio.com
Date: June 25
Subject: Purchase #651388

Dear Ms. Dupont,

We have received your order for the Stellar Hi-Fi Home Entertainment Stereo System (Item #651388) but we regret to inform you that Stellar Audio is ------- to ship your purchase at this moment. **131.** -------. However, it is on backorder and we will receive more by July 10. We are sorry **132.** that this ------- you. You can cancel your order if you want to. -------, the system will be delivered **133.** **134.** to the address you listed by July 25 at the latest. Please feel free to contact me at Groberts@stellaraudio.com for any question.

Sincerely,

Greta Roberts

---

131. (A) about
(B) unable
(C) always
(D) unexpected

132. (A) We have begun the process of delivering your order.
(B) The item you have ordered is no longer being manufactured.
(C) The stereo system you ordered is currently not in stock.
(D) We were unable to process your credit card for payment.

133. (A) inconvenient
(B) inconveniencing
(C) inconveniently
(D) inconveniences

134. (A) Otherwise
(B) Accordingly
(C) Nevertheless
(D) Indeed

Question 135-138 refer to the following announcement.

Dear Client:

We are sending you this message because we are concerned that an error may have occurred during the ------- (135.) of your most recent order with Valentinafashions.com. The on-line store cannot correct a mistyped quantity or determine whether you accidentally ordered the wrong item. ------- (136.). If you receive another email like this, your order may ------- (137.). If you think you made a mistake when you sent your on-line order, please contact us as soon as possible, so that we do not ship the wrong items. ------- (138.) mistake can be corrected by accessing your online account on our Web site.

135. (A) motivation
(B) transmission
(C) review
(D) retrieval

136. (A) Please check the quantity and item and resend your order.
(B) Your satisfaction with your order is guaranteed.
(C) Please take a moment to review the product that you received.
(D) All transactions are processed using our secure online server.

137. (A) be deleting
(B) to be deleted
(C) have been deleted
(D) have been deleting

138. (A) His
(B) Their
(C) Other
(D) Any

Questions 139-142 refer to the following e-mail.

To: Adrian Gonzalez
From: J.P. Howell
Date: March 12
Subject: New Copy Machine

Dear Mr. Gonzalez,

If you purchased or leased your copy machine over three years ago, it may be time to consider trading it in for new technology. We guarantee that our new model, Fro204, will be more -------. **139.**

You can reduce your office expenses by replacing your old, less efficient machines with a new one. -------. With a new photocopier, your office will become more productive as you will be able **140.** to get more work done in less time. Pro204 can also perform multiple tasks ------- printing, faxing, **141.** copying and scanning.

If you have any questions about Pro204 or other models, you can ------- the brochure I attached **142.** to this e-mail, or contact one of our sales representatives.

Regards,

J.P. Howell

139. (A) achievable
(B) portable
(C) reliable
(D) detectable

140. (A) We have sent a technician to assist you in repairing your photocopier.
(B) A catalog of our products can be sent to you upon request.
(C) This special offer will be valid by the end of the month.
(D) You will agree that copy machines are critical to office productivity.

141. (A) as well
(B) such as
(C) of these
(D) sort of

142. (A) consult
(B) discard
(C) approve
(D) revise

Questions 143-146 refer to the following flyer.

National Outdoor Sculpture Competition & Exhibition

Are you looking for a chance to display your thought-provoking and extraordinary sculptures? ------- (143.), this is the perfect competition for you! Please download and fill out the registration form at www.NOSCE.com, and email us together with ------- (144.) of your work. ------- (145.). Any applications received after this date will not be considered. Up to 14 sculptures are selected for the exhibition and compete for cash prizes. The images you send in will be critical to selecting entries. ------- (146.) entrants will be notified two months after the deadline date.

---

143. (A) Nevertheless
 (B) If so
 (C) After that
 (D) Instead

144. (A) descriptions
 (B) photographs
 (C) requirements
 (D) developments

145. (A) The deadline for applying is September 30.
 (B) More information can be found on the Web site.
 (C) The outdoors provides a relaxing environment to showcase your work.
 (D) We will carefully select each sculpture for the exhibition.

146. (A) Inviting
 (B) Invites
 (C) Invitation
 (D) Invited

PART 7

Direction: In this part you will read a selection of texts, such as magazine and newspaper articles, letters, e-mails, and instant messages. Each text or set of texts is followed by several questions. Select the best answer for each question and mark the letter (A), (B), (C), or (D) on your answer sheet.

Questions 147-148 refer to the following information on a product container.

Pridex Industries

Do you enjoy the great taste of Pridex Industries's products? Now you can receive Pridex chips, candy bars, and cookies for free! Just register at www.pridexind.com and enter the codes from Pridex product wrappers to get points. After you get enough points, we send you a voucher for the product of your choice.

For quality foodstuffs, choose Pridex
Your code: 484DBE83

147. What type of merchandise does the company sell?
(A) Computers
(B) Snacks
(C) Books
(D) Musical instruments

148. How can consumers get points?
(A) By filling out a questionnaire about Pridex merchandise
(B) By sending proofs of purchase
(C) By submitting a code on a website
(D) By writing a new slogan for the company

*어휘 NOTE

Questions 149-150 refer to the following article.

Chamber Improves Website

Atlas Chamber of Commerce announced that they upgraded the website to allow enrolled businesses to find other enrolled businesses by accessing its extensive directory on the site. "There was plenty of information for Atlas businesses to use, but it was difficult for businesses to find information about other businesses", Tiffany Billings, a local enrolled business member, said. "With the new directory search function, if an enrolled business needs consultation services for advertising, they can find local firms, addresses and phone numbers, and websites and e-mail addresses. The Chamber's Commercial Growth Committee really helped with this update." Technical support for the website will be undertaken by MegaCom, an enrolled Atlas Business. Previously available information from the site such as local event schedules and job postings will still be available to the general public, but only enrolled local businesses will be able to gain access to the directory by using an assigned password.

149. Why did the Chamber update its website?
    (A) To advertise career counseling
    (B) To give details about a conference schedule
    (C) To assist local businesses in working together
    (D) To notify general public of consulting services

150. What is indicated about the directory?
    (A) It is serviced by an international company.
    (B) It was recommended by MegaCom.
    (C) It is open only to enrolled businesses.
    (D) It will be updated on a monthly basis.

Questions 151-152 refer to the following text message chain.

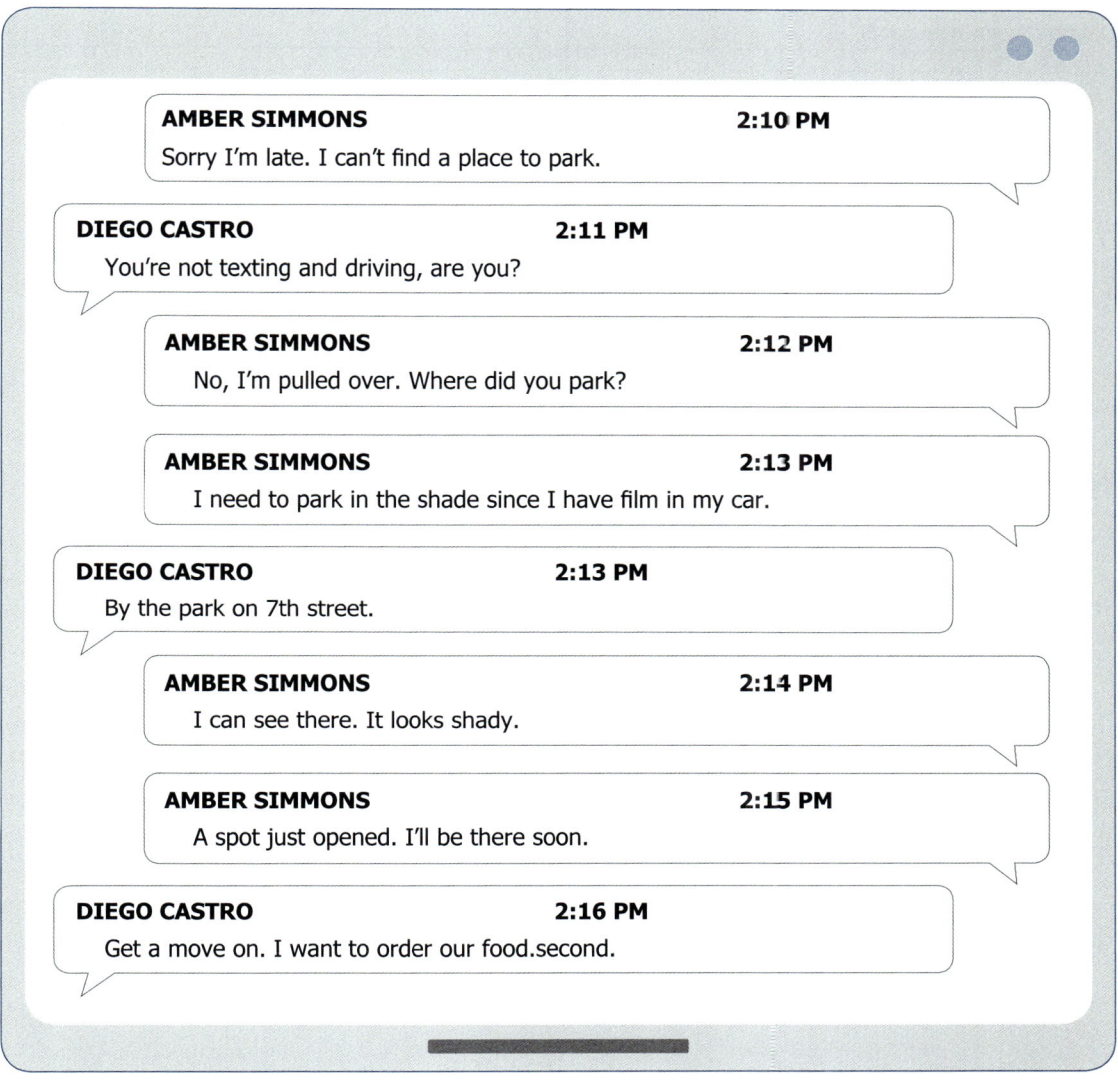

151. What is Ms. Simmons most likely trying to do?
(A) Find a restaurant's location
(B) Order a meal for take-out
(C) Schedule an appointment
(D) Secure a place for her car

152. At 2:16 p.m, what does Diego Castro mean when he writes, "Get a move on"?
(A) Ms. Simmons should schedule a moving company.
(B) Ms. Simmons should hurry to a location.
(C) Ms. Simmons should call when she arrives.
(D) Ms. Simmons should relate her food order.

Questions 153-154 refer to the following information from a website.

http:// www.nama.com

The National Argentinian Marketing Association is honored to have Felix Rodriguez as their keynote speaker at the association's 12th yearly convention, being held from May 12 to May 14 in Buenos Aires. Mr. Rodriguez helped get Bueno Marketing Consultants started nearly one decade ago with the help of his partner Hector Villanova, a former accountant. Rodriguez's company has had much success and is a shining example of how good marketing can help companies. Bueno Marketing Consultants has assisted companies ranging from food and beverage producers to electronics manufacturers in increasing their sales. Mr. Rodriguez's speech is largely influenced by his book, "Think Locally, Market Globally," published by Manzana Publications last year.

153. What is the purpose of the information?
(A) To promote a book about local culture
(B) To detail a company's achievements
(C) To notify readers of a speaker at a convention
(D) To give information on registration

154. What is Felix Rodriguez's occupation?
(A) Publishing executive
(B) Electronics manufacturer
(C) Public accountant
(D) Marketing consultant

Questions 155-157 refer to the following letter.

January 18

Paul Daniels
8744 Merit Road
Milford, DE 19963

Dear Mr. Daniels,

We have finished processing your application and it is my pleasure to tell you that we will be issuing an increase in credit to your Maltese Bank Platinum Card ending with the numbers 4497. You will have $20,000.00 in total credit on the card from February 4. The account number of the card will not change, but the expiration date will be extended. You will need to activate the new card upon receiving it by going to www.maltesebank.com/platinum/activate.

Regards,

Lynette Givens
Account Manager
1-800-555-4488

155 Why was the letter sent to Mr. Daniels?
(A) To inform him about an approved application
(B) To verify receipt of a payment
(C) To promote a newly available credit card
(D) To request a statement for an account

156. What information is shown in the letter?
(A) A payment date
(B) A bank address
(C) A partial card number
(D) An expiration date

157. What is Mr. Daniels advised to do?
(A) To pay to activate a card
(B) To properly dispose of his old card
(C) To visit the Maltese Bank website
(D) To bring additional documents to the bank

Questions 158-160 refer to the following note.

From the Editor-in-Chief

The upcoming March issue of Midwest Kitchen will be the third-year anniversary issue of our publication. It's hard to believe that much time has passed since we began sharing the best recipes and cooking tips that Midwestern chefs and others around the nation have to offer. Just two months ago, our total subscribers reached 500,000, with more subscribers joining every month. At last year's Kitchen and Cooking Convention, we received the award for most innovative cooking publication. In my role as editor-in-chief of this magazine, I can't tell how much I appreciate our team of writers, photographers, and contributors, as well as our sponsors and our increasingly larger group of subscribers, who have helped our publication succeed over the last three years. Thank you.

Thomas Swift

158. What is a purpose of Mr. Swift's note?
(A) To show appreciation
(B) To offer a subscription
(C) To contribute a recipe
(D) To request funds

159. What is indicated about Midwest Kitchen?
(A) It is looking for a new editor.
(B) It will cease publication soon.
(C) It is becoming more popular.
(D) It has decreased subscription prices.

160. Why does Mr. Swift mention the Kitchen and Cooking Convention?
(A) Because he signed recipe books at the event
(B) Because he presented a new cooking methed there
(C) Because the organizers sponsor the magazine
(D) Because the publication was praised there

Questions 161-164 refer to the following letter.

Corn County Medical Center
213 Jespersen Avenue
Milwaukee, WI 53022

July 5

Mark Commer
424 Henders Road
Madison, WI 53532

Dear Mr. Commer,

We appreciate your applying for the position of charge nurse at Corn County Medical Center. Your interview will take place on Thursday, July 12 at 10:30 a.m. We will hold the interview at the Williams Clinic instead of the main medical center. The committee interviewing you will be made up of Sebastian Lexor, head of operations, and Miriam Naren, the head nurse. Dr. Lexor and Mrs. Naren are in charge of all nurses at the medical center.

As we discussed during our phone conversation, it is usually very difficult to find a parking spot near the clinic. At this time, the clinic also has no guest parking lot, so you would have to secure a parking space on the street. It would be a much better idea if you take the bus.

Let me know if you need more information before your interview.

Regards,

Layla Hempel
Personnel director

161. What is suggested about Mr. Commer?
(A) He will visit the hospital when the interview is finished.
(B) He will see Ms. Hempel at Williams Clinic.
(C) He has talked to Ms. Hempel on the phone before.
(D) He is interested in working at the check-in desk.

162. What is indicated about Mrs. Naren?
(A) She is currently working for Williams Clinic.
(B) She will take part in Mr. Commer's interview.
(C) She is being trained to become a doctor.
(D) She arranged a schedule for Mr. Commer's interview.

163. The word "secure" in paragraph 2, line 2 is closest in meaning to
(A) Guard
(B) Attach
(C) Obtain
(D) Borrow

164. What does Ms. Hempel suggest that Mr. Commer do?
(A) To use public transportation
(B) To make use of a guest parking lot
(C) To provide reference contact information
(D) To confirm a reservation

Questions 165-167 refer to the following e-mail.

From :	Beth Tempton <btempton@healthstrong.com>
To :	Richard Lang <rlang@ healthstrong.com >
Subject :	Sales Workshop
Date :	May 23

Hi, Richard,

I just found out about a great chance for you to get involved in a workshop as we talked about. —[1]—. Unlike previous workshops, we want to direct these at both sales staff with more experience and sales staff who recently started.

Like other workshops, these will be held over the course of one month, with each workshop lasting for two hours. —[2]—. Since you work in the research and development department, your knowledge would make you a great addition to our training team if your schedule permits. —[3]—.

Lilly Heeman and Dirk Tently will be leading the workshops for the first two weeks. However, we had a schedule problem with Stephanie Wrigley from product testing, as she will be in Geneva until the first week of August. Her co-worker, Maryanne Broderick said that she can take over Stephanie's workshop by herself. If you're able, I'd like you to join Maryanne for the final session. I think Maryanne and you would make a great team for the last workshop. —[4]—.

Best regards,

Beth Tempton

Sales Director

165. According to the e-mail, how is the upcoming sales workshop different from the ones before?
(A) It has four conductors rather than one.
(B) Every session will take more time.
(C) Not as many topics will be discussed.
(D) It is designed for all sales staff.

166. Who is NOT mentioned as a possible trainer?
(A) Beth Tempton
(B) Lilly Hetman
(C) Dirk Tently
(D) Maryanne Broderick

167. In which of the positions marked [1], [2], [3], and [4] does the following sentence best belong?

"The workshops will be held from 1 p.m. until 3 p.m. every Thursday in July, with each one being conducted by several department specialists."

(A) [1]
(B) [2]
(C) [3]
(D) [4]

Questions 168-171 refer to the following article.

Transportation Routes Changing After Road Construction

May 31 – Drivers should prepare to find alternative routes as road construction will cause some streets to close down in Lawrence from tomorrow.

The Transportation Department initiated the construction process, which will be completed over the course of three stages, with the Worryfree Roads program. The first stage of the work, which is expected to last about two months, includes repaving part of Alderidge Street from Farrer Avenue to Highway 22. —[1]—.

Stage two of the construction process, the longest of the three, is tentatively scheduled to start in August. —[2]—. The work is intended to accommodate two lanes, doubling it from its current one lane in order to decrease traffic congestion which has risen since the Silver Shopping Center opened a year ago. The ramp will also be made safer by reducing the sharp curves.

—[3]—. Olivia Petrova, a resident of Prairie Road, which is about 700 meter from Exit 4B, is following the progress of the construction with great interest. "It's wonderful that the ramp will finally be rebuilt" she says. Even though she's pleased about the ramp, she'd like to see the construction completed sooner than the three months that the stage will take to complete. "It'd be nice if it could be done sooner," she says.

The third stage includes various work which will not affect traffic as much as the previous stages. —[4]—. In this phase, signs will be replaced so that they are more visible at night and repainting traffic markings on the road with reflective paint. The Lawrence Transit Commission estimates that the costly but necessary construction will be finished within six months, but the schedule is tentative and subject to change depending on weather conditions.

168. What is NOT an intended result of the construction?
(A) To alleviate traffic jams near a mall
(B) To increase the visibility of road signs in the dark
(C) To decrease the cost of parking in Lawrence
(D) To deal with concerns about safety

169. The word "following" in paragraph 4, line 1, is closest in meaning to
(A) Obeying
(B) Monitoring
(C) Proceeding
(D) Reporting on

170. How long is the second stage expected to last?
(A) One month
(B) Two months
(C) Three months
(D) One year

171. In which of the positions marked [1], [2], [3], and [4] does the following sentence best belong?

"Work during this stage will increase the size of the exit ramp for Treeton Drive from Route 58 (Exit 4B)."

(A) [1]
(B) [2]
(C) [3]
(D) [4]

Questions 172-175 refer to the following online chat discussion.

Olivia Byrne	[11:11 a.m.]	Has anyone else had a chance to take a look at Terrence O'Hara's proposal for his next novel? I was hoping to get others' opinions since I really think it's promising.
Bridget Stamp	[11:13 a.m.]	I did and it definitely caught my eye. I'm very interested in getting it published, but Mark didn't think that it would be very marketable.
Mark Boughton	[11:15 a.m.]	Yeah, I don't think the story sounds very accessible. I think that if we published it, it would become successful in some groups, but overall, I think it would bomb. It seems to be a much different theme than his last novel.
Bridget Stamp	[11:17 a.m.]	I agree that it is moving in a different direction. I think the sci-fi themes for the proposal seem more prevalent than his previous novels. Although his old fans might not like it, it could attract new readers.
Olivia Byrne	[11:18 a.m.]	What if we try a different approach to releasing it? Rather than releasing it as a straightforward novel, we could release the first chapter in some literary and sci-fi journals and see what kind of response it gets.
Mark Boughton	[11:20 a.m.]	That's an interesting idea. Which magazines or journals do you think would be best?
Bob Copeland	[11:21 a.m.]	I can get in touch with a couple of contacts at Future Times Journal of Sci-Fi and Fiction Monthly. I'm sure they'll be interested.
Olivia Byrne	[11:23 a.m.]	That sounds great, Bob. I'll call Terrence now and see if he's interested in releasing a chapter in some journals first. Let me know what your contacts say after you talk to them.

172. Where most likely do the writers work?
(A) A literary journal
(B) A publishing firm
(C) An educational institute
(D) A science museum

173. What is indicated about Terrence O'Hara?
(A) He's had his work in magazines before.
(B) He writes primarily science fiction stories.
(C) He works with multiple publishing houses.
(D) He has published novels before.

174. At 11:15 a.m., what does Mark Boughton mean when he writes, "it would bomb"?
(A) A publication would be profitable.
(B) Critics will find the book enjoyable.
(C) The novel has too much violence.
(D) A publication would be a commercial failure.

175. What will Olivia Byrne probably do next?
(A) Discuss a plan with a writer
(B) Contact some magazine editors
(C) Schedule a meeting with some contacts
(D) Edit a proposal for a novel

*어휘 NOTE

Questions 176-180 refer to the following e-mails.

* E-mail *

To :	dapplebaum@cordis.com
From :	gretrand@huxleyinternational.ca
Subject :	Interview
Date :	October 15
Attachment:	Employment policy manual

Dear Mr. Applebaum,

I want to thank you for coming to our booth at the Vancouver Career Fair two weeks ago. Your experience and your present position at Cordis Systems are remarkable. I'm happy you decided to forward your resume and application for the job we talked about.

Our human resources director looked over your credentials and wants you to visit our headquarters for an interview within the next two weeks. Please tell me which of these times works best with your schedule.

    Wednesday, October 21, 11:00 a.m. or 3:00 p.m.

    Friday, October 23, 10:00 a.m. or 2:00 p.m.

    Tuesday, October 27, 10:30 a.m. or 11:30 a.m.

Before coming to our office, we'd like you to peruse the policy manual that I've attached so that you may ask any questions about our procedures. Feel free to contact me if you have any questions about the interview.

Sincerely,

Gertrude Retrand

To :	gretrand@huxleyinternational.ca
From :	dapplebaum@cordis.com
Subject :	Re: Interview
Date :	October 16

Dear Mrs. Retrand,

I very much appreciate the chance to interview at Huxley International. It'll be an exciting challenge to direct a team after so many years as a consultant. As for the interview time, my afternoons are usually more free, so I can come to your headquarters for the interview at 3:00 p.m.

I had a question about something you said at the career fair, actually. You said you would like some references and recommendation letters concerning my experience. It's no problem to do this, but can you let me know how many I should bring to the interview?

Thanks again for this opportunity. I'm looking forward to meeting you again next week.

176. How did Mr. Applebaum likely learn about the job opening of Huxley International?
(A) From a colleague
(B) From an online posting
(C) From the company's bulletin board
(D) From a job fair

177. What is Mr. Applebaum instructed to do before his interview?
(A) Review the company's history
(B) Write a reference letter
(C) Read through a handbook
(D) Undergo a background check

178. When will Mr. Applebaum's interview probably be?
(A) On Tuesday
(B) On Wednesday
(C) On Thursday
(D) On Friday

179. Why is Mr. Applebaum seeking a new job?
(A) Because he wants to head a team
(B) Because he wants to move to a new town
(C) Because he would like to work in a new field
(D) Because he wants to work in a full-time position

180. What information does Mr. Applebaum request?
(A) The location of the headquarters
(B) The number of references he should bring
(C) The duties of his new position
(D) The names of employees he will manage

*어휘 NOTE

Questions 181-185 refer to the following e-mails.

E-mail Message

To : Larry Baird
From : Moira Lovett
Date : Mar 18
Subject : Silverson Electronics Workshop

Dear Mr. Baird,

I am preparing a team-building workshop for my employees at Silverson Electronics and I was thinking of hosting it at the Biltmore Hotel. My co-worker, Mr. Piazza held a gathering at your hotel earlier this year and he was very pleased with the hospitality and service of your staff and you, as well as the hotel itself.

The Silverson Electronics team-building workshop is scheduled to be on May 2 around 9 a.m. I will need a big conference room and the workshop will last about five and a half hours. At most, there will be 40 people coming. A majority of them plan on staying overnight at the hotel. We will be taking a break during the workshop for lunch, so I would like a package for a half day that includes a lunch buffet. Also, we will need a sound system with four microphones for the workshop, as well as a projector and screen.

Thanks in advance for helping.

Moira Lovett

TO : Moira Lovett
FROM : Larry Baird
DATE : Mar 19
SUBJECT: RE: Silverson Electronics Workshop
ATTACHMENT: Buffet Menu options

Dear Ms. Lovett,

We're honored that you would choose our hotel to host Silverson Electronics workshop. Our hotel has four options for rooms and catering, all including wireless Internet.

<u>The Biltmore Option</u>: $70 / guest – Reservation for a full day in a conference room – Up to 10 hours
A Breakfast buffet, lunch buffet, and light refreshments are included along with sound and video equipment. Free valet parking is available for attendees.

<u>The Executive Option</u>: $55 / guest – Reservation for a full day in a conference room – Up to 10 hours
Sound and video equipment are included. Guests may use our parking facilities free of charge.

<u>The Preferred Option</u>: $45 / guest – Reservation for a half day in a conference room – Up to 6 hours
A Lunch buffet is included with sound and video equipment. Guests may use our parking facilities free of charge.

<u>The Robbins Option</u>: $30 / guest – Reservation for a half day in a conference room – Up to 6 hours
Light refreshments will be made available at the start and conclusion of the conference. Sound and video equipment are supplied and guests may use our parking facilities free of charge.

Please look through the attached buffet menu and feel free to ask me any questions you may have.

Larry Baird

181. What is the purpose of the first e-mail?
(A) To fix a conflict in a schedule
(B) To ask about conference facilities
(C) To confirm a hotel reservation
(D) To request a guest list

182. What is suggested about the workshop?
(A) A movie will be presented at the beginning.
(B) Attendees are hired by a company.
(C) It was initially scheduled at a later date.
(D) It will have one presenter.

183. What is indicated about Mr. Baird?
(A) He was suggested by a colleague of Ms. Lovett.
(B) He has not worked at the hotel long.
(C) He was employed by Silverson Electronics before.
(D) He put together Biltmore Hotel's buffet menu.

184. What is NOT mentioned as a feature of the conference options?
(A) Access to the Internet in the conference room
(B) Complimentary parking for conference attendees
(C) Audiovisual equipment for the conference room
(D) Discounted room rates for attendees

185. What package best meets Silverson Electronics' wishes?
(A) The Biltmore option
(B) The Executive option
(C) The Preferred option
(D) The Robbins option

Questions 186-190 refer to the following Web page, brochure, and e-mail.

---

http://www.premiumtours.com/washingtondc

Premium Tours

Premium Tours makes it our mission to bring you to the best local food favorites in historic Washington D.C., Baltimore and Pittsburgh areas. Come with our knowledgeable guides as they tell you about the culture and history of each area while walking to restaurants and trying the best food from all of them.

Penn Quarter (Washington D.C.)

Time: From Monday to Friday, 5:30 p.m. to 8:00 p.m. (not available on weekends.)

Dress: Clothes and footwear that are appropriate for walking are recommended.

Food: Participants will be enjoying a variety of tastes throughout the tour. The first restaurant will serve appetizers. At the second location, participants can meet Jacques Zieman, owner of the restaurant and chocolate connoisseur, and sample his favorite chocolates. The following restaurant will feature a partial dinner, and dessert will be served at the final location.

Price: $60 per person

Included: Food, complimentary bottled water, a city map and a detailed pamphlet featuring the restaurants and stores from the tour.

Premium Tours – Penn Quarter Restaurants
Restaurants are listed below in the order in which they will be visited on the tour.

Restaurant/Store	Location
1. Stan's Pizza	**644 Hill Avenue** • Featuring Chicago style pizza
2. Sweet Life	**113 George Street** • International gourmet food shop
3. Bread & Butter	**129 George Street** • The Restaurant combines Mediterranean cuisine with live music in the evening • Reservations required
4. Sucre Bleu	**495 North 15th Street** • The finest cakes and desserts • Doesn't operate on Thursdays
5. Penn Quarter Creamery	**490 North 15th Street** • High quality ice cream and sundaes • Participants visit here if Sucre Bleu is not open.

* E-mail *

To: Premium Tours <inquiries@ premiumtours.com>
From: Lena Tomaski <ltomaski@speedmail.com>
Date: May 16
Subject: Question about tours

Hi,

I'm very interested in going on one of your tours, but the page that shows which restaurants are visited on the tours seems to be down. I'm very interested in trying some restaurants in the Washington D.C. area. I'm a huge ice cream lover, so if possible, I'd like to go on a tour which includes ice cream. Please let me know when would be the best time to join your Penn Quarter tour and give me more information about the restaurants.

Sincerely,

Lena Tomaski

---

186. What is stated about Premium Tours?
(A) They offer tours of historic homes.
(B) They provide week-long tours.
(C) They provide tours on the holidays.
(D) They provide tours in different areas.

187. In the Web page, the word "complimentary" in paragraph 6, line1, is closest in meaning to?
(A) supplement
(B) extra
(C) free
(D) appreciative

188. What is suggested about the Penn Quarter tour?
(A) It takes place twice a day.
(B) It offers attendees foods from around the world.
(C) The guide is a resident of Penn Quarter.
(D) The attendees receive free transportation.

189. Where will tour participants meet Mr. Zieman?
(A) At Sweet Life
(B) At Bread & Butter
(C) At Sagarmatha
(D) At Sucre Bleu

190. On what day will Ms. Tomaski most likely go on a Premium Tour?
(A) Monday
(B) Wednesday
(C) Thursday
(D) Friday

Questions 191-195 refer to the following article, website, and article.

WELCOME TO THE NEIGHBORHOOD, PLAIN GLASS THEATER

The Plain Glass Theater company has opened their doors to the general public and our students after renovating the Cornwell Theater, only half a kilometer from Ellington College's campus.

The theater will be Plain Glass Theater's permanent home after moving from venue to venue after its founding twelve years ago. The renewed facility, which once housed a community center, is truly a great fit for the company. Gordon DeLaren, art director says that the renovations were definitely worth the wait. "The Cornwell Theater is a spacious and elegant facility that allowed the company to maintain both artistic and administrative staff under one roof for the first time. It was less expensive to renovate this existing space than to construct a brand-new building. Being close to Ellington College is also a nice advantage. We hope we can provide quality entertainment for the arts-loving students of the school."

"Secret Summer," a new play written by Clark Katz, will be the company's first production at the new building. The play opens on Saturday, February 12 and will begin with a speech by the play's director. More information can be found at www.plainglasstheater.com.

Plain Glass Theater

Buy Tickets

Purchase tickets	Homepage	Upcoming productions	About Us	Contact

TICKET PRICES:
- General public — $40
- Supporting members — $30
- Students — $25
- Children under 10 years old — $12

A valid and current Student ID card is required to receive a student discount at the Plain Glass Theater ticket office.

PLAIN GLASS THEATER OPENED WITH ITS SUCCESSFUL DEBUT PLAY

"Secret Summer", the first production at Plain Glass Theater was an excellent presentation of the performing arts for all in attendance. During a short introductory speech, Kurt Hedaya, said he was pleased that so many came out to support the arts community and delivered his gratitude to Ellington College since a majority of the audience was from the college.

The play, which lasted 3 hours with a thirty minute intermission, starred Emilia Snell as barista who happens to learn that she has the power to read minds. The play addressed serious, potentially difficult yet universally relevant subjects in a moving, humorous and totally engrossing way. It is set to be performed by Plain Glass Theater until March 30.

191. What is indicated about the theater?
(A) It was founded by Mr. Katz.
(B) It did not have a stable location.
(C) It has had productions in many countries.
(D) It has changed its name.

192. In the first article, the word "space" in paragraph 2, line 10, is closest in meaning to?
(A) Distance
(B) Privacy
(C) Available place
(D) Period of time

193. What does Mr. DeLaren NOT mention as an advantage of the Cornwell Theater?
(A) A history with the community
(B) Proximity to potential customers
(C) A good amount of space
(D) Decent restoration expenses

194. What most likely is Kurt Hedaya's job?
(A) An art director of a theater
(B) An actor in a play
(C) A director of a play
(D) A theater reviewer

195. What is indicated about the audience for the performance on February 12?
(A) Many of them received discounted tickets.
(B) They thought the play was too long.
(C) Some of them left during intermission.
(D) Many brought their children along.

Questions 196–200 refer to the following advertisement, e-mail, and notice.

Riverview Apartments
Now Leasing!

New leases come with lower rates!
(A minimum of a one-year rent is required)

One-bedroom apartment: $900/month
Two-bedroom apartment: $1150/month
All utilities are included with the monthly lease payment

A laundry area, a recreation area, and a fully furnished lobby are all accessible to tenants.

244 West River Road
Brooklyn Center, MN 55429
416-555-0142
www.riverviewapartments.com

To :	Rita Adler
From :	Eric Jansen
Subject :	New tenant
Attachment :	Apartment-55

Dear Ms. Adler:

All of the documents have been completed for Harvey Lang. He will come by the office this morning to sign a lease for one year, and he plans on paying his first month's rent with a personal check for $900. You'll find the documents and his rent payment on your desk later today. He also plans to register with the tenants association immediately.

Please let our maintenance department know that the apartment has to be ready by June 2. I've attached a detailed work order to this e-mail. Make sure that the maintenance staff notice that Mr. Lang wants the room to be painted beige.

There are three more apartments that are still vacant on the third, sixth, and seventh floors. I'm meeting with some potential tenants this afternoon to show them the two bedroom apartments, and another potential tenant tomorrow for the one bedroom. Once these are leased, we will be at full occupancy.

Thanks.

Regards,

Eric Jansen

Notice from the Riverview Apartments Tenants Association
July 1

Greetings, fellow tenants. Below is a tentative schedule for our upcoming meeting scheduled on July 7.

New tenant introduction: Any new members of our association will be asked to introduce themselves to the group.

Upcoming parking lot renovations: We'll be giving information about the renovations to be done to the parking lot and alternate parking places for tenants.

Update to community pool rules: The rules for the community pool have changed. Come find out how it will be changed and give your thoughts on it.

Construction notices: There will be renovations in apartments 340, 680, and 723 for new tenants through the month of July. We'll discuss what tenants can expect from this.

---

196. What is suggested about Mr. Lang?
(A) He will lease a one-bedroom unit.
(B) He is extending his lease for an extra year.
(C) He will vacate the apartment in May.
(D) He requested access to the lobby.

197. What is Ms. Adler asked to do?
(A) Approve some paperwork
(B) Provide details to maintenance employees
(C) Schedule a meeting with Mr. Jansen
(D) Persuade potential tenants to sign a lease

198. According to the notice, the word, "tentative" in paragraph 1, line 1, is closest in meaning to,
(A) indefinite
(B) hesitant
(C) experimental
(D) specific

199. What will Mr. Lang be expected to do at a meeting?
(A) Talk about himself to other members
(B) Vote on changing rules for an apartment complex's facilities.
(C) Be assigned an alternate parking spot
(D) Present updates for a Web site

200. What is indicated about Riverview Apartments?
(A) Monthly rent is expected to increase soon.
(B) They will be no vacancy after the renovations.
(C) The tenants are unhappy with the state of the community pool.
(D) Many of its tenants do not own automobiles.

Stop! This is the end of the test. If you finish before time is called, you may go back to Parts 5, 6, and 7 and check your work.

동시토익 실전 WORKBOOK

101. Because classes are limited only to 12 students, we need a quick response for you to take this course.

해석]

102. Please allow at least six business days for delivery of your order.

해석]

103. Ms. Taylor asked that her people attend both the team building workshop this week and the training session next month.

해석]

104. All the supplies you ordered online will be shipped from our Hong Kong distribution center within 24 hours.

해석]

105. Tiffy Bath announced that its products have been removed from duty-free shelves in Japan and China.

해석]

106. Interviewers agreed that Ronald Belisario is the most qualified of all the applicants for the supervisory position.

해석]

107. The intended market for the book is people who already have experience and want to develop their cooking skills further.

해석]

108. All the facilities in the factory must be inspected frequently to detect signs of excessive wear or damage.

해석]

109. Various community events have been planned by cities all over the county during the week of May 11 to May 18.

해석]

110. The spokesman has specified that the chairman will appoint a director this week and wait for approval from the board.

해석]

*어휘 NOTE

111. The best security advice would be to avoid details about personal information such as names, birth of date and the like.

해석]

112. Cardmax will expand regionally opening a new branch in Boston to defend its market share in the east.

해석]

113. Whenever customers apply for a mobile phone contract, they will be subject to a credit check before their application is approved.

해석]

114. Mr. Crawford's exhibition called Boat Stories has attracted many first-time visitors and he made this his most popular exhibition to date.

해석]

115. The city will offer more than twice as many jobs to young people this year as it had offered a year ago.

해석]

116. North Ridge College announced this morning that Ms. Rosa Parks, former dean of St. John's College, was named the new dean.

해석]

117. Make your product readily available to the general public to strengthen the company's recognition in the market.

해석]

118. Please be assured that every employee has until October 5 to decide whether to attend next month's training session.

해석]

119. Unexpected glitches in the system have become rare due to adequate and regular maintenance.

해석]

120. Polynet Corp. announced today that it will expand its international business further by setting up subsidiaries in Korea and Japan.

해석]

*어휘 NOTE

121. Additional materials relevant to the discussions at the last staff meeting will be posted on the intranet no later than tomorrow morning.

해석]

122. This quarter Mega Tele's exports exceeded 40 billion dollars for the first time, thanks to a sharp increase in demand for semiconductors.

해석]

123. Starting next month, Nokicell Inc., will be providing affordable smart phones that will improve the quality and ease of Internet access.

해석]

124. Laptops, tablets, or smart phones provided to you by your employer should be used for work-related tasks only.

해석]

125. Last month, the recreation magazine's readership topped 1 million for the first time.

해석]

126. Competitive salaries as well as generous bonuses will be awarded to sales representatives for big sales.

해석]

127. Hatter Footwear predicted a 20 percent rise in the total volume produced, owing to the expansion of the manufacturing facility.

해석]

128. A person or an organization that sells something is referred to as the vendor.

해석]

129. Biowill Chemicals makes plastics, chemicals and energy derived from renewable crops rather than petroleum.

해석]

130. The amount of work we do may vary slightly from week to week.

해석]

*어휘 NOTE

TEST 09

동시토익 CONTEMPORARY **TOEIC**

TEST 09

READING TEST

In the Reading test, you will read a variety of texts and answer several different types of reading comprehension questions. The entire Reading test will last 75 minutes. There are three parts, and directions are given for each part. You are encouraged to answer as many questions as possible within the time allowed.

You must mark your answers on the separate answer sheet. Do not write your answers in your test book.

Part 5

Directions: A word or phrase is missing in each of the sentences below. Four answer choices are given below each sentence. Select the best answer to complete the sentence. Then mark the letter (A), (B), (C), or (D) on your answer sheet.

101. Gracia's Restaurant _____ opened a new restaurant in Fullerton.
 (A) successfully
 (B) successful
 (C) successes
 (D) success

102. Part-time workers are scheduled to work more _____ five hours and then be given thirty-minute work-free meal period.
 (A) from
 (B) than
 (C) as
 (D) of

103. The speaker stated that laws should be as _____ as possible to take account of various circumstances, time and places.
 (A) flexing
 (B) flexed
 (C) flexible
 (D) flexibility

104. The critic who saw Impossible wrote in his column that _____ was a two-thumbs-up movie.
 (A) its
 (B) its own
 (C) itself
 (D) it

105. Mr. Gonzalez expects that the final construction phase of the main building should be completed _____ next month.
 (A) at
 (B) by
 (C) of
 (D) on

106. Mr. Ed Simon _____ his proposals to directors in a plausible fashion.
 (A) explained
 (B) inserted
 (C) decided
 (D) believed

107. AX Energy _____ reports on their oil reserves on a weekly basis.
 (A) publisher
 (B) publishing
 (C) publishes
 (D) publishable

108. All of the packages which are received from customers must be labeled _____.
 (A) correctly
 (B) correcting
 (C) correctable
 (D) corrected

109. International students can choose from all regular courses offered _____ the University of California provided they meet the necessary qualifications.
(A) by
(B) about
(C) after
(D) off

110. We offer free magazines to our hotel guests in _____ with Peacock Publishing Company.
(A) cooperate
(B) cooperated
(C) cooperation
(D) cooperates

111. If your purchase is not delivered to your home within a week of purchase, you will have your shipping charge _____.
(A) posted
(B) refunded
(C) priced
(D) changed

112. Old colleagues of Nick Punto have been amazed by how _____ his new business has become successful.
(A) strongly
(B) tightly
(C) quickly
(D) usually

113. We must regard any statement about this issue as gossip _____ it is confirmed by the Senate.
(A) next
(B) until
(C) without
(D) from

114. Santa Barbara City Council members finally set the budget for the next fiscal year after _____ debate.
(A) length
(B) lengthy
(C) lengthen
(D) lengthwise

115. Stephenson's Warmite, in business _____ the mid-1950s, provides high quality light-weight equipment.
(A) since
(B) while
(C) along
(D) toward

116. The reselling of tickets _____ through our website at prices above face value is strictly prohibited by law.
(A) valued
(B) fined
(C) signed
(D) acquired

117. It is _____ that Carl Crawford will be promoted to senior vice president of Belco Enterprise.
(A) probable
(B) constant
(C) endless
(D) qualified

118. _____ supervising and managing office personnel, she is responsible for overseeing all the reports to the management.
(A) In addition to
(B) Provided that
(C) As well
(D) In order that

119. Nolasco, Inc. has developed a profitable business model in emerging countries, while maintaining a _____ share of domestic market.
(A) prepared
(B) defensive
(C) significant
(D) cooperative

120. Middle and senior managers in mining companies improve their leadership competencies with an _____ on safety.
(A) emphasize
(B) emphasis
(C) emphasized
(D) emphasizes

GO ON TO THE NEXT PAGE

121. _____ purchasing a car, it is beneficial to use a car leasing option if you are using the car strictly for work.
(A) Away from
(B) Except for
(C) Next to
(D) Rather than

122. For travelers eager _____ the ancient history of the city, the hotel is ideally situated in the center of the city.
(A) explore
(B) will explore
(C) exploring
(D) to explore

123. Since demand in a part of your business is increasingly outgrowing your staff or resources, the decision to outsource some jobs is a natural _____.
(A) another
(B) most
(C) one
(D) either

124. Given that last year's conference sold out, it is anticipated that this year's conference enrollment will _____ last year's.
(A) surpass
(B) surpassing
(C) surpassed
(D) surpassingly

125. This organization's _____ is to teach, inform, and guide the public to respect and appreciate the nature around us.
(A) inquiry
(B) structure
(C) transfer
(D) objective

126. The cost of destruction of unsold stamps, including _____ stamps, is a regular item in the Postal Service's budget.
(A) commemorate
(B) commemorates
(C) commemoration
(D) commemorative

127. Ramirez Airlines, now struggling with financial difficulties, has yet to make a decision about _____ operations in China.
(A) suspending
(B) to suspend
(C) suspends
(D) suspend

128. It was reported to a senior executive that there had been an _____ large money transfer to a financial institution.
(A) outwardly
(B) easily
(C) unsecurely
(D) unusually

129. With only a few days remaining before the inspection from the outside, the factory supervisor has _____ to be prepared for it.
(A) not
(B) finally
(C) yet
(D) already

130. Mr. Ito will make a presentation at the meeting with potential investors because he knows the new line of product better than _____.
(A) each
(B) whichever
(C) much
(D) most

PART 6

Direction: Read the texts that follow. A word, phrase, or sentence is missing in parts of each text. Four answer choices for each question are given below the text. Select the best answer to complete the text. Then mark the letter (A), (B), (C), or (D) on your answer sheet.

Questions 131-134 refer to the following memo.

The Teleworld Media's service center is in charge of ensuring that the business phones ------- **131.** properly. If you have something wrong with any phone in your office, submit a repair request form though our website. Please make sure to include in your form a complete description of the -------. **132.** Upon receipt of your form, our service center representative will provide you with a detailed estimate of the service required and will list all parts to be replaced. You will be ------- contacted, **133.** within 24 hours, and the repair will begin upon approval. -------. **134.** If, for any reason, you are not able to be home during the scheduled time, our representative will reschedule the appointment at your earliest convenience.

131. (A) functional
 (B) to function
 (C) are functioning
 (D) functionally

132. (A) payment
 (B) meeting
 (C) event
 (D) problem

133. (A) collectively
 (B) periodically
 (C) promptly
 (D) randomly

134. (A) All repaired parts are guaranteed for one year after the time of repair.
 (B) The technician will also contact you one hour before arriving.
 (C) Our schedules are now fully booked and will let you know when they are able to visit you.
 (D) The service center is staffed by knowledgeable employees.

Question 135-138 refer to the following e-mail.

To: Hellen Outdoor Furniture customers
From: Elian Herrera
Date: July 26
Subject: Apologies

Dear Mr. Ethier,

Please note that our summer sale insert delivered with Tuesday's newspaper contains a -------. The **135.** sale price for the five-piece set of lawn furniture is $400, not $100. -------. However, this price is **136.** still quite a deal since the set is manufactured from solid oak and will last for decades. We hope that you will be able to take ------- of this. Moreover, to further apologize for the incorrect price, **137.** we will give the first ten customers to purchase the dining room sets an additional fifteen percent off the already low sale price. We're looking forward to ------- you at the store soon. **138.**

Yours sincerely,

Elian Herrera
Managing Director
Hellen Outdoor Furniture

135. (A) declaration
(B) correction
(C) schedule
(D) misprint

136. (A) Bring in the coupon to save even more on your next purchase.
(B) Our summer sale will take place over the entire month of August.
(C) A separate piece of furniture will be on sale during our fall sale.
(D) We are sorry if this has disappointed you at all.

137. (A) advantage
(B) service
(C) merit
(D) improvement

138. (A) visiting
(B) hiring
(C) seeing
(D) calling

Questions 139-142 refer to the following letter.

March 23

Dear Mr. Hamilton,

Thank you for your order through www.raymondretail.com. ------ (139). We ------ (140) to providing customers with unique, content-packed products. If you don't like our products for any reason, you will be issued a ------ (141). All the orders may be cancelled at any time by submitting a written cancellation request to our customer service department. If you have ------ (142) questions, please call us at 1-800-555-5429. We hope you find our product to your complete satisfaction.

Rosa Parks
Regional Sales Representative

139. (A) Unfortunately, there has been an issue with your purchase.
(B) Your order will be processed as soon as we confirm your payment.
(C) Your account details have been updated as entered.
(D) We have received your cancelation request and will process it immediately.

140. (A) are committed
(B) would be committing
(C) were committed
(D) will have committed

141. (A) discount
(B) replacement
(C) warranty
(D) refund

142. (A) furthering
(B) furthered
(C) further
(D) furthers

Questions 143-146 refer to the following e-mail.

Dear Ms. Bellevue,

This is in response to your ------- 143. about renovating the cabinets in your kitchen. If you are available next week, one of our design specialists ------- 144. you many samples of the kitchen cabinets.

------- 145. I'm quite certain that you will find something that suits your style. We offer everything from plain white cabinets to give your kitchen a clean look, or varnished wood cabinets to give your kitchen a more ------- 146. atmosphere. We also use only the finest materials to manufacture our cabinets, so you can be sure that your kitchen cabinets will last for years to come.

If you'd like to browse some of our selection before meeting with our specialist, you can visit our Web site at www.stiltoninteriors.com. Thank you and I look forward to receiving your response.

Regards,

Leslie Oberman
General Manager
Stilton Interiors

143. (A) inquiry
(B) article
(C) complaint
(D) examination

144. (A) did show
(B) can show
(C) are showing
(D) were showing

145. (A) I have to check the schedules of our specialists.
(B) Your kitchen should make you feel comfortable.
(C) We have a large variety of different designs for our cabinets.
(D) The cleanliness of your kitchen is our top priority.

146. (A) invitation
(B) invite
(C) inviting
(D) invited

PART 7

Direction: In this part you will read a selection of texts, such as magazine and newspaper articles, letters, e-mails, and instant messages. Each text or set of texts is followec by several questions. Select the best answer for each question and mark the letter (A), (B), (C), or (D) on your answer sheet.

Questions 147-148 refer to the following advertisement.

Smart Stationery

12 Orange Grove Parkway
Rio Caballo, NM

Relocation Clearance

Save money on
- Desks
- File cabinets
- Conference tables

The sale only lasts until the final day at the current location, so rush to Smart Stationery by July 1.

Store Hours: 9:00 a.m. - 8 p.m.
Monday through Saturday
(Closed from July 2 to July 4.)

New store address: (opening on July 5)
550 Plains Street
Rio Caballo, NM

147. Why is Smart Stationery having a sale?
(A) It is selling last year's merchandise.
(B) It is changing its store's location.
(C) It is changing its name.
(D) It is shutting down its operations.

148. When is the final day of the sale?
(A) July 1
(B) July 2
(C) July 3
(D) July 5

Questions 149-150 refer to the following e-mail.

---

* E-mail *

To : Company staff <stafflist@delawind.com>
From : Robert Young <ryoung@delawind.com>
Subject : Notice
Date : November 2

Dear Employees,

I am writing to make sure you know that employee pay dates have been changed. This is due to our acquisition in September of NanoArts, which has led to some shifting of employees between departments.

Payments to employees will be made on the 1st and 16th of each month starting in December. If either date is on a weekend or day off, payments will be distributed on the working day before that date.

Your reported work hours should still be turned in to Fatima Ali.

Regards,

Robert Young
Managing Director

---

149. Why did Mr. Young send the e-mail?
(A) To report that an acquisition has been postponed
(B) To clarify a change in payment distribution
(C) To introduce a new accounting director
(D) To explain a procedure for requesting days off

150. What are staff asked to do?
(A) To verify payment details with Mr. Young
(B) To go to a conference on December 16th
(C) To turn in their work hours in the same way
(D) To double check their payments every month

Questions 151-152 refer to the following excerpt from a brochure.

Karsten Museum of History

The Karsten Museum of History has worked
with our community for years to compile and retain information
about people, companies, and artistic organizations in our community.
The museum houses many hand-drawn and printed maps from our town's history.
The museum's picture collection, with over 3,000 historical images,
can be found on the museum's website.
Copies of any pictures are also able to be bought
on the website for a nominal fee.

---

151. What is the information concerning?
(A) An informational institution
(B) A citizen's group
(C) A residential project
(D) A information station for tourists

152. What is able to be bought?
(A) Directories of local businesses
(B) Images depicting historical events
(C) Old issues of magazines
(D) Local artists' paintings and sculptures

Questions 153-155 refer to the following advertisement.

THG   The Heartful Gallery

We hope you will join us for our yearly Home and Gardening Craft Sale and Festival on Saturday, March 3. —[1]—. Any earnings will be used to maintain the gallery and bring new and exciting exhibits. Admission to the gallery will be free while the sale is ongoing.

—[2]—. The Heartful Gallery has been a part of our community for 25 years. The building showcases a unique gallery of sculptures and many paintings from well-known artists from around the world. —[3]—.

While the Home and Gardening Craft Sale and Festival is happening, patrons of the gallery gift shop will receive a 20 percent discount on all purchases. The gallery is open from 8 am to 7 pm, Monday to Saturday and 12 pm to 4 pm, Sunday. —[4]—.

Our ongoing exhibit, The Life and Photography of Brandon Call, is open to the public until March 28. More information can be found at www.heartfulgallery.com.

---

153. What is being advertised?
(A) A grand opening
(B) A fund-raising event
(C) A presentation by Nancy Heartful
(D) A painting sale

154. What is NOT scheduled to happen at the Heartful Gallery on March 3?
(A) Gallery visitors will receive complimentary admission.
(B) Gallery gift shop purchases will be discounted.
(C) The Gallery will close at 4 pm.
(D) Photographs will be exhibited.

155. In which of the positions marked [1], [2], [3], and [4] does the following sentence best belong?

"Local gardens and nurseries will have beautiful floral arrangements available for viewing and purchase."

(A) [1]
(B) [2]
(C) [3]
(D) [4]

Questions 156-157 refer to the following text message chain.

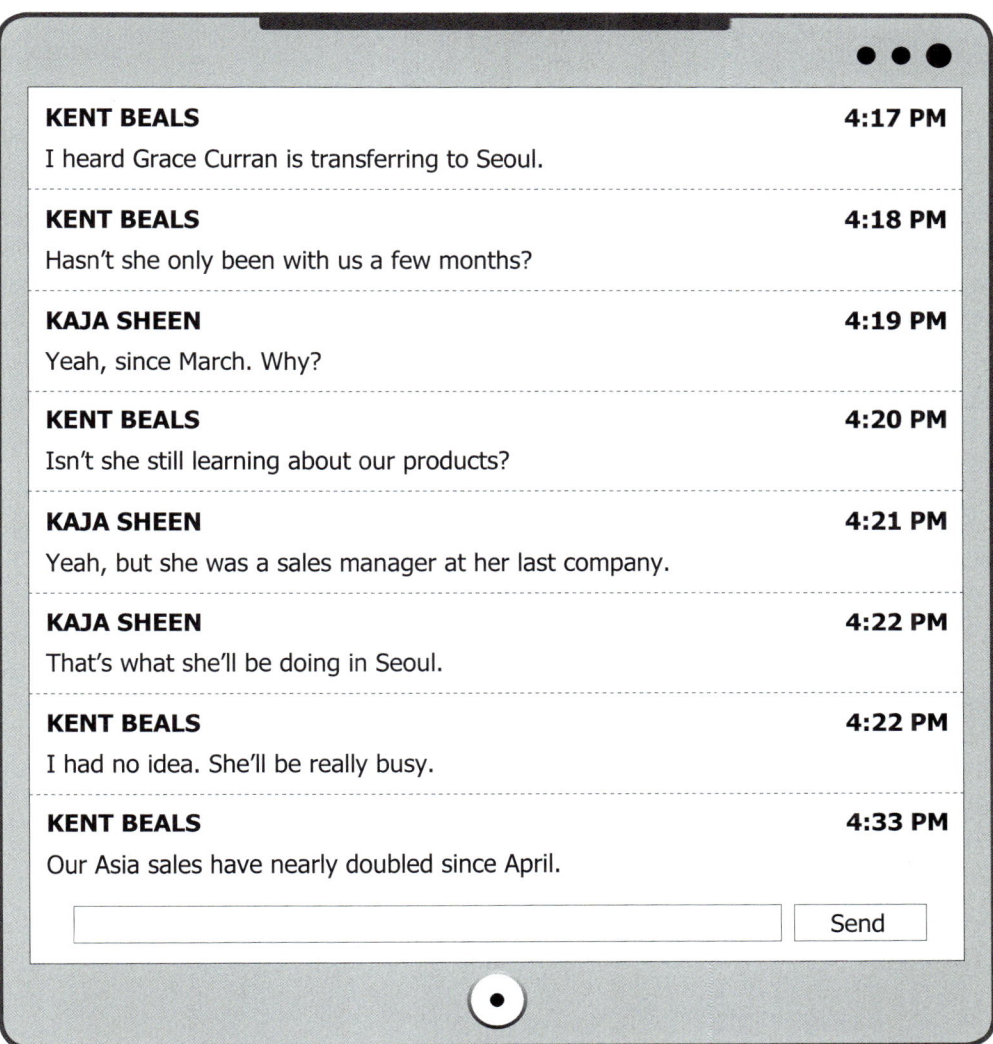

156. What is indicated about Grace Curran?
(A) She's been hired by another company.
(B) She is unhappy in her position.
(C) She is still in training.
(D) She has previous management experience.

157. At 4:22 p.m., what does Mr. Beals mean when he says, "I had no idea"?
(A) He didn't know what Ms. Curran will do in Seoul.
(B) He was uninformed about the Asian market.
(C) He didn't know about Ms. Curran's past work experience.
(D) He didn't know how long Ms. Curran was with the company.

Questions 158-160 refer to the following memo.

MEMO — Primo Inn

The Primo Inn will now wash the towels and sheets in our guest rooms on a daily basis only if the guest requests such service, as automatic daily laundry service makes up the majority of the hotel's electric and water use. We are instituting this new policy to keep our pledge to have our practices in the hotel be environmentally friendly. Please make sure you inform guests about this new procedure when they check in. Ensure that guests know that sheets will be replaced with new sheets every four days unless the guest asks that sheets be washed on a requested schedule while they stay with us. Guests will also have these notices posted in their rooms, as well as a guest guide explaining the hotel's other guest services.

158. For whom is the notice most likely intended?
(A) Inn customers
(B) Inn reception staff
(C) Cleaning employees
(D) Repair workers

159. According to the notice, why has a new procedure been instituted?
(A) To raise inn guest satisfaction
(B) To improve new staff performance
(C) To decrease consumption of utilities
(D) To lower the occurrence of repairs

160. What are inn staff instructed to do?
(A) To inform guests they may ask for special laundry service
(B) To give complete invoices to guests
(C) To make sure guest rooms have extra sheets and towels
(D) To tell guests about raised room rates

* 어휘 NOTE

Questions 161-163 refer to the following letter.

Houston Daily Journal

July 12

Michael Soto
25 Bighorn Drive
Houston, TX 77003

Dear Mr. Soto,

Since you are a long-time subscriber of the Houston Daily Journal, we would like to take this opportunity to let you know about a new feature in our Sunday paper. We will be featuring a calendar of happenings around Houston, including local entertainment and concerts, as well as theater and film reviews. Discount coupons for community businesses, such as stores and restaurants, will also be provided.

Because of your continued support, you are able to receive the Sunday paper for one month at no cost. To keep receiving the Sunday paper, you would need to pay the small extra fee of $6.20 per month added on to your regular bill.

You can also participate in our Friends of Houston plan where you can receive a free month of the Houston Daily Journal whenever someone you know lists your name as a referral for our paper. For more information, feel free to call our offices at 555-3345.

Regards,

Dwight Tomlin
Dwight Tomlin
Subscription Manager
Houston Daily Journal

161. What is the purpose of the letter?
(A) To give reduced prices for entertainment options
(B) To describe a new service to a current subscriber
(C) To request that a subscriber pay an invoice
(D) To interest a business in promotional space

162. What will NOT be included in the Sunday paper of Houston Daily Journal?
(A) Reduced prices at local stores
(B) Film and theater reviews
(C) Recipes from community restaurants
(D) Schedules of community events

163. What will happen if Mr. Soto chooses to keep receiving the Sunday paper after August?
(A) People he knows will receive a discount on the paper.
(B) The cost of delivery will be reduced.
(C) He will get a voucher for a free meal at a restaurant.
(D) His monthly bill will include the additional service charge.

Questions 164-167 refer to the following online chat discussion.

Online Chat

Morgan Caine [2:55 p.m.] Does anyone know if the SharpCopy photocopier by conference room G has been fixed yet? I know this morning that it just kept getting paper jams and that IT said they would send someone to fix it.

Jolene Griffin [2:56 p.m.] I just walked by there a minute ago. It looks like they had to call someone in SharpCopy to come work on it. They're still trying to fix it.

Stephanie Gazio [2:57 p.m.] I've been waiting to use it too. I'll go check on it right now since I'm close to it and I'll let you know.

Morgan Caine [2:59 p.m.] IT said that they would have it fixed by now. This isn't the first time we've had problems with that copier. We really should get a new color photocopier. I have an important meeting with a client at 4:00 and I'd really rather not use black and white copies.

Jolene Griffin [3:01 p.m.] You could get some copies made at the print shop down the street. They're usually not busy around this time.

Morgan Caine [3:02 p.m.] Well, if the copier's not fixed in the next ten minutes, I don't think I'll have a choice.

Stephanie Gazio [3:03 p.m.] I asked the technician from SharpCopy how long it will take to fix and he said that he'll have it fixed by 3:30. He just needs to get a part from his truck first.

Morgan Caine [3:04 p.m.] In that case, I guess I'd better go to that print shop. Better safe than sorry. Does anyone need anything while I'm out?

Stephanie Gazio [3:05 p.m.] If you don't mind, I'll come with you to the print shop. I just want to get it done so that I won't have to worry even if it takes longer to fix the photocopier.

Morgan Caine [3:07 p.m.] Sure thing. I'll meet you in the lobby in about two minutes.

164. What is indicated about the SharpCopy photocopier?
(A) It can make color copies.
(B) It is going to be replaced.
(C) It was recently purchased.
(D) It needs to be taken to the factory for repairs.

165. What is suggested about Stephanie Gazio?
(A) She has a meeting later today.
(B) She works in the IT department.
(C) She left her desk during the conversation.
(D) She will make black and white copies.

166. At 3:02 p.m., what does Morgan Caine mean when he writes, "I don't think I'll have a choice"?
(A) He needs to use black and white copies.
(B) He has to delay a meeting with a client.
(C) He has to visit a local store.
(D) He will wait for the photocopier to be fixed.

167. What will Morgan Caine probably do next?
(A) Meet a colleague at a building entrance
(B) Speak with a technician
(C) Contact his clients
(D) Make a reservation at a restaurant

* 어휘 NOTE

Questions 168-171 refer to the following flyer.

The Perth Residential Committee invites you to attend one of our New Neighbor Gatherings.

Presentation Schedule

Time		
1:00 p.m.	Public transportation and you: Around the city (Room 204)	
2:00 p.m.	Places to live in Perth (Room 202)	Sanitation and recycling services (Room 209)
3:00 p.m.	Financial services and banks around Perth (Room 207)	Perth's Company Association and starting your own business (Room 209)
4:00 p.m.	Recreation in and around Perth: Where to have fun and meet people (Room 204)	

The presentations concerning public transportation and recreation are attended the most among visitors, so we recommend arriving early to these presentations to ensure you have a seat.

All presenters use English for the presentation, but brochures in Korean, Tagalog, and Thai are available upon request. Refreshments are also provided at the gathering.

When the last presentation has concluded, we invite all participants to take a walking tour of downtown and uptown of Perth. The tour is free of charge and guided by one of Perth's council members, who has lived in Perth nearly all his life.

More information can be found at www.newneighbors.co.au/perth

168. At whom is the flyer likely directed?
(A) Perth city council members
(B) People that recently moved to Perth
(C) Perth concert promoters
(D) People traveling through Perth

169. Where are the most popular presentations held?
(A) In room 202
(B) In room 204
(C) In room 207
(D) In room 209

170. What is suggested about the Perth Residential Committee?
(A) It offers information in multiple languages.
(B) It will soon renovate the city council chambers.
(C) It has information booths around the city.
(D) It offers tax incentives to residents.

171. According to the flyer, what can participants do after the gathering?
(A) Go to a dinner party
(B) Register on a website
(C) Register for free classes
(D) Take a city tour

Questions 172-175 refer to the following article.

Employee of the Month: Philip Haynesman

Philip Haynesman, who moves to the head of the insurance fraud department next month, has had many positions at Penley Insurance over his 29 years here. —[1]—. "I don't think any employee has worked in as many departments as Philip has," said company CEO Sylvia West.

The beginning of Mr. Haynesman's career in insurance was as a file clerk for six months at Good Friends Insurance Brokerage in Sacramento through a temporary staffing agency. —[2]—. Mr. Haynesman took over the job as a field agent in Penley's Berkley office, attending to customers in person for three years. Following this, Mr. Haynesman moved to the insurance adjustment department at the Los Angeles office and became the senior insurance adjuster after one year.

Mr. Haynesman did not end there, though. He recalled, "The experience of working with customer profiles and figures intrigued me and I wanted to do more work with them. My colleague in Los Angeles, Martha Bragg, suggested I try to get into the fraud department. But first, I would need my degree in fraud management and Martha suggested her old school, Century University in Los Angeles, where she had gotten her degree. I had to take out a student loan and continue working, but I received my diploma in fraud management in four years in four years, just as Martha had done some years ago." —[3]—.

After completing his fraud management degree at Century University, Mr. Haynesman was moved to the insurance fraud department at the main office of Penley Insurance. —[4]—. He was appointed the assistant supervisor by Barry Corns, the director of the insurance fraud department, after five years. As Mr. Corns is about to transfer to the industrial insurance division, he has suggested that Mr. Haynesman take over his position. "It's hard to believe," said Mr. Haynesman. "So many years ago, I was just handling insurance files and now I'm managing the fraud department at Penley's main office."

172. What is a purpose of the article?
(A) To detail the variety of positions a staff member has had
(B) To explain a new insurance benefits program
(C) To describe how staff can enroll in special training courses
(D) To report that a new company CEO has been selected

173. What is indicated about Mrs. Bragg?
(A) She is a temporary insurance adjuster.
(B) She was consulted about Mr. Haynesman.
(C) She majored in fraud management.
(D) She has worked as a professor.

174. What is NOT mentioned about Los Angeles?
(A) Penley Insurance has an office there.
(B) Century University is located there.
(C) Mr. Corns was a resident there.
(D) Mr. Haynesman was employed there.

175. In which of the positions marked [1], [2], [3], and [4] does the following sentence best belong?

"His interest in the insurance field grew during his time there and he decided to pursue a permanent occupation in insurance."

(A) [1]
(B) [2]
(C) [3]
(D) [4]

Questions 176-180 refer to the following flyer and e-mail.

Beautify Your Neighborhood with Free Trees

The Roseburg Nature Committee is going to give 1500 complimentary tree saplings to the citizens of Roseburg on March 14 to create more green areas in our densely built metropolitan area. The committee will hold this event in the parking lot of the Hempstead Valley Shopping Center, where it was held last year, from 11 a.m. to 3 p.m. Trees will be given to residents on a first-come, first-served basis.

To receive your complimentary tree, you need to bring identification that has your name and address on it, such as an electricity bill or a driver's license. People that live outside of Roseburg may also buy a sapling. The prices range from $15 to $30 depending on the varieties. Any funds raised during this event will support the Roseburg Nature Committee in its mission to promote the preservation of nature through the planting of trees. The committee also educates the public on planting and caring for trees.

For more information about the committee's activities, including nature classes and volunteer opportunities, please visit www.roseburgnature.org/committee.

---

* E-mail *

To:	c.meade@hrw.com
From:	janice_warden@roseburgnature.org
Date:	March 27
Subject:	RE: The tree I bought
Attachment:	Oregon Ash Care Directions

Dear Mr. Meade,

I'm happy to provide help with the tree sapling that you bought at the give-away event on March 14 and thank you for supporting the committee with your purchase. If I understand correctly, you followed the directions for planting your Oregon Ash sapling and the directions for caring for it given to you by our staff, but it doesn't seem to be doing well. To assist you further, I've attached detailed directions for caring for your tree, which also includes online resources for your specific tree. If you can email me some pictures of the sapling and information about how much water you're giving it and how much sunlight it receives, as well as the location of the tree, I can give you more detailed feedback. Alternatively, you're also welcome to come to one of our nature classes to talk to one of our volunteer specialists.

Best regards,

Genevieve Denham
Community Program Director
Roseburg Nature Committee

176. What information is NOT mentioned in the flyer?
(A) The reason for the give-away
(B) The documents that are required
(C) The varieties of trees available
(D) The committee's mission

177. What is suggested about Roseburg?
(A) Its buildings are close together.
(B) It has a newly built shopping center.
(C) It is opening several new parking areas.
(D) It is developing a garden at Hempstead Valley.

178. What is implied about Mr. Meade?
(A) He did not receive directions for caring for his sapling.
(B) He is not a resident of Roseburg.
(C) He has previously attended a nature class.
(D) He cannot volunteer for the committee.

179. Why did Ms. Denham write the e-mail?
(A) To provide some pictures
(B) To respond to a concern
(C) To complain about a schedule
(D) To give an updated class timetable

180. What does Ms. Denham suggest that Mr. Meade do?
(A) Change the location of his tree
(B) Bring the tree to the nature committee
(C) Inform her further about his tree
(D) Request a refund for his tree

Questions 181-185 refer to the following letter and e-mail.

January 28

Ms. Megumi Tanaka
Hayamiki Corportation
8-2-3 Nakahara-ku, Kawasaki-shi
Kanagawa, Japan

Dear Ms. Tanaka,

Cromo Tech Disposals is the foremost leader in assisting companies with the recycling of their unusable and damaged electronics. We maintain multiple facilities in five countries around the world to ensure efficient and inexpensive collection of your materials by keeping shipping distance and fuel consumption low.

Considering that your company is one of the fastest growing companies in Japan, we know that your choice of how to recycle your unneeded electronics matters greatly, especially as you are the corporation's Preservation Management Director. Please take a look at the enclosed pamphlet concerning Cromo Tech Disposals' safe and sustainable electronic waste recycling programs. For further assurance regarding the quality of our services, I encourage you to call or write any of the clients identified on the back page of the brochure. You may also contact me or Sasuke Hiroshi in our Tokyo office should you wish to talk about your corporation's specific requirements for recycling.

Best regards,

Hilary Grace
Account Management Director

Enclosure

From:	Megumi Tanaka <mtanaka@hayamiki.co.jp>
To:	Simon Mann <smann@retainindustries.co.jp>
Subject:	Cromo Tech Disposals
Date:	February 27

I'm the Preservation Management Director at Hayamiki Corporation in Kanagawa. I wanted to ask you about your experience with Cromo Tech Disposals since our company is contemplating working with it to recycle much of our unusable electronic equipment.

I saw that your company employs Cromo Tech Disposals with your offices around the world. If you wouldn't mind, I'd like to know what your experience with it at your Tokyo branch has been. I'm mostly interested in their ability to pick up materials on schedule, but any information you can give me would be appreciated.

Regards,

Megumi Tanaka

Preservation Management Director

181. What is the purpose of the letter?
(A) To explain a change in disposal procedures
(B) To publicize a service for recycling
(C) To inquire about an electronics sale
(D) To suggest contacting a sales consultant

182. According to the letter, how does Cromo Tech Disposals increase its energy efficiency?
(A) It uses recycled paper products.
(B) It transports goods in vehicles that use less fuel.
(C) It operates facilities close to its clients.
(D) It reconditions staff computers.

183. Who most likely is the regional associate for Cromo Tech Disposals?
(A) Hilary Grace
(B) Megumi Tanaka
(C) Simon Mann
(D) Sasuke Hiroshi

184. Where did Ms. Tanaka most likely obtain Mr. Mann's e-mail address?
(A) From a Japanese company database
(B) From a co-worker of Ms. Grace
(C) From Cromo Tech Disposals' homepage
(D) From Cromo Tech Disposals' reference list

185. What concerns Ms. Tanaka about Cromo Tech Disposals?
(A) The kinds of products it recycles
(B) The services it offers exclusively
(C) The dependability of its pick ups
(D) The number of service failures it has

Questions 186-190 refer to the following announcement, leaflet, and e-mail.

Rewards Club Raises Calasnack's Revenues.

Snack food and beverage producer, Calasnack, showed a 20% increase in profits last month. This is a vast improvement from the reported drop in sales in the last quarterly report. The implementation of the Munchies rewards club, started in June, is credited with the increase. The Munchies rewards clubs allows customers to collect points by purchasing Calasnack products and exchange them for exclusive rewards.

Currently, only snack food items, such as Calasnack potato chips, mixed nuts, and candy bars, produced by Calasnack carry the newly designed green "M" logo. However, the rewards program has been so effective that Calasnack will begin placing the "M" logo on many of the company's soft drinks starting in October as well. One such soft drink is the company's new diet soda, Calasoda, currently on sale. During the promotional period, customers can obtain ten times points from its soft drinks.

T-shirts, personal music players, snowboards, and computer games are just some of the rewards available. Of course, some of the rewards are more in demand than others. "Most of our customers don't like to exchange the points for the reward until they collect 500," said company representative Theodore Chips. "They can get most popular ZYX product with those points".

Earn rewards with Munchies Points!

With every Calasnack product with the green "M" logo (pictured below) you buy,
earn 10 points you can use towards the great prizes below.
Collect Munchies Points!!!

Points needed	Rewards
100	Munchies T-shirt
300	Snack Attack Family Computer Game
500	Music player from ZYX Electronics
700	Zoomer A2 snowboard

* E-mail *

To:	Keith Delarocha <kdelerocha@ragemail.com>
From:	Munchies Rewards <stservice@ calasnack.com>
Subject:	Your recently redeemed Munchies Points

Dear Mr. Delarocha,

I'm writing regarding the Munchies points which you recently redeemed. According to your order form, you wanted to redeem 700 points and we have already processed your request. However, part of the points was from Calasoda and was actually worth 100 points. This means that you actually sent us 790 points. To show our appreciation to you for being our customer, we've added 10 points to those that you sent and we will send you a Munchies T-shirt with your other prize. Thanks again!

Regards,

Rina Smith
Calasnack Loyalty Program Representative

---

186. What can be inferred about Calasnack's sales last quarter?
(A) They surpassed their prior record.
(B) They met their company goals.
(C) They were not correctly estimated.
(D) They were going down.

187. In the announcement, the word "vast" in paragraph 1, line 1, is closest in meaning to?
(A) considerable
(B) brief
(C) consistent
(D) fast

188. What will Calasnack begin in October?
(A) Create new logos
(B) Offer sales on multiple snacks
(C) Acquire new snacks from local companies
(D) Give points for the company's other goods

189. According to Mr. Chips, in which products are most customers interested?
(A) T-shirts
(B) Computer games
(C) Music players
(D) Snowboards

190. What is most likely true about Ms. Delarocha?
(A) She wanted to have a music player.
(B) She sent her request for a prize after October.
(C) She is an employee of Calasnack.
(D) She will receive all prizes.

*어휘 NOTE

Questions 191-195 refer to the following e-mails and schedule.

E-mail Message

From: fred.dickens@homeprofessionals.com
To: realestateagents@netlisting.org
Subject: March 4, 3:20 p.m.
Date: Rochelle Tan

Dear Netlisting subscribers,

Next month there will be an all-day symposium led by a well-known real estate agent, Rochelle Tan. Some of you may have read some of her four books concerning the real estate business to help you in your own work in the field.

The date of the symposium will be April 9 and the event will be held at the Royalton Convention Hall, located at 485 North Star Drive, across the street from the Manor Hotel. An admission pass will cost $200.00.

Any participants that refer other participants will have $20.00 credited to their admission cost. Not only that, but a copy of Ms. Tan's book, Selling Houses and Success (Himmel Expert Publishing), a $30.00 value will be provided.

If you have any questions, just ask me or Phil Stannis, the other event organizer at the convention hall at 488-555-0855.

Fred Dickens

From: phil.stannis@homeprofessionals.com
To: realestateagents@netlisting.org
Subject: March 4, 3:53 p.m.
Date: Re: Rochelle Tan

Dear Netlisting subscribers,

Fred Dickens made a small mistake in his e-mail to everyone earlier. The cost of admission for Ms. Tan's symposium was listed as $200.00, but it is $175.00. We apologize for the mistake. For those who plan to attend, I highly suggest getting back from the intermission on time, as the information given by Ms. Tan will be invaluable for those selling houses in the coming months.

Looking forward to seeing you there.

Phil Stannis

Real Estate in the Coming Year
Hosted by: Rochelle Tan

Symposium Schedule

11:00 a.m. – 11:30 a.m.: *Know Your Neighborhood* – A look at being informed about your region and matching your clients with the neighborhood that's best for them.

11:30 a.m. – 12:00 p.m.: *Renting Vs. Buying* – A presentation about the advantages and disadvantages for renting or buying property and how each will help clients.

12:00 p.m. – 12:30 p.m.: Intermission

12:30 p.m. – 1:00 p.m.: *Help Yourself with Home Inspections* – A helpful advice session about how hiring a home inspector can help you find problems before they become bigger.

1:00 p.m. – 1:30 p.m.: *Open Forum* – A chance for the audience to ask Ms. Tan any questions they have relating to the real estate and property management field.

---

191. In the first e-mail, the word "concerning" in paragraph 1, line 2, is closest in meaning to
(A) worrying
(B) except
(C) regarding
(D) versus

192. How much credit will a mailing list subscriber receive for referring another participant?
(A) $6.00
(B) $20.00
(C) $30.00
(D) $40.00

193. Who sent the second e-mail?
(A) An economics publication company
(B) A real estate information provider
(C) An event organizer
(D) A featured presenter

194. What will Ms. Tan do at the end of her symposium?
(A) Sign copies of her books
(B) Hold a drawing for prizes
(C) Host a question and answer session
(D) Hand out complimentary copies of her books

195. Which part of the symposium does Phil Stannis think will be helpful to subscribers?
(A) Know your neighborhood
(B) Renting Vs. Buying
(C) Help Yourself with Home Inspections
(D) Open forum

Questions 196-200 refer to following press release, e-mail, and schedule.

= Press Release=

February 26

Rakliss Media will be opening two new branch offices in Tunis and Sousse on Tuesday, March 3. Along with these openings, Rakliss will also take over Oceanview Telecommunications, a Web design company based in Bizerte at the end of February. Rakliss Media's CEO, Mohammed al-Qari stated that the company hopes to better build its reputation in Tunisia with these efforts.

Rakliss Media was founded by Rahim Ali after he decided to leave his job at Jetspeed Industries ten years ago. Having worked there for six years, he felt ready to return home to Sfax, where he started his telecommunications business with financial assistance from some friends and relatives. Mr. Ali's plan was to specialize in data transmission systems using high-speed optical cable networks. The strategy was fruitful: Rakliss Media's system was soon adopted across the nation, and the company has grown to become one of the most innovative and respected firms of its kind.

Even with its impressive record of success, the company's modest offices are still located right where they were founded a decade ago, and the business has not lost its spirit of innovation. The product development team introduced a new rooting system that can transmit information almost twice as fast as earlier models.

---

* E-mail *

From:	Samson Tagobe
To:	Fatima Alfarsi
Subject:	August 20
Date:	Congratulations

Dear Fatima,

It is my pleasure to notify you of the board of directors' decision to name you as a winner of one of Rakliss' annual employee awards. You are receiving this award because of your commitment and expertise that you have shown during your time with our company. Having been among the company's very first group of employees, you have greatly helped Rakliss move from a small telecommunications company to the leading media company that we are today. Additionally, the leadership qualities you have shown over the years, most recently as the leader of the product development team, are extraordinary.

In honor of you and the other award winners, a reception will be held at our headquarters on Friday, August 30 at 5:00 p.m. You will receive your award during the reception after the dinner. Also, you may be pleased to know that the manager of your branch in Goroka will be hosting the dinner. Rakliss Media truly thanks you for all of the hard work over the years. I look forward to seeing you at the dinner.

Samson Tagobe
HR director, Rakliss Media

10th Annual Rakliss Media Staff Awards Dinner

We invite you to attend this year's Rakliss Media Staff Awards Dinner, where we will celebrate the diligence and commitment of some of our best employees. We hope you enjoy the selection of food at the buffet. Below is a schedule of the events planned for this special occasion.

5:30 – 6:00: Greeting and Seating

6:00 – 7:00: Dinner

7:00 – 7:30: A History of Rakliss Media presented by Vice President Michael Wahlen

7:30 – 8:00: Award Presentations

8:00 – 8:15: Closing

Hosted by: Thomas Ryan

Thank you for coming and enjoy your dinner.

---

196. What is NOT mentioned as an activity Rakliss Media is involved in?
(A) Opening new branches
(B) Acquiring a company
(C) Providing training courses
(D) Releasing new merchandise

197. How long did Mr. Ali work at Jetspeed Industries?
(A) For 3 years
(B) For 6 years
(C) For 10 years
(D) For 16 years

198. Where will Ms. Alfarsi probably be on August 30?
(A) In Sfax
(B) In Bizerte
(C) In Tunis
(D) In Sousse

199. What is suggested about Ms. Alfarsi?
(A) She will be promoted to manager.
(B) She will receive a salary bonus.
(C) She has worked with Rakliss Media for ten years.
(D) She plans to start her own firm.

200. What is Thomas Ryan's position at Rakliss Media?
(A) CEO
(B) Vice President
(C) Research & Development Director
(D) Branch Manager

Stop! This is the end of the test. If you finish before time is called, you may go back to Parts 5, 6, and 7 and check your work.

동시토익 실전 WORKBOOK

101. Gracia's Restaurant successfully opened a new restaurant in Fullerton.

해석]

102. Part-time workers are scheduled to work more than five hours and then be given thirty-minute work-free meal period.

해석]

103. The speaker stated that laws should be as flexible as possible to take account of various circumstances, time and places.

해석]

104. The critic who saw Impossible wrote in his column that it was a two-thumbs-up movie.

해석]

105. Mr. Gonzalez expects that the final construction phase of the main building should be completed by next month.

해석]

106. Mr. Ed Simon explained his proposals to directors in a plausible fashion.

해석]

107. AX Energy publishes reports on their oil reserves on a weekly basis.

해석]

108. All of the packages which are received from customers must be labeled correctly.

해석]

109. International students can choose from all regular courses offered by the University of California provided they meet the necessary qualifications.

해석]

110. We offer free magazines to our hotel guests in cooperation with Peacock Publishing Company.

해석]

*어휘 NOTE

111. If your purchase is not delivered to your home within a week of purchase, you will have your shipping charge refunded.

해석]

112. Old colleagues of Nick Punto have been amazed by how quickly his new business has become successful.

해석]

113. We must regard any statement about this issue as gossip until it is confirmed by the Senate.

해석]

114. Santa Barbara City Council members finally set the budget for the next fiscal year after lengthy debate.

해석]

115. Stephenson's Warmite, in business since the mid-1950s, provides high quality light-weight equipment.

해석]

116. The reselling of tickets acquired through our website at prices above face value is strictly prohibited by law.

해석]

117. It is probable that Carl Crawford will be promoted to senior vice president of Belco Enterprise.

해석]

118. In addition to supervising and managing office personnel, she is responsible for overseeing all the reports to the management.

해석]

119. Nolasco, Inc. has developed a profitable business model in emerging countries, while maintaining a significant share of domestic market.

해석]

120. Middle and senior managers in mining companies improve their leadership competencies with an emphasis on safety.

해석]

121. Rather than purchasing a car, it is beneficial to use a car leasing option if you are using the car strictly for work.

해석]

> **★ 어휘 NOTE**

122. For travelers eager to explore the ancient history of the city, the hotel is ideally situated in the center of the city.

해석]

123. Since demand in a part of your business is increasingly outgrowing your staff or resources, the decision to outsource some jobs is a natural one.

해석]

124. Given that last year's conference sold out, it is anticipated that this year's conference enrollment will surpass last year's.

해석]

125. This organization's objective is to teach, inform, and guide the public to respect and appreciate the nature around us.

해석]

126. The cost of destruction of unsold stamps, including commemorative stamps, is a regular item in the Postal Service's budget.

해석]

127. Ramirez Airlines, now struggling with financial difficulties, has yet to make a decision about suspending operations in China.

해석]

128. It was reported to a senior executive that there had been an unusually large money transfer to a financial institution.

해석]

129. With only a few days remaining before the inspection from the outside, the factory supervisor has yet to be prepared for it.

해석]

130. Mr. Ito will make a presentation at the meeting with potential investors because he knows the new line of product better than most.

해석]

*어휘 NOTE

TEST 10

동시토익 CONTEMPORARY **TOEIC**

TEST 10

READING TEST

In the Reading test, you will read a variety of texts and answer several different types of reading comprehension questions. The entire Reading test will last 75 minutes. There are three parts, and directions are given for each part. You are encouraged to answer as many questions as possible within the time allowed.

You must mark your answers on the separate answer sheet. Do not write your answers in your test book.

Part 5

Directions: A word or phrase is missing in each of the sentences below. Four answer choices are given below each sentence. Select the best answer to complete the sentence. Then mark the letter (A), (B), (C), or (D) on your answer sheet.

101. Ms. Sanders _____ her book about how to build and sustain a creative workplace culture next month.
(A) will finish
(B) to finish
(C) finishing
(D) finished

102. Victoria College's _____ new program will be starting at the upcoming semester.
(A) innovation
(B) innovative
(C) innovator
(D) innovated

103. Mr. Taylor's revised personnel report provides added enhancements over his _____ version.
(A) earlier
(B) lowest
(C) sudden
(D) added

104. A Spanish seafood restaurant that has been under construction for many months is _____ opening tomorrow.
(A) final
(B) finality
(C) finals
(D) finally

105. Mr. Schumaker will be conferring with all the managers from the company over the next _____ months.
(A) of
(B) few
(C) some
(D) within

106. Crawford Enterprise has an opening _____ a regional sales coordinator in our Seattle office.
(A) off
(B) for
(C) through
(D) across

107. Please be assured that free _____ to the museum on the first Sunday of every month does not include the special exhibitions in the Stuart Hall.
(A) connection
(B) movement
(C) admission
(D) exchange

108. Over five years of experience in our foreign branches is a _____ for a new branch manager in Singapore.
(A) requirement
(B) require
(C) requiring
(D) required

109. To try to protect its steel industry, the United States raised import tariffs but, unsurprisingly, _____ did its trading partners.
(A) still
(B) even
(C) so
(D) but

110. Children under 18 are not required to have government-issued identification _____ boarding planes.
(A) such as
(B) when
(C) although
(D) in addition

111. These easy-to-use solutions have been meeting the asset management _____ of local businesses and organizations of all sizes.
(A) to need
(B) has needed
(C) needs
(D) needing

112. The management took an immovable stance _____ negotiations with the labor union over the contract terms.
(A) because
(B) once
(C) during
(D) later

113. With Ethier Mobile shipping 1.3 million compact cars last quarter, its sales this year are _____ 19 percent from a year earlier.
(A) as
(B) up
(C) even
(D) about

114. Ms. Vedder, _____ has conducted more than 1,500 seminars and workshops across Australia over her 30-year career, will be the first presenter.
(A) she
(B) her
(C) who
(D) we

115. The employee manual describes _____ office supplies should be ordered, stored, and distributed.
(A) could
(B) with
(C) this
(D) how

116. Norwak Airlines is pleased to announce that they will fly three times a day from Seoul to Los Angeles _____ in July.
(A) begin
(B) begins
(C) beginning
(D) was begun

117. After _____ considering the terms and conditions of the proposal, the board found it to be worthwhile.
(A) care
(B) caring
(C) careful
(D) carefully

118. _____ for the 24th annual theater awards must be submitted by email to Linda Morris by May 7 at the latest.
(A) Authorities
(B) Nominations
(C) Occurrences
(D) Performances

119. Ellis and his teammates can _____ expect a bonus of approximately $20,000 if his team wins the project.
(A) each
(B) another
(C) any
(D) which

120. The Internet will be intermittently unavailable between 5 a.m. and 10 a.m. on Saturday, May 10 _____ scheduled regular maintenance.
(A) due to
(B) instead of
(C) even though
(D) now that

GO ON TO THE NEXT PAGE

121. The street on First Avenue is too _____ to allow a cyclist to safely pass the vehicle out of the door zone.
(A) narrow
(B) narrows
(C) narrowly
(D) narrower

122. _____ from clients will be handled in strict confidence and will not be revealed to third parties.
(A) Correspond
(B) Corresponds
(C) Corresponded
(D) Correspondence

123. Ed Smith _____ medical records of hospital and clinic patients in a manner consistent with medical and legal requirements.
(A) realizes
(B) proceeds
(C) responds
(D) compiles

124. The North Ridge University has changed the admission policy to attract highly _____ students.
(A) competent
(B) competence
(C) competency
(D) competently

125. Please make sure to turn off all the lights before you leave the office at the end of the day, unless instructed _____.
(A) accordingly
(B) otherwise
(C) indeed
(D) meanwhile

126. Whereas most of the candidates met the deadline for application, _____ missed it.
(A) much
(B) a few
(C) whose
(D) either

127. It was the unpredictable weather over three _____ years, which resulted in the cancellation of the August Festival.
(A) atmospheric
(B) consecutive
(C) refreshed
(D) deliberate

128. It is mandatory to _____ all safety rules and instructions while in the factory.
(A) adhere
(B) observe
(C) comply
(D) dedicate

129. Jay Kim Foundation began _____ the idea of giving women an opportunity to pursue their career in whatever field they want to work in.
(A) toward
(B) regarding
(C) with
(D) over

130. Had Sordino Studios not given Brandon League an opportunity to work together, our company _____ so.
(A) should do
(B) will be doing
(C) has done
(D) would have done

PART 6

Direction: Read the texts that follow. A word, phrase, or sentence is missing in parts of each text. Four answer choices for each question are given below the text. Select the best answer to complete the text. Then mark the letter (A), (B), (C), or (D) on your answer sheet.

Questions 131-134 refer to the following letter.

Ricky Nolasco
Apt. # 304
1798 Kingsway Blvd.
Alexandria, VA 22314

Dear Mr. Nolasco,

At Nora Eye Care Center, our primary goal is to provide you with quality and thorough eye care services with the latest technology. You can schedule an ------- for an eye exam online anytime
131.
or call 703-555-8997 during office hours. -------. The Web site makes it ------- to find useful
132. **133.**
information about our clinic, such as doctors' profiles and directions to the clinic. You can also browse the huge ------- of glasses frames and contact lenses that we have available. We hope to
134.
see you at our clinic soon!

Yours sincerely,

Nora Eye Care Center

131. (A) interview
 (B) assignment
 (C) appointment
 (D) order

132. (A) Please visit our Web site for more information about us.
 (B) Our office hours have recently changed on the weekend.
 (C) Taking care of your vision is very important.
 (D) We have the largest selection of glasses in the region.

133. (A) able
 (B) early
 (C) easy
 (D) likely

134. (A) collected
 (B) collectable
 (C) collects
 (D) collection

Question 135-138 refer to the following announcement.

Award-winning advertising firm, The Dayton Agency, is looking to fill openings for several managerial positions in its customer relations department. The company, which has created advertisements and commercials for businesses throughout the country, has its headquarters in Charlotte, North Carolina and is currently planning to employ up to eight managers who are ------- of handling the needs and requests of multiple clients. The number of ------- for the
      135.   136.
company has increased since the company has been expanding its operations further across the country. At this time, the company has opened new branches in Illinois, Nevada, and Wyoming. The candidates hired for the managerial positions ------- with the rest of a team to ensure actions
                                                                       137.
on the plan are completed and targets are met. -------.
                                               138.

135. (A) capably
     (B) capabilities
     (C) capability
     (D) capable

136. (A) locations
     (B) instructions
     (C) reports
     (D) schedules

137. (A) had worked
     (B) will work
     (C) worked
     (D) has been working

138. (A) The expansion has been handled by several teams around the country.
     (B) Contract management is a very important responsibility for managers.
     (C) The Wyoming branch in particular has been doing very well with its action plan.
     (D) More details for this position are available at www.daytonads.com/employment.

Questions 139-142 refer to the following e-mail.

To: lexinez@jokemail.come
From: woodrow@heightsinn.com
Subject: Heights Hotel Chicago Branch
Date: May 20
Attachment: Pamphlet

Dear Mr. Inez,

Following up on our recent telephone conversation, I am writing to ------- your reservation from May 25 to May 28 for six people. -------. You might need to ------- this number when you check in. I suggest writing it down and keeping it in your wallet in case that you are not able to access your email upon arrival. Attached are your booking details and our hotel brochure you requested on the phone. If you have ------- request, please feel free to call us again. Thank you and we look forward to welcoming you and your guests to our hotel.

Sincerely,

Woodrow Wilson
Customer Services

---

139. (A) associate
(B) confirm
(C) cancel
(D) propose

140. (A) As I mentioned to you before, your reservation number is WSV248S.
(B) This is the maximum amount of guests allowed in one room.
(C) More details about hotel facilities can be obtained from the concierge.
(D) I will be contacting you again later this week regarding this matter.

141. (A) presenting
(B) present
(C) have presented
(D) be presented

142. (A) formal
(B) primary
(C) additional
(D) temporary

Questions 143-146 refer to the following e-mail.

To: All Santa Maria College alumni
From: Lary Donovan
Date: November 13
Subject: Directory Update
Attachment: Contact Info

-------. We want to make sure we have the latest contact information for all alumni. Your phone
143.
number and e-mail address are included in this information. Can you review the attached form and

fill it in if ------- has changed. Also, anyone who wants to receive the newsletter from our college
144.

can write down your home or work address on the form if you have not ------- done so. If you did
145.

not provide your contact information when your original ------- was created, please check the box
146.

next to "not done". We greatly appreciate your assistance in this matter.

143. (A) Thank you for your interest in Santa Maria College.
(B) You are graciously invited to the upcoming alumni reunion.
(C) We are currently updating our alumni records.
(D) We understand that your privacy is very important to you.

144. (A) another
(B) either
(C) anyone
(D) whatever

145. (A) much
(B) hardly
(C) later
(D) already

146. (A) listing
(B) schedule
(C) invoice
(D) announcement

PART 7

Direction: In this part you will read a selection of texts, such as magazine and newspaper articles, letters, e-mails, and instant messages. Each text or set of texts is followed by several questions. Select the best answer for each question and mark the letter (A), (B), (C), or (D) on your answer sheet.

Question 147-148 refer to the following information.

Please carefully follow these directions on operating your new CloudTek X5 digital camera, as well as transmitting pictures to your home computer. CloudTek customer service associates are available to assist you from 9 to 5 on the weekdays should you need further explanation on any directions. A listing of all service centers with phone numbers is printed on page 12.

147. Where is the most likely place for this information to be found?
(A) In a telephone directory
(B) In a product catalog
(C) In an owner's manual
(D) In an employee handbook

148. According to the information, how do CloudTek associates offer assistance?
(A) By explaining directions
(B) By repairing broken products
(C) By listing common problems
(D) By describing product features

Questions 149-150 refer to the following notice.

Bowie Electronics

Visitors to our store:

Bowie Electronics of Robin Grove will be offering free delivery for any items brought in for repair or service from April 10. When bringing in a product, we ask that you tell us whether you would like to pick it up at the store, or have it delivered to your home or place of business. This service is only available for those in the Robin Grove area.

149. What are visitors asked to do?
(A) To update contact information
(B) To reserve goods quickly
(C) To secure any valuables
(D) To select a choice

150. What will happen on April 10?
(A) An old location will be closed.
(B) A new service will be available.
(C) A store will undergo repairs.
(D) A sale will end.

Questions 151-152 refer to the following text message chain.

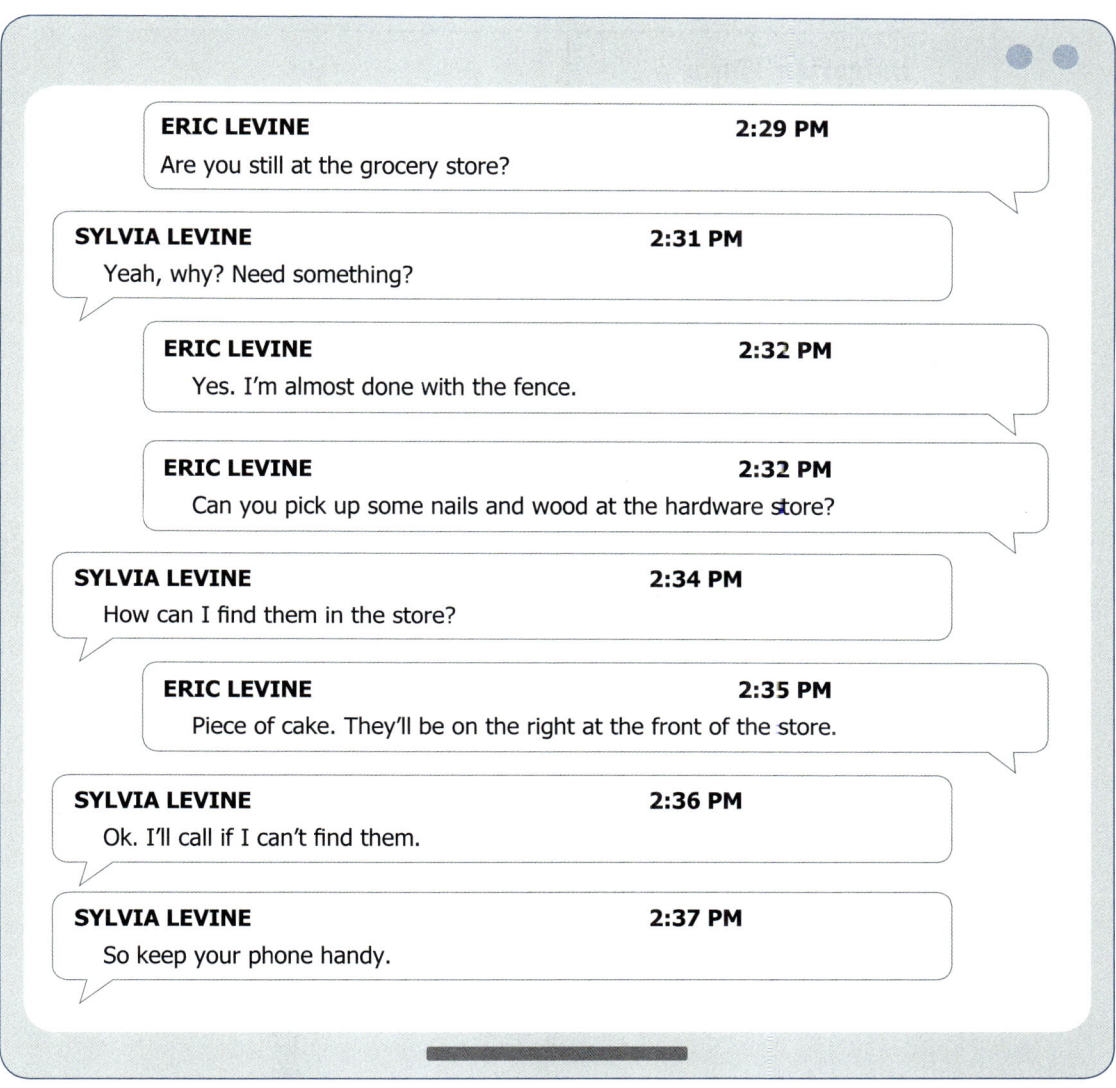

151. What does Eric Levine Request?
 (A) Some building supplies
 (B) A few grocery items
 (C) A computer upgrade
 (D) Directions to a store

152. At 2:37, what does Sylvia Levine mean when she writes, "keep your phone handy"?
 (A) Text her at a later time
 (B) Change her contact number
 (C) Make sure a phone is nearby
 (D) Keep a phone battery charged

Questions 153-154 refer to the following news article.

**Bulgarian Times
Economy and Finance**

Macedex sponsoring Balkan Dance Party

Sofia (March 3) - Macedex, Bulgaria's most widely used bank, will be celebrating 40 years in business this year. In observance of this achievement, Macedex will promote this year's Balkan Dance Party, a free concert festival, at Rodino Amphitheater on March 21. Macedex has stated that the festival will be filmed and broadcast in its entirety on television in Bulgaria. To ensure entry, tickets may be picked up for free at any Macedex bank branch before the concert.

---

153. What is being commemorated?
(A) The achievement of a musician
(B) The renovation of an amphitheater
(C) The birthday of a bank employee
(D) The anniversary of a financial organization

154. What is indicated about the Balkan Dance Party?
(A) It will be open only to Macedex customers.
(B) It will be broadcast all around a country.
(C) It will be held in early summer.
(D) It will feature an award ceremony.

Questions 155-157 refer to the following article.

Citizens Upset Over Travel Book

Objections have been raised against "The Minnesota Hiking Guide" by the citizens and city council of Apple Rapids. The objections concern the latest volume of the guide published earlier this year. The guide gives an extremely negative review of the town's oldest and most well-loved lodging and restaurant. —[1]—.

Mark Grant, a member of Apple Rapids' city council, has demanded that all bookstores in Minnesota cancel their book orders. In the previous volume of the guide, the writer lauded North Star Inn for being "the pinnacle of small town lodging and dining." —[2]—. This praise came only two years before the current version of the guide was published, with the manager and chef having been unchanged.

"The Inn provides a great example of small town living, but the editors of the hiking guide seem more accustomed to roadside motels." Mayor Stein found the review to be needlessly harsh and hostile. —[3]—. "North Star Inn has been a popular gathering place for locals and visitors to our town. Our town's economy could be greatly harmed by a review like the one in the guide. The guide's editors have not returned any phone calls wishing to discuss the issue." —[4]—. The Minnesota Hiking Guide has been published for nearly 25 years, with new volumes being released every few years.

---

155. Why are citizens of Apple Rapids angry?
(A) They were asked to leave a hotel.
(B) A town lodging was reviewed negatively.
(C) A state park has been damaged.
(D) The number of campers has declined.

156. What is implied about The Minnesota Hiking Guide?
(A) It was a best-selling guide book.
(B) It was first published in Apple Rapids.
(C) It can affect the decisions of visiting tourists.
(D) It doesn't review conditions of roadside motels.

157. In which of the positions marked [1], [2], [3], and [4] does the following sentence best belong?

"North Star Inn, which has been in business in Apple Rapids for over 70 years, received a ranking of only half a star in the travel guide's latest volume."

(A) [1]
(B) [2]
(C) [3]
(D) [4]

Questions 158-160 refer to the following advertisement.

The Galacite Inn

Thanks for staying at the Galactic Inn. We'd like to make your stay as comfortable as possible. While here, feel free to try our new restaurant, Steak Planet.

The restaurant is open on weekdays from 11 a.m. to 11 p.m. and on weekends from 10 a.m. to 12 a.m. Guests of the hotel may order room service from the normal menu or the children's menu any time the restaurant is open. If the restaurant is closed, please use the special room-service menu, including exclusive desserts and wines, until 3 a.m.

Guests of the hotel are also welcome to a free buffet dinner, with food from chef Hurt, from 5 p.m. to 7 p.m. this Sunday. This flyer is required for guests to gain entrance to the buffet area.

---

158. At what time does the restaurant open on Saturdays?
(A) 10:00 a.m.
(B) 11:00 a.m.
(C) 12:00 a.m.
(D) 5:00 p.m.

159. What is NOT indicated about the room service menu?
(A) It includes desserts and wines.
(B) It features choices that are not as expensive as the restaurant.
(C) It has food that is made especially for children.
(D) It is available at Steak Planet.

160. What will the Galactic Inn offer its guests?
(A) A tour of the city
(B) Free wine sampling
(C) A complimentary dinner
(D) A chance to meet a TV personality

Questions 161-163 refer to the following e-mail.

To :	All Employees <employee.list@pommesindustries.com>
From :	H. Gagnon <hgagnon@pommesindustries.com>
Subject :	Re: Spring has sprung
Date :	April 3

All Pommes Industries employees are invited to join us in celebrating the arrival of spring on April 15 from 1:00 to 6:00 in the fourth floor conference room.

We will be providing snacks and beverages for your enjoyment. Lunch will also be served, with a selection of grilled and baked chicken dishes, fresh fruit and vegetables, gourmet crackers and cheeses, and custard for dessert. Musical entertainment will be provided by Patrick Epstein, who will provide his services as a DJ.

All employees who would like to come to this complimentary party have to register by signing the form located outside the office of Sylvia Fanson and Katrina van Patton, our personnel specialists on the second floor by April 10 at the latest. Ideas and questions are welcome, so all Pommes Industries staff should feel free to come by my office or e-mail me to talk about the party.

Hope to see everyone there!

Henri Gagnon
Head of Employee Relations

161. What is the reason for the e-mail?
(A) To encourage staff attendance at an event
(B) To announce the location of a conference
(C) To remind staff of an upcoming holiday
(D) To reserve a catering service

162. What is NOT indicated about the party?
(A) It is arranged by the company.
(B) It is an annual occurrence.
(C) It will include music.
(D) It will take place inside.

163. Who should be contacted for more information?
(A) Patrick Epstein
(B) Sylvia Fanson
(C) Katrina van Patton
(D) Henri Gagnon

Questions 164-167 refer to the following online chat discussion.

Jessica Fisher	[10:06 a.m.]	The supervisor at the building site just called me and said that they're ready to start knocking down the walls, but that they need the revised construction plans before they can do anything.
Stanley Abrell	[10:08 a.m.]	I just talked with the manager of the engineering department and the manager is going to send me the revised plans in a few minutes. They just finished updating it this morning.
Jessica Fisher	[10:09 a.m.]	Great. Can you print it out and bring it to the construction site by 11:00?
Stanley Abrell	[10:10 a.m.]	Actually, I have a presentation to do with the marketing department at 11:30 p.m., so I don't think I can go to the construction site today. Is there anyone else available to take it there?
Ryan Burke	[10:12 a.m.]	I'll take care of it, Stanley. When will you have the revised plans printed out?
Stanley Abrell	[10:13 a.m.]	I just got an email with the revised plans from Timothy Howard. I'll start printing them out now, so they should be ready in about ten minutes. Do you know how to get to the construction site?
Ryan Burke	[10:14 a.m.]	I've been there once before, but I wasn't the one driving there. Do you think you could give me some directions?
Jessica Fisher	[10:15 a.m.]	I have a map with directions from here to the construction site. I'll forward it to Stanley now for him to print out for you.
Ryan Burke	[10:16 a.m.]	Thanks, Jessica.
Stanley Abrell	[10:17 a.m.]	I got it. How about you stop by my office at about 10:30 to pick everything up, Ryan?
Ryan Burke	[10:17 a.m.]	Will do, Stanley.
Jessica Fisher	[10:18 a.m.]	Please make sure that you get to the site as soon as you can, Ryan. When I talked to the supervisor, he was a little upset that he didn't have the plans yet.

164. What is the main topic of the discussion?
(A) Scheduling the beginning of construction
(B) Revising plans for construction
(C) Delivering updated construction plans
(D) Choosing a site for a new building

165. What is indicated about Ryan Burke?
(A) He is acquainted with the construction supervisor.
(B) He recently started working with the company.
(C) He previously worked in construction.
(D) He will visit a construction site later.

166. At 10:17 a.m., what does Stanley Abrell mean when she writes, "I got it"?
(A) He arrived at the site.
(B) He received the email from Ms. Fisher.
(C) He accepted Mr. Burke's gratitude.
(D) He had the revised plan delivered.

167. What will Stanley Abrell probably do next?
(A) Speak with the construction manager
(B) Print out some materials
(C) Get in touch with a client
(D) Make plans to deliver a package

Questions 168-171 refer to the following information.

WoodWorks Home Furnishing Assembly Set

The expert artisans of WoodWorks craft your home furnishing sets based on designs found in the world's premier galleries and exclusive pieces. —[1]—.

Even with these beautiful designs, our furniture is still simple to put together. All you will need to set up your new furnishing are some household tools. —[2]—.

Each assembly set comes with all furniture parts, sandpaper, and easy-to-follow directions. The only thing not included is the oil finish, so that you may choose the finish that best suits your style. —[3]—. Descriptions of each kind of stain are below.

Finishing Recommendations
Each assembly set includes enough water-based wood varnish to complete your furnishing, although the final oil finish must also be applied. During the finishing process, patience is required. Completely remove any blemishes like glue or fingerprints with sandpaper and a moist cleaning cloth. Ensure your work area has no dust. Work slowly and make sure each coat of the finish has dried thoroughly before applying another layer. —[4]—.

Wood Stain Choices

Standard Stain:	175 Most WoodWorks customers select this type, which gives the wood a rich brown hue similar to walnut.
Deep Stain:	This rich stain gives your furnishings a classic, deep-brown color that emits sophistication.
Dark Stain:	For a more modern style, this stain gives your furnishing a lustrous black finish.

168. Where would this information most likely appear?
(A) In a gallery pamphlet
(B) In a catalog of merchandise
(C) In a promotion for a housekeeping service
(D) In a magazine article

169. What is NOT included with each kit?
(A) Furniture parts
(B) sandpaper
(C) Oil Finish
(D) Wood Stain

170. What stain do most customers choose?
(A) Standard stain
(B) Natural stain
(C) Deep stain
(D) Dark stain

171. In which of the positions marked [1], [2], [3], and [4] does the following sentence best belong?

"When you order, please select which style of wood stain you would like."

(A) [1]
(B) [2]
(C) [3]
(D) [4]

Questions 172-175 refer to the following letter.

May 16

Serena Kim
2455 First Avenue
Portland, OR 97201

Dear Ms. Kim,

We wish to express our thanks to you for choosing QuickCom as your Internet service provider. An installation specialist will visit your house at 2 p.m. on May 19. We ask that someone be at your house during this time. As our specialists have many appointments, please confirm your appointment the day before the scheduled installation by calling our service center at (888) 555-3386.

As for your agreement with QuickCom, we will provide your Internet service at a special price of $20 per month for a period of 18 months. Your first bill will also include an initial charge of $40 for the installation fee. Following this period, the normal rate of $30 per month will begin. Should you choose to cancel your service prior to the end of this period, you will be charged an $80 early termination fee for breaking our contract. We have enclosed a copy of the agreement for you to retain.

We send bills by mail on the first day of the month and request payment by the fifteenth. You may choose to pay through the mail, on our website, or at one of our customer service offices. Thank you again for choosing QuickCom.

Regards,

Theodore Poulain
QuickCom Customer Service Director

172. Where is Ms. Kim installing an Internet connection?
(A) At her home
(B) At her workplace
(C) At her market
(D) At her restaurant

173. In paragraph 2, line 4, the word "breaking" is closest in meaning to
(A) dividing
(B) destroying
(C) violating
(D) separating

174. According to the letter, why would Ms. Kim incur an additional charge?
(A) For breaching a contract
(B) For cancelling her appointment
(C) For sending a payment too late
(D) For using the service too often

175. When will Ms. Kim's first payment to QuickCom be due?
(A) May 16
(B) May 19
(C) June 1
(D) June 15

Questions 176–180 refer to the following Website and e-mail.

http://www.cda.co.ca

Career Development Academy

Workshops for Advancing your Career

10 July - Successful Business Practices The CEO of Lorken Production gives advice on how to make your company more successful by implementing sustainable business practices. She will also explain how it helped her own company increase sales and profits.	**17 July - Organization: The Key to Success** Learn how to get the most out of your work with organizational coach, Glenn Baxter as he gives a presentation on how to set priorities when organizing projects in your business and scheduling work in order to improve productivity.
24 July - Succeeding With Your Pitch If you're an entrepreneur who has great ideas, you'll need to know how to pitch those ideas successfully to get them funded. Author of Get Your Ideas Off the Ground, Greg Diamond, can help you do this with his 6-step plan for successful pitching.	**31 July - Making the Most of the Future** Media expert Ivana Bauer leads a workshop on how your business can increase its online presence to increase its marketing reach and attract more customers. Course materials are included in the workshop fee.

Workshops for advancing your career are held at the Career Development Academy every Tuesday from 7:00 p.m. to 9:00 p.m. These are open to the public. You can register online at www.cda.co.ca/enrollment.

---

* **E-mail** *

To: gbaxter@mailtime.co.ca
From: floragordon@gordonmanufacturing.co.ca
Date: 26 July
Subject: Thanks again!

Dear Mr. Baxter,

I wanted to tell you how much I appreciated your time you took to talk with me after your presentation. I found your ideas to be extremely useful, and I'd like to ask you to give a presentation at my company, Gordon Manufacturing, so that my employees may also learn from your ideas. You said that you'll be traveling for much of August, so I was hoping we could schedule a time in September. Please let me know when you would be available. I hope to hear back from you soon.

Sincerely,
Flora Gordon
CEO, Gordon Manufacturing

176. What is indicated about the workshops for advancing careers?
(A) They take place two times a week.
(B) They are taught by university instructors.
(C) They are held at several places.
(D) Enrollment is open to everyone.

177. Which seminar would be most useful for a business owner who wanted to learn about advertising online?
(A) Successful Business Practices
(B) Organization: The Key to Success
(C) Succeeding with Your Pitch
(D) Making the Most of the Future

178. What is stated about Mr. Diamond?
(A) He has recently started his own business.
(B) He is going on tour in August.
(C) He is a member of Career Development Academy
(D) He has authored a book.

179. Why did Ms. Gordon send the e-mail?
(A) To schedule a training session
(B) To enroll in a workshop
(C) To share a travel itinerary
(D) To suggest a seminar topic

180. What is Ms. Gordon most likely interested in doing at Gordon Manufacturing?
(A) Teaching her staff how to use an operating system
(B) Increasing her company's online presence
(C) Enhancing time management skills of her employees
(D) Attracting more funding for a new project

Questions 181-185 refer to the following e-mail and note.

E-mail Message

To :	Patrick Barwurton <barwurton08@supraline.com>
From :	Wu Lenwei <lenwei04@supraline.com>
Subject :	September 3
Date :	Lunch with Turro representatives

I'm really looking forward to our lunch with the Turro representatives at Sawatdee. Every review that I've read says that it's one of the best restaurants in town, even though it opened just a few months ago. I was informed that the clients from Turro really enjoy Thai food, so I really hope that this restaurant will give them a good feeling about our company. The only issue is that it will take a while to get to the restaurant from work.

There's one more problem, which is that my car is still being fixed at the garage on 1st Street. Right now, I'm not sure how I can get to 20th Street for the meeting. I think I could take the subway, but I know that the trains are usually very crowded around that time. I suppose I could just check out the train from the platform and if it's too crowded, I'll take a cab to the restaurant. Everything for the meeting has been taken care of, except that I haven't been able to drive to the copy shop for the blueprint copies.

If I do need to take the subway, which line do you think I should take? I know there are two lines, but I don't know which would be faster and less crowded. If you have any idea, I'd appreciate the advice.

Regards,

Wu

Supraline Industries
55 3rd Street
Boston, MA 02127

September 4

Wu,

I really appreciate all the time and efforts you put in to secure the new account. Don't worry. It'll be my pleasure to take care of the rest. It's no problem for me to handle it, as my car is working fine. If you want, I'll see you on the 11th, and I can easily pick you up to bring to the restaurant.

Patrick

181. Why did Ms. Lenwei send the e-mail?
(A) To ask for a co-worker's help
(B) To suggest a recently opened restaurant
(C) To request driving directions to a meeting place
(D) To postpone a reservation

182. What is NOT stated about Sawatdee?
(A) It started operating recently.
(B) It is not close to Supraline Industries.
(C) It provides complimentary appetizers.
(D) It has received many good reviews.

183. Where is Sawatdee?
(A) On 1st Street
(B) On 3rd Street
(C) On 11th Street
(D) On 20th Street

184. In the note, the word "rest" in line 2 is closest in meaning to
(A) Pause
(B) Reminder
(C) Remainder
(D) Establishment

185. What will Patrick Barwurton do before the meeting with the Turro representatives?
(A) Pick up copies
(B) Update an itinerary
(C) Reserve a table
(D) Go on a business trip

Questions 186–190 refer to the following webpage and e-mails.

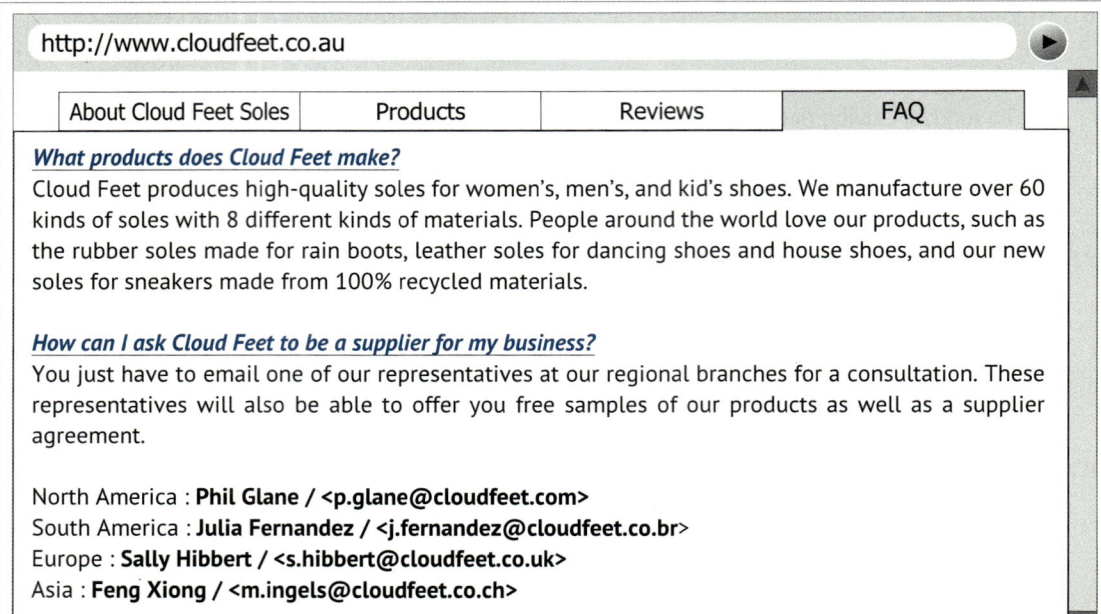

http://www.cloudfeet.co.au

| About Cloud Feet Soles | Products | Reviews | **FAQ** |

What products does Cloud Feet make?
Cloud Feet produces high-quality soles for women's, men's, and kid's shoes. We manufacture over 60 kinds of soles with 8 different kinds of materials. People around the world love our products, such as the rubber soles made for rain boots, leather soles for dancing shoes and house shoes, and our new soles for sneakers made from 100% recycled materials.

How can I ask Cloud Feet to be a supplier for my business?
You just have to email one of our representatives at our regional branches for a consultation. These representatives will also be able to offer you free samples of our products as well as a supplier agreement.

North America : **Phil Glane** / <p.glane@cloudfeet.com>
South America : **Julia Fernandez** / <j.fernandez@cloudfeet.co.br>
Europe : **Sally Hibbert** / <s.hibbert@cloudfeet.co.uk>
Asia : **Feng Xiong** / <m.ingels@cloudfeet.co.ch>

E-mail Message

To : Sally Hibbert <s.hibbert@cloudfeet.co.uk
From : Charles Ryu cling@accel.co.jp
Date : 20 October
Subject : Request for consultation

Dear Ms. Hibbert,

I work for a Tokyo-based athletic shoe company called Accel as the marketing manager. I recently went to the Athletic Apparel Expo in Paris, France and was impressed by the Supranex sneakers which had the Cloud Feet logo on their sole. The soles seemed to perform much better than the latex material my company uses now.

I was hoping to contact a Cloud Feet representative about receiving some samples and possibly making a contract, and I would like to know what is the next step I should take. I emailed the regional representative for Asia, but my email kept getting returned with a notice saying that the address was not valid.

Sincerely,

Charles Ryu
Purchasing manager, Accel

E-mail Message

To : Charles Ryu cling@accel.co.jp
From : Tony Weng Xia <tonywx@cloudfeet.co.ch>
Date : 21 October

Dear Mr. Ryu,

We deeply apologize for the frustration you had to experience and thank you for your interest in our products. There have been some changes in our staffing. Now I represent Asia region for Could Feet. I have a business trip to Tokyo scheduled for next week to meet our clients there. If you let me know what time you are available and what kind of soles you are interested in other than those for your sneakers, I'll make sure to bring samples when I come to see you.

Best Regards,

Tony Weng Xia
Representative, Cloud Feet

---

186. What is stated about Cloud Feet?
  (A) It produces high-quality rain boots.
  (B) It manufactures parts only for children's footwear.
  (C) It does business with companies in many countries.
  (D) It sends a catalogue to clients every month.

187. What is most likely true about Ms. Hibbert?
  (A) She is employed by Accel.
  (B) She can give samples to potential clinets.
  (C) She has been to Tokyo.
  (D) She met Mr. Ryu in Paris, France.

188. What type of materials does Mr. Ryu most likely want to use for his company's products?
  (A) Leather
  (B) Recycled
  (C) Rubber
  (D) Latex

189. In the first email, the word "step" in paragraph 2, line 2 is closest meaning to
  (A) action
  (B) recommendation
  (C) footprint
  (D) degree

190. What is suggested about Mr. Xia?
  (A) He has been with Cloud Feet for a long time.
  (B) He has been transferred from other regions.
  (C) He is a replacement for Mr. Xiong.
  (D) Mr. Ryu is already his client.

Questions 191-195 refer to the following flyer, e-mail, and article.

The 10th Biannual Uptown Art Fair
April 9 - 11

The Uptown Art Fair, brought to you by the Metropolitan Arts Council, is back by popular demand.

Please find a partial schedule of events below:

- Friday, April 9, 6 p.m. / Forrester Museum of Art
  The opening of Meredith Parilla's new exhibit of photography, Shutter Down and Tune Out. The exhibit will run until April 23.
  Museum hours are from 9 a.m. to 8 p.m. during the weekdays, and from 11 a.m. to 6 p.m. on the weekends.

- Saturday, April 10 and Sunday April 11, 9 a.m. to 7 p.m. / Uptown Community Center
  Games and craft-making activities for kids.

- Saturday, April 10, 5 p.m. / Miller Street Park Outdoor Theater
  (Rain relocation: Lamps Concert Hall.)
  A musical performance by the Burkino Teenage Chore, who gave a great performance last year.

- Saturday, April 10 and Sunday April 11, 11 a.m. to 8 p.m. / Uptown Junction Square
  Various food trucks and local artists will be selling food and art pieces at the food and crafts market.

- Sunday, April 11, 4 p.m. to 7 p.m. / Tourian Theater
  An Obscure Camera, a new play by Carroll Bady will be performed by the Tourian Theater players.

---

* E-mail *

To :	Mary Wildenburg <mwildenburg@uaf.org>
From :	Saban Azizov <sabanaz@bwt.org.za>
Subject :	Uptown Art Fair
Date :	April 14

Dear Ms. Wildenburg,

I wanted to let you know how much we appreciated bringing the music of our native South Africa to the Uptown Art Fair. It would've been better if more people could have enjoyed the performance, but we had no choice but to play indoors because of the rainy weather. Even with that, the audience was great. Also, it seems like many of them bought some of our albums and some asked what Web sites they could use to download our music after the show.

We would be honored to play at any other future festivals. Thanks again.

Regards,

Saban Azizov
Manager
Burkino Teenage Chore

Uptown Art Fair a Huge Success

SANDUSKY (April 13) – The Uptown Art Fair this spring had bigger crowds than ever, with the organizers calling the festival the most successful one yet. Despite the rain, many attendees waited in long lines to sample the international cuisine offered by the food trucks, some of which needed to be moved from their original location in Uptown Junction Square because of limited space. "At first, I was worried about changing locations," stated food truck owner Reggie Lopez, "But I think that many of our customers on Sunday ate at our food truck while they were waiting to see An Obscure Camera."

Festival organizers have already begun planning events for the next festival in the fall. "Most of the locations will be the same, but we may have to find a new place for games and craft-making activities since the venue we usually use will be undergoing renovations in the fall" said Scarlett Anthony of the Metropolitan Arts Council. "Considering how much fun the festival was this time, the fall festival will definitely be something to look forward to."

191. What is the event that is NOT scheduled to be taking place at 5 p.m. on Sunday?
(A) A dance competition
(B) An arts and crafts activity
(C) A photography exhibit
(D) A food market

192. Why did Mr. Azizov send Ms. Wildenburg an email?
(A) To ask for directions to a theater
(B) To postpone a concert
(C) To give her thanks
(D) To recover a lost item

193. What is suggested about Burkino Teenage Chore?
(A) It performed at the fair for the first time.
(B) It played in the Lamps Concert Hall.
(C) It is currently on tour in South Africa.
(D) It has many visitors to its online store.

194. Where most likely was Mr. Lopez food truck close to?
(A) Forrester Museum of Art
(B) Miller Street Park Outdoor Theater
(C) Lamps Concert Hall
(D) Tourian theater

195. What will happen to Uptown Community Center in the fall?
(A) It will change its hours of operation.
(B) It will house the arts and crafts section for the festival.
(C) It will begin to offer classes for the community.
(D) It will be renovated.

Questions 196-200 refer to the following article, report, and review.

Executive Interview

Lusk Company, the corporation which holds a chain of hotels throughout Asia, has seen its profits rise smoothly with the efforts of Sun Yiping. Mr. Yiping talked to us, in his office overlooking Shenzhen Park in Hong Kong, about the company's ongoing business plans and its financial status.

Q. What makes Lusk Company's hotels different from those of other hotel chains?
   A. We have spent a lot of time customizing our hotels to the needs of guests on business trips, as they are the majority of our guests. For these guests, comfort and access to business services is key. So, our rooms are larger than average and we ensure that our business equipment is easily available and accessible to all of our guests.

Q. Can you tell us about any projects that helped the company flourish over the past year?
   A. We bought a hotel in Kyoto in February, built a new restaurant at our hotel in Kuala Lumpur, completely restored a majority of the guest rooms at our Seoul location, and completed plans for construction of a hotel in Bangkok. Our annual profits rose by seven percent because of these endeavors.

Lusk Company Annual Financial Report
SUMMARY

A rise in corporate travel throughout Asia, driven in part by favorable economic conditions, resulted in greater occupancy in almost every Lusk Hotel, making this year quite profitable even though our room rates remained unchanged. The recent postponement of a plan to construct a new hotel will not affect our positive financial performance.

Figure A: ESTIMATED PROFITS BY LOCATION
(Units listed are in million US dollars)

	1st Quarter	2nd Quarter	3rd Quarter	4th Quarter
Hong Kong	20	8	7	2
Seoul	11	12	11	2
Kuala Lumpur	13	11	6	2
Kyoto	3	7	8	3
Total	47	38	32	9

http://www.realhotelreviews.com

Reviewer Name: Christophe Luccardi
Name of Hotel: Lusk Hotel
Length of Stay: 3 nights
Rating: 5/5

Comments: My stay at Lusk Hotel was excellent, as it always is. I've stayed at multiple Lusk Branches and have always been pleased with the service and facilities at every branch. The stay was even better this time, as my room seemed to have been recently renovated, so it was completely clean. The staff were also extremely helpful. I had to make a reservation for an upcoming convention and the staff told me that since that is during the off-season, they could upgrade my room at no charge. I'll definitely continue to stay at Lusk hotels.

196. In the article, the word "customizing" in paragraph 2, line 2, is closest in meaning to
(A) reflecting
(B) publicizing
(C) streamlining
(D) tailoring

197. Where has Lusk Company decided to delay a project?
(A) In Kyoto
(B) In Kuala Lumpur
(C) In Hong Kong
(D) In Bangkok

198. According to the report, why has Lusk Company been profitable
(A) The hotel has had more guests.
(B) A fee for using business supplies was increased.
(C) Some hospitality services have been eliminated.
(D) The prices for rooms were increased.

199. At which branch did Mr. Luccardi most likely stay?
(A) At the Hong Kong branch
(B) At the Seoul Branch
(C) At the Kuala Lumpur branch
(D) At the Kyoto branch

200. During which time period will Mr. Luccardi most likely attend a convention?
(A) Between January and March
(B) Between April and June
(C) Between July and September
(D) Between October and December

Stop! This is the end of the test. If you finish before time is called, you may go back to Parts 5, 6, and 7 and check your work.

동시토익 실전 WORKBOOK

101. Ms. Sanders will finish her book about how to build and sustain a creative workplace culture next month.

해석]

102. Victoria College's innovative new program will be starting at the upcoming semester.

해석]

103. Mr. Taylor's revised personnel report provides added enhancements over his earlier version.

해석]

104. A Spanish seafood restaurant that has been under construction for many months is finally opening tomorrow.

해석]

105. Mr. Schumaker will be conferring with all the managers from the company over the next few months.

해석]

106. Crawford Enterprise has an opening for a regional sales coordinator in our Seattle office.

해석]

107. Please be assured that free admission to the museum on the first Sunday of every month does not include the special exhibitions in the Stuart Hall.

해석]

108. Over five years of experience in our foreign branches is a requirement for a new branch manager in Singapore.

해석]

109. To try to protect its steel industry, the United States raised import tariffs but, unsurprisingly, so did its trading partners.

해석]

110. Children under 18 are not required to have government-issued identification when boarding planes.

해석]

111. These easy-to-use solutions have been meeting the asset management needs of local businesses and organizations of all sizes.

해석]

*어휘 NOTE

112. The management took an immovable stance during negotiations with the labor union over the contract terms.

해석]
_____

113. With Ethier Mobile shipping 1.3 million compact cars last quarter, its sales this year are up 19 percent from a year earlier.

해석]
_____

114. Ms. Vedder, who has conducted more than 1,500 seminars and workshops across Australia over her 30-year career, will be the first presenter.

해석]
_____

115. The employee manual describes how office supplies should be ordered, stored, and distributed.

해석]
_____

116. Norwak Airlines is pleased to announce that they will fly three times a day from Seoul to Los Angeles beginning in July.

해석]
_____

117. After carefully considering the terms and conditions of the proposal, the board found it to be worthwhile.

해석]
_____

118. Nominations for the 24th annual theater awards must be submitted by email to Linda Morris by May 7 at the latest.

해석]
_____

119. Ellis and his teammates can each expect a bonus of approximately $20,000 if his team wins the project.

해석]
_____

120. The Internet will be intermittently unavailable between 5 a.m. and 10 a.m. on Saturday, May 10 due to scheduled regular maintenance.

해석]
_____

121. The street on First Avenue is too narrow to allow a cyclist to safely pass the vehicle out of the door zone.

해석]
_____

＊어휘 NOTE

122. Correspondence from clients will be handled in strict confidence and will not be revealed to third parties.

해석]

123. Ed Smith compiles medical records of hospital and clinic patients in a manner consistent with medical and legal requirements.

해석]

124. The North Ridge University has changed the admission policy to attract highly competent students.

해석]

125. Please make sure to turn off all the lights before you leave the office at the end of the day, unless instructed otherwise.

해석]

126. Whereas most of the candidates met the deadline for application, a few missed it.

해석]

127. It was the unpredictable weather over three consecutive years, which resulted in the cancellation of the August Festival.

해석]

128. It is mandatory to observe all safety rules and instructions while in the factory.

해석]

129. Jay Kim Foundation began with the idea of giving women an opportunity to pursue their career in whatever field they want to work in.

해석]

130. Had Sordino Studios not given Brandon League an opportunity to work together, our company would have done so.

해석]

* 어휘 NOTE

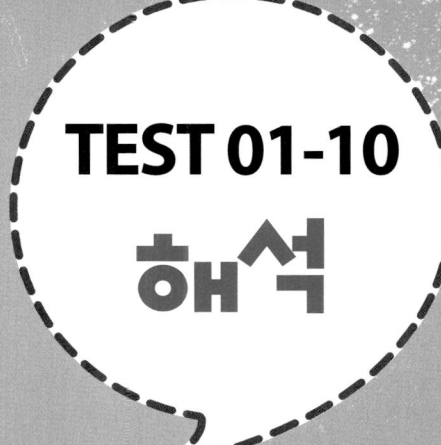

동시토익 CONTEMPORARY TOEIC

TEST 1

PART 5

101. 일단 따뜻한 날씨가 도래하면, 난방장치들을 좋은 상태로 유지하기 위해서 보관소에 두세요.

102. Jergen Bank에서 계좌를 개설 할 때, 신규 계좌를 소지하신 분들은 새 신용카드를 신청 할 수 있습니다.

103. 영업이사가 다른 지점을 방문해야 했기 때문에 Horner씨는 직접 판매 홍보를 주주들에게 선보였습니다.

104. Blines는 이메일로 그의 숙박과 비행편 예약에 대한 확인을 받지 못했습니다.

105. Harrison's Sports는 개점 바로 직후 이 지역에서 가장 인기 있는 스포츠 용품 가게가 되었습니다.

106. Olley사의 모든 직원들은 다음주 목요일 새로운 의료 보건 프로그램에 등록하는 것에 관한 세미나에 참석해야 합니다.

107. 모든 직원은 그들이 6월 10일까지 의료 보험 수당을 위해 등록을 해야 한다는 것을 알고 있습니다.

108. Kline University의 대강당은 그 학교를 졸업한 유명 건축가에 의해 설계되었습니다.

109. Carltec사의 노트북 컴퓨터는 출시 시에 저렴하게 가격이 매겨졌지만, 호평을 받고 나서 회사는 가격을 인상했습니다.

110. Lawson Daily 신문사의 편집자에게 보내는 편지들은 출판 전에 편집자에 의해 검토된다.

111. 그의 경력 내내, Ian Carter는 이 업계에서 가장 유명한 마케팅 컨설턴트가 되기를 열망했다.

112. Caring Airways은 캐나다에서 가장 저렴한 국내 항공편을 제공합니다.

113. Mantel Pharmaceuticals사는 최근 임상 실험의 결과 때문에 새로운 진통제를 출시하지 않을 방침입니다.

114. Fisher씨는 그가 Lester Automotive에서 그렇게 헌신적이고, 열정적인 팀과 일하게 되어 영광이었다고 그의 직원들에게 전했습니다.

115. 최근 소비자 보고서에 따르면, Everton Industries는 올해에 가장 평점이 높은 오븐 토스터기를 생산해 오고 있습니다.

116. Overton Party Supplies사는 Xenor Technologies 시상식을 위해서 대여되었던 모든 것들이 반납되었다고 알렸습니다.

117. 저희의 폭 넓은 조사 덕분에, 저희 연구는 이전 연구들보다 판매율을 좀더 정확하게 예측할 수 있었습니다.

118. 일정이 겹쳐서 다음주 지부장의 방문이 다음달까지 미뤄진 상태입니다.

119. Revel Bohem의 거실가구 신규라인은 Revel사의 디자인 부서와 아티스트인 Teresa Gile간의 공동 노력의 결과입니다.

120. 업그레이드가 된 웹사이트에서 당신은 런던에서 열릴 다가오는 미술품과 골동품 판매로 연결해주는 직접 링크가 걸린 달력을 발견 하실 수 있습니다.

121. 신분증에 주소 정보를 아직 업데이트 하지 못하신 Telville의 신규 입주자들은 벌금의 대상이 될 수 있습니다.

122. 회계정책이 변경된 이후에 Thilsen사의 마케팅 부서를 위해 더 큰 규모의 예산이 할당되었습니다.

123. Lyle's Sandwiches의 고객 만족도는 그 지역 어떤 음식점보다 높았습니다.

124. 지난 시의회 회의에서 Dale Harper의원은 Fairley의 커뮤니티 센터를 개조하지 않을 것이라는 시의회의 결정을 발표했습니다.

125. 지원자들은 그 직책에 뽑혔는지 아닌지를 면접 본 2주 이내에 통보 받을 것입니다.

126. 연구팀은 현재 Philtert사의 최신 속 쓰림 치료제의 효율성을 측정하기 위해서 연구조사를 실시하고 있습니다.

127. Halico사는 이달 초 Island Telecom사를 인수한 덕분에 국내에서 가장 규모가 큰 광대역 공급자가 되었습니다.

128. Champlain의 모든 주민들은 지역 예술가인 Beverly Summers에 의해 가르쳐 지는 무료 그림 수업에 참여하도록 환영되는 바입니다.

129. 신형 Operton 세단의 연비는 얼마나 자주 몰아지느냐에 따라 달라집니다.

130. 11월 30일까지 등록한 회원들만 1월에 전국 대회에 참가 할 수 있습니다.

PART 6

Questions 131-134 편지

Troyer에게

이 편지는 우리가 5월 4일에 발송한 200개의 음료수 잔 중에 15개가 거부된 것에 관한 것입니다. 저희는 모든 Valsin Glassware 제품들의 품질을 보장합니다. 따라서 (제품의) 결함은 (고객뿐만 아니라) 심지어 저희에게도 항상 받아들일 수 없는 것으로 간주됩니다. 저희는 언제나 저희의 가장 소중한 고객 중에 한 분으로서 귀하의 거래에 감사 드립니다. 따라서 우리는 고객님에게 파손된 유리잔에 대한 총비용을 환불해 드리겠습니다. 저희가 파손된 물품을 검사해보고 제조과정을 개선할 수 있도록, 파손된 물품을 저희에게 다시 보내주실 것을 요청 드리는 바입니다. 당신이 편리한 시간에 가급적 빨리 해주시기 바랍니다.

Questions 135-138 광고문

피아노 연주를 배우고 싶다면 오늘 당장 BTR에 등록하세요.

Bradwell Recreation Center(BTR)에서는 모든 시민들이 Rita Masterson의 피아노 수업에 등록하는 것을 환영하는 바입니다. Masterson는 International Arts Academy에서 공부를 했고, 25년 동안 피아노를 연주해 왔고 학생들을 지도해 왔습니다.

그녀의 경력 중에 스튜디오 음악가로 활동해 왔고, Girgio Amatano, Wesley Kines, the Decker Brothers 밴드를 포함한 우리 시대에 가장 유명한 음악가들 중 몇몇과 공연해 왔습니다.

Masterson은 어떤 수준의 학생도 여러 다른 음악 스타일로 피아노를 치는 것을 지도할 수 있습니다.

그녀는 클래식 소나타에서부터 재즈 피아노 독주에 이르기까지 모든 것을 연주 할 수 있는 자격이 충분한 사람입니다. 단체 수업은 3월 4일부터 가능하고 일대일 레슨은 3월 10일부터 시작됩니다. 좀더 자세한 일정을 원하시면 555-3085로 전화 주세요.

Questions 139-142 이메일

수신: 회사 직원
발신: Rita Kim
날짜: 9월 12일
제목: Announcement

친애하는 동료들에게

저는 오늘 아침에 제 직책에서 사임하려는 은퇴의사를 이사회에 알렸습니다. 이 자리에 근무하는 마지막 날은 11월 20일이 될 것입니다.

인선위원회가 소집되고 있으며, 인사과에서는 적당한 제 후임자가 조만간 찾아질 수 있을 것이라고 예상하고 있습니다. 인선 위원회 패널 자리를 위해 심사를 받고 싶다면 12월 20일까지 당신의 상사에게 얘기하세요.

관리자들은 그날(12월20일) 패널 위원들을 뽑게 될 것입니다. 몇몇은 제 은퇴 후에 계획이 무엇인지를 궁금해 하신다는 것도 알고 있습니다. 현재로선 제가 제 가족들과 더 자주 함께 할 수 있도록 Gordon University에서 시간 강사로 강의를 할 예정입니다.

Rita Kim
Staunton, Inc.

Questions 143-146 편지

4월 15일
Dr. Sylvia Lucas
58122 ND, Fargo, Fillings Street 888가

Dr. Lucas 에게

다시 한번 Serton Custodial 서비스에 대한 당신의 문의에 감사를 드립니다. 현재 저희 직원 중 한 명이 서비스에 대한 견적을 내도록 준비해두었습니다.

Serton Custodial은 Elm Grove 지역 의료시설에 청소 용역 서비스를 제공하는 일을 전문으로 하고 있습니다. 저희는 가장 안전하고도 가장 친 환경적인 청소용 화학물질과 방법들만 사용하고 있습니다.

당신이 요청한 바대로, 저희 직원 중 한 명이 4월 18일에 귀하의 시설물을 청소하는데 요건들을 판단하기 위해서 당신의 사무실을 방문할 것입니다. 이 평가에 근거해서 저희 청소 서비스에 대한 최종 가격 견적이 영업일 기준 하루 이내에 제공될 것입니다. 저희는 당신과 함께 일하기를 고대하는 바입니다.

Questions 147-148 초대장

귀하의 Galestorm Theater에 대한 후원을 감사 드리고자, 제12회 연례 Galestorm Theater Festival에 귀하를 초대하는 바입니다.

3월 24일 금요일
Lakeside Hotel
동쪽 별관
Greenton Drake가
6833번지

으후 5시 30분 식사
전채요리, 주요리, 음료 및 케이크

오후 7시 음악 및 댄스
탱고인 들의 공연

오후 8시 30분 감사행사
극장의 주요 기부자에 대한 특별 감사인사

3월 2일까지 몇몇의 손님과 함께 참석할 것인지를 알려주세요. 이를 위해서 www.galestormtheater.com 웹사이트를 방문해주세요.

147. 이 행사의 목적은 무엇입니까?
(A) 회사의 상품을 광고하기 위해서
(B) 참석자들을 회의에 환영하기 위해서
(C) Galestorm Theater에 기부한 기부자를 예우하기 위해서
(D) 직원의 성과를 축하하기 위해서

148. 행사에 참석하기 전에 초대손님은 무엇을 해야 합니까?
(A) 질문지에 응답해야 한다.
(B) 아트수업에 등록해야 한다.
(C) 기부금을 내야 한다.
(D) 웹사이트를 방문해야 한다.

Questions 149-150 공지문

시민들은 주목하세요

Annual Tarburg Reuse - Recycle Fest가 4월 24일 오전 10시부터 오후 6시까지 Postman Park에서 열립니다. 이 행사는 Tarburg Neighborhood Association에서 후원하고 있습니다. 이 행사에서, 지역 주민들은 자신에게서 더 이상 사용하지 않는 물건을 제거하고 (사용하지 않은 물건을 처분하고) 전자제품, 주방 용품, 컴퓨터와 같은 주민들이 사용할 있는 물건들을 얻어갈 수 있습니다. 일부 물건들의 경우 경매가 진행될 것이고, 판매되지 않으면 그들은 재활용될 것입니다. 당신의 기증은 당신의 집과 우리 주변 환경을 모두 계속 깨끗하게 만드는데 도움이 될 것입니다.

당신 차에 실을 수 없는 대형 품목이 있다면, 저희가 도와 드리겠습니다. 트럭이 귀하의 물품을 싣고 가도록 준비하려면 555-6788으로 Ted Booker에게 전화주세요. 재활용 물건들을 정리하는데 자원봉사자로 참여를 원하시는 분들은 555-4338로 Gil Ronson에게 전화주세요.

149. Tarburg 시민들은 무엇을 하도록 요구 받고 있는가?
(A) 재활용 통을 특정 지역에 두는 것
(B) 원치 않는 물건을 기증하는 것
(C) 사용되지 않을 때 컴퓨터를 끄는 것
(D) 축제에 등록하는 것

150. 시민들은 왜 Booker씨에게 전화해야 하는가?
(A) 트럭을 재활용하는 것을 도우려고
(B) Tarburg Neighborhood Association에 가입하려고
(C) Postman Park에 자리를 예약하려고
(D) 물품을 옮기는데 도움을 요청하려고

Questions 151-152 문자메시지 대화

CONNOR BERNARD	11:02 AM
Dana, 다음 주 화요일 오후에 바빠요?	

DANA HAAS	11:03 AM
2시에 직원회의가 있어요. 왜요?	

CONNOR BERNARD	11:04 AM
얼마나 걸려요?	

DANA HAAS	11:05 AM
한 시간 정도요. 확실한 건 확인해봐야 해요.	

CONNOR BERNARD	11:05 AM
영업직 인터뷰 관련해서 도와줄 수 있어요?	

DANA HAAS	11:06 AM
물론이요. 회의 끝나고 나서요.	

CONNOR BERNARD	11:07 AM
잘됐네요. 그러면 일단 3시반으로 인터뷰를 잡아놓을게요.	

DANA HAAS	11:08 AM
좋아요. 그때 봐요.	

151. Bernard씨는 무엇과 관련하여 도움을 필요로 하나요?
(A) 후보를 인터뷰 하는 것
(B) 직원 미팅을 개최하는 것
(C) 컨벤션을 기획하는 것
(D) 동료에게 연락하는 것

152. 11시 6분에 Haas씨가 "Of course"라고 쓸 때 무엇을 의미하고 있는가?
(A) Haas씨는 일정을 확인해볼 것이다.
(B) Haas씨는 영업직을 수락할 것이다.
(C) Haas씨는 Bernard씨에게 도움을 줄 것이다.
(D) Haas씨는 직원회의를 연기할 것이다.

Questions 153-154 이메일

수신: Wesley Dawkins 〈wesleyd33@titannet.com〉
발신: 선적부서 〈donotreply@liquistpharmacy.com〉
날짜: 11월 22일 오후 3시 45분
제목: 귀하의 최근 구매

인터넷에서 의약품을 구입하는 가장 손쉬운 곳인 Liquist Pharmacy에서 거래해주셔서 대단히 감사 드립니다. 이 이메일은 귀하의 가장 최근 주문 배송을 확인하고자 보내는 것입니다. 처방된 의약품은 주문이 완료된 지 하루 안에 보내질 것입니다. 아래 구매 세부사항들을 확인해 주세요.

주문번호 #: 853694
주문 날짜 및 시간: 11월 22일 오후 3시 42분
배송지 주소: 40223 KY, Louisville, Hines Street 2433가, Wesley Dawkins,
구입 품목: Dr. Harry Burns가 처방전을 내린 Vimitor 한 병
총 금액: $20.42, 신용카드로 결제 (카드 끝자리 3285)

만약 이 처방약의 리필이 필요하시면, 자동 주문과 배송을 설정하기 위해서 1-800-555-1414 저희 고객 서비스 센터로 전화해 주세요. 저희 웹사이트인 www.liquistpharmacy.com에 등록함으로써 다음 번 주문 시에 할인을 받으실 수 있습니다.

153. Dawkins의 주문에 대해서 유추 할 수 있는 것은?
(A) 회사에 의한 할인을 받았다.
(B) 11월 23일까지 아마도 배송될 것이다.
(C) 의사에 확인을 받아야 한다.
(D) 처방전이 필요 없는 의약품을 포함하고 있다.

154. Dawkins씨는 왜 고객 서비스 부서로 연락하도록 요청되는가?
(A) 주문 변경을 하려고
(B) 그의 배송 주소를 확인하려고
(C) 약사와 상담하려고
(D) 자동 서비스를 준비하려고

Questions 155-157 이메일

수신: 회사 직원 〈employees@partnersdrug.com〉
발신: Vera Mackey 〈vmackey@partnersdrug.com〉
제목: Cambert Kids Camp
날짜: 5월 24일

Partners Drug은 이번 6월에 Cambert Kids Camp를 준비하는데 도움을 주려고 합니다. 이 캠프는 비영리 단체에 의해 운영되며 참가비용을 최소한으로 해서 더 많은 지역 아이들이 캠프에 참가 할 수 있도록 Partners Drug사와 다른 기업들에게 후원을 요청하고 있습니다. 연령대가 4세부터 11살에 이르는 아이들이 캠프에 참가하며, 저희 몇 몇 직원들도 그들의 자녀들을 해마다 캠프로 보낸다고 알고 있습니다.

저희 Cambert Kids Camp 기부 운동은 내일 시작될 것이고, 저희 본사 건물의 로비에 박스가 놓여질 것입니다. 미술품이나아동용 게임, 수영 관련 물품과 자외선 차단제 등은 특히나 감사히 받겠습니다. 풋볼과 배드민턴과 같은스포츠용 장비도 당연히 큰 도움이 되겠습니다.

6월 29일까지 박스가 로비에 있을 것입니다. 기부금 또한 가능합니다. 기부금은 3층에 있는 회계부서의 Becky Hansen에게 전달해 주시기 바랍니다.

Bill Carlson
Partners Drug사의 봉사활동 담당자

155. 이메일의 목적은 무엇인가?
(A) 선물 교환을 준비하려고
(B) 캠프를 위한 할인을 제공하려고
(C) 지역 단체에 후원을 요청하려고
(D) 아이들을 위한 휴가 장소를 제안하려고

156. 아마도 상자에 담기지 않을 물건은?
(A) 크레용
(B) 서양장기 세트
(C) 야구 방망이
(D) 생수

157. 이메일에 따르면, Hansen은 무엇을 담당하고 있는가?
(A) 기부금을 모으는 것
(B) 등록된 아이들을 이동시키는 것
(C) 아이들 장난감을 수거 하는 것
(D) 직원 참여를 독려 하는 것

Questions 158-160 공지문

Summerville 대중교통 위원회
주말 Blue line 서비스 공지

6월 12일 금요일 오전 6시경부터 Blue Line 역 공사로 Summerville Park과 University Street간 서비스에 변경사항이 있습니다. 공사가 진행되는 동안에 Blue Line은 두 지역으로 운행될 것입니다. 첫 번째 구간은 Summerville Park에서 Carrer Drive까지 운행될 것이고, 두 번째 구간은 Hanter Museum에서 University Street까지 운행될 것입니다. Carrer Drive와 Hanter Museum역 사이에 있는 Marston 역에서는 선로 공사가 진행 될 것이기 때문에 이 두 역간은 기차가 운행될 수 없을 것입니다. 이 두 역 사이에 이동할 필요가 있는 승객들을 위해 무료 셔틀버스를 운행합니다. Blue Line은 7월 14일 일요일 오전 11시부터 평상시처럼 운행되고, 다른 모든 노선들은 이번 공사 중에도 정상으로 운영될 것입니다.

158. 어떤 역에서 공사가 예정되어 있나요?
(A) Summerville Park Station
(B) Marston Station
(C) Hanter Museum Station
(D) Carrer Station

159. 서비스 변경에 대해서 언급되어 있는 것은 무엇인가요?
(A) 모든 기차 노선이 변경될 것이다.
(B) 기차 요금 상승을 부추길 것이다.
(C) 영구적인 것은 아니다.
(D) 서비스 변경이 예상되지 못한 것이었다.

160. 안내문에 따르면, 셔틀버스의 목적은 무엇인가요?
(A) 두 역간 이동을 돕기 위해서
(B) 기차 탑승객의 수를 줄이기 위해서
(C) 시외 고객들에게 서비스를 제공하기 위해서
(D) 인기가 덜한 목적지에 교통수단을 제공하기 위해서

Questions 161-163 이메일

수신: hwilton@miltonmfg.com
발신: totoole@orangeplanning.com
날짜: 1월 12일
제목: Re: 서비스에 관한 문의

저는 방금 귀하의 Orange Planning사의 서비스에 대한 문의를 받았으며 기꺼이 도와드리고자 합니다. Orange Planning사는 귀사의 주요 제품들을 위한 생산라인의 생산량을 높이기 위해 귀사인 Milton Manufacturing와 함께 일하는데 아주 관심이 있습니다. —[1]—

Orange Planning사는 지난 20년간 전 세계 여러 기업들을 위한 기술 컨설팅 서비스를 제공해 오고 있습니다. 우리와 함께 일해온 회사에는 모스크바의 Babushka Mart, Orlando의 Pitchfork Industries와 홍콩의 Hord Robotics사 등이 있습니다. —[2]—

귀사가 저희 Orange Planning을 선택해 주시면, 그 결과에 귀하가 만족할 것이라는 것을 보장합니다. 저희는 특히나 기업들의 프로젝트를 그들의 예산 내에서 마감 시한 전에 마무리하는 것에 있어서 좋은 기록을 가지고 있기 때문에 저희 함께 일했던 모든 업체들은 매우 두드러진 결과를 얻어 왔습니다. —[3]—

—[4]— 좀 더 협력하는 건에 이야기를 하고 싶으시면, 466-555-3755번으로 저에게 전화주세요. 귀하가 궁금해 하는 모든 점을 기쁘게 해결해드리겠습니다. 귀하의 전화를 기다리겠습니다.

Tom O'Toole
Orange Planning사의 고객 지원 팀장

161. O'Toole은 왜 이메일을 보내는가?
(A) Milton Manufacturing와 미팅 시간을 확인하려고
(B) 업체가 사업 관계를 도모할 것을 권장하려고
(C) 생산 시설로 오는 길을 알려주려고
(D) 생산의 새로운 절차를 설명해 주려고

162. Orange Planning사에 대해서 언급된 것은?
(A) 최근에 여러 시설물을 지었다.
(B) 비용이 다른 컨설팅 회사만큼 비싸지 않다.
(C) 여러 나라의 기업들과 거래를 해왔다.
(D) 본사는 모스크바에 있다.

163. [1], [2], [3], [4]로 표시된 자리 중에 다음 문장이 들어가기에 가장 적합한 곳은?

"우리는 이러한 기업들과 다른 업체들이 그들의 생산시설에서 더 효율적이고 더 빨라지도록 도와 왔습니다."

(A) [1]
(B) [2]
(C) [3]
(D) [4]

Questions 164–167 인터넷 채팅 대화

Sienna Reynolds [3:30 p.m.]
명함 받는 것에 대해 제가 누구에게 얘기를 해야 하는지 아는 분 계시나요? 제가 여기 온지 일주일 정도밖에 안됐지만, 고객에게 주려면 명함이 필요하다고 들었는데요, 제가 아직 받지를 못해서요.

Jason Welch [3:32 p.m.]
사실 그건 당신이 직접 해야 하는 거예요. 저희 회사가 명함을 위해 가는 인쇄회사는 사실 3곳이 있습니다.

Sienna Reynolds [3:33 p.m.]
그러면 제가 직접 명함비용을 지불해야 한다는 말인가요? 저는 회사가 그런 비용은 내준다고 생각했어요.

Jason Welch [3:35 p.m.]
아니요. 당신이 지불하지 않아요. 회사는 각 인쇄회사와 이미 계정을 튼 상태고요, 각 회사는 우리 회사에 고지서를 보내요.

Sienna Reynolds [3:36 p.m.]
네. 그러면 제가 선택할 수 있는 것이 어떤 것이 있죠?

Shamarr Murphy [3:37 p.m.]
Highland Document Printing을 추천합니다. 제가 이 회사에서 받은 명함이 품질이 굉장히 좋았고요, 주문품을 매우 빨리 배송해줬어요.

Jason Welch [3:38 p.m.]
저도 Highland에서 제걸 만들었어요. 다른 옵션은 Ace Print Shop과 Coastal Printers예요. Ace는 가장 품질이 좋은데 인쇄하고 배송하는 데 너무 오래 걸려요. Highland는 만약 당신이 빨리 받고 싶다면, 더 이상 따를 자가 없습니다.

Sienna Reynolds [3:40 p.m.]
그렇군요. 두 분, 제가 제 명함 주문하기 전에 여러분 명함을 봐도 괜찮을까요?

Jason Welch [3:41 p.m.]
물론이죠. 5분 후에 제 사무실에 들르면 제걸 볼 수 있어요.

Shamarr Murphy [3:42 p.m.]
저도 Jason사무실에 갈 거라서요, Sienna 두 군데 따로따로 방문할 필요 없겠네요.

164. 대화의 주요 주제는?
(A) 화물을 고객에게 배송하는 것
(B) 명함을 구하는 것
(C) 청구서를 어디에 보낼 지
(D) 수당 패키지를 선택하는 것

165. Highland Document Printing에 대해 언급된 것은?
(A) 이 회사는 주문을 빨리 처리한다.
(B) 이 회사는 대화자들 회사에 가까이 위치해있다.
(C) 이 회사는 최고의 제품을 만든다.
(D) 디자인 선택의 폭이 넓다.

166. 3시 38분에 Jason Welch 씨가 "Highland can't be beaten"라고 쓸 때 무엇을 의미하고 있는가?
(A) Highland는 주문에 대해 가장 빠른 대응력을 가지고 있다.
(B) Highland는 최고의 이용후기들을 보유하고 있다.
(C) Highland는 다른 두 회사보다 더 비싸다.
(D) Highland는 대부분의 직원들이 선택하는 곳이다.

167. Shamarr Murphy는 다음 무엇을 할 가능성이 가장 높은가?
(A) 명함을 주문할 것이다.
(B) 미팅을 위한 서류를 준비할 것이다.
(C) 사무실에서 동료들을 만날 것이다.
(D) 주문과 관련하여 고객에게 연락할 것이다.

Questions 168–171 광고문

EnviroOffice
V5K 1N9, British Columbia, Vancouver
Victoria Street 243번지
(604) 555-4486

사무실에서 아름다운 식물들을 키우기를 원하지만, 가꾸기에 충분한 시간이 없으신가요? 그렇다면 EnviroOffice를 고려해 주세요. 저희는 크고 작은 사무실에 적합한 이 지역에서 최고의 다양한 식물들을 보유하고 있습니다. 식물들을 판매할 뿐만 아니라 저희가 판매하는 모든 식물에 대해 최소한의 비용만 받고 돌봄 서비스도 제공해 드리고 있습니다. 우리는 이국적인 식물들뿐만 아니라 일반적인 식물들도 재고로 가지고 있기 때문에 당신이 저희 가게를 나설 때 귀하의 사무실에 적합한 무엇인가를 가지고 가실 거라고 확신합니다. 1년 이상 저희 서비스를 신청하시면, 저희 전문가들이 만든 무료 꽃꽂이도 제공해 드리고 있습니다. 당신 사무실을 식물들로 꾸미는 것은 귀하의 근무 공간을 좀 더 상쾌하게 만들어 드릴 것입니다. 그러니 저희 상품이나 서비스에 관해서 좀더 알고 싶으시거나 무료 견적서를 받아 보시려면 오늘 당장 전화주세요.

168. 무엇이 광고 되는가?
(A) 주택 조경 회사
(B) 행사용 꽃 장식 전문 회사
(C) 정원 관리에 관한 전문 잡지
(D) 식물을 판매하고 돌보는 서비스

169. EnviroOffice가 이 공지에서 광고하지 않은 것은?
(A) 무료 견적서
(B) 수입 식물 배송
(C) 사무실을 위한 식물 관리
(D) 다양한 식물 종

170. 첫 번째 단락의 두 번째 줄 "consider"와 의미상 가장 가까운 것은?
(A) 간주하다
(B) 밝히다
(C) 생각해보다
(D) 향상시키다

171. 어떤 특별행사가 언급되어 있는가?
(A) 관리하지 않아도 되는 식물들
(B) 무료 꽃꽂이
(C) 이국적인 식물에 대한 할인
(D) 반값에 과실수 제공

Questions 172-175 이메일

발신: Henry Connors <hconnors@prostaffing.com>
수신: Kimberly Stevens <kimstevens@qpost.com>
제목: 등록
날짜: 6월 26일

Kimberly에게

귀하의 이력서와 대학교 성적표를 받았으니 귀하의 정보를 Pro Staffing system에 입력시킬 수가 있게 되었습니다.

—[1]— 이 시점에서 귀하의 교육과 자격에 맞고, 저희가 채우고자 하는 임시직 일자리가 여러 개 있습니다. 그 일자리 가운데 두 개는 텔레마케팅 자리로, 하나는 유통회사에서의 행정 보조직이고 나머지 하나는 치과 진료소의 접수 담당자 자리입니다. —[2]— 이 인턴근무 동안에 근무 성과가 좋으면 신문사의 보조 편집자 자리로써 정규직 제안 받을 것입니다. 귀하가 저널리즘에서 막 취득한 학위 덕분에, 이 일자리가 당신에게는 아주 그만 일 것입니다. —[3]— 유일한 문제는 그 자리는 Hastings 지역으로, 그곳은 Rochester의 당신의 집에서 꽤 먼 거리에 있다는 것입니다. 통근을 하실 의향이 있으신가요? 임시직들은 귀하가 사시는 곳에 가까이 위치해있습니다. 만약 통근 시간에 대해 개의치 않으신다면 저희는 또한 다른 자리들도 찾아드릴 수 있습니다. —[4]—

저희는 세 통의 추천서를 필요로 하구요, 그리고 나서 귀하가 일할 수 있는 회사들과 접촉을 시작할 수 있습니다. 추천서는 상급자나 교사, 혹은 전 동료 직원들에게서 받으시면 됩니다. 이메일이나 팩스로 서류들을 보내주시고, 추천인들의 연락처를 꼭 포함시켜 보내주세요. 등록 과정에서의 다음 단계는 귀하가 저희 고용 상담사와 인터뷰를 하는 것입니다. 우리가 인터뷰 시간을 잡을 수 있도록 저에게 전화 주시기 바랍니다.

Henry Connors
Pro Staffing

172. Stevens에 대해서 유추 할 수 있는 것은?
(A) 그녀는 자격이 있는 기자이다.
(B) 그녀는 최근에 졸업했다.
(C) 그녀는 Pro Staffing사에서 근무한다.
(D) 그녀는 Connors씨에게 소포를 보냈다.

173. 접수 담당자 일자리에 대해서 사실은 것은?
(A) Rochester 근처에 위치해 있다.
(B) 정규직 자리로 이어진다.
(C) 유연한 근무 시간을 가진다.
(D) 유통회사에서 일하는 것이다.

174. Connors가 Stevens에게 요청하지 않은 것은?
(A) 추천서 보내기
(B) 약속 날짜 잡기
(C) 통근을 할 의향이 있는지 확인하기
(D) 서명된 서류 제출하기

175. [1], [2], [3], [4]로 도시된 자리 중에 다음 문장이 들어가기에 가장 적합한 곳은?

"저희는 또한 정규직 일자리도 가지고 있지만, 귀하가 여기서는 석 달간 인턴으로 근무하게 될 것입니다."

(A) [1]
(B) [2]
(C) [3]
(D) [4]

Questions 176-180 웹사이트와 양식

http://www.valorfootwear.com/businessprogram			
Valor Footwear의 기업 프로그램			
소개	기업 프로그램	카달로그	연락처

직장에서 당신의 직원들을 계속 안전하게 만들기를 원하나요? Valor Footwear는 당신의 사업환경에 맞는 신발과 부츠를 당신의 직원들이 확실히 구비하도록 도울 수 있습니다.

Valor Footwear는 병원, 공장, 호텔 및 식당과 같은 많은 일터를 위한 다양한 스타일을 제공합니다. 모든 신발은 미끄럼 방지 밑창을 장착할 수 있습니다. 저희는 또한 어떤 신발이 귀하의 사업환경에 최적인지를 판단할 수 있게 돕도록 무료 상담을 제공합니다. 또한 당신의 직원들이 어떤 신발이 직장에서 착용하기에 적절한지를 쉽게 확인할 수 있도록 귀하의 회사를 위한 맞춤형 웹사이트도 제작할 수 있습니다.

계정을 만들 준비가 되셨다면, 당신이 해야 하는 모든 것은 당신 사업체의 니즈에 대한 짧은 설문서를 작성하기 위해 아래 버튼을 클릭하는 것입니다(아래 버튼을 클릭만 하시면 됩니다). 저희 고객 계정 전문가 중 한 명이 Valor Footwear의 계정을 만들어 드리고 귀하가 궁금하실 수 있는 질문에 답해드리기 위해 이틀 안에 연락을 드릴 것입니다.

Valor Footwear 기업프로그램에 등록하세요

이름: Gregory Sample
회사: International Eateries, Inc.   직책: 운영이사
연락처: 618-555-1229
이메일주소: gsample@intleateries.com
선호하는 연락수단 (하나만 표시):
이메일 ☐   전화 ☑   방문 ☐   모두 가능 ☐
저희에게 오늘 연락하신 이유는?

저는 여러 개의 식당 운영을 담당하고 있으며 이번에 모든 직원들이 미끄럼 방지 밑창이 달린 신발을 착용하도록 요구하는 정책을 도입했습니다. 식당에 적합한 5개 다른 스타일의 신발 조합을 짜도록 귀사의 컨설턴트가 도와주시기를 희망합니다. 저는 가능하다면 4월 2일까지 맞춤형 웹사이트를 구축하기를 원합니다. 또한 저희 회사의 각 직원들이 신발을 한 켤레씩 고르면 청구서가 직원이 아닌 회사로 바로 전달되도록 청구 시스템을 만들고 싶습니다.

〈제출〉

176. 이 웹사이트는 누구를 대상으로 하나요?
  (A) 전문 요리사
  (B) 패션 디자이너
  (C) 의류 제조업체
  (D) 비즈니스 매니저

177. 이 양식에 따르면 최근 International Eateries에서는 어떤 변화가 있었나요?
  (A) 경영진이 새로운 정책을 구축했다.
  (B) 마케팅 활동이 시작됐다.
  (C) 새로운 지점이 개장되었다.
  (D) 직원 유니폼이 변경되었다.

178. 많은 International Eateries 직원들은 4월에 아마도 무엇을 할 것이 기대되고 있는가?
  (A) 안전기술에 대한 교육을 받는 것
  (B) 새로운 설비를 사용하는 것
  (C) 인터넷에서 제품을 구매하는 것
  (D) 새로운 주문접수 시스템을 배우는 것

179. Sample씨는 웹사이트에서 언급되지 않은 어떤 서비스를 요구하고 있나요?
  (A) 적합한 신발을 추천하는 것
  (B) 청구시스템을 구축하는 것
  (C) 맞춤형 웹사이트를 만드는 것
  (D) 신발의 스타일을 바꾸는 것

180. Valor Footwear는 Sample씨의 양식에 대해 어떻게 대응할 가능성이 가장 높은가?
  (A) Valor Footwear는 그에게 개인용 제품 카다로그를 보낼 것이다.
  (B) Valor Footwear는 매니저가 얼마를 청구 받을 지를 계산해 줄 것이다.
  (C) Valor Footwear는 몇몇 식당의 검사 일정을 잡을 것이다.
  (D) Valor Footwear는 컨설턴트를 시켜서 48시간 안에 그에게 연락할 것이다.

Questions 181-185 일정표와 메모

Hindelmintz Industires
안전 워크샵
3월 15일

10:00 – 10:50	당신의 근무지역을 계속 정리하는 것: 직장에서 안전을 보장할 가장 쉬운 방법 Workplace Operations Committee 이사, Dietrich Packer 발표
11:00 – 11:50	작업장에서의 안전 필수사항: 검토와 관행 제조 감독관, Samuel Rochard 발표
12:00 – 1:00	점심
1:00 – 1:50	공장 기계의 유지보수 및 사용법 고위 기술자 Patricia Long 발표
2:00 – 2:50	유해물질을 관리 및 처분하는 법 Lampwick Occupational Safety Department의 고위 검사관, Olivia Mackie 발표
3:00 – 3:50	Renner Factory Instruments사의 기계 작동 시연 Renner Factory Instruments 대표, Emily Slattery 발표

날짜: 3월 7일
발신자: Jessica Woodard
수신자: 제조시설의 전 직원
내용: 안전 워크샵 일정 변경사항

이 메시지는 다가오는 안전 워크샵에 대한 변경사항을 여러분들에게 알려 드리는 것입니다. Renner Factory Instruments 대표가 그날 오후에 다른 일정이 있어서 좀 더 이른 시간에 워크샵을 진행할 예정입니다. 그녀의 워크샵은 이제 1시에 열릴 것이며, 오후에 다른 워크샵들이 원래 예정되었던 것보다 각각 한 타임씩 뒤로 밀려서 열릴 것입니다.

공장 작업장이나 주변 사무실에서 근무하는 모든 직원들은 이번 안전 워크샵에 반드시 참석해야 합니다. 또한 연구개발부서의 일부 직원들도 참석할 예정입니다. 이번 교육 전반에 걸쳐 질문이나 의견 혹은 우려사항이 있으시면 언제든 저에게 연락 주시기 바랍니다.

협조해주셔서 감사합니다.

—Jessica

181. 워크샵의 주요목적은 무엇인가요?
  (A) 직원들이 정확하게 업무시간을 보고하는 것을 돕는 것
  (B) 매니저들이 그들의 부하직원들과 커뮤니케이션을 더 잘하도록 돕는 것
  (C) 새로운 운영시스템을 시연하는 것
  (D) 직원들에게 안전관행과 절차를 교육시키는 것

182. Rochard씨의 업무 중 하나일 가능성이 높은 것은?
 (A) 회사 제품을 위한 소책자를 만드는 것
 (B) Hindelmintz Industires사의 제품 생산을 관리하는 것
 (C) 신제품을 위한 광고를 제작하는 것
 (D) 고객의 질문과 항의를 처리하는 것

183. 워크샵 일정은 왜 변경되고 있는가?
 (A) 발표자가 그날 다른 약속이 있다.
 (B) 발표자가 건강상의 이유로 교체되어야 했다.
 (C) 워크샵 장소가 변경되어야 할 필요가 있다.
 (D) 워크샵이 Hindelmintz Industires사의 다른 행사와 겹쳤다.

184. 누구의 발표는 다른 시간대로 변경되지 않을 까요?
 (A) Long씨의 발표
 (B) Mackie씨의 발표
 (C) Slattery씨의 발표
 (D) Packer씨의 발표

185. 메모에서 2번째 문단 3번째줄의 "expected"가 의미상 가장 가까운 것은?
 (A) 수용가능한
 (B) 다가오는
 (C) 의무적인
 (D) 일관적인

Questions 186-190 2개의 이메일과 영수증

발신: draymond@treetechnology.com
수신: nate.amos@webpost.com
날짜: 11월 10일
제목: 구매번호 #186550

Amos씨에게
725불짜리 데스크 탑 컴퓨터와 모니터 주문이 완료 되었습니다. 거래해 주셔서 대단히 감사하며 구매품에 만족하시기를 바랍니다. 데스크 탑 컴퓨터와 함께 키보드와 마우스가 포함되어 있으며, 모니터에는 리모컨이 딸려 있습니다. 구매 비용이 700불이 넘었기 때문에, 무료로 HDMI 케이블도 보내드립니다.

주문품은 Carbondale에 있는 저희 물류센터로부터 발송될 것이며 주문하신 물건에 대한 예상된 배송 날짜는 11월 20일입니다. 하지만, 이 주문은 5불만 추가하면 빠른 배송을 받아 보실 수 있습니다. 이렇게 업그레이드를 하시면, 주문품은 6일 더 일찍, 11월 14일에 도착하게 됩니다. 이 서비스를 신청하시려면, 11월 12일이나 이전에 배송을 업그레이드 하겠다는 의향을 저희에게 알려주시기 바랍니다. 이 기한이 지나면 이 옵션은 더 이상 이용하실 수가 없습니다. 이 정보와 다른 업데이트된 정보들이 당신의 온라인 계정에 표시될 것이지만, 인쇄된 영수증에는 표시되지 않을 것입니다.

Diane Raymond
고객 지원부
Tree Technology
Elk Springs, CO

발신: nate.amos@wepost.com
수신: draymond@treetechnology.com
날짜: 11월 11일
제목: Re: 구매번호 #186550

Raymond씨에게
저는 당신이 언급한 빠른 배송 편을 이용하고 싶습니다.

그리고 제가 새 집으로 이사 중이기 때문에, 배송은 제 사무실로 보내주시기 바랍니다. 이 주소는 제 주문서에 비용 청구지에 명시된 주소와 같습니다. 제가 주문 할 때 입력했던 배송지 정보는 무시하시기 바랍니다.

Nate Amos

Tree Technology 최고의 기술을 위한 당신의 최상의 선택 구매번호 #186550	
물품	가격
Tech+ 데스크탑 컴퓨터	$560
고성능 마우스	$20
고성능 키보드	$45
Ultraview HDMI 모니터	$100
Ultraview HDMI 전선줄	$0
소계	$725
배송 및 처리	$3
총계	$728
청구서 발송 주소	634 Ashley St. Pittsfield, MA
배송 주소	880 Prospect Ave Gloversville, MA
구매해 주셔서 감사합니다!	

186. 첫 번째 이메일이 전송된 한가지 이유는 무엇인가?
 (A) 주문을 취소하려고
 (B) 배송 계약을 변경하려고
 (C) 배송이 늦어지는 이유를 설명하려고
 (D) 제한된 기한에 제공되는 행사를 제시하려고

187. 첫 번째 이메일에서 2번째 문단, 5번째 줄의 "reflected"가 의미상 가장 가까운 것은?
 (A) 표시되다
 (B) 고려되다
 (C) 복제되다
 (D) 반품되다

188. Amos 아마도 언제 주문품을 받겠는가?
 (A) 11월 10일
 (B) 11월 12일
 (C) 11월 14일
 (D) 11월 20일

189. 인쇄된 영수증에는 어떤 정보가 나와있지 않나요?
(A) 청구 주소
(B) 제품 비용
(C) 긴급 배송 비용
(D) 주문 번호

190. 구매품은 어디로 배송될 가능성이 가장 높은가?
(C) Carbondale
(B) Elk Springs
(C) Pittsfield
(D) Gloversville

Questions 191-195 기사문, 이메일 및 웹페이지

10월 8일 어떻게 인생을 가장 값지게 살 것인가?

Style Life사의 사장인 Amanda Thibido씨는 5년 전에 이 질문에 대해서 궁금해 했습니다. "제가 기차에서 한 사람과 얘기를 나누던 중이었어요. 그는 유명한 바이올린 연주가인 Sun Ling의 전기에 완전히 빠져 있더군요. 그녀의 스토리는 그 남자에게 자신의 과거를 돌아보게 만들었어요. 그것은 어떻게 하면 우리가 우리 자신의 스토리를 유명인이나 잘 알려진 사람들의 삶과 연결시킬 수 있을지를 생각하게 만들었어요. 저는 이것이 정말로 사람들을 도와줄 수 있을 거라 생각했어요."

여행에서 돌아온 후에, Thibido씨는 여러 상과 명성, 그리고 전 세계 수백만 방문자들을 얻게 된 블로그인 IntertwinedLives.com을 시작했습니다. 이 블로그는 매주 업데이트 되고 이미 유명인들의 수천 개의 스토리가 올라와 있습니다. "사람들이 진정으로 이 스토리에 공감하기 때문에 이 사이트가 성공적이라고 저는 생각해요"라고 Thibido씨는 얘기합니다. "사람들은 유명인의 스토리를 읽을 때 자기 자신의 삶을 되돌아 보게 됩니다".

Thibido의 웹사이트는 너무나 많은 방문객들을 유치하게 되었고, 그래서 Humans Being이라는 제목의 잡지도 발간할 예정입니다. 이 새 월간지는 인상적인 일반 사람들뿐만 아니라 과거나 현재의 유명인들에 관한 영감을 주는 스토리들을 담을 예정입니다. 독자들이 그들의 삶이 유명인들의 삶과 똑같이 마찬가지로 성취감을 주는 삶이라는 것을 깨달았으면 하는 게 Thibido씨의 바람입니다. 웹사이트 www.intertwinedlives.com/remarkablepeople에는 향후 게재될 스토리에 관한 제안 양식뿐만 아니라 구독관련 정보도 나와 있습니다.

발신: ptorn@stylelife.com
수신: athibido@stylelife.com
제목: 희소식
날짜: 10월 20일

Thibido씨 안녕하세요.

신문 기사의 출간이 굉장히 도움이 된 것으로 보인다는 것을 당신에게 알려주고자 합니다. 구독 수는 거의 두 배가 되었습니다. 엄청난 일이죠! 웹사이트 IntertwinedLives.com에는 현재 기사에 링크가 걸려있어서 일부 열혈 독자들이 잡지 구독을 예약주문하고 있는 것으로 보입니다. 저희 웹사이트에 처음 방문하는 첫 방문객들도 대거 들어왔습니다. 당신이 알아야 할 또 한가지는 영화 배우들, 특히 Ivan Sloan에 대한 스토리

를 올려달라는 많은 건의들이 들어오고 있다는 점입니다. 우리는 그에 대한 스토리를 다음 기사에 내봐야겠네요.

Peter Torn
수석 편집장

IntertwinedLives.com			
홈	자료실	Human Beings	의견

이름: Teri Wilson
IntertwinedLives.com은 어떻게 알게 됐나요? (해당하는 모든 것을 고르세요)
_____ 웹사이트
___X__ 인쇄물 (신문, 잡지 등)
_____ 친구나 지인
_____ 기타

추천하는 사람:
Owen Rocha

제안하는 이유:
Rocha씨는 Burns 타운의 시장입니다. 그는 십대 때 이민자로써 이 나라에 왔으며 교육을 잘 받지 못했습니다. 그는 역경을 헤쳐나갔고, 근면성과 친근한 성격 때문에 사회에서 출세하게 되었습니다. 그를 만나는 모든 사람들은 그가 굉장히 감동을 주는 인물이라는 데에 동의합니다.

191. 기사문의 목적은 무엇인가?
(A) 여행 목적지를 제안하려고
(B) Thibido의 업적을 소개하려고
(C) 인터넷 작가들에게 조언을 해주려고
(D) Ling의 커리어에 대해서 자세히 설명하려고

192. 기사에서 1번째 문단, 5번째 줄의 "renowned"가 의미상 가장 가까운 것은?
(A) 잘 알려진
(B) 선택된
(C) 후보로 지명된
(D) 회복된

193. 이메일에서 Torn이 기사에 대해서 무엇을 언급하고 있는가?
(A) 기사는 유명한 바이올린 연주가가 추천했다.
(B) 기사는 잡지에 재출판 되었다.
(C) 기사는 구독자 수를 늘려주고 있는 것으로 보인다.
(D) 기사가 토크 쇼에 등장했다.

194. Sloan에 대해서 언급 되어 있는 것은?
(A) 그는 Torn에게 의견을 주었다.
(B) 그는 Style Life사에서 근무한다.
(C) 그에 대해서 쓴 글이 Human Being에 나올 것이다
(D) 그는 IntertwinedLives.com 웹사이트에 올라온 스토리의 주제였다.

195. Teri Wilson에 대해 사실일 가능성이 가장 높은 것은?
(A) Teri Wilson은 IntertwinedLives.com의 오랜 독자다.
(B) Teri Wilson은 10월 8일자 기사를 읽었다.
(C) Teri Wilson은 Ivan Sloan의 삶에 관심이 있다.
(D) Teri Wilson는 Human Beings를 구독하고 있다.

Questions 196-200 기사문, 이메일 및 메모

업계 보고서

3월 18일– Hyde and David Marketing사는 조만간 고용하는 직원 수를 늘릴 것입니다. 회사 대변인인 Susie Ellis씨는 변화해가는 기업 관행에 적응하고자 회사는 최소한 25명을 추가 고용하겠다고 밝혔습니다.

"우리는 여전히 상품과 서비스를 홍보하는데 전통적인 수단에 지나치게 의존하고 있습니다. 하지만 온라인 마케팅의 중요성은 분명히 높아지고 있습니다." 라고 대변인이 말했습니다. " 이것 때문에, 창의적이고 마케팅 분야에 자격을 갖춘 그리고 새로운 매체에 경험도 있는 숙련된 직원들을 찾아야 합니다."

Hyde and David사는 적격인 지원자를 찾기를 희망하면서이 지역에서 열릴 취업 박람회에 참여 할 것입니다. 시카고에서 있을 다음 박람회들은 4월 2일에는 Henley Convention Hall에서 5월 4일에는 Park Community College에서 열릴 예정입니다.

Hyde and David사는 오하이오주 콜럼버스에 본사를 두고 있으며 현재 230명의 직원을 보유하고 마케팅 서비스와 상담을 제공하고 있습니다.

수신: ⟨lgaines@hoopmail.com⟩
발신: ⟨chong@ hydeanddavidmarketing.com⟩
날짜: 5월 5일
제목: 후속 내용

Gaines씨에게

어제 취업박람회에서 당신을 만나서 정말로 반가웠습니다. 당신이 David and Hyde Marketing사에서 일하는 것에 관심을 가져주어서 저는 기쁘며, Sundin School of Arts에서 만든 당신의 포트폴리오 또한 좋았습니다.

저희 디자인부서 이사님인 Hillary Kline씨와 몇몇 그녀의 직원들과 인터뷰를 위해서 와 주시기 바랍니다. 이것이 가능하다면, 오전 8시부터 오후 3시 사이에 어떤 시간이 당신에게 가장 편한지를 알려주세요.

곧 당신의 연락을 듣기를 고대하고 있습니다.

Cindy Hong
직원 채용 부서장

마케팅 직원들을 위한 메모
이번 달 마케팅 워크샵은 우리 광고활동을 위한 새로운 미디어의 사용에 초점을 맞출 것이며 6월 14일에 열릴 것입니다. 이 워크샵은 최근에 입사한 몇몇 직원들의 발표를 선보일 것이므로 아직 그들과 인사를 하지 않았다면 워크샵에서 편하게 그들에게 자신을 소개하세요(신입사원들과 인사하세요). 발표 제목과 발표자 이름은 아래와 같습니다.

소셜 네트워킹: 반발을 막는 것 – Lyle Gaines
전문적인 온라인 미디어 상호작용 – Amy Fiore
블로그와 마케팅 – Judah Reid

196. Ellis씨가 온라인 마케팅에 대해서 언급하고 있는 것은?
(A) 전통적인 마케팅보다 더 중요하다.
(B) 대학생들 사이에 공통 관심사였다.
(C) 전통적인 마케팅보다 실행하는데 더 저렴하다.
(D) 기업들이 다양한 기술을 지닌 직원을 찾게 만들고 있다.

197. 기사문에 따르면, Hyde and David Marketing사는 무엇을 하려고 준비하고 있는가?
(A) 시카고에서 열리는 행사에 대표를 파견하는 것
(B) 전문가들에게 보너스 지급을 올려 주는 것
(C) 고용 정책에 변화를 주는 것
(D) 본사를 개조 하는 것

198. 이메일을 보낸 이유는 무엇인가?
(A) 일자리 제안을 위해서
(B) 미팅 날짜를 잡기 위해서
(C) 이력서를 제출하기 위해서
(D) 작품 샘플을 요청하기 위해서

199. Hong은 아마도 Gaines씨를 어디에서 만났을까요?
(A) Park Community 대학에서
(B) Henley Convention Hall에서
(C) Hyde and David Marketing사의 본사에서
(D) Sundin School of Arts에서

200. Lyle Gaines에 대해 언급된 것은?
(A) Lyle Gaines는 최근에 Hyde and David Marketing에 고용되었다.
(B) Lyle Gaines는 대학에서 우수졸업을 했다.
(C) Lyle Gaines는 콜럼버스시, 오하이오주에 거주한다.
(D) Lyle Gaines는 Amy Fiore의 친구다.

TEST 2

PART 5

101. 지난달 건축가 Diane Lewis는 Hilldale 공립도서관 디자인으로 칭찬받았습니다.

102. 반품 및 교환에 대한 조건들은 모든 구매된 물품의 영수증 뒷면에 인쇄되어 있습니다.

103. 모든 주거 신청자들은 Goals Bank에 계좌를 개설할 때 주소지 증명서가 있는 신분증을 제공하셔야 합니다.

104. 저희 자원봉사자들의 노고덕분에 Manley Art Museum의 복원을 위한 자금을 마련하는 목표가 달성되었습니다.

105. 당신이 퇴근 할 때 사무실에 다른 직원들이 없으면, 반드시 문을 잠가 주세요.

106. 새 태블릿 컴퓨터는 4월 6일에 모든 IT 부서직원들에게 보급될 것입니다.

107. Ms. Harkin은 Mr. Vogon의 짧은 부재중에 임시로 인사과를 책임질 것입니다.

108. Flagstaff에 있는 본점을 제외하면 이 나라에 남아있는 Gilly's 후라이드 치킨 가게는 더 이상 없습니다 ⇒ 본점 빼고 다 없어졌습니다.

109. 저작권이 있는 자료의 복사는 출판업자의 서면 허가가 없다면 금지됩니다.

110. 승객들은 비행기가 이착륙하기 전에 안전벨트가 단단히 매졌는지를 확인해 주셔야 합니다.

111. Nelson Lenses사는 광범위한 양의 선택범위를 자랑합니다. 그래서 당신은 분명히 당신이 원하는 것을 구할 수 있을 것입니다 ⇒ 상품이 다양해서 당신이 원하는 것을 찾을 것입니다.

112. Round Table에서 식사하시는 모든 분들은 세 개의 코스요리를 주문하든지 그저 전체요리만 주문하든지 상관 없이 최고의 서비스를 받을 자격이 있습니다.

113. 시장과 그의 아내는 Karl Ingram이 신문에 내려고 찍은 그들의 사진에 만족하였습니다.

114. Johnson 의료센터의 사명은 각각의 환자와 직접 그들의 요구를 해결해 줄 수 있는 의료 전문가를 연결시켜주는 것입니다.

115. 직원 매뉴얼은 제품을 파손시키는 것 없이 물건을 선적하는 것을 위한 포장 기술을 상세히 설명해 놓았습니다 ⇒ 제품을 파손시키지 않고 물건을 선적하는 기술을 설명해놓았다.

116. 최신 기술을 제품에 적극적으로 통합함으로써 Polton Computers는 시장 점유율을 높였습니다.

117. 월요일에 직업 개발 세미나에 참석을 원하신다면 당신의 매니저와 얘기하세요.

118. 이번 주말에 Calvin Booksellers서점에서 모든 섹션에 있는 책들이 최대 70 퍼센트까지 할인 판매됩니다.

119. 대인 커뮤니케이션 세미나는 모든 부서의 생산성을 높이는데 일조 한 것으로 보입니다.

120. Science Monthly Journal의 기사들은 출판 에디터의 서면 동의 없이 재인쇄 될 수 없습니다.

121. 사원들은 이번 주에 발표된 메모에 의해 영업부서에 나온 공석에 대해 공지 받았습니다 ⇒ 이번 주 발표된 메모를 통해 공석에 대해 알게 되었습니다.

122. 만약 당신이 어떤 Livwell 매장에서나 쓸 수 있는 특별 상품권을 받고 싶다면, 그저 로비에 비치된 간단한 설문 조사를 작성해 주면 됩니다.

123. 버스 노선의 최근 변경사항에 관한 안내문들이 모든 Belleton Public Transit 버스 정류장에 눈에 띄게 게시되어 있습니다.

124. Menoly Metals 연구원들은 공사에 사용될 아주 강력한 강철을 만들기 위해서 통계적으로 견고한 연구 방법을 사용합니다.

125. Polver사의 겨울 코트 신규라인에 대한 높은 수요를 고려해서, 회사는 생산을 늘리기 위해 추가 공장 직원들을 고용했습니다.

126. 고객들의 편의를 증진하기 위해서, Liberty Inn은 교통과 쇼핑에 편리한 접근을 제공합니다.

127. Bill's 자동차 수리 점은 주로 다른 경쟁사보다 차를 더 빨리 수리하기 때문에 높은 수준의 고객 만족도를 가지고 있습니다.

128. 대다수의 작업장 부상은 제대로 된 안전 교육과 감독만 있다면 쉽게 예방할 수 있습니다.

129. Telson 보험사는 자사의 성공을 주로 영업부와 고객서비스부서 직원들의 헌신의 공으로 돌리고 있습니다.

130. 기록이 완벽하도록 확실히 하기 위해서, 회계부서 직원들은 타 부서에게 지출 보고서를 요청하는데 있어서 주도적으로 일을 해야 한다.

PART 6

Questions 131-134 메모

여러분은 보통 근무시간 보고서가 여러분이 업무를 끝내고나서 한 주가 끝날 때 보고되어야 한다는 것을 잘 알고 있습니다. 하지만 9월 첫 주에는 다소 변경될 것입니다. 그 주 동안 저희 회계 소프트웨어가 업데이트를 거칠 것입니다. 이로 인해, 9월 5일과 6일을 포함하는 근무 시간 보고서는 늦어도 9월 4일까지 제출해 주셔야 하며, 이것은 많은 직원들이 아직 모든 시간의 근무를 실제로는 끝내지 않았을 것임을 의미합니다. 그러므로 이 두 날짜에 해당되는 근무시간을 미리 예상해 주셔야 합니다. 만약 당신이 실질적으로 근무한 시간을 반영하기 위해서 근무기록표를 조정해야 할 필요가 있다면, 당신의 직속상관에게 나중에 요청하시면 됩니다.

Questions 135-138 서신

6월 10일
Harry Burton
IA 50647, Janesville, Illinois Avenue 9847
Burton씨에게

우리는 귀하가 Economics Monthly 잡지에 "Careers in Financial Consultation" 제목으로 기고하신 기사에 아주 흡족해 하고 있습니다.

편집자는 그 기사를 희희 8월호에 포함하고자 원하지만 현재 상태로는 기사가 희희의 글자수 제한 요건을 준수하지 않습니다. 엄밀히 말하자면, 기사가 너무 길어서 희희 Hopeful Advice 코너에 실을 수 없습니다. 가능하면 2,500 단어로 줄여야 합니다. 우리는 당신이 주니어 편집자인 Cecilia Fine와 협의하여 작업하도록 해드리겠습니다. 기사는 적절한 길이로 7월 15일까지 제출해 주셔야 합니다.

혹시 궁금하신 점이 있다면 저에게 알려주세요. 555-0086로 전화하시면 저에게 연락됩니다.

투고 담당 편집자 Tory Hillman.

Questions 139-142 이메일

수신: hbolker@emailcity.com
발신: renewal@womenstime.com
제목: 귀하의 구독 연장
날짜: 2월 28일

Bolker씨에게

이 글은 당신의 Feminine Galaxy Magazine 구독이 3월 31일 자로 만기가 될 것이라는 것을 상기시켜 드리는 안내글입니다. Feminine Galaxy가 귀하의 우체통으로 계속 배송되길 원하신다면, 구독을 갱신해주셔야 합니다.

귀하는 희희의 소중한 고객이시기 때문에, 한 해 전체를 위해 20불이라는 할인된 가격을 제공하는 바입니다. 또한 일찍 연장하시면 Home Styles와 Cars and Motors 같은 Harley & Company 출판사의 다른 잡지들의 경우도 이 할인된 요금을 누릴 수 있는 자격을 갖추게 됩니다. 이 행사는 제한된 기간 동안에만 이용가능합니다. 희희 웹사이트 www.wandapublishing.com에 방문하셔서 3월 20일까지 갱신 신청서를 작성해주시기만 하면 됩니다.

Questions 143-146 설명문

얼룩 제거하기

당신의 Forrester Furniture에 잘 지워지지 않는 얼룩을 없애기 위해 필요한 것은 약간의 베이킹 소다, 식초 그리고 부드러운 천뿐입니다. 심지어 가장 강력한 얼룩도 없애려면 단지 이 간편한 지시사항만 따르면 됩니다. 베이킹 소다 한 스푼을 준비하시고, 그것을 반 스푼의 식초와 한 스푼의 물에 섞어주세요. 베이킹 소다가 식초에 완전히 용해될 때까지 이 용액을 저어주세요. 다음은 이 용액을 천 위에 묻히시고 부드럽게 얼룩진 곳에 문지르세요. 천에 흰색 점이 남아 있다면 일단 얼룩진 곳이 마르고 난 뒤 베이킹 소다를 제거하기 위해 진공청소기를 이용하세요. 그리고 나면, 얼룩이 싹 사라진 것을 당신은 발견할 것입니다.

Questions 147-148 메시지

수신: Jamie Shwartz   오후 1시
발신: Trent Railway 승객 지원부

여행 공지: Trent 철로 47B 기차에 변경사항이 있습니다. 세부사항은 아래를 참고하세요.

Train 47B
Chicago역에서 Chattanooga역까지

지연
원래 출발 시간: 오후 1시 35분
신규 출발 시간: 오후 1시 50분
원래 도착 시간: 오후 9시 20분
신규 도착 시간: 오후 9시 35분
탑승구: 8번 플랫폼
하차 플랫폼: 9번 플랫폼

귀하의 목적지에서 다른 기차로 갈아 타실 경우에는 안내 데스크 직원에게 말씀하세요.

147. 왜 문자가 발송됐는가?

(A) 기차 일정의 변경을 알리기 위해서
(B) 탑승권 구매를 확인하기 위해서
(C) 승객에게 취소를 알리기 위해서
(D) 환승 기차에 관한 정보를 주기 위해서

148. Schwartz씨에 대해 언급되어 있는 것은?

(A) 그는 정시에 환승역에 도착 하지 못했다.
(B) 그는 시카고에서 출발 할 것이다.
(C) 그는 플랫폼에서 누군가를 만날 것이다.
(D) 그는 기차표를 Chattanooga에서 구입했다.

Questions 149-150 전단지

Hurley 항공사   저렴한 요금!

Hurley Airways 항공편을 이용하는 12인 이상의 단체는 이코노미 요금에서 20퍼센트 할인 받을 수 있습니다. 5인 이상의 가족들도 15퍼센트 할인 받을 수 있습니다. 이 할인행사에 자격을 갖추기 위해서는 9월과 10월 사이에 항공편을 이용하셔야 합니다.

이 요금들은 귀하의 여행 당일 티켓 판매대에서는 구입 할 수 없다는 것을 명심해 두십시오. 할인된 요금에 항공권을 구입하려면 비행기는 사전에 예약해야 합니다. 귀하의 단체가 확실히 할인을 받으려면 적어도 일주일 전에 희희 웹사이트 www.hurleyairways.com에서 항공권을 구입해야 합니다. 항공편, 가격, 수하물 규정 등에 관한 세부 정보는 인터넷에서 확인 바랍니다.

149. Hurley Airways에 대해서 언급되어 있는 것은?
 (A) 항공사는 9월에 적은 항공편을 운항할 계획이다.
 (B) 30여개 이상의 도시를 운항한다.
 (C) 가족 요금을 할인해 준다.
 (D) 추가 화물에 대해서는 가격을 부과하지 않는다.

150. 승객들은 무엇을 하도록 권고되고 있는가?
 (A) 신용카드로 결제 하기
 (B) 주말 항공편 이용을 피하기
 (C) 비행 당일 전에 항공권을 구매하기
 (D) 티켓 판매처에 할인에 대해서 문의하기

Questions 151-152 문자메시지 대화

ANNE BLACK	7:45 AM

Amy, 저는 같은 사무실에서 일하는 Anne입니다.

ANNE BLACK	7:46 AM

회사에 출근할 때 Preston Street으로 운전해서 가시지요?

AMY CNEY	7:47 AM

맞아요, 왜요?

ANNE BLACK	7:47 AM

오늘 출근할 때 좀 태워주실 수 있나요?

ANNE BLACK	7:48 AM

원래 Tina가 태워주는데, 오늘 아프다고 하네요.

AMY CNEY	7:48 AM

보통 때라면 당연히 승낙할 텐데요, 오늘 제 차가 카센터에 가있어요.

AMY CNEY	7:49 AM

좋으시다면 같이 택시를 타도 될 것 같아요.

ANNE BLACK	7:50 AM

좋아요. Preston도로 모퉁이 4번가에서 (택시타고 가시다가) 저를 태워주시겠어요?

AMY CNEY	7:51 AM

네, 7시 15분까지 거기로 갈게요.

151. 이들은 주로 무엇에 대해 논의하고 있는가?
 (A) 하루 휴가를 내는 것
 (B) 아픈 동료에게 연락하는 것
 (C) 출근할 방법을 찾는 것
 (D) 점심먹으러 어디를 갈지

152. 7시 48분에 Black씨가 "Can I catch a ride"라고 쓸 때 무엇을 의미하고 있는가?
 (A) Black씨는 Carney씨의 차를 빌리길 원한다.
 (B) Black씨는 Carney씨가 자기를 태워줄 것을 원한다.
 (C) Black씨는 Carney씨와 함께 버스를 타길 원한다.
 (D) Black씨는 Carney씨를 태워주고 싶어한다.

Questions 153-154 기사

Cidra Cavings씨는 곧 개봉될 SF 스릴러 Galactic Strife에 주연을 맡았습니다. 그녀는 우주 정거장을 수리하는 임무를 맡은 우주비행사, Vanna Humphrey역을 맡았는데, 우주 정거장의 한 직원이 기이하게 행동하는 것을 발견하면서 예상치 못한 전개가 이루어집니다. Jeremy Hill이 감독한 이 흥미로운 영화는 영화 보는 내내 관람객들이 손에 땀을 쥐게 만들 것입니다. 3월 13일 수요일에 극장가에 개봉될 것입니다.

153. Cidra Cavings는 누구인가?
 (A) 영화 감독
 (B) 과학자
 (C) 여배우
 (D) 우주 비행사

154. 기사문에 따르면, 3월 13일에 무슨 일이 있겠는가?
 (A) 영화평이 출간될 것이다.
 (B) 영화가 개봉 될 것이다.
 (C) 셔틀이 출발할 것이다.
 (D) 감독이 인터뷰를 할 것이다.

Questions 155-158 기사

탐험
해안가의 보석
Olivia Haverdash 작성

19세기에 세워졌지만 Svensen Lighthouse는 Sweden 남부 해안을 여행하는 여행객들에게는 엄청난 인기를 얻어왔습니다. 그 고전적인 원형 구조물은 이층 타워 정상에 밝은 번쩍거리는 불빛이 나옵니다. 타워는 150년 넘게 이용 중이며 빨간색 줄무늬에 야광 흰색 페인트가 칠해져 있습니다. 타워는 여러 차례 복원되었고 1910년대에 높이가 10미터(30피트) 높아졌습니다. 가장 최근에는 작년 말에 복원을 했고 이 아름다운 스웨덴의 해안지역으로 사람들을 유치하고 있습니다.

그 건축물이 방문객들을 다시 허용한 이래로 관광객들은 대규모로 스웨덴의 이 지역으로 오고 있습니다. 지난 9월에는 등대 소유주에 의해 국제적인 예술 박람회를 개최되기도 했습니다. 그는 예술 애호가이며 매년 예술 행사를 열기를 바라고 있습니다. 그렇지만 연간 아무 때나 등대를 방문하셔도 항상 좋습니다. Sheila Comstock씨는 거의 매일 관광객들을 이 해안으로 데려 오고 있으며 "많은 사람들이 이런 종류의 투어를 좋아하며 이런 스타일의 구조물을 또한 매우 좋아한다"고 그녀가 말합니다. Comstock씨는 Sundsvall에서 버스를 타는 것이 등대를 찾아오기 가장 손쉬운 방법이며, 또한 이 나라의 경치를 즐길 수도 있다고 덧붙였습니다.

등대는 6월에 방송되는 Svensen 지역에 관한 TV 프로그램에도 나올 것입니다. www.swedenlh.sw 에 가시면 스웨덴의 등대에 관한 더 많은 정보를 찾아보실 수 있습니다.

155. Svensen Lighthouse에 대해서 언급되어 있는 것은?
 (A) 현재 선박들을 안내하는 것을 지원하고 있다.
 (B) Sundsvall 소유의 부동산이다.
 (C) 150년 동안 같은 모습으로 남아있다.
 (D) 지어진 이래로 관광객들을 허용하고 있다.

156. Comstock씨는 누구일 가능성이 가장 높은가?
 (A) 여행 전문 기자
 (B) 배 선장
 (C) TV 프로그램 사회자
 (D) 관광 가이드

157. Comstock씨는 Svensen 등대에 오는 방문객들이 무엇을 할 것을 제안하고 있습니까?
 (A) 버스로 그곳을 방문할 것
 (B) 9월에 그 지역을 방문할 것
 (C) 미리 예약을 할 것
 (D) 웹사이트를 방문 할 것

158. 6월에 무슨 일이 있겠는가?
 (A) 구조물이 개조에 들어 갈 것이다.
 (B) 특별 투어가 있을 것이다.
 (C) 다큐멘터리가 TV에서 방영될 것이다.
 (D) 국제 예술 박람회가 개장할 것이다.

Questions 159-161 이메일

수신: Harper Manufacturing 직원들
발신: Alphonse Grave
제목: 연례 건의사항 요청
날짜: 7월 14일

Harper Manufacturing사는 최고의 고용 경험을 직원들에게 제공하려고 노력하지만 우리는 여전히 일부 분야에서는 개선이 필요하다는 것을 압니다. —[1]— 그래서 우리는 규정, 관리, 우리가 제조하는 물품, 사원 복지 및 마케팅과 같은 분야에서 우리가 무엇을 할 수 있는지에 대한 여러분의 의견을 해마다 받고자 합니다. —[2]—

여기서 근무하는 것이 사원들에게 만족스럽도록 확실히 만들고 싶습니다. 그래서 사원 관리부서에서 7월 30일까지 직장 만족 설문지를 작성해서 제출 하도록 요청하는 바입니다. 설문지 양식은 여기에 클릭을 하시면 Jacob's Consultation 웹사이트에서 받으실 수 있습니다. —[3]—

여러분의 답변들은 비밀로 부쳐질 것이며, 응답자가 누구인지를 알 수 있는 정보는 양식 어디에도 없음을 알려드립니다. 작성된 질문지는 Jacob's Consultation에 컨설턴트에게 바로 전달될 것입니다. —[4]—

혹시 궁금한 점이 있으면 전화나 이메일로 알려주세요.

Alphonse Grave
사원 관리 이사

159. Harper Manufacturing에 대해서 언급 되어 있는 것은?
 (A) 회사는 직원들에게 해마다 설문지를 작성하도록 요청한다.
 (B) 회사는 데이터 베이스와 정보를 관리한다.
 (C) 설문지의 답변을 공개한다.
 (D) 사원들에게 훌륭한 복리후생을 제공한다.

160. 이메일에 따르면, 7월 30일까지 무슨 일이 발생할까?
 (A) 신상품이 제조된다.
 (B) 복리후생이 변경된다.
 (C) 직원들은 회사 홈페이지에 접속할 것이다.
 (D) 설문조사의 결과가 공개될 것이다.

161. [1], [2], [3], [4]로 표시된 자리 중에 다음 문장이 들어가기에 가장 적합한 곳은?

"그들이 결과를 검토한 후에, 사원 관리부서와 결과를 의논할 것입니다."
 (A) [1]
 (B) [2]
 (C) [3]
 (D) [4]

Questions 162-165 인터넷 채팅 대화

Marshall Dennis [1:20 p.m.]
오늘 Paula Castillo를 보신 분 있나요? 신임 시장님에 대한 그녀의 기사에 대해 업데이트(어떻게 되어 가는지에 대한 소식)가 필요해서요.

Dane Houston [1:21 p.m.]
제가 오늘 아침에 Paula Castillo와 얘기했어요. 시장님의 이전 동료와 인터뷰를 하기 위해 외근 나가는 중이었어요. 점심식사시간 후에 돌아온다고 얘기했습니다.

Marshall Dennis [1:22 p.m.]
정확히 언제인지는 모르나요? 수석편집장이 기사가 언제 인쇄 가능한지 알고 싶어합니다.

Dane Houston [1:23 p.m.]
죄송해요, 상관님. 거기까지는 모르겠습니다. 아침에 일정이 꽉 차있고, 점심시간 후에나 돌아올 거라고만 얘기했습니다. 제가 아는 한, 오늘 오후 늦게 신임 시장과 인터뷰가 있는 것 같습니다.

Elle Goldberg [1:25 p.m.]
제가 방금 시장님 비서와 확인해봤어요. Castillo가 3시에 시청 집무실에서 Brian Greenwood와 만날 거랍니다. Dennis, 당신이 Castillo와 얘기를 나누려면 Castillo가 사무실에 2시 전에는 도착해야겠네요.

Marshall Dennis [1:27 p.m.]
맞아요, Elle. 그녀가 돌아오면 제 사무실로 오라고 얘기해주세요. Castillo가 시장에게 그의 계산안에 대한 질문을 꼭 하도록 당부하고 싶어서요.

Elle Goldberg [1:28 p.m.]
제가 알기로 이미 그 문제에 대한 질문을 Castillo가 준비한 것 같던데요. 그렇지만, 그녀가 돌아오면 당신이 이 문제를 꼭 살피기를 원한다고 알리겠습니다.

Marshall Dennis [1:30 p.m.]
고마워요. 그런데 Dane, 제 사무실에 와줄 수 있나요? 내일 자에 실을 수 있도록 페스티벌 관련 당신 기사에 대한 최종 편집을 하고 싶어서요.

Dane Houston [1:31 p.m.]
네, 바로 가겠습니다.

162. 대화자들은 어떤 회사에 근무할 가능성이 가장 높은가?
(A) 출판사
(B) 마케팅 회사
(C) 신문사
(D) 컨설팅 회사

163. Brian Greenwood는 누구일까요?
(A) 새로 선출된 공직자
(B) 신문사 기자
(C) 예산관련 컨설턴트
(D) 비서

164. 1시 23분에 Dane Houston씨가 "she had a packed morning" 라고 쓸 때 무엇을 의미하고 있는가?
(A) Castillo씨가 집에서 점심을 싸왔다.
(B) Castillo씨는 아침에 근무하지 않을 것이다.
(C) Castillo씨는 오늘 아침에 일찍 일어났다.
(D) Castillo씨는 점심시간까지 매우 바쁘다.

165. Marshall Dennis에 대해 언급된 것은?
(A) Dennis는 한 번에 여러 개의 기사를 작성한다.
(B) Dennis는 시청과 긴밀한 관계로 일한다.
(C) Dennis는 관리직책에 있는 사람이다.
(D) Dennis는 Houston의 작업이 마음에 들지 않는다.

Questions 166-168 편지

Porton Monorail
2월 2일
친애하는 승객 여러분

모노레일 운영비가 계속해서 상승하기 때문에 우리는 2월 15일부터 요금을 인상하지 않을 수 없게 되었습니다. 성인, 대학생, 취학아동 요금은 7 퍼센트 인상될 것이고 7세 이하의 어린이들은 여전히 요금을 지불할 필요가 없을 것입니다.

이 요금 인상으로 인해 고객들께서 겪으실 불편에 사과 드립니다. 하지만 이것이 6년 만에 처음으로 요금 인상을 하는 것이라는 점을 알아주시기 바랍니다. 요금으로 버는 모든 수익은 직원들의 급여와 정기적으로 모노레일을 유지 관리하는데 들어갑니다.

Porton Monorail 이용해 주셔서 여러분들께 대단히 감사 드립니다.

166. Porton Monorail에 대해서 유추 할 수 있는 것은?
(A) 공사로 인해 노선을 변경 할 것이다.
(B) 6년 전에 요금을 인상했었다.
(C) 승객들에게 제안을 요청할 것이다.
(D) 최근에 서비스 이용객들이 줄었음을 목격하고 있다.

167. 대학생들에 대해서 언급되어 있는 것은?
(A) 그들은 학교로부터 할인 카드를 받을 수 있다.
(B) 그들의 요금은 성인요금과 동일한 비율로 오를 것이다.
(C) 학생 요금을 받기 위해서는 신분증을 갱신해야 한다.
(D) 더 이상 그들에게 특별요금은 제공 되지 않을 것이다.

168. 공지에 따르면, 요금을 통해 얻어진 수익은 쓰여진 방식 중의 하나는 무엇인가?
(A) 직원들을 보상하는데
(B) 노선 수를 늘리는 데
(C) 기차역을 복구하는 데
(D) 서비스를 홍보하는데

Questions 169-171 공지문

Hector Rodriguez씨 Chapala 시청에서 강연

수상경력을 가진 작가이자 Quatro Perro사의 대표이사인 Hector Rodriguez씨가 4월 4일에 Chapala 시청에서 강연을 할 것입니다. 이번 강연은 재계에 영향을 미치는 법에 초점이 맞춰질 것입니다. 연설 후에 Rodriguez씨는 시청의 남관에서 그의 책 중 어느 책이건 (가지고 오시면) 사인을 해줄 것입니다. 입장료는 없지만 자리가 제한되어 있는 관계로 참가자들께서는 4월 1일까지 등록을 하셔야 합니다. 등록이나 정보를 얻고자 원하시면 주최자인 Maria Ortega (mortega@chapalacity.go.mx)에게 이메일을 주세요.

Rodriguez씨는 Hernandez Industries사에서 영업 사원으로 첫 직장을 시작하였고 승진도 빨랐습니다. Hernandez사에서 10년간 근무한 후에 자신의 회사를 차렸고 큰 성공을 얻게 되었습니다. 그의 신간 서적인 Stand Tall and Succeed는 4월 3일부터 서점에서 이용 가능할 것입니다.

169. 어떤 이벤트가 홍보되는가?
(A) 회사 개업식
(B) 회사의 성공 축하연
(C) 수상자 축하연
(D) 비즈니스관련 강연

170. Hector Rodriguez씨에 대해서 언급되어 있는 것은?
(A) 회사 창업을 준비 중에 있다.
(B) 웹사이트에 기사를 기고한다.
(C) Chapala 시청을 자주 방문한다.
(D) 여러 권의 책을 집필했다.

171. 행사 전에 참가자들은 무엇을 하도록 요구 받는가?
 (A) Hector Rodriguez씨에게 이메일을 쓰는 것
 (B) 입장표를 구매 하는 것
 (C) Maria Ortega씨에게 연락 하는 것
 (D) 시청 청사 남관으로 가는 것

Questions 172-175 기사

7월 10일– Lorville Association of Developing Culture (LADC)는 Harold Miller를 2년에 한번 열리는 제5회 아마추어 그림 공모전에 수상자로 선정했다는 성명서를 발표했습니다. Miller씨의 그림 "Letters Upon Letters"와 대회에 참가한 분들의 작품들이 8월 10일부터 28일까지 LADC 갤러리에서 전시될 것입니다. 전시회 첫날에 개회식이 열릴 것이며, 그곳에서 Miller씨가 그의 성과를 인정해서 수여되는 2,000달러의 상금을 LADC 의장인 Nancy Mael씨로부터 받을 것입니다. —[1]—

LADC는 또한 웹사이트에서 그림들을 볼 수 있도록 할 것인데, 이는 협회에서 이전에는 한 번도 하지 않았던 것입니다. —[2]— "저희는 온라인 갤러리가 더 많은 사람들에게 지역의 재능 있는 아마추어 화가들의 그림들을 즐길 수 있게 해 줄 것을 희망합니다"라고 Mael씨가 말했습니다. —[3]—

갤러리가 8월 30일부터 9월 28일까지 연례 가을 휴식기 동안에는 열지 않는 다는 것을 주민들께서는 기억해주시기 바랍니다. 갤러리의 새 시즌은 음대 교수인 Dr. James Haver씨의 재즈음악 역사에 대한 강연과 함께 9월 30일에 시작됩니다. —[4]—

172. 기사의 목적이 아닌 것은?
 (A) 대회 우승자를 발표하기 위해서
 (B) 웹사이트의 업데이트를 홍보하기 위해서
 (C) 협회 이사장의 이력을 설명하기 위해서
 (D) 곧 있을 강연을 알리기 위해서

173. Miller씨에 대해서 언급되어 있는 것은?
 (A) 그는 미술 강사이다.
 (B) 그는 6월에 그림 대회를 심사 할 것이다.
 (C) 그는 8월 10일 갤러리 행사에 참여 할 것이다.
 (D) 그는 문화단체에서 근무 한다.

174. 갤러리에 대해서 기사가 언급하고 있는 것은?
 (A) 주민들에게 미술 수업을 제공한다.
 (B) 이전 대회의 그림들이 웹사이트에 게재될 것이다.
 (C) 최근에 개조를 했다.
 (D) 이번 그림 전시회는 이번 시즌 마지막 전시회다.

175. [1], [2], [3], [4]로 표시된 자리 중에 다음 문장이 들어가기에 가장 적합한 곳은?

 "전시회에 별도 입장료는 없지만 LADC를 후원하는 기부금은 감사히 받겠습니다."

 (A) [1]
 (B) [2]
 (C) [3]
 (D) [4]

Questions 176-180 지침서와 기사

Mara & Associates
소개표지 만들 때 참고하시 길 바랍니다.

설문조사 잠재 응답자에게 배포되는 각 설문 조사지의 첫 페이지는 소개표지가 되어야 합니다. 소개표지는 참가자들의 응답의 가치와 중요성을 설명함으로써 설문조사에 참여를 유도할 기회를 조사관들에게 제공합니다. 소개표지는 이해하기 쉬워야 하며, 그래서 쉬운 언어로 작성되어야 하고 응답자들에게 아래 나열된 정보를 제공해야 합니다.

- 조사가 시행되는 이유
- 누가 조사를 시행하고 있으며 질문지를 만들었는지
- 설문지에 응답하는 것의 중요성
- 설문조사가 얼마나 긴지 (예: 2페이지)
- 설문조사를 마치는데 얼마나 걸릴지
- 작성된 설문지가 언제까지 제출되어야 하는지
- 답변이 기밀로 처리될 지의 여부와 무엇을 위해 사용될 지

Mara & Associates
P.O. Box 564388 · Atlanta, GE 30312

8월 6일

Lupita Rose
2983 Delouise Drive
Monroe, LA 71212

Rose씨에게:

Strong Life Exercise Equipment는 Strong Life제품을 인터넷에서 구매하는 소비자를 설문조사하기 위해 Mara & Associates를 고용했습니다. 귀하는 6월 18일에 Strong Life 제품을 온라인에서 구매하셨기 때문에 이 설문지 중 하나를 받아보시도록 특별히 선정되셨습니다. 귀하가 작성해주신 설문지는 인터넷 상에서 운동기구를 구매할 때 고객분들은 무엇이 중요하다고 생각하는지를 저희가 배울 수 있게 도와줄 것입니다.

2페이지 짜리 설문지에 있는 질문에 답하시고 기한인 9월 30일까지 돌려보내주세요. 귀하의 편의를 위해 저희 주소가 적힌 요금별납 봉투를 동봉하였습니다. 모든 설문조사는 기밀로 유지될 것이기 때문에 귀하의 이름이나 연락처와 같은 개인정보는 기재하지 말아주세요. 모든 설문응답에 대한 요약본이 11월 30일에 공개될 것입니다. 만약 (요약본의) 인쇄본을 받아보시길 원하신다면 설문지 마지막 페이지에서 이 사항을 표시하는 박스에 표시해주시기 바랍니다.

Mara & Associates

동봉

176. Mara & Associates는 어떤 종류의 회사일 가능성이 높은가요?
(A) 생물학 연구 단체
(B) 운동 제품 제조사
(C) 소비자 리서치 기관
(D) 기업 교육 컨설팅 회사

177. 지침서는 Mara & Associaties 직원들에 의해 작성된 소개표지에 대해 무엇을 암시하고 있는가?
(A) 소개표지는 한 페이지로 구성된다.
(B) 소개표지는 다양한 언어로 제공될 수 있다.
(C) 소개 표지는 일반적으로 기밀 정보를 포함한다.
(D) Mara & Associates의 조직강령을 전달한다.

178. 서신에 따르면 Rose씨는 최근에 무엇을 했나요?
(A) Rose씨는 공석에 대한 지원서를 제출했다.
(B) Rose씨는 잘못된 제품에 대해 항의했다.
(C) Rose씨는 인터넷에서 제품을 구매했다.
(D) Rose씨는 마케팅 회사를 고용했다.

179. 지침서에 언급된 정보 중 서신에 포함되어 있지 않은 것은?
(A) 양식이 제출되어야 하는 마감 일자
(B) 설문조사가 몇 페이지로 구성되어 있는지
(C) 설문조사를 제작한 업체
(D) 설문지를 작성하는데 걸리는 시간

180. 서신에 따르면 Rose씨는 무엇을 요청할 수 있나요?
(A) 향후 구매에 대한 할인
(B) 설문조사의 결과
(C) 영수증의 사본
(D) 제품 카달로그

Questions 181-185 기사와 이메일

Inglewood University의
건축과 다시 성공가도를 달리다
Marilyn Nedson 기자

Inglewood (1월 10일) – 5년 연속 Inglewood University의 프로젝트가 명망 있는 Mitchell-McBrien 메달 중 하나에 후보로 선정되었습니다. 건축학과 학생들에 의해 설계된 Ballard Building이 Best Design 카테고리에 후보로 발표되었습니다.
이 메달은 건축분야에 업적을 기리기 위해 전세계 젊은 건축가들에게 수여됩니다. 이 메달을 수여하는 기관은 건축분야에 신예 건축가들을 독려하려는 주목적을 가지고 설립되었습니다. 이 메달은 모두가 받고 싶어하는 메달입니다.

"현장에 있는 실제 전문가들과 함께 작업하는 것은 학생들이 소중한 경험을 쌓게 해주고 학생들이 추구하는 직업이 실제 어떤 모습인지를 볼 수 있게 해줍니다"라고 Neighbors씨가 얘기합니다.
Ballard Building은, 이전에 후보로 올랐던 Inglewood의 다른 프로젝트와 마찬가지로 이 프로그램에 참여했던 학생들에 의해 만들어졌습니다. 이 학생들의 멘토인, Polysum Design의 건축가 Nia Varice씨는 이 프로젝트의 시작 때부터 학생들과 함께 작업해왔습니다. Nia Varice씨는 프로그램 초창기부터 그녀의 시간을 할애해 줄 만큼 너그러웠지만 그녀의 제자들이 후보지명이 된 것은 이번이 처음입니다. "보통 저에게 보상은 젊

Inglewood University의 학장인 Ian Neighbors씨는 Inglewood 학생들이 여러 번 후보로 선정된 이유가 이 대학의 멘토링 프로그램인 Inglewood Mentors에 기인한다고 생각하고 있습니다. 이 프로그램의 목적은 건축과 학생들을 이미 현장에서 일하고 있는 건축가들과 연결시켜서 1년의 기간 동안 프로젝트와 관련하여 학생들을 지원해 주는 것입니다.

은이들과 일을 한다는 것 자체였습니다(젊은이들과 일하는 것 만으로 보람이었습니다)" Varice씨가 말합니다. "이 상에 그들이 후보지명이 된 것은 훨씬 더 신이 나네요". 수상자들은 3월 5일에 발표될 예정입니다. Ballard Building의 완성된 설계를 보고 싶은 분들은 Inglewood University 도서관에 방문해주시기 바랍니다. 그 곳에서 2월말까지 전시될 것입니다.

수신자: Nia Varice ⟨nvarice@polysumdesign.com⟩
발신자: Jerry Ling ⟨jling@somemail.com⟩
주제: 굉장한 소식
날짜: 3월 6일

Dear Nia,

오늘 Lancing Herald에 난 Ballard Building 관련 기사를 읽었습니다. 축하 드립니다. Inglewood의 건축과도 매우 기쁘겠지만 당신 회사도 마찬가지로 매우 기쁘겠네요. 여러 얘기도 나눌 겸 곧 한번 만났으면 합니다. Polysum사가 새로운 Sonitor Planetarium 작업을 하고 있다는 소식도 들었습니다. 언제든 시간 나시면, 어떻게 진행되고 있는지도 들어보고 그리고 멘토링에 대해서도 당신에게 조언을 들어보면 좋을 것 같습니다.

Jerry

181. Mitchell-McBrien Medals에 대해 언급된 것은?
(A) 이 메달은 3년마다 수여된다.
(B) 이 메달은 현재 Inglewood University 도서관에 전시되어 있다.
(C) 이 메달은 국적을 가리지 않고 전세계 학생들에게 수여된다.
(D) 이 메달은 훌륭한 멘토에게 수여된다.

182. Inglewood Mentors 프로그램에 대해 언급된 것은?
(A) 학생들이 전문가의 지원을 받게 해준다.
(B) 학생들에게 자금을 지원해준다.
(C) 학생들이 다른 학생들에게 멘토 역할을 하게 해준다.
(D) 공동 프로젝트를 위해서 다양한 대학의 학생들을 연결해준다.

183. Varice씨에 대해 언급된 것은?
(A) Varice씨는 Inglewood University에서 학위를 받았다.
(B) Varice씨는 그녀 자신의 건축회사를 설립했다.
(C) Varice씨는 심사 받은 모든 프로젝트의 멘토역할을 했다.
(D) Varice씨는 프로그램이 시작했을 때부터 멘토역할을 해왔다.

184. Ling씨가 Varice씨를 축하하는 이유는?
(A) Varice씨는 잡지에서 주목 받은 건축가였다(잡지에 그녀에 대한 집중 기사가 났다)
(B) Varice씨가 연봉인상을 받았다.
(C) Varice씨와 함께 작업한 학생들에게 상이 수여되었다.
(D) Varice씨의 회사가 큰 규모의 지원금을 받았다.

185. Ling씨는 누구일까요?
(A) Varice씨의 감독관
(B) Varice씨의 학생
(C) Polysum Design의 직원
(D) Inglewood Mentors의 자원봉사자(멘토)

Questions 186–190 발표문, 회원가입양식 및 기사

The Society for Arts Preservation은
'A Night with the Stars'의
첫 발표에 귀하를 모시고자 합니다.

출연 Bradley Kowalski
6월 13일 목요일 오후 8시
Candlelight Theater

유명 영화배우인 Bradley Kowalski는 여러 나라로의 여행과 존경 받는 감독들과의 작업 그리고 음악가 Sheila Son과의 협력작업 등을 포함한 그의 45년간의 배우생활에 대해 이야기를 할 것입니다.

입장료 – 12불
학생요금 – 9불

프레젠테이션 이후 리셉션: 오후 9시 30분부터 오후 11시(사전예약 필수)
The Society for Arts Preservation의 지원담당자에게 1-800-555-8663로 전화하셔서 예약하세요.

오늘 회원으로 가입하셔서 The Society for Arts Preservation(TSAP)를 후원해 주세요.

후원자들은 아래와 같은 혜택을 누릴 수 있습니다.
TSAP 행사에 입장료 면제(A Night with the Stars 프레젠테이션은 제외)
행사 이후에 열리는 리셉션에 별도 예약이 필요 없습니다.
저희 월간지 Arts Preservation Now가 귀하의 가정으로 직접 배송됩니다.
개인 회원은 연회비가 40불이며 가족 회원은 연회비가 60불입니다.
이름 _____
주소 _____
전화번호 _____
회원등급선택 및 결제 _____

작성된 양식은 다음 주소로 보내주세요:

97211 OR, Portland, Washington 가 808, TSAP, 지원 담당자, Barbara Lueck

---

Bradley Kowalski씨와의 멋진 밤
– Arts Preservation Now 수석 편집장, Cooper Cohn

이번 달 "A Night with the Stars"는 우리 멤버들 덕분에 TSAP의 지금껏 가장 큰 행사가 되었습니다. Bradley Kowalski씨는 많은 웃음을 자아내면서 그의 강연 중에 Andrew Geddes과의 얘기 등 많은 멋진 얘기들을 들려주었습니다. Kowalski씨는 강연과 리셉션이 너무 즐거웠고 향후에 다시 한번 출연하고 싶다고 얘기했습니다. TSAP가 이런 행사를 마련할 수 있는 것은 우리 회원들의 지원 덕분입니다. 저희 회원들은 "A Night with the Stars"의 리셉션이나 다른 많은 행사에 우대권을 받게 되므로 저희 회원들은 다시 회원가입 재등록을 하실 것을 잊지 마시기 바랍니다.

186. 이 광고는 무엇에 대한 것인가?
(A) 영화
(B) 극장 개장
(C) 강연
(D) 콘서트

187. 6월 13일 이벤트에 관해서 언급되어 있는 것은?
(A) The Society for Arts Preservation회원은 강연 입장료 12불을 내야 합니다.
(B) 예약은 TSAP 웹사이트에서 가능합니다.
(C) 질의 응답시간이 있습니다.
(D) TSAP 후원자들만 참여 할 수 있습니다.

188. 6월 13일 행사 이후에 리셉션에 참여를 원하면 어떻게 해야 합니까?
(A) Bradley Kowalski의 비서에게 얘기를 해야 한다.
(B) Candlelight Theater에서 표를 구매해야 한다.
(C) Sheila Son에게 얘기해야 한다.
(D) Barbara Lueck에게 전화해야 한다.

189. 기사문, 첫 번째 문단, 두 번째 줄의 "largely"가 의미상 가장 가까운 것은?
(A) 널찍하게
(B) 주로
(C) 크게
(D) 듬성듬성하게

190. 이 기사는 어디에 등장했을 가능성이 가장 높은가?
(A) 전국 예술관련 신문
(B) 극장의 웹사이트
(C) 조직의 월간 잡지
(D) 행사에 관한 팜플렛

Questions 191–195 이메일, 정보 및 이메일

발신: Suda Hunsuk ⟨shunsuk@portmobile.com⟩
수신: Paj Poonpratin ⟨ppoonpratin@tomindustries.com⟩
날짜: 11월 19일
제목: 귀하의 주문

Poonpratin씨에게

저희 Port Mobile사는 귀하의 이동통신 서비스 제공업자로서 저희 회사를 선택해 주셔서 대단히 감사합니다. 귀하의 휴대폰과 서비스에 관한 자세한 구매 내역은 아래와 같습니다.

제품명	주문량	서비스
Patti	6	National Advantage
Moody	12	Country Light
Phatta	6	Fast Lane
Hoot	2	Top Speed

저희는 저희 Chiang Rai 대리점에서 5일 이내에 전화를 보내드릴 것입니다. 전화를 받으시면, 이 전화를 사용해서 (+66 351) 555-4868로 전화 주셔서 기기를 활성화 시키셔야 합니다. 고객님이 요청 하신 대로 월정액은 귀하의 Tom Industries 신용카드로 청구됩니다. 선결제 서비스를 이용하는 전화들은 잔액이 4불 이하로 떨어지면 전화로 문자를 받게 될 것입니다. 추가 적립은 웹사이트나 전화를 통해 충전될 수 있습니다.

거래에 다시 한번 감사의 말씀 전하며 앞으로도 계속해서 귀하에게 서비스를 제공할 수 있게 되기를 희망합니다.

Suda Hunsuk
Port Mobile

법인 고객 분들을 위한 이동 통신 서비스 상품들은 아래와 같습니다. 무제한 데이터 용량과 무제한 국내 전화 통화의 혜택이 있는 상품을 이용하시는 고객들은 주말에는 무료 해외 전화 이용이 가능합니다.

서비스 특징

서비스	전화량		데이터	요금 (월별)
	국내	해외		
Top Speed	무제한	600 분	무제한	60 불
National Advantage	무제한	200 분	6 기가바이트	40 불
Country Light	250분	0 분	12 기가바이트	25 불
Fast Lane (선불)	0 분	0 분	0 기가바이트	0 불

추가 요금 (시간과 데이터의 월간 이용량 초과시 청구됨)

추가 해외 전화	추가 데이터	추가 국내전화
분당 0.25 불	기가바이트당 5.00 불	분당 0.10 불

수신자: Paj Poonpratin <ppoonpratin@tomindustries.com>
발신자: Country Light <customerservice@countrylight.com>
날짜: 1월 7일
주제: 회신: 서비스 변경

Poonpratin씨에게,

귀하의 전화에 서비스를 업그레이드 하는 것과 관련하여 저희에게 연락주셔서 감사합니다. 1월 10일부터 귀하의 서비스는 National Advantage로 업그레이드될 것입니다. 귀하의 거래에 대한 감사의 뜻으로, 지난 달 귀하의 계정에 사용된 추가 기가바이트에 대한 10불의 요금은 공제될 것입니다. 이는 다음 청구서에 반영될 것입니다. 저희 서비스를 애용해 주셔서 다시 한번 감사 드립니다.

Leonard Magnotta
Country Light 고객지원 직원

191. Poonpratin씨는 어떻게 기기를 활성화시키라고 지시 받았는가?
(A) 기기를 매장에 가지고 옮으로써
(B) 전화로 번호를 누름으로써
(C) 문자 메시지를 보냄으로써
(D) 인터넷 상점을 방문함으로써

192. 두 번째 지문(정보문)에서 제공된 것은 무엇인가?
(A) 서비스별 요금
(B) 기기 사양
(C) 배송 옵션
(D) 회사 정보

193. 고객들이 주말에 무료 해외 전화를 걸 수 있도록 허용하는 것은 어떤 상품인가?
(A) Top Speed
(B) National Advantage
(C) Country Light
(D) Fast Lane

194. 누가 계정 정보를 자동으로 문자 메시지로 받게 되는가?
(A) Patti 전화기 소유자
(B) Moody 전화기 소유자
(C) Phatta 전화기 소유자
(D) Hoot 전화기 소유자

195. 지난 달 Poonpratin씨의 서비스 사용에 대해 언급된 것은?
(A) Poonpratin씨는 이전에 Fast Lane 서비스를 사용했다.
(B) Poonpratin씨는 추가 데이터 2GB를 사용했다.
(C) Poonpratin씨는 서비스에 대해 요금을 청구 받지 않았다.
(D) Poonpratin씨는 국내 전화를 추가로 사용했다.

Questions 196-200 지침서, 양식 및 이메일

Gorland Business 혁신 Convention – 발표자 안내서

제안서 제출하기:
제안서 양식을 이용해서 웹사이트에서 기획서 보내기
제안서는 다음 같은 사항을 갖추어야 합니다.
- 프레젠테이션이나 강연 요약
- 발표자의 프로필
- 발표자와 연락하는 방법

기억하세요:
- 컨벤션 제안서는 4월 4일부터 접수 받으며 접수 마감은 4월 23일 입니다. 이 규정에 예외는 없습니다.
- 특정 상품에 대한 마케팅 발표(마케팅을 위한 발표)는 용납되지 않습니다.
- 귀하의 제안서가 수락되면 3주 이내에 연락이 갈 것입니다.

발표자들이 반드시 지켜야 할 사항:
- 귀하의 제안서에 설명된 주제에 관해서 전문가 수준으로 발표해 주세요.
- 귀하의 발표를 위해 필요하신 시청각 장비를 준비하기 위해 적어도 발표 3주 전에 행사 주최자와 상의하세요.

프레젠테이션 제안서 제출 양식

발표자 이름: Frank Conning　　　　직업: 선임 마케팅 이사
회사: Electron Corp.　　　　　　　날짜: 4월 29일
E-mail: fconning@electroncorp.com　전화번호: 683-555-8863
프로필: 첨부된 파일을 참고하세요

발표 주제: 디지털 세대의 성공

발표요약: 많은 고객들은 회사의 웹사이트를 방문하며 이것이 그 기업에 대한 첫 인상을 만들어줍니다. 하지만 회사들은 상품과 서비스를 홍보하는데 웹사이트를 어떻게 하면 최대한 이용할 수 있는지에 대한 지식이 부족합니다. 이번 발표는 어떻게 기업들이 인터넷을 이용해서 고객들을 성공적으로 유치 하느냐를 보여 줄 것입니다.

발표 형식: ___ 패널 토론　　　___ 컨벤션 이전 세미나
　　　　　　 X　컨벤션 발표　　 X　나는 발표자 안내서를 검토해 봤다.

수신자: Frank Conning 〈fconning@electroncorp.com〉
발신자: Jill Avery 〈javery@gbi.org〉
날짜: 5월 2일
주제: 당신의 제안서

Conning씨에게,

저희가 올해 컨벤션을 위해 귀하의 발표제안서를 수락할 수 없음에도 불구하고, Gorland Business Innovation Association는 여전히 이 제안서의 주제가 선견지명이 있고 흥미롭다고 생각합니다. 만약 가능하다면, 저희는 컨벤션 한달 후인 8월에 GBIA에서 개최를 준비하고 있는 엑스포, 공개토론에 귀하를 포함시키고 싶습니다. 엑스포 공개토론에 한 가지 장점은, 당신이 원한다면 토론 중에 귀하의 회사를 자유롭게 홍보할 수 있다는 점입니다. 관심 있으시면 본 메일로 저에게 답장해주시기 바랍니다.

Jill Avery
총괄매니저
Gorland Business Innovation Association

196. 지침서의 목적은 무엇인가?
(A) 컨벤션에서 회사가 상품을 팔려면 무엇을 해야 하는지 목록을 작성하려고
(B) 발표를 더 잘 하기위한 조언을 하기 위해서
(C) 컨벤션 등록 설명을 하기 위해서
(D) 장래 발표자에게 컨벤션 요건에 대해 설명해주기 위해서

197. 컨벤션 발표자들은 무엇을 하도록 요구되는가?
(A) 컨벤션 주최자와 협의하는 것
(B) 오리엔테이션에 가는 것
(C) 안내서의 사본에 서명해서 보내는 것
(D) 추천 목록을 제출 하는 것

198. Conning씨는 누구인가?
(A) Gorland Business Innovation Convention 직원
(B) 한 기업에 이사
(C) 세미나 참가자
(D) Electron Corp 회사 고객

199. 왜 Conning씨의 제안서가 아마도 거부될까요?
(A) 그의 회사 상품을 광고해서
(B) 요구된 정보를 담고 있지 않아서
(C) 마감이 지나서 제출되어서
(D) 작년 컨벤션에 제출된 것이어서

200. 8월에 열릴 공개토론에 주제는 무엇일까요?
(A) 인터넷 마케팅의 사용을 개선하는 것
(B) 잠재고객을 대상으로 한 발표의 질을 개선하는 것
(C) 엑스포 환경에서 업체를 선보이는 것
(D) 환경친화적인 사업 관행을 활용하는 것

TEST 3

PART 5

101. Elling Web Radio는 온라인을 통해서 음악 애호가들에게 온라인 음악 서비스를 제공하게 되어서 흥분됩니다.

102. Sherley Banking Services는 인터넷 뱅킹을 제공하고 고객들이 온라인으로 다양한 지원 서비스를 받을 수 있도록 하고 있습니다.

103. Cold Rock사의 최신 겨울 신상 재킷은 가게에 거의 출시되자 마자 모두 품절 되었습니다.

104. 공사 보조금을 받기 위한 서류 작업은 모든 항목들이 작성되기 전에 실수로 제출 되었습니다.

105. Holbrook Books Online은 아주 단기간에 가장 인기 있는 온라인 서점 중 하나가 되었습니다.

106. Isen Industries사의 많은 직원들은 정규직 일자리를 제공 받기 전에 인턴으로 경력을 시작했습니다.

107. Headley Credit Card에 대한 당신의 신청서를 처리하는 것을 위해 2주 내지 3주 정도를 허용하세요 ⇒ 감안하세요.

108. 귀하는 다음주 말까지 수정된 사업 계획서를 마케팅 팀장에게 제출해 주셔야 합니다.

109. 여러 발표자들의 일정이 Expo 일정과 겹치기 때문에 Kitchen Appliance Expo가 미뤄졌습니다.

110. 최근 연구에 따르면, 중국에서 해마다 대략 백만 명의 사망 건이 담배로 야기되고 있다.

111. Nelson씨는 주주 총회에 맞춰 도착하는 것을 확실히 하기 위해서 기차를 탈 것입니다.

112. 당신의 사업을 효율적으로 운영하고 싶을 때는, 당신의 회계사와 협의할 필요가 있습니다.

113. 감독직에 지원을 원하는 어떤 사람도 그들이 심사 대상이 되는지 여부를 알아내기 위해서 직속 상관에게 얘기해야 한다.

114. Dolton Tech사의 신상 휴대용 컴퓨터들은 사람들의 눈을 사로잡는 광고 캠페인 때문에 상승된 인기를 목격했습니다.

115. 1월 1일부터, 모든 매니저들은 적어도 세 번의 직업개발세미나에 참석하도록 요구되는 바입니다 ⇒ 참석해야 합니다.

116. 신상 디지털 카메라에 대한 고객 관심을 높이고자 하는 마케팅 부서의 최근 시도는 부분적으로는 성공적이었습니다.

117. 두 살이나 그 미만의 아이들은 물놀이 시설에 입장이 무료이고 회원카드나 손님용 입장권을 제시할 필요가 없습니다.

118. TravelSmart 웹사이트를 통해서 예약된 모든 예약은 Landing Hotel 음식점에서 할인 혜택을 받을 자격을 갖춥니다 ⇒ 웹사이트에서 예약하면 할인을 받을 수 있습니다.

119. 이 도표는 지난 한해 동안에 회사 간부들에 의해 수행된 출장의 비용을 보여주고 있다 ⇒ 회사 간부들이 사용한 출장 경비를 보여주고 있다.

120. 휴가 요청을 할 때, 귀하의 사원증 번호가 서류 상에 분명히 인쇄되도록 확인해 주세요.

121. 초과근무 수당에 대한 새로운 절차는 내년도 회계연도에 시행될 것 입니다.

122. 자전거 도로를 포함시키는 Main Street의 확장은 4월에 완료될 것입니다.

123. 태양 에너지의 지속적인 연구를 지원하기 위해서, Upton Laboratories에서는 Earth First Association 협회로부터 보조금을 지원받았습니다.

124. 아름다운 현대식 호텔일 뿐만 아니라 이 호텔은 기분 좋은 서비스를 제공하는 훌륭한 직원을 보유하고 있습니다.

125. 재무부서에서 취합해 둔 올해 회계연도의 자세한 수치들은 3월 1일에 공개된 연례 보고서에서 찾아 보실 수 있을 것입니다.

126. 재 개장 행사에 앞서서, Jarling Community Center는 주와 연방 안전 위원회에 의한 검사를 받았습니다.

127. 응답자의 3분의 1 이상이 HIV 연구가 진단법과 의약 및 백신 개발의 발전에 상당히 기여했다고 말했습니다.

128. 마케팅 부서의 다른 사원들처럼, 이사인 Sylvia Gorn은 이 지역에서 열린 모든 마케팅 회의에 참석해왔습니다.

129. 모든 레스토랑 직원들은 보건부의 검사에 대비하여 자신의 근무 지역을 면밀히 점검하는 것을 확실히 해야 합니다 ⇒ 꼭 점검해야 합니다.

130. 귀하의 대금이 받아진 후에(귀하의 대금을 받고 나서) 귀하의 온라인 청구서 상에 있는 지불되어야 할 총 금액은 그에 상응하게 조정될 것입니다.

PART 6

Questions 131–134 이메일

Mr. Eisen 에게

Sacramento Small Business Society (SSBS)는 저희 협회에 대한 귀하의 지원을 수락하였습니다.

귀하의 가게가 고객서비스에 대한 명성, 상업적 성과, 현재 회원의 추천 등이 좋았기 때문에 귀하의 입회를 승인했습니다.

당신의 회원 가입을 확정하기 위해서는 저희 웹사이트 www.ssbs.org 에서 즉시 당신의 계정을 등록해 주세요.

귀하가 변경하기 전까지 귀하의 계정 ID는 Sacramento Attire이고 패스워드는 SA9866입니다. 등록 직후에 바로 회원으로서 혜택이 활성화 될 것입니다 ⇒ 혜택을 받으실 수 있습니다. 회원들에게 저희가 제공하는 서비스에 대한 세부 사항은 웹사이트에서 찾아 보실 수 있습니다.

귀하의 저희 협회 회원가입이 매우 보람 있다고 귀하가 생각하게 될 것임을 SSBS는 확신합니다.

Questions 135-138 브로셔 발췌문

경치 좋은 Shireton을 방문하셔서 저희 아름다운 시의 모습을 볼 수 있도록 다섯 개 중의 하나의 도보 여행을 떠나보세요. Shireton 관광청에 의해 제공되면서, 각각의 투어는 경험 많은 가이드에 의해 진행되며, 여행자들께 도시의 환상적인 곳을 보여드릴 것입니다.

가장 많이 선택 되는 투어는 이 도시의 문화 예술지구 중의 한 곳인 Selby Plaza를 지나는 것입니다. Selby Plaza에는 시립 예술 박물관과 빼어난 건축양식으로 유명한 몇 개의 호텔뿐만 아니라 세 개의 독자적으로 운영되는 화랑들이 있습니다. 전체적으로 이 투어는 약 세 시간 가량 걸리며, Plaza에서 가장 큰 식당 중의 하나에서 저녁식사를 하는 것으로 마무리가 됩니다. 몇몇 식당들은 투어 참가자들에게 할인을 제공하기도 합니다. 어떤 식당이 할인행사에 참여하는지를 가이드에게 꼭 물어보세요.

오늘 당장 Shireton 관광청에 방문하시거나 555-3756번으로 전화 주셔서 투어를 신청을 하세요.

Questions 139-142 이메일

발신: customercare@webshop.com
수신: hcollins@kld.com
날짜: 4월 24일
제목: 구매 #684633

Collins씨에게

귀하의 구매(#684633)가 처리 되었습니다. 귀하의 계정에 적혀있는 주소로 구매하신 두 개의 품목을 발송했으며 7영업일 이내에 도착 할 것입니다. 유감스럽게도, 당신의 세 번째 구매품은 발송하지 못했습니다. 은색의 Lansing Bluetooth 헤드셋은 5월 14일 이후에야 배송 가능합니다. 이로 인해 당신이 겪을지 모르는 어떠한 불편에 대해서도 우리는 사과를 드리는 바입니다. 이 제품이 나오기 전에 당신 주문에서 이 부분을 취소하고 싶다면 service@jollystore.com으로 저희 고객지원부서에 알려주시기 바랍니다. 그렇지 않다면, 재고가 들어오는 데로 당신 주문의 이 마지막 부분을 발송할 것입니다.

귀하의 애용에 대단히 감사 드립니다.

Georgia Smith
Customer Care Associate, Web Shop

Questions 143-146 발표문

Bradford Gallery는 Humans of Brasilia라는 제목이 붙은 Belinda Hartness의 최신 콜렉션 전시회를 개최할 것입니다. 이번 전시회는 도시 생활과 도시 생활을 살고 있는 사람들의 생생한 이미지를 보여줄 것이며 2월 12일부터 3월 1일 까지 화랑에서 전시될 것입니다.

그녀가 뉴욕, 파리, 방콕에서 보낸 그녀의 젊은 시절 때문에 대도시들은 Harness씨 사진의 주 초점이 되고 있습니다.

Hartness씨는 시카고에 있는 Score Museum에서 큐레이터로 근무하고 있습니다. Hartness씨는 그녀의 독특한 카메라 앵글로 유명세를 타면서, 전 세계 박물관에서 그녀의 작품을 전시해왔습니다. 프랑스 파리에서 열린 그녀의 마지막 전시회는 비평가들의 찬사를 받았습니다.

PART 7

Questions 147-148 광고

원예 회사

Acorn Valley에 있는 저희 회사는 숙련되고, 유능한 접수계원을 모집하고 있습니다. 지원자는 손님을 맞이하기, 전화를 걸고 받기, 메시지를 남기기 등과 같은 다양한 업무를 해야 할 것입니다. 복사기나 팩스 및 다른 사무 기계를 잘 다루는 기술뿐만 아니라 뛰어난 파일 정리 기술이 반드시 있어야 합니다.

지원자는 그래픽 디자인 경력자라야 합니다. 시급은 14불에서 16불입니다.

147. 어떤 일자리가 나왔는가?
(A) 서비스 직원
(B) 조경사
(C) 접수계원
(D) 비서

148. 이 자리에는 어떤 경험이 요구되지 않는가?
(A) 서류 파일 정리
(B) 원예 기술
(C) 전화 활용
(D) 그래픽 디자인

Questions 149-150 광고

Nightingale
노래 메시지

Nightingale Singing Telegram 소속 예술가들은
사람들의 특별한 날을 축하해 주거나
재미있는 방식으로 축하를 전해 주는 일을 해왔습니다.
저희 Nightingale은 생일 파티, 기념행사, 졸업파티 등
아주 다양한 행사에
노래로 메시지를 전달할 수 있는 아주 좋은 방법입니다.
저희는 또한 소속 엔터테이너들이 깜짝 등장하는 서비스도 제공합니다.

당신도 Nightngale이 될 수 있다고 생각하세요?

기타나 아코디언과 같은 악기들을 연주 할 수 있는
지원자들은 뽑힐 가능성이 아주 높습니다.
그냥 저희에게 당신의 능력이 담긴 짧은
비디오 영상을 보내주세요. 비디오 영상은 연락처와 함께 61101 IL, Rockford, Gerald Silver, 사서함 43번으로 보내주세요.

149. 광고의 목적은 무엇인가?
(A) 특별행사를 공고하기 위해서
(B) 연극단을 소개하기 위해서
(C) 지원자를 모집하기 위해서
(D) 신규 회사를 홍보하기 위해서

150. Nightingale에서 일하는 예술가들에 대해서 언급된 것은?
  (A) 그들은 여러 현장으로 일하러 갑니다.
  (B) 그들은 근무복을 구입해야 합니다.
  (C) 그들은 곧 대학을 졸업할 것입니다.
  (D) 그들은 파티에서 비디오 녹화를 합니다.

Questions 151-152 메모

공지

수신: 직원들
발신: 회계부서
날짜: 8월 8일
제목: 근무시간 보고

급여 지급을 좀더 시간 내에 원활하게 할 수 있도록, 경리부에서는 온라인으로 근무시간을 보고하는 새로운 시스템을 시행하고자 합니다. 9월 3일부터 직원들은 매주마다 근무한 시간을 회사에서 관리하는 웹사이트에 보고해야 합니다. 인사과에서는 8월 23일 회의실 24호에서 전 직원에게 정보를 시스템에 어떻게 입력하는지를 교육 할 것입니다. 회의실 24호 근처에 외부에 게시된 목록에서 교육 시간을 선택해 주십시오.

151. 이 공지의 목적은 무엇입니까?
  (A) 지급을 받았음을 확인하기 위해서
  (B) 직원들에게 연기된 배송에 대해서 알려주기 위해서
  (C) 직원들에게 신규 절차를 알리기 위해서
  (D) 직원들에게 웹사이트 등록을 요청하기 위해서

152. 왜 직원들은 8월 23일에 회의실로 가야 합니까?
  (A) 경리부와 회의를 갖기 위해서
  (B) 신규 시스템에 대한 수업을 듣기 위해
  (C) 급여 자동 입금 프로그램에 등록하기 위해
  (D) 승진을 위한 새로운 프로세스를 배우기 위해

Questions 153-155 광고

Donna's Donuts
Havelin시 Main Street 89번지
635-555-4684

당신이 Donna's Donuts에서 도넛을 한 입 먹은 후라면 결코 다른 가게에서는 도넛을 사고 싶어하지 않을 것입니다. 저희 가게는 Main Street 바로 중심에 위치하며, 모든 연령대가 즐기는 먹을 거리, 마실 거리를 제공합니다. 우리는 지역 학교 학생들을 위한 개인 스터디룸 또한 갖추고 있습니다.

Donna's Donuts 가게에서 아래와 같은 것들을 찾아 보실 수 있습니다.
• 현지 업체들의 재료들로 우리 가게에서 만들어진 50여 종 이상의 다양한 도넛들
• 다양한 향을 가진 커피와 차
• 곡물 머핀과 시리얼 바와 같은 건강한 아침 식사 메뉴
• 모든 고객들께 제공되는 무선 인터넷 무료 접속

월요일부터 토요일, 오전 8시부터 오후 8시까지 영업.
6월부터 9월까지 하계기간 동안 9시 30분 까지 영업.
매주 목요일, 5세 미만 아이들은 정상가에서 50% 할인된 가격에 무료 주스를 제공받을 수 있어요.

153. Donna's Donuts에 대해서 언급된 것은 무엇인가?
  (A) 도너츠들이 매장에서 만들어진다.
  (B) Donna's Donuts의 음식은 지역 식료품가게에서 구입가능하다.
  (C) Donna's Donuts는 가족이 운영한다.
  (D) Donna's Donuts는 신규 지점을 오픈했다.

154. 광고에 따르면, 6월에는 무슨 일이 있겠는가?
  (A) 영업 시간의 변경된다.
  (B) 스터디 룸을 더 이상 이용 할 수 없다.
  (C) 가게는 대학생들을 고용한다.
  (D) 음료 메뉴가 바뀐다.

155. 할인에 대해서 언급된 것은?
  (A) 할인은 조식에만 적용된다.
  (B) 어떤 종류의 도너츠도 할인된다.
  (C) 할인은 재방문하는 고객들에게만 적용된다.
  (D) 일주일에 하루만 할인된다.

Questions 156-157 문자메시지 대화

TERRY CLAYBURGH	9:13 AM
Kali, 당신 사무실로 옮길 준비가 다 됐나요?	

KALI KEMPER	9:14 AM
아직이요. 그렇지만 일단 시작은 잘 했습니다.	

TERRY CLAYBURGH	9:15 AM
시작이요? 이사하시는 분들이 10시까지 거기로 갈 예정이에요.	

KALI KEMPER	9:16 AM
10시요? 저는 오후나 되서야 오는 줄 알았어요.	

KALI KEMPER	9:17 AM
그때까지는 도저히 끝낼 수가 없는데요.	

TERRY CLAYBURGH	9:18 AM
저도 지금은 완전히 바쁜 상태예요.	

TERRY CLAYBURGH	9:19 AM
그렇지만 20분 후에는 짐 싸는 걸 거들기 위해 갈 수 있습니다.	

KALI KEMPER	9:20 AM
정말 고마워요, Terry.	

156. Kali Kemper에 대해 언급된 것은?
  (A) Kemper씨는 근무하는 자리를 옮길 것이다.
  (B) Kemper씨는 Clayburgh의 부하직원이다.
  (C) Kemper씨는 현재 발표문 작업을 하고 있다.
  (D) Kemper씨는 일정표를 잃어버렸다.

157. 9시 18분에 Terry Clayburgh씨가 "I've got my hands full now"라고 쓸 때 무엇을 의미하고 있는가?
 (A) Clayburgh씨는 이사 박스를 옮기고 있다.
 (B) Clayburgh씨는 전화로 얘기 중이다.
 (C) Clayburgh씨는 그때 매우 바쁘다.
 (D) Clayburgh씨는 Kemper씨의 사무실로 가고 있는 중이다.

Questions 158–160 이메일

발신: fredad@fredassandwiches.com
수신: aaronlee@webpost.com
날짜: 4월 15일
제목: 이번 주
Lee씨에게

당신이 저희 레스토랑을 자주 찾는 단골이기 때문에, 다음 주에 Freda's Sandwiches에서 "5불의 Hero Special"을 다시 선보인다는 소식을 들으시면 기뻐하실 것입니다. 이것은 당신이 정상가 9불짜리 큼직한 hero sandwich를 단돈 5불에 먹을 수 있다는 것을 의미합니다.

이번 특별가에는 아래 모든 종류의 샌드위치가 다 포함됩니다.

닭고기	소고기	채식
Five Alarm Chicken	Blue Cow	Mondo Avacado.
Indian Chicken Curry	Classic Cheesesteak	Artichoke Avalanche
Chinese Chicken	The Bullhorn	Cheesy Cheese and Such.
	Cow Over the Moon	

손님들이 많은 점심시간에 예약을 하려면 저희 www.fredassandwiches.com 을 방문해 주세요. 이 할인가는 4월 20일부터 4월 26일까지만 유효합니다.

다음 주에 뵙겠습니다!

Freda Dee
주인 겸 수석 요리사
Freda's Sandwiches

158. 왜 이메일을 보냈는가?
 (A) 새롭게 출간되는 요리책을 홍보하려고
 (B) 신메뉴 샌드위치를 홍보하려고
 (C) 레스토랑으로 오는 길을 안내하려고
 (D) 판촉 행사에 대한 세부사항을 제공하려고

159. Lee씨에 대해서 언급된 것은?
 (A) 그는 Freda's Sandwiches에서 일한 적이 있다.
 (B) 그는 Freda's Sandwiches를 친구에게 추천했다.
 (C) 그는 Freda's Sandwiches의 단골 고객이다.
 (D) 그는 Freda's Sandwiches에서 점심을 예약했다.

160. Freda's Sandwiches에 대해서 언급된 것은?
 (A) 오전에는 열지 않는다.
 (B) 넓은 좌석이 있다.
 (C) 웹사이트에서 예약을 받는다.
 (D) 품질로 유명하다.

Questions 161–163 편지

Sharpton Commercial Consultation

5월 19일
Lawrence Sturdevant
30003 GE, Atlanta
Heights Avenue 8655번지
Sturdevant씨에게

귀하가 9월 10일부터 9월 12일까지 오클라호마 Tulsa에서 Sharpton Commercial Consultation이 주최하는 컨퍼런스에서 발표할 프레젠테이션을 확인하고자 이 편지를 보냅니다. 귀하의 발표는 9월 11일 입니다.

컨퍼런스가 열리는 곳의 2층에 위치한 Hollings Grace Convention Hall에서 컨퍼런스 끝난 후 오후 7시에 있는 저녁식사와 환영회에 당신을 초대 하고 싶습니다. —[1]—

제 비서인 Gloria Bingham씨가 Tulsa에 머무르는 동안 귀하의 숙소를 준비해 놓았습니다. —[2]— Plaza Hotel은 편리하고 편안한 숙소입니다. 회의장에서 걸어 갈 수 있는 거리에 있습니다.

저희 법무부와 홍보부에서 발표 전에 당신의 프레젠테이션 내용을 인가해야 함을 잊지 마세요. —[3]—

저희 회사는 온라인 마케팅 기술에 관한 당신의 작업에 대해서 좋은 얘기를 많이 들었습니다. 따라서 당신을 직접 만나서 당신의 작업에 대해서 좀 더 알고 싶습니다. —[4]—

Harriet Manning
Harriet Manning
선임 이사, Employee Advancement Techniques.

161. Sturdevant씨는 어디에서 발표를 할 것인가?
 (A) 호텔에서
 (B) 컨벤션 센터
 (C) 회사 본사에서
 (D) 법률회사에서

162. 편지에서 언급되지 않은 것은?
 (A) 컨퍼런스 일정
 (B) 사교 모임
 (C) 머무를 곳
 (D) 발표 날짜

163. [1], [2], [3], [4]로 표시된 자리 중에 다음 문장이 들어가기에 가장 적합한 곳은?

"가능하면 빨리 저희 사무실로 귀하가 발표할 내용의 완성된 사본을 보내주세요."

(A) [1]
(B) [2]
(C) [3]
(D) [4]

Questions 164–167 광고

Borland 직업개발소

만일 귀하가 경력을 위해서 가치 있는 경험과 교육을 받고 싶으시면, Borland Career Development Center에서는 2월 2일부터 바쁜 일정이 있는 분들을 위한 세미나와 강의를 제공합니다.

- 신규 강좌: 주말 이틀 일정의 세미나들
- 신규 강좌: 아무 때나 접근 가능한 온라인 강의
- 추가 저녁 강의는 주중, 주말 모두 가능함

Borland는 금융, 경영, 마케팅 분야의 일자리를 위한 직업개발의 최고의 장소입니다. 우리는 경쟁력 있는 가격에 초보자, 중급자, 고급자를 위한 경험 있고, 자격이 있는 강사들이 강의하는 수업을 제공합니다.

Borland는 올 해 고등교육 위원회로부터 받은 창의력이 있는 강의 대상을 포함하여 여러 상을 수상한바 있습니다.

제공되는 수업, 수업료, 비용에 관한 추후 세부사항은 www.borland-center.edu에 방문함으로써 찾아 보실 수 있습니다. 아니면 간단히 (684)555-0686로 전화해서 등록하시면 됩니다.

164. 이 광고의 목적은 무엇인가?
(A) 새로운 일정을 홍보하기 위해서
(B) 저렴해진 등록비를 알려주기 위해서
(C) 신입 강사를 모집하기 위해서
(D) 최근 경영진의 교체를 설명하기 위해서

165. Borland는 어떻게 변화 되었는가?
(A) 모든 수업 일정을 야간으로 변경함으로써
(B) 웹사이트에 기반한 수업을 제공함으로써
(C) 경영관리 프로그램들에만 집중함으로써
(D) 다양한 회사에서 세미나를 준비함으로써

166. Borland에 대해서 언급되지 않은 것은?
(A) 비지니스와 관련된 수업을 제공한다.
(B) 다양한 수준의 학생들을 돕는다.
(C) 전문 강사들을 고용한다.
(D) 학생들이 일자리 찾는 것을 도와준다.

167. 웹사이트를 방문하는 이유로 이 광고에서 언급된 것은?
(A) 주말 동안 세미나에 등록하기 위해서
(B) 수업료를 찾아보기 위해서
(C) 센터가 제공하는 상을 받기 위해서
(D) 강사들의 자질을 검토하기 위해서

Questions 168–171 편지

Salkin 출판사
97220 OR, 포틀랜드, Harrodson로 896번지

9월 15일

친애하는 투자자들에게

Salkin 출판사의 경영위원회는 Cole Publishing사에 의해 제안된 합병안을 수락하기로 결정했습니다. 합병이 성사되려면, 출판과 통신업계에 규제를 만드는 연방 통신위원회뿐만 아니라 저희 투자자 대다수가 이 합병을 승인해야 합니다. —[1]—.

경영위원회는 이번 합병이 회사에 도움이 될 것이라고 확신합니다. 비록 회사가 지난 2년간 예상했던 만큼 수익이 나지는 않았지만, 우리는 이번 합병을 계기로 상황을 반전시킬 가능성이 있다고 믿고 있습니다. —[2]—. Cole Publishing사는 비소설 부문에서 성공한 출판사이며 저희 회사와 나란히 베스트 셀러에 여러 책을 올리고 있습니다. 그리고 그들은 우리가 해왔던 것처럼 전자출판분야에도 노력을 기울이기 시작했고 성공적입니다. Salkin 출판사는 11월 14일 본사에서 투자자들의 합병 승인 여부를 결정하기 위해서 우리 투자자들을 위한 회의를 열 것입니다. —[3]—.

우리는 Cole Publishing사와의 합병 계약서 사본과 외부 컨설팅 업체에서 실시한 Cole Publishing의 재무 및 마케팅 조사 결과도 이 편지와 함께 동봉했습니다. —[4]—. 우리는 귀하가 결정을 내리기 전에 이 자료들을 살펴보실 것을 요청합니다.

전체 이사회를 대표해서 이 문제에 대한 귀하의 참여에 감사 드립니다.

Bill Carlin
경영위원장

동봉물

168. 이 편지는 무엇을 권고하고 있는가?
(A) 새로운 경쟁업체에 도전할 것을
(B) 한 회사와의 합병을 승인할 것을
(C) 인터넷 투표에 대해 논의할 것을
(D) 부서의 작업을 늘릴 것을

169. 양 측 회사에 대해서 사실인 것은?
(A) 두 회사 모두 전자출판 상품을 가지고 있다.
(B) 두 회사 모두 Minneapolis에 본사를 두고 있다.
(C) 두 회사 모두 최근 출판에 성공을 거두지 못했다.
(D) 두 회사 모두 픽션 소설책을 낸다.

170. 편지와 함께 동봉된 것은?
(A) Cole Publishing의 컨설팅 회사에 관한 세부사항
(B) Cole Publishing의 재무 상황에 대한 조사보고서
(C) Salkin 출판사 본사로 오는 길에 대한 안내
(D) Salkin 출판사의 최신 출간 목록

171. [1], [2], [3], [4]로 표시된 자리 중에 다음 문장이 들어가기에 가장 적합한 곳은?

"Cole Publishing의 투자자들도 11월 20일 Minneapolis 본사에서 유사한 결정을 내릴 것입니다."
(A) [1]
(B) [2]
(C) [3]
(D) [4]

Questions 172-175 인터넷 채팅 대화

Clay Hutchman [4:07 p.m.]
영업부서에 컴퓨터 업데이트 작업이 어떻게 되어가나요? 우리는 내일 회계부서 컴퓨터들 시작할 예정입니다.

Donna Caviezel [4:08 p.m.]
약간의 문제가 있었습니다. 컴퓨터 중의 하나가 바이러스에 걸린 걸 발견했습니다. 우리가 바이러스를 제거하기 전에 3개의 다른 컴퓨터에 전염이 되었어요. 아직 컴퓨터 10대 업데이트 작업을 해야 합니다.

Clay Hutchman [4:09 p.m.]
10개나요? 최소 5시간은 걸리겠네요. 바이러스는 어디에서 온 거죠?

Donna Caviezel [4:10 p.m.]
Kate Surjik씨가 자기 이메일로 바이러스가 온 걸, 먼저 스캐닝을 하지 않고 열었답니다. 그렇지만 우리가 찾아내서 다행이에요. 하마터면 다시 원점으로 돌아갈 뻔 했습니다.

Clay Hutchman [4:12 p.m.]
어쨌건, 영업팀 컴퓨터가 다 업데이트되려면 오늘 야근할 사람이 몇 명 필요하겠네요. 야근할 수 있는 분 있나요?

Donna Caviezel [4:14 p.m.]
아시겠지만, 저는 안되겠네요. 언니(혹은 동생)랑 콘서트에 가기로 했어요. 준비하려면 여기서 5시 정각에는 나가야 합니다.

Omar Hooks [4:16 p.m.]
저는 괜찮아요, Clay. 오늘밤 10시까지는 남아있을 수 있습니다. 그때까지 모든 컴퓨터를 업데이트할 수 없으면, 전부 끝내기 위해 내일 일찍 오겠습니다.

Clay Hutchman [4:17 p.m.]
고마워요, Omar. 감사 드립니다. 제가 피자를 주문해놓을게요. 피자 위에 특별히 올리고 싶은 게 있나요?

Omar Hooks [4:18 p.m.]
페퍼로니하고 소시지만 있으면 됩니다. 감사해요.

172. 이들은 어느 부서에서 일할 가능성이 가장 높은가?
(A) 영업부서
(B) 회계부서
(C) IT(정보통신) 부서
(D) 물류부서

173. 회계부서에 있는 컴퓨터에 대해 언급된 것은?
(A) 이 컴퓨터들이 바이러스를 다운받았다.
(B) 이 컴퓨터들은 최근에 구매되었다.
(C) 이 컴퓨터들은 아직 업데이트 작업을 해야 한다.
(D) 이 컴퓨터들은 영업부서 컴퓨터보다 빠르다.

174. 4시 16분에 Omar Hooks씨가 "I can stick it out"라고 쓸 때 무엇을 의미하고 있는가?
(A) Hooks씨는 파손된 컴퓨터의 문제를 고칠 것이다.
(B) Hooks씨는 저녁까지 계속 일할 수 있다.
(C) Hooks씨는 지금 회계부서 컴퓨터 작업을 시작할 수 있다.
(D) Hooks씨는 잘못 끼어있는 컴퓨터 부품을 제거할 수 있다.

175. Kate Surjik씨에 대해 사실일 가능성이 가장 높은 것은?
(A) Surjik씨는 영업부서에서 일한다.
(B) Surjik씨는 최근에 이 회사에서 일하기 시작했다.
(C) Surjik씨는 많은 이메일을 받는다.
(D) Surjik씨는 자기 컴퓨터에 바이러스 백신이 설치되어 있지 않다.

Questions 176-180 서신과 정보

Singer Publications
883 Alameda Street
Norman, OK 73070

6월 19일
Diana Ballard
144 Switzer Canyon Drive
Flagstaff, AZ 86001

Ballard씨에게,

우리의 Singer Tour Guide Series에 당신이 새로운 기고가로 함께 일하게 되어 기쁩니다. 당신이 서명한 계약서에 근거하여, 당신은 여행가이드 총괄 에디터에 의해 이미 승인된 작업을 자세하게 설명해주는 청구서를 전송해야 합니다. 청구서에 당신의 연락처, 당신이 작업하고 있는 시리즈명 그리고 담당에디터의 이름을 기재하시기 바랍니다. 저에게 청구서를 보내주시면 제가 회계부서로 전달하겠습니다. 저희 이미지 부서가 사용하는 별도의 청구서 양식이 있기 때문에 당신의 사진에 대한 청구서를 제출하는 방법에 대해서는 Lafferty씨에게 상의하셔야 합니다. 부서에서 아직 안 보냈다면 곧 당신에게 이 양식을 보낼 거라 생각합니다.

Amanda Neeson

Singer Publications				
기 진행 중인 프로젝트 팀				
시리즈 명	Travel & Tales Picture Diaries	Singer Tour Guide Series	** Around the Globe Series
상급 에디터	elly Daniels	Eva Gideon	Roy Becker
이미지 에디터	Melissa Franco	Damon Lafferty	Melissa Frano
행정 관리자	Harriet Barry	Amanda Neeson	Samuel Coogan

** Franco씨가 다른 출판물, 즉 곧 새로운 호가 출시될 Travel & Tales Picture Diaries에 집중할 수 있도록, Becker씨 및 Coogan 씨와 함께 일할 신규직원을 뽑을 예정임을 다시 한번 알려드립니다.

176. 이 편지는 무엇을 설명하고 있는가?
(A) 작업료를 받는 방법
(B) 여행 사진을 제출하는 방법
(C) 배정된 기사를 출판하는 방법
(D) 프로젝트 자리에 지원하는 방법

177. 서신에서 언급되지 않은 것은?
(A) Neeson씨는 계약직 작가들로부터 청구서를 받는다.
(B) Neeson씨는 여행사진을 위한 프로젝트를 감독한다.
(C) Ballard씨는 최근에 집필 프로젝트를 마쳤다.
(D) Ballard씨는 자신이 쓴 글을 위한 사진을 찍었다.

178. 서신의 첫 번째 문단, 일곱 번째 줄에서 "suspect"가 의미상 가장 가까운 것은?
(A) 믿는다
(B) 희망한다
(C) 불신한다
(D) 비난한다

179. Gideon씨에 대해 사실인 것은?
(A) Gideon씨는 최근에 Singer Publications에서 일하기 시작했다.
(B) Gideon씨는 많은 프로젝트에서 Franco씨와 함께 일한다.
(C) Gideon씨는 이미 Ballard씨와의 계약을 승인했다.
(D) Gideon씨는 행정관리자를 교육시킨다.

180. 도표와 함께 제공된 정보에 따르면 프로젝트 배정이 어떻게 바뀔까?
(A) The Travel & Tales Picture Diary팀이 새로운 프로젝트를 맡을 것이다.
(B) 각 팀의 총괄 에디터가 새로운 프로젝트에 돌아가며 투입될 것이다.
(C) 네 번째 프로젝트 팀이 결성되고 있다.
(D) 팀들 중 한 팀은 새로운 이미지 에디터를 맞을 것이다.

Questions 181–186 정보 및 서신

작품 대여를 위한 정책과 절차

Bolivian Institute of Arts(BIA)에 소장되어 있는 작품들은 박물관, 대학 및 기관들에 한해서만 전시 및 연구의 목적을 위해 대여가 가능합니다. 작품의 대여를 신청하기 위해서는 서면 요구서가 BIA의 상급 큐레이터에게 전달되어야 합니다. 또한 작품을 대여하는 어떤 기관도 작품을 대여해주는 기관으로써 BIA를 적절하게 표기하여야 합니다. 대여는 최대 12개월까지 가능합니다.

BIA의 소장 위원회는 작품대여를 위한 모든 신청서를 철저하게 검토하고 나서 총괄이사에게 추천을 할 것이며, 총괄이사는 그리고 나서 최종 결정을 내릴 것입니다. 대여 신청의 처리는 최고 4주까지 소요될 수 있습니다. BIA가 상당한 양의 (대여) 신청을 받고 있으며, 물품을 이송하기 위해 보통 요구되는 준비작업이 굉장히 많기 때문에, 작품이 필요로 되는 시점에서 최소 6개월 전에 신청서를 제출하셔야 합니다.

The Portuguese Museum of Fine Arts
948 R. da Liberdade
리스본, 포르투갈

3월 23일

Ms. Camila Amparo
P.O. Box 67336
코차밤바, 볼리비아

Amparo씨에게,

The Portuguese Museum of Fine Arts는 South American Modern Art라는 제목으로 전시회를 준비하고 있으며, 저희가 이미 소장하고 있는 예술작품과 함께 Bolivian Institute of Arts에 소장되어 있는 작품들을 전시할 수 있도록 작품 대여를 위해 저희 박물관에게 승인을 해주시기를 희망하는 바입니다. 몇몇 현지 기업들이 전시회를 위한 자금을 제공할 것입니다. 또한 저희는 기념품점에서 판매하기 위해서, 저희가 대여하는 작품에 대한 포스터 크기의 인쇄물을 제작하고 싶습니다.

저희가 대여하고자 하는 작품은 아래와 같으며, 저희는 이들이 볼리비아의 예술활동을 보여주는 훌륭한 본보기라고 믿고 있습니다.

1. Ascension, Veronica Baros의 사진작품
2. Rios Blanco Y Negro, Jose Ochoa의 수채화 작품
3. Chiquitos, Arturo Francisco의 조각품

박물관의 웹사이트에 나와 있는 요구조건에 따라서, 건물 규모, 각 별관의 온도 및 습도 수준, 보안규정 및 설비, 보관, 조명을 포함한 저희 시설의 물리적 특성에 관한 정보를 기재하였습니다. 질문이 있으시거나 추가 정보가 필요하시면 저에게 연락 주시기 바랍니다.

Adriana Mendes, 상급 디렉터

181. 정보에 따르면, Bolivian Institute of Arts에 대해 사실인 것은?
(A) BIA는 작품대여에 대한 신청을 별로 많이 받지 않는다.
(B) BIA는 최대 3개의 작품을 대여해 준다.
(C) BIA는 개인에게 작품을 대여해주지 않는다.
(D) BIA는 최대 6개월간 대여를 해준다.

182. 대여 결정과정에 대해 언급되지 않은 것은?
(A) 결정과정은 다수의 사람을 거친다.
(B) 결정하는데 한달 미만의 시간이 걸린다.
(C) 대여하는 기관에 대한 정보가 고려된다.
(D) 볼리비아에 초점을 맞추는 전시회에 우선권이 주어진다.

183. Amparo씨는 누구인가?
(A) 상급 큐레이터
(B) 기관의 위원회 멤버
(C) 총괄 이사
(D) 전시회에 자금을 지원하는 업체 관계자

184. 특별전시회에 대해 언급된 것은?
(A) 이 전시회는 대여작품만을 선보인다.
(B) 이 전시회는 다양한 종류의 예술작품을 선보인다.
(C) 이 전시회는 작가들의 프로필을 선보인다.
(D) 이 전시회는 12개월간 열린다.

185. 포스터에는 무엇이 인쇄될까요?
(A) 포르투갈 사진
(B) 예술작품 관리에 대한 설명
(C) 대여해주는 박물관에 대한 언급
(D) 남미의 지도

Questions 186-190 편지, 정보 및 이메일

8월 10일

Arkson씨에게

당신은 Serene Astronomy Society (SAS)의 원로회원이기 때문에, 우리 학회가 관리 되는 방식을 바꿀 수 있는 선택을 하는데 당신의 참여를 요청합니다. 다음주 후반에 우리는 현재 출판을 위해서 운용하는 자금이 새 망원경을 구입하는데 사용 될 수 있는지 여부를 결정 짓는 투표 용지를 당신에게 보낼 것입니다. Clayton 천문관은 더 이상 저희에게 Mount Aster 망원경을 이용할 시간을 제공해줄 수 없습니다. 그러므로 우리 제안서가 승인되지 않으면 Mount Aster 토론은 인솔자에 의한 토론으로만 구성될 것입니다.

우리가 이 자금을 망원경 구매에 할당하기 위해서는 6개월 동안 임시적으로 잡지 Galaxy Visions 인쇄를 중단해야 하지만, 새 망원경은 우리 단체에게는 대단히 도움이 될 것입니다. 우리 단체가 어떻게 운영될 것인가와 관련된 이 문제에 대한 귀하의 도움에 감사합니다.

Haley Franz
이사, Serene Astronomy Society

Serene Astronomy Society
회원들을 위한 서비스들

• The Astronomer's Friend – 저희 이메일 소식지는 SAS에 관한 뉴스, 월간 일정, 천문학 분야의 시사문제들을 전해드립니다.
• Galaxy Visions – 저희 잡지는 매달 당신에게 배달되며 별자리 관찰에 관한 조언, 천문과학과 관련된 소식들, 천문학에 관한 신간 서적 서평들을 주요내용으로 다룹니다.
• Mount Aster Discussions – Clayton 천문관에 연구원으로 있는 Gladys McDonald씨가 천문관의 Mount Aster Telescope에서 천체를 관찰하고 이야기를 나누기 위한 토론을 매주 주최합니다.

수신자: SAS Members ⟨members@sereneastronomysociety.org⟩
발신자: Steve Azzara ⟨sazzara@sereneastronomysociety.org⟩
날짜: 9월 2일
주제: 새로운 진행자

회원 여러분께,

Gladys McDonald씨가 저희 기관의 멤버로써 탈퇴할 것을 저희에게 알려왔음을 공지하게 되어 유감입니다. 그녀의 탈퇴이유는 다른 먼 지역으로 이주함에 따라서 저희 협회에서 그녀의 의무를 이행할 수 없을 것이기 때문입니다.

그러나 McDonald씨의 동료인 Taylor Vasquez씨가 이 역할을 자청하였으며 9월 5일부터 SAS Research Center에서 McDonald씨의 임무를 맡을 예정임을 알려드리게 되어 기쁩니다.

Steve Azzara
Galactic Study Association 이사

186. 편지의 목적은 무엇인가?
(A) 운영진의 교체를 보고하기 위해서
(B) 프로세스의 변화를 설명하기 위해서
(C) 회원들에게 잡지 구독을 권장하기 위해서
(D) 투표에 관심을 불러일으키기 위해서

187. Arkson은 무엇을 하도록 요구되고 있는가?
(A) 장비 구매를 지지하도록
(B) 단체 캘린더를 훑어 보도록
(C) 미팅 날짜를 변경하도록
(D) 새로운 회합장소를 추천하도록

188. 편지에서 두 번째 단락, 세 번째 줄의 "concerns"와 가장 가까운 의미의 단어는 무엇인가?
(A) 복잡하게 만들다
(B) 걱정하게 만들다
(C) 관련되다
(D) 호기심을 자극하다

189. 6개월 동안 SAS를 통해서 이용이 불가해질 가능성이 있는 것은?
(A) 인하된 장비 비용
(B) 천문 잡지들의 서평
(C) 천문학자들에 대한 소식들
(D) 다른 회원들과의 만남의 기회

190. Taylor Vasquez씨는 9월 5일부터 무엇을 관리할까?
(A) The Astronomer's Friend
(B) Galaxy Visions
(C) Mount Aster Discussions
(D) SAS의 예산

Questions 191-195 계약서, 청구서 및 고객 설문지

Victorin Rentals

장비 렌트 계약서   날짜: 5월 10일

Victorin Rentals와 Cornwell Company의 이 계약은 5월 29일에 행사용 가구를 대여 한다는 내용입니다. 가구는 66046 KS Lawrence, Heston Avenue 668에 위치한 Cornwell Company 행사 장소로 직접 배달될 것입니다. 5월 29일 오후 3시에 배달될 것이고 5월 30일 오전 9시에 픽업해서 반납할 준비가 되어 있어야 합니다. 그날 행사를 위해서 회사 측에서 고용한 행사 진행자 Claire Dinsley씨는 배달 및 픽업을 위해 현장에 있겠다고 말했습니다.

의자와 테이블은 Victorin Rentals사의 직원들에 의해 배송 당일 늦어도 오후 3시 30분까지는 설치가 될 것입니다. Cornwall Company는 늦어도 오전 9시에 픽업할 수 있도록 대여 가구들을 준비해 놓기로 합의했습니다. 만약 대여된 장비가 제시간에 청소되어 있지 않거나 접혀지지 않고 쌓아놓지 않았다면 추가 요금이 발생 할 것입니다.

Victorin Rentals

당신의 서비스를 위해 저희를 선택해주셔서 감사합니다.

대여 품목	수량	비용/개당	소계
접의식 의자	49	2불	98불
LS9 타입 테이블	7	9불	63불
배송료			40불
총계:			201불

배송주소: 520 Heston Ave Gloversville, MA
대여자: Claire Dinsley   영업 직원: Steven Finworth

Victorin Rentals

고객님께

Victorin Rentals은 귀하의 거래에 대단히 감사 드립니다. 저희가 서비스를 더욱 향상 시킬 수 있도록 이 질문지를 시간 내서 작성해 주세요.

	매우 좋음	좋음	보통	형편없음
대여 물품 상태		×		
의견:	배달된 가구들은 청결했고 상태도 괜찮았습니다.			
배달 및 물품 준비				×

의견:	처음에 배달 직원들은 Heston Avenue가 아닌 Vine Street 사무실로 갔습니다. 그들은 이 실수를 알아차리고 나서 저희 행사 장소로 왔지만, 30분이 늦었습니다. 배송 담당자 Nancy Lester씨는 모든 것들이 빨리 준비되도록 도왔으므로 이것은 큰 문제가 되지는 않았습니다. Lester씨는 또한 배달이 늦었기 때문에 그 서비스 비용을 환불해 드린다고 말했습니다.
Victorin Rentals사에 대한 전반적인 만족도	×
의견:	저는 분명히 다른 행사를 위해 7월에 Victorin Rentals사를 다시 이용할 것입니다. 서비스는 대체로 좋았고 이 지역에서 가장 대여료도 저렴합니다.
고객:	Claire Dinsley

191. Claire Dinsley의 직업은 무엇인가?
(A) 전문 행사 담당자
(B) 가구 수송업자
(C) 배송 매니저
(D) 장비 대여 회사를 위한 중개인

192. Cornwell Company에 대해서 언급되어 있는 것은?
(A) 이전에도 Victorin사로부터 대여 한 적이 있다.
(B) 새 가구를 살 계획이다.
(C) 여러 개의 사무실을 가지고 있다.
(D) 본사를 이전할 것이다.

193. 계약서 첫 번째 문단, 네 번째 줄에 "pick up"이 의미상 가장 가까운 것은?
(A) 고장
(B) 후속조치
(C) 회수
(D) 따라잡기

194. 예상되는 환불 금액은 얼마인가?
(A) 9불
(B) 40불
(C) 63불
(D) 98불

195. Victorin Rentals에 대한 설문지에서 언급되어 있는 것은?
(A) Victorin Rentals는 Cornwell사 행사를 관리하도록 Steven Finworth씨를 파견했다.
(B) 물품 대여 가격이 다른 회사만큼 비싸지 않은 편이다.
(C) 배송팀은 물품들을 회수하는데 정시에 오지 않았다.
(D) 질이 좋지 않은 물품들을 제공했다.

Questions 196-200 이메일, 설문조사 및 편지

발신: Michael Higgins
수신: 개발부 직원들
날짜: 3월 27일
제목: Business Innovation Convention

저는 다음달 Maldives의 Business Innovation Convention에서 저희 전시를 담당할 개발부 스텝들에게 Blue Clam Hotel에서 단체로 머무를 방을 다음 주 말 까지 예약해야 한다는 것을 상기시키고자 이 이메일을 보냅니다. 예약 최종 일은 4월 4일 화요일입니다. 법인카드를 이용할 수 있는 직원들은 가능한 빨리 예약해 주세요.

4월 4일까지 예약을 완료하지 못하면 호텔 객실 요금이 $110에서 $220으로 큰 폭으로 오를 것입니다.

Michael Higgins
Atlas Laboratories 사 전무 이사

Blue Clam Hotel에 묵어주셔서 감사합니다. 다음 번 방문을 더 좋은 체류로 만들기 위해 저희가 할 수 있는 것이 있다면 알려주시기 바랍니다.

투숙객 이름: Robert Paulson
체류 날짜: 4월 21일 – 4월 23일

객실의 청결정도는?
___ 매우 만족 X 만족 ___ 불만족 ___ 매우 불만족
호텔 시설의 만족도는?
___ 매우 만족 ___ 만족 X 불만족 ___ 매우 불만족
호텔 직원들의 서비스는?
___ 매우 만족 ___ 만족 ___ 불만족 X 매우 불만족

기타 사항:
저는 컨벤션 기간중에 여기에 묵었으며 저의 방에 만족했습니다. 그러나 체류기간 동안 비즈니스 센터가 공사중이었고 서류를 인쇄할 방법이 없었습니다. 길을 따라 내려가서 인쇄소를 이용해야 했습니다. 최악은 제가 객실에 대해 잘못된 요금을 청구받았는데, 체크인 담당 직원이 이것을 어떻게 수정해야 할지 몰라 했다는 점입니다. 관리자가 자리에 없었기 때문에 저는 이 문제를 해결하기 위해 나중에 연락을 달라고 요청했습니다. 다시 이곳에 머물지 않을 것 같습니다.

Blue Clam 호텔

4월 29일

Robert Paulson
개발부
Atlas Laboratories
94246 캘리포니아, 새크라멘토
DeLuca Drive 289번지

Paulson씨 에게

귀하의 청구서를 처리하는데 발생한 실수에 대해서 매우 유감스럽게 생각합니다. 귀하의 말처럼 당신의 객실료가 the Business Innovation Convention 특별객실료가 되어야 하는데 저희가 귀사의 신용카드에 일반 요금으로 결제해 버렸습니다. 일부 신입 프런트 직원들이 Convention 객실료로 손님을 체크인하는 일에 익숙치 않아서 일어난 실수입니다.

귀하가 요청한 대로 귀사의 회계부의 경비보고서에 기록할 수 있도록 정정된 청구서를 보내드립니다. 기타 다른 것도 필요하시면 저에게 연락주세요. 다시 한번 the Blue Clam Hotel에 묵어 주신 것 감사드립니다.

Fatima Benzi
매니저

---

196. 왜 Higgins씨가 호텔 예약을 서둘러 해줄 것을 요청했는가?
(A) 숙박료를 할인 받기 위해서
(B) Banes씨와의 계약을 이행하기 위해서
(C) 회사 신용카드의 유효기한이 지날 것이기 때문에
(D) 호텔에 남아 있는 객실이 많지 않기 때문에

197. 이메일에서 첫 번째 단락의 첫 번째 줄 "block"과 가장 가까운 의미의 단어는 무엇인가?
(A) 장애물
(B) 단체
(C) 디자인
(D) 구조

198. Paulson씨에 대해 언급되어 있는 것은 무엇인가?
(A) 그는 해마다 Business Innovation Convention에 간다.
(B) 그는 Atlas Laboratories사의 회계부에서 근무한다.
(C) 그는 호텔 객실 요금을 자신의 신용카드로 결제 했다.
(D) 그는 4월 4일까지 호텔 예약을 했다.

199. Paulson씨가 Benzi씨에게 무엇을 보내 달라고 요청했나?
(A) 온라인으로 객실을 예약하는 것에 대한 설명
(B) 호텔에 무료 숙박을 위한 쿠폰
(C) 호텔 예약 절차의 세부사항들
(D) 호텔 경비의 요약 자료

200. Benzi씨에 대해 언급된 것은?
(A) Benzi씨 또한 컨벤션에 참가했다.
(B) Paulson씨가 체크인을 할 때 Benzi씨는 호텔에 없었다.
(C) Benzi씨는 이 지역에 많은 호텔을 관리한다.
(D) Benzi씨는 고객의 항의사항에 대해 개인적으로 대응을 한다.

TEST 4

PART 5

101. 신작영화 Halfway Down의 감독은 이 영화가 영화의 기초가 되는 원작과는 아주 다르다고 말했습니다.

102. Mayner씨는 Windhill Distribution and Supply사와의 계약을 손쉽게 따냈다.

103. TV 출연 요리사인 Carol Brinn는 당신의 가족 전체를 만족시킬 만한 채식 식사를 어떻게 만드는지를 목요일에 보여줄 것입니다.

104. 새 장비 구매에 대한 매니저의 요청이 승인을 받는다면, 물류창고는 효율성을 최고 50퍼센트까지 높일 것입니다.

105. Fulton Enterprises사의 모든 직원은 세금 환급금의 전부나 혹은 일부를 그들이 선택한 자선단체에 기부할 선택권이 있습니다.

106. Hovink 박사가 양자물리학에서의 그의 업적으로 Bellvue상을 수상했다.

107. 지원서 처리에 관한 어떠한 문의사항도 인사과로 전달될 것을 우리는 요청 드립니다.

108. Tale Industries의 CEO인 Hillary Long은 혼자서 임원자리를 위한 후보자 명단을 마무리 할 것입니다.

109. Hotshop.com사는 당신의 주문 완료 후에 구매를 확인하는 이메일을 보낼 것입니다.

110. 레스토랑이나 다른 식당에서 고객과의 미팅으로 인해 나온 어떠한 지출도 세금 환급을 신청할 때 공제받을 수 있습니다.

111. 초과 근무수당 지불 양식은 이달 말 전에 Argyle씨에게 제출 될 필요가 있습니다 ⇒ 제출되어야 합니다.

112. Stalkin Foods는 인스턴트 먹거리에 높아가는 수요를 맞추기 위해서 더 많은 공장 직원을 고용했습니다.

113. 저희 파일에 따르면, 스페인에서 Dillon Electronics 사업허가증은 1월 2일에 만기 될 것입니다.

114. Linus Construction사는 현재 고층 아파트 단지가 될 타워를 짓고 있습니다.

115. 시민들이 그를 Portville의 시장으로 뽑았을 때, Potter씨의 교육에 대한 열정이 주요 요인이었습니다.

116. Port Industries는 거의 10년 동안 가정용의 쓰레기 처리 제품들을 제조하고 있습니다.

117. Longview Bank는 10년 전 창립이래로 십만 명 이상의 고객들에게 대출을 제공해왔습니다.

118. 신차 Helo Ultra 세단의 성공은 광고대행사 Lobed Ad Agency가 제작한 특별한 마케팅 캠페인의 공으로 돌려졌습니다.

119. 사업 대출에 대한 상환금은 모두 받았고 처리되었습니다.

120. Senti Electric Company사는 올해 목표를 달성한 것처럼 보이지만 모든 데이터가 마무리 될 때 까지는 단지 추정으로 간주되어야 합니다.

121. Steven Bilk 작가의 최신 소설을 읽는 대부분의 독자들은 매우 이해하기가 쉬운 소설임을 알게 될 것입니다.

122. Stockton News사의 직원들은 어떤 직원에게 연락해야 할 지 불확실 때마다 업데이트가 된 사원 주소록을 이제 참고 하실 수 있습니다.

123. 많은 손님들은 굉장히 다양한 음식들 때문에 Buena Cabeza를 찾습니다.

124. Skyhigh Industries의 직원들은 Baker Business Solutions사의 컨설턴트와 인터뷰를 할 때 유익한 의견을 제공했습니다.

125. 빡빡한 예산으로 여행하는 여행객들은 국내 기차 여행이 비행기편으로 여행하는 것보다 훨씬 덜 비싸다는 것을 알고 있어야 합니다.

126. 많은 젊은이들은 콘텐츠를 인터넷에 게재하는 것에 익숙하지만 개인 정보를 게재하는 것이 그들을 신원도용 사기에 취약하게 만든다는 것을 알아둬야 합니다.

127. Manderly Enterprises사는 회사의 유럽 시장 쪽으로의 확장을 도와줄 컨설턴트를 구하고 있습니다.

128. Hillbrook와 Lakeside 축구 클럽은 작년 플레이오프 동안 서로 만났고 올 해 챔피언 게임에서도 다시 만날 것입니다.

129. 기타리스트 Frank Lenster씨는 Excel Instruments사에 의해 생산된 전자기타 제품라인을 대중화시킨 것에 대해 공을 인정 받고 있습니다.

130. Master Audio사의 최신 MP3 플레이어는 Portal Electronics 전자 대리점에서만 독점 판매 합니다.

PART 6

Questions 131-134 광고

가전제품이나 전자제품에 있어서 최상의 거래를 찾고 있다면, Galactic Home Super Store에 오시기 바랍니다. HDTV나 프로젝터와 같은 대형가전 혹은 전자제품의 구매에 한시적으로 무료 배송과 설치가 제공되고 있습니다.

이 행사에 자격을 갖추시려면 귀하가 구입하는 제품은 적어도 총 액수가 200달러는 되어야 합니다. 고객들은 일주일에 한번만 무료 배송을 받을 수 있습니다.

이 행사나 아니면 저희가 보유하고 있는 다른 어떤 제품에 대해서도 질문이 있으시면 www.galactichome.com으로 저희 홈페이지를 방문해주시거나, 당신의 지역에 있는 Galactic Home Super Store 매장을 방문해주세요. 자질이 뛰어난 저희 고객서비스 전문가들이 당신이 가지고 있는 어떤 질문에도 답변해줄 것입니다.

Questions 135-138 편지

Nordic씨에게

아래는 1월 6일 월요일에 우리가 말씀 드렸던 저희 Hydrolife 정수기 제품의 구매 및 설치 가격입니다.

전반적으로 설치 인건비를 포함하여 제품을 구입하려면 비용은 1,590 불이 될 것입니다.

하지만 이것은 단지 견적비용임을 명심하세요. 실제 가격은 인건비와 설치 작업에 걸리는 시간에 따라 높아질 수도 낮아 질 수도 있습니다. 그렇지만, 가격차이는 견적액 대비 위로건 아래로건 최대 50불 이내 일 것입니다.

구매를 진행하고자 원하신다면, 우리가 약속을 잡을 수 있도록 저에게 연락주세요. 감사합니다.

Pat Gilley

Questions 139-142 기사

JAKARTA (10월 19일) – 11월부터 Indonesian Architecture Monthly는 그들 출판물의 모바일 버전을 출시할 것입니다. 모바일 버전은 휴대폰 이용자들에게만 제공되는 특집 내용뿐만 아니라 인쇄판의 모든 내용을 포함할 것입니다.

이 월간 잡지의 인쇄판은 인도네시아 건축물의 구조, 빌딩, 혁신 및 여타 다른 건축적 요소들을 다룹니다.

모바일 버전은 이 컨텐츠를 한층 더 개선할 것입니다. 모바일 버전은 독자들이 가상으로 인도네시아의 가장 아름답고, 흥미로운 건축 구조물들을 걸어 다니며 둘러보게 해 드릴 것입니다.

Indonesia Architecture Monthly 잡지의 모바일 버전은 4불입니다. 추가 정보를 원하시면 www.indonesiaarchitecture.com를 방문하세요.

Questions 143-146 기사

Barton – 5월 28일 (OH 연합뉴스) – Burke Sports Equipment사의 Barton 지점, Steve Lopez 매니저는 그의 뛰어난 판매 실적으로 본사에서 선정하는 올 해의 가장 뛰어난 우수사원으로 선정되었습니다.

그의 성과를 축하 하기 위해서, Barton 지점은 5월 24일 가게에서 축하연을 열었습니다.

게다가, 그는 전국의 우수사원 수상자들을 기리는, Seattle 에서 열릴 회사의 전국 행사에 참석 할 것입니다.

작년에 매장이 오픈한 이래로 Lopez는 Barton 지점에서 근무했습니다. 이 지점은 주로 그의 노력 덕분에 성공적으로 운영되어 왔습니다. 그는 Seattle로의 여행을 분명히 즐길 거라고 확신하고 있습니다.

PART 7

Questions 147-148 청구서

Speed-Up Industries
08650 NJ Trenton, Hadlock Avenue가 289
(609) 555-0852

송장 번호 #: 984163
날짜: 4월 23일
고객:

Daniel McCormick
55 Paulson Stree
Buffalo, NY 14220
(716) 555-3568

제품	제품번호	수량	비용
Desktop PC	35796	1	599.99 달러
Laser printer	98633	1	49.99 달러
Monitor	76598	1	329.99 달러
		소계	979.97 달러
		판매세	63.70 달러
		운임	20.00 달러
		계약금	450.00 달러
		총계	613.67 달러

147. Speed-Up Industries가 판매하는 것은 무엇인가?
(A) 안전 용품들
(B) 컴퓨터 장비
(C) 오디오 시스템
(D) 가정용 가구류

148. McCormick씨에 대해서 언급되어 있는 것은?
(A) 그의 물건을 4월 23일에 배송 받을 것이다.
(B) Speed-Up Industries 업체로부터 연장된 보증서를 구매했다.
(C) 구매품에 대해 할인을 받았다.
(D) 총비용에서 일부를 지불했다.

Questions 149-150 공지문

Barton 시립 도서관
05822 VT Barton, 12th Avenue 가 298
(802) 555-2986
회원 이름: Felix Grimes   도서관 아이디: 3574668

7월 25일

Grimes씨에게

저희 기록에 따르면, 귀하께서는 아래 나열된 책 한 권을 반납 하지 않으셨습니다.

Summer Back East by Charles Thorn
대출일: 4월 30일   반납일: 6월 30일

우리는 이 책에 대해서 두 번의 공지를 보냈습니다. Barton 지역 시립 도서관 중 어디건 이 책을 반납해 줄 것을 저희는 요청드리는 바입니다. 또한 책이 연체되는 기간 동안 매일 0.3불씩 가산금이 붙을 것이라는 것을 상기 시켜드리고자 합니다. 당신의 총 연체료는 7월 25일자로 7.20불입니다. 신속하게 이 문제를 처리해 주시면 감사하겠습니다.

149. 이 공지문의 주요목적은?
(A) 지역사회 행사를 홍보하기 위해서
(B) 대출절차의 차이점을 발표하기 위해서
(C) 신규 도서관의 개장을 광고하기 위해서
(D) 회원이 문제를 해결할 것을 요청하기 위해서

150. 도서관에 대해서 무엇이 언급되어 있는가?
(A) Grimes씨로부터 자금을 받았다.
(B) 이전에도 Grimes씨에게 연락하려 했었다.
(C) Grimes씨를 고용할 것을 고려하고 있다.
(D) Grimes씨와 구매제품을 교환했다.

Questions 151–153 광고문

Morton 식료품점
83719 ID, Boise, Bailey 가 86
(208) 555-6433
www.mortongrocery.com

Morton 식료품점은 귀하의 특별 행사와 파티를 위한 음식과 모듬 요리를 구하기 위한 훌륭한 장소입니다. 저희 요리들은 회사 야유회, 생일 파티, 축하 파티, 및 기타 등등의 모든 종류의 행사에 안성맞춤입니다. 아래 가장 잘 팔리는 다양한 요리들이 있습니다.

Veggie Party (8–10인용) 당신의 손님을 만족시킬 것이 분명한, 신선하게 잘라 놓은 채소와 다양하고 맛있는 소스의 특별한 결합. $15

Crazy Cookies (12–15인용) 저희 빵집에서 갓 구어 낸 맛있는 쿠키. 당신이 어떤 종류의 쿠키를 원하는지 만 알려주세요. 그러면 저희가 그대로 준비해드립니다. $12

Luxurious Lunch (10–13인용) 여러 가지 신선 육, 치즈, 미식가들이 선택하는 빵을 포함합니다. 칩과 음료수 또한 포함되어 있습니다. $35

Main Dish Mania (7–9인용) 다양한 종류의 소고기, 치킨, 돼지고기 및 채소용 메인 요리를 갖춘 정식요리. 요청 시에 맞춤형 요리구성도 가능합니다. $38–55

5개 이상의 요리를 주문하시면 10% 할인을 받으실 수 있습니다. 주문은 이틀 전에 미리 해주셔야 합니다.

151. 광고에 목적은 무엇인가?
(A) 식료품점의 오픈을 알리기 위해서
(B) 행사용 출장 요리의 메뉴 종류를 설명하기 위해
(C) 레스토랑의 새로운 주요리를 홍보하기 위해
(D) 개별 포장된 요리들을 홍보하기 위해

152. 어떤 요리가 음료를 포함하고 있나요?
(A) Veggie Party
(B) Crazy Cookies
(C) Luxurious Lunch
(D) Main Dish Mania

153. 고객들은 Morton 식료품점에서 어떻게 할인을 받을 수 있나요?
(A) 인터넷으로 요리를 주문함으로써
(B) 행사 전에 요리를 주문함으로써
(C) 최소한 다섯 접시를 주문함으로써
(D) 메인 요리 중 하나를 주문함으로써

Questions 154–155 정보문

이사 및 관리

식물을 새로운 장소로 옮길 때는 목적지에 안전하게 도착해서 새로운 장소에서 잘 자랄 수 있도록 조심하는 것이 중요합니다. 식물들을 윗부분만 들어서 옮기면 식물 자체나 식물의 뿌리에 피해를 줄 수도 있기 때문에 식물들은 화분과 함께 옮겨져야 합니다. 종이 다른 식물들은 다른 물주기 방식을 요합니다. 당신이 구매한 식물에 어떻게 물을 줄 지를 자세하게 설명해주는 안내책자가 가게 정문에서 무료로 제공됩니다.

154. 이 정보는 주로 누구를 위한 것인가?
(A) 식물을 구매한 고객
(B) 컨테이너 판매원들
(C) 가게 직원들
(D) 수선 직원들

155. 무료로 이용가능 한 것은?
(A) 포장
(B) 운송
(C) 모종
(D) 안내용 팜플렛

Questions 156–158 이메일

수신: list@corpco.com
발신: Anna Nanders
날짜: 5월 24일 2시 40분
제목: 컴퓨터 지원 요청 #35124

여러분 안녕하세요

컴퓨터 지원부 매니저인 Greg Kinderman씨는 많은 직원들이 인터넷이나 이메일 계정에 연결하는 것과 관련해 어려움을 겪고 있다고 저에게 말했습니다. 여러 직원들이 이 문제에 관해서 부서로 연락을 해왔고 기술자들이 오늘 아침부터 문제 해결을 위해서 작업 중에 있으며 오후 4시까지는 해결될 것입니다. 본사에 있는 저희는 이런 문제를 겪지 않았지만 Porville에 경리부와 마케팅 부서에게는 문제가 되고 있다는 것을 알고 있습니다. 혹시 여러분이 이들 부서의 직원들에게 연락할 필요가 있다면 전화로 연락하시기 바랍니다. Kinderman씨로부터 문제가 해결되었다는 소식을 들으면 모든 분들께 다시 한번 소식을 전하겠습니다.

156. 누가 본 이메일을 받았을 가능성이 가장 높은가?
(A) 본사 직원
(B) Porville의 마케팅 직원들
(C) 컴퓨터 지원부의 매니저들
(D) 회계부서 직원들

157. 이메일에 따르면 Kinderman씨의 직원들은 무엇을 하려고 하는가?
(A) 본사로 연락하기
(B) 직원들을 인터넷에 다시 연결 시키기
(C) 이메일의 바이러스에 대해서 직원들에게 경고하기
(D) 소포를 Porville로 보내기

158. 이메일 수신자들은 무엇을 하도록 권고 받고 있는가?
(A) Kinderman씨에게 컴퓨터 문제에 대해 말하기
(B) 서류를 제출하기 위해 회계부서에 보고하기
(C) 컴퓨터를 동료들과 공유하기
(D) 의사소통을 위한 대체 방법 이용하기

Questions 159-160 문자메시지 대화

HUGH RUDOLPH 3:15 PM
Molly, 다음 주 휴가 때문에 신나나요?

MOLLY CASADO 3:17 PM
그렇습니다. Bahamas에 어서 가고 싶네요.

HUGH RUDOLPH 3:18 PM
Bahamas요? 신나겠네요.

HUGH RUDOLPH 3:19 PM
거기서 뭘 할 계획이에요?

MOLLY CASADO 3:20 PM
그냥 쉬려고요. 최근 회사에서 너무 정신이 없었어요.

HUGH RUDOLPH 3:21 PM
좋은 생각이네요. 휴가가 있는 동안 누가 당신 계정을 관리하나요?

MOLLY CASADO 3:22 PM
저희 직계 이사님이요.

MOLLY CASADO 3:23 PM
제가 없는 동안 긴급한 사항은 다 처리해 주신다고 했습니다.

159. Cadado씨의 계정에 대해 언급된 것은?
(A) 잠시 계정이 중단될 것이다.
(B) 이 계정들은 사업에 중요하다.
(C) 이 계정을 관리하는 데는 많은 시간이 든다.
(D) 이 계정들은 그의 상관에 의해 관리될 것이다.

160. 3시 17분에 Casado씨가 "I can't wait to get to the Bahamas"라고 쓸 때 무엇을 의미하고 있는가?
(A) Casado씨는 곧 출발할 예정이다.
(B) Casado씨의 휴가가 연기되었다.
(C) Casado씨는 지금 숙박시설을 찾을 수가 없다.
(D) Casado씨는 여행계획에 매우 신이나 있다.

Questions 161-163 기사

지역 슈퍼마켓이 새로운 웹사이트를 선보입니다

PHILADELPHIA (5월 10일)— Bangles Groceries사는 온라인 쇼핑을 위한 새 웹사이트를 제작했습니다. 새로운 서비스는 iMart라고 불리며 6월부터 서비스에 들어갈 것입니다.

—[1]— "iMart는 아주 간단하며 사용도 편리합니다"라고 Bangles 대변인 Jake Resis씨가 말했습니다. "쇼핑객들은 인터넷에서 식료품 목록을 만들고, 저희 인터넷 광고에서 주간 특가상품을 살펴볼 수 있으며 사이트에서 쿠폰도 다운받을 수 있습니다." 주문이 완료 되고 결제가 이뤄지면, 쇼핑객들은 물건을 받아가기 위해 슈퍼마켓에 들리기만 하시면 됩니다. —[2]—

—[3]— New Hope에 사는 Laura Kline씨는 이 서비스를 정말 기다려왔다고 얘기합니다. "이 서비스로 인해 저는 상당한 시간을 절약 할 수 있을 거예요"라고 말합니다. "보통 퇴근 후에 쇼핑하는데 한 시간 이상 걸립니다. 제가 iMart를 이용하면, 인터넷에서 식료품을 고르고, 집에 가는 길에 찾아가기만 하면 됩니다." Kline씨는 그녀의 전화로 주문할 수 있도록 iMart가 스마트폰 용 앱을 만들어 준다면 또한 매우 기쁠텐데요. —[4]— 하지만 Resis씨는 Bangles사가 아직은 스마트폰 용 앱을 만들 계획이 없다고 밝혔습니다.

"이 시점에서, 우리는 다른 무언가를 시도하기 전에 이 서비스가 제대로 운영되는 것을 확실히 하고 싶습니다"라고 Resis씨가 말합니다. 현재로선 9월에 배달서비스를 iMart에 추가할 계획입니다.

161. iMart의 특징으로 언급되지 않은 것은?
(A) 일부 품목에 대해 할인을 받는 것
(B) 식료품 쇼핑의 목록을 만드는 것
(C) 전화로 식료품을 선택 하는 것
(D) 인터넷으로 물품 결제를 하는 것

162. Bangles Supermarkets은 언제 배달 서비스를 제공할 것인가?
(A) 5월에
(B) 6월에
(C) 8월에
(D) 9월에

163. [1], [2], [3], [4]로 표시된 자리 중에 다음 문장이 들어가기에 가장 적합한 곳은?

"Bangles는 주문품을 찾아가실 때 고객들이 이용할 수 있는 지정된 주차공간도 마련해놓을 것입니다."

(A) [1]
(B) [2]
(C) [3]
(D) [4]

Questions 164-167 이메일

수신: Gregory Tomlin 〈gtomlin@hertzairways.com〉
발신: Hillary Kwon 〈hkwon@ausmail.com〉
제목: 5월 항공편
날짜: 1월 3일

Tomlin씨에게

우선 저는 Hertz Airways 항공사와의 기분 좋은 기억들이 많았음을 밝히고 싶으며, 그것이 제가 이 글에서 설명하고 있는 상황이 더욱 놀라웠던 이유입니다. 지난 5월 27일 LA에서 시애틀까지의 비행(HA242) 동안 비행기 착륙을 지연시키는 문제가 있었습니다. 제가 이용한 항공기가 마침내 시애틀에 착륙했을 때, 제가 갈아타야 하는 Minneapolis행 비행기는 이미 떠난 상태였습니다. —[1]— Hertz Airway 항공사의 관계자와 얘기를 나눈 후에, 저는 Piscine Hotel 무료 이용권을 받았고, 교통편이 제공되었습니다.

제가 Piscine Hotel에서 겨우 하루를 묵었음에도 불구하고, 굉장히 불쾌하고 불만족스러운 경험이었습니다. —[2]— 저에게 제공된 이용권은 만료일이 지났다고 하여 호텔 내 식당에서 거부되었습니다. 저는 식사비용으로 23.97불을 결제해야 했습니다. —[3]— 제 방에 돌아 왔을 때, 너무 추웠고 온도 조절장치는 고장이 나 있었습니다.

저는 제가 과거에 받았던 훌륭한 서비스 때문에 Hertz Airways 항공사를 이용했습니다. 하지만, 이번 Piscine Hotel에서의 경험은 저의 좋았던 기억을 퇴색시켰고 저는 귀하의 항공사가 그 호텔과의 어떠한 사업 관계도 중단하기를 제안하는 바입니다. —[4]—

항공사 직원이 저에게 준 이용권(#6513873)을 가지고 결제 할 수가 없었기 때문에 Piscine Hotel에서의 저녁 식사에 대해 정산해 주시면 감사하겠습니다. 다음 번 제가 Hertz Airways 항공사를 선택하게 되면 제가 이전에 경험했던 동일한 양질의 서비스가 제공 되기를 기대 합니다.

Hillary Kwon
53051 WI, Milwaukee Hillside 가 2877

164. Kwon씨가 그녀의 이메일에서 암시하고 있는 것은?
 (A) 그녀는 보통 여행사를 통해서 항공권을 예약한다.
 (B) 호텔 객실을 예약 하려고 준비 중이다.
 (C) 그녀는 종종 Hertz Airways 항공사를 이용한다.
 (D) 그녀는 현재 호텔 업계에서 근무하고 있다.

165. Piscine Hotel은 어디에 위치하는가?
 (A) LA
 (B) Seattle
 (C) Minneapolis
 (D) Milwaukee

166. Kwon씨는 Tomlin씨로부터 무엇을 요청했는가?
 (A) 청구서
 (B) 환승 정보
 (C) 음식점 추천
 (D) 식당에서의 비용 보상

167. [1], [2], [3], [4]로 표시된 자리 중에 다음 문장이 들어가기에 가장 적합한 곳은?

"이후에 저는 호텔의 fitness center를 이용하려고 했으나, 개조 수리 중이었습니다."
 (A) [1]
 (B) [2]
 (C) [3]
 (D) [4]

Questions 168-171 웹페이지

One Stop Sport Shop

| 안내 | 메인 | 매장들 | 제품 | 수리 및 관리 |

One Stop Sport Shop 안내

One Stop Sport Shop(OSSS)의 1호점은 10년 전에 David Avenue 746번지에서 수년 동안 농구 경기를 함께 했던 Parker Kenny와 Steve Stern씨에 의해 설립되었습니다. 그들 주변의 스포츠 용품 가게들은 Levert 주민들 사이에서 아주 인기 있던 캠핑 장비, 래프팅 장비와 같은 어드벤쳐 스포츠 용품들에 초점을 두었습니다. 그래서 다른 취미를 가지고 있던 사람들은 선택의 폭이 거의 없었습니다. 1호점 오픈 후에 또 다른 가게가 Cork Street 298에 개장했습니다. 그리고 나서 OSSS는 Levert 외곽 지역에서 성공을 하게 되었고, 지금은 농구, 야구, 조깅 장비를 찾는 사람들에게는 국내 최고의 가게가 되었습니다.

지금 OSSS는 올림픽 야구 선수 출신의 William Shaugnessy씨가 직접 디자인한 신규 의류라인, One Stop Sports Wear를 선보이게 되어 자랑스럽습니다. 전 매장에서 판매가 될 것이며 저희 웹사이트에서도 주문이 가능합니다.

저희 본점만이 다른 매장에서는 이용 할 수 없는 수리 및 관리 서비스를 제공하고 있음을 참고하세요. 수리 및 보수 서비스는 신발 수선, 러닝머신 보수관리, 야구 글러브 관리 등을 포함하고 있습니다. 추가 정보를 원하시거나 서비스 일정을 잡으시려면 저희 사이트 **수리 및 관리**를 클릭하세요.

168. OSSS의 소유주들에 대해서 언급되어 있는 것은?
 (A) 그들이 스포츠 의류를 디자인 했다.
 (B) 그들은 스포츠 활동에 함께 참여했다.
 (C) 그들은 열렬한 조깅 마니아 들이다.
 (D) 그들은 OSSS 체인을 매각할 계획이다.

169. 첫 번째 단락, 첫 번째 줄의 "established"가 가장 의미상 가까운 것은?
 (A) 나타내다
 (B) 경쟁하다
 (C) 도입하다
 (D) 복구하다

170. OSSS에 대해서 언급되어 있는 것은?
(A) 어드벤쳐 스포츠 용품을 취급하지 않는다.
(B) Levart 외곽에는 가게를 소유하고 있지 않다.
(C) 웹사이트에서 더 이상 물건을 판매하지 않는다.
(D) Cork Street에 매장은 문을 닫았다.

171. 무엇이 David Avenue 매장에서만 OSSS 고객들에게 제공되는가?
(A) 스포츠 의류
(B) 선수용 신발
(C) 조깅 용품
(D) 장비 수리

Questions 172-175 인터넷 채팅 대화

Elias Reily [10:05 a.m.]
여러분 안녕하세요. 중요한 고객이 동경에서 방문하는데요, 일주일 정도 여기에 머물 것입니다. 고객이 여기 머무는 동안, 하루 저녁 정도는 특별한 것을 마련해주고 싶은데요. 좋은 생각 있나요?

Penelope Dean [10:07 a.m.]
다음주에 여러 행사가 있어요. 그 분이 어떤 걸 좋아하는 좀 알고 계시나요? 다음주에 스포츠경기도 있고 Uptown에서 재즈 페스티벌도 있어요.

Elias Reily [10:09 a.m.]
그 분이 야구에 대해 얘기를 많이 하긴 합니다. Burton Cobras팀에 투수인 Tyler Boone의 광팬이라고 알고 있어요. 다음주에 야구경기도 있나요?

Penelope Dean [10:10 a.m.]
있고 말고요, 운이 좋으시네요. 목요일에 그 투수를 볼 수 있는 경기가 있는 것 같아요. 서두르면 아직 티켓을 구할 수 있습니다.

Travis Doran [10:13 a.m.]
재즈 페스티벌에 대해 말이 나와서 말인데요, 제 친구가 사실 기획자 중의 한 사람이에요. 만약 대비해서 제가 무료 티켓을 몇 개 구할 수 있습니다.

Elias Reily [10:14 a.m.]
고마워요, Penelope 그리고 Travis, 그것도 좋겠네요. 재즈 페스티벌이 무슨 요일인지 아세요?

Travis Doran [10:16 a.m.]
제가 생각하는 게 맞다면, 주말 행사고, 금요일 저녁에 시작해서 일요일 오후에 끝날 거예요. 제가 주말 통행증(티켓)을 몇 개 확실히 구할 수 있습니다.

Elias Reily [10:17 a.m.]
음, 그 분이 토요일 오후에 떠나요. 주말 티켓은 필요 없을 것 같아요. 괜찮다면 금요일 저녁 티켓을 구해줄 수 있나요?

Travis Doran [10:18 a.m.]
물론이에요. 저를 믿으셔도 됩니다.

172. 대화의 주제는 무엇인가?
(A) 회사 모임 일정을 잡는 것
(B) 음악 페스티벌을 기획하는 것
(C) 주말 계획을 잡는 것
(D) 중요한 고객을 접대하는 것

173. Tyler Boone에 대해 언급된 것은?
(A) Boone씨는 다음주 운동경기를 관람할 것이다.
(B) Boone씨는 리그에서 최고의 투수다.
(C) Boone씨는 동경으로 전근을 갈지도 모른다.
(D) Boone씨는 재즈 페스티벌에 참석할 것이다.

174. 10시 18분에 Travis Doran씨가 "You can count on me"라고 쓸 때 무엇을 의미하고 있는가?
(A) Doran씨는 재즈 공연에 참석할 것이다.
(B) Doran씨는 통계자료를 정확하게 보고할 것이다.
(C) Doran씨는 행사 티켓을 구할 것이다.
(D) Doran씨는 금요일 저녁에 고객을 만날 것이다.

175. 재즈 페스티벌에 대해 언급된 것은?
(A) 이 공연은 3일 동안 열린다.
(B) 이 공연은 이 지역 주변에서 많은 사람들을 끌어들인다. (이 공연에 많은 사람들이 온다)
(C) 공연 티켓은 구하기 힘들다.
(D) 공연이 야구경기와 같은 날이다.

Questions 176-180 평가카드와 이메일

고객 설문

Oak Grove Hotel

저희 서비스의 수준을 유지하고 개선 할 수 있도록 귀하께서 이 짧은 설문지를 작성해 주시면 감사하겠습니다.

	아주 좋음	평균 이상	보통	아주 나쁨
1. 호텔 외관		x		
2. 객실 상태	x			
3. 음식		x		
4. 직원 서비스		x		
5. 피트니스 센터와 사우나			x	

의견:

이전에 Maine주를 방문하는 동안 Oak Grove Hotel에 여러 번 투숙했을 때, 저는 항상 유쾌한 경험을 했습니다. 하지만 이번에는 그리 좋지 않았습니다. 제 방 냉장고의 냉동고가 작동하지 않았습니다. 게다가 직원은 저희가 호텔에서 체크 아웃 하는데 유별나게 오랜 시간을 소요했고, 호텔 입구에서 택시가 대기 중이었기 때문에 이것은 매우 짜증스럽기까지 했습니다.

손님: Carol Weatherbee
집주소: 15215 PA, Pittsburgh, Steel Street 755가

이메일 주소: carolw@treemail.com

수신: Carol Weatherbee <carolw@treemail.com>
발신: Theodore Crimmel <tcrimmel@oakgrovehotel.com>
날짜: 10월 3일
회신: 귀하의 최근 방문

Weatherbee씨에게

설문지를 작성해 주신 것에 감사 드리며, 귀하가 겪었던 불편에 대해 듣게 되어 죄송합니다. 귀하께서 겪으신 문제에 대해 만회하기 위해, 저희 호텔에서 무료로 1박을 묵으실 수 있는 쿠폰을 보내드립니다. 이 쿠폰은 1년 뒤에 만기됩니다. 저는 또한 앞으로 손님들을 제대로 체크 아웃 시켜드리도록 확실히 하기 위해서 저희 리셉션 직원과 체크 아웃 절차에 대해서 얘기를 나누었습니다.

Theodore Crimmel
Oak Grove Hotel Manager

176. 질문지의 목적은?
 (A) 공석을 위한 지원서를 모으기 위해서
 (B) 어떤 직원들이 봉급인상을 받을 만 한지 알아내기 위해서
 (C) 고객 활동에 대해 매니저에게 세부사항을 전달하기 위해서
 (D) 숙박에 대한 고객들의 의견을 알아보기 위해서

177. 호텔의 어떤 면을 Weatherbee씨는 가장 높게 평가 했는가?
 (A) 그녀가 머문 객실의 상태
 (B) 피트니스 시설의 상태
 (C) 음식점 직원
 (D) 호텔 외관

178. Weatherbee씨에 대해 언급되어 있는 것은?
 (A) 그녀는 다른 호텔에 고용되어 있다.
 (B) 그녀는 매달 여행을 다닌다.
 (C) 그녀는 이전에도 Oak Grove Hotel에 묵었던 손님이다.
 (D) 그녀는 Maine 주에 산다.

179. Crimmel씨는 그녀의 이메일에서 Weatherbee씨에게 무엇을 제공했는가?
 (A) 음식점 상품권
 (B) 무료 숙박권
 (C) Maine 주립 공원 무료 투어
 (D) 사우나 무료 이용권

180. Theodore Crimmel씨는 직원과 관련하여 어떤 불만에 대해 얘기했는가?
 (A) 냉장고가 작동하지 않았다.
 (B) 객실 열쇠가 작동하지 않았다.
 (C) TV 화질이 형편 없었다.
 (D) 체크아웃을 마치는데 너무 오래 걸렸다.

Questions 181-185 광고 및 이메일

영양관리 및 진료를 위한 Aurora Center
605 N Horsecreek Road, Dubois, WY 82513
307-555-2277

신규고객을 위한 정보

Aurora Center for Nutrition and Medical Care (ACNMC)에 방문해 주셔서 감사합니다. 저희는 지난 30년동안 환자들과 고객들에게 식이요법 및 생활습관에 대한 조언을 제공함으로써 Dubois지역과 그 주변 지역이 더 건강해지도록 도와왔습니다. 저희는 또한 저희 고객들이 맛있고 몸에 좋은 음식으로 식사습관을 개선하도록 돕기 위해 Twilight Garden의 전직 셰프인 Jennifer Church가 이끄는 요리교실도 제공했습니다.

저희 웹사이트 www.acnmc.com하셔서 진료예약을 잡거나 수업에 등록하실 수 있습니다. 이 지역에서 일어나고 있는 여러 행사에 대한 정보나 더 건강한 삶을 살기 위한 정보를 얻기 위해서 저희 인터넷 게시판을 꼭 방문해주시기 바랍니다. 여러분은 또한 Dubois 및 주변지역에 있는 여러 식당과 소매점에서 최고 10% 할인혜택을 받기 위해 이용 가능한 ACNMC Healthy Living Card에 가입하실 수 있습니다.

질문이 있으시면 언제든 ACNMC의 매니저인 Zoe Philips에게 연락하시길 바랍니다.

http://www.acnmc.org/bulletinboard

Aurora Center for Nutrition and Medical Care 인터넷 게시판

홈	게시판	의사진	영양사

요리교실: 당신의 건강한 식단에 양념을 뿌리세요, 4월 14일 오후 4시

소금섭취를 줄이는 것이 당신의 음식으로부터 풍미를 앗아갔나요? 저희가 허브나 양념을 가지고 풍미를 다시 가져오도록 도와드릴 수 있습니다. 이 허브와 양념은 당신의 음식에 강한 맛을 다시 가져다 줄 것입니다.

[센터의 키친 교실이 수리 중이기 때문에 이 수업은 394 Meckern Street에 있는 Apollo's Dining에서 열릴 것임을 숙지하시기 바랍니다.]

Wiseworth Shopping Center에서 지금 맛볼 수 있는 새로운 테이크아웃 샐러드

Brett's Better Groceries의 사장인 Brett Mars씨는 5월초부터 바로 먹을 수 있는 샐러드를 제공할 것이며, 이는 몰에서 쇼핑하는 동안 여러분들에게 빠르고 건강한 대안책을 제공해줄 것입니다.

Marciana 묘목장이 정원터를 나눠드립니다

자신의 채소나 꽃을 재배하는 것은 건강식품을 구하고 약간의 운동을 할 수 있는 훌륭한 방법입니다. Marciana Nursery Center는 여러분 자신의 정원터를 가지고서 여러분이 직접 시작해볼 수 있도록 도와줄 것입니다. 이 무상 정원터는 빨리 사라지므로 여러분의 구획을 예약하기 위해서 Barry Magnuson에게 서둘러 전화하세요.

181. 전단지에 따르면 Aurora Center for Nutrition and Medical Care에서 이용 가능한 것은?
(A) 더 나은 식단선택을 위한 조언
(B) 무료 지역사회 운동 교실
(C) 구매를 위한 다양한 허브와 양념
(D) 할인된 가격에 제공되는 일일 비타민 영양제

182. ACNMC 고객들은 특정 식당에서 어떻게 할인을 받을 수 있나요?
(A) Bret's Better Groceries에서 자주 쇼핑을 함으로써
(B) ACNMC에 의해 발급된 카드를 보여줌으로써
(C) 식당 개업일에 방문함으로써
(D) 무료상담을 받음으로써

183. Apollo's Dining에서 누가 수업을 인솔할까요?
(A) Zoe Philips
(B) Brett Mars
(C) Jennifer Church
(D) Barry Magnuson

184. ACNMC 행사는 4월에 어디에서 열릴까요?
(A) Twilight Garden 식당에서
(B) Wiseworth Street에서
(C) 394 Meckern Street에서
(D) 605 N Horsecreek Road에서

185. Marciana Nursery Center의 정원터에 대해 언급된 것은?
(A) Dubois 시민들 사이에서 인기가 좋다.
(B) 현지 기업들을 위한 채소를 재배하기 위해 사용된다.
(C) 명목상의 요금을 내면(아주 싼 값에) 임대 가능하다.
(D) 꽃을 키울 목적으로만 사용될 수 있다.

Questions 186–190 광고 및 이메일들

Rolfson 가족 사진

Rolfson 가족 사진으로 당신의 특별한 행사를 기억에 남게 만드세요!

여러 사진전의 수상자인 Dean Rolfson 사진작가와 함께하시면 귀하의 다음 번 축하 행사는 더욱더 좋아질 수 있을 것입니다. 저희 가격은, Charleston에 있는 저희 스튜디오에서 20마일 이내에 있는 장소의 경우 모든 출장비가 포함된 채로, 5시간에 500불, 9시간에 700불로 저렴합니다. 당신은 30장의 출력된 사진들과 모든 디지털 사진을 받을 것입니다. 추가 편집이나, 확대, 추가 출력 및 20마일이 넘는 지역으로 출장도 추가요금을 내시면 이용가능 합니다.

더 많은 정보를 위해 저희 웹사이트에 방문하실 수 있습니다. 웹사이트에는 사진 견본들과 저희가 언제 서비스가 가능한지를 보여주는 일정표가 있습니다. 당신은 또한 저희 이전 고객들이 저희 서비스에 관해 올려주신 게시글이나 어린이들을 위한 무료월간사진수업에 대해 더 찾아보실 수 있습니다

수신: Henry Lovett 〈hlovett@lovettaccounting.com〉
발신: Dean Rolfson dean@rolfsonfamilyphoto.com
날짜: 7월 19일
제목: 회신 : Lovett Accourting 저녁모임

Lovett씨에게

7월 2일자 귀사의 저녁모임에 대해 500불의 대금을 보내주셔서 감사합니다.

행사 관련 사진들은 매우 훌륭합니다. 당신은 저희 웹사이트 www.rolfsonfamilyphoto.com/pictureselection에서 어떤 30장의 사진이 출력되기를 원하는지 선택하실 수 있습니다.

게다가 당신이 회사 로비에 걸 대형 단체 사진을 출력해 달라고 말씀하신 것도 기억합니다. 아래 대형 사진 출력에 대한 요금이 나와 있습니다.

치수	40 x 30 cm	65 x 50 cm	80 x 60 cm	100 x 85 cm
장 당 가격	12.50 불	20.00불	30.00불	45.00불

수신자: All staff 〈staff@lovettaccounting.com〉
발신자: Henry Lovett 〈hlovett@lovettaccounting.com〉
날짜: 8월 3일
주제: 회사 사진

여러분,

지난달 Beverly Hotel에서 열렸던 회사 만찬에서 찍은 모든 사진을 스캔해서, 여러분이 언제든 친구나 가족들에게 보여줄 수 있도록 웹사이트에 올려놨다는 것을 달려드리게 되어 기쁩니다. 저희는 또한 단체 사진도 받았으며 로비에 걸려있습니다. 여러분들이 사진에서 모든 사람을 잘 볼 수 있도록 가장 큰 사이즈를 선택했습니다. 만찬 중에 찍은 작은 사진들도 빌딩 주변에 걸려있습니다.

Henry Lovett

186. 광고에 따르면 Rolfson씨는 추가비용을 내면 어떤 서비스를 제공하나요?
(A) 사진확대
(B) 사진촬영 수업
(C) 사진촬영술에 대한 상담
(D) 디지털 사진

187. Rolfson 웹사이트에서 이용 가능한 것으로 광고에 언급되지 않은 것은?
(A) Rolfson씨가 수상한 모든 상의 목록들
(B) 이전 고객들로부터의 평가들
(C) Rolfson씨의 사진 갤러리
(D) Rolfson씨의 작업 가능한 일정

188. 7월 2일 파티에 대해서 언급되어 있는 것?
(A) 행사가 Lovett Accounting의 본사에서 열렸다.
(B) 행사는 Charleston에서 20 마일 이내에서 열렸다.
(C) 행사가 Lovett씨에 의해 조율되었다.
(D) 행사는 영상발표를 포함했다.

189. 두 번째 이메일, 첫 번째 문단, 세 번째 줄에 "opted for"가 의미상 가장 가까운 것은?
(A) 자격을 줬다
(B) 찾았다
(C) 선택했다
(D) 고려했다

190. Lovett씨가 낸 추가 비용은 얼마일까요?
(A) 12.50불
(B) 20.00불
(C) 30.00불
(D) 45.00불

Questions 191-195 기사, 서신 및 설문조사

Stark Grove News

7월 20일

숙박 리뷰: Mallister Hotel
평가자 : Patrick Stuckey

6월에 개조 공사를 한 Mallister Hotel은 10번가와 11번가 사이에 있는 Central Avenue에 아주 좋은 위치를 가지고 있습니다. 이 호텔은 대형 쇼핑몰 가까이에 있으며, 도보로 5분 거리에 conference 센터도 있어서 사업차 방문하는 혹은 여행을 목적으로 방문하는 고객들에게 매우 편리합니다. 아이들을 동반한 고객들은 호텔의 수영장과 놀이터의 가치를 분명히 높이 살 것입니다.

호텔은 지하 주차장에 충분한 주차공간을 제공하며 호텔 로비는 아름답고 편안합니다. 이례적으로 좁긴 하지만 객실들은 요금이 저렴하며 실내 장식이 따뜻한 색상과 예쁜 가구들로 꾸며져 있어 산뜻합니다.

업무상 묵는 분들은 현재 객실에 무선 인터넷 연결이 되지 않아 불편할 수도 있습니다. 하지만 호텔 주인이 제가 이번 달 숙박하는 동안 저와 얘기를 나누었는데, 이러한 상황이 개선될 것이라고 말해 주었습니다. 지금은 호텔 내 비즈니스 센터에서만 인터넷 연결이 가능합니다.

심지어 이런 약간의 단점에도 불구하고 Mallister Hotel은 많은 투숙객들이 만족스러운 것 이상이라고 생각할 만한 훌륭한 호텔입니다.

Stark Grove News
독자들에게서 온 편지들

8월 2일

편집장에게

7월 20일자 최근 리뷰에서, 저는 당신의 평가자가 전반적으로 저희 호텔에 만족스러워 한 것으로 보여서 매우 기쁩니다. 특히나 객실과 로비에 있는 우리 디자이너가 한 장식들을 만족스러워 해서 매우 기쁩니다.

귀사의 평가자는 저희 객실에 무선 인터넷이 연결 되지 않아서 업무상 출장 온 분들이 이것을 불편하게 느낄 것이라고 언급했습니다. 이 문제가 지금 처리되고 있고 9월 1일부터 모든 객실이 무선 공유기를 통해 인터넷에 연결 될 것이라는 것을 알리게 되어 저는 매우 기쁩니다.

Simon Greyson
Mallister Inn 사장

Mallister Hotel을 이용해주셔서 감사합니다. 여러분의 숙박을 좀 더 낫게 만들기 위해 저희가 할 수 있는 일이 있다면 의견란에 써서 알려주세요.

투숙객 이름: Nichelle Faris
객실 번호: 238

1. 객실 만족도는?
___ 매우 만족 _X_ 만족 ___ 불만족 ___ 매우 불만족

2. 호텔 시설에 대한 만족도는?
___ 매우 만족 ___ 만족 _X_ 불만족 ___ 매우 불만족

3. 호텔 아침식사에 대한 만족도는?
_X_ 매우 만족 ___ 만족 ___ 불만족 ___ 매우 불만족

4. 의견
제 방은 매우 편안하고 깨끗했습니다. 그러나 무선인터넷 신호가 너무 약했고 조금 느렸습니다. 또한 실내 놀이터가 저녁 7시에 폐쇄되는 것을 알게되어 실망했습니다. 이 시간은 너무 이르다고 생각합니다. 더 늦게까지 오픈했으면 합니다.

191. 이 기사는 Mallister Inn의 위치에 대해서 무엇을 언급하고 있는가?
(A) 상업지구와 근접해 있다.
(B) 대학 근처에 있다.
(C) 버스 정류장까지 걸어가는 것이 용이하다.
(D) 컨퍼런스 센터의 바로 옆에 있다.

192. 기사에서 첫 번째 단락, 일곱 번째 줄의 "value"와 가장 의미상 가까운 것은?
(A) 비슷하다
(B) 인정하다
(C) 지불하다
(D) 참가하다

193. 평가자는 객실의 어떤 특징을 이례적이라고 생각하는가?
(A) 객실의 디자인
(B) 객실의 가구
(C) 객실 비용
(D) 객실 크기

194. 이 편지의 목적은 무엇인가?
(A) 평가서를 제출하기 위해서
(B) 어떤 것에 대해 항의하기 위해서
(C) 새로운 세부사항을 언급하기 위해서
(D) 신입사원을 채용하기 위해서

195. Faris씨에 대해 언급된 것은?
   (A) Faris씨는 자녀와 함께 체류한 것 같다.
   (B) Faris씨는 Mallister Hotel에 다시 체류할 것이다.
   (C) Faris씨는 영화를 다운받기 위해 와이파이를 사용했다.
   (D) Faris씨는 퇴실 전에 호텔주인과 얘기를 나눴다.

Questions 196 – 200 기사, 이메일 및 기사

6월 16일 – Clarkton시 외곽의 Mulberry Mall에서는 7월 초부터 9월 말까지 로비에서 사진작가 Kim Taggert씨의 사진전을 선보일 것입니다. 쇼핑몰의 소유주인 Sharon Bittle씨는 수년 동안 이 지역 예술가들을 후원해 왔으며 로비는 종종 예술작품을 감상할 좋은 장소이곤 했습니다.

"저는 쇼핑몰의 로비가 사람들이 모이기에 좋은 장소라고 생각합니다. 그래서 Clarkton 출신의 재능 있는 예술가들의 작품을 전시할 훌륭한 장소가 될 거라 생각했습니다"라고 Bittle씨는 말했습니다. 그녀는 누구든 와서 예술작품을 감상하도록 환영한다고 말합니다. "우리는 또한 모든 분들이 다양한 문화적 경험을 해보기 위해서 한번쯤 와 보셔야 할, Prai라는 태국 음식점을 포함한 몇몇 새로운 식당들을 식당가에 추가로 오픈했습니다."

수신: Sandra Luce ⟨scluce@mullmail.com⟩
발신: Sharon Bittle ⟨sbittle@mulberrymall.com⟩
날짜: 9월 20일
제목: 귀하의 전시회

Luce씨 에게

저는 10월부터 Mulberry Mall의 로비에서 당신의 그림들을 전시하게 되어서 매우 기쁩니다. 커뮤니티 센터 전시회에서의 당신의 작품들이 매우 훌륭하다고 저는 생각했으며, 심지어 더 많은 사람들이 쇼핑몰에서 당신의 작품을 감상할 수 있을 것입니다.

우리가 로비에서 그림들을 배치하는 것을 기획할 수 있도록 각각의 그림들의 치수를 알아야 합니다. 9월말 전에 저에게 알려주시면 감사하겠습니다.

Sharon Bittle
Mulberry Mall 주인

Try Thai at Prai
By Ed Bennett

Mulberry Mall에서 개점한 가장 최근 식당 중의 하나인 Prai는 이 지역 다른 식당에서는 찾아보기 힘든 맛과 문화적 경험을 방문객들에게 선사합니다. 저는 태국음식에 대해 많은 경험이 없는데, Prai의 직원들은 제가 무엇을(무슨 음식을) 시도해볼 지를 결정하는데 매우 도움이 되었습니다.
저는 Panaeng 카레와 밥을 강력히 추천하며, 디저트로는 망고를 추천합니다. 식당은 기분좋게 장식되어 있고, 창문으로 현지 예술가들의 작품이 전시되어 있는 것을 볼 수 있습니다. 설사 한번도 태국음식을 먹어본 적이 없다 하더라도 겁먹지 마세요. Prai에서 태국음식을 먹어보시기 바랍니다.

196. 첫 번째 기사문은 무엇을 설명하는가?
   (A) 쇼핑몰의 로비가 어떻게 사용되는지
   (B) 쇼핑몰에서의 신규 가게
   (C) 한 사진작가의 전시회
   (D) 개조된 갤러리

197. Bittle씨에 대해서 무엇이 언급되어 있는가?
   (A) 그녀는 화가이다.
   (B) 그녀는 사진 수업을 듣고 있다.
   (C) 그녀는 벽화 제작을 위탁했다.
   (D) 그녀는 현지 예술가들의 육성을 지원한다.

198. Bittle씨는 방문객들이 쇼핑몰에서 무엇을 하도록 초대하고 있는가?
   (A) 로비에서 무료 스낵을 즐길 것
   (B) 쇼핑몰에 있는 은식점에서 식사 할 것
   (C) Taggert씨를 위한 축하연에 올 것
   (D) 쇼핑몰의 새로운 예술용품 가게를 방문할 것

199. Luce씨에 대해 언급되어 있는 것은?
   (A) 그녀는 많은 화랑에서 전시회를 열어왔다.
   (B) 그녀는 Clarktor 주민이다.
   (C) 그녀는 초상화 화가다.
   (D) 그녀는 Mills씨의 지인이다.

200. Prai에 대해 언급된 것은?
   (A) Prai는 매우 인기 있어 졌다.
   (B) Prai는 신규고객에게 할인을 제공한다.
   (C) Prai는 카레요리로 상을 받았다.
   (D) Prai는 창문에서 로비 전망을 가진다.

TEST 5

PART 5

101. 이 편지와 함께 동봉된 워크샵 일정을 당신은 발견할 것입니다 ⇒ 일정을 동봉했으니 확인하세요.

102. Michael Balik의 신간 소설은 지난주에 출간되었고 평론가들은 그 책에게 아주 긍정적인 평을 주었습니다.

103. 교대 근무 조 책임자 자리는 뛰어난 대인관계 화술뿐만 아니라 뛰어난 조직력을 요구합니다.

104. Gilby Hotel에서는 여전히 손님들에게 최고의 고객 서비스를 제공하는 동시에 가장 저렴한 숙박비도 제공합니다.

105. Kindet Technology의 직원들은 내년에 적어도 20일간의 휴가를 받을 것입니다.

106. Prince George 카운티와 Charles City 카운티를 연결하는 다리는 구조적 파손 가능성 때문에 추후 통보가 있을 때까지 여전히 폐쇄되어 있을 것이다.

107. 신제품 x90 경주용 차는 Horser Motors와 Tolvir Automotive사에 의해 공동으로 생산되었습니다.

108. 모든 투자자 전문잡지들의 11월 호 기사들은 Held씨의 많은 인용구를 싣고 있는데, 그 인용구들 중 몇 개는 특히 흥미롭습니다.

109. 새 전자레인지의 출시와 함께, Dalk Electronics사는 이 지역에서 경쟁사들 보다 시장 점유율을 높였습니다.

110. 메트로폴리탄 교향악단은 주로 일반인들로부터의 기부로 자금이 조달됩니다.

111. Michelle Kim과 Daniel Heely는 지난 달에 열린 Boise 직업 박람회에서 그 둘이서만 모든 지원자들을 면접했습니다.

112. Halicart는 시내 중심가에 많은 멕시코 음식점을 가지고 있는 것으로 유명하다 ⇒ 멕시코 음식점이 많기로 유명합니다.

113. 도서관 회원들은 연체나 분실한 책에 대해서 발생된 벌금을 다른 책을 대출하기 전에 꼭 지불해야 합니다 ⇒ 벌금을 내야만 책을 대출할 수 있습니다.

114. 무료 경품을 받기 위해서, 당신은 구매를 하거나, 잔금을 이체하거나, 혹은 현금인출을 함으로써, 당신의 Discover Titanium 카드를 먼저 활성화시켜야 합니다.

115. 지난주 학자금 대출과를 방문했던 학생들의 대부분은 학자금 신청서를 작성하는데 있어서 도움을 필요로 했습니다.

116. 그의 동료와 가족들에게는 굉장히 실망스럽게도, Jackson씨는 조기퇴직을 신청했습니다.

117. 계약서의 조건은 이용자들이 중도 해지를 할 경우 취소 수수료를 지불해야 한다고 명시하고 있습니다.

118. 일주일 내내 해가 비칠 것이라는 사실은 이 추운 겨울 동안 기온이 더 따뜻해질 것이라는 걸 의미하지는 않습니다.

119. 증가하는 운영비 때문에, Reddon사는 직원들이 일 할 수 있도록 허용되는 추가 근무 시간을 제한하기 시작할 것입니다.

120. 대표이사인 Paul Settler는 주주총회에서 결함이 있는 TV에 대한 리콜을 발표하는 결정을 침착하게 논의했습니다.

121. Victory Coffee Shop은 새로운 과일 스무디를 선보인 이래로 젊은이들 사이에 점점 더 인기 있는 장소가 되었습니다.

122. 생산성 개선 프로그램의 최근 개발은 많은 전문가들에 의해 전례 없는 것으로 간주되고 있다.

123. Cybob는 지난 5년간 스마트폰을 위해 가장 널리 사용되는 운영체계중의 하나였습니다.

124. Lightspeed News의 새로운 온라인 서비스와 함께, 구독자들은 그들에게 흥미로운 주제가 출판될 때마다 문자 메시지를 받습니다.

125. Latent Software사의 파일 전송 소프트웨어는 올 3월 이후에 생산된 Latent 스마트폰과 호환됩니다.

126. 온라인 게임 배급업체인 Joinus는 때때로 고객들의 관심을 불러 일으키기 위해서 대대적인 할인행사를 개최합니다.

127. 임시 대기실은 도로 오른편 공항 출입문을 약간 지나서 위치해 있다.

128. 송장들은 한달 기준으로 모든 Grove Cable Services 고객들에게 우편으로 보내집니다.

129. 5월에 혁신적인 광고 캠페인을 시작한 이래로 Morton Refrigerators사의 판매량은 향상되어 왔습니다.

130. 처음 출시되었을 때 많은 이용자들이 신고했던 문제점들에도 불구하고 Norse Playbox는 지금껏 최고의 비디오 게임기로 평가 받았습니다.

PART 6

Questions 131–134 광고

Paulina's Hiar Salon and Manicure는 4월 16일 토요일에 기념일을 축하하기 위해 지역모임을 개최할 것입니다. 이 지역의 모든 분들은 (경품이 있는) 게임, 음식, 음료 및 오랜 경력의 저희 전문가로부터 스타일 조언을 받기 위해 오후12시에서 5시까지 저희 매장에 들려주시기 바랍니다. 커트나 파마, 염색과 같은 헤어 서비스에 대해 25% 할인을 받을 수 있는 쿠폰 또한 받아가실 수 있습니다. 방문객 한 분당 1개의 쿠폰만을 나눠드릴 것입니다. 이번 모임 후 한달 동안 이 쿠폰은 유효할 것입니다. 더 자세한 사항은 555-6833으로 전화 주시기 바랍니다.

Questions 135–138 메모

일전에 포장담당 층에 있는 저희 직원 중 한 명이 우리가 시리얼 봉투를 밀봉하기 위해 사용하는 기계에 온도조절기가 제대로 작동하지 않는다는 것을 알아챘습니다.

계기판은 그 기계가 실제보다 더 뜨거운 것처럼 보여주고 있습니다. 이 문제에도 불구하고 기계 자체는 제대로 작동하는 것으로 보입니다.

장비 기술자가 방문해서 기계를 살펴보고 조절기 관련 문제를 해결하도록 일정을 잡아놨습니다. 그는 오늘 오후 3시쯤에 현장에 도착할 것입니다. 수리가 끝날 때까지 봉투가 제대로 밀봉되고 있는지 확실히 하기 위해 모든 봉투를 면밀히 검사해주시기 바랍니다.

제대로 밀봉되지 않은 봉투를 보시면, 시리얼이 나중에 다시 포장될 수 있도록 이 봉투들을 따로 분리해주시기 바랍니다.

Questions 139-142 메모

수신: 직원들
발신: Haley Griggs
제목: Workshops
날짜: 3월 4일

인사과에서 사용중인 시스템이 현재 업데이트 중입니다. 이 시스템을 사용중인 모든 관련 매니저들이 이 변경 사항을 숙지하는 것은 매우 중요하기 때문에, 직원들의 근무시간을 보고하는 일은 담당하는 분들은 교육 세미나 중 하나에 참석해 주셔야 합니다.

세미나는 3월 8일부터 10일까지 3일 동안 오후 2시부터 3시까지로 예정되어 있습니다.

저희 IT 관리자에게 어느 날짜가 귀하에게 가장 좋은지를 inftech@preeton.com으로 알려주세요. 당신이 이 날짜에 오실 수가 없으면 hgriggs@preeton.com으로 저에게 이메일을 주세요. 단체 교육에 참여 하지 못하는 분들은 제가 직접 개별적으로 교육 시킬 것입니다.

Questions 143-146 기사

Red Hot Barbecue 오마하에 열기를 끌어올리다

알라바마에 있는 최고의 바비큐 식당인 Red Hot Barbecue가 그들의 다양한 자극적인 음식을 오마하에 가지고 왔습니다.

원래 식당의 배치가 변경되어야 했습니다. 새로운 디자인을 위해서 식당 주인들은 업타운 지역의 노점상으로부터 영감을 얻어냈습니다. 새로운 오마하 Red Hot Barbecue 지점은 Wimbley Drive 89번지에서 2주전에 오픈했으며 너무 작아서 모든 음식은 테이크아웃만 가능합니다.

맛있는 바비큐 샌드위치와 고기 모듬요리는 바비큐 매니아들과 자극적인 음식을 좋아하는 사람들을 분명히 만족시킬 것입니다. 또한 이 식당은 다양한 전문 샐러드와 사이드 메뉴 등을 가지고 있습니다.

Questions 147-148 공지

공지

수신: Hill County 병원 직원
발신: Sylvester Trent, 건물 관리소장
날짜: 3월 7일
제목: 임박한 공사

4월 2일부터 4월 7일까지 정문 주차장에 공사가 있어서 이용할 수 없습니다. 평상시에 동문 주차장에 주차를 하셨던 직원들은 Vern Avenue에 공영 주차장을 이용해 주시기 바랍니다. Hill County Hospital 직원들께는 무료 주차권을 발급해 드립니다. 또한 셔틀버스가 주차장에서 병원 남동 별관까지 운행됩니다. 무료 이용권을 받으시려면, 내일 오전 8시와 오후 4시 사이 사원 등록증과 차량등록증을 Haverson Building 내 경리부로 가져오시기 바랍니다.

147. 무엇이 안내 되고 있는가?
 (A) 지역의 도로 폐쇄
 (B) 무료 셔틀 버스의 종결
 (C) 사원 등록증의 등록 절차
 (D) 주차장의 임시 변화

148. 언제 주차 이용권이 배포되는가?
 (A) 3월 7일
 (B) 3월 8일
 (C) 4월 2일
 (D) 4월 7일

Questions 149-150 편지

Riverton 도서관
9월 2일
Kim Burns
Valley Drive 982번지
89503 NV Reno

Burns씨에게

저희 기록에 따르면, 10월 3일 자로, 귀하의 회원자격이 더 이상 유효하지 않습니다. 향후 1년 더 저희 도서관에서 책을 대출하기를 원하시면, 도서관 카드와 현주소가 있는 신분증을 들고 안내데스크로 오셔서 회원 자격을 갱신하십시오. 귀하는 비밀번호 다섯 자리를 변경해야 하지만, 회원번호는 변경되지 않을 것입니다. 책이나 기타 물품에 미지급된 연체금이 있다면, 갱신 시에 납부되어야 합니다.

Riverton 도서관 회원 곤리부 Steven Kimball 드림

149. 이 편지는 왜 쓰여졌나요?
 (A) 신규 도서관 프로그램을 홍보하기 위해서
 (B) 신규 비밀번호를 확인하기 위해서
 (C) 회원 가입을 위한 절차를 설명하기 위해서
 (D) 회원 갱신 방법을 설명하기 위해서

150. Burns씨는 안내데스크에 무엇을 가져오도록 지시 받고 있는가?
 (A) 그녀의 현 주거지 증명서
 (B) 그녀의 최근 사진
 (C) 연체된 도서곤 물품
 (D) 그녀의 신규 회원 번호

Questions 151-152 문자메시지 대화

JESSICA HEIDECKER	1:16 PM
Frank, 내일 고객들과 만날 시간이 있나요?	

JESSICA HEIDECKER	1:17 PM
PLR Labs이 당신의 잡지 광고를 마음에 들어 해서 인터넷 광고를 위한 아이디어를 받기를 원합니다.	

FRANK DURDEN	1:19 PM
내일이요? 저는 목요일에 만난다고 생각했는데요.	

FRANK DURDEN	1:20 PM
내일까지는 전체 광고안을 만들 수가 없는데요.	

JESSICA HEIDECKER	1:21 PM
전체 제안서는 필요 없어요.	

JESSICA HEIDECKER	1:22 PM
그들은 단지 아이디어를 좀 얻어서 그들의 이사에게 전달하고 싶어 합니다.	

FRANK DURDEN	1:23 PM
아이디어 일부요? 문제도 아니죠.	

JESSICA HEIDECKER	1:24 PM
좋아요, 내일 2시에 로비에서 그들과 만납시다.	

151. Frank Durden씨의 잡지 광고에 대해 언급된 것은?
(A) 이 광고는 페이지 전면을 차지했다.
(B) 이 광고는 상을 받았다.
(C) 고객들은 이 광고가 좋다고 생각했다.
(D) 이 광고는 목요일까지 완성 가능하다.

152. 1시 23분에 Durden씨가 "No sweat"이라고 쓸 때 무엇을 의미하고 있는가?
(A) 온도가 매우 차갑다.
(B) Durden씨는 오늘 열심히 일하지 않았다.
(C) Durden씨는 새로운 아이디어를 전혀 가지고 있지 않다.
(D) Durden씨는 그 요청과 관련하여 전혀 문제가 없다.

Questions 153-155 전단지

즐거운 행사에 참여하세요!
행사: Hans Mixler 감독의 신작 영화 Hawk's Ascent 전세계 첫 상영
장소: 오리건 주 Portland, Gaverton 극장
시간: 8월 14일 일요일. 버스가 오후 4시에 사원 주차장을 출발합니다.
잠정 복귀 시간: 오후 11시 30분
가격: 일인당 30불이며 7시 공연에 교통비, 저녁 식사비, 입장료가 포함된 가격입니다. 출발 전 버스에 탑승 할 때 지불해 주셔야 합니다. Chez Rouge에서 저녁식사를 할 수 있고 스낵 및 음료는 영화 시작 전 구내 매점에서 구입 할 수 있습니다.

공지: 함께 보실 분들은 동쪽 휴게실에 놓여진 서식을 사용해서 등록하시면 됩니다. 서식은 8월 8일 오후 4시 30분까지 게재 될 것입니다.

153. 어떤 종류의 행사가 홍보되고 있는가?
(A) 관광 여행
(B) 캠핑 여행
(C) 영화 상영
(D) 하이킹

154. 참가자들은 어디에서 행사를 위한 결제를 해야 하나요?
(A) Gaverton Theater에서
(B) 동쪽 휴게실에서
(C) 접수처에서
(D) 버스에서

155. 여행 가격에 포함 되어 있는 것은?
(A) 점심
(B) 저녁
(C) 음료
(D) 스낵

Questions 156-158 웹페이지

Zimmerman Furniture

30년 간 최고급 사무. 주택 가구 공급처

Zimmerman Furniture 온라인 계정에 등록하고자 하시면 여기를 클릭하세요.

등록하시면 많은 혜택들이 있습니다. 가령

- 이메일로 발송되는 할인 행사에 대한 최신 소식
- 가입고객에게만 제공되는 할인 코드
- 웹사이트에서의 보다 빠른 주문 처리

귀하의 등록 정보를 입력하는 방법은 쉽고 겨우 몇 분이 소요됩니다. 단지 귀하의 연락처와 신용카드 정보를 입력하시면 됩니다. 저희는 최신 암호 기술을 사용해서 저희 고객 정보를 안전하게 보호해 드린다는 점을 안심하셔도 좋습니다.

156. 웹 페이지의 목적은 무엇인가?
(A) 고객이 등록하도록 장려하기 위해서
(B) 새로운 가게 오픈 소식을 알리고자
(C) 배송 날짜를 확인하기 위해서
(D) 구매 정보를 요청하기 위해서

157. 회원의 혜택으로 언급되지 않은 것은?
(A) 빠른 주문 처리
(B) 할인가를 위한 특별 코드
(C) 할인 소식 공지
(D) 할인된 배송 서비스

158. Zimmerman Furniture사에 대해서 언급된 것은?
(A) 가족 소유의 회사다.
(B) 최신 보안 조치를 사용하고 있다.
(C) 전세계로 배송한다.
(D) 품질에 대한 높은 평판을 가지고 있다.

Questions 159-160 이메일

수신: Chris Barrett 마케팅 이사
발신: Tricia Wallace CFO
제목: Aaron Copsy
날짜: 8월 27일

Chris씨에게

저는 최근에 귀하의 부서가 지난 한달 동안에 여러 신규 계약을 따냈으며 귀하의 팀이 일손이 부족하다는 것을 들었습니다.

저는 당신의 마케팅 팀에 캠페인 디자이너 직책에 Aaron Copsy씨를 추천하고자 합니다. 제가 지난 6개월간 그를 인턴으로 고용했기 때문에 그가 매우 부지런하고 지적이라는 것을 저는 알고 있습니다. 그뿐 아니라 그는 독창성이 뛰어나고 혼자서 뿐만 아니라 팀으로도 일을 잘 수행합니다.

Copsy씨는 최근에 마케팅 학위를 따고 대학을 졸업했으며 저희 Carnet 회사 내 그 분야에서 일을 시작해보고 싶어합니다. 그가 귀하의 팀에 유용한 인재가 될 것임을 저는 확신합니다. 혹시 궁금한 질문이 있으면 언제라도 저에게 연락 주세요.

Tricia Wallace
CFO
Carnet, Inc.

159. 이메일을 보낸 이유는 무엇인가?
(A) 신규 채용 절차를 설명하기 위해서
(B) 추천을 하려고
(C) 신규 계약에 대한 세부 사항을 요청하기 위해서
(D) 미팅 장소를 추천하려고

160. 이메일에서 Wallace씨에 대해 언급하고 있는 것은?
(A) 그녀는 마케팅 부서와 프로젝트 작업을 할 것이다.
(B) Barrett씨 밑에서 일한다.
(C) 그의 직업을 바꿀 계획이다
(D) 6개월간 Copsy씨와 함께 근무 했었다.

Questions 161-164 광고

**Steve Shores와 함께
호주 오지를 탐험하세요!**

호주 오지의 야생미를 보고 싶고, 원주민의 생활을 알고 싶으시면, 오늘 Koala Tours의 오지 탐험 투어 가운데 하나를 신청하세요. 저희 여행사에서는 일년 내내 Mungo 국립공원, Ayers Rock, 다른 호주 전역 명소들의 투어를 제공합니다. 모든 투어는 전문적이고 경험이 많은 가이드에 의해 진행됩니다. 우리는 또한 우리의 전문 셰프들이 준비하는 요리를 제공해 드립니다. 아래 몇 가지 투어 상품이 소개되어 있습니다.

도보 탐험: 베이스 캠프 산장에서 숙박
    4박 5일 – AU 800달러부터
    7박 8일 – AU 1150달러부터

오지 탐험: 초원 전역에 텐트 숙박
    4박 5일 – AU 600달러부터
    7박 8일 – AU 800달러부터

귀하의 전체 여행을, 귀하가 계신 곳에서부터 비행기를 타고 호주까지 오는 것까지 책임져 주는 사파리 패키지상품으로 예약하셔도 됩니다. 인기 있는 탐험에는 사전 등록을 권합니다. 좀더 세부사항과 사진들은 저희 웹사이트 www.koalatours.co.au에서 보실 수 있습니다.

161. Mungo 국립공원에 대해서 언급되어 있는 것은?
(A) Ayers Rock 근처이다.
(B) 여행 가이드가 거기 살고 있다.
(C) 베이스 캠프 산장이 거기에 위치해 있다.
(D) 일년 내내 손님들에게 개장된다.

162. 광고에 따르면, Koala Tours에서 제공 하는 것은?
(A) 숙소의 선택
(B) 가이드에 대한 교육
(C) 하루 동안의 탐험
(D) 오지 요리 수업

163. Koala Tours에 대해 언급되지 않은 것은?
(A) 사전 등록을 권고한다.
(B) 투어 패키지에 비행편도 제공한다.
(C) 전문 셰프를 고용한다.
(D) 신규 매니저 찾고 있다.

164. 광고에서 1번째 문단, 3번째 줄의 "attractions"이 의미상 가장 가까운 것은?
(A) 매혹적임
(B) 관광지
(C) 매력
(D) 대우

Questions 165-167 기사

Bayden 지역의 아름다운 역사적 랜드마크 중에 하나인 Sphere Theater는 심각하게 훼손되었고 복원이 필요합니다. 공연 문화 센터는 무려 100년이나 우리 도시에 있었으며 많은 훌륭한 오래된 극장 시설을 갖춘 이 지역 역사의 일부분입니다. —[1]— 아름답게 디자인된 로비는 극장이 처음 건립되었을 때를 떠올리게 해주는 예술적인 석조물을 특징으로 합니다. Deidre Mallister나 Mark Hintz와 같은, 수년 동안 Sphere 극장에서 존연을 해왔던 유명 공연가들의 사진들과 아름다운 벽화들이 벽을 장식하고 있습니다. —[2]—

관광객의 수가 과거에는 훨씬 많았으며, 극장의 공연물 수도 마찬가지로 많았었으나, 이 숫자는 현격하게 하락했습니다. 극장은 지속적으로 사용가능 하도록 하기 위해서 대대적인 복원이 필요합니다. 대대적인 복원을 위해서, Bayden 시민, 사업주들, 그리고 지역 대표들로 구성된 Sphere Theater Revival Society가 계획을 수립하게 위해 함께 모였습니다. —[3]— 이 복원 프로젝트는 향후 6개월 간 진행될 것이며, 이 Society는 Sphere Theater 극장을 이전 영광스런 모습으로 복원하기 위한 기금 마련에 애쓰고 있습니다.

Sphere Theater Revival Society는 Bayden과 이 복원 사업에 관심이 있는 주변 지역의 시민들을 위한 특별 설명회 열고자 합니다. —[4]— 복원 계획, 기부 방법 및 기타 정보는 www.sphere theaterrevival.com에서 찾아 보실 수 있습니다.

165. 이 기사문은 주로 무엇에 관한 것인가?
(A) 도시의 독특한 건물 투어
(B) 최근 열린 선거의 결과
(C) 곧 있을 도시 사업에 관한 설명
(D) 극장에서의 공연 일정

166. Sphere Theater에 대해서 유추 할 수 있는 것은?
(A) Bayden에서 가장 유명한 건물이다.
(B) 후원자들에게 무료 티켓을 제공한다.
(C) 더 이상 공연을 위해 사용되지 않는다.
(D) 이전에 유명 예술가들이 출연했다.

167. [1], [2], [3], [4]로 표시된 자리 중에 다음 문장이 들어가기에 가장 적합한 곳은?
"이 미팅들은 Bayden Community Center에서 이달 첫 번째 목요일을 시작으로 매달 열릴 예정입니다."
(A) [1]
(B) [2]
(C) [3]
(D) [4]

Questions 168–171 인터넷 채팅 대화

Celia Ashforth [9:32 a.m.]
우리가 최근에 출시한 아동복에 대한 지난달 매출수치 복사본 가지고 있는 분 있나요? 오늘 오후에 제가 발표가 있는데요, 이 수치들을 넣어야 해서요.

Marisa Dawkins [9:33 a.m.]
회사의 인터넷 공유 하드드라이브에 매출보고서가 전부 다 있습니다. 로그인 ID와 비밀번호만 있으면 됩니다. 있으세요?

Celia Ashforth [9:35 a.m.]
가지고는 있는데요, 제 ID하고 비밀번호가 일치하지 않는다는 메시지가 계속 뜹니다. 왜 그러는지 모르겠어요. 저는 회사에 입사한 이래로 같은 ID와 비번을 사용해 왔거든요.

Kevin McClure [9:37 a.m.]
그래서 그런 거예요. 새 보안규정에 대해 이메일 못 받으셨어요? 모두 다 3개월마다 비밀번호를 변경해야 해요. 당신이 비밀번호를 변경하지 않았다면 당신 ID는 제한된 접근권한만 가지게 되고, 그렇게 되면 인터넷 하드드라이브를 사용할 수 없게 됩니다.

Celia Ashforth [9:38 a.m.]
맞아요, 기억이 나네요. 제가 계속 미뤄오다가 완전히 잊어버렸네요. 그러면, 지금 비밀번호를 변경하려면 어떻게 해야 하나요?

Kevin McClure [9:40 a.m.]
비밀번호 재설정 요청서를 IT부서에 제출해야 합니다. IT부서에서 처리하고 나서 대략 하루 뒤에 임시 비밀번호를 당신에게 이메일로 보내줄 거예요.

Celia Ashforth [9:42 a.m.]
아주 성가시네요. 저는 오늘 오후에 지난달 매출 보고서가 필요한데요. 제가 복사본을 구할 수 있게 도와주실 수 있는 분이 있나요?

Marisa Dawkins [9:43 a.m.]
제가 당신 자리로 가서 제 계정을 가지고 인터넷 하드드라이브에 접속을 할게요. 그러면 당신이 보고서를 다운받을 수 있으니까요. 앞으로 몇 일 동안 필요할지 모르는 다른 서류들도 다 다운받으시면 되겠네요.

Celia Ashforth [9:45 a.m.]
고마워요, Marisa. 한 15분쯤 후에 와주실 수 있나요? 먼저 비밀번호를 처리하기 위해 IT부서에 가려고 합니다.

168. Celia Ashforth에 대해 언급된 것은?
(A) Ashforth씨는 이날 오후 회의에 참석할 것이다.
(B) Ashforth씨는 오늘 늦게 발표를 할 것이다.
(C) Ashforth씨는 IT부서에서 일한다.
(D) Ashforth씨는 자기 이메일에 접속할 수가 없다.

169. 지난 3개월 동안 어떤 규정이 변경되었는가?
(A) 직원들은 항상 ID 배지를 착용해야 한다.
(B) 직원들은 정기적으로 비밀번호를 업데이트해야 한다.
(C) 직원들은 다른 직원을 위해 로그인할 수 없다.
(D) 방문객들은 반드시 직원과 동행해야 한다.

170. 9시 38분에 Celia Ashforth씨가 "it completely slipped my mind"라고 쓸 때 무엇을 의미하고 있는가?
(A) Ashforth씨는 자기 비밀번호를 기억하지 못한다.
(B) Ashforth씨는 IT부서가 어디 있는 지를 모른다.
(C) Ashforth씨는 새로운 절차를 따라야 한다는 것을 잊어버렸다.
(D) Ashforth씨는 약속을 기재할 수 없다.

171. Marisa Dawkins씨는 오전 10시에 무엇을 할 가능성이 가장 높은가?
(A) IT직원과 얘기를 나눌 것이다.
(B) 공유 하드드라이브에서 자료를 다운받을 것이다.
(C) 파일에 접근함으로써 직원을 도와줄 것이다.
(D) 자신의 회사 비밀번호를 업데이트할 것이다.

Questions 172-175 기사

서점에서의 음악이 판매에 어떤 영향을 미치는가?
Sander Magrue
Jamestown 경영대학

서점에서 나오는 음악이 당신이 어떻게 쇼핑을 하는지를 변화 시킬지 궁금해 한 적이 있는가? 과연 음악이 고객에게 서점을 좀 더 둘러보게 한다든가 혹은 심지어 책을 더 사게 만들까? Jamestown 경영대학교 학생들에 의한 연구는 서로 다른 음악 곡목 표를 사용하는 12개 서점에서, 하나는 빠른 곡조의 음악, 하나는 중간 템포의 음악 그리고 하나는 느린 음악을 틀어주면서 한달 동안 고객들의 행동을 조사 했습니다. —[1]—

서점들은 모든 지역마다 지점을 갖고 있는 프랜차이즈 형태였습니다. —[2]— 연구 결과를 일관성 있게 만들려는 노력의 일환으로써, 연구용으로 선정된 각 서점들은 20대 청년들이 밀집된 대학가 근처에 위치했습니다.

이 연구는 고객들이 서로 다른 곡목 표를 사용하는 각각의 서점에서 얼마나 많은 시간을 보내는지를 살펴 보았습니다. 쇼핑이 끝나고 난 후 고객들은 얼마나 많은 책을 구입했는지를 알아보는 질문을 받았습니다. —[3]— 그리고 정확하게 자료를 수집하고 제대로 통계를 분석했는지 확인하기 위해서 저 자신을 포함한 Jamestown 경영대학교의 교직원들이 이 연구를 감독했습니다.

—[4]— 연구 결과에 따르면 빠른 템포의 음악을 트는 서점의 고객들은 쇼핑하는데 더 짧은 시간을 썼으며, 반면에 중간 템포와 느린 템포의 음악을 들려주는 서점들은 쇼핑 시간에 별반 차이를 보이지 않았습니다. 게다가 높은 템포의 음악을 들려주는 가게 손님들이 평균적으로 더 많은 책을 구매했습니다. 2학년에 재학중인 Jenny Baek 학생은 높은 템포의 음악은 소비자들로 하여금 책 쇼핑을 더 빨리 하게 만들고, 따라서 하나하나의 구매를 심사숙고 하는 데는 시간을 덜 쓰게 만든다는 가설을 도출했습니다. 이것이 결국 쇼핑시간은 덜 쓰고, 더 많은 구매를 하는 결과를 내는 것입니다.

172. 이 기사문에 무슨 정보가 언급되어 있는가?
(A) 얼마나 많은 고객들이 조사 받았는지
(B) 얼마나 많은 시간이 자료를 수집하는데 소요되었는지
(C) 각 고객이 몇 권의 책을 구매했는지
(D) 가게에서 음악이 얼마나 시끄럽게 틀어졌는지

173. 저자는 이 연구에서 어떤 역할을 했는가?
(A) 그는 고객들을 설문 조사했다.
(B) 그는 학생들을 관리했다.
(C) 그는 가게에서 쇼핑했다.
(D) 그는 가설을 세웠다.

174. 기사문에 따르면, 가게에서 무엇이 음악의 템포에 의해 영향을 받는가?
(A) 고객들이 가게에 머무르는 시간
(B) 고객들이 가장 많이 찾는 섹션
(C) 고객과 직원 사이에 상호관계
(D) 고객만족의 정도

175. [1], [2], [3], [4]로 표시된 자리 중에 다음 문장이 들어가기에 가장 적합한 곳은?

"모든 가게는 쇼핑 구역이 5000에서 7000 평방미터의 규모입니다."
(A) [1]
(B) [2]
(C) [3]
(D) [4]

Questions 176-180 편지와 이메일

Smithson씨에게

당신의 감사 프로세스를 지원하도록 Eco Consulting사와 계약을 체결하셔서 저희는 매우 기쁩니다. 우리는 감사가 끝날 무렵에는 귀사가 환경 보호 조항에 있어서 최신수준으로 업데이트 되어 있을 것을 보장해드립니다.

논의한 바대로, 귀사의 절차가 대기 환경과 물 절약, 쓰레기 처리를 규제하는 현 정부 기준을 잘 준수하도록 확인하기 위해서 감사작업을 할 것입니다. 저희는 일반 관행, 배기 가스 배출량, 수질 정화, 쓰레기 처리 및 재활용 절차, 이 네 가지 부분을 검사할 것입니다. 우리는 귀사의 전반적인 관리에 등급을 마킬 뿐만 아니라 이 네 가지 부문에서의 실적을 평가 할 것입니다.

당신이 저희 서비스를 요청했을 때 8월 첫 3주 동안 감사가 진행될 것을 요청했습니다. 이 일정은 우리에게 적당합니다. 우리가 달리 통보 받는 게 없다면, 이 일정에 맞춰 감사를 진행할 것입니다.

Ms. Hines
Eco Consulting

수신: Dean_Smithson@coltautoparts.com
발신: Alan_Shore@coltautoparts.com
제목: 3분기 일정
날짜: 6월 18일
첨부: 잠정 일정표.pdf

Smithson씨에게

8월, 9월, 10월의 회사 일정에 관한 초안이 이 이메일에 첨부되어 있습니다. 운송부서 직원들은 MTK 자동차사의 주문량에 따라 이 세달 동안 초과근무를 해야 할 수도 있을 것 같습니다. 저희는 금요일까지 주문이 들어 올 거라 예상하고 있으며, 금요일에 이 일정을 확인해 드릴 수 있을 것입니다.

지난 대화에서, 당신은 9월에 안전 세미나 시간을 추가하고자 일정을 변경 할 수도 있을 거라 말씀하셨습니다. 그래서 저는 일정표에 이미 그 사항을 입력했습니다만 200c더 추가하고 싶은 것이 있으십니까? 다음주 초에 지역 매니저들에게 완성된 일정표를 보낼 수 있도록 준비하고자 합니다.

Alan Shore

176. Hines씨는 왜 편지를 썼는가?
 (A) 유망 고객을 끌어들이기 위해서
 (B) 정보 요청에 답장하려고
 (C) 잠정적인 일정을 확인하기 위해서
 (D) 절차상의 변경을 보고하기 위해서

177. Eco Consulting사는 어떤 서비스를 제공하는가?
 (A) 운송 및 선적부서에서 일할 직원 채용하기
 (B) 업체의 재무 관행 기획하기
 (C) 해로운 화학물질과 쓰레기의 처리
 (D) 기업들의 정부 규제 준수여부에 등급 매기기

178. 이메일에 따르면 다음 달에 운송부서에서 무슨 일이 일어날 가능성이 높은가?
 (A) 일부 직원들이 평상시 보다 많은 시간 근무를 할 것이다.
 (B) 일부 차량들이 점검을 받을 것이다.
 (C) 직원들은 처리 절차에 대해 교육을 받을 것이다.
 (D) 회사 일정표가 직원들에게 배포될 것이다.

179. Shore씨는 그 주가 끝나기 전에 무엇을 하기를 희망하고 있는가?
 (A) Eco Consulting사와의 계약서를 검토하기
 (B) 공식적인 회사 일정표를 마무리 하기
 (C) 환경 절차에 대한 감사를 시작하기
 (D) MTK Automotive사로부터 물품을 주문하기

180. Smithson씨는 이 이메일에 대한 답장에서 아마도 무엇을 언급하겠는가?
 (A) 생산 공장들이 공장가동을 늘릴 준비가 되어 있어야 한다.
 (B) 회사 감사가 일정표에 들어가야 한다.
 (C) 안전 세미나가 9월로 일정이 잡혀야 한다.
 (D) 일정을 변경하기 위한 절차가 개선 되어야 한다.

Questions 181-185 e-mail and survey.

수신자	Danielle McCourt ⟨dmccourt @ femail.com⟩
발신자	서비스 직원 ⟨customerservice @ malachibusinessservices.com⟩
날짜	8월 17일
주제	최근 주문

McCourt씨에게,

Malachi Business Services에서 저희 목표는 저희 고객에게 최고의 사무용품과 서비스를 제공하는 것입니다. 이 목적을 위해 저희와 거래를 하는데 있어서의 고객들의 경험을 주기적으로 물어봅니다. 저희 기록에 따르면 귀하는 8월 3일 저희로부터 제품을 구매하셨습니다. 이 설문조사는 작성하는데 단 5분정도가 소요됩니다. 8월 31일까지 설문조사를 작성해주시면 저희가 다음 구매금액에서 20% 할인을 받으실 수 있는 무료이용권을 기쁘게 보내드리겠습니다.

설문조사를 작성하기 위해서 아래 링크를 클릭해주세요:
www.malachibusinessservices.com/questionnair

감사합니다.

> www.malachibusinessservices.com/questionnaire
>
> 이 설문을 작성하기 위해 시간을 내주셔서 대단히 감사합니다. malachibusinessservices.com에서 가장 최근에 한 주문건에 대해 가장 적절한 답변을 선택해주세요.
>
> 1. 제출일: August 20
>
> 2. 웹사이트 이용의 만족도는?
> ☐ 매우 만족   ☐ 만족   ☐ 불만족   ☑ Very Dissatisfied
>
> 3. 얼마나 자주 malachibusinessservices.com에서 쇼핑을 하나요?
> ☐ 하루에 한번   ☐ 한 주에 한번 ☐ 한 달에 한번
> ☐ Once every three months ☐ Once a year
>
> 4. 당신의 마지막 구매품은?
> ☐ 프린터   ☐ 문구용품   ☑ Shipping supplies
> ☐ 컴퓨터   ☐ 컴퓨터 부품   ☐ Desk organization
>
> 의견란 :
> 저는 최근 malachibusinessservices.com에서의 구매에 매우 만족했습니다. 보통 저는 일년에 몇 번정도 사무실 펜이나 종이를 구매하기 위해 사이트를 이용합니다. 그런데 이번에 우리 프린터에 문제가 생겨서 빠르게 새것을 구매해야 했습니다. 저는 사이트의 직원 중 한 명과 상담을 했고 제가 저희 사무실 상황에 대해 알려준 정보를 기반으로 직원분이 프린터를 추천해주었습니다. 그녀가 추천해준 프린터는 이전 것보다 훨씬 잘 작동합니다. 익일배송도, 저희가 빠르게 업무에 복귀할 수 있었기 때문에 매우 좋았습니다.

181. Malachi Business Services에 대해 언급된 것은?
 (A) 최근에 웹사이트를 업데이트했다.
 (B) 이 지역에 많은 지점을 가지고 있다.
 (C) 정기적으로 고객 의견을 묻는다.
 (D) 경쟁사들 사이에서 가장 저렴한 가격을 가지고 있다.

182. 이메일에 따르면 첫 번째 문단, 첫 번째 줄에 "aim"이 의미상 가장 가까운 것은?
 (A) 세트
 (B) 지시
 (C) 요구조건
 (D) 의향, 의도

183. McCourt씨에 대해 사실인 것은?
 (A) McCourt씨는 그녀의 계좌정보를 변경했다.
 (B) McCourt씨는 다음 주문건에 대해 판촉행사 혜택을 받을 것이다.
 (C) McCourt씨는 8월 3일 전에는 Malachi Business Services에서 쇼핑한 적이 없다.
 (D) McCourt씨는 주문품을 예상보다 늦게 받았다.

184. McCourt씨가 그녀의 최근 주문에 대해 언급하고 있는 것은?
  (A) 주문품을 받는데 너무 오래 걸렸다.
  (B) McCourt씨는 추천해준 것에 대해 매우 감사하고 있다.
  (C) 주문품이 다른 주소로 배송됐다.
  (D) McCourt씨는 무료배송에 대해 만족해 했다.

185. McCourt씨는 정기적으로 무엇을 구매하는가?
  (A) 문구 용품
  (B) 프린터
  (C) 책상 정리 용품
  (D) 컴퓨터

Questions 186–190 안내문, 공지 및 이메일

이번달
Alley Cat Books에서 젊은이들을 위한 신간 소식

To the Lighthouse, My Friend, Patrick Fox 지음
한 그룹의 친구들에 대한 미스터리 스릴러 시리즈 중 첫 1편은 해안 마을을 배경으로 펼쳐지며 예상치 못한 반전을 담고 있다.

Giant Heads and More Below, Martin Glint 지음
작가의 아름답게 읽혀나가는 문체로 Glint는 Easter Island 여행과 그 섬 원주민들과의 경험 대해서 이야기한다. 수업 토론을 위한 가이드도 들어있음.

Not My Crown, Sally Alex 지음
Almiar왕이 사라지고 난 후에, 그의 외아들이 왕위를 이어받는데 우스꽝스러운 결과로 이어진다. 독자들은 자신이 웃음을 참을 수 없음을 발견하게 될 것이다.

Oceanside Blues, Leila Moody 지음
생각하게 만드는 이 책은 소설부분 Layton 상을 수상한 작가가 지인들과 친구들에 관한 이야기를 통해서 어떻게 과거가 우리에게 영향을 미치는 지를 보여준다.

7월 10일 금요일
Writers Monthly Magazine 잡지사의 수석 에디터 Marshall Cartman씨는 Darland Booksellers(Forest Drive 229)에서 작가들, Patrick Fox, Martin Glint, Sally Alex와 함께 하는 패널 토론을 진행할 것입니다. 이 작가들은 올해 초 Alley Cat Books에서 첫 작품들을 출판했고, 출판하기까지의 경험에 대해서 이야기를 나눌 것입니다. 세 명의 작가들은 관객과의 질의 응답 시간을 가질 것이며 그 이후에 책 사인회도 가질 것입니다.

수신인: Marshall Cartman 〈mcartman@writersmagazine.net〉
발신인: Daniella Quintero 〈dquintero@alleycatbooks.com〉
날짜: 7월 2일 화요일
주제: 일정 문제

Cartman씨에게,

행사가 얼마 남지 않은 시점에서 이 사항에 대해 알려드리는 것에 대해 죄송합니다만 저희 작가 중 한 분인 Martin Glint씨가 다음주 금요일 열릴 다가오는 당신의 공개토론에 참석하지 못할 예정입니다. 그 시간대에 한 대학에서 낭독회 일정을 이전에 잡아놓았고, 이 일정에 계약상 묶여있는 상황이라고 그는 저희에게 알려왔습니다. 그러나 저희는 Loathsome Balance 라는 제목의 책을 최근에 출간한 대체 작가, Victor Smallwood를 제안하게 되어 기쁩니다. 이 책도 Smallwood씨의 첫 번째 출판이며 이번 공개토론의 주제에 기여할 수 있을 것입니다. 이번 행사와 관련하여 어떤 일이건 제가 지원할 수 있다면 언제든 저에게 연락 주시기 바랍니다.

Daniella Quintero
Alley Cat Books 홍보이사

186. 안내문의 모든 책들의 공통점은 무엇인가?
  (A) 소설 작품들이다.
  (B) Easter Island지역 출판사에서 출간되었다.
  (C) 젊은이들을 겨냥한 책들이다.
  (D) 각 작가들의 첫 작품들이다.

187. 7월 10일 행사의 주제는 무엇인가요?
  (A) 어떻게 서점들이 책 판매고를 높일 수 있을 것인가
  (B) 어떻게 작가들이 책을 출판할 수 있는가
  (C) 어떻게 잡지 에디터의 직업을 구하는가
  (D) 어떻게 수업 계획표를 짜는가

188. Cartman씨는 이벤트에서 무엇을 할 것인가?
  (A) 독자들에게 책 사인을 해 준다.
  (B) 수업 관리의 조언을 제공한다.
  (C) 패널들과 토론을 진행한다.
  (D) 보안을 관리 한다.

189. Leila Moody에 대해 언급되지 않은 것은?
  (A) Leila Moody씨는 수상경력이 있는 작가다.
  (B) Leila Moody씨는 행사에서 책 사인회에 참여할 것이다.
  (C) Leila Moody씨는 Alley Cat Books를 통해 책을 출판했다.
  (D) Leila Moody씨는 최근에 젊은사람들을 위한 책을 출판했다.

190. 어떤 책의 작가가 행사에 참석하지 못할까?
  (A) To the Lighthouse, My Friend
  (B) Giant Heads and More Below
  (C) Not My Crown
  (D) Loathsome Ealance

Questions 191–195 이메일, 일정표 및 이메일

수신: William Harvest〈wharvest@zeamail.co.nz〉
발신: Katie Simm 〈ksimm@nzaw.org〉
제목: Auckland Convention
날짜: 6월 2일
첨부: 세미나 일정표

Harvest씨에게

뉴질랜드 작가 협회에 의해 여러분에게 제공되는 5주년 연례 Writer's

Convention에 귀하의 등록이 완료되었습니다. 하지만 일정상에 몇 가지 변경 사항이 생겨서 6월 20일까지 필요한 정보와 함께 이 이메일에 응답해 주셔야 합니다.

유감스럽게도 당신이 등록하신 세미나 중에 하나인, Belinda Corrs에 의해 발표될 "Relatable Character Creation"이 최소되었습니다. 이 세미나는 Victor Hines씨에 의해 발표될 "Making Characters Readers Like"으로 대체 되었습니다. 이 세미나에 참석을 원하시면 이메일을 통해서 당신이 원하는 바를 확인해 주세요.

또한 귀하의 두 개 세미나 일정이 겹쳤습니다. Dylan Burgers씨의 세미나는 지금 토요일 오전 대신에 토요일 오후로 옮겨졌습니다. 이것은 당신이 이미 등록한 Evelyn Praymore씨의 발표와 시간이 겹친다는 것을 의미합니다. 그러니 어떤 세미나를 참석하는 것을 선호하시는지 결정하셔서 저희에게 알려 주세요.

Katie Simm, Convention 기획자

뉴질랜드 작가 협회(NZAA)
5주년 연례 Convention(7월 15 ~16일)
뉴질랜드, 오클랜드

토요 세미나		
시간	세미나 명	추최 측
11:15 – 12:10	뉴질랜드 풍 만들기 셀프 출판 및 입문과정	Odette Lafleur 작가 Alvin Bright 출판업자
12:30 – 1:30 점심 휴식		
1:50 –3:00	뉴질랜드 문학세계	Evelyn Praymore 소설가
	광범위한 독자층을 위한 글쓰기	Dylan Burgers TV 극작가

일요 세미나		
시간	세미나 명	추최 측
10:00 – 1:00	독자에게 먹히는 스토리	Mallory Stonch
	가벼운 어휘를 쓰면 호감도를 떨어뜨림	문학 판매 분석가 Liz Trill 시인
	1:15 – 2:15 점심 휴식	
2:40 – 5:00	독자가 선호하는 캐릭터 만들기	Victor Hines, 영문학 교수
	온라인 독자 확보하기	Sally Gosh, 기자

수신인: Berta West 〈bwest@jawharppublications.com〉
발신인: William Harvest 〈wharvest@zeamail.co.nz〉
날짜: 7월 18일
주제: 다시 한번 감사 드립니다

Berta씨,

제가 작가 학회에 참석할 수 있도록 당신과 Jaw Harp Publications에서 등록비를 내주신데 대해 감사 드립니다. 저의 소설을 쓰는 데 제가 사용할 수 있을 것 같은 많은 것을 그곳에서 배웠습니다. 제 소설뿐만 아니라, 인터넷을 사용해 저의 글에 대한 관심을 불러일으키기 위해서 학회에서 배웠던 것들 중 일부를 써먹어 보리라 결심했습니다. 인터넷 문학 사이트에 단편 소설 중 일부를 기고하는 것뿐만 아니라 블로그도 시작해볼 계획입니다. 아이디어가 있으시면 저에게 알려주세요.

William Harvest

191. 이메일의 목적은 무엇인가?
(A) 협회 행사에 참석을 확인하기 위해서
(B) 곧 있을 컨벤션 홍보를 위해서
(C) 위원회 가입을 유도하기 위해서
(D) 컨벤션 일정상의 변경을 알려주기 위해서

192. 첫 번째 이메일에 2번째 단락, 3번째 줄의 "via"와 가장 의미상 가까운 것은?
(A) 위해서
(B) 통해서
(C) 향해서
(D) 관해서

193. 어떤 워크숍이 원래 일요일로 예정되어 있었는가?
(A) Relatable Character Creation
(B) New Zealand in the Literary Universe
(C) Historical characters in fiction
(D) A Nation of Narratives

194. 이메일에서 Harvest씨에 대해 언급된 것은?
(A) Harvest씨는 자기가 원했던 모든 발표에 참석할 수는 없었다.
(B) Harvest씨는 현재 출판사들에게 자신의 책을 보내고 있다.
(C) Harvest씨는 학회 등록비를 직접 지불하지 않았다.
(D) Harvest씨는 몇몇 발표자에 대해 실망했다.

195. Harvest씨는 학회에서 누구의 발표에 참석했을 가능성이 가장 높은가?
(A) Alvin Bright
(B) Thomas Gaines
(C) Liz Trill
(D) Sally Gosh

Questions 196–200 정보, 이메일 및 메모

Chrosin
의학 기계
영업점

필라델피아 주 피츠버그
피츠버그는 Chrosin사가 시작된 곳이고 여전히 회사 본사가 위치한 곳이기도 합니다. 이 지점에 600명 이상의 직원들이 제품 검사 및 개발, 홍보, 판매, 관리부에 고용되어 있습니다.

메인 주 포츠머스
저희의 새롭게 개조된 생산 공장이 Portsmith시에 위치하며 제품을 제조하고 전세계로 선적하는 일을 담당하는 250명의 직원들을 보유하고 있습니다.

프랑스 파리
파리 지사는 유럽 사업의 허브역할을 합니다. 400명 이상의 직원들이 북미 이외의 지역에서 근무하고 있으며 그들 중 대부분이 파리에서 일하고 있습니다.

홍콩 홍콩
홍콩은 환태평양의 아시아 시장을 위해서 가장 최근에 생긴 영업 지점입니다. 홍콩 사무소는 우리가 이 지역에서 시장 확대를 꾀하고 있기 때문에 앞으로 더욱 중요해 질 것입니다.

수신: Becca Neilsen
발신: Pierre Dumont
날짜: 8월 2일
제목: 전근

친애하는 Becca씨에게

저는 귀하가 유럽 지사에서 저희와 함께 근무 할 것이라는 소식에 기쁩니다. 저는 귀하가 저희 사무소에 유용한 인재가 될 것이라고 확신합니다. 8월 4일 오후 3시에, 당신이 있는 지역시간으로는 오전 9시에 직원 미팅이 있습니다. 저는 신상품에 대한 마케팅 계획안에 대해서 이야기를 나누고자 이 미팅 동안 당신에게 전화를 드리고 싶습니다. 이 시간이 가능한지 알려주세요.

귀하가 본사에서 전근 오는 것을 원활하도록 저희가 할 수 있는 일이 있으면, 거리낌없이 저에게 말씀해 주시면 기꺼이 돕겠습니다.

모든 지사 직원들에게 보내는 메모:

Becca Nielsen씨를 위한 송별회가 유럽으로 떠나기 이틀 전인 다음 금요일, 9월 2일에 열릴 예정입니다. 파리지사는 Nielsen씨가 이미 그들에게 제공해준 지원에 대해 감사하고 있으며 그녀가 그들의 팀에 합류할 것을 고대하고 있습니다. 우리는 분명히 그녀의 열정과 헌신을 그리워할 것입니다. 그녀가 경영진에서 지원업무를 하는 것 대신에 직접 자신의 팀을 이끌게 되어 매우 흥분되어 있다는 것을 우리는 알고 있습니다. Nielsen씨에게 작별인사를 하기 위해 꼭 송별파티에 와주시기 바랍니다.

196. 정보에서, 세 번째 문단, 첫 번째 줄의 "hub"가 의미상 가장 가까운 것은?
 (A) 배포
 (B) 해결책
 (C) 공장
 (D) 중심

197. 회사의 아시아 태평양 사업에 대해 유추될 수 있는 것은?
 (A) 유럽 사업보다 더 성공적이다.
 (B) Dumont씨가 관리를 맡고 있다.
 (C) 사업이 성장 할 것이다.
 (D) 매우 성공적이지는 않다.

198. Neilsen이 현재 근무 하는 곳은 어디인가?
 (A) 피츠버그
 (B) 포츠미스
 (C) 파리
 (D) 홍콩

199. Nielsen씨에 대해 메모가 언급하고 있는 것은?
 (A) Nielsen씨는 그녀의 새로운 직책에 대해 불만이다.
 (B) Nielsen씨의 전근은 승진을 내포한다.
 (C) Nielsen씨의 출장비는 정산이 될 것이다.
 (D) Nielsen씨는 부서를 바꾸고 있다.

200. Nielsen씨는 얼마 동안 파리지사를 지원해왔는가?
 (A) 1주
 (B) 2주
 (C) 3주
 (D) 4주

TEST 6

PART 5

101. Delay씨는 그의 법대과정을 끝냈지만, Dylan씨는 아직 그녀의 법대과정을 끝내지 못했다.

102. 저희가 제공하는 여러 다른 마감재를 사용함으로써 당신의 단순한 목공작업을 향상시키실 수 있습니다.

103. 과거 유명한 외과의사였던 Dr. Capuano은 이제 그의 시간을 환자를 돌보는 것과 미래의 의사들을 교육하는 데 나눠 쓰고 있습니다.

104. Lim & Kim Group은 사람들이 은퇴를 위해 필요로 하는 수익율을 얻을 수 있는 투자를 하도록 돕는 일에 최선을 다하고 있습니다.

105. 7명의 다른 전문가들이 시간제 요금으로 상담에 응할 것입니다.

106. 태양열 에너지 활용의 효율성은 적절한 방식으로 정기적으로 확인될 필요가 있습니다.

107. 재해의 발생 수는 70년대 이래로 3배이상 증가했음에도 불구하고, 보고된 사망자수는 반 이하로 줄었습니다.

108. 그 공장에 상당한 손실을 야기한 것처럼 보이는 폭발에 대한 보고서들이 막 발표되었습니다.

109. 저희 회사는, 당신이 회계 시스템을 유지관리하도록 지속적으로 지원할 것입니다.

110. Ralf Reed 기념 병원의 간호사직을 위해 심사를 받기 위해서 지원자들은 어떤 교대근무시간에도 근무할 수 있어야 합니다.

111. 작년 동기간과 비교할 때, 상장된 시멘트 업체들은 올 상반기에 수익증가를 경험했습니다.

112. 우리는 내빈 여러분들이 기념식이 시작하기 30분전에 착석하실 것을 요청했습니다.

113. Withrow 교수는 사업기획서를 제출하기 전에 기획서가 간결하고 현실성이 있는 지 학생들이 확인할 것을 당부했습니다.

114. Funn Sports는 내년에 스포츠 상품 사업을 신흥시장으로 확장할 것입니다.

115. 당신이 우리에게 준 $500의 보증금은, 아파트가 검사를 통과했을 경우에만 당신에게 반환될 것입니다.

116. 고객들에게 보다 나은 서비스를 제공하기 위해서, 저희는 재고량을 20% 증가시킬 계획이며, 이는 우리에게 더 많은 공간이 필요하다는 것을 의미합니다.

117. 대다수의 고소득자들은 향후 수개월간 그들의 부동산투자 포트폴리오를 확장할 작정이라고 말할 가능성이 크다.

118. 현재 Scandi Household는 신규고객들에게 구입품의 25% 할인을 제공하는 판촉행사를 제공하고 있습니다.

119. 당신의 사업이 성공할 수 있도록 지원하기 위해서, 저희는 당신이 특별한 고객서비스를 제공하도록 도와줄 교육과정도 제공합니다.

120. Mr. Karst가 자리를 비운 동안에는 그에게 온 모든 편지와 소포를 그의 비서에게 보내주시기 바랍니다.

121. 도움이 필요한 아이들을 위해 프로그램을 만들고 지원하는 것을 목표로 하는 Ronald Charities은 독립적인 비영리 조직입니다.

122. 결국, 향후 3개월 동안 누가 정리해고될 지 최종 결정을 해야 하는 사람은 Goodwill씨입니다.

123. Jerry Hairston이 CEO로 승진했을 때 즘에는, 회사가 자본 구조를 재조정하는 작업을 이미 시작한 상태였습니다.

124. 모든 사업부문의 많은 기업가들이 금년 세미나에 참석할 것이며, 그 중 일부는 현시대 최고의 비즈니스 리더들입니다.

125. 재계의 거물인 Blanchett씨는 그녀의 새 책에서 세계 자본주의의 불안정성에 대해 썼습니다.

126. Sienna씨는 지난 달에 자기 자신의 사업을 시작하기로 결심했고, 그 이후로 사업시작을 준비해오고 있습니다.

127. 보건국은 환자에 관한 디지털 정보가 기밀로 유지될 수 있도록 하기 위해서 강력한 보안조치를 취해야 합니다.

128. Togo Food Company는 최상의 품질의 재료만이 그들 제품에 사용됨을 보장합니다.

129. 당신의 이름이 쓰여진 연간 주차권을 구입시에 자동차 창문의 왼쪽 아래부분에 직접 부착하세요.

130. 올해 진행된 워크샵을 평가하는 데 있어서의 시간상의 제약 때문에, 우리는 참석자들로부터 12월 워크샵에 대한 신속한 피드백을 받을 필요가 있습니다.

PART 6

Questions 131-134 기사

Gerald Art Gallery 졸업생 작품 전시

6월 4일– Holy Cross 대학의 Gerald Art Gallery에서 연례 "4학년생의 미술작품" 전시회를 열 예정입니다.

이 연례 전시회에 참석하는 미대생들은 시각 예술학부 부교수인 Michael Beatty 교수가 강의하는 수업을 들었습니다. 그는 작년 Visual Art Award의 수상자로써 잘 알려져 있습니다.

전시회 사전 티켓은 www.geraldag.com에서 인터넷으로 구매 할 수 있습니다. 인터넷 티켓 판매는 행사 4시간 전에 끝납니다. 만약에 매진되지 않는 다면, 티켓은 현장 매표소에서 구입 할 수 있습니다. 10인 이상의 단체 할인권에 대한 정보는 714-555-2401로 전화주세요.

Questions 135-138 이메일

발신: Elizabeth Warren
수신: 전직원
날짜: 8월 16일
제목: Larry Page

Larry Page씨는 지난주에 CEO 자리를 사임하겠다고 밝혔습니다. 여러분 대부분이 알다시피 그는 CHCI에 고위 기업 홍보관 자리를 수락했습니다.

의미 있는 방식으로 지역사회에 기여하는 것이 그가 오랫동안 품어왔던 꿈이었습니다. 심지어 그렇다 할지라도, 그가 떠나면 우리 모두는 그를 그리워할 것이라는 것을 잘 알고 있습니다.

Kaufmann에서의 그의 23년간의 노고와 헌신을 기리기 위해서 멋진 송별회가 8월 30일 금요일에 주 회의실에서 있을 것입니다. 우리는 Page씨와의 추억에 대한 개인적인 이야기를 나누는 것뿐만 아니라 Page씨를 축하해주기를 원하는, 행사에 참여할 연사를 찾고 있습니다. 관심 있으시면 저희 상관에게 연락 주시기 바랍니다.

우리는 Page씨의 앞으로의 커리어에 있어서 성공과 행운을 기원합니다.

Elizabeth Warren

Questions 139-142 광고

당신의 사업체를 위한 Terwilliger Financial의 최상의 서비스

당신의 회사를 위해 금융서비스 회사로부터 받을 수 있는 최상의 서비스를 원하신다면, Terwilliger Financial보다 더 멀리 보실 필요가 없습니다(먼 곳에서 찾을 필요 없이 Terwilliger Financial에게 맡기시면 됩니다). 회사를 키우고 회사의 안정성을 도모하기 위해 저희 고객들이 필요로 하는 바로 그 서비스를 제공하기 위해 저희 회사의 모든 직원들은 최선을 다하고 있습니다.

저희가 제공하는 고객 서비스 가운데는 재무 컨설팅, 효율성 컨설팅 및 세금처리 등이 있습니다. 저희 서비스를 좀 더 개선하기 위해 저희는 최근에 웹사이트를 업그레이드했습니다. 저희 인터넷 서비스는 더 큰 유연함과 편리성을 고객들에게 제공하고 있습니다.

이 변화 무쌍한 세상에서 어떻게 전략적으로 자금과 거래를 관리하는지 알고 싶으시면 우리에게 연락주세요.

Questions 143-146 발표

4월 1일부터 Victoria 대학은 GOMA Art Gallery에서 해마다 후원하는 포스터 디자인 경연대회를 주최할 것입니다. 경연대회는 현재 대학을 다니는 재학생들에게만 참가 자격이 주어집니다. 모든 출품작들은 참가자의 원본 작품이어야 합니다. 복사본이거나, 혹은 지원자의 작품이 아니라고 판단되는 참가작품은 참가 자격이 박탈될 것입니다.

"Naturally digital"이라는 주제를 잘 표현한 포스터를 제출하는 학생이 대회를 우승할 것입니다.

참가에 관심이 있는 학생들은 4월 20일까지 대회 주최측에게 이메일을 보냄으로써 등록하셔야 합니다. 출품작품 제출 마감 시한은 5월 10일 입니다. 참가작들은 5월 20일 홍콩에서 열리는 다가오는 국제 디지털 포럼에서 심사 될 것입니다.

PART 7

Questions 147-148 문자 메시지

From: Ellen Ting
1월 21일, 오후 2시 10분

제 열차가 막 기차역에 도착했는데 기사가 역에 없네요. 부탁 좀 들어주세요. 기사가 저를 데리러 곧 올 것인지 알아보기 위해 기사에게 연락 좀 해주세요. 제가 오래 기다려야 하는지 알고 싶습니다. 감사합니다. 회사에서 뵐게요.

147. 이 문자 메시지의 목적은?
(A) 교통편 준비에 대해 알아보기 위해서
(B) 건물 위치에 대해 문의하기 위해서
(C) 고객과의 미팅을 연기하기 위해서
(D) 여행 일정을 보고하기 위해서

148. Ting씨는 어디에서 굿자를 보냈나요?
(A) 공항 버스
(B) 자신의 자택
(C) 기차역
(D) 직장

Questions 149-151 광표

사업체 매물

Brenda's Bakery and Cakery는 매물가 50만 달러 혹은 최고 제시가에 매물로 나와 있습니다(50만 달러에 매물로 나왔지만, 이 보다 높은 가격을 제시하는 사람이 있을 경우 그 가격에 매각하겠다는 의미). 이 성공적인 식당은 Headerton 외곽의 아주 인구밀도가 높은 지역에 위치하고 있기 때문에 많은 고객들이 매일마다 찾아옵니다. 많은 식당과 154c공원뿐만 아니라, Martin 쇼핑 센터와 매우 가까이에 있습니다. 모든 자재, 가구 그리고 장비들도 상점과 함께 (매물에) 포함되어 있습니다.

고객들을 위한 더 넓은 좌석을 만들고 소매영업을 위한 더 많은 공간을 추가함으로써 154d이 상점의 수익성은 한층 더 상승될 수 있습니다. 고객을 위한 테라스를 추가하는 것 또한 옵션입니다.

Atlas Business Realty에 Peter Lydon(plydon@atlasbr.ca)에게 연락함으로써 부동산이 가지고 있는 더 많은 정보와 사진들을 받아보실 수 있습니다.

149. 어떤 종류의 상점이 매물로 나왔는가?
(A) 식료품 상점
(B) 커피 상점
(C) 제과점
(D) 요리 용품 판매점

150. Brenda's 에 대해 언급되지 않는 것은?
  (A) 아침 일찍 문을 연다.
  (B) 많은 고객들을 가지고 있다.
  (C) 공원들 가까이에 있다.
  (D) 수익성이 높은 상점이다.

151. 이 안내문에 상점을 위한 가능한 변화는 어떤 것이 제안되어 있는가?
  (A) 재료가 개선될 수 있다.
  (B) 광고가 더 넓게 퍼질 수 있다.
  (C) 판매 구역은 더 넓어 질 수 있다.
  (D) 상품이 변경될 수 있다.

Questions 152–153 잡지 목차

목 차

24번째, 3월호

9	In-Grow-Diets	Bob Treston은 여러분만의 허브를 키우는 것을 위한 아이디어를 제공해준다.
13	Treats from Trees	객원 기고가들이 어떤 종류의 과일 나무가 당신에게 최선이 될지에 대한 조언을 준다.
21	Tips and Hints	Helen Nguyen는 어떻게 퇴비를 십분 활용하는지를 보여준다.
24	Essentials	Nick Rogerson은 당신의 마당을 최대한 푸르게 만드는 방법을 자세히 설명해 준다.
28	Chef Glenda Anore	Southside Kitchen의 요리사는 집에서 키울 수 있는 채소들을 가지고 어떻게 맛있는 파스타 요리를 만들 수 있는지를 보여준다.
32	Coming Up	다음 4월호에 무엇이 실릴 것인지 살펴본다.

152. 이 잡지의 주제는 무엇인가?
  (A) 요리
  (B) 정원 가꾸기
  (C) 운동
  (D) 카메라

153. 어느 페이지에서 아마도 독자들이 요리법을 찾을 수 있을까?
  (A) 13쪽
  (B) 21쪽
  (C) 28쪽
  (D) 32쪽

Questions 154–155 문자메시지 대화

TIM HARDEN	8:40 AM
공항버스가 우리 건물 앞에서 몇 시에 정차하는지 아세요?	
EMMY BOWEN	8:41 AM
보통 30분마다요. 왜요?	
TIM HARDEN	8:41 AM
제가 15분째 기다리고 있는데 아직 나타나질 않네요.	
EMMY BOWEN	8:42 AM
버스가 종종 늦어요.	
EMMY BOWEN	8:43 AM
비행은 몇 시 인데요?	
TIM HARDEN	8:44 AM
12시 15분이요. 그런데 제가 짐을 맡겨야 해요.	
TIM HARDEN	8:45 AM
그리고 요즘 보안검열이 시간이 꽤 걸린다고 들었거든요.	
EMMY BOWEN	8:46 AM
맞아요. 그런데 시간 맞출 수 있을 거예요. 버스가 분명 금방 올 거예요.	

154. Harden씨에 대해 언급된 것은?
  (A) Harden씨는 휴가를 내고 있다.
  (B) Harden씨는 택시를 부를 것이다.
  (C) Harden씨는 짐을 가지고 이동하고 있다.
  (D) Harden씨는 공항에서 Bowen씨를 만날 것이다.

155. 8시 46분에 Bowen씨가 "the bus will be there in a second" 라고 쓸 때 무엇을 의미하고 있는가?
  (A) 버스는 예약을 요한다.
  (B) 버스가 곧 도착할 것이다.
  (C) 버스가 굉장히 빨리 달린다.
  (D) Harden씨는 손을 흔들어서 버스를 세워야 한다.

Questions 156–157 편지

LandWorks Yard Services
14 Philip Road
Perth, Austrlia

2월 15

Nelson Foley
Australia, Perth, Kings Street 768번지
New Sun Networks

Foley씨에게,

LandWorks Yard Services와의 지속적인 거래에 감사 드립니다. 계절이 바뀌는 가운데, 저희는 모든 서비스를 연중 내내, 심지어 겨울에도 제공한다는 것을 기억해주세요. LandWorks Yard Services는 겨울 동안 다음과 같은 다양한 서비스를 제공합니다.

- 잔디나 포장된 구역으로부터 눈과 얼음 제거하기
- 실외식물과 관목들을 추위로부터 보호하기
- 저온에 민감한 식물들을 모아서 우리 실내 묘목장에 보관하기

가격과 다른 정보에 대한 보다 자세한 내용을 원하시면 주저 말고 저희에게 연락 주세요.

Larry Green
LandWorks Yard Services

156. 이 편지는 왜 쓰여졌는가?
(A) 정원관리 서비스에 대해 물어보기 위해서
(B) 눈 치우는 새 장비를 설명하기 위해
(C) 고객들의 지속적인 거래를 장려하기 위해
(D) 정원관리 자재의 구매를 위한 견적서를 제공하기 위해

157. LandWorks Yard Services에 대해 유추할 수 있는 것은?
(A) 사업을 확장할 준비 중이다.
(B) 저장 시설을 관리하고 있다.
(C) 호주에 3개의 점포를 가지고 있다.
(D) 그들의 빌딩이 리모델링 중이다.

Questions 158-160 일정표

6월

월	화	수	목	금	토
2 월요일 밤 영화 오후 7:00 70년대 영화	3 기부자들의 오찬 오전 11:30	4 아이들의 시간 오후 4시 "신나는 지구"	5	6	7
9 월요일 밤 영화 오후 7:00 암흑기의 예술	10 발표 오후 2시 Tien Trahn Postmodern 갤러리 큐레이터	11	12 직원 모임 (모든 전시는 마감됨)	13	14
16 월요일 밤 영화 오후 7:00 현대 사진 전쟁	17 아이들의 시간 오후 4시 "희귀한 화석들"	18	19	20 발표, 오후 5시 Praja Khan Fresco 복원 전문가	21
23 월요일 밤 영화 오후 7:00 르네상스 시대의 장인들	24 조각기법 세미나 오후 6시, (초보자 환영)	25 워크샵 오전 11시, "인상파 화법" (좌석예약 필수)	26	27 기부자들의 오찬 오전 11:30	28

158. 어떤 단체가 이 일정표를 공개했을까?
(A) 대학원
(B) 회의장
(C) 박물관
(D) 도서관

159. 어떤 행사를 위해 참석자들이 사전에 등록해야 하는가?
(A) 그림 워크샵
(B) 아이들을 위한 과학 활동
(C) 포스트 모던 예술에 대한 강의
(D) 조각 기법 세미나

160. 일주일 1번씩 무엇이 열리는가?
(A) 발표
(B) 직원 모임
(C) 영화 상영
(D) 아이들을 위한 교육 시간

Questions 161-164 인터넷 채팅 대화

Frank Noonan [10:13 a.m.]
모두들 안녕하세요? Dennis Bonifant씨가 최근에 저희 신규라인 음료 마케팅활동을 구축을 위한 프로젝트를 이끌도록 배정되었습니다. 그의 팀에서 함께 일할 자원자를 저는 찾고 있습니다.

Angela Viracola [10:14 a.m.]
몇 명이나 찾고 있나요? 저가 하고 싶지만 지금은 다른 프로젝트로 너무 바빠서요. Larry Carrol이 이전에 Dennis와 프로젝트 작업을 같이 했다고 생각되는데요.

Larry Carrol [10:16 a.m.]
맞아요, 제가 했었어요. Dennis는 저와 함께 작년 전국 음료 컨벤션에서 함께 발표를 했었어요. 저는 기꺼이 그와 함께 다른 프로젝트를 맡아서 하고 싶습니다.

Frank Noonan [10:18 a.m.]
좋아요. 잘됐네요. Denis도 사실 이번 건에 대해 당신과 다시 한번 작업하고 싶다고 물어왔어요. 저는 최소 두 분 정도 더 확보하려고 했었는데요.

Larry Carrol [10:19 a.m.]
Linda McAvoy와 Rose Condor가 이번 활동을 도울 적임자일 것 같은데요.

Linda McAvoy [10:21 a.m.]
제가 이쪽 프로젝트에 경험이 많지는 않지만, 마케팅 활동을 기꺼이 돕고 싶습니다. Larry가 생각하기에 제가 도울 수 있다고 한다면, Larry의 판단을 믿겠습니다. Rose는 오늘 아침에 고객과 미팅 중인데, 오후에는 돌아올 거예요.

Frank Noonan [10:23 a.m.]
사실 제가 방금 Rose에게 전화를 받았는데요, 고객이 미팅을 오후로 미뤘답니다. 그래서 현장에 머물렀다가 오후에 고객을 만날 거라고 합니다. 사무실에는 내일 돌아온다고 합니다. Larry씨, 그때(내일) 마케팅활동에 대해 Rose에게 얘기해주시겠어요?

Larry Carrol [10:25 a.m.]
네, 좋습니다. 내일 아침 오자마자 Rose에게 얘기하겠습니다.

161. 이들은 어떤 업계에서 일할 가능성이 가장 높은가?
(A) 광고
(B) 음료수 생산
(C) 환대(호텔)
(D) SNS

162. Frank Noonan씨가 찾고자 하는 것은?
(A) 컨벤션 일정표
(B) 마케팅 활동을 위한 지원
(C) 고객의 전화번호
(D) 사무실 위치

163. 10시 14분에 Angela Viracola씨가 "I'm up to my neck in other projects"라고 쓸 때 무엇을 의미하고 있는가?
(A) Viracola씨는 다른 작업에 깊게 관여하고 있다.
(B) Viracola씨는 그녀의 직업을 잃을 지도 모른다.
(C) Viracola씨는 추가 프로젝트를 맡고 싶어한다.
(D) Viracola씨는 마감시한을 맞출 수 없을 것이다.

164. Rose Condor씨에 대해 언급된 것은?
(A) Condor씨는 Denis Bonifant씨와 전에 일해본 적이 있다.
(B) Condor씨는 다른 마케팅 활동 작업을 해본 적이 있다.
(C) Condor씨는 일주일 내내 사무실 밖에 있을 것이다.
(D) Condor씨는 미팅 일정이 재조정되었다.

Questions 165-167 메모

발신:	Simon Locklear, 행정 비서장
수신:	회사 직원들
제목:	연례 회의
날짜:	9월 15일

Alternative Automotive의 연례 회의가 9월 22일 다가오는 월요일 개최될 예정입니다. 우리 회사가 지난 12개월 동안 보여온 성장을 감안하면 이 회의에 오고 싶어하는 많은 사람들이 있습니다. —[1]— 예상 참석자가 많은 관계로, 회사는 올해의 회의를 Alternative Automotive 본사에서 Oak Grove Convention Hall로 옮기기로 결정했습니다. —[2]—

직원들이 놓치면 안 될 행사는 오후 7시경 시작할 컨퍼런스 후에 친목 모임입니다. 회사 회장인 Amanda Fealy는 손님들과 어울릴 것이며 다과와 음료도 무료로 제공될 것입니다. —[3]— 직원들은 안내데스크에서 신분확인증을 보여줘야 하므로 꼭 신분증을 함께 챙겨오세요. —[4]— 더 많은 정보가 필요하다면, 저에게 연락주세요.

165. 왜 이 공지가 방송되었는가?
(A) 회의 일정표의 순서를 변경하기 위해서
(B) 회사 주주들의 참석을 요청하기 위해서
(C) 행사장소 변경에 대해 직원들에게 알리기 위해서
(D) 회사 행사로 오늘 길을 알리려고

166. 회의 참석자들이 요청 받은 것은 무엇인가?
(A) 경영진 위원회를 위한 후보자를 선출하는 것
(B) 얼마나 많은 사람들이 그들의 일행에 포함되는지 명시하는 것
(C) 더 많은 정보를 위해 Fealy씨에게 연락 하는 것
(D) 안내 데스크에서 신분증을 보여주는 것

167. [1], [2], [3], [4]로 표시된 자리 중에 다음 문장이 들어가기에 가장 적합한 곳은?

"8월 30일 제가 모두에게 보낸 일정표를 포함한 나머지 회의 일정은 동일합니다."
(A) [1]
(B) [2]
(C) [3]
(D) [4]

Questions 168-171 기사

업계 선두인 Revton
작성자: Gerald Shall, 경제 기자

SHEFFIELD (6월 10일) - Progressive Electronics Multinational(PEM)의 연구 부서가 취합한 업계 보고서 통계자료는 이 회사가 처음으로 MP3 플레이어 분야에서 선두가 될 것이라는 것을 보여줍니다. 그 결과, 원래 Sheffield에서 설립된 이 회사는, 주요 라이벌인 Technological Marvels, LLC(TML), 15년 전에 설립되었으며 지난 2년간 명실 상부한 MP3 플레이어 업계 1위를 수성했던 이 회사의 자리를 차지하게 될 것입니다. —[1]—

—[2]— PEM의 수익은 지난 5년 동안 평균 15% 증가했습니다. 3년 전 이사회의 의장으로써 Jillian Carter를 지명한 덕분에, 회사의 판매는 한층 더 상승했습니다.

—[3]— 회사는 지난 1년간 완전히 새로운 플레이어는 고작 3개만을 출시 했을 뿐입니다. 사실 그들의 경쟁사들이 광고비를 삭감했을 때, 이 회사는 반사이익을 얻게 되었습니다. —[4]— 첨단 장비를 사용해서 생산 비용을 낮추는 방법을 찾음으로써 PEM은 이전 해와 동일한 광고 예산을 유지할 수 있었습니다.

168. 이 기사의 목적은 무엇인가?
(A) 조직의 경영상의 변화를 예상하기 위해서
(B) 새로운 MP3 플레이어를 광고하기 위해서
(C) 회사의 성취를 발표하기 위해서
(D) 어떻게 전자 기기가 작동하는지 설명하기 위해서

169. PEM의 수익에 대해서 언급되어 있는 것은?
(A) Carter씨에 의해 발표되었다.
(B) 지난 5년 동안 낮았었다.
(C) 올해 업계에서 가장 높을 것이라고 예상된다.
(D) 올해 평소보다 더 늦게 발표될 것이다.

170. 기사에 따르면, 얼마나 오래 TML은 사업을 해오고 있는가?
(A) 2년
(B) 3년
(C) 5년
(D) 15년

171. [1], [2], [3], [4]로 표시된 자리 중에 다음 문장이 들어가기에 가장 적합한 곳은?

"수익 증가는 PEM의 신제품 출시와 무관합니다."

(A) [1]
(B) [2]
(C) [3]
(D) [4]

Questions 172-175 광고

Daesung Z22 자동화 조립 장치: 부품들

Daesung Z22 자동화 조립 장치는 제조 시설의 조립라인의 일부분으로 부품들을 들어올리거나 정확하게 설치할 수 있습니다. 자동화 조립 장치는 2개의 관절을 가진 사람의 신체 일부와 유사한데, 조인트가 하나는 아래에 하나는 중간에 있습니다. 두 개의 조인트는 왼쪽과 오른쪽으로 움직일 수 있습니다. 팔 끝에 있는 것은 부품이 정확하게 자리를 잡도록 확실히 하기 위해 회전할 수도 있을 뿐만 아니라(회전축), 아래 위로 움직임이 가능한 막대입니다(수직 축). 막대의 끝에는 어떠한 공장 환경에서도 적절한 조립이 가능하도록 손잡이나 흡입 컵 같은 여러 가지의 도구들이 붙여질 수 있습니다.

Z22는 최대 5kg까지 들어 올리기가 가능하고 초당 50cm의 속도로 이동이 가능합니다. 총 도달 가능한 거리는 직경 200cm 입니다. Z22는 또한 안전 지침을 충족시켜주면서 어떤 자재들도 오염되는 것을 막도록 로봇에 딱 맞춰질 수 있는 덮개를 포함합니다.

Daesung Z22 자동화 조립 장치: 사양

연결부위	회전
아래 부분	180도
중간	180도
축	한도
수직	초당 50cm
회전	360도

172. Daesung Z22는 어디에서 사용될 가능성이 가장 높은가?

(A) 직업 학교에서
(B) 하수 처리 시설에서
(C) 제조 공장에서
(D) 발전소에서

173. 자동화 조립 장치는 얼마나 많은 연결부위를 가지고 있는가?

(A) 1
(B) 2
(C) 3
(D) 4

174. 1번째 문단, 5번째 줄에 있는 "assorted"가 의미상 가장 가까운 것은?

(A) 분류된
(B) 발전된
(C) 안전한
(D) 다양한

175. 덮개에 대하여 언급되어 있는 것은?

(A) 안전 지침을 준수하는 것을 돕는다.
(B) 지름이 200cm 이다.
(C) 추가 도구를 보관하는데 사용될 수 있다..
(D) 지퍼로 잠근다.

Questions 176-180 이 메일과 양식

수신:	부서장들
발신:	Oliver Martin
날짜:	8월 2일
제목:	자기 개발 세미나

지난 6개월 동안 고용된 직원들이 SecuriPath Logistics에 대해 더 깊은 이해를 도울 수 있는 자기 개발 세미나가 인사부에 의해 만들어 졌습니다. 다른 부서의 직원들이 이끄는 세미나에 참석하는 것의 장점을 당신 직원들이 숙지하도록 모든 부장님들이 확실히 해주시기를 바랍니다.

세미나에 참석하는 직원들이 그들의 마지막 교육에 참석하고 나서 작성한 평가서를 제출해 주신다면 또한 감사하겠습니다. 이 양식은 세미나가 종료된 후에 각 세미나실의 출구 가까이에 있을 것입니다.

아래는 세미나의 시간표로, 모든 세미나는 Beek 빌딩의 2층 회의장에서 열릴 것입니다. 모든 참석한 직원들에게는 무료 점심이 제공될 것입니다.

부서	발표자	날짜	시간
회계	Michelle Patton	8월 18일	오후12:00 - 오후12:45
광고	Nigel Kent	8월 25일	오전11:30 - 오후12:15
연구개발	Nam Sudara	9월 5일	오후12:00 - 오후12:45
영업	Betty Sebastian	9월 11일	오전11:30 - 오후12:15

Oliver Martin
인사부장

자기개발 세미나 평가지

직원 성명: Anita Berkin

어느 세미나에 참석하였나요?

✓ 회계   ✓ 광고   ✓ 연구개발   ___ 영업

당신은 어느 세미나가 가장 흥미롭다고 생각했습니까? 이유도 설명해주세요.

연구개발의 진행자는 으리가 써볼 수 있도록 신제품의 샘플을 나누어 주었습니다. 그것은 세미나에 훨씬 더 관심이 가게 만들었으며, 어떻게 저 부서가 일을 하는지를 쉽게 이해하게 해 주었습니다.

세미나가 개선될 수 있는 어떤 방법이 있을까요?

상당수의 저희 동료들과 저는 우리 부서가 이달 마지막 수요일 11시 30분까지 미팅을 가졌었기 때문에 8월 25일 세미나에 제시간에 갈 수 없었습니다. 인사부는 다음 세미나를 정할 때 모든 부서 직원들 스케줄이 겹치지 않도록 꼭 확인해 주셨으면 합니다.

176. 왜 이 이메일이 보내졌는가?
(A) 부장들이 평가에 참여하도록 요청하기 위해서
(B) 회의장의 변경을 알리기 위해서
(C) 직원들이 행사에 참석하도록 장려할 것을 부장들에게 요청하기 위해서
(D) 공석의 새로운 리스트를 발표하기 위해서

177. 이 모든 세미나에 대해 사실인 것은?
(A) 부장님들은 반드시 모든 세미나에 참석해야 한다.
(B) 직원들은 참석 전에 등록을 해야 한다.
(C) 세미나는 모두 오전 11시30분에 시작한다.
(D) 참석하는 직원은 음식을 제공 받을 것이다.

178. Anita Bekin에 대해 언급되어 있는 것은?
(A) 그는 1년이 안 되는 기간 동안 SecuriPath Logistics에서 일을 했다.
(B) 그녀의 상사는 Oliver Martin이다.
(C) 그녀는 회계 부서 소속이다.
(D) 그녀는 Beek 빌딩에서 일한다.

179. 세미나 기간에 누가 샘플을 나누어 주었는가?
(A) Michelle Patton
(B) Nigel Kent
(C) Nam Sudara
(D) Betty Sebastian

180. Anita Berkin은 어느 세미나에 늦게 도착하였는가?
(A) 회계 세미나
(B) 광고 세미나
(C) 연구 개발 세미나
(D) 영업 세미나

Questions 181-185 웹페이지와 이메일

http://www.fittonflavor.com/ads

| 홈 | 연락 | 주문 | 사용후기 |

당신의 회사를 FittonFlavor.com에서 홍보하세요!

FittonFlavor.com은 Fitton지역에 주민들과 주변지역에서 Fitton에 방문하시는 분들에게 가장 인기 있는 웹사이트 중에 하나이며, Fitton의 식료품 쇼핑과 식당에 대한 조언과 정보를 제공해 드리고 있습니다.

우리는 당신의 사업을 우리 사이트에 광고할 4가지 디자인을 제공합니다:

디자인 1	디자인 2
이 디자인은 페이지 상단에 배너 광고형식으로 독자들이 다른 어떤 것보다 당신의 업체 이름을 먼저 보게 됩니다. (이미지나 사운드는 포함할 수 없음)	당신의 광고가 특집기사의 중앙에 작은 사이즈로 게재되며, 하나의 사운드와 이미지가 텍스트와 함께 포함가능 합니다.
디자인 3	디자인 4
이 디자인은 당신의 업체를 홍보하는 배너광고가 특집기사 옆에 세로로 놓여지는 형태입니다. (이미지나 사운드는 포함할 수 없음)	이것은 가장 큰 디자인으로 한 페이지의 반을 당신의 업체를 홍보하도록 할당해드리며, 텍스트와 함께 여러 개의 이미지와 사운드 옵션을 사용할 수 있습니다.

발신: Priya Latesh <priyalatesh@bombayeatery.com>
수신: Troy Bauer <tbauer@fittonflavor.com>
제목: Bombay 레스토랑의 홍보
날짜: 3월 14일

Bauer씨에게

FittonFlavor.com에서 다시 한번 당신의 광고 서비스를 이용하기 위해 물어볼 것이 있습니다. 저는 다시 한번 절반의 페이지 디자인을 게시하길 원합니다. 최근 저희 레스토랑의 리모델링을 보여주는 2개의 새로운 사진을 보낼 것인데, 텍스트와 사운드는 우리의 이전 광고와 동일하게 넣어주세요. 제가 사진을 제출하기 전에 사진이 얼마나 커야 하는지 저에게 알려주시기 바랍니다.

Priya Latesh
주인
Bombay Eatery

181. Bauer씨는 어디에서 일하고 있는가?
(A) 식당 자재 유통업체
(B) 광고 컨설팅 회사
(C) 제과점
(D) 음식과 관련된 인터넷 사이트

182. 디자인 1에 대하여 언급되어 있는 것은?
(A) 저렴하다.
(B) 눈에 띄는 곳에 위치해 있다.
(C) 가장 많은 텍스트를 포함할 수 있다.
(D) 방문객들이 다운로드 받을 수 있다.

183. Latesh씨는 아마도 어떤 광고 디자인에 관심이 있는가?
(A) 디자인 1
(B) 디자인 2
(C) 디자인 3
(D) 디자인 4

184. Bombay Eatery에 대하여 언급되어 있는 것은?
(A) 새로운 점포로 옮기고 있다.
(B) 현재 할인된 메뉴가 있다.
(C) 이전에 FittonFlavor.com가 광고를 해 준 적이 있다.
(D) 공사하는 동안 계속 영업할 것이다.

185. Latesh씨는 이미지와 관련하여 무엇에 관해 문의하고 있는가?
(A) 이미지의 크기를 어떻게 정할지
(B) 누가 사진을 찍을 것인지
(C) 몇 개의 이미지를 보내야 하는지
(D) 사진 안에 무엇이 있어야 하는지

Questions 186-190 기사문, 이메일 및 광고

DETROIT (9월 4일)-회사의 언론보도에 따르면, Marlon 자동차는 다음 달부터 오랫동안 인기를 얻어온 Skylark 쿠페 생산을 중단할 것입니다.

10년 전에 출시된 이 차는 독특한 디자인과 많은 사랑을 받아온 안전 기능을 가지고 있으며, 이러한 점들은 이 차를 국내에서 가장 잘 팔리는 차 중 하나로 만들어주었습니다.

하지만 이 차도 최근 몇 년간 역시 판매가 부진 했으며 Marlon사는 추가로 두 개의 다른 차종도 단종 시키기로 결정했습니다. Marlon의 대표 이사인 Lars Storch씨는 더 많은 고객들이 더 넓은 공간을 갖춘 편안한 큰 차를 찾고 있어서 소형차들의 판매가 부진 하다고 말했습니다. "자동차 구매자들이 대체로 더 넓은 공간을 요구하고 있으며 우리는 고객들에게 원하는 것을 제공 해야 할 필요가 있습니다"라고 최근에 Storch 씨가 말했습니다.

Marlon 대리점들은 기존 재고를 처리하고 내년도 Halo를 포함한 신차를 위한 공간을 마련하기 위해서 조만간 가격 인하를 할 것으로 예상됩니다.

발신자: Evelyn Carson 지사장 ecarson@marlon.com
수신자: Marlon Automotive 영업 이사들
〈saleslist@marlon.com〉
날짜: 10월 15일
제목: 재고 정리 세일

영업 담당 이사와 감독관에게

저는 당신들 모두가 연말 재고정리 세일을 준비하는데 아무런 문제가 없을 거라고 확신합니다. 이번 세일은 다음 달 1일에 시작될 것입니다. Skylark, Crimson, and Laker 차종들에 대한 할인 폭이 25퍼센트 임을 기억하세요. 몇몇 지점들은 또한 내년 차량(내년 출시될 신차)의 테스트 모델을 구비할 것입니다. 그리고 반드시 전국적으로 방송될 TV와 라디오 광고들을 검토하세요. 광고들은 현재 Marlon Automotive 웹사이트에 올려져 있습니다.

그리고 내년도 신차들을 전시장 중앙에 두어야 하는 것을 꼭 기억하시기 바랍니다.

Evelyn

Marlon사의 연말 재고정리 세일

Janesville Marlon 대리점은 11월부터 연말 재고정리 세일을 개최할 것입니다. 오셔서, 올해 모델에 대해 저희가 제공하는 저렴한 가격을 직접 보시기 바랍니다.

Skylark	25% 할인
Crimson	25% 할인
Laker	25% 할인

저희는 또한 이 지역에서 시승을 할 수 있도록 내년도 모델을 구비하고 있는 유일한 대리점입니다. 저희 지점은 Marlon의 전국적인 TV광고에서도 등장합니다. Marlon사의 최상의 신규 차량을 보시려면 오늘 바로 Janesville Marlon을 방문하세요!

186. 왜 기사문이 쓰여졌는가?
(A) 자동차 제조사의 차종 변경을 발표하기 위해서
(B) 회사 간부의 프로필(신상)을 알리기 위해서
(C) 회사의 삭감을 보고하기 위해서
(D) 설문조사 결과를 발표하기 위해서

187. 기사문에 따르면, 왜 Skylark 세단 판매량이 감소하였는가?
(A) 고객들이 디자인에 대한 다른 바람을 가지고 있기 때문에
(B) 차가 너무 비싸서
(C) 경쟁사들이 이 지역에 더 많은 대리점을 가지고 있기 때문에
(D) 차들이 그리 안전하지 않기 때문에

188. 기사에서 네 번째 문단, 첫 번째 줄에 "mark down"이 의미상 가장 가까운 것은?
(A) 긁다
(B) 파악하다
(C) 깎다
(D) 평가하다

189. 25퍼센트 할인에 대해서 언급 되어 있는 것은?
(A) 전국적으로 광고가 나갈 것이다.
(B) 앞으로 몇 달 후에 할인율이 더 높아질 것이다.
(C) 모든 차종에 대해 할인이 제공되고 있다.
(D) 매년 연말에 할인이 이루어질 것이다.

190. Janesville Marlon 대리점에 대해 언급된 것은?
(A) 이 대리점은 Marlon의 신차와 중고차를 모두 판매한다.
(B) 구매자들은 보험에 대해 할인을 받는다.
(C) 이 대리점은 이 지역에서 가장 큰 대리점이다.
(D) 쇼핑객들은 그곳에서 Halo차를 시승할 수 있다.

Questions 191-195 웹사이트와 이메일들

http://www.joycewei.ma

도서 정보	작가 정보	출연과 발표	Wei씨의 작품에 대한 칭찬

캐나다 일정

- 10월 2 – 3일: Wendtz 극장 – Halifax
  2개의 강의 모두 오후 8시에 시작될 것입니다. 티켓을 구매하거나 더 많은 정보를 찾기 위해 www.wendztheater.com을 방문하세요.

- 10월 5일: Upton 대학 – Ottawa
  이 강의는 오후 6시에 시작될 것이고, Wei씨는 오후 7시 30분에 책 사인회를 가질 것입니다.

- 10월 7일: Onyx 대강당 – Calgary
  이 출연에 대한 정보는 매표소에 (403) 555-7716으로 전화함으로써 얻을 수 있습니다.

- 10월 16일: Porthal 호텔과 컨벤션 홀 – Victoria
  9월 24일까지 객실을 예약한 PHCH의 투숙객들은 만약 그들이 Wei씨의 강의에 참석하기 위한 티켓을 구매 한다면, 객실에 대해 20%의 할인을 받을 것입니다. 할인을 받기 위해서는 Darryl Nern에게 (250) 555-1164로 전화 하세요.

Wei씨의 출연일정을 잡고 싶으시다면 spool@joycewei.ma로 Stephanie Pool에게 이메일을 보내 주세요.

발신: tnguyen@traverse.edu
수신: spool@joycewei.ma
날짜: 10월 10일
제목: 1월 학회

Pool씨에게,

저는 Onyx 대강당에서 열린 Wei씨의 최근 강연에서 그녀를 만날 수 있었습니다. 우리가 만났을 때, 제가 기획하는 학회에 그녀가 강의할 수 있는지 물어보았습니다. 그녀는 아주 흥미로워 했지만, 그녀가 시간이 나는지 확인하기 위해 당신과 얘기해보라고 말했습니다.

올해의 Science and Technology 학회는 1월 14일부터 17일까지 Quebec의 Montreal에 있는 Wendel 호텔에서 열릴 예정이며 학회의 스폰서는 Audacious Industrial사 입니다. Wei씨가 1월 15일 오후에 발표를 하는 것이 가능할까요? 그날의 강연 주제가 마침 업계에서의 로봇공학의 미래라서요.

Audacious Industrial는 그녀의 참석에 대한 소정의 사례비뿐만 아니라 Wei씨를 위한 여행경비와 숙소비용을 모두 부담할 수 있을 것입니다. 늦어도 11월 10일까지 Wei씨의 강연이 가능한지 여부를 저에게 알려주시고 궁금하신 점은 무엇이든 편하게 물어주세요.

Tien Nguyen

수신인: Harold Kim 〈hkim@mail4you.com〉
발신인: Porthal Hotel 〈service@porthalhotel.com〉
날짜: 9월 20일
제목: 귀하의 예약

Kim씨에게,

저희는 10월 14일부터 10월 17일까지 Porthal Hotel에 귀하의 예약을 확인해드리게 되어 기쁩니다. 귀하가 예약하실 때 입력하신 무료이용권 번호에 따라서 귀하의 객실요금에 20%할인을 적용해드렸습니다. 저희 컨벤션홀에서 열리는 행사에 대한 당신의 티켓 또한 예약되었습니다. 당신의 방문을 더욱 편안하게 만들어드리기 위해 저희가 할 수 있는 일이 있다면 언제든 알려주시기 바랍니다.

Hayden Burrell
Porthal Hotel 및 컨벤션홀 매니저

191. Wei씨는 아마도 누구인가?
(A) 작가
(B) 과학자
(C) 광고주
(D) 컨벤션 기획자

192. 웹사이트에서 5번째 문단, 1번째 줄의 "appearance"가 의미상 가장 가까운 것은?
(A) 발표
(B) 외관
(C) 인상
(D) 인물, 수치

193. Nguyen씨는 어디에서 Wei씨를 만났는가?
(A) Halifax에서
(B) Ottawa에서
(C) Calgary에서
(D) Victoria에서

194. Nguyen씨의 이메일의 목적은 무엇인가?
(A) 행사에서 프리젠테이션을 요청하는 것
(B) 위원회 멤버를 위해 결제를 처리하는 것
(C) 호텔 예약이 변경될 것을 요청하는 것
(D) 곧 있을 행사에 입장을 위해 결제하는 것

195. Harold Kim에 대해 언급된 것은?
(A) Kim씨는 Darryl Nern씨와 얘기를 나눴었다.
(B) Kim씨는 Stephanie Pool에게 이메일을 보냈다.
(C) Kim씨는 Tien Nguyen의 동료다.
(D) Kim씨는 일월에 학회에 참석할 것이다.

Questions 196–200 정보와 이메일들

Essense
MP3 플레이어 수리 및 교체 관련 보증

모든 Essense MP3 플레이어는 구매한 날짜로부터 12개월 동안 사용할 수 있는 품질보증을 포함하고 있습니다. 만약 이 기간 동안 어떠한 결함이나 손상을 경험 한다면, 상품을 교체하거나 수리하는 것이 가능합니다.

추가 1년 더 품질 보증 기간을 연장하고 싶은 고객들은 MP3 플레이어를 구매한지 1년 이내에 Essense Premium Guarantee Package를 구매하실 수 있습니다. Essence Premium Guarantee Package의 가격은 모델 별로 다양합니다.

더 많은 정보는 www.essenseaudio.com/premium에서 찾아보시거

나 1-800-555-1122에 전화하시면 됩니다.

수신: maintenance@essenseaudio.com
발신: gbeakman@speedcom.net
날짜: 5월 18일
제목: 청구번호 #1865BU651

저는 제 MP3 플레이어 교체가 어떻게 진행되고 있는지 알고 싶습니다. (청구번호#1865BU651)

저는 5월 15일 Essense 매장에서 청구서를 제출했고, 점원은 Premium Guarantee Package 때문에 제 기기가 무료로 교체될 것이라고 전해 주었습니다. 그는 또한 누군가가 저에게 클레임 청구가 처리되고 있음을 알려주는 이메일을 그 다음날 보낼 것이라고 언급했습니다. 매장으로부터 저의 플레이어가 발송된 지 지금 4일이 지났고 저는 처리가 되고 있는지에 대한 어떠한 이메일도 받지 못했습니다. 제 MP3 플레이어가 어떻게 되고 있는지 저에게 알려주시고, 대략 언제 저의 집으로 배송되는지 예상일을 알려주세요.

감사합니다.

Gloria Beakman

수신인: gbeakman@speedcom.net
발신인: maintenance@essenseaudio.com
날짜: 5월 18일
제목: 회신: 청구번호 1865BU651

Beakman씨에게,

저희에게 이메일을 보내셔야 했던 수고에 대해 사과 드립니다. 귀하의 수리 상태에 대해 알려주는 이메일을 귀하가 받지 못한 이유는 수리 신청서에 이메일 주소가 gbeakman@speedcom.com로 적혀있었기 때문입니다. 만약 이 사항이 저희 기술자에 의해 행해진 것이라면 저희가 사과 드립니다.

귀하의 MP3 플레이어는 수리가 되었고 현재 배송준비 단계입니다. 문제는 헤드폰 잭과의 연결과 관련되어 있었습니다. 이번에 진행된 수리 건은 완료 후 90일간 보증되므로 만약 다시 Essence 기기에 문제가 생기면 알려주시기 바랍니다.

Paul Astin
Essence Audio 고객지원 직원

196. 이 정보는 아마 누구를 위한 것인가?
 (A) 최근에 Essense MP3 플레이어를 구매한 사람들
 (B) Essense 오디오 기술자들
 (C) Essense MP3 플레이어를 구매하길 원하는 고객들
 (D) Essense Audio 가게 점원들

197. 정보에서 두 번째 문단, 세 번째 줄의 "vary"가 의미상 가장 가까운 것은?
 (A) 탁월하다
 (B) 다르다
 (C) 퍼뜨리다
 (D) 반영한다

198. Beakman씨에 대해 사실일 가능성이 가장 높은 것은?
 (A) 그녀는 Essense Audio에 채용이 되었다.
 (B) 그녀는 1년이 안 되는 기간 전에 MP3를 구매했다.
 (C) 그녀 기기의 첫 번째 품질보증은 기간이 만료되었다.
 (D) 그녀의 기기는 한 달도 더 전에 교체 되었다.

199. Beakman씨의 수리 신청서에 대해 언급된 것은?
 (A) 신청서가 기술자에 의해 분실되었다.
 (B) 신청서는 Beakman에게 다시 보내질 것이다.
 (C) 신청서가 일부 부정확한 정보를 가지고 있었다.
 (D) 신청서가 다른 부서로 발송되었다.

200. 요구된 어떤 정보가 Beakman씨에게 제공되지 않았는가?
 (A) 수리 상태
 (B) 기술자의 이름
 (C) Beakman씨가 방문해야 하는 매장
 (D) 배송 도착 날짜

TEST 7

PART 5

101. 저희 서비스에 대해 어떻게 생각하시는지 알려주시고 개선사항에 대한 제안사항을 남겨주시기 위해서 잠시 시간을 내주시기 바랍니다.

102. 스낵바에 있는 어떤 음식물이든 거의 떨어져 가면, 주방직원 중 한 명에게 알려주시기 바랍니다.

103. 지게차를 작동하는 작업자들은 그 기계에 의해 부상을 당할 수 있으므로, 항시 매우 주의를 기울여야만 합니다.

104. 인사과 직원들은 매우 철저하게 지원서를 검토하는데, 이는 일반적으로 2주가 소요됩니다.

105. 호텔은 모든 투숙객들이 오후 2시 이후에 체크인하고, 오전 11시 이전에 체크아웃해줄 것을 정중히 요청합니다.

106. 복잡하고 예측 불가능한 시장에서의 마케팅 담당자들은, 미리 계획할 수 있어야 하며, 또한 주변환경의 변화에 신속하게 대처할 수 있어야 합니다.

107. 내일 있을 취업면접은 오전 10시 정각에 시작되므로, 면접자들은 시간을 엄수해야 합니다.

108. 상황이 급해서 제가 호텔 청구서를 받았을 때 꼼꼼히 살펴 볼 기회가 없었습니다.

109. 저희 식료품점은 한 캔 당 겨우 6불에 영국에서 수입된 구운 콩을 제공할 것입니다.

110. 명상이 어떻게 집중력을 강화하는지를 연구하는 연구조사에서 정량적 및 정성적 방법이 함께 사용되었습니다.

111. 소비자 중심 교육 프로그램을 이수한 사람들은 추후에 관리직에 심사대상이 될 수 있습니다.

112. 버터와 마가린을 다른 재료로 대체함으로써, 당신은 당신이 만든 제과제품에서 포화지방산을 제거할 수 있습니다.

113. 팀원들이 주말 내내 예산 요약표 작업을 하긴 했지만, 예산 요약표가 우리 기준을 충족시킬 만큼 충분히 좋지는 않았습니다.

114. 우리 신형 휴대전화 판매량은 지난 5개월에 걸쳐서 월 5%의 꾸준한 비율로 증가해 왔습니다.

115. Fresh Scent의 비누는 꽤 오랫동안 사용할 수 있어서, 다른 일등 브랜드들보다 가격이 덜 비싼 셈입니다.

116. Northampton Community college는 정신 건강 문제와 관련하여 다른 사람들을 돕는 것을 즐기는 사람들을 지원하기 위해 만들어진 무료 과정에 현지 주민들을 초대하고 있습니다.

117. 비상등으로써 에너지 효율성이 좋은 LED 전구가 정전 시 자동으로 작동하므로, 당신은 전구를 켤 필요가 없습니다.

118. 세법에 관한 자문을 구하는 소기업주들은 저희 회계사들 중 한 명과 상담하실 수 있습니다.

119. 고객분들이 제품의 하자나 결함을 경험하시고 저희가 돈을 환불해줄 것을 요청하신다면, 저희는 구입일로부터 30일 이내에 전액 환불을 해드릴 것입니다.

120. 프로젝트 비서는, 작업의 높은 질과 정확성을 보장해주면서, 행사 조직과 관련된 지원을 제공할 것입니다.

121. 휘발유 가격이 계속해서 증가하는 가운데, 분석가들은 소비자들이 다른 분야에서 지출을 줄일 것이라고 예상하고 있습니다.

122. 모든 짐들은 당신의 출발예정시간으로부터 최소 60분 전에 탑승 수속이 되어야 합니다.

123. 이 최근 연구는 Kang씨가 제안한 사업을 위한 대규모 시장이 더 이상 존재하지 않음을 보여줍니다.

124. 공사를 시작하기 전에 당신이 작업하고 있는 모든 건축설계들이 건축법을 준수하고 있는지 확인하세요.

125. 5월 12일, 수요일부터, 유명한 조각가인 Robert Maki는 시청 안에 있는 Bellevue City Art Gallery에서 전시회를 가질 것입니다.

126. 우리가 사용하는 운영 체제는 새로운 소프트웨어와 호환이 되지 않는다. 따라서, 업데이트할 필요가 있습니다.

127. 어떤 구매자든지 직접 모든 가구를 조립할 수 있도록 하기 위해서, 당사의 DIY 가구에는 자세한 제품 설명서가 딸려 나옵니다.

128. Model T에 대한 상당히 높은 수요가 Chalm Corporation을 디트로이트에 있는 보다 큰 공장으로 옮기도록 촉발했습니다.

129. 전문가의 도움을 받으면서 지속적인 스트레스를 관리해야 합니다. 지속적인 스트레스는 제대로 관리되지 않으면, 장기적인 우울증을 야기할 수 있습니다.

130. 동부해안에 다섯 개의 상점을 더 개점한 것은, 사무 용품 분야 선두업체로써의 Mega Office의 위치를 또한 더욱 확고하게 해줄 것입니다.

PART 6

Questions 131-134 편지

11월 2일

티켓을 소지하신 분들께

센트럴파크에서 열릴 예정인 8월 콘서트 시리즈를 변경 할 수 밖에 없다는 사실을 귀하에게 알리게 되어 저희는 매우 유감스럽습니다.

일기예보에 따르면 강력한 폭풍이 다음주에 몰려온다고 합니다. 따라서 저희는 다음주 공원에서 있을 야외 공연들을 나중에 기상 상태가 좋아질 때까지 연기하려고 합니다.

콘서트 티켓을 소지하신 분들은 두 가지 옵션이 있습니다: 전액 환불을 받거나 추후 공연에 티켓을 사용하실 수 있습니다. 공연 일정을 다시 잡는 대로 정확한 공연 날짜를 알려드리겠습니다. 전액 환불을 원하시면 (213) 555-1234로 저희 직원 중 한 명에게 연락주세요.

David Drummond
매니저

Questions 135-138 이메일

수신: dunger@mapleglademc.org
발신: gcandell@biolectric.com
날짜: 12월 2일

Unger씨에게

오늘 아침에 전화 주셔서 감사합니다. 당신과의 대화는 아주 유익하고 저에게 많은 도움이 되었습니다.

우리가 논의한 벤처사업은 이 지역 의료계뿐만 아니라 다른 분야에까지 광범위한 파급효과를 가질 것이라고 저는 믿습니다. 저희와 함께 일하는 것은 Maple Glade Medical Center에게 도움이 될 것이라고 저는 확신합니다. 저는 이미 두 회사의 여러 임원들과 얘기를 나눴고, 그들도 또한 우리가 매우 긍정적인 방향으로 함께 공조할 수 있을 거라 믿고 있습니다. 제가 공식적인 제안서의 초안을 당신에게 보낼 것입니다. 제가 제안서에 추가하길 원하는 사항이 있으시다면 알려주시기 바랍니다.

George Candell
연구개발팀 이사, Biolectric

Questions 139-142 편지

2월 16일
Zack Greinke
NZ Enterprise
New Zealand, Wakatipu 9349
우편번호 2376

Greinke씨에게

저는 이 편지를 귀사의 직원 중에 한 명인 Mary Smith씨가 저에게 제공했던 훌륭한 서비스에 대한 감사의 표시로서 쓰고 있습니다. 그녀는 상대하기에 너무나 유쾌했고, 그래서 저는 몇 초 만에 거래를 마무리 할 수 있었습니다.

그녀는 제가 구매하려는 기계 브랜드에 대해서 시간에 맞게 유익한 조언을 제공해 주었습니다. 그녀는 저에게 제품에 관한 모든 중요한 정보도 알려주었습니다. 그리고 나서 그녀는 회사에 결제 수단과, 그 기계가 호주에 언제까지 배송될 것으로 예상하면 되는지에 관련하여 모든 정보를 제가 제대로 챙겼는지 확인해주었습니다.

저는 그녀의 이례적인 수고에 대해서 Mary를 칭찬하고자 합니다.

Clayton Kershaw

Questions 143-146 기사

Long Beach, 6월 15일 – Doris Florist는 Long Beach Road 223가에 새로운 가게를 막 오픈 했으며, 그곳은 그녀의 이전 점포에서 조금 아래로 내려오는 곳이고 새로 생긴 좀더 넓은 빌딩에 위치해 있습니다.

가게 주인인 Doris Kresky는 편리한 곳에 위치한 가게자리를 임대하고 사업을 확장할 기회를 놓치고 싶지 않았다고 말했습니다.

Long Beach Road 가게는 이미 영업 중이지만 정식 개원식이 7월 1일 토요일 오전 11시에 대박 할인행사와 함께 열릴 예정입니다. 다양한 식물들이 당일 배송이 가능합니다. 과일 선물 바구니, 풍선 부케와 다른 선물용 상품들을 포함한 새로운 품목들이 새 가게에 진열되어 있습니다.

Questions 147-148 듣기

6월 14 – 18일 C룸의 시간표					
	월요일 6월 14일	화요일 6월 15일	수요일 6월 16일	목요일 6월 17일	금요일 6월 18일
오전 9:00		아이들의 함께 책 읽는 시간	어린이들의 이야기책 제작 활동	아이들의 함께 책 읽는 시간	
오전 10:00	수석 사서 Susan Pakowski의 발표				공상 소설 클럽 모임
오전 11:00			도서관 기금모금 도서 판매	도서 판매 여름 독서 프로그램 파티	
오후 12:00		아이들의 함께 책 읽는 시간			젊은 시인 모임
오후 1:00				직원 회의	
오후 2:00	무료 경력 컨설팅 워크샵				

147. C룸은 아마 어디에 위치 하는가?
(A) 경력 컨설팅 사무실
(B) 극장
(C) 지역사회 도서관
(D) 어린이 탁아 센터

148. 책 만들기 활동과 같은 날에는 무슨 행사가 잡혀있나요?
(A) 도서관 기금모금 도서 판매
(B) 아이들의 함께 책 읽는 시간
(C) 젊은 시인 모임
(D) 공상 소설 클럽 모임

Questions 149-151 이메일

발신: Ellen Funt 〈ellenf@currentcooking.com〉
수신: 〈subscribers@currentcooking.com〉
제목: 회원들을 위한 새로운 기능
날짜 : 11월 2일

안녕하세요, CurrentCooking.com의 구독자 여러분!

Current Cooking 인터넷 잡지사에 있는 저희는 우리 웹사이트를 구독자들에게 더 도움이 되게 개선했다는 것을 알려드리게 되어 매우 기쁩니다. 오늘부터 구독자들은 유명 요리사들의 흥미로운 요리법을 인터넷 교육용 비디오로 보실 수 있습니다. 당신은 또한 최첨단 주방 장비의 시연과 평가도 보실 수 있습니다. 유명 요리사들과 미식가들의 인터뷰 또한 선보입니다. 그리고 물론 여러분들은 여전히 우리 사이트에서 기사에 나와 있는 정보와 뉴스를 보실 수 있습니다.

여러분들의 모든 요리와 주방의 니즈를 위해서 오늘 CurrentCooking.com에 들어오셔서 확인해보세요!

Ellen Funt
편집장

149. 이 이메일의 목적은 무엇인가?
(A) 업그레이드된 서비스를 알리기 위해서
(B) 새로운 웹사이트를 광고하기 위해서
(C) 일자리를 위한 지원자들을 모집하기 위해서
(D) 회원들의 의견을 요청하기 위해서

150. 이 이메일은 누구를 겨냥해서 쓰여졌는가?
(A) 웹 마스터
(B) 요리사
(C) 사진작가
(D) 잡지 기자

151. Current Cooking 웹사이트의 기능으로서 언급된 것이 아닌 것은?
(A) 인터뷰
(B) 광고
(C) 제품 평가
(D) 요리법 설명

Questions 152–153 영수증

Eagle's Place
32789 FL, 올란도 Front Street 242번지
689-555-0558

3월 10일	오전 10:05
과학소설 – 페이퍼백	
Galactic Zombie Hunter, Sylvester Stanks	7.99
비소설 – 양장본	
Recycling and Home Decoration, Freda Biltz	15.99
소계	23.98
세금 – 6.5%	1.55
합계	25.53
받은 현금	26.00
거스름돈	0.47

환불 및 교환 정책

환불과 교환은 원래 구매 날짜의 2주 이내에 상점으로 다시 가져온 신규 구매품에 대해서만 적용됩니다. 손상된 제품이나 영수증이 없는 제품은 일체 반품이 수락되지 않을 것입니다. 중고 코너에서 구매한 제품에 대해서는 어떠한 반품도 받지 않지만 4주 이내에 원래 영수증과 함께 다시 가지고 오신 중고제품의 경우 교환은 가능합니다.

152. Eagle's Place는 어떤 종류의 상점인가?
(A) 연구실 자재 상점
(B) 실내 장식 상점
(C) 책방
(D) 사냥 장비 매장

153. 상점의 정책에 대해 사실인 것은?
(A) 모든 상품은 구매한지 2주 이내에 반품이 가능하다.
(B) 반품 되는 모든 구매품에는 6.5%의 제품진열 요금이 발생한다.
(C) 모든 교환 품목은 반드시 새것의 상태여야만 한다.
(D) 모든 교환 품목은 반드시 영수증이 동반되어야 한다.

Questions 154–156 정보

Illuminate T-24A 프린터를 구매해 주셔서 감사하며 저희는 당신의 프린터와 함께 샘플 사이즈의 잉크 카트리지를 3개 넣어드렸습니다. 샘플 사이즈 잉크는 장기간 사용을 위해 만들어진 것이 아니기 때문에 샘플 사이즈 카트리지가 설치 되자 마자 바로 정식 사이즈 잉크 카트리지를 구매하는 것을 추천합니다. 새로운 카트리지는 Illuminate Web site인 www.illuminateprinters.com에서 직접 구매가 가능합니다. 어떤 주도 주문한지 일주일 이내에 고객들이 받아보실 것을 보장해드리며 그렇지 않으면 지불금은 환불될 것입니다. 주문할 때, 총 주문 금액의 30%에 해당하는 우대고객 할인을 받기 위해서 결제하는 동안 코드 28874를 입력하세요. 또한 대부분의 사무 용품 가게에서 대체 잉크 카트리지를 구매하실 수도 있지만 우대고객 할인은 불가능 합니다.

새로운 프린터에 관한 어떠한 질문이나 우려가 있으시다면 항시 대기중인 우리의 지원센터 기술자들에게 1-800-555-0152로 전화 주세요. 우리 영업점은 주중에 오전 8시부터 오후 8시까지 1-800-555-4845로 연락하실 수 있습니다.

154. 누구를 위하여 이 공지는 쓰여졌는가?
(A) 인쇄 기술자
(B) 웹사이트 디자이너
(C) 최근 구매한 프린터를 가지고 있는 사람들
(D) 영업 사원

155. 잉크 주문에 대하여 무엇을 약속하는가?
(A) 만약 배송이 늦는다면, 고객의 비용은 면제된다.
(B) 영업 사원들은 항시 대기 중이다.
(C) 잉크 카트리지는 1년은 족히 잉크를 공급한다.
(D) 기술자들은 고객들에게 신속하게 답신 전화를 한다.

156. 어떻게 고객들은 할인을 받을 수 있는가?
(A) 지원 센터에 전화 함으로써
(B) 인터넷 상점에서 코드를 사용함으로써
(C) 지역 사무용품점을 방문함으로써
(D) 무료이용권을 보냄으로써

Questions 157-158 문자메시지 대화

ROBERT DOMAN	3:12 PM
포크리프트 장비 운전 자격증 받았다면서요.	
ROBERT DOMAN	3:13 PM
어떻게 (그렇게 힘든 일을) 해냈어요?	
LAURA PAGE	3:15 PM
모든 안전절차과정을 배우기 위해 수업을 들어야 했어요.	
ROBERT DOMAN	3:16 PM
엄청난 시간이 걸렸겠네요.	
LAURA PAGE	3:17 PM
그렇지는 않아요. 인터넷으로 모두 들었습니다.	
ROBERT DOMAN	3:18 PM
인터넷으로 할 수 있어요? 얼마나 들었어요?	
LAURA PAGE	3:19 PM
약간 비쌌지만 회사에서 정산해주었어요.	
LAURA PAGE	3:20 PM
관심 있으시면 인사과에 문의해보세요.	

157. Laura Page씨에 대해 언급된 것은?
 (A) Page씨는 인터넷 수업을 듣고 있다.
 (B) Page씨는 최근에 새로운 일(직장)을 시작했다.
 (C) Page씨는 Doman씨의 동료다.
 (D) Page씨는 인사과에서 일한다.

158. 15시 16분에 Doman씨가 "That must have taken ages"라고 쓸 때 무엇을 의미하고 있는가?
 (A) 강의를 수료하는데 오랜 시간이 걸렸다.
 (B) 참가자들은 특정 연령이어야 한다.
 (C) Doman씨도 자격증에 관심이 있다.
 (D) Doman씨는 비용이 걱정된다.

Questions 159-160 웹페이지

The Gildem Company

이름 : Dalek Prapesh
물품 번호 : KT55
물품 구매일 : 5월 3일

고객님의 상품평에 감사드립니다. 당신의 의견은 The Gildem Company에 있는 저희들에게 큰 의미를 가지며 저희는 고품질 상품으로 고객들을 만족시키고자 노력하고 있습니다. 아래의 모든 양식을 작성하고 난 뒤, 고객 만족 팀으로 설문지를 제출하기 위해 '양식 보내기'를 클릭해주세요.

당신이 구매한 Gildem 품목의 개수	☐ 0	☒ 1-3	☐ 3개 이상
Gildem 품목의 만족도	☐ 높음	☒ 적절함	☐ 낮음
추후 다른 Gildem 품목을 구매할 가능성	☐ 높음	☐ 가능성 없음	☒ 가능함
당신이 구매한 Gildem 품목에 대한 세부사항을 포함한 기타 의견	제가 6년전에 구매했던 Gildem 스피커는 성능이 좋았습니다. 제가 며칠전에 구매한 Gildem MP3 플레이어(KT55)는 같이 딸려 나온 헤드폰으로 들으면 음질이 열악했습니다. 그래서 저는 헤드폰을 교체했습니다.		

양식 보내기

159. 설문조사의 목적은 무엇인가?
 (A) 직원들의 업무를 평가하기 위해서
 (B) 광고에 대한 의견을 모으기 위해서
 (C) 회사의 제품을 향상시키기 위해서
 (D) 웹사이트의 기능을 평가하기 위해서

160. Gildem Company는 어떤 종류의 회사인가?
 (A) 일용직 직업 소개소
 (B) 개보수 공사 회사
 (C) 전자제품 제조사
 (D) 디자인 상담 회사

Questions 161-163 기사

새로운 주차 요금 시행
10월 22일
Graham Postman

Peach Valley의 도심지로 오는 방문객의 증가가 주차난의 결과를 초래함에 따라서 도로교통국는 새로운 주차 요금을 시행하는 걸 고려 중에 있습니다. "매일 밤 이용 가능한 주차 공간을 찾는 것이 점점 더 어려워지고 있습니다."라고 위원회 멤버인 Travis Heinz는 이야기 했습니다. —[1]— 많은 방문객들이 시간당 주차비를 부과하는 유료주차장을 피하려 함에 따라 주민들은 주차 공간을 찾는데 애를 먹고 있습니다. 무료 노상 주차를 찾는 방문객들이 또한 주차공간을 찾아서 시내 지역을 돌아다님에 따라서 교통 체증을 가중시키고 있습니다. —[2]—

—[3]— 현재, 시의 노상주차의 요금은 오전 8시부터 오후 5시까지만 적용되고 있으며 이 시간 이후로는 전혀 요금이 부과되지 않습니다." 이 시스템은 저녁시간의 주차를 악몽으로 만들고 있습니다." Heinz씨가 말했습니다. "다른 도시들처럼 24시간 내내 요금을 부과하는 시스템을 채택하는 것이 도움이 될 수 있습니다."

이번 주차 규제의 변경은 당국이 주차 미터기를 업그레이드 했던지난 달 이래로 두 번째 입니다. —[4]— 이 미터기는 현재 운전자들이 동전과 신용카드 중 아두거나 사용해서 요금을 지불할 수 있도록 하고 있습니다.

161. Peach Valley에 대하여 암시되고 있는 것은?
(A) 이곳의 거리는 상태가 열악하다.
(B) 대중교통을 위한 자금을 마련하기 위해 세금을 올려야 한다.
(C) 교통 정체와 관련된 문제를 겪고 있다.
(D) 주차장들은 도시 거주자들에게는 무료다.

162. 교통국 위원회는 무엇을 고려하고 있는가?
(A) 주차 공간의 수를 늘리는 것
(B) 업그레이드된 신호등을 설치 하는 것
(C) 더 많은 주차 관리인을 고용하는 것
(D) 저녁에 주차 요금부과를 시행하는 것

163. [1], [2], [3], [4]로 표시된 자리 중에 다음 문장이 들어가기에 가장 적합한 곳은?

"Peach Valley 시내는 많은 새로운 식당, 극장 그리고 상점들이 생겨나면서 점점 사람이 많아지고 있습니다."
(A) [1]
(B) [2]
(C) [3]
(D) [4]

Questions 164-167 인터넷 채팅 대화

Alexandra Peters [2:44 p.m.]
여러분, 안녕하세요. 연구개발팀이 오늘 오후 직원회의에서 내년도 신차 기능에 대한 진척사항을 공개할 예정입니다. 가고 싶으신 분 계시나요?

Fraser Isaac [2:46 p.m.]
그들이 해온 작업을 저는 보고 싶습니다. 또한 이번 주가 Monique Hardy씨의 여기(우리 회사)에서 보내는 첫 주라서 Monique Hardy씨가 참석하면 좋을 것 같습니다.

Monique Hardy [2:47 p.m.]
맞아요, 저 너무 가고 싶습니다. 이미 연구개발팀 몇 분을 만나봤어요. 그들이 해온 작업을 보는 것은 좋은 기회일 거예요. 그들이 공개할 기능에 대해서 아는 게 있는 분 있나요?

Alexandra Peters [2:48 p.m.]
전혀 모르겠어요, Monique. 그렇지만 그 발표가 디자인 부서에서의 당신의 업무에 도움이 될 거라고 확신합니다. 미팅은 오후 4시반에 Conference Room D에서 열릴 거예요.

Monique Hardy [2:49 p.m.]
네, 알겠습니다. 그런데 사실 회의실이 어디 있는지를 제가 아직 몰라요.

Fraser Isaac [2:50 p.m.]
상관없어요, Monique. 어디 있는지 제가 안내해드릴게요. 그런데 미팅 바로 전에는 제가 바쁠 것 같아요. 제가 지금 들러서 회의실 가능 방법을 알려드려도 될까요?

Monique Hardy [2:52 p.m.]
네, 그렇게 해주시면 너무 감사하죠.

Manuel Hoult [2:54 p.m.]
저도 가고 싶지만, 제가 준비해야 하는 고객과의 저녁 미팅이 있네요(제가 고객하고 저녁 미팅이 있어서 준비를 해야해요). 누가 (회의 내용을) 메모해주거나 아니면 저를 위해 발표를 녹음해줄 수 있나요?

Alexandra Peters [2:55 p.m.]
제 비서가 저랑 같이 참석해서 메모를 할 거예요. Manuel, 미팅 끝나고 메모한 복사본을 당신에게 꼭 전달해줄게요.

164. 오늘 오후에 열리는 연구개발팀 발표의 주제는 무엇인가?
(A) 새로운 회의실 디자인
(B) 최근의 마케팅 활동
(C) 연간 매출 수치 검토
(D) 신차의 특징

165. Monique Hardy씨에 대해 언급된 것은?
(A) Hardy씨 연구개발팀으로 옮길 것이다.
(B) Hardy씨는 과거에도 Fraser Isaac과 일했었다.
(C) Hardy씨는 최근에 이 회사에서 일하기 시작했다.
(D) Hardy씨는 오후 늦게 고객을 만날 것이다.

166. 2시 48분에 Alexandra Peters씨가 "Beats me"라고 쓸 때 무엇을 의미하고 있는가?
(A) Peters씨는 연구개발팀에 물어볼 것이다.
(B) Peters씨도 답을 알지 못한다.
(C) Peters씨는 직장에서 부상을 당했다.
(D) Peters씨도 발표작업을 해왔다.

167. Fraser Isaac씨는 Monique Hardy씨에게 무엇을 해줄 것을 제안하고 있는가?
(A) 그녀를 위해 발표를 녹음해줄 것을
(B) 고객 미팅을 조정할 것을
(C) 미팅에서 메모를 할 것을
(D) Hardy씨에게 위치를 알려줄 것을

Questions 168-171 평론

Stewton Gazette　　　　　　　　　　　　오락 부문

No Strings Attached
Annie Newfam, 평론가

금요일 밤, Yann Curset의 작품인 새로운 뮤지컬 No Strings Attached가 연례 봄맞이 프로그램 시리즈로 Wheaton Theater Company에서 상연을 시작했습니다. 이 뮤지컬은 세계적으로 유명한 음악가가 되기 위해 그녀의 인생 내내 많은 장애물을 극복한 첼로리스트의 삶에 기반한 것입니다.

영화 작품 Keep Your Chin Up에서의 연기로 전세계적으로 인정받은 Hera Constant는 유명한 첼로리스트, Aria Nordak의 역할을 아주 실감나게 연기합니다. Wheaton Theater Company의 단골 출연자인 Marcus Galisotn 또한 Nordak의 지원을 아끼지 않는 남편 역할인 Jacob Edmond로써 놀라운 연기를 보여주고 있습니다.

No Strings Attached는 Wheaton Theater Company가 빈번하게 보여줘 왔던 가벼운 코미디물 보다 훨씬 더 극적이고, 긴장감 넘치는 작품입니다. 심지어 2시간 30분의 공연시간에도 불구하고, 연기자들은 청중들을 극의 세계로 끌어들입니다. 엉성한 무대장식과 절제된 의상 또한 청중들이 연극 속으로 빠져들게 만듭니다.

Stewton에서 성장한 Continent Theatrical Award의 수상자인 Moira Yarco가 No Strings Attached의 연출을 맡았습니다.

티켓 판매와 상영시간 정보를 원하시면 814-555-1157로 극장 매표소에 연락하시면 됩니다.

168. 누가 이 뮤지컬을 썼는가?
(A) Hera Constant
(B) Moira Yarco
(C) Yann Curset
(D) Marcus Galiston

169. No Strings Attached은 Wheaton Theater Company의 보통의 공연들과 어떻게 다른가?
(A) 세계적으로 유명한 실제 인물의 인생에 관한 것이다.
(B) 관현악단 전체가 참여하고 있다.
(C) 훨씬 극적이고 진지하다.
(D) 전부 현지인들이 캐스팅되었다.

170. 어떻게 상영시간에 대한 정보를 얻을 수 있나?
(A) 인터넷 사이트를 방문함으로써
(B) e-mail 을 보냄으로써
(C) 매표소로 전화함으로써
(D) 팜플렛을 집어감으로써

171. No Strings Attached에 관해 유추할 수 있는 것은?
(A) 뮤지컬은 훈련된 음악가들에 의해 공연된다.
(B) 뮤지컬은 최근에 상을 받았다.
(C) 배우들은 화려한 복장을 하고 있다.
(D) 봄에만 공연을 한다.

Questions 172-175 기사

8월 18일 – Live 4 Health 광고에 도움을 준 Glass Tiger Studios는 존경 받는 Calenbach Award의 후보로 지명되었습니다. 이 상은 지난 25년간 혁신을 보여준 애니메이션 회사들과 예술 출판 회사들에게 수여되어 왔습니다. Glass Tiger Studios는 거의 1500개의 자격을 갖춘 업체들 가운데 선택된 방콕에서는 첫 번째, 유일한 애니메이션 회사입니다. —[1]— 올해의 모든 수상자들이 발표되는 시상식이 9월 20일 독일의 베를린에서 열릴 예정입니다.

제품 포장 작업을 해왔습니다." 라고 Pranathat씨는 덧붙였습니다. "그리고 우리는 우리 작업이 고객들의 기대를 넘어 설수 있록 고객들과 주의 깊게 의사소통을 합니다."

—[3]— 후보자의 명단이 공개되고 나서 Glass Tiger Studios에게 일을 맡기고자 하는 업체들이 줄을 섰습니다. "우리가 지금 보고 있는 이 모든 신규사업들과 관련하여, 더 많은 만화영화 제작자와 디렉터들을 고용하지 않고서는

—[2]— "우리는 최종 후보가 되어 아주 영광스럽습니다. 이것은 우리 직원들이 얼마나 자능있고 창조적이며 기술력이 뛰어난지를 보여주기 때문입니다." Glass Tiger Studios의 상임이사인 May Pranathat은 이야기 했습니다.

"우리는 다른 여러 가지도 하지만, 그 중에서도 아동서적, 패션 잡지,

이 수요를 채우는 것이 불가능합니다. 그래서 우리는 사람을 고용하는 작업을 시작 했습니다." —[4]—

Glass Tiger Studios의 웹사이트는 이 회사에 대한 더 자세한 내용을 담고 있습니다. Calenbach Award 에 관한 더 많은 정보는 www.calenbachaward.org에서 찾아보실 수 있습니다.

172. 이 기사의 목적은 무엇인가?
(A) 지명 절차를 설명하기 위해서
(B) 명망 있는 시상식을 발표하기 위해서
(C) 제품 포장 직의 빈자리를 광고하기 위해서
(D) 한 회사의 성과를 자세히 설명하기 위해서

173. Calenbach Award에 대하여 언급되어 있는 것은?
(A) 이 상은 잡지 출판업자에게 자금을 지원 받았다.
(B) 이 상은 예전에 방콕 회사에게 수여된 적이 있다.
(C) 이 상은 매년 몇몇의 회사들에게 수여된다.
(D) 이 상은 20년 전에 처음으로 시상 되었다.

174. 이 기사에 따르면, Pranathat씨는 무엇을 계획하고 있는가?
(A) 더 많은 직원을 채용하는 것
(B) 광고를 다시 디자인 하는 것
(C) 회사 웹사이트를 업데이트 하는 것
(D) 방콕의 시상식에 가는 것

175. [1], [2], [3], [4]로 표시된 자리 중에 다음 문장이 들어가기에 가장 적합한 곳은?

"Glass Tiger studios는 많은 고객들로부터 점점 큰 관심을 받아왔습니다."
(A) [1]
(B) [2]
(C) [3]
(D) [4]

Questions 176-180 구인광고와 편지

Fresh Delivery의 Cape Town 사무실은 현재 물류창고 관리직을 위한 입사지원을 받고 있습니다. Fresh Delivery는 30년 이상 남아프리카에서 고품질의 농산품 배송 및 처리분야에 있어서 선두주자였습니다. 저희 고객에는 전국의 식료품점, 식당 그리고 기타 업체들이 있습니다.

물류 창고 관리자는 신규 직원을 교육하고, 일정표를 작성하고, 창고 직원들의 업무 퀄리티를 관리하는 등의 다양한 임무를 수행합니다. 입사 지원자는 1년 간의 관리직 경험을 포함하여, 이 분야에서 최소 5년의 경력을 보유해야 합니다.

때때로, 중요한 배송이 있는 경우에 창고 관리자는 야간 및 주말 근무가 요구될 것입니다. 지원자들은 또한 NPL 재고 관리 시스템을 사용하는

데 있어서 풍부한 경험을 가지고 있어야 합니다.

이러한 요건을 충족하는 관심 있는 지원자들은 자기소개서와 이력서 그리고 최소한 2개의 추천서를 8001 South Africa, Cape Town, Empire Avenue 15번지 Fresh Delivery사의 Lydia Herron씨에게 보냄으로써 지원하실 수 있습니다.

6월 15일

Ms. Lydia Herron
8001 Cape Town, Empire Avenue 15가
Fresh Delivery

Herron씨에게,

귀하의 시설 창고 관리자로 입사 지원하는 Shelley Moon를 추천하며 글을 쓰는 것은 저에게는 큰 기쁨입니다. Moon씨는 Fernley에서 근무한 10년 중 6년을 저의 감독하에서 일했으며 7년 전 임시직에서 정규직으로 인사 발령되었습니다.

Moon씨는 특히 창고 절차에 대한 지식과 민감한 화물을 다루는 것과 관련하여 이 자리에 딱 맞는 자격을 갖추었습니다. NPL 시스템은 수년 동안 우리 회사에서 사용 되어왔고, Moon씨는 NPL을 사용하는데 아주 능숙하며 새로운 직원들이 NPL 사용을 배우도록 도와왔습니다. 그녀는 또한 Thurston 대학에서 행정학 학사학위를 얻기 위해 공부하고 있으며, 기술적인 지식에 초점을 맞춘 추가 수업도 듣고 있습니다.

Moon씨는 이 직책을 위해 필요한 모든 요건을 갖추고 있고 훌륭한 직원이기 때문에, Moon씨가 당신의 회사에 자산이 될 것이라는게 저의 의견입니다. Moon씨에 대해 아무 질문이라도 물어보고 싶다면 저에게 연락해 주세요.

Charles Robbins
Charles Robbins
선창 담당 매니저
Fernley, Inc.

---

176. Fresh Delivery에 대해서 언급되어 있는 것은?
(A) 남아프리카에서 최근에 운영을 시작했다.
(B) 상당히 다양한 컴퓨터 프로그램을 제공한다.
(C) 식료품 체인점을 관리한다.
(D) 주로 식료품을 취급한다.

177. 구인광고에 따르면, 창고 관리자는 무엇을 기꺼이 해야 하는가?
(A) 안전 세미나에 참석하는 것
(B) 때때로 주말에 근무하는 것
(C) 무거운 물건을 옮기는 것
(D) 1년 동안 근무하는 것에 동의하는 것

178. Robbins씨는 왜 편지를 썼는가?
(A) 직원에 대해 긍정적인 의견을 표현하기 위해서
(B) 면접을 연기하기 위해서
(C) 지원자들에 대해 질문을 하기 위해서
(D) 새로운 회사 시스템을 소개하기 위해서

179. Moon씨에 대해 유추 할 수 있는 것은?
(A) 그녀는 이전에 Fresh Delivery에서 근무했었다.
(B) 그녀는 Thurston 대학의 교수이다.
(C) 그녀는 재고관리시스템에 대해 잘 안다.
(D) 그녀는 Fresh Delivery의 임시직에 지원했다.

180. Moon씨는 Fernley에서 얼마나 오래 근무 하였는가?
(A) 1년
(B) 5년
(C) 6년
(D) 10년

Questions 181-185 이메일들

수신:	Henry Ritter
발신:	Marcia Jones
참조:	Patrick Collins, Roberta Botlin
날짜:	11월 13일
제목:	전화 회의

당신은 제가 Baron Textiles의 남동부 사무실에서 4일전에 일하기 시작한 것을 알고 있을 거라 생각합니다. 저의 임무 중 하나는 매주 우리 영업에 관련한 전화 회의에 참여하는 것입니다. 그러나 오늘 오후 저는 전화가 계속 끊겨서 대부분의 대화내용을 듣는데 어려움을 겪었습니다. 제 상사는 저에게 Patrick Collins와 Roberta Botlin도 북부 지점에서 동일한 문제를 겪었다고 알려줬습니다. 이것은 다른 지점에서도 마찬가지로 문제가 될 가능성이 있습니다.

지점 사무실의 직원들이 본사 직원들과의 회의에 보다 더 잘 참가할 수 있도록 전화 미팅을 위한 더 좋은 장비를 가질 수 있는 방법이 있을까요?

Marcia Jones
남동부 지점, 영업
Baron Textiles

수신:	Marcia Jones, Patrick Collins, Roberta Botlin
발신:	Henry Ritter
날짜:	11월 18일
제목:	전화기 관련 업데이트

Marcia, Patrick, Roberta씨에게

저는 어제 새 전화기 3대를 주문했으며 11월 24일까지 당신들의 각각 사무실로 아마 배송될 것입니다. 우리는 이 전화기들을 테스트해보고, 여러분들의 의견을 수집할 것입니다. 여러분이 이 전화기가 만족스럽다고 생각할 경우, 필요한 만큼의 많은 전화기를 구매 하기 위한 추가적인 자금을 배정해 놓았습니다. 저는 11월 30일 Marcia의 지점에 방문해서 그녀의 영업 회의 전에 전화기를 어떻게 사용해야 하는지 사용법에 대해 그녀에게 알려줄 것입니다. 미팅 이후에 그녀의 의견을 들을 것입니다.

12월 7일에는 Patrick과 Robert의 사무실에도 동일한 이유로 방문할 것입니다. 상품평들을 보면 Cleartone 전화기가 수신력이 매우 좋다고 합니다. 이는 사무실의 소음 또한 아마 증폭 시켜 줄 수도 있다는 걸 의

미합니다. 전화기를 확인한 후에, 이것이 문제가 된다면, 우리는 통신 장비를 위한 다른 옵션을 찾아 볼 것입니다.

저희가 이 문제를 해결하기 위해 노력하는 동안 인내해 주셔서 감사합니다.

Henry Ritter
IT 컨설턴트
Baron Textiles

181. 첫 번째 이메일의 목적은 무엇인가?
(A) 문제를 신고하기 위해서
(B) 이전을 요청하기 위해서
(C) 분쟁을 해결하기 위해서
(D) 통신기기를 시판하기 위해

182. Jones씨에 대하여 언급되어 있는 것은?
(A) 그녀는 IT업체에서 근무하고 있다.
(B) 그녀는 Ritter씨의 상사와 토론을 가졌다.
(C) 그녀는 11월 13일에 Baron Testiles에서의 첫 번째 회의에 참여하려 했었다.
(D) 그녀는 11월 18일에 전화 회의에 참석했다.

183. 만약 Cleartone 전화기가 만족스럽다면 Ritter씨는 무엇을 할 것이라고 암시하고 있나요?
(A) 다른 전화기 모델과의 성능을 검사하는 것
(B) 제조회사로부터 가격 할인을 요청하는 것
(C) 그의 매니저와 공급업체를 변경하는 것을 논의하는 것
(D) 다른 지점을 위하여 더 많은 전화기를 구매 하는 것

184. 두 번째 이메일에서 Cleartone 전화기에 대하여 언급되어 있는 것은?
(A) 이 전화기는 그 업계에서 가장 인기 있는 전화기 모델이다.
(B) 이 전화기는 판매처에 의해 공급된 유일한 전화기이다.
(C) 이 전화기는 주변 소리를 더 크게 만들지도 모른다.
(D) 이 전화기는 즉시 주문하기는 불가능할 지 모른다.

185. 12월 7일 Henry씨는 아마 어디에 있을까요?
(A) 남동부 사무실
(B) 북부 사무실
(C) 본사 사무실
(D) 판매 워크샵

Questions 186-190 회사 사보 기사, 이메일 및 일정표

Wentford 산업 사보
8월 22일

Wentford Industries에 있는 우리들은 Janet Flanders가 올해의 매니저로 선정되어 오타와에서 열린 올해의 경영 컨퍼런스에서 상을 받은 것을 알리게 되어 기쁩니다. Flanders는 9년 전 벤쿠버 지점에서 인턴으로 시작해서 그녀의 근면성과 업무에 대한 열의 덕분에 빠르게 경영진의 자리에까지 올라왔습니다. 대학에서 학위를 받고 나서, Flanders는 토론토에 있는 본사에서 정규직을 수락하게 되었고, 그곳에서 지금도 일하고 있습니다.

Flanders는 유능하고 정감 있는 고객관리 매니저라는 것을 입증해왔을 뿐만 아니라, 고객 불만을 처리하는 우리의 방법을 개선함으로써 Wentford Industries 고객들의 만족도를 높이는데 일조해왔습니다. 그녀의 노력 덕분에 고객들 사이에서 Wentford의 평판은 압도적으로 긍정적인 것이 되었습니다. 그녀는 8월 25일 컨퍼런스에서 다른 수상자들과 함께 상을 받을 것이며 그 곳에서 Wentford 대표이사님의 우리 과거에 대한 연설뿐만 아니라 몇몇 개발관련 발표도 진행이 될 것입니다. Flanders에게 그녀의 성과에 대해 축하를 보내는 바입니다!

발신: Laura Myers ⟨lmyers@wentfordind.com⟩
수신: Janet Flanders ⟨jflanders@wentfordind.com⟩
제목: 안녕하세요
날짜: 8월 26일

Janet에게,

올해 제가 컨퍼런스에 갈 수 없는 것에 대해 사과를 드립니다. 하지만 당신도 제가 Minneapolis로 전근을 가게 된 것이 참석을 불가능하게 만들었음을 이해하리라 확신합니다. 수상 축하 드려요! 저에게 컨퍼런스에서 찍은 사진 좀 보내주실 수 있나요? Taylor Cobbin이 그곳에서 굉장한 발표를 했다고 들었습니다. 볼 수 있었다면 좋았을 텐데요.

여기서 저의 일은 자리를 잡아가고는 있지만 영업은 분명히 힘든 부서네요. 그렇지만 제가 마침내 부서 전체를 감독할 자리에 오르게 되었다는 것은 정말 멋진 일입니다.

저는 9월에 당신이 있는 지역에 갈 예정이에요. 그래서 이번 상도 축하할 겸 제가 점심을 사는 게 어떨까요?

Laura

Wentford Industries 경영 컨퍼런스
8월 25일

일정(변경될 수 있음):

오후 3:00 – 3:40: Wentford의 역사 – 발표자 Gregory Burns

오후 4:00 – 4:40: 직원과의 효과적인 의사소통 – 발표자 Taylor Cobbin

오후 5:00 – 5:40: 권한위임을 통한 생산성 제고 – 발표자 Sam Warner

오후 5:40 – 7:00: 중간 휴식 및 저녁식사 (Sally's Catering 제공)

오후 7:00 – 8:00: Arthur Sorensen에 의한 시상식

186. 기사에 따르면, Flanders씨는 어떤 과정을 개선했는가?
(A) 불만족한 고객들을 다루는 것
(B) 고객 만족 설문조사
(C) 컨퍼런스 등록
(D) 부서간의 적절한 의사소통을 확실히 하는 것

187. Myers씨에 대해 언급되어 있는 것은?
(A) 그녀는 사진 찍는 것을 좋아한다.
(B) 그녀는 다른 회사로 옮길 것이다.
(C) 그녀는 많은 인턴들을 담당하고 있다.
(D) 그녀는 영업부를 관리하고 있다.

188. 9월에 Myers씨는 아마도 어느 도시를 방문할까요?
(A) Minneapolis
(B) Toronto
(C) Vancouver
(D) Ottawa

189. Myers씨가 보고 싶었던 발표는?
(A) Wentford의 역사
(B) 직원과의 효과적인 의사소통
(C) 권한위임을 통한 생산성 제고
(D) 시상식

190. Gregory Burns는 누구인가?
(A) 컨퍼런스 기획자
(B) 수상자
(C) 출장뷔페 업체
(D) 회사 임원

Questions 191-195 이메일, 목록 및 영수증

수신: Raymond Grace 〈raygrace@heat.com〉
발신: Angelo Martinez 〈amartinez@amazebooks.com〉
날짜: 10월 14일
제목: 추천
첨부: 4개의 책

Grace씨에게

첨부파일에 나와있는 4개의 책을 당신이 좋아할 것이라 믿습니다. 이 선정 도서들은 당신의 과거 구매기록을 토대로 추천된 것입니다.

당신이 주문한 책이 재고가 있다면 주문한 책은 당일 발송되며, 영업일 기준으로 4일 이내에 당신이 원하는 주소에 도착할 것임을 기억해 주세요. 아직 출시되지 않은 책들은 10% 할인가에 미리 주문하실 수 있으며 이 책들이 출시될 때 원하는 주소로 배송될 것입니다.

독서를 멈추지 마세요!

Angelo Martinez
Amaze Books

우리 책들을 둘러보려면 여기를 클릭하세요.

신간 도서

Vegetable Party
지은이: Rachel Griggs
출판사: Symphonic Publications
가격: 15.60달러 (배송비 별도)

전 가족이 좋아할 신선하고 몸에 좋은 수십 가지의 야채 요리의 요리법

상태: 재고 있음

The Trees of National Parks
지은이: Robin Pride
출판사: Natural Birth
가격: 32.50달러 (배송비 별도)

전국의 주립공원과 국립 공원의 나무들을 소개하는 식물도감을 주요 내용으로 하는 방대한 책. 당신이 나무를 식별 할 수 있도록 삽화가 꽉차게 포함되어 있습니다.

상태: 재고 있음

The Home Guide to Furniture Restoration
지은이: Walter Verus
출판사: Symphonic Publications
가격: 23.40달러 (배송비 별도)

작가는 쉽게 이해할 수 있는 방식으로 집필을 했으며, 심지어 가구 리폼 경험이 전혀 없는 사람들도 집에서 가구 리폼을 쉽게 할 수 있게 만들어 줍니다.

상태: 11월에 출시됨. 지금 미리 주문 하세요

Antiquing and You
지은이: Francis O'Gladdery
출판사: P. Newton 출판
가격: 18.40달러 (배송비 별도)

Antiquing and You는 진짜 골동품을 찾거나 구입하는데 필요한, 쉽게 따라 할 수 있는 설명을 제공해줍니다.

상태: 재고 있음

인터넷 구매 영수증

주문일: 12월 10일 월요일
고객명: Raymond Grace

항목	가격
Vegetable Party	$15.60
The Sailor and the Element	$16.80
The Home Guide to Furniture Restoration	$23.40
배송 및 처리 비용	$5.60
총 금액	$63.70

Amaze Books을 이용해주셔서 감사합니다!

191. 이 이메일은 왜 쓰여졌는가?
(A) 주문을 확인하기 위해서
(B) 고객들에게 가게 이전을 알리기 위해서
(C) 이전 주문품에 대한 평가를 요청하기 위해서
(D) 추천 상품을 홍보하기 위해서

192. Grace씨에 대해서 언급되어 있는 것은?
(A) 그는 출판사 직원이다.
(B) 그는 책 추천을 요청했다.
(C) 그는 이전에 Amaze Books에서 책을 구매한 적이 있다.
(D) 그는 현재 주문품이 배송되기를 기다리고 있다.

193. The Trees of National Parks에 대해서 언급되어 있는 것은?
 (A) 이 책은 많은 그림을 포함하고 있다.
 (B) 이 책은 작가의 서명이 들어있다.
 (C) 이 책은 무료 배송을 포함한다.
 (D) 이 책은 시리즈물의 일부다.

194. Grace씨는 언제 주문품을 받을 가능성이 가장 높은가?
 (A) 10월 18일
 (B) 10월 22일
 (C) 12월 10일
 (D) 12월 14일

195. Grace씨의 주문과 관련하여 사실인 것은?
 (A) 배송처리가 업그레이드 되었다.
 (B) 사전예약주문 할인의 자격을 갖추지 못했다.
 (C) 또 하나의 주문과 별도로 이루어졌다.
 (D) 그의 사무실로 배송될 것이다.

Questions 196 – 200 웹사이트 정보와 이메일들

Elevate Financial

뉴스	예금	재무	구인

Dream Savings Plan은 당신이 돈을 절약 할 수 있는 가장 새로운 방법입니다.

Elevate Financial의 최신 저축 예금인 Dream Savings Plan은 저희 기존 Select Savings Plan보다 고객들에게 더 많은 혜택을 드립니다. 혜택 가운데는 높은 금리와 돈을 이체하는 여러 가지 옵션이 있습니다.

이번 상품 홍보기간에만, 저희는통상적으로 부과했던 예금전환 요금 없이 전 고객들에게 Select Savings Plan에서 Dream Savings Plan으로 갈아 탈 수 있는 기회를 드리고 있습니다. 또한, 이 상품은 첫 1년 동안 연간 서비스 이용료 3불로 고객들에게 제공 되고 있습니다. 첫 1년 이후에는 연간 이용료가 Dream Savings Plan의 경우 연간 5불로 인상됩니다.

이 특별 홍보이벤트는 6월 말까지 유효합니다.

수신: accountcare@elevatefinancial.com
발신: ktrump@mercurybroadband.com
제목: 예금계좌 문제
날짜: 6월 17일

제가 일주일 전에 Dream Savings Plan을 개설했을 때, 제 기존 Select Savings Plan에 남아있는 잔고가 상품을 개설한 후에 새 예금계좌로 이동한다고 들었습니다. 하지만 제가 방금 예금 계좌에 로그인 했더니 Dream Savings Plan에 아무런 돈도 남아 있지 않았습니다. 제 Select Savings Plan에서 Dream Savings Plan으로 언제 돈이 이체되는지를 알고 싶습니다.

가급적 빠른 시일 내에 어떻게 된 일인지를 알려주세요.

Karen Trump

수신인: ktrump@mercurybroadband.com
  accountcare@elevatefinancial.com
발신인: accountcare@elevatefinancial.com
제목: 회신: 예금계좌 문제
날짜: 6월 18일

Trump씨, 이번 문제와 관련하여 저희에게 연락 주셔서 감사합니다. 저희 기록에 따르면 고객님은 최근 계좌를 Dream Savings Plan으로 변경하셨습니다. 새로운 계좌를 개설하고 나서 자금이 이체되는 데는 보통 10일 정도가 걸립니다. 이는 고객님의 금융을 안전하게 유지하도록 하기 위해 취해지는 계좌 확인 및 보안조치 때문입니다. 돈을 인출할 필요가 있으시면 당분간 이전 계좌를 이용해주시기 바랍니다. 다른 문제가 있으시면 언제든 연락 주시기 바랍니다.

Sharon House
Elevate Financial 고객 계좌 전문가

196. 웹사이트 정보의 목적은 무엇인가?
 (A) 서비스 요금 인상을 설명하려고
 (B) 새로운 저축 상품을 홍보하려고
 (C) 온라인 뱅킹 절차를 설명하려고
 (D) 신규 지점 오픈을 알리려고

197. 서비스 이용료에 대해서 언급된 것은?
 (A) 고객들은 신규 계좌를 개설 할 때 이 이용료를 내야 한다.
 (B) 처음에는 이용료가 평상시보다 저렴할 것이다.
 (C) 다른 은행이 청구하는 이용료만큼 높지 않다.
 (D) 고객들은 2년 동안만 이 이용료를 지불하게 된다.

198. Trump씨에 대해서 사실일 가능성이 가장 높은 것은?
 (A) 그녀는 새로운 은행을 찾고 있다.
 (B) 그녀의 서비스 요금이 인상되었다.
 (C) 그녀는 계좌 변경에 대한 요금을 부과 받지 않았다.
 (D) 그녀는 현재 Select Savings Plan으로부터 자금을 인출할 수 없는 상태다.

199. 이메일의 첫 번째 단락의 첫 번째 줄 "balance"와 가장 가까운 의미의 단어는 무엇인가?
 (A) 금액
 (B) 조화
 (C) 수단
 (D) 안정성

200. Trump씨의 Dream Savings Plan 계좌는 언제 그 안에 자금이 들어갈까요?
 (A) 6월 10일
 (B) 6월 20일
 (C) 6월 27일
 (D) 6월 28일

TEST 8

PART 5

101. 학급이 12명의 학생들로 제한되어 있기 때문에, 당신이 이 과정을 수강하기 위해서는 저희는 빠른 회신을 필요로 합니다.

102. 당신의 주문 물품 배송을 위해서 최소한 영업일 기준으로 6일을 감안해주시기 바랍니다.

103. Taylor씨는 그녀의 부하직원들이 이번 주에 있을 팀 빌딩 워크샵과 다음 달에 있을 교육과정을 모두 참석하도록 요구했습니다.

104. 당신이 인터넷으로 주문한 모든 용품들은 홍콩 유통센터에서 24시간 이내에 선적이 될 것입니다.

105. Tiffy Bath는 그들의 제품이 일본과 중국의 면세점에서 철수되었음을 발표했습니다.

106. Ronald Belisario가 모든 관리직 지원자들 중에서 가장 자격이 뛰어나다는 사실에 면접관들이 동의했습니다.

107. 그 책이 목표하는 시장은 이미 요리 경험이 있으며 요리 기술을 보다 발전시키고자 하는 사람들입니다.

108. 과도한 마모나 손상의 조짐을 발견해 내기 위해서 공장 내 모든 설비는 자주 점검되어야 합니다.

109. 다양한 지역행사가 카운티 전역에 걸쳐서 5월 11일부터 18일까지 일주일 동안 (진행되도록) 시에 의해 계획되어 왔습니다.

110. 의장님께서 이번 주에 이사를 임명한 후에 이사회의 승인을 기다릴 것이라고 대변인이 명시했습니다.

111. 최상의 보안을 위한 조언은, 이름, 생일 등과 같은 개인 정보에 대한 세부사항을 피하라는 것입니다.

112. Cardmax는 동부지역에서의 시장점유율을 방어하기 위해서 보스턴에 새로운 지점을 개점하면서 지역적으로 확장할 것입니다.

113. 고객들이 휴대전화 약정서를 신청할 때마다, 고객들은 신청서가 승인되기 전에 먼저 신용조회를 받게 될 것입니다.

114. 보트 스토리라는 제목의 Crawford씨의 전시회는 수많은 첫 방문객들을 유치했으며, 그는 이 전시회를 지금껏 가장 인기 있는 전시회로 만들었습니다.

115. 이 도시는 1년전보다 두 배 이상 많은 일자리를 올해 젊은이들에게 제공할 것입니다.

116. North Ridge College는 St. John's College의 전 학장이었던 Rosa Parks씨가 신임 학장으로 임명되었음을 오늘 아침에 발표했습니다.

117. 시장 내에서의 회사 인지도를 강화시키기 위해서 귀사의 제품이 일반대중들에게 바로 이용 가능하게 만들어야 합니다 ⇒ 당신의 제품을 대중들이 바로 접할 수 있게 만들어야 합니다.

118. 모든 직원들은 다음달에 열릴 교육과정의 참석여부를 10월 5일까지 결정하셔야 함을 유념해주시기 바랍니다.

119. 충분하고 정기적인 유지관리보수로 인해서, 예기치 못한 시스템 고장은 보기 드물게 되었습니다.

120. Polynet사는 한국과 일본에 자회사를 설립함으로써, 그들의 해외 사업을 한층 더 확장시킬 것이라고 오늘 발표했습니다.

121. 지난 직원 회의에서 논의된 사항들과 관련된 추가자료가 늦어도 내일 오전까지 인트라넷에 게재될 것입니다.

122. 반도체에 대한 급격한 수요증가 덕택에, 이번 분기에 Mega Tele의 수출은 처음으로 400억 달러를 초과했습니다.

123. 다음달부터 Nokicell사는 인터넷 사용 품질과 편의성을 개선해줄 저렴한 가격의 스마트폰을 공급할 예정입니다.

124. 회사에서 당신에게 제공한 노트북, 태블릿, 스마트폰은 업무에 관련된 일에만 사용되어야 합니다.

125. 지난 달에, 오락용 잡지의 구독자수가 처음으로 1백만명을 넘어섰습니다.

126. 후한 상여금뿐만 아니라 상당히 높은 급여가 큰 판매 건들에 대해 영업사원들에게 수여될 것입니다.

127. 제조시설의 확장으로 인해서, Hatter Footwear는 총 생산량이 20% 증가할 것으로 예측했습니다.

128. 원가를 판매하는 사람이나 조직은 판매처로 불립니다.

129. Biowill Chemicals사는 석유 대신에 재생 가능한 곡물에서 추출된 플라스틱, 화학제품, 에너지를 생산합니다.

130. 우리가 하는 업무량은 매주 약간씩 다를 수 있습니다.

PART 6

Questions 131-134 이메일

수신: MichelleDupont@alphamail.com
발신: Groberts@stellaraudio.com
날짜: 6월 25일
제목: 구매번호 651388

Dupont씨에게

저희가 Stellar Hi-Fi Home Entertainment Stereo System (물품번호 651388)에 대한 귀하의 주문을 받았으나 Stellar Audio에서 지금은 귀하의 주문품을 발송할 수 없음을 알려드리게 되어 유감입니다. 귀하가 주문하신 스테레오 시스템은 현재 재고가 없는 상태입니다. 그러나 이 제품이 이월주문 상태에 있으며 7월 10일까지는 저희가 더 많은 물량을 받을 수 있습니다. 이것이 당신에게 불편을 드리게 되어 죄송합니다. 원하시면 주문을 취소하실 수도 있습니다. 그렇지 않다면, 이 시스템은 늦어도 7월 25일까지 귀하가 입력하신 주소로 배송이 될 것입니다. 질문 있으시면 주저 마시고 Groberts@stellaraudio.com으로 저에게 연락 주시기 바랍니다.

Questions 135-138 공지

고객님께

귀하가 가장 최근 Valentinafashions.com에서 하신 주문의 전송과정에서 에러가 발생했을지도 모른다는 우려 때문에 이 메시지를 보내는 바입니다. 인터넷 상점은 잘못 입력된 수량을 수정해 드릴 수가 없으며, 귀하가 실수로 잘못된 물품을 주문했는지를 판단할 수도 없습니다. 귀하가 주문하신 제품과 수량을 확인해 주시고, 주문을 다시 한번 보내주세요. 본 메일과 같은 종류의 이메일을 또 받게 되시면, 귀하의 주문이 삭제되었을지도 모릅니다. 귀하가 인터넷 주문을 넣을 때 실수 했다고 생각되시면 저희가 잘못된 물품을 선적하지 않도록 가능한 한 빨리 저희에게 연락을 취하십시오. 어떠한 실수도 웹사이트에서 귀하의 인터넷 계정으로 접속함으로써 수정 하실 수 있습니다.

Questions 139-142 이메일

수신: Adrian Gonzalez
발신: J.P. Howell
날짜: 3월 12일
제목: 새 복사기

Gonzalez씨에게

지난 3년 전에 복사기를 사셨거나 대여하셨다면 새로운 기술을 위해서 보상 판매를 이용하는 것을 고려해 보실 때입니다. 저희는 저희 신규 모델인 Pro204가 더 믿을 만 하다는 것을 보장합니다.

오래되고, 효율성이 떨어지는 기계를 신형 기계로 교체 함으로써 사무실 비용을 절감할 수 있습니다. 복사기가 사무실의 생산성을 위해서 중요한 도구라는 점에 동의하실 것입니다. 새로운 복사기와 함께라면, 더 적은 시간에 당신은 더 많은 업무를 처리 할 수 있을 것이므로 당신의 사무실은 생산성이 높아질 것입니다. Pro204는 인쇄, 팩스, 복사, 스캔과 같은 여러 기능을 수행 할 수 있습니다.

Pro204나 다른 모델에 대해서 질문이 있으시다면 제가 이 이메일에 첨부한 안내책자를 참고하시거나 아니면 저희 영업사원에게 연락주세요.

Questions 143-146 전단지

전국 야외 조각 경진대회 및 전시회

귀하의 생각을 하게 만드는, 특별한 조각품을 전시할 기회를 찾고 있습니까? 만약 그렇다면, 이것은 당신을 위한 완벽한 대회입니다. www.NOSCE.com에서 등록 양식을 다운로드 받아서 작성하시고, 저희에게 당신의 작품 사진과 함께 이메일로 보내주세요. 신청 마감일은 9월 30일입니다. 이날 이후에 접수된 모든 신청서는 심사대상이 되지 않을 것입니다. 최대 14개의 조각품들이 전시회에 나갈 것이며, 상금을 위해서 경합을 벌일 것입니다. 당신이 보낸 사진들이 출품작을 선정하는데 있어서 아주 중요합니다. 초대된 출품작들은 접수 마감 2달 후에 공지를 받을 것입니다.

Questions 147-148 제품 포장지

Pridex Industries

Pridex Industries 제품의 훌륭한 맛을 즐기십니까? 지금 당신은 Pridex 칩, 캔디 바 그리고 쿠키를 무료로 받을 수 있습니다! 단지 www.pridexind.com에 등록하시고 포인트를 받기 위해 Pridex 제품 포장지에 있는 코드를 입력하기만 하면 됩니다. 당신이 충분한 포인트를 모으면, 우리는 당신이 선택한 제품을 구매할 수 있는 무료이용권을 당신에게 보내드립니다.

품질 좋은 먹거리를 원하신다면 Pridex을 선택하세요.

당신의 코드 번호: 484DBE83

147. 이 회사는 어떤 종류의 상품을 판매하나요?
 (A) 컴퓨터
 (B) 스낵
 (C) 책
 (D) 음악 악기

148. 어떻게 고객들은 포인트를 받을 수 있나요?
 (A) Pridex 제품에 대해서 설문지를 작성함으로써
 (B) 구매 증거(영수증 등)를 보냄으로써
 (C) 웹사이트에 코드를 제출함으로써
 (D) 회사를 위한 새로운 슬로건을 만듦으로써

Questions 149-150 기사

Chamber Website를 개선하다

Atlas 상공부는 등록된 업체들이 웹사이트에 있는 대규모 주소록에 접속함으로써 다른 등록된 업체들을 찾아볼 수 있게 만들기 위해서 웹사이트를 업그레이드 했다고 발표했습니다. "Atlas 회사들이 사용할 수 있는 많은 정보가 있긴 했지만 업체들이 다른 업체들에 대한 정보를 찾기는 어려웠습니다" 현지역 등록된 기업 회원인 Tiffany Billings가 이야기 했습니다. "새로운 주소록 검색 기능 덕분에, 만약 등록된 업체가 광고를 위한 상담 서비스를 필요로 한다면, 그들은 지역의 업체들, 주소, 전화번호와 인터넷 혹은 이메일 주소를 찾을 수 있습니다. Chamber's Commercial Growth Committee가 이 업데이트 작업에 큰 도움을 주었습니다. "웹사이트의 기술 지원은 Atlas Business에 등록된 업체인 MegaCom이 맡을 것입니다. 이전에 사이트에서 이용 가능했던 현지 행사 일정이나 구인광고와 같은 정보는 여전히 일반대중에게 공개 될 것이지만, 등록된 현지 업체들만이 배정된 비밀번호를 사용해서 주소록에 접속할 수 있을 것입니다.

149. 왜 상공부는 웹사이트를 업데이트 했는가?
 (A) 직업 상담을 광고하기 위해서
 (B) 회의 일정에 대하여 세부사항을 주기 위해서
 (C) 현지 업체들이 함께 일하는 걸 돕기 위해서
 (D) 일반 대중들에게 상담 서비스를 알리기 위해서

150. 주소록에 대하여 언급되어 있는 것은?
(A) 세계적인 회사가 서비스한다.
(B) MegaCom에 의해서 추천 되었다.
(C) 등록된 회사들에게만 공개된다.
(D) 매월 갱신 될 것이다.

Questions 151-152 문자메시지 대화

AMBER SIMMONS	2:10 PM

늦어서 죄송해요. 주차 공간을 찾을 수가 없네요.

DIEGO CASTRO	2:11 PM

지금 운전하면서 문자 보내는 건 아니죠?

AMBER SIMMONS	2:12 PM

아니에요. 차를 잠깐 세워놨어요. 어디 주차했어요?

AMBER SIMMONS	2:13 PM

차에 필름이 있어서 저는 그늘에 주차를 해야 해요.

DIEGO CASTRO	2:13 PM

7번가 공원 옆이요.

AMBER SIMMONS	2:14 PM

거기가 보이네요. 그늘이 진 것 같은데요.

AMBER SIMMONS	2:15 PM

자리가 막 하나 났네요. 곧 거기로 갈게요.

DIEGO CASTRO	2:16 PM

서두르세요. 음식 주문하고 싶어요.

151. Simmons는 무엇을 하고 있나요?
(A) 식당 위치를 찾고 있다.
(B) 테이크 아웃을 위해 음식을 주문하고 있다.
(C) 약속을 잡고 있다.
(D) 자신의 차를 위한 공간을 확보하고 있다.

152. 2시 16분에 Diego Castro씨가 "Get a move on"이라고 쓸 때 무엇을 의미하고 있는가?
(A) Simmons씨는 이삿짐 센터와 날을 잡아야 한다.
(B) Simmons씨는 장소로 오기 위해 서둘러야 한다.
(C) Simmons씨는 도착했을 때 전화를 해줘야 한다.
(D) Simmons씨는 자신이 주문할 음식을 전달해줘야 한다.

Questions 153-154 웹사이트의 정보

http:// www.nama.com

National Argentinian Marketing Association은 부에노스 아이레스에서 5월 12일부터 14일까지 열릴 협회의 12번째 연례 컨벤션에서 기조연설가로 Felix Rodriguez를 모시게 되어 매우 영광입니다. Rodriguez씨는 전직 회계사였던 그의 파트너 Hector Villanova의 도움을 받으며 거의 10년 전 Bueno Marketing Consultants을 시작하는데 크게 일조했습니다. Rodriguez의 회사는 큰 성공을 거두어 왔으며, 좋은 마케팅이 어떻게 회사를 도울 수 있는지의 훌륭한 예시가 되고 있습니다. Bueno Marketing Consultants는 식품과 음료 제조사에서부터 전자 업체에 이르기까지 다양한 회사들이 그들의 판매를 신장시키도록 지원해왔습니다. Rodriguez씨의 연설은 작년 Manzana 출판사에 의해 출판된 그의 저서인 "Think Locally, Market Globally"에 주로 의거합니다.

153. 이 정보의 목적은 무엇인가?
(A) 지역 문화에 대한 책을 홍보하려고
(B) 회사의 업적을 자세히 설명하려고
(C) 독자들에게 컨벤션 연사에 대해 알리려고
(D) 등록에 관한 정보를 주려고

154. Felix Rodriguez의 직업은 무엇인가?
(A) 출판사 임원
(B) 전자제품 제조업자
(C) 공인 회계사
(D) 마케팅 컨설턴트

Questions 155-157 편지

1월 18일

Paul Daniels
19963 DE Milford
Merit Road 8744

Daniels씨에게,

우리는 당신의 신청서 처리를 끝냈고, 끝자리 번호가 4497인 당신의 Maltese Bank Platinum Card 신용한도 상향조정을 승인할 것임을 당신에게 알리게 되어 기쁩니다. 당신은 2월 4일 부로 카드에 총 2만 달러의 신용한도를 가지게 될 것입니다. 카드의 계좌 번호는 변경되지 않을 거지만, 만료 일자는 연장될 것입니다. 당신은 신규 카드를 수령 하자마자 www.maltesebank.com/platinum/activate에 방문하셔서 카드를 활성화 하셔야 할 것입니다.

Lynette Givens
회계 담당자
1-800-555-4488

155. 왜 Daniels씨에게 편지가 보내졌는가?
(A) 그에게 승인된 신청 건에 대해 알리기 위해서
(B) 대금을 받았음을 확인해 주기 위해서
(C) 신규 이용 가능한 신용카드를 홍보하기 위해서
(D) 계좌의 내역서를 요청하기 위해서

156. 이 편지에 어떤 정보가 있는가?
(A) 지불 날짜
(B) 은행 주소
(C) 카드 번호 일부
(D) 만기 날짜

157. Daniels씨는 무엇을 하도록 권고되고 있는가?
  (A) 카드를 활성화시키기 위해 지불하는 것
  (B) 그의 이전 카드를 제대로 버리는 것
  (C) Maltese Bank 웹사이트를 방문하는 것
  (D) 추가 문서를 은행으로 가져 오는 것

Questions 158-160 쪽지

편집장으로부터

다가오는 Midwest Kitchen의 3월 호는 우리 출판사의
3주년을 기념하는 특집호가 될 것 입니다.
Midwestern 요리사들과 전국의 다른 요리사들이 제공하는
최고의 요리법들과 요리 팁을 공유하기 시작한지
이렇게나 많은 시간이 흘렀다는 것이 믿기지 않습니다.
딱 2달 전에, 우리의 총 구독자 수는
50만 명에 이르렀습니다.
매달 더 많은 구독자들이 가입하는 가운데 말이죠.
그리고 지난해의 167Kitchen and Cooking Convention에서
우리는 최고 혁신적인 요리 잡지로 상을 받았습니다.
이 잡지의 편집장으로써의 저는 우리의 작가, 사진작가
그리고 기고가뿐만 아니라
우리의 후원자들, 그리고 지난 3년간 우리 잡지가 성공하도록
도와줬던 점점 더 늘어나고 있는 우리 구독자들에게
어떻게 감사의 말을 전해야 할지 모르겠습니다. 감사합니다.

Thomas Swift

158. Swift씨의 메모의 목적은 무엇인가?
  (A) 감사의 뜻을 보여주기 위해
  (B) 구독을 제안하기 위해
  (C) 요리법을 기고하기 위해
  (D) 기금을 요청하기 위해

159. Midwest Kitchen에 대하여 언급되어 있는 것은 무엇인가?
  (A) 새로운 편집자를 찾고 있다.
  (B) 곧 출판을 중단할 것이다.
  (C) 훨씬 더 인기 있어지고 있다.
  (D) 구독료를 내렸다.

160. 왜 Swift씨는 Kitchen and Cooking Convention을 언급하였는가?
  (A) 그 행사에서 그가 요리책에 사인을 해줬기 때문에
  (B) 그곳에서 그가 새로운 요리 방법을 발표했기 때문에.
  (C) 그 행사 기획자들이 잡지를 후원하기 때문에
  (D) 자기네 출판물이 그곳에서 칭찬을 받았기 때문에

Questions 161-164 편지

Corn County Medical Center
213 Jespersen Avenue
Milwaukee, WI 53022

7월 5일

Mark Commer
5353 WI , Madison
Henders Road 2424

Commer씨에게,

우리는 당신이 Corn County Medical Center의 수간호사 자리에 지원해 주신 것을 감사 드립니다. 당신의 면접은 7월 12일 목요일 오전 10시 30분에 있을 예정입니다. 우리는 메인 병원 대신에 Williams Clinic에서 면접을 시행할 것입니다. 당신을 인터뷰할 위원회는 사업 본부장인 Sebastial Lexor와 수간호사인 Miriam Naren로 구성될 것입니다. Lexor 박사와 Naren씨는 병원의 모든 간호사들을 담당하고 있습니다.

우리가 전화상 논의 했듯이, 병원 가까이에 주차공간을 찾는 것은 보통 아주 어렵습니다. 현재, 병원은 또한 손님용 주차 공간을 가지고 있지 않습니다. 그래서 당신은 도로의 주차 공간을 확보 해야만 합니다. 버스를 이용하는 것이 훨씬 좋을 것입니다.

만약 당신이 인터뷰 전에 더 많은 정보가 필요하다면, 알려주세요.

Layla Hempel
인사 부장

161. Commer씨에 대해서 언급되어 있는 것은 무엇인가?
  (A) 그는 면접이 끝날 때 병원을 방문할 것이다.
  (B) 그는 Williams 병원에서 Hempel씨를 볼 것이다.
  (C) 그는 이전에 전화로 Hempel씨와 이야기를 했었다.
  (D) 그는 안내데스크에서 일하는데 관심이 있다.

162. Naren씨에 대해서 언급되어 있는 것은?
  (A) 그녀는 현재 Williams 병원에서 근무 중이다.
  (B) 그녀는 Commer씨의 면접에 참석할 것이다.
  (C) 그녀는 의사가 되기 위해서 교육을 받고 있는 중이다.
  (D) 그녀가 Commer씨의 면접 일정을 잡았다.

163. 2번째 단락 2번째 줄의 "secure"과 의미상 가장 가까운 것은?
  (A) 경계하다
  (B) 붙이다
  (C) 확보하다
  (D) 빌리다

164. Hempel씨는 Commer씨가 무엇을 할 것을 제안 하는가?
  (A) 대중 교통을 이용하는 것
  (B) 손님용 주차 공간을 이용하는 것
  (C) 추천인 연락처를 제공하는 것
  (D) 예약을 확인 하는 것

Questions 165-167 이메일

발신: Beth Tempton ⟨btempton@healthstrong.com⟩
수신: Richard Lang ⟨rlang@ healthstrong.com ⟩
제목: 판매 워크샵
날짜: 5월 23일

안녕하세요 Richard씨.

우리가 이야기 했던 워크샵에 당신이 참여할 좋은 기회를 제가 방금 알게 되었습니다. —[1]— 이전 워크샵과 달리, 이번 워크샵은 경력이 많은 영업사원들과 최근에 시작한 영업사원들 모두 대상으로 하기를 원합니다.

다른 워크샵들처럼, 각 워크샵이 2시간 동안 지속되는 가운데, 전체 한 달 기간에 걸쳐서 진행될 것입니다. —[2]— 당신이 R&D 부서에서 일하기 때문에, 당신의 일정만 허용한다면, 당신의 지식은 당신을 우리 교육팀에 훌륭한 추가인원으로 만들어 줄 것입니다. —[3]—

Lilly Heeman과 Dirk Tently는 처음 2주 동안 워크샵을 이끌 것 입니다. 그런데 Stepthanie Wrihley씨가 8월 첫째 주까지 제네바에 있어야 하기 때문에, 제품 테스트 부서에 있는 그녀의 일정에 차질이 생겼습니다. 그녀의 동료인 Maryanne Broderich씨가 Stephanie의 워크샵을 혼자서 맡아 줄 수 있다고 이야기 했습니다. 만약 당신이 가능하다면, 저는 당신이 마지막 워크샵을 위해 Maryanne과 함께 해주기를 원합니다. Maryanne과 당신이 마지막 워크샵을 위한 아주 훌륭한 팀이 될 거라 저는 생각합니다. —[4]—

Beth Tempton
영업 부장

165. 이메일에 따르면, 이전의 워크샵과 다가오는 판매 워크샵이 어떻게 다른가?
(A) 이번 워크샵은 한 명이 아닌 여러 명의 진행자가 있다.
(B) 각 워크샵의 시간이 더 길다.
(C) 이전만큼 많은 주제가 논의되진 않을 것이다.
(D) 모든 영업사원을 위해 만들어졌다.

166. 가능한 진행자로써 언급되지 않은 사람은?
(A) Beth Tempton
(B) Lilly Heeman
(C) Dirk Tently
(D) Maryanne Broderick

167. [1], [2], [3], [4]로 표시된 자리 중에 다음 문장이 들어가기에 가장 적합한 곳은?

"각각의 워크샵이 몇 명의 부서 전문가들에 의해 진행되는 가운데, 7월 매주 목요일에 오후 1시부터 오후 3시까지 열릴 것입니다."
(A) [1]
(B) [2]
(C) [3]
(D) [4]

Questions 168-171 기사

도로 공사 이후의 교통 노선의 변경

5월 31일– 내일부터 도로공사로 인해 Lawrence의 몇몇 도로가 통제 될 것이므로 운전자들은 대체 노선을 찾을 준비를 해야 합니다.

교통부는 Worryfree Roads 프로그램과 함께 3단계의 과정으로 완료 될 공사에 착수했습니다. 이 작업의 첫 번째 단계는 2개월 동안 지속될 예정으로, Farrer Avenue부터 Highway 22까지의 Alderidge Street의 일부 도로를 재포장하는 것입니다. —[1]—

공사 프로세스의 두 번째 단계는, 세 단계 중에 가장 오랜 시간이 걸리는 공사로, 잠정적으로 8월에 시작할 예정입니다. —[2]— 이 공사는 1년 전 176aSilver 쇼핑 센터가 개장한 이래 상승되어 왔던 교통 혼잡을 해소하기 위해 현재 하나의 차선에서 두 배로 키워 2개의 차선으로 늘리기 위해 마련되었습니다. 이 램프는 경사로의 커브를 더 완만하게 만 듦으로써 176d 더 안전하게 만들어질 것입니다.

—[3]— 4B 출구로부터 대략 700미터 떨어진 Prairie Read의 주민인 Olivia Petrova는 큰 관심을 가지고 이 공사의 진행을 지켜보고 있습니다. "이 경사로가 마침내 재 공사가 된다니 참 잘됐네요."라고 그녀가 이야기 했습니다. 그녀는 램프와 관련해 기뻐했지만 공사가 원래 예정되어 있는 3개월 보다는 더 빨리 완성되는 것을 보고 싶어 합니다. "더 빨리 끝날 수 있다면 좋을 텐데요"라고 그녀가 덧붙였습니다.

세 번째 단계는 이전 단계만큼 교통에 크게 영향을 끼치지는 않을 다양한 작업들을 포함합니다. —[4]— 이 단계에서, 교통 표지판들은 밤에 더욱 잘 보이게 하기 위해서 교체가 될 것이고, 야광 페인트로 도로 위의 교통 표시와 주행선들을 다시 칠할 것입니다. Lawrence Transit Commission은 많은 비용이 들지만 꼭 필요한 이 공사가 6개월 이내에 종료될 것이라고 예상하고 있습니다만, 그 일정은 잠정적인 것이고, 날씨 상태에 따라 변경 될 수 있다고 합니다.

168. 그 공사의 결과로 의도되지 않은 것은 무엇인가?
(A) 쇼핑몰 주변의 교통 혼잡을 완화시키는 것
(B) 야간에 도로 표지판의 가시성을 높이는 것
(C) Lawrence의 주차 비용을 내리는 것
(D) 안전에 대한 우려를 해결하는 것

169. 4번째 단락, 첫 번째 줄의 "following"과 가장 의미상 가까운 것은?
(A) 준수하다
(B) 지켜보다
(C) 진행하다
(D) 보고하다

170. 얼마나 오래 두 번째 단계가 지속될 예정인가?
(A) 한 달
(B) 두 달
(C) 석 달
(D) 일 년

171. [1], [2], [3], [4]로 표시된 자리 중에 다음 문장이 들어가기에 가장 적합한 곳은?

"이 단계 동안의 작업으로 58번 도로(출구 4B)에서 Treeton Drive로 빠지는 출구 램프가 확장될 것입니다."

(A) [1]
(B) [2]
(C) [3]
(D) [4]

Questions 172-175 인터넷 채팅 대화

Olivia Byrne [11:11 a.m.]
Terrence O'Hara씨의 다음 소설 제안서 읽어보신 분 있나요? 제가 보기에는 너무 좋은 것 같아서 다른 분들의 의견도 들어보고 싶습니다.

Bridget Stamp [11:13 a.m.]
저 읽어봤는데요, 확실히 제 눈을 사로잡았어요. 저는 이 책을 출판하고 싶은데, Mark는 시장성이 별로 없다고 생각하던데요.

Mark Boughton [11:15 a.m.]
맞아요, 저는 잘 읽히는 얘기는 아니라고 생각해요. 만약 저희가 출간을 하면, 몇 몇 그룹에서는 성공적일 테지만, 전반적으로 볼 때 대 실패가 될 거라고 생각합니다. 지난번 이 작가의 소설과는 매우 다른 주제인 것 같습니다.

Bridget Stamp [11:17 a.m.]
이 소설이 좀 다른 방향으로 가고 있다는 데는 저도 동감합니다. 이 제안서에는 작가의 이전 소설들과 비교해서 SF주제가 주를 이루고 있다고 생각해요. 예전 팬들은 좋아하지 않을 지 몰라도 새로운 독자를 끌어드릴 수는 있을 것 같아요.

Olivia Byrne [11:18 a.m.]
이 소설을 발표하는데 좀 다른 접근방식을 시도하면 어떨까요? 그대로 소설로 출간하는 것 대신, 다른 문예잡지나 SF잡지에 첫 장을 발표하고 어떤 반응을 얻는지 살펴보면 어떨까요?

Mark Boughton [11:20 a.m.]
흥미로운데요. 어떤 잡지가 좋을 거라고 생각하세요?

Bob Copeland [11:21 a.m.]
Future Times Journal of Sci-Fi나 Fiction Monthly에 있는 아는 분들에게 연락해 볼 수 있습니다. 관심 있어 할거라고 생각해요.

Olivia Byrne [11:23 a.m.]
좋은 생각이에요, Bob. 제가 지금 Terrence에게 전화해서 우선 잡지에 한 챕터를 공개하는 게 괜찮은지 물어볼게요. 잡지사 아는 분들과 얘기하고 나서 그들이 뭐라고 얘기하는지 저에게 알려주세요.

172. 이들은 어디에서 일할 가능성이 가장 높은가?
(A) 문예 잡지
(B) 출판사
(C) 교육 기관
(D) 과학 박물관

173. Terrence O'Hara에 대해 언급된 것은?
(A) O'Hara씨는 이전에도 잡지에 글을 발표한 적이 있다.
(B) O'Hara씨는 주로 SF 소설을 집필한다.
(C) O'Hara씨는 여러 개의 출판사와 일한다.
(D) O'Hara씨는 예전에 소설책을 출판한 적이 있다.

174. 11시 15분에 Mark Boughton씨가 "it would bomb"이라고 쓸 때 무엇을 의미하고 있는가?
(A) 출판사가 수익을 낼 것이다.
(B) 비평가들은 책이 재미있다고 생각할 것이다.
(C) 이 소설은 너무 심한 폭력성을 담고 있다.
(D) 출판은 상업적인 실패일 것이다.

175. Olivia Byrne씨는 아마도 다음에 무엇을 할까?
(A) 작가와 계획에 대해 논의한다.
(B) 잡지 편집장들에게 연락한다.
(C) 몇 몇 아는 사람들과 미팅을 잡는다.
(D) 소설책을 위한 제안서를 편집한다.

Questions 176-180 기메일들

수신: dapplebaum@cordis.com
발신: gretrand@huxleyinternational.ca
제목: 면접
날짜: 10월 15일
첨부: 채용 정책 메뉴얼

Applebaum씨에게

2주전 벤쿠버 채용 박람회에서 우리 부스를 찾아준 것에 대해 감사를 드리고 싶습니다. 당신의 경력과 현재 Cordis Systems에서의 지위는 대단합니다. 우리가 이야기했던 직책에 당신이 신청서와 이력서를 보내기로 결정 하셔서 저는 대우 기쁩니다.

우리 인사 관리자가 당신의 자격을 검토 했고 당신이 2주 이내에 면접을 위해 우리의 본사를 방문하기를 원합니다. 이 시간대 중 언제가 당신의 일정과 가장 잘 맞는지를 저에게 알려주세요.

10월 21일 수요일, 오전 11시 또는 오후 3시
10월 23일 금요일, 오전 10시 또는 오후 2시
10월 27일 화요일, 오전 10시 30분 또는 오전 11시 30분

우리 사무실로 오시기 전에, 제가 첨부한 정책 매뉴얼을 정독하시기를 바랍니다. 그래야 저희 정책에 대해 궁금한 것이 있으시면 질문하실 수 있을 테니까요. 면접에 대하여 궁금한 점이 있으시면 저에게 주저하지 말고 연락주세요.

Gertrude Retrand

수신: gretrand@huxleyinternational.ca
발신: dapplebaum@cordis.com
제목: 답신: 인터뷰
날짜: 10월 16일

Retrand씨에게

Huxley International에서 면접을 볼 기회를 주셔서 감사합니다. 굉장

히 오랜 시간 컨설턴트로써 일해오다가 이렇게 한 팀을 이끈다는 것은 흥미로운 도전이 될 것입니다. 면접 시간에 대해 말하자면, 저는 보통 오후시간이 훨씬 자유롭습니다. 그래서 저는 오후 3시에 면접을 위해 당신의 본사로 갈 수 있습니다.

저는 사실 직업 박람회에서 당신이 말한 것에 대하여 궁금한 것이 있었습니다. 저의 경력에 관련하여 추천인과 몇 개의 추천서를 원한다고 이야기 하셨는데요. 준비하는 것은 전혀 문제가 없는데, 면접에 몇 개를 가지고 가야 하는지 알려줄 수 있으신지요?

다시 한번 이 기회를 주셔서 감사합니다. 다음주에 당신을 다시 만나길 고대하고 있습니다.

176. 어떻게 Applebaum씨는 Huxley International의 일자리에 관하여 알게 되었는가?
(A) 동료로부터
(B) 인터넷 게시글로부터
(C) 회사의 게시판에서
(D) 채용 박람회에서

177. Applebaum씨는 그의 면접 전에 무엇을 하도록 지시 받았는가?
(A) 회사 역사를 검토하기
(B) 추천서 쓰기
(C) 소책자 읽어보기
(D) 신원조사를 받기

178. 언제 Applebaum씨의 면접이 있을 것인가?
(A) 화요일
(B) 수요일
(C) 목요일
(D) 금요일

179. 왜 Applebaum씨는 새로운 직업을 구하고 있는가?
(A) 팀을 이끌기를 원하기 때문에
(B) 새로운 지역으로 이사하기를 원하기 때문에
(C) 새로운 분야에서 일하고 싶어하기 때문에
(D) 정규직으로 일하고 싶어 하기 때문에

180. 어떤 정보를 Applebaum씨가 요청하는가?
(A) 본사의 위치
(B) 그가 가져가야 할 추천서의 숫자
(C) 그의 새 직책의 임무
(D) 그가 관리할 직원들의 이름

Questions 181-185 이메일들

수신: Larry Baird
발신: Moira Lovett
날짜: 3월 18일
제목: Silverson Electronics Workshop

Baird씨에게

저는 Silverson Electronics의 저의 직원들을 위해 팀 빌딩 워크샵을 준비하고 있으며 워크샵을 Biltmore Hotel에서 개최할 생각을 하고 있었습니다. 저의 동료인 Piazza씨가 올해 초에 당신의 호텔에서 모임을 개최했었고, 그가 호텔 자체뿐만 아니라 당신과 당신 직원들의 서비스와 환대에 매우 만족해 했습니다.

Silverson Electronics사의 팀 빌딩 워크샵은 5월 2일 오전 9시경에 예정되어 있습니다. 저는 큰 회의실이 필요하고, 워크샵은 5시간 30분 가량 지속될 예정입니다. 최대한으로 잡아서 40명이 올 것입니다. 그들 중에서 다수의 사람들이 호텔에서 그날 밤 투숙할 계획입니다. 저희는 점심식사를 위해서 워크샵 동안 쉬는 시간을 가질 예정이라서, 점심 뷔페가 포함된 반나절 짜리 패키지를 원합니다. 또한, 우리는 프로젝터와 스크린뿐만 아니라 워크샵을 위해 4개의 마이크가 갖춰진 사운드 시스템이 필요합니다.

도움 주실 것을 미리 감사 드립니다.

Moira Lovett

수신: Moira Lovett
발신: Larry Baird
날짜: 3월 19일
제목: RE: Silverson Electronics Workshop
첨부: 뷔페 메뉴 옵션

Lovett씨에게

당신이 저희 호텔을 Silverson Electronics 워크샵 장소로 선택하려 하신다니 영광입니다. 저희 호텔은 객실과 식사에 대해 4가지의 옵션이 있으며 모든 옵션에는 무선 인터넷이 포함됩니다.

The Biltmore Option: 일인당 70달러 − 회의장 1일 예약 − 최대 10시간
아침 뷔페, 점심 뷔페 및 가벼운 다과가 음향, 비디오 장비와 함께 제공됩니다. 참가자들을 위한 무료 대리주차도 가능합니다.

The Executive Option: 일인당 55달러 − 회의장 1일 예약 − 최대 10시간
음향, 비디오 장비가 포함되어 있습니다. 손님들은 주차시설을 무료로 이용하실 수 있습니다.

The Preferred Option: 일인당 45달러 − 회의장 반나절 예약 − 최대 6시간
점심 뷔페가 음향, 비디오 장비와 함께 포함되어 있습니다. 손님들은 주차시설을 무료로 이용하실 수 있습니다.

The Robbins Option: 일인당 30달러 − 회의장 반나절 예약 − 최대 6시간
가벼운 다과가 회의의 시작과 마지막에 제공됩니다. 음향, 비디오 장비가 제공되며, 손님들은 우리 주차시설을 무료로 이용하실 수 있습니다.

첨부된 뷔페 메뉴를 살펴봐주시고 어떤 질문도 편하게 물어보세요.

Larry Baird

181. 첫 번째 이메일의 목적은 무엇인가?
(A) 스케줄이 겹치는 것을 해결 하기 위해서
(B) 회의 시설에 대해서 물어보기 위해서
(C) 호텔 예약을 확인하기 위해서
(D) 게스트 리스트를 요청하기 위해서

182. 워크샵에 대해서 언급되어 있는 것은?
(A) 시작할 때 영화가 상영될 것이다.
(B) 참석자들은 한 회사에 고용되어 있다.
(C) 워크샵이 원래는 더 늦게 열리도록 예정되어있다.
(D) 워크샵에 발표자는 한 명일 것이다.

183. Baird씨에 대해 언급되어 있는 것은?
(A) 그를 Lovett씨의 동료가 추천했다.
(B) 그는 호텔에서 오래 일하지 않았다.
(C) 그는 Silverson Electronics에 의해 이전에도 고용되었다.
(D) 그는 Biltmore Hotel의 뷔페 메뉴를 만들었다.

184. 회의 옵션의 특징으로써 언급된 것이 아닌 것은 무엇인가?
(A) 회의장에서의 인터넷 연결
(B) 회의 참석자들을 위한 무료 주차
(C) 회의장에서의 시청각 장비
(D) 참석자들을 위한 할인된 객실 요금

185. Silverson Electronics의 바람을 가장 충족하는 패키지는 무엇인가?
(A) The Biltmore 옵션
(B) The Executive 옵션
(C) The Preferred 옵션
(D) The Robbins 옵션

Questions 186-190 웹페이지, 브로셔 및 이메일

---

http://www.premiumoutings.com/washingtondc

Premium Tours

Premium Tours는 당신을 역사적인 워싱턴 D.C, 볼티모어 그리고 피츠버그 지역에서 최고의 현지 식당으로 데려다 주는 것을 우리의 임무로 생각합니다. 우리의 박식한 가이드가 함께 하면, 그들은 맛있는 식당으로 걸어가는 동안 그리고 최고의 음식을 맛보는 동안에 당신에게 그 지역의 역사와 문화에 대해 설명해 줄 것입니다.

Penn Quarter (워싱턴 D.C.)

시간: 월요일부터 금요일까지, 오후 5시30분부터 오후 8시까지 (주말 동안에는 여행 일정이 없습니다.)

복장: 걷는 데 적절한 의류와 신발이 추천됩니다.

음식: 참석자들은 여행 내내 다양한 맛을 즐기게 될 것입니다. 첫 번째 식당은 전체요리를 제공합니다. 두 번째 식당에서 참가자들은 식당의 사장이며 초콜릿 감정가인 Jacques Zieman를 만날 수 있으며, 그가 좋아하는 초콜릿을 시식하게 될 것입니다. 다음 식당은 많

지 않은 양의 저녁식사를 선보임이며, 마지막 식당에서 디저트가 제공될 것입니다.

포함 품목: 음식, 무료 생수, 지도, 여행에서 만나는 식당과 가게들을 설명해주는 자세한 팜플렛.

가격: 1인당 60달러

Premium Outings – Penn Quarter 식당들

식당들은 투어에서 방문하는 순서대로 아래에 나열되어 있습니다.

식당/상점	위치
1. Stan's Pizza	**644 언덕 거리** • 시카고 스타일의 피자를 특징으로 함.
2. Sweet Life	**113 George가** • 전세계 미식가들의 음식
3. Bread & Butter	**129 George가** • 저녁에 라이브 뮤직과 함께 하는 최고의 지중해식 음식 • 예약 필수
4. Sucre Bleu	**495 북부 15번가** • 최고의 케이크와 후식 • 목요일은 쉽니다.
5. Penn Quarter Creamery	**490 북부 15번가** • 수준 높은 아이스 크림과 선대 아이스크림 • 참석자들은 만약 Sucre Bleu가 열지 않았다면, 이곳을 방문할 것입니다.

수신인: Premium Tours ⟨inquiries@ premiumtours.com⟩
발신인: Lena Tomaski ⟨ltomaski@speedmail.com⟩
날짜: 6월 16일
제목: 투어관련 질문

안녕하세요,

저는 귀사의 투어에 참여하는데 관심이 있는데요, 투어 중에 어떤 식당을 방문하는 지를 보여주는 페이지가 다운된 것으로 보입니다. 저는 워싱턴 DC 지역에 식당에 가보고 싶습니다. 저는 아이스크림 매니아라서요, 가능하다면 아이스크림을 포함하는 투어에 가고 싶습니다. Penn Quarter 투어에 참여하기에 가장 좋은 시간은 언제 인지와 식당에 대한 더 자세한 정보를 알려주셨으면 합니다.

Lena Tomaski

186. Premium Tours에 대해서 언급되어 있는 것은?
(A) 역사적인 집(유명한 사람들이 살았던 집) 견학을 제공한다.
(B) 일주일짜리 여행을 제공한다.
(C) 휴일에도 여행을 제공한다.
(D) 여러 다른 지역에서 여행을 제공한다.

187. 웹페이지 여섯 번째 문단, 첫 번째 줄의 "complimentary"가 의미상 가장 가까운 것은?
(A) 보충의
(B) 여분의
(C) 무상의
(D) 감사하는

188. Penn Quarter 투어에 대해서 언급되어 있는 것은?
    (A) 하루에 두 번 열린다.
    (B) 참석자들에게 세계 전역의 음식을 제공합니다.
    (C) 가이드는 Penn Quarter의 거주민이다.
    (D) 참석자들은 무료 교통편을 제공 받는다.

189. 투어 참석자들은 어디에서 Zieman씨를 만날 것인가?
    (A) Sweet Life에서
    (B) Bread & Butter에서
    (C) Sagarmatha에서
    (D) Sucre Bleu에서

190. Tomaski씨는 어느 요일에 Premium Tour에 참여할 가능성이 가장 높은가?
    (A) 월요일
    (B) 수요일
    (C) 목요일
    (D) 금요일

Questions 191-195 기사, 웹사이트 및 기사

Plain Glass Theater, 이웃이 된걸 환영합니다

Plain Glass Theater는 Ellington 대학의 캠퍼스로부터 겨우 0.5킬로미터 떨어진 곳에 위치한 Cornwell Auditorium을 개조해서, 일반 대중들과 우리 학생들에게 문을 열었습니다.

이 극장은, 12년 전 창립이래로 이곳 저곳 이사를 다녔던 Plain Glass Theater의 영구적인 보금자리가 될 것입니다. 한때 지역문화회관이 입주해 있기도 했던 이 수리된 시설은 이 회사에 딱 안성맞춤 입니다. 아트 디렉터인 Gordon DeLaren씨는 이 공사가 분명히 (오랜 시간을) 기다릴만한 가치가 있는 공사라고 이야기 했습니다. "Cornwell Theater는 회사가 처음으로 예술활동 담당직원과 행정직원을 한 지붕아래 보유할 수 있게 해주는 넓고 우아한 시설입니다. Ellington 대학과 가까이 있는 것 또한 좋은 장점입니다. 우리는 그 학교에 예술을 사랑하는 학생들을 위해 수준 높은 공연을 제공할 수 있기를 희망합니다."

Clark Katz가 쓴 새로운 연극인 "Secret Summer"는 새로운 건물에서의 회사의 첫 번째 작품이 될 것입니다. 이 연극은 2월 12일 토요일 공개되며 이 연극 연출자의 연설로 시작할 것입니다. 더 많은 정보는 www.plainglasstheater.com에서 찾아 보실 수 있습니다.

Plain Glass Theater
티켓을 구매하세요

티켓 구매	홈페이지	다음 작품	극단 소식	연락처

티켓 가격:	일반 고객	40달러
	후원 회원	30달러
	학생	25달러
	10살 이하 어린이	12달러

Plain Glass Theater 티켓 판매처에서 학생 할인을 받기 위해서는 현재 유효한 학생신분증이 요구됩니다.

Plain Glass Theater, 데뷔 연극과 함께 성공적으로 오픈

Plain Glass Theater의 첫 번째 작품인 "Secret Summer"는 그 자리에 모인 모든 사람을 위한 공연예술의 훌륭한 상연이었습니다. 짧은 소개연설 동안 Kurt Hedaya씨는 예술사회를 지원해주기 위해 이렇게 많은 분들이 모여서 기쁘다고 말하며 청중들의 대부분이 Ellington College에서 오신 분들이었기 때문에 이 대학에도 감사의 뜻을 전달했습니다. 30분의 중간휴식 시간과 함께 3시간 상연된 이 공연에는 Emilia Snell이 출연했으며, 사람의 마음을 읽는 힘을 가졌음을 우연히 알게 되는 바리스타 역을 맡았습니다. 이 연극은 진지하면서, 매우 어려울 수 있으나 누구나 공감할 수 있는 주제를 감동적이고, 유머러스하면서 전체적으로 몰입하게 만드는 방식으로 다루어졌습니다. 3월 30일까지 Plain Glass Theater에 의해 상연될 예정입니다.

191. 극장에 대해서 언급되어 있는 것은?
    (A) 이 극장은 Katz씨에 의해 창립되었다.
    (B) 이 극장은 안정된 장소를 가지지 못했었다.
    (C) 이 극장은 많은 나라에서 공연을 했었다.
    (D) 이 극장은 이름을 변경했다.

192. 이 기사에서, 2번째 단락의 10번째 줄에 있는 단어 "space"와 의미상 가장 가까운 것은?
    (A) 거리
    (B) 사생활
    (C) 이용 가능한 장소
    (D) 기간

193. Cornwell Theater의 장점으로써 DeLaren씨가 언급한 것이 아닌 것은?
    (A) 지역사회와의 역사
    (B) 잠재 고객들과의 근접성
    (C) 넓은 공간
    (D) 적절한 복원 비용

194. Kurt Hedaya씨의 직업은 무엇인가?
    (A) 극장의 아트 디렉터
    (B) 연극에 출연하는 배우
    (C) 연극의 연출자
    (D) 극장 평론가

195. 2월 12일 공연을 위해 모인 청중들에 관해 언급된 것은?
    (A) 청중들 중 많은 사람들이 할인 티켓을 받았다.
    (B) 청중들은 연극이 너무 길다고 생각했다.
    (C) 청중들 중 일부는 중간 휴식시간에 자리를 떴다.
    (D) 많은 청중들이 자녀를 동반했다.

Questions 196-200 광고, 이메일 및 공지

Riverview Apartments
현재 임대 중!

저렴한 임대료로 나오는 신규 임대!

(최소 1년의 임대가 요구됨)

원룸 아파트: 월세 900불
투룸 아파트: 월세 1150불
모든 공과금은 월세 임대료에 포함되어 있습니다.

세탁소, 레크리에이션 시설, 시설이 완비된 로비는
모두 세입자들이 이용 가능합니다.

**55429 MN, Brooklyn Center,
West River Road 24번지**
416-55-0142
www.riverviewapartments.com

수신: Rita Adler
발신: Eric Jansen
주제: 신규 세입자
날짜: 5월 4일
첨부: 아파트-55

Adler씨에게

Harvey Lang씨를 위한 모든 서류들이 작성되었습니다. 그는 1년짜리 임대 계약을 하러 오늘 아침에 사무실로 들를 것이고 첫 달 집세 900불을 개인 수표로 결제할 것입니다. 서류와 집세는 오늘 오후에 귀하의 책상 위에 있을 것입니다. 그는 또한 바로 세입자 협회에 등록할 계획입니다.

아파트가 6월 2일까지는 준비가 돼 있어야 한다는 점을 관리부서에 알려주세요. 저는 이 이메일에 자세한 작업 순서를 첨부했습니다. Mr. Lang씨가 방을 베이지 색으로 칠해 주기를 원한다는 것을 관리실 직원이 분명히 알게 해 주세요.

여전히 비어 있는 아파트가 3층, 6층, 7층에 세 개가 더 있습니다. 저는 오늘 오후에 몇 분의 계약 희망자와 만나서 그들에게 투 룸 아파트를 보여 줄 것이고, 내일은 원 룸 아파트를 보실 다른 계약 희망자를 만나기로 했습니다. 일단 이 아파트들이 리스가 되고 나면, 빈집이 없이 전부 임대 되는 것입니다.

감사합니다.
Eric Jansen

Riverview Apartments 세입자 협회 공지문
7월 1일

세입자 여러분들 반갑습니다. 아래 사항은 7월 7일 다가 오는 미팅의 잠정적인 일정입니다.

새로운 세입자 소개: 저희 협회의 어떤 새로운 세입자도 자신을 소개하도록 요청 받을 것입니다.

다가오는 주차장 공사: 저희는 주차장에서 진행될 공사와 세입자들을 위한 대체 주차공간에 대한 정보를 제공할 것입니다.

공용 수영장 수칙 업데이트: 공용 수영장에 대한 수칙이 수정되었습니다. 오셔서 어떻게 변경이 되는지 확인해주시고 그에 대한 여러분의 생각도 들려주세요.

공사 통지: 7월 한달 동안 내내 아파트 340호, 680호, 723호에서 새로운 세입자를 위한 공사가 있을 것입니다. 세입자분들이 이로부터 무엇을 예상할 수 있는 지(에로 인한 여파가 무엇인지)를 저희는 논의할 것입니다.

---

196. Lang씨에 대해서 언급되어 있는 것은?
(A) 그는 원룸 아파트를 계약 할 것이다.
(B) 그는 집 계약을 1년 더 연장 할 것이다.
(C) 그는 5월에 아파트를 비워야 한다.
(D) 그는 로비 사용권한을 요청했다.

197. Adler씨는 무엇을 하도록 요청 받고 있는가?
(A) 일부 서류를 승인해야 한다.
(B) 세부 사항을 관리실 직원에게 제공해야 한다.
(C) Jansen씨와 만남 일정을 잡아야 한다.
(D) 세입 희망자들에게 계약하도록 설득해야 한다.

198. 공지 첫 번째 단락, 첫 번째 줄의 "tentative"가 의미상 가장 가까운 것은?
(A) 분명히 규정되지 않은
(B) 망설이는
(C) 실험적인
(D) 구체적인

199. Lang씨는 미팅에서 무엇을 할 것으로 예상되는가?
(A) 다른 멤버들에게 자신에 대해 얘기할 것이다.
(B) 아파트 단지 시설의 변경되는 수칙에 대해 투표할 것이다.
(C) 대체 주차 공간을 배정받을 것이다.
(D) 웹사이트의 업데이트를 발표할 것이다.

200. Riverview Apartments에 대해 언급된 것은?
(A) 월 임대료가 곧 오를 전망이다.
(B) 공사 후에 빈 집이 없을 것이다.
(C) 세입자들은 공용 수영장 상태에 불만이다.
(D) 세입자 중 많은 사람들이 차량을 소유하고 있지 않다.

TEST 9

PART 5

101. Gracia's Restaurant은 Flluerton에 신규 레스토랑을 성공적으로 개점했습니다.

102. 시간제 직원들은 5시간 이상 근무하고 나서 업무 없이 30분 동안의 식사 시간을 제공받도록 일정이 짜여 있습니다.

103. 다양한 상황, 시간, 장소 등을 감안하기 위해서는 법이 가능한 한 융통성이 있어야 한다고 발표자는 언급했습니다.

104. Impossible을 본 비평가는 그의 칼럼에서 그 영화는 두 엄지를 치켜 올릴만한 영화라고 썼다.

105. Mr. Gonzalez는 본관의 최종 공사 단계가 다음달까지 완료될 것이라고 예측합니다.

106. Mr. Ed Simon은 이사들에게 그의 제안서에 대해 그럴 듯하게 설명했다.

107. AX energy는 석유 매장량에 대한 보고서를 주간 단위로 발행합니다.

108. 고객들로부터 접수되는 모든 소포에는 정확하게 라벨이 부착되어야 합니다.

109. 유학생들은 필수 자격요건을 갖추고 있다면, University of California에 의해 제공되는 모든 정규수업 중에서 고를 수 있습니다 ⇒ 모든 정규수업 중에서 아무거나 골라서 들을 수 있습니다.

110. 저희는 Peacock 출판사와 협력하여 당 호텔의 고객들에게 무료 잡지를 제공합니다.

111. 당신이 구매한 물품이 구입 후 1주일 이내에 집으로 배송되지 않는다면, 당신은 운송료 환불을 받으실 겁니다.

112. Nick Punto의 오랜 동료들은 그의 신규 사업이 그렇게 빨리 성공한 것에 대해 경이로워했습니다.

113. 상원의원에 의해서 확인이 될 때까지는 우린 이 문제와 관련한 어떤 이야기도 소문으로 간주해야 합니다.

114. Santa Barbara 시의원들은 장시간의 논의 끝에 드디어 차기 회계연도의 예산을 결정했습니다.

115. 1950년대 중반부터 운영중인 Stephenson's Warmite에서는 고품질의 경량 장비를 제공합니다.

116. 웹사이트에서 구입된 티켓을 액면가보다 높은 가격으로 되파는 행위는 법적으로 엄격하게 금지되어 있습니다.

117. Carl Crawford가 Belco Enterprise의 수석부사장으로 승진될 것 같습니다.

118. 사무실 직원을 관리, 감독할 뿐만 아니라, 그녀는 경영진에 올리는 일체의 보고서 관리를 책임집니다.

119. Nolasco사는 국내 시장에서 상당한 점유율을 유지하는 동시에 신흥국가에서 수익성이 높은 비즈니스 모델을 개발했습니다.

120. 광업회사의 중, 상급 관리자들은 안전을 강조하면서 그들의 지도자적인 역량을 강화시킵니다.

121. 차를 직장용으로만 사용한다면, 차를 구입하는 것보다는 임대하는 것이 이익이 됩니다.

122. 그 도시의 고대 역사를 살펴볼 수 있기를 간절히 바라는 여행객들을 위해서, 그 호텔은 도시 중심부 이상적인 곳에 위치해 있습니다.

123. 당신 사업의 일부에서 수요가 점점 더 당신의 직원이나 자원보다 커지고 있기 때문에, 일부 업무를 외부에 위탁하기로 한 결정은 당연한 결정일 것입니다.

124. 작년의 컨퍼런스가 매진되었다는 사실을 고려하면, 올해의 컨퍼런스 등록인원은 작년보다 더 많을 것으로 예상됩니다.

125. 이 조직의 목적은 일반 대중들이 우리 주변의 자연을 존중하고 감사함을 느끼도록 가르치고, 알리고, 지도하는 것이다.

126. 기념 우표를 포함해서 판매되지 않은 우표를 폐기하는 비용은 우편서비스 예산에 정기적인 항목입니다 ⇒ 항상 들어있는 항목입니다.

127. 현재 재정적으로 어려움을 겪고 있는 Ramirez 항공사는 중국에서의 사업을 중지할 지 아직 결정하지 못했습니다.

128. 금융기관으로 유례없이 큰 송금이 있었다는 사실이 최고 중역에게 보고되었습니다.

129. 외부 검사가 겨우 며칠밖에 남지 않은 가운데, 공장 감독관은 아직도 검사를 받을 준비를 해야 했다 ⇒ 아직 준비가 되어 있지 않았다.

130. Mr. Ito가 대부분의 직원들보다 신규제품에 대해서 잘 알고 있기 때문에, 그가 미래 투자자들과의 회의에서 프레젠테이션 할 것입니다.

PART 6

Questions 131–134 메모

Teleworld Media's service center는 사업용 전화들이 제대로 작동하고 있는지 확인 할 책임이 있습니다.

만약 당신 사무실 전화기에 잘못된 점이 있다면, 수리 요청서를 저희 웹사이트를 통해서 보내주세요. 수리요청서에는 문제에 대한 완전한 설명을 반드시 포함시켜주세요.

수리요청서를 받자마자, 저희 서비스 센터 직원이 귀하에게 필요한 서비스의 자세한 견적을 제공해 드릴 것이며 검사 받거나 교체될 모든 부품들은 목록을 작성해 드릴 것입니다. 고객님은 24시간 이내에 즉시 연락을 받으실 수 있으며 수리는 인가 받는 즉시 시작될 것입니다. 기술자는 또한 도착하기 한 시간 전에 당신에게 연락을 취할 것입니다. 어떤 이유에서건 만약 당신이 예정된 시간 동안 집을 비우게 된다면 저희 직원은 당신에게 편한, 가급적 빠른 시간에 약속을 다시 잡아줄 것입니다.

Questions 135–138 이메일

수신: Hellen Outdoor Furniture 고객들
발신: Elian Herrera
날짜: 7월 26일
제목: 사과문

Ethier씨에게

화요일 신문에 함께 끼어 보낸 여름 세일 광고지에 오타가 있으니 참고해 주세요. 다섯 피스로 구성된 정원용 가구 세트의 판매가가 100불이 아니라 400불입니다. 이번 일로 실망시켜 드렸다면 죄송합니다. 그렇지만 이 가구 세트는 오크 나무로만 만들어졌고 수십 년간 끄떡 없을 것이므로 이 가격도 여전히 아주 좋은 가격입니다. 당신이 이번 기회를 십분 활용하시기를 바랍니다. 또한, 잘못된 가격에 대해 사과하기 위해 이 식탁 세트를 구매하시는 첫 10분의 고객분들께 이미 저렴한 가격에서 추가 15% 할인을 제공할 것입니다. 저희 가게에서 고객님을 곧 만나 뵙기를 바랍니다.

Elian Herrera
관리 이사
Hellen Outdoor Furniture

Questions 139-142 편지

3월 23일

Hamilton씨에게

고객님이 www.raymondretail.com를 통해서 주문해 주신데 감사 드립니다. 저희가 결제를 확인하자 마자 귀하의 주문이 바로 처리될 것입니다. 저희는 고객들에게 독특하면서 실속 있는 제품들을 제공하는데 최선을 다하고 있습니다. 어떤 이유로라도 저희 제품이 맘에 들지 않으면, 환불을 받으실 수 있습니다. 저희 모든 상품들은 한 달 이내에는 언제든 환불을 보장해 드리고 있습니다. 모든 주문은 저희 고객 센터로 서면 취소 신청서를 보냄으로써 언제라도 취소될 수 있습니다. 좀 더 궁금한 사항이 있으시면 1-800-555-5429로 전화 주세요. 귀하가 저희 제품이 완전히 만족스럽다고 느끼시기를 바랍니다.

Rosa Parks
지역 영업 대표

Questions 143-146 이메일

Bellevue씨에게,

당신의 부엌 찬장을 개조하는 것과 관련한 당신의 문의에 대해 답변 드립니다. 다음주에 시간이 되신다면, 저희 디자인 전문가 중 한 명이 당신에게 다양한 부엌 찬장 샘플을 보여드릴 수 있습니다.

저희는 매우 다양한 찬장 디자인을 보유하고 있습니다. 당신의 스타일에 맞는 찬장을 발견하시리라 확신합니다. 당신의 부엌을 깔끔하게 보이게 해 줄 일반적인 하얀 찬장에서부터, 당신의 부엌에 더욱 매력적인 분위기를 선사해 줄 니스칠이 된 목재 찬장에 이르기까지 저희는 모든 종류를 제공합니다. 저희는 찬장을 제조하기 위해 최상의 자재만을 사용하기 때문에 당신은 수년 간 저희 제품을 사용할 수 있다는 점을 신뢰하셔도 좋습니다.

저희 전문가와 만나기 전에 저희 제품을 살펴보고 싶으시면, www.stiltoninteriors.com으로 저희 웹사이트에 방문해주시기 바랍니다. 감사 드리며, 답장 기다리겠습니다.

Questions 147-148 광고

Smart Stationery	본 할인은 현 매장에서 마지막 날까지만 진행되므로 7월 1일까지 Smart Stationery로 서둘러 오세요.
12 Orange Grove Parkway, Rio Caballo, NM	영업 시간: 오전 9:00 - 오후 8:00. 월요일부터 토요일까지 (7월2일부터 7월4일까지 닫습니다.)
점포이전 정리세일	
할인 대상 책상 파일 캐비넷 회의 테이블	새로운 상점 주소: (7월 5일 오픈) 550 Plains Street Rio Caballo, NM

147. 왜 Smart Sationery는 할인을 하고 있는가?
 (A) 작년 제품을 판매할 것이다.
 (B) 매장 위치를 바꿀 것이다.
 (C) 상점이름을 바꿀 것이다.
 (D) 사업을 접을 것이다.

148. 언제가 이 세일의 마지막 인가?
 (A) 7월 1일
 (B) 7월 2일
 (C) 7월 3일
 (D) 7월 5일

Questions 149-150 이메일

수신인: 회사 전 직원 〈stafflist@delawind.com〉
발신인: Robert Young 〈ryoung@ delawind.com〉
날짜: 11월 2
제목: 공지

직원 분들에게,

직원 급여 지급 날짜가 변경되었다는 것을 여러분에게 알리기 위해 편지를 씁니다. 이것은 9월에 있었던 NanoArts사의 인수 때문이며, 인수는 부서간 직원들의 이동으로 이어졌습니다.

12월부터 직원들 급여지불은 매달 1일과 16일에 이루어질 것입니다. 만약 이 두 날짜가 쉬는 날이거나 주말이라면, 급여는 해당일 이전 영업 일에 배포될 것입니다.

당신의 근무 시간보고는 여전히 Fatima Ali에게 제출되어야 합니다.

Robert Young
관리부장

149. 왜 Young씨는 이메일을 썼는가?
(A) 인수가 연기되었다는 것을 알리기 위해서
(B) 급여 배포의 변경사항을 명확하게 설명하기 위해서
(C) 새로운 회계 이사를 소개하기 위해서
(D) 휴가를 요청하는 절차를 설명하기 위해서

150. 직원들은 무엇을 하도록 요구되고 있는가?
(A) Young씨와 함께 급여 지불 세부사항을 확인하는 것.
(B) 12월 16일에 회의에 가는 것
(C) 같은 방법으로 그들의 근무 시간을 제출 하는 것
(D) 매달 그들의 급여를 재확인 하는 것

Questions 151–152 브로셔 발췌문

Karsten 역사 박물관

Karsten 역사 박물관은 우리 지역사회의 인물, 회사 그리고 예술 단체에 대한 정보를 취합하고 보관하기 위해 수년 동안 우리 지역사회와 함께 일해왔습니다. 박물관은 우리 마을의 역사에 대한 많은 수작업의 그리고 인쇄판의 지도를 소장하고 있습니다. 3000개가 넘는 역사적인 이미지들을 포함한 박물관의 소장사진들은 박물관의 웹사이트에서 찾아보실 수 있습니다. 모든 사진들의 복사본은 소정의 요금만 내시면 웹사이트에서 구매할 수 있습니다.

---

151. 이 발췌문은 무엇에 관한 정보인가?
(A) 정보 기관
(B) 시민 단체
(C) 주거관련 프로젝트
(D) 관광객들을 위한 정보센터

152. 무엇이 구매 될 수 있는가?
(A) 현지 기업들의 명단
(B) 역사적인 사건들을 보여주는 이미지들
(C) 잡지의 예전 발행물
(D) 현지 예술가들의 그림과 조각들

Questions 153–155 광고

THG The Heartful Gallery

3월 3일 토요일에 우리의 연례 Home and Gardening Craft Sale and Festival에 여러분이 참여해 주시길 바랍니다. —[1]— 모든 수익금은 갤러리를 유지하고, 새롭고 흥미로운 전시회를 유치하는 데에 사용될 것입니다. 판매가 진행되는 동안 갤러리 입장은 무료입니다.

—[2]— The Heartful Gallery는 25년동안 우리 지역사회의 한 부분이었습니다. 이 건물은 세계 전역의 유명한 예술가들의 많은 그림과 조각들의 독특한 예술작품들을 보여줍니다. —[3]—

Home and Gardening Craft Sale and Festival이 진행되는 동안, 갤러리 선물가게의 고객들은 모든 상품에 대해 20% 할인을 받을 것입니다. 갤러리는 월요일부터 토요일까지 오전 8시에서 오후 7시까지, 일요일은 오후12시에서 오후 4시까지 열릴 것입니다. —[4]—

현재 진행 중인 The Life and Photography of Brandon Call 전시는 3월 28일까지 대중에게 공개됩니다. 더 많은 정보는 www.heartfulgallery.com에서 찾아보실 수 있습니다.

---

153. 무엇이 광고되고 있는가?
(A) 개장
(B) 기금 모금 행사
(C) Nancy Heartful의 발표
(D) 미술품 판매

154. Heartful Gallery에서 3월 3일에 일어날 예정이 아닌 것은 무엇인가?
(A) 갤러리 방문객들은 무료 입장 허가를 받을 것이다.
(B) 갤러리 선물 가게 상품구매가 할인될 것이다.
(C) 갤러리는 오후 4시에 닫을 것이다.
(D) 사진들이 전시가 될 것이다.

155. [1], [2], [3], [4]로 표시된 자리 중에 다음 문장이 들어가기에 가장 적합한 곳은?

"지역 화원과 묘목장들은 감상하거나 구매하실 수 있는 아름다운 꽃꽂이들을 구비해놓을 것입니다."

(A) [1]
(B) [2]
(C) [3]
(D) [4]

Questions 156–157 문자메시지

KENT BEALS   4:17 PM
Grace Curran씨가 서울로 전근 간다고 들었어요.

KENT BEALS   4:18 PM
Curran씨가 저희 회사에 겨우 몇 달 다니지 않았나요?

KAJA SHEEN   4:19 PM
맞아요, 3월부터요. 왜요?

KENT BEALS   4:20 PM
우리 제품에 대해서도 아직 배우는 단계 아닌가요?

KAJA SHEEN   4:21 PM
맞아요, 그런데 전 직장에서 영업부장이었어요.

KAJA SHEEN   4:22 PM
그 일을 서울에서도 하게 될 거고요.

KENT BEALS   4:22 PM
저는 몰랐어요. Curran씨가 매우 바빠지겠네요.

KENT BEALS   4:33 PM
우리 아시아 매출이 4월 이래로 거의 두 배로 증가했어요.

156. Grace Curran씨에 대해 언급된 것은?
(A) Curran씨는 또 다른 회사에 고용되었다.
(B) Curran씨는 직장에 만족하지 못하고 있다.
(C) Curran씨는 아직 교육을 받고 있다.
(D) Curran씨는 이전 관리직 경력을 가지고 있다.

157. 4시 42분에 Beals씨가 "I had no idea"라고 쓸 때 무엇을 의미하고 있는가?
(A) Beals씨는 Curran씨가 서울에서 무슨 일을 할 지 알지 못했다.
(B) Beals씨는 아시아 시장에 대해 모르고 있었다.
(C) Beals씨는 Curran씨의 과거 경력에 대해 모르고 있었다.
(D) Beals씨는 Curran씨가 회사에 얼마나 다녔는지를 모르고 있었다.

Questions 158-160 메모

Primo Inn

매일 이루어지는 자동 세탁 서비스가 호텔의 전기 및 수도 사용의 대부분을 차지함에 따라, Primo Inn은 이제 고객이 요청하는 경우에만, 매일 객실의 시트와 타월을 세탁할 것입니다. 우리 호텔에서의 관행들이 환경 친화적이도록 만들겠다는 우리의 약속을 지키기 위해 우리는 이 정책을 실행하고 있습니다. 고객들이 체크인을 할 때, 여러분은 고객들에게 이 새로운 절차에 대해 꼭 알려주시기 바랍니다. 만약 투숙객들이 그들이 머무르는 동안 시트가 특정한 일정에 맞게 세탁되도록 요청하지 않는다면, 시트는 4일마다 새로운 시트로 교체될 것이라는 것을 투숙객들이 숙지하도록 꼭 확실히 해주세요. 투숙객들은 또한 객실 안에서 호텔의 여타 고객 서비스들을 설명하고 있는 투숙객 가이드뿐만 아니라 이와 관련된 공지사항들이 게시되어 있는 것을 보게 될 것입니다.

158. 누구를 위해 이 공지가 의도 되었을 가능성이 가장 높은가?
(A) 숙박업체 고객들
(B) 숙박업체의 접수담당자
(C) 청소 직원
(D) 수리 직원

159. 공지에 따르면, 왜 새로운 절차는 시행되었는가?
(A) 숙박업체 고객 만족을 향상시키기 위해서
(B) 신규직원 실적을 향상시키기 위해서
(C) 공공서비스 소비를 줄이기 위해서
(D) 수리의 발생 건수를 줄이기 위해서

160. 직원들은 무엇을 하도록 지시 받았는가?
(A) 투숙객들에게 그들이 특별 세탁 서비스를 요청할 수 있다는 것을 알려주는 것
(B) 완전한 청구서를 투숙객들에게 주는 것
(C) 객실에 새 시트와 타월이 구비되어 있는지 확인 하는 것
(D) 객실요금 인상에 대해 투숙객들에게 알려 주는 것

Questions 161-163 편지

Houston Daily Journal

7월 12일

Michael Soto
25 Bighorn Drive
Houston, TX 77003

Soto씨 에게,

당신은 휴스턴 데일리 잡지의 장기 구독자이기 때문에, 우리는 이번 기회를 통해 당신에게 일요일 신문의 새로운 특집에 대해 알려드리고 싶습니다. 우리는 극장과 영화의 리뷰뿐만 아니라 지역 엔터테인먼트와 공연을 포함한 휴스턴 주변의 행사들을 담은 달력을 제공할 것입니다. 상점과 식당 같은 지역 업체들의 할인 쿠폰 또한 제공될 것입니다.

당신의 계속적인 지원으로 당신은 한달 간 무료로 일요일 신문을 받아 보실 수 있습니다. 일요일 신문을 계속해서 받기 위해서는, 당신의 정상 요금에 추가되는 매달 6.20달러의 소정의 추가요금만 지불하시면 됩니다.

당신은 또한 언제든지 당신이 알고 있는 누군가가 우리 신문을 소개한 사람으로써 당신의 이름을 적을 때마다 휴스턴 데일리 잡지를 무료로 1개월 동안 받아보실 수 있는 우리의 Friends of Houston 행사에 참여하게 됩니다. 더 많은 정보를 위해서, 주저하지 마시고 우리 사무실로 전화주세요. 555-3345

Dwight Tomlin
Dwight Tomlin
구독 관리자
휴스턴 데일리 잡지

161. 이 편지의 목적은 무엇인가?
(A) 유흥활동에 대한 가격인하를 제공하기 위해서
(B) 현재 구독자들에게 새로운 서비스를 설명하기 위해서
(C) 구독자들이 청구서의 금액을 지불하길 요청하기 위해서
(D) 홍보 공간에 대해 회사들의 관심을 끌기 위해서

162. 휴스턴 데일리 잡지의 일요일 신문에 포함되어 있지 않은 것은 무엇인가?
(A) 지역 상점에서의 할인가격
(B) 영화와 극장의 리뷰
(C) 지역 식당의 요리법
(D) 지역 행사의 일정

163. 8월 이후에 만약 Soto씨가 일요일 잡지를 계속 받기를 선택한다면 무슨 일이 일어날 것인가?
(A) 그가 아는 사람들이 신문에 대해 할인을 받을 것이다.
(B) 배송 가격이 줄어들 것이다.
(C) 그는 식당에서의 무료 식사를 위한 상품권을 받을 것이다.
(D) 그의 월 고지서가 추가적인 서비스 요금을 포함할 것이다.

Questions 164–167 인터넷 채팅 대화

Morgan Caine [2:55 p.m.]
G회의실 옆에 있는 SharpCopy 복사기가 수리되었는 지 아시는 분 있나요? 오늘 아침에는 계속 종이가 끼어서 IT부서에서 수리하기 위해 사람을 보내주기로 했거든요.

Jolene Griffin [2:56 p.m.]
제가 1분 전에 그 앞을 지나왔는데요. IT부서 사람들이 SharpCopy사에 연락해서 사람을 부르려는 것 같았어요. 아직 고치는 중입니다.

Stephanie Gazio [2:57 p.m.]
저도 복사기 써야 해서 기다리고 있어요. 제가 복사기에 가까우니까 지금 가서 확인해보고 알려줄게요.

Morgan Caine [2:59 p.m.]
IT부서에서는 지금쯤이면 다 고쳐놨을 거라고 하던데요. 이 복사기가 말썽을 부린 게 이번이 처음이 아니에요. 정말 새 칼라 복사기를 사야해요. 저는 4시에 고객하고 중요한 미팅이 있는데 흑백 복사본은 정말 쓰고 싶지 않아요.

Jolene Griffin [3:01 p.m.]
길 아래에 있는 복사집에서 복사하실 수 있어요. 이 시간대에는 보통 한가해요.

Morgan Caine [3:02 p.m.]
네, 앞으로 10분 안에 복사기가 고쳐지지 않으면, 그럴 수 밖에 없겠네요.

Stephanie Gazio [3:03 p.m.]
제가 SharpCopy에서 온 기술자에게 고치는데 얼마나 걸릴지 물어봤더니 3시반까지는 고칠 거라고 하던데요. 먼저 트럭에서 부품을 가지고 와야 한다고 합니다.

Morgan Caine [3:04 p.m.]
그렇다면, 그 복사집으로 가는 게 낫겠네요. 미안한 것 보다는 (복사를 못해서 미안한 상황이 되는 것 보다는) 안전한 게 낫죠. 제가 나가는 김에 필요한 거 있으신 분 있나요?

Stephanie Gazio [3:05 p.m.]
괜찮으시면 제가 복사집에 같이 갈게요. 혹시 복사기 고치는데 오래 걸리더라도 걱정할 필요 없게 저도 (복사집에서) 일을 처리하고 싶습니다.

Morgan Caine [3:07 p.m.]
물론이죠. 한 2분 후에 로비에서 만나요.

164. SharpCopy 복사기에 대해 언급된 것은?
 (A) 이 복사기는 칼라복사를 할 수 있다.
 (B) 이 복사기는 교체될 것이다.
 (C) 이 복사기는 최근에 구매되었다.
 (D) 이 복사기는 수리를 위해 공장으로 가져가야 한다.

165. Stephanie Gazio씨에 대해 언급된 것은?
 (A) Gazio씨는 오늘 늦게 미팅이 있다.
 (B) Gazio씨는 IT부서에서 일한다.
 (C) Gazio씨는 이 대화 중에 자리를 뜨고 다른 곳에 갔었다.
 (D) Gazio씨는 흑백 복사를 할 것이다.

166. 3시 02분에 Morgan Caine씨가 "I don't think I'll have a choice"라고 쓸 때 무엇을 의미하고 있는가?
 (A) Caine씨는 흑백 복사를 써야 한다.
 (B) Caine씨는 고객과의 미팅을 연기해야 한다.
 (C) Caine씨는 주변 매장을 이용해야 한다.
 (D) Caine씨는 복사기가 고쳐지는 것을 기다릴 것이다.

167. Caine씨는 아마도 다음에 무엇을 할까?
 (A) 건물 출입문에서 동료와 만난다.
 (B) 기술자와 얘기한다.
 (C) 고객에게 연락한다.
 (D) 식당에 예약을 한다.

Questions 168–171 전단지

Perth Residential Committee는 당신을 우리의 새 이웃 모임에 초대 합니다.

발표 일정

오후1:00	대중교통과 당신: 도시 주변 (204호)	
오후2:00	Perth에서 살만한 장소 (202호)	위생시설과 재활용 서비스 (209호)
오후3:00	금융 서비스와 Perth 주변의 은행 (207호)	Perth의 기업협회와 창업에 관하여 (209호)
오후4:00	Perth와 그 주변의 레크리에이션: 재미있게 놀 수 있는 장소와 사람들을 만날 수 있는 장소 (204호)	

대중교통과 레크리에이션 관련 발표시간에 방문객 중에 가장 많은 사람들이 참석합니다. 그러므로 이 발표들에서 자리를 꼭 잡기 위해서는 일찍 오실 것을 추천 드립니다.

모든 발표자들은 영어를 사용합니다. 그러나한국어, 타갈로그어, 태국어로 된 책자가 요청 시에 이용 가능합니다. 다과 또한 모임에 제공됩니다.

마지막 발표가 마무리 되고 나서 우리는 모든 참가자들이 Perth의 다운타운과 업 타운을 도보 여행하도록 초대되는 바입니다. 이 투어는 무료이고 거의 평생을 Perth에서 지낸 Perth의 시의회 멤버에 의해 안내됩니다.

더욱 많은 정보는 www.newneighbors.co.au/perth에서 찾아보실 수 있습니다.

168. 이 전단지는 아마도 누구를 대상으로 할까요?
 (A) Perth시의 시의회 멤버들
 (B) 최근에 Perth로 이사온 사람들
 (C) Perth 콘서트 기획자들
 (D) Perth를 지나면서 여행하는 사람들

169. 어느 곳에서 가장 인기 있는 발표가 열리는가?
(A) 202호
(B) 204호
(C) 207호
(D) 209호

170. Perth Residential Committee에 대해 무엇이 언급되어 있는가?
(A) 위원회는 여러 언어들로 정보를 제공하고 있다.
(B) 위원회는 곧 시의회 회의실을 공사할 것이다..
(C) 위원회는 도시 주변에 정보 부스를 가지고 있다.
(D) 위원회는 세금혜택을 거주민들에게 제공한다.

171. 전단지에 따르면, 참가자들은 모임이 끝난 후 무엇을 할 수 있는가?
(A) 저녁 파티에 간다.
(B) 웹사이트에 등록한다.
(C) 무료 수업에 등록한다.
(D) 도시 투어를 한다.

172. 이 글의 목적은 무엇인가?
(A) 직원이 가졌던 다양한 직책을 설명하는 것
(B) 새로운 보험 수당 프로그램에 대해 설명하는 것
(C) 어떻게 직원들이 특별 훈련 코스에 등록할 수 있는 지 설명하는 것
(D) 새로운 CEO가 선정되었다는 것을 알려주는 것

173. Bragg씨에 대하여 무엇이 언급되어 있는가?
(A) 그녀는 임시 보험 조정자이다.
(B) 그녀는 Haynesman씨와 관련하여 문의를 받았다.
(C) 그녀는 보험 사기 관리를 전공했다.
(D) 그녀는 교수로써 일했다.

174. 로스앤젤레스에 대하여 언급되지 않은 것은?
(A) Penley Insurance는 그곳에 사무실을 가지고 있다.
(B) Century University가 그곳에 위치하고 있다.
(C) Corns씨는 그곳의 거주자였다.
(D) Haynesman씨는 그곳에서 일했었다.

175. [1], [2], [3], [4]로 표시된 자리 중에 다음 문장이 들어가기에 가장 적합한 곳은?

"그곳에서의 시간 등안 그의 보험 분야에 대한 관심이 커졌고, 그는 보험 업계에서 정규직을 찾아보기로 결심했다."
(A) [1]
(B) [2]
(C) [3]
(D) [4]

Questions 172-175 기사문

올해의 직원 : Philip Haynesman

다음달 보험사기 담당 부장 직으로 이동할 Philip Haynesman은 Penley Insurance에서 29년간 많은 직위를 거쳐왔다. —[1]— "나는 어떤 직원도 Philip만큼 많은 부서에서 일을 했던 직원은 없다고 생각합니다"라고 회사 CEO인 Sylvia West가 말했다.

Haynesman의 보험 업계 경력의 시작은 임시직 채용업체를 통해서 세크라멘토에 있는 Good Friends Insurance Brokerage에서의 6개월간의 문서 정리직원으로써 이었다. —[2]— Haynesma은 Penley의 Berkley 지점에서 현장파견직으로서의 직책을 맡았고, 3년동안 직접 고객들을 돌보아왔다. 이후에 Haynesman씨는 로스앤젤레스 지점의 보험 조정부서로 옮겼고 1년 후에 고위직 보험 조정자가 되었다.

그러나 Haynesman씨는 거기서 멈추지 않았다. 그는 "고객의 프로필과 수치들을 가지고 일하는 경험은 나를 흥미진진하게 만들었고, 나는 그와 관련한 더 많은 일을 하고 싶었다. 로스앤젤레스에 있는 동료인 Martha Bragg는 사기담당 부서를 경험해볼 것을 제안했다. 그러나 처음에는 사기관리 분야에 대한 학위가 먼저 필요했고, Martha는 그녀의 모교인 Los Angeles에 있는 Century University를 제안했다. 나는 학자금 대출을 얻고, 지속적으로 일도 해야 했지만 4년 후에는, Martha가 몇 년 전에 그랬던 것처럼, 보험 사기 관리 졸업장을 받게 되었다"고 상기했다. —[3]—

그의 보험 사기 관리 학위를 Century University에서 완료한 후에, Haynesman씨는 Penley Insurance 본사의 보험 사기 부서로 이동했다. —[4]— 그는 5년 후, 보험 사기 부서장 Barry Corns에 의해 부 감독관으로 지명되었다. Corns씨가 산업 보험 분야로 이동할 예정이었기 때문에, Corns씨는 Haynesman씨가 그의 자리를 맡을 것을 제안 했다. "믿기 힘든 일이다." Haynesman씨가 말했다. "꽤 오래 전에, 나는 단지 보험 파일을 다뤘다. 그러나 지금 나는 Penley의 본사에서 보험 사기 부서를 관리하고 있다."

Questions 176-180 전단지 및 이메일

무상 배포되는 나무로 당신의 동네를 아름답게 꾸미세요.

Roseburg Nature Committee는 건물이 빼곡히 들어차있는 우리의 대도심 지역에 더 많은 녹지를 형성하기 위해 3월 14일 Roseburg 시민들에게 1500개의 무상 묘목을 제공할 것입니다. 위원회는 오전11시부터 오후3시까지, 작년에도 같은 행사가 열렸었던 Hempstead Valley Shopping Center 주차장에서 이번 행사를 개최할 것입니다. 나무는 선착순으로 주민들에게 배포될 것입니다.

무상으로 나무를 받으려면 전기세 고지서나 운전면허증과 같이 자신의 이름과 주소가 적혀있는 신분증을 가지고 오셔야 합니다. Roseburg 외부에 거주하는 분들은 나무를 구입하실 수 있습니다. 가격은 품종에 따라 15불에서 30불 사이 입니다. 이 행사 동안 모금된 자금은 나무심기를 통해 자연의 보존을 장려하는 임무를 수행하는데 있어서 Roseburg Nature Committee를 지원해줄 것입니다. 이 위원회는 또한 나무를 심고 가꾸는 것에 대해 일반 대중에게 알려주고 있습니다.

네이쳐 클래스나 자원봉사 기회와 같은 위원회 활동에 대한 자세한 내용을 원하시면 www.roseburgnature.org/committee를 방문하세요.

수신인: c.meade@hrv.com
발신인: janice_warden@roseburgnature.org
날짜: 3월 27일

제목: 회신: 제가 구매한 나무
첨부: Oregon Ash 가꾸기 설명서

Meade씨에게,

3월 14일 배포행사에서 당신이 구매한 묘목에 대해 도움을 제공해드리게 되어 기쁘며, 이 구매로 저희 위원회를 후원해주신 것에 감사 드립니다. 제가 제대로 이해했다면, 당신은 저희 직원에 의해 제공된 Oregon Ash 묘목 심기 설명서와 나무 가꾸기 설명서를 모두 잘 따랐는데, 나무가 잘 자라지 않는다는 말씀이시죠. 당신을 좀 더 도와드리기 위해 당신의 나무를 가꾸는 법에 대한 자세한 설명서를 첨부했으며, 여기에는 인터넷 자료들도 포함되어 있습니다. 저에게 묘목 사진과 함께, 물을 얼만큼 주고 계신지, 나무가 햇빛을 얼마나 받고 있는지, 나무를 어디에 두셨는지와 같은 정보를 이메일로 보내주시면 제가 좀 더 자세한 답변을 드릴 수 있을 것입니다. 혹은 대안으로, 저희 네이쳐 클래스에 오셔서 자원봉사로 일하시는 전문가와 얘기해 보시는 것도 환영입니다.

Genevieve Denham
지역사회 프로그램 디렉터
Roseburg Nature Committee

176. 전단지에 언급되지 않은 정보는?
(A) 무상배포의 이유
(B) 요구되는 서류
(C) 나눠주는 나무들의 품종
(D) 위원회의 임무

177. Roseburg에 대해 언급된 것은?
(A) 도시의 건물들이 서로 가깝게 붙어있다.
(B) Roseburg에는 신축 쇼핑몰이 있다.
(C) 몇 개의 새로운 주차장을 오픈할 것이다.
(D) Hempstead Valley에 정원을 개발하고 있다.

178. Meade씨에 대해 언급된 것은?
(A) 묘목을 가꾸는 법에 대한 설명서를 받지 못했다.
(B) Roseburg의 주민이 아니다.
(C) 네이쳐 클래스에 이전에 참석했었다.
(D) 위원회를 위한 자원봉사를 할 수 없다.

179. Denham씨가 이메일을 쓴 이유는?
(A) 사진을 제공하기 위해서
(B) 우려사항에 답해주기 위해서
(C) 일정에 대한 불만을 표현하려고
(D) 업데이트된 수업 일정표를 제공하려고

180. Denham씨는 Meade씨가 무엇을 할 것을 제안하고 있는가?
(A) 나무의 위치를 바꿔볼 것
(B) 나무를 위원회에 가지고 올 것
(C) 자신에게 나무에 대해 더 알려줄 것
(D) 나무에 대해 환불을 요청할 것

Questions 181–185 편지와 이메일

1월 28일

Ms. Megumi Tanaka
Hayamiki Corportation
8-2-3 Nakahara-ku, Kawasaki-shi
Kanagawa, 일본

Tanaka씨에게,

Cromo Tech Disposals는 사용할 수 없는 손상된 전자제품의 재활용에 있어서 기업들을 지원하는 가장 유명한 선두기업입니다. 우리는 배송 거리와 연료 소비를 낮게 유지함으로써 당신의 자재의 효율적이고 저렴한 수거를 확실히 하기 위해서 세계 전역 5개국에 다수의 시설을 보유, 관리하고 있습니다.

당신의 회사가 일본에서 가장 빠르게 성장하는 회사들 중의 하나라는 것을 고려해볼 때, 우리는 불필요한 전자제품을 어떻게 재활용할 지에 대한 당신의 선택이 아주 중요하다는 것을 알고 있습니다. 당신이 회사의 보수관리 부장이기 때문에 특히 더 그러할 것입니다. Cromo Tech Disposal의 안전하고 지속가능한 전자 폐기물 재활용 프로그램과 관련하여 동봉된 팜플렛을 살펴봐 주세요. 저희 서비스 품질에 대해 좀 더 안심하실 수 있도록 하기 위해, 저희는 당신이 브로셔의 마지막 페이지에 나와있는 저희 고객분들에게 전화 혹은 서면으로 연락해보실 것을 장려하는 바입니다. 또한 당신은 재활용을 위한 당신의 회사의 특별 요구조건에 대하여 이야기 하기를 원한다면, 저나 우리의 도쿄 사무실의 Sasuke Hiroshi에게 연락 하실 수 있습니다.

Hilary Grace
회계이사

동봉

보낸사람: Megumi Tanaka ⟨mtanaka@hayamiki.co.jp⟩
받는사람: Simon Mann ⟨smann@retainindustries.co.jp⟩
제목: Cromo Tech Disposals
날짜: 2월 27일

저는 카나가와에 위치한 Hayamiki Corporation사의 보존관리 이사입니다. 저희 회사가 사용불가한 많은 전자제품들을 재활용하기 위해서 Cromo Tech Dispoals사와 함께 일하는 것에 대해 고려하고 있기 때문에, Cromo Tech Disposals와 함께한 당신의 경험에 대해서 여쭤보고 싶습니다.

당신의 회사가 세계 전역의 지사들에서 Cromo Tech Disposals를 고용하고 있는 것을 제가 보았습니다. 실례가 되지 않는다면, 저는 당신의 도쿄지점에서 이 회사와 함께한 당신의 경험이 어떠했는지 알고 싶습니다. 저는 이 회사가 일정에 맞춰 자재를 수거할 수 있는 지가 가장 궁금합니다만 당신이 저에게 줄 수 있는 어떤 정보도 감사히 받겠습니다.

Megumi Tanaka
보존 관리 부장

181. 이 편지의 목적은 무엇인가?
(A) 폐기절차의 변경을 설명하기 위해서
(B) 재활용을 위한 서비스를 광고하기 위해서
(C) 전자제품 판매에 대해 문의 하기 위해서
(D) 판매 상담원에게 연락해 볼 것을 제안하기 위해서

182. 편지에 따르면, Cromo Tech Disposals는 어떻게 그들의 에너지 효율을 향상시키는가?
(A) Cromo Tech Disposals는 재활용된 종이 제품을 사용한다.
(B) Cromo Tech Disposals는 연료를 더 적게 사용하는 차량으로 제품을 수송한다.
(C) Cromo Tech Disposals는 그들의 고객들과 가까이에 시설을 운영한다.
(D) Cromo Tech Disposals는 직원 컴퓨터를 수리해서 재사용한다.

183. 누가 Cromo Tech Disposals의 지역담당자인가?
(A) Hilary Grace
(B) Megumi Tanaka
(C) Simon Mann
(D) Sasuke Hiroshi

184. Takaka 씨는 Mann 씨의 이메일 주소를 어디서 얻었는가?
(A) 일본 회사 데이터베이스에서
(B) Grace씨의 동료로부터
(C) Cromo Tech Disposals의 홈페이지에서
(D) Cromo Tech Disposal의 소개 목록에서

185. Cromo Tech Disposals에 대하여 Tanaka씨는 무엇을 걱정하는가?
(A) Cromo Tech Disposals이 재활용하는 제품의 종류
(B) Cromo Tech Disposals만이 제공하는 서비스
(C) Cromo Tech Disposals이 물건을 수거하는 것에 대해 믿을만한지
(D) Cromo Tech Disposals이 몇 회나 서비스 오류를 범했는지

Questions 186-190 발표와 전단지 및 이메일

Rewards Club이 Calasnack의 매출을 올리다

스낵과 음료 생산업체인 Calasnack은 지난달 수익에서 20%의 상승을 보여주었다. 이것은 지난 분기 보고됐던 매출의 하락세로부터 엄청난 향상이다. 6월에 시작한 Munchies 보상 클럽의 시행에 성장의 공이 돌려지고 있다. Munchies 보상 클럽은 고객들이 Calasnack제품을 구매함으로써 포인트를 적립하게 해주며, 이 포인트들을 고급 보상품과 교환하게 해준다.

현재는 Calasnack에 의해 생산된 Calasnack 감자칩, 혼합 땅콩 그리고 캔디 바 같은 오직 스낵 제품들만 최근 만들어진 초록색 M 로고를 가지고 있다. 그러나 보상 프로그램이 너무 효과적임에 따라서 Calasnack은 M로고를 10월부터 회사의 많은 청량음료에도 역시 새겨 넣을 것이다. 이런 청량음료 중 하나가 7월에 출시된 이후로 현재도 할인판매중

인 회사의 새로운 다이어트 소다인 Calasoda입니다. 판촉기간 동안 소비자들은 청량음료로 10배의 포인트를 받을 수 있습니다.

티셔츠, 뮤직 플레이어, 스노우보드 그리고 컴퓨터 게임 등은 받아갈 수 있는 보상품들 중의 단지 일부이다. 물론, 보상품들 중 몇몇은 다른 것들 보다 더 수요가 많다(더 인기가 있다). "우리 고객들의 대부분은 그들이 500 포인트를 모을 때까지 보상 포인트를 교환하려고 하지 않는다"라고 회사 직원인 Theodore Chips가 이야기했다. "그들은 이 포인트로 가장 인기 있는 ZYX 제품을 얻을 수 있다."

Munchies 포인트로 보상품을 얻으세요

당신이 구매한 모든 초록색 M 로고(아래 사진에 나와있는)가 붙은 Calasnack 제품마다 아래에 나온 멋진 경품을 위해 당신이 사용할 수 있는 10포인트를 받게 됩니다.
Munchies 포인트를 모으세요!

필요 포인트	보상품
100	Munchies 티셔츠
300	Snack Attack Family 컴퓨터 게임
500	ZYX 전자의 뮤직 플레이어
700	Zoomer A2 스노우 보드

수신인: Keith Delarocha 〈kdelerocha@ragemail.com〉
발신인: Munchies Rewards 〈stservice@calasnack.com〉
제목: Your recently redeemed Munchies Points
Delarocha씨에게,

당신이 최근 사용하신 Munchies 포인트와 관련해서 편지 드립니다. 당신의 주문서에 따르면 700포인트를 사용하길 원하셨고 저희가 당신의 요청을 이미 처리한 상태입니다. 그런데 포인트 중의 일부가 Calasoda의 포인트였으며 사실 100포인트에 해당하는 것이었습니다. 이는 결국 당신이 저희에게 790포인트를 보내셨다는 말이 됩니다. 저희 고객이 되어 주신 것에 대한 저희의 감사의 표시로 이미 보내주신 포인트에 10포인트를 저희가 보태서 다른 경품과 함께 Munchies T-shirt를 보내드릴 것입니다. 다시 한번 감사 드립니다.

Rina Smith
Calasnack 고객보상 프로그램 직원

186. Calasnack의 지난 분기 매출에 대하여 무엇이 유추될 수 있는가?
(A) 매출이 이전 기록을 능가했다.
(B) 매출이 회사 목표를 달성했다.
(C) 매출이 정확히 계산되지 않았다.
(D) 매출이 하락 하고 있었다.

187. 발표에서 첫 번째 문단, 첫 번째 줄의 "vast"가 의미상 가장 가까운 것은?
(A) 상당한
(B) 간략한
(C) 일관적인
(D) 신속한

188. Calasnack은 10월에 무엇을 시작할 것인가?
(A) 새로운 로고를 만든다
(B) 다양한 스낵에 대해 할인을 제공한다
(C) 현지업체들로부터 새로운 스낵을 매입한다
(D) 회사의 다른 상품들을 위해 포인트를 지급한다

189. Chips씨에 따르면, 고객들은 어떤 상품에 가장 흥미를 가지는가?
(A) 티셔츠
(B) 컴퓨터 게임
(C) 뮤직 플레이어
(D) 스노우 보드

190. Delarocha에 대해 사실일 가능성이 가장 높은 것은?
(A) Delarocha씨는 뮤직플레이어를 받고 싶어했다.
(B) Delarocha씨는 10월 이후에 경품 신청서를 보냈다.
(C) Delarocha씨는 Calasnack의 직원이다.
(D) Delarocha씨는 모든 경품을 받을 것이다.

Questions 191–195 이메일들 및 일정표

수신: fred.dickens@homeprofessionals.com
발신: realestateagents@netlisting.org
날짜: 3월 4일 오후 3시 20분
제목: Rochelle Tan

Netlisting 구독자들에게,

다음달 유명한 부동산 중개인인 Rochelle Tan에 의해 이끌어질 일일 심포지움이 있을 것입니다. 여러분들 중 일부는 부동산 분야에서의 여러분의 일을 도와줄, 부동산업에 관련한 그녀의 4개의 책 중 일부를 읽어보셨을지도 모르겠습니다.

심포지움의 날짜는 4월 9일이며 이 행사는 Manor Hotel로부터 맞은편 거리인 North Star Drive 485에 위치한 Royalton Convention Hall에서 열릴 것입니다. 입장료는 200달러 입니다.

다른 참가자들을 소개하는 (데리고 오는) 참가자들은 그들의 입장료에서 20달러를 차감해드립니다. 그것뿐만 아니라 Himmel Expert 출판사에서 나온 30달러 상당의 Tan씨의 책인 Selling Houses and Success가 제공될 것입니다.

질문이 있으시면 저나 컨벤션 홀의 다른 행사기획자인 Phil Stannis에게 488-555-0855로 물어주세요.

Fred Dickens

보내는이: phil.stannis@homeprofessionals.com
받는이: realestateagents@netlisting.org
날짜: 3월 4일 오후 3시 53분
제목: 회신 : Rochelle Tan

Netlisting 구독자님,

Fred Dickens가 이전에 모두에게 보낸 그의 이메일에서 작은 실수가 있었습니다. Tan씨의 심포지움의 입장료는 200달러로 적혀있었지만, 그것은 175달러입니다. 이 실수에 대해 사과 드리는 바입니다. 참석계획이신 분들은, Tan씨에 의해 제공될 정보가 향후 몇 달간 집을 파실 분들에게 매우 귀중한 정보가 될 것이기 때문에 중간 휴식시간 후에 시간 맞춰서 돌아오실 것을 강력히 권해드립니다.

그곳에서 당신을 뵙길 바랍니다.

Phil Stannis

내년도 부동산
Rochelle Tan 진행

심포지엄 일정

오전 11:00 – 오전 11:30: 당신의 동네를 파악해라 – 당신의 지역에 대해 숙지하고, 고객들을 그들에게 최적인 동네와 연결해주는 것을 논의한다.

오전 11:30 – 오후 12:00: 임대와 매입 비교 – 집을 임대하는 것과 사는 것의 장단점과 각각이 어떻게 고객에게 도움이 되는지에 대한 발표.

오후 12:00 – 오후 12:30: 중간 휴식시간

오후 12:30 – 오후 1:00: 홈 인스펙션(고장난 곳이 있는지 전문가의 도움으로 점검하는 것)은 당신에게 반드시 도움이 된다 – 홈 인스펙션 전문가를 고용하는 것이 어떻게 문제가 커지기 전에 발견하도록 도와주는지를 설명해주는 유용한 조언으로 가득한 발표.

오후 1:00 – 오후 1:30: 공개 포럼 – 부동산 및 부동산 관리 분야와 관련하여 청중들이 가지고 있는 질문들을 Tan씨에게 물어볼 수 있는 기회.

191. 첫 번째 이메일에 첫 번째 단락, 두 번째 줄의 "concerning"이 의미상 가장 가까운 것은?
(A) 걱정스러운
(B) 제외하고
(C) 관련하여
(D) 에 대조적으로

192. 메일 명단에 있는 구독자들(메일을 받는 구독자들)은 다른 참가자를 추천한 것에 대해 얼마의 공제액을 받는가?
(A) 6달러
(B) 20달러
(C) 30달러
(D) 40달러

193. 두 번째 이메일은 누가 보낸 것인가?
(A) 경제 잡지 출판사
(B) 부동산 정보 제공자
(C) 행사 기획자
(D) 특별 연사

194. Tan씨는 심포지엄 후반에 무엇을 할까요?
(A) 그녀의 책에 사인해줄 것이다.
(B) 경품을 위한 추첨을 할 것이다.
(C) 질의 응답시간을 가질 것이다.
(D) 그녀의 책을 무료로 나눠줄 것이다.

195. Phil Stannis씨는 심포지엄에 어느 부분이 구독자에게 도움이 될 것이라고 생각하는가?
 (A) 당신의 동네를 파악해라
 (B) 임대와 매입 비교
 (C) 홈 인스펙션은 당신에게 반드시 도움이 된다
 (D) 공개 포럼

Questions 196-200 언론보도자료, 이메일 및 일정표

= 기사 보도=

2월 26일

Rakliss Media는 Tunis와 Sousse에 3월 3일 2개의 새로운 지사를 오픈 할 것입니다. 개점과 함께 2월말에는 Bizerte에 본사를 두고 있는 웹디자인 회사인 197bOceanview Telecommunications를 또한 인수할 것입니다. Rakliss Media의 대표이사인 Mohammed al-Qari는 이러한 노력과 함께 회사가 Tunisia 지역에서 더 좋은 평판을 쌓을 수 있기를 희망한다고 발표했습니다.

Rakliss Media는 Rahim Ali씨가 10년전 Jetspeed Industries에서의 직책을 그만두기로 결정하고 나서 창립되었습니다. 6년간 그곳에서 일하고 나서 Rahim Ali씨는 고향인 Sfax에서 돌아갈 준비가 되었다고 생각했고, 그 곳에서 몇몇 친구들과 친척들로부터 받은 자금을 가지고 그의 통신사를 창립했습니다. Ali씨의 계획은 고속 광케이블망을 사용해서 데이터 전송 시스템을 전문으로 만드는 것이었습니다. 이 전략은 성과가 있었습니다: Rakliss Media의 시스템은 곧 전국적으로 채택이 되었고 이 회사는 동종 업체 중에서 가장 혁신적이고 신뢰받는 회사로 성장했습니다.

이러한 인상적인 성공에도 불구하고 이 회사의 평범한 사무실은 여전히 10년 전에 창립되었던 바로 그곳에 여전히 위치하고 있으며 이 회사는 혁신 정신을 잃지 않아 왔습니다. 제품개발팀은 이전 모델보다 거의 두 배 빠르게 정보를 전송할 수 있는 새로운 루팅 시스템을 도입했습니다.

보내는이: Mohammed al-Qari
받는이: Fatima Alfarsi
날짜: 8월 20일
제목: 축하 합니다.

Fatima 에게,

Rakliss의 연례 직원상 중 하나의 수상자로써 당신을 지명할 이사회의 결정을 당신에게 알리게 된 것은 나에겐 기쁨입니다. 우리의 회사와 함께한 시간 동안 당신이 보여준 전문성과 헌신 때문에 당신은 이상을 받을 것입니다. 당신은 Rakliss의 초창기 멤버 중 한 명이었으면서, 당신은 Rakliss가 작은 전자통신회사에서 오늘날 선두 미디어 회사로 성장한 데 크나큰 도움이 되었다고 할 수 있습니다. 또한 당신이 몇 년간 보여준 리더십 능력은, 가장 최근 제품개발 팀의 리더로써의 능력은 대단합니다.

당신과 다른 수상자들을 기념하여, 환영식이 8월 30일 금요일 오후 5시 우리 본사에서 열릴 것입니다. 당신은 저녁식사 이후에 환영식 동안 수상하게될 것입니다. 또한 Goroka에 있는 당신의 지점 매니저가 저녁만찬을 진행할 임을 알게 되면 기쁠 것 같습니다. Rakliss media는 수년 간의 당신의 모든 노고에 진심으로 감사 드립니다. 저녁 만찬에서 뵙기를 고대합니다.

Samson Tagobe
인사과 이사 Rakliss Media

제 10회 연례 Rakliss Media 직원 시상만찬

몇몇 최고의 직원들의 근면성과 노고를 기념하게 될 올해 Rakliss Media Staff Awards Dinner에 참석해주시도록 여러분을 초대하는 바입니다. 뷔페로 제공되는 음식들을 여러분이 즐기실 수 있기를 바랍니다. 이번 특별 행사를 위해 계획된 일정은 아래와 같습니다.

 5:30 - 6:00: 환영 인사 및 착석
 6:00 - 7:00: 저녁식사
 7:00 - 7:30: Michael Wahlen
   부사장의 연설 - Rakliss Media의 역사
 7:30 - 8:00: 시상식
 8:00 - 8:15: 폐회

 진행: Thomas Ryan

오셔서 만찬행사를 즐겨주실 것에 대해 감사 드립니다.

196. Rakliss Media가 관여하고 있는 활동으로써 언급되지 않은 것은 무엇인가?
 (A) 새로운 지점 개점
 (B) 회사 인수
 (C) 교육 과정을 제공하는 것
 (D) 새로운 상품을 출시하는 것

197. Ali씨는 Jetspeed Industries에서 얼마나 오래 근무 했나?
 (A) 3년동안
 (B) 6년동안
 (C) 10년 동안
 (D) 16년 동안

198. Alfarsi는 8월 30일 어디로 갈 것인가?
 (A) Sfax
 (B) Bizerte
 (C) Tunis
 (D) Sousse

199. Alfarsi씨에 대해 언급된 것은?
 (A) Alfarsi씨는 매니저로 승진될 것이다.
 (B) Alfarsi씨는 보너스를 받을 것이다.
 (C) Alfarsi씨는 Rakliss Media에서 10년간 일했다.
 (D) Alfarsi씨는 자신의 회사를 창립할 계획이다.

200. Rakliss Media에서 Thomas Ryan의 직책은?
 (A) 대표이사
 (B) 부사장
 (C) 연구개발 이사
 (D) 지점 매니저

TEST 10

PART 5

101. Ms. Sanders는 창의적인 직장문화를 구축하고 유지하는 방법에 관한 책을 다음 달에 완성할 것입니다.

102. Victoria College의 혁신적인 신규 프로그램은 다가올 학기에 시작될 것입니다.

103. Mr. Taylor의 수정된 인사 보고서가 이전 보고서보다 훨씬 향상된 내용을 제공합니다.

104. 여러 달 동안 공사 중이었던 스페인 해산물 레스토랑이 드디어 내일 개점할 것입니다.

105. Mr. Schumaker은 향후 수 개월 동안 회사의 모든 관리자들과 협의할 것입니다.

106. Crawford Enterprise에는 시애틀 사무실에서 근무할 현지 영업 직원에 대한 공석이 하나 있습니다.

107. 매달 첫 번째 일요일에 사용할 수 있는 박물관 무료 입장권에는 Stuart Hall에서의 특별전시회는 포함되지 않음을 주의하세요.

108. 5년 이상의 해외 지점 경력이 신임 싱가폴 지점장직을 위한 필수자격요건입니다.

109. 자국의 철강산업을 보호하기 위해서 미국은 수입관세를 올렸고 아니나 다를까, 미국의 교역국들도 마찬가지로 수입관세를 올렸다.

110. 18세 미만은 비행기 탑승 시 정부 발행 신분증을 제시할 필요가 없습니다.

111. 사용하기 편리한 이 솔루션은 모든 규모의 현지 기업과 조직의 자산관리 요구사항을 충족시켜주어 왔습니다.

112. 계약조건을 놓고 노조와 협상하는 동안, 경영진은 부동의 입장을 취했다.

113. Ethier Mobile가 지난 분기에 1,300,000대의 소형차를 선적한 가운데, 올해 이 회사의 매출은 1년 전보다 19% 상승한 상태입니다.

114. 30년간 호주 전역에서 1,500여개의 세미나와 워크샵을 개최해온 Vedder씨가 첫 번째 발표자가 될 것입니다.

115. 직원용 소책자는 사무용품이 어떻게 주문, 보관, 배분되는 지를 상세히 설명하고 있습니다.

116. Norwak 항공사는 7월부터 서울-로스앤젤레스 노선을 하루 3회 운항한다는 사실을 발표하게 되어 기쁩니다.

117. 그 제안서의 조건들을 세심하게 고려한 후에, 이사회는 그 제안서가 가치가 있다고 생각했습니다.

118. 제 24회 연극상에 대한 후보추천은, 늦어도 5월 7일까지 Linda Morris에게 이메일로 제출되어야 합니다.

119. 그의 팀이 그 프로젝트를 따낸다면, Ellis와 그의 팀원들은 대략 2만달러의 보너스를 각기 기대할 수 있습니다.

120. 예정된 정기점검으로 인하여, 5월 10일 토요일 오전 5시에서 10시 사이에 간헐적으로 인터넷 사용이 불가할 것입니다.

121. 1번가에 길이 너무 좁아서 자전거 타는 사람들이 차량의 문 옆으로 안전하게 지나갈 수 없습니다.

122. 고객과의 서신은 극비로 다뤄질 것이며, 제 3자에게 공개되지 않을 것입니다.

123. Ed Smith는 의료적, 법적 요건에 맞는 방식으로 병원 및 환자의 기록을 취합합니다.

124. North Ridge University는 아주 유능한 학생들을 유치하기 위해서 입학정책을 수정했습니다.

125. 별도의 지시가 없다면, 퇴근하면서 사무실을 나서기 전에 모든 조명이 꺼져 있는 지 확인해주시기 바랍니다.

126. 대부분의 후보들이 지원서 마감 기일을 맞춘 반면에, 몇몇은 마감일을 넘겼습니다.

127. 3년 연속으로 예측할 수 없는 날씨였으며, 이는 8월 축제를 취소하는 결과를 야기했습니다.

128. 공장에 있는 동안 모든 안전 규정과 지침을 준수하는 것은 의무사항입니다.

129. Jay Kim 재단은 여성들에게 그들이 일하고 싶어하는 어떤 분야에서도 직장생활을 할 수 있는 기회를 제공하겠다는 생각으로 시작했습니다.

130. Sordino Studios가 Brandon League에게 함께 일할 기회를 주지 않았더라면, 당사에서 그렇게 했을 것입니다 ⇒ 당사에서 함께 일할 기회를 주었을 것입니다.

PART 6

Questions 131-134 편지

Nora eye care Center
22314 VA, Alexandria, Duke 가 3773
(703) 555-8997
www.noraecc.com

Nolasco씨에게

Nora Eye Care Center에서 우리의 주된 목적은 귀하에게 최신 기술을 이용해서 우수하고 철저한 눈 관리 서비스를 제공해 드리는 것입니다. 인터넷으로 아무 때나 안과 검진 약속을 잡으시거나 근무시간에 703-555-8997으로 전화 주셔도 됩니다. 좀 더 정보를 얻으시려면 저희 웹사이트 www.noraecc.com을 방문해 주실 것을 권합니다. 웹사이트는 안전하고 사용이 간편하도록 만들어 졌습니다. 저희 웹사이트는 의사의 프로필이나 병원 약도와 같은 병원에 대한 유용한 정보를 찾는 걸 쉽게 만들어줍니다. 또한 저희가 구비하고 있는 매우 다양한 안경테나 컨택 렌즈를 둘러보실 수 있습니다. 병원에서 곧 만나 뵙기를 바랍니다.

Nora Eye Care Center

Questions 135-138 발표

수상 경력에 빛나는 광고회사인 The Dayton Agency는 고객지원부서 관리직 몇 개의 공석에 사람을 뽑고 있습니다. 전세계 업체들을 위해 광고를 만들어 온 이 기업은 North Carolina주 Charlotte시에 본사를 두고 있으며 여러 고객들의 니즈와 요청을 처리할 수 있는 최고 여덟 명의 매니저를 고용할 계획입니다. 이 기업은 전국적으로 사업활동을 확장해 왔기 때문에 회사의 지사 수도 늘어났습니다. 현재 일리노이, 네바다 및 와요밍 주에 새로운 지사를 오픈했습니다. 관리직에 고용될 후보는 계획안이 완수되고 목표가 달성되는 것을 확실히 하기 위해 팀의 다른 멤버들과 일하게 될 것입니다. 이 자리에 대한 좀더 자세한 사항은 www.daytonads.com/employment에서 확인하실 수 있습니다.

Questions 139-142 이메일

수신: lexinez@jokemail.com
발신: woodrow@heightsinn.com
제목: Heights Hotel 시카고 지점
날짜: 5월 20일
첨부: 팜플렛

Inez씨에게

최근 저희의 전화통화에 대한 후속조치로서, 5월 25일부터 5월 28일까지 여섯 분을 위한 귀하의 예약을 확인하고자 이메일을 쓰는 바입니다. 제가 이미 말씀 드린 대로, 귀하의 예약번호는 WSV248S입니다. 체크인 하실 때 이 번호를 제시하셔야 할지도 모릅니다. 도착 시에 이메일에 접속할 수 없을 때를 대비해서, 이 번호를 적어두시고 지갑에 보관해 주실 것을 제안 드립니다. 첨부된 것은 예약관련 세부사항과 고객님이 전화로 요청하신 저희 호텔 안내서입니다. 추가 요청이 있으시면 언제든 저희에게 다시 연락주세요. 감사 드리며 저희는 고객님과 고객님의 손님들을 저희 호텔로 모실 것을 고대하고 있습니다.

Woodrow Wilson
고객서비스팀

Questions 143-146 이메일

수신 : Santa Maria College 동문   발신: Lary Donovan
날짜: 11월 13일   제목: 주소록 업데이트
첨부: 연락처

우리는 현재 저희 동문 기록을 업데이트 중입니다. 저희가 저희 모든 동문들의 최신 연락 정보를 가지고 있는지를 확인하고자 합니다. 여러분의 전화번호와 이메일 주소가 이 정보에 포함되어 있습니다. 첨부된 양식을 검토해 주시고, 만약 둘 중 하나라도 변경되었으면 다시 기입해 주실 수 있으신지요? 또한, 저희 대학으로부터 학교 소식지를 받아보기를 원하시는 분들은 누구든지, 만약 이미 해둔 상태가 아니라면, 양식에 집주소와 직장주소를 써주시면 됩니다. 만약 원래 동문 명단이 만들어졌을 때 여러분의 연락처를 제공하지 않으셨다면 'not done' 문구 바로 옆에 있는 박스에 체크해 주시기 바랍니다. 협조해 주셔서 대단히 감사합니다.

PART 7

Questions 147-148 정보

당신의 새로운 CloudTek X5 디지털 카메라의 작동하는 것 뿐만 아니라 동영상을 당신의 집 컴퓨터로 옮기는 것에 관련하여이 지시사항을 조심스럽게 따라주세요. 혹시 어떤 지시사항에 관해 추가적인 설명이 필요하다면 CloudTek 고객 서비스 직원들이 평일 9시부터 5시까지 당신을 돕기 위해 대기하고 있습니다. 모든 서비스 센터의 목록이 전화번호와 함께 페이지 12에 적혀져 있습니다.

147. 이 정보를 찾을 수 있는 가장 가능성이 높은 장소는 어디일까?
(A) 전화번호부
(B) 제품 카타로그
(C) 사용자 설명서
(D) 직원 안내서

148. 이 정보에 따르면, CloudTek의 직원들은 어떻게 도움을 줄 수 있는가?
(A) 지시사항을 설명함으로써
(B) 고장난 제품을 수리함으로써
(C) 흔한 문제를 목록으로 정리함으로써
(D) 제품 특징들을 설명함으로써

Questions 149-150 공지

Bowie Electronics

우리 상점의 손님여러분:

Robin Grove의 Bowie Electronics는 4월 10일부터 수리나 서비스를 위해 맡겨진 물건을 위해 무료 배송을 제공합니다. 제품을 가지고 오실 때, 물건을 상점에서 찾아가실지, 아니면 집이나 사무실로 배송시키실지를 저희에게 알려주실 것을 요청 드립니다. 이 서비스는 Robin Grove지역의 계시는 분들에게만 이용 가능합니다.

149. 손님들은 무엇을 하도록 요청 받는가?
(A) 연락처 정보를 업데이트 하는 것.
(B) 상품을 빨리 예약하는 것.
(C) 어떠한 귀중품도 안전하게 보관하는 것.
(D) 선택사항을 결정하는 것

150. 4월 10일날 어떤 일이 일어날 것인가?
(A) 예전 지점이 문을 닫을 것이다.
(B) 새로운 서비스가 이용 가능할 것이다.
(C) 상점이 수리 중에 있을 것이다.
(D) 할인행사가 종료될 것이다.

Questions 151-152 문자 메시지

ERIC LEVINE	2:29 PM
아직 식료품점에 있어요?	

SYLVIA LEVINE	2:31 PM
네, 왜요? 모 필요하세요?	

ERIC LEVINE	2:32 PM
네. 저는 울타리작업이 거의 끝났어요.	

ERIC LEVINE	2:32 PM
철물점에서 못이랑 목재 좀 찾아다 줄 수 있어요?	

SYLVIA LEVINE	2:34 PM
매장에서 물건을 어떻게 찾죠?	

ERIC LEVINE	2:35 PM
아주 쉬워요. 가게 정문에서 바로 오른쪽에 있을 거예요.	

SYLVIA LEVINE	2:36 PM
좋아요. 만약 못 찾으면 전화할게요.	

SYLVIA LEVINE	2:37 PM
그러니까 전화 잘 챙기고 있으세요.	

151. Eric Levine씨는 무엇을 요청하고 있는가?
   (A) 약간의 건축 자재
   (B) 몇 개의 식료품
   (C) 컴퓨터 업데이트
   (D) 매장 약도

152. 2시 37분에 Sylvia Levine씨가 "keep your phone handy"라고 쓸 때 무엇을 의미하고 있는가?
   (A) 나중에 자기에게 문자를 보내라
   (B) 연락처를 변경해라
   (C) 전화기를 가까운 곳에 두어라
   (D) 전화기 건전지를 충전해 두어라

Questions 153-154 기사

Bulgarian Times
경제 및 금융

발칸 댄스 파티를 지원하는 Macedex

Sofia (3월3일) – Bulgaria에서 가장 널리 이용되는 은행인 Macedex는 올해 사업40주년을 기념합니다. 이 성취를 기념하여 Macedex는 3월 21일 Rodino Amphitheater에서의 무료 콘서트 페스티벌인 올해의 발칸 댄스 파티를 홍보할 것입니다. 이 콘서트는 올해의 발칸 뮤지션상에 2회 수상자인 Gregor Petroff를 포함한 발칸 주의 많은 유명한 뮤지션들의 참여화 함께 오후 7시경에 시작할 계획입니다. Macedex는 이행사가 전체가 촬영이 되고 불가리아의 텔레비전으로 방영될 것이라고 발표했습니다. 참석하기 위해서는 콘서트 이전에 Macedex 은행 지점에서 무료로 티켓을 받아가실 수 있습니다.

153. 무엇이 기념되고 있는가?
   (A) 뮤지션의 성취
   (B) 원형극장의 공사
   (C) 은행 직원의 생일
   (D) 금융기관의 기념일

154. 발칸 댄스 파티에 대해 무엇이 나타나 있는가?
   (A) 그것은 오직 Macedex 고객들에게만 열려있다.
   (B) 그것은 모든 나라 전체에 방송될 것이다.
   (C) 그것은 초여름에 개최될 것이다.
   (D) 그것은 시상식을 포함할 것이다.

Questions 155-157 기사

시민들, 여행책자에 불쾌감 보여

시민들과 Apple Rapids의 시의회에 의해 "The Minnesota Hiking Guide"에 대한 이의가 제기되었다. 그 이의는 올해 초 출판된 여행책자의 최신판에 관한 것이다. 이 여행책자는 도시의 가장 오래되고 가장 사랑 받는 숙소와 식당에 대해 매우 부정적인 평가를 주었다. —[1]—

Apple Rapids의 시의회 멤버인 Mark Grant는 미네소타의 모든 서점이 그들의 책 주문을 취소하도록 요구했다. 이 책자의 이전 판에서 저자는 North Star Inn을 "작은 마을의 숙소와 식당으로써의 절정판"이라고 극찬했다. —[2]— 이러한 극찬은 이 책자의 현재 버전이 출판되기 겨우 2년전에, 호텔의 매니저와 요리사가 변경되지 않은 상태에서 나온 것이다.

"이 숙소는 작은 마을 생활의 훌륭한 예시를 제공하고 있는데, 이 책자의 편집자들은 도로변 모텔들에 훨씬 더 익숙한 것으로 보입니다." 시장인 Stein은 이 평가가 불필요하게 냉혹하고 적대적이라고 생각했다. —[3]— "North Star Inn은 지역민과 우리 도시의 방문객들을 위한 인기 있는 모임 장소였다. 우리 도시의 경제는 이 가이드의 이번과 같은 평가로 인해 매우 나빠질 수 있다. 이 책자의 편집자들은 이 문제를 토의하길 원하는 어떠한 전화에도 답하지 않았다." —[4]— The Minnesota Hiking Guide는 수년 마다 새로운 버전이 출판 되는 가운데 거의 25년 동안 출판되어 왔다.

155. 왜 Apple Rapids의 시민들이 화나있는가?
   (A) 그들은 호텔을 떠나라고 요청 받았다.
   (B) 마을의 숙박시설이 부정적인 평가를 받았다.
   (C) 주립 공원이 피해를 입었다.
   (D) 야영객의 숫자가 줄었다.

156. The Minnesota Hiking Guide에 관하여 암시되는 것은?
   (A) 그것은 베스트 셀러인 가이드 책 이였다.
   (B) 그것은 Apple Rapids에서 최초로 출판되었다.
   (C) 그것은 방문 여행객들의 결정에 영향을 미칠 수 있다.
   (D) 그것은 길가의 모텔들의 상태를 리뷰하지 않았다.

157. [1], [2], [3], [4]로 표시된 자리 중에 다음 문장이 들어가기에 가장 적합한 곳은?

"Apple Rapids에서 70년 넘게 운영되고 있는 North Star Inn은 이 여행 책자의 최신판에서 오직 별 반 개의 점수를 받았다."

(A) [1]
(B) [2]
(C) [3]
(D) [4]

Questions 158–160 광고

The Galacite Inn

Galactic Inn에 묶어 주셔서 감사합니다. 우리는 당신의 방문을 가능한 편안하게 만들어 드리고 싶습니다. 이곳에 있는 동안, 우리의 새로운 식당인 Steak Planet을 편하게 방문해 주세요.

식당은 주중 오전 11시부터 오후 11시까지, 그리고 주말에는 오전 10시부터 자정 12시까지 열려있습니다. 호텔의 손님들은 식당이 열려있는 동안은 언제든지 일반 메뉴나 어린이 메뉴를 룸서비스로 주문할 수 있습니다. 만약 식당이 닫힌다면, 새벽 3시까지 다른 곳에서는 찾아볼 수 없는 우리 식당만의 디저트와 와인을 포함하고 있는 특별 룸서비스 메뉴를 이용하세요.

호텔 투숙객들은 또한 이번 주 일요일 오후 5시부터 7시까지 요리사 Hurt의 요리가 제공되는 무료 저녁 뷔페에 초대됩니다. 투숙객들이 뷔페 식당으로 들어오기 위해서는 이 전단지가 요구됩니다. (전단지를 들고 오셔야 입장하실 수 있습니다.)

158. 토요일에 식당은 몇 시에 문을 여는가?
(A) 오전 10시
(B) 오전 11시
(C) 오전 12시
(D) 오후 5시

159. 룸서비스 메뉴에 대하여 언급되지 않은 것은?
(A) 디저트와 와인을 포함한다.
(B) 식당만큼 비싸지 않은 음식들을 포함하고 있다 (choice는 '선택물'의 의미로써 선택할 수 있는 음식들을 의미한다)
(C) 특별히 어린이들을 위해 만들어진 음식을 포함한다.
(D) Steak Planet(식당)에서 이용 가능하다.

160. Galactic Inn은 투숙객들에게 무엇을 제공할까?
(A) 도시 관광
(B) 무료 와인 시음
(C) 무료 저녁식사
(D) TV 유명인과 만날 기회

Questions 161–163 이메일

수신: 전직원 <employee.list@pommesindustries.com>
발신: H. Gagnon <hgagnon@pommesindustries.com>
제목: 회신: 봄이 왔습니다
날짜: 4월 3일

모든 Pommes Industries직원들은 4층 회의장에서 4월 15일 1시부터 6시까지 봄의 도착을 축하하는데 우리와 함께하도록 초대 되는 바입니다.

우리는 스낵과 음료수를 여러분이 즐길 수 있도록 제공할 것입니다. 다양한 석쇠에 구운 치킨 요리, 오븐에 구운 치킨요리, 신선한 과일과 채소, 미식가들이 즐기는 크래커와 치즈 그리고 디저트용 커스터드와 함께 점심식사가 제공될 것입니다. DJ로써 활약할 Patrick Epstein에 의해 음악연주도 제공이 될 것입니다.

이 무료 파티에 오고 싶은 고든 직원들은 늦어도 4월 10일까지 우리 인사 전문가인 Sylvia Fanson과 Katrina van Patton의 2층 사무실 바깥에 위치한 양식에 서명함으로써 등록을 해야만 합니다. 의견과 질문들을 환영합니다. 모든 Pommes Industries 직원들은 파티에 대해 논의하기 위해서 주저하지 마시고 저의 사무실로 오시거나 이메일을 보내주세요.

모든 분들을 그곳에서 뵙기를 바랍니다!

Henri Gagnon
직원 관리 부서장

161. 이 이메일의 목적은 무엇인가요?
(A) 직원들이 행사에 참석할 것을 장려하는 것
(B) 회의 장소를 발표하는 것
(C) 직원들에게 다가오는 휴일을 상기시켜 주는 것
(D) 출장 뷔페 서비스를 예약하는 것

162. 파티에 대해 언급되지 않은 것은?
(A) 회사에 의해 마련되고 있다.
(B) 연례 행사다.
(C) 음악을 포함할 것이다.
(D) 실내에서 열릴 것이다.

163. 더 많은 정보를 위해 누구에게 연락해야 하나요?
(A) Patrick Epstein
(B) Sylvia Fanson
(C) Katrina van Patton
(D) Henri Gagnon

Questions 164–167 인터넷 채팅 대화

Jessica Fisher [10:05 a.m.]
공사현장에 감독관이 방금 저에게 전화를 해서 벽을 철거할 준비가 되었다고 전했는데요, 뭐든 시작하기 전에 수정된 공사 계획안이 필요하다고 합니다.

Stanley Abrell [10:08 a.m.]
제가 방금 기술부서 매니저와 얘기했는데요, 몇 분 후에 저에게 수정안을 보낼 거라고 합니다. 오늘 아침에 막 업데이트 작업을 끝냈다고 합니다.

Jessica Fisher [10:09 a.m.]
잘됐네요. 수정안을 인쇄해서 11시까지 공사현장에 가져다 줄 수 있나요?

Stanley Abrell [10:10 a.m.]
제가 사실 11시반에 마케팅 부서에서 발표가 있어요. 그래서 오늘은 현장에 갈 수 없을 것 같습니다. 현장에 수정안을 가져다 주실 수 있는 분 계시나요?

Ryan Burke [10:12 a.m.]
Stanley, 제가 할게요. 수정안 인쇄는 언제 할건가요?

Stanley Abrell [10:13 a.m.]
제가 방금 Timothy Howard한테 수정안을 이메일로 받았습니다. 바로 인쇄 시작할거니까 10분후면 준비가 될 거에요. 공사현장에 어떻게 가는지는 아세요?

Ryan Burke [10:14 a.m.]
이전에 한번 가본 적이 있습니다만, 제가 운전을 했던 게 아니라서요. 약도를 좀 주실 수 있나요?

Jessica Fisher [10:15 a.m.]
제가 여기서 현장에 가는 길을 보여주는 지도를 가지고 있어요. Stanley가 인쇄할 수 있도록 Stanley에게 지금 전달할게요.

Ryan Burke [10:16 a.m.]
고마워요, Jessica.

Stanley Abrell [10:17 a.m.]
받았습니다. Ryan, 10시반쯤 모두 챙기러 제 사무실에 오시는 게 어때요?

Ryan Burke [10:17 a.m.]
그럴게요, Stanley.

Jessica Fisher [10:18 a.m.]
Ryan, 가능한 빨리 현장에 가주세요. 저하고 얘기했을 때 감독관이 아직 수정안을 받지 못해서 기분이 약간 상해 있었어요.

164. 토론의 주제는 무엇인가?
(A) 공사 시작의 일정을 잡는 것
(B) 공사 계획을 수정하는 것
(C) 업데이트된 공사 계획안을 전달 하는 것
(D) 신규 건물을 위해 부지를 선정하는 것

165. Ryan Burke씨에 대해 언급된 것은?
(A) Burke씨는 공사장 감독관과 아는 사이다.
(B) Burke씨는 최근에 이 회사에서 일하기 시작했다.
(C) Burke씨는 이전에 건설부문에서 일했었다.
(D) Burke씨는 나중에 공사현장에 방문할 것이다.

166. 10시 17분에 Stanley Abrell씨가 "I got it"이라고 쓸 때 무엇을 의미하고 있는가?
(A) Abrell씨는 현장에 도착했다.
(B) Abrell씨는 Fisher씨로부터 이메일을 받았다.
(C) Abrell씨는 Burke씨의 감사인사를 받아줬다.
(D) Abrell씨는 수정안을 전달했다.

167. Stanley Abrell씨는 아마도 다음에 무엇을 할까요?
(A) 공사현장 매니저에게 얘기를 할 것이다.
(B) 자료들을 인쇄할 것이다.
(C) 고객에게 연락할 것이다.
(D) 물건을 전달할 계획을 세울 것이다.

Questions 168-171 정보

목재 작품 가정용 가구 조립 세트

WoodWorks의 전문 공예가들은 세계에서 아주 유명한 갤러리나 최고급 가구의 디자인을 기반으로 여러분의 가정용 가구 세트를 만듭니다. —[1]—

심지어 이 아름다운 디자인과 함께 우리 가구는 여전히 조립하기에도 간단합니다. 여러분이 새로운 가구를 만들기 위해 필요할 것들은 가재 도구들 뿐입니다. —[2]—

각 조립 세트들은 모든 가구 부품, 사포 그리고 따라하기 쉬운 설명서와 함께 제공됩니다. 오직 하나 포함되지 않은 것은 마무리 오일인데, 그래서 여러분은 여러분의 스타일에 딱 맞는 마감을 선택할 수 있습니다. —[3]— 각 착색의 종류별 설명은 아래에 나열되어 있습니다.

마감작업 조언
최종 유성 오일은 따로 칠해져야 하지만, 각 조립세트는 마무리 작업을 하기 위한 충분한 수성 니스를 포함하고 있습니다. 작업을 마무리 하는 동안, 인내가 요구 되어집니다. 풀 또는 손자국 같은 어떠한 흠집도 사포나 촉촉한 청소용 천으로 완벽히 제거하세요. 당신의 작업지역에 먼지가 없도록 확인하세요. 작업은 천천히 그리고 착색의 각 칠은 다른 덧칠을 하기 전에 완전히 마른 것을 꼭 확인하세요. —[4]—

착색 선택
표준 착색: 대부분의 WoodWorks 고객들이 이 착색을 선택하는데, 월 넛과 유사한 진한 갈색의 분위기를 줍니다.
짙은 착색: 이 짙은 착색은 당신의 가구에게 고전적이고, 세련미를 내뿜는 짙은 갈색을 만들어 줍니다.
어두운 착색: 더욱 현대적인 스타일을 위해 이 착색은 당신의 가구에게 윤기 나는 검은 마감효과를 준다.

168. 이 정보는 어디에서 보여질 가능성이 가장 높은가?
(A) 미술관 팜플렛
(B) 상품의 카탈로그
(C) 가사 서비스 판촉물
(D) 잡지 기사

169. 각각의 조립용 세트에 포함되지 않는 것은?
(A) 가구 부품
(B) 사포
(C) 마무리 오일
(D) 나무 착색

170. 어떠한 착색을 가장 많은 고객들이 선택하는가?
(A) 표준 착색
(B) 천연 착색
(C) 짙은 착색
(D) 어두운 착색

171. [1], [2], [3], [4]로 표시된 자리 중에 다음 문장이 들어가기에 가장 적합한 곳은?

"주문할 때, 어떤 종류의 나무 착색이 좋은 지 선택해 주세요."
(A) [1]
(B) [2]
(C) [3]
(D) [4]

Questions 172–175 편지

5월 16일

Serena Kim
2455 First Avenue
Portland, OR 97201

Kim씨에게,

당신의 인터넷 서비스 공급 업체로써 Quickcom을 선택해 주신 것에 대해 감사의 말씀을 전하고 싶습니다. 설치전문가가 5월 19일 오후 2시에당신의 집을 방문할 것입니다. 이 시간에 누군가가 집에 계실 것을 요청드립니다. 우리 전문가가 (고객방문) 약속이 많기 때문에, 우리 서비스 센터에 (888) 555-3386 으로 전화하셔서 예정된 설치일 전날에 당신의 약속을 확인해 주세요.

QuickCom과의 당신의 계약에 대해 말하자면, 우리는 당신의 인터넷 서비스를 18개월동안 20달러라는 특별 가격으로 제공해 드립니다. 당신의 첫 번째 고지서는 설치비로 40달러의 초기 요금을 포함할 것입니다. 이 기간 이후에는 매달 30달러의 정상가가 적용될 것입니다. 만약 당신이 이 기간이 끝나기 전에 당신의 서비스를 취소하기로 선택하신다면, 당신은 우리 계약을 위반한 것에 대한 80달러의 조기 해지 비용을 청구 받을 것입니다. 우리는 당신이 보관할 계약서 사본을 동봉했습니다.

우리는 매달 첫째 날에 우편으로 고지서를 발송하며 15일까지 요금납부를 요청 드립니다. 당신은 우편이나, 웹사이트, 고객 서비스 사무실 납부 중 하나를 선택해서 요금을 납부하는 것을 선택 할 수 있습니다. 다시 한번 QuickCom을 선택해 주셔서 감사합니다.

172. 김씨는 어디에서 인터넷을 설치하려고 하는가?
(A) 그녀의 집
(B) 그녀의 작업장
(C) 그녀의 시장
(D) 그녀의 레스토랑

173. 2번째 문단, 4번째줄에서 "어기다"와 가장 의미상 가까운 것은?
(A) 나누다
(B) 파괴하다
(C) 위반하다
(D) 분리하다

174. 편지에 따르면, 왜 김씨는 추가 요금을 내게 될 수 있는가?
(A) 계약을 위반하는 것 때문에
(B) 그녀의 약속을 취소하는 것 때문에
(C) 요금납부를 너무 늦게 보내는 것 때문에
(D) 서비스를 너무 자주 사용하는 것 때문에

175. 언제가 김씨의 QuickCom 요금납부 첫 번째 기한인가?
(A) 5월 16일
(B) 5월 19일
(C) 6월 1일
(D) 6월 15일

Questions 176–180 웹사이트 및 이메일

http://www.cda.co.ca

Career Development Academy
(직업개발 훈련소)

커리어 발전을 위한 워크샵

7월 10일 성공적인 사업행행 Lorken Production사의 대표이사는 지속가능한 사업행행을 실행함으로써 당신의 회사를 더욱 성공하게 만드는 법에 대해 자문을 해줍니다. 또한 이러한 것이 자신의 회사가 매출과 수익을 올리는데 어떻게 도움을 주었는지도 설명할 것입니다.	7월 17일 조직: 성공의 열쇠 기업코치인 Glenn Baxter씨가 당신의 회사에서 프로젝트를 관리할 때, 그리고 생산성 재고를 위해 작업일정을 짤 때 어떻게 우선순위를 설정하는지에 대한 발표를 할 때 당신의 작업으로부터 최대치를 얻어내는 법을 배우세요.
7월 24일 당신의 홍보법으로 성공하는 법 만약 당신이 좋은 아이디어를 가지고 있는 기업가라면, 당신은 그 아이디어가 지금지원을 성공적으로 받기 위해서 그 생각들을 홍보하는 법을 알아야 합니다. '당신의 아이디어를 뜨게 만들기'의 작가인 Greg Diamond는 성공적인 홍보법을 위한 6단계 계획안으로 당신이 이를 달성하도록 도울 수 있습니다.	7월 31일 미래를 십분 활용하기 미디어 전문가인 Ivana Bauer씨는 마케팅이 더 많은 사람들에게 전달되고 더 많은 고객을 끌어들이기 위해서 인터넷 상의 활동을 어떻게 보강할 지에 대한 워크샵을 진행합니다. 워크샵 등록비에 강의 교재가 포함되어 있습니다.

커리어 발전을 위한 워크샵은 Career Development Acadmy에서 매주 화요일 오후7시부터 9시까지 개최됩니다. 워크샵은 일반인에게 공개됩니다. www.cda.co.ca/enrollment에서 인터넷으로 등록하실 수 있습니다.

수신인: gbaxter@mailtime.co.ca
발신인: floragordon@gordonmanufacturing.co.ca
날짜: 7월 26일
제목: 다시 한번 감사 드립니다!

Baxter씨에게,

발표 후에 저와 얘기를 나누기 위해 내주신 시간에 대해 얼마나 감사 드리는지 전하고 싶었습니다. 저는 당신의 아이디어가 매우 유용하다고 생각하며, 저의 직원들도 당신의 아이디어로부터 배울 수 있도록 당신이 저희 회사, Gordon Manufacturing에서 발표를 해주십사 요청을 드리고 싶습니다. 8월 대부분을 출장 중이실 거라 하셔서 9월에 시간을 잡았으면 합니다. 언제 시간이 되시는지 알려주시기 바랍니다. 곧 회신을 받기를 바랍니다.

Flora Gordon
대표이사, Gordon Manufacturing

176. 커리어 발전을 위한 워크샵에 대해 언급된 것은?
(A) 워크샵은 일주일에 두 번 열린다.
(B) 워크샵은 대학 강사들이 가르친다.
(C) 워크샵은 여러 장소에서 열린다.
(D) 등록은 모든 사람에게 오픈되어 있다.

177. 인터넷에서 광고를 하는 것에 대해 배우고 싶은 기업인을 위해 가장 유용한 세미나는?
(A) 성공적인 사업관행
(B) 조직: 성공의 열쇠
(C) 당신의 홍보법으로 성공하는 법
(D) 미래를 십분 활용하기

178. Diamond씨에 대해 언급된 것은?
(A) Diamond씨는 최근 자신의 사업을 시작했다.
(B) Diamond씨는 8월에 여행을 갈 것이다.
(C) Diamond씨는 Career Development Academy의 회원이다.
(D) Diamond씨는 책을 한 권 집필했다.

179. Gordon씨는 왜 이메일을 보냈는가?
(A) 교육과정 일정을 잡으려고
(B) 워크샵에 등록하려고
(C) 여행일정표를 공유하려고
(D) 세미나 주제를 제안하려고

180. Gordon씨는 Gordon Manufacturing사에서 무엇을 하는 것에 가장 관심이 있을까?
(A) 직원들에게 운영시스템 사용하는 법을 가르치는 것
(B) 회사의 인터넷 상의 입지를 넓히는 것
(C) 직원들의 시간관리 기술을 연마하는 것
(D) 새로운 프로젝트를 위해 더 많은 자금을 유치하는 것

Questions 181-185 이메일과 쪽지

수신: Patrick Barwurton 〈barwurton08@supraline.com〉
발신: Wu Lenwei 〈lenwei04@supraline.com〉
날짜: 9월 3일
제목: Turro 대표자와 함께 점심

나는 Sawatdee에서 Turro 대표자와 함께할 점심식사를 굉장히 고대하고 있습니다. 그 식당이 단지 몇 달 전에 개업을 했음에도 불구하고, 내가 본 모든 리뷰들은 그곳이 이 지역의 최고 식당중의 하나라고 이야기 합니다. 나는 Turro사의 우리고객들이 타이 음식을 즐긴다고 들었습니다. 그래서 나는 이 식당이 그들에게 우리 회사에 대해 좋은 느낌을 줄 수 있기를 진심으로 희망합니다. 유일한 문제는 회사에서 식당으로 가는 데 시간이 좀 걸릴 것이라는 점입니다.

한가지 더 문제가 있습니다. 내 차가 여전히 1번가의 정비소에서 수리 중입니다. 지금으로서는 어떻게 미팅을 위해 20번가로 갈 수 있을지 잘 모르겠습니다. 지하철을 탈 수 있겠지만 지하철이 그 시간쯤에는 보통 매우 붐빈다고 알고 있습니다. 플랫폼에서 살짝 전철을 확인해보고, 만약 너무 붐빈다면 레스토랑으로 택시를 타고 갈려고 나는 생각하고 있습니다. 청사진(도면)을 찾아오기 위해 복사가게에 가는 것을 처리하지 못한 것을 제외하고는 미팅에 대한 모든 준비는 완료되었습니다.

만약 내가 지하철을 타야 한다면, 제가 몇 호선을 타야 할까요? 나는 2개의 라인이 있다는 것을 알고 있습니다만, 어떤 라인이 덜 붐비고 더 빠른지 알지 못합니다. 만약 당신이 알려준다면, 조언에 감사하겠습니다.

Wu

Supraline Industries
55 3rd Street
보스톤, MA 02127

9월 4

Wu,

나는 새로운 고객을 확보하기 위해 당신이 드린 모든 시간과 노력에 진심으로 감사 드립니다. 걱정마세요. 나머지는 제가 기꺼이 처리하겠습니다. 제 차가 정상적으로 작동하기 때문에, 그것을 처리하는 데에는 문제가 없습니다. 원하시면, 11번가에서 뵙죠. 제가 손쉽게 당신을 태워서 식당으로 이동할 수 있습니다.

Patrick

181. 왜 Lenwei씨는 이 메일을 보냈는가?
(A) 동료의 도움을 요청하기 위해서
(B) 최근 개점한 식당을 제안하기 위해서
(C) 미팅 장소로의 운전용 약도를 요청하기 위해서
(D) 예약을 연기하기 위해서

182. Sawatdee에 대해 언급되지 않은 것은?
(A) 최근에 영업을 시작 했다.
(B) Supraline Industries와 가깝지 않다.
(C) 무료 전체요리를 제공한다.
(D) 많은 좋은 리뷰를 받았다.

183. Sawatdee 식당은 어디에 있는가?
  (A) 1번가
  (B) 3번가
  (C) 11번가
  (D) 20번가

184. 두 번째 지문에서, 2번째 줄의 "rest"와 가장 의미상 가까운 것은?
  (A) 멈춤
  (B) 상기시켜 주는 연락
  (C) 나머지
  (D) 확립

185. Patrick Barwurton은 Turro 대표자와 미팅 전에 무엇을 할 것인가?
  (A) 복사본을 찾아오는 것
  (B) 여행 일정표를 업데이트 하는 것
  (C) 테이블을 예약하는 것
  (D) 출장을 가는 것

Questions 186-190 웹페이지와 이메일들

Http://www.cloudfeet.co.au			
About Cloud Feet Soles	Products	Reviews	FAQ

Cloud Feet는 어떤 제품을 만드나요?
Cloud Feet는 여성용, 남성용, 그리고 아동 신발을 위한 고품질 밑창을 생산합니다. 저희는 8개 종류의 자재로 60 종의 밑창을 제조하고 있습니다. 레인부츠를 위한 고무 밑창, 무용화나 실내화를 위한 가죽 밑창, 그리고 100% 재활용된 자재로 만든 운동화를 위한 새로운 밑창과 같은 저희 제품들을 전세계 사람들이 애용하고 있습니다.

저는 어떻게 하면 Cloud Feet가 저의 사업에 납품업체가 되게 요청할 수 있나요?
당신은 상담을 받기 위해서 우리 지역 지사에 있는 대표자 중 한 명에게 이메일을 보내셔야 합니다. 이 대표들은 납품업체 계약서뿐만 아니라 당신에게 무료 샘플을 제공해줄 수 있을 것입니다.

북미 : Phil Glane / ⟨p.glane@cloudfeet.com⟩
남미: Julia Fernandez / ⟨j.fernandez@cloudfeet.co.br⟩
유럽: Sally Hibbert / ⟨s.hibbert@cloudfeet.co.uk⟩
아시아: Feng Xiong / ⟨m.ingels@cloudfeet.co.ch⟩

수신인: Sally Hibbert ⟨s.hibbert@cloudfeet.co.uk⟩
발신인: Charles Ryu ⟨cling@accel.co.jp⟩
날짜: 10월 20일
주제: 상담 요청

Hibbert씨에게,

저는 Accel이라 불리는 동경에 본사를 둔 신발회사에 마케팅 부장으로 일하고 있습니다. 최근 프랑스, 파리에서 열린 Athletic Apparel 박람회에 가서 밑창에 Cloud Feet 로고가 박혀있는 Supranex 운동화를 인상 깊게 봤습니다. 현재 저희 회사가 사용하고 있는 라텍스 자재보다 이 밑창이 훨씬 성능이 좋은 것으로 보였습니다.

저는 샘플도 받고 가능하면 계약도 할 겸 Cloud Feet 대표에게 연락을 취하고 싶었습니다. 그리고 제가 취해야 할 다음 단계가 무엇인지도 알고 싶었고요. 제가 아시아 지역 대표에게 이메일을 보냈으나 주소가 유효하지 않다는 공지문과 함께 이메일이 계속 반송되었습니다.

Charles Ryu
구매담당 부장, Accel

수신인: Charles Ryu ⟨cling@accel.co.jp⟩
발신인: Tony Weng Xia ⟨tonywx@cloudfeet.co.ch⟩
날짜: 10월 21일

Ryu씨에게,

저희는 당신이 겪어야 했던 혼란에 대해 깊이 사과 드리며, (동시에) 저희 제품에 관심을 가져주셔서 감사 드립니다. 저희 직원배정 상에 약간의 변화가 있었습니다. 현재 제가 Cloud Feet의 아시아 지역을 대표하고 있습니다. 제가 다음주에 저희 고객을 만나기 위해 잡혀있는 동경 출장이 있습니다. 언제가 시간이 괜찮으신지 그리고 당신의 운동화를 위한 밑창 외에 어떤 종류의 깔창에 관심이 있으신지 알려주시면, 제가 꼭 당신을 만나러 올 때 샘플을 가지고 가겠습니다.

Tony Weng Xia
Cloud Feet 대표

186. Cloud Feet사에 대해 언급된 것은?
  (A) Cloud Feet사는 고품질 레인부츠를 생산한다.
  (B) Cloud Feet사는 아동용 신발을 위한 부품만을 제조한다.
  (C) Cloud Feet사는 많은 국가에 있는 회사들과 거래를 한다.
  (D) Cloud Feet사는 매달 고객들에게 카달로그를 배포한다.

187. Hibbert씨에 대해 사실일 가능성이 가장 높은 것은?
  (A) Hibbert씨는 Accel에 고용된 사람이다.
  (B) Hibbert씨는 잠재고객에게 샘플을 제공할 수 있다.
  (C) Hibbert씨는 동경에 가본 적이 있다.
  (D) Hibbert씨는 프랑스 파리에서 Ryu씨를 만났다.

188. Ryu씨는 자신의 회사 제품을 위해 어떤 종류의 자재를 사용할 가능성이 가장 높은가?
  (A) 가죽
  (B) 재활용품
  (C) 고무
  (D) 라텍스

189. 첫 번째 이메일에 두 번째 단락, 두 번째 줄에 "step"이 의미상 가장 가까운 것은?
  (A) 조치
  (B) 추천
  (C) 발자국
  (D) 정도

190. Xia씨에 대해 언급된 것은?
(A) Xia씨는 오랫동안 Cloud Feet에서 근무해왔다.
(B) Xia씨는 다른 지역에서 전근을 왔다.
(C) Xia씨는 Xiong씨의 후임자다.
(D) Ryu씨는 이미 Xia씨의 고객이다.

Questions 191–195 전단지, 이메일 및 기사

제 10회 반기 Uptown Art Fair
4월 9일–11일

Metropolitan Arts Council에 의해 여러분에게 선사되는 The Uptown Art Fair가 많은 요구에 의해 다시 돌아옵니다.

행사의 부분 일정은 아래에서 찾아 보세요.

- 4월 9일 금요일 오후 6시 / Forrester Museum of Art
  Meredith Parilla의 새로운 사진 전시 Shutter Down and Tune Out의 오프닝. 이 전시는 4월 23일까지 진행될 것입니다.
  박물관 시간은 주중 동안에는 오전 9시부터 오후 8시까지, 주말에는 오전 11시부터 오후 6시까지입니다.

- 4월 10일 토요일과 4월 11일 일요일 오전 9시부터 오후 7시 / Uptown Community Center
  아이들을 위한 게임과 공예 체험 활동

- 4월 10일 토요일 오후 5시 / Miller Street Park Outdoor Theater
  (우천시 이동장소: Lamps Concert Hall)
  작년에 훌륭한 공연을 했던 Burkino Teenage Chore에 의한 음악 공연.

- 4월 10일 토요일과 4월 11일 일요일 오전 11시부터 오후 8시/ Uptown Junction Square
  다양한 푸드 트럭과 지역 예술가들이 음식과 공예품을 마켓에서 판매 합니다.

- 4월 11일 일요일 오후 4시부터 오후 7시/ Tourian Theater
  Carroll Bady가 만든 새로운 연극인 An Obscure Camera가 Tourian Theater의 연극배우들에 의해 공연됩니다.

수신: Mary Wildenburg <mwildenburg@bwt.org>
발신: Saban Azizov <sabanaz@burkinoork.com>
제목: Uptown Art Fair
날짜 :4월 1일

Ms. Wildenburg에게

남아프리카 토착 음악을 Uptown Art Fair에 초대해 준 것에 얼마나 우리가 감사하는지 전하고 싶었습니다. 더 많은 사람들이 공연을 즐길 수 있더라면 더 좋았을 테지만, 비 오는 날씨 때문에 실내에서 공연을 할 수 밖에 없었네요. 그럼에도 불구하고 청중들은 굉장했습니다. 또한, 많은 이들이 우리 앨범을 구매해주신 것 같습니다. 몇몇은 공연 이후에 우리 음악을 다운로드 할 수 있는 웹사이트를 물어보기도 했습니다.

우리는 향후 또 다른 어떤 페스티벌에서도 연주할 수 있다면 영광일 것입니다. 다시 한번 감사합니다.

Saban Azizov
관리자
Burkino Teenage Chore

Uptown Art Fair 대 성공

SANDUSKY (4월 13일) – 이번 봄에 Uptown Art Fair는, 기획자들이 이번 페스티벌을 지금껏 가장 성공적인 페스티벌이었다고 얘기하는 가운데, 이전 보다 더 많은 관중을 불러모았습니다. 비가 오는 날씨에도 불구하고 많은 사람들이 푸드 트럭에서 제공하는 세계 음식들을 맛보기 위해 긴 줄을 서서 기다렸습니다. 푸드 트럭 중에 일부는 제한된 공간 때문에 원래 장소였던 Uptown Junction Square에서 (다른 곳으로) 옮겨져야 했습니다. "처음에 저는 장소를 변경하는 것에 대해 걱정했습니다"라고 푸드 트럭 운영자인 Reggie Lopez씨가 말했습니다. "그러나 일요일에 많은 손님들이 An Obscure Camera를 보기 위해 기다리면서 저의 푸트 트럭에서 음식을 사먹었던 것 같습니다".

페스티벌 기획자들은 가을에 열릴 다음 페스티벌 행사들을 이미 기획하기 시작했습니다. "대부분의 장소는 동일하겠지만 저희가 (게임이나 공예활동을 위해) 보통 사용하는 공간이 이번 가을에 공사에 들어가기 때문에 게임과 공예 활동을 위한 새로운 공간을 찾아야 할 지 모릅니다"라고 Metropolitan Arts Council의 Scarlett Anthony씨가 말했습니다. "이번에 페스티벌이 얼마나 재미있었는지를 고려해보면, 가을 페스티벌도 분명히 고대할 만한 것이 될 것입니다"라고 말했습니다.

191. 일요일 오후 5시에 열릴 예정이 아닌 행사는 무엇인가?
(A) 춤 경연
(B) 아트공예 활동
(C) 사진 전시회
(D) 음식 마켓

192. 왜 Azizov씨가 Wildenburg씨에게 이메일을 보냈는가?
(A) 강당으로 가는 길을 물어보기 위해서
(B) 콘서트를 연기하기 위해서
(C) 그녀에게 고마움을 전하기 위해서
(D) 잃어버린 물건을 되찾기 위해서

193. Burkino Orchestra에 대하여 무엇이 언급되고 있는가?
(A) 이 행사에서 처음으로 공연을 했다.
(B) Lamps Concert Hall에서 공연했다.
(C) 지금 남아프리카에서 투어공연 중이다.
(D) 이들의 인터넷 상점에 많은 방문객이 오고 있다.

194. Lopez 푸드 트럭은 어디에 가까이 있었을 가능성이 가장 높은가?
(A) Forrester Museum of Art
(B) Miller Street Park Outdoor Theater
(C) Lamps Concert Hall
(D) Tourian theater

195. Uptown Community Center에는 이번 가을 무슨 일이 발생할까?
(A) Uptown Community Center는 운영시간을 변경할 것이다.
(B) Uptown Community Center는 페스티벌을 위해 예술 및 공예 부문을 센터 내에 둘 것이다.
(C) Uptown Community Center는 지역사회를 위한 수업을 제공하기 시작할 것이다.
(D) Uptown Community Center는 수리가 될 것이다.

Questions 196-200 기사, 보고서 및 후기

| 월간 호텔 뉴스 | 10월 |

독점 인터뷰

아시아 전역에 호텔 체인을 가지고 있는 회사인 Lusk Company는 그들의 이익이 Sun Yiping의 노력으로 완륭하게 상승한 것을 보아왔습니다. Yiping 씨는 홍콩의 Shenzhen Park를 내려다 보는 그의 사무실에서 회사의 현재 진행중인 사업 계획과 그들의 재무 상태에 대해서 우리에게 이야기 했습니다.

Q. Lusk Company의 호텔이 다른 호텔 체인들과 다른 점은 무엇입니까?
A: 출장을 다니는 고객들이 우리 고객의 대부분을 차지하기 때문에 우리는 그들의 요구에 맞게 우리 호텔을 맞춤화시켜 조정하는데 많은 시간을 써왔습니다. 이런 고객들에게는 안락함과 업무 서비스의 사용이 중요합니다. 그래서 우리 객실은 평균보다 더 크며, 우리는 업무설비를 쉽게 이용할 수 있게, 그리고 모든 고객들이 접근할 수 있도록 확실히 준비합니다. 다른 호텔 체인은 이렇게 하지 않습니다.

Q. Lusk Company는 고객들에게 최고의 서비스를 계속해서 제공하는 것을 확실히 하기 위해서 무엇을 하나요?
A: 우리 고객들의 만족은 주로 우리 직원의 직업 만족도에 달려있습니다. 그래서 우리는 우리 직원들 모두에게 급여를 잘 지불하고 후한 수당을 제공합니다. 모든 승진은 (외부 인사가 아닌) 현 직원들에게 제공되며, 직원들이 우리 업계에 대한 그들의 지식을 함양하도록 돕기 위해 외부기관 교육을 위한 (수업료를) 지불해주는 것뿐만 아니라 (내부) 교육도 제공합니다.

Q. 지난 한 해 동안 회사가 번창하는데 도움을 주었던 프로젝트에 대해 우리에게 말해줄 수 있나요?
A: 우리는 2월에 교토에 있는 호텔을 매입했고, 쿠알라룸푸에 있는 우리 호텔에 새로운 식당을 지었고, 서울 지점의 객실 대부분을 완전히 수리했으며, 방콕에 호텔을 건설할 계획을 마무리 했습니다. 이러한 노력으로 우리의 연간 수익이 7% 상승했습니다.

Lusk Company 연례 재무 보고서
요약

아시아 경제의 활성화에 따른 이 지역 전역에 걸친 출장의 증가는 Lusk Hotel 거의 전 지점에서의 객실이용률 증가로 이어졌으며, 객실요금을 올리지 않았음에도 불구하고 올해 수익성을 꽤 높여주었습니다. 최근 신규호텔 공사의 연기도 우리의 긍정적인 재무실적에 영향을 미치지는 않을 것입니다.

수치 A: 지점별 추정되는 수익
(나열된 숫자 단위는 100만 미국 달러임)

	1분기	2분기	3분기	4분기
홍콩	20	8	7	2
서울	11	12	11	2
쿠알라룸프	13	11	6	2
교토	3	7	8	3
합계	47	38	32	9

---

http://www.realhotelreviews.com

후기 작성자: Christophe Luccardi
호텔 이름: Lusk Hotel
체류 기간: 3박
평가등급: 5/5

의견: Lusk Hotel에서의 투숙은 늘 그렇듯이 훌륭했습니다. 저는 여러 Lusk Branches에서 묵어봤으며 항상 모든 지점의 서비스와 시설에 만족해왔습니다. 이번에는 저의 객실이 최근에 공사를 했던 것으로 보여서 완전히 깨끗했기 때문에 더 좋았습니다. 직원들도 매우 도움이 되었습니다. 제가 컨벤션 때문에 예약을 해야 했었는데 이 기간이 비성수기 기간이라 무료로 저의 객실을 업그레이드 시켜줄 수 있다고 직원들이 얘기해줬습니다. 저는 의심의 여지없이 계속해서 Lusk 호텔을 이용할 것입니다.

196. 기사의 두 번째 문단, 두 번째 줄에 "customizing"가 의미상 가장 가까운 것은?
(A) 반영하다
(B) 홍보하다
(C) 간소화하다
(D) 맞춤형으로 조정하다

197. Lusk Company가 프로젝트를 연기하기로 결정한 곳은?
(A) 교토
(B) 쿠알라룸프
(C) 홍콩
(D) 방콕

198. 보고서에 따르면, Lusk Company는 왜 수익성이 좋았는가?
(A) 호텔에 더욱 많은 고객이 왔다.
(B) 업무 장비를 이용하는 요금이 증가 했다.
(C) 일부 고객응대 서비스가 없어졌다.
(D) 객실 요금이 증가 했다.

199. Luccardi씨는 어느 지점에서 투숙했을 가능성이 가장 높은가?
(A) Kong 지점
(B) Seoul 지점
(C) Kuala Lumpur 지점
(D) Kyoto 지점

200. Luccardi씨는 어느 기간 동안 컨벤션에 참석했을 가능성이 가장 높은가?
(A) 1월과 3월 사이
(B) 4월과 6월 사이
(C) 7월과 9월 사이
(D) 10월과 12월 사이

Test 1

101	B	102	A	103	D	104	D	105	A
106	C	107	C	108	C	109	B	110	A
111	C	112	C	113	A	114	C	115	B
116	C	117	C	118	D	119	D	120	B
121	B	122	C	123	B	124	A	125	B
126	A	127	C	128	A	129	C	130	D
131	B	132	C	133	C	134	A	135	D
136	C	137	C	138	B	139	A	140	C
141	D	142	B	143	D	144	C	145	A
146	B	147	C	148	D	149	B	150	D
151	A	152	C	153	B	154	D	155	C
156	D	157	A	158	B	159	C	160	A
161	B	162	C	163	B	164	B	165	A
166	A	167	C	168	D	169	B	170	C
171	B	172	B	173	A	174	D	175	B
176	D	177	A	178	C	179	B	180	D
181	D	182	B	183	A	184	D	185	C
186	D	187	A	188	C	189	C	190	C
191	B	192	A	193	C	194	C	195	B
196	D	197	A	198	B	199	A	200	A

Test 2

101	A	102	B	103	D	104	C	105	A
106	A	107	D	108	D	109	A	110	A
111	C	112	B	113	D	114	C	115	A
116	D	117	C	118	B	119	D	120	D
121	A	122	D	123	A	124	D	125	D
126	A	127	D	128	B	129	B	130	A
131	C	132	C	133	A	134	B	135	A
136	B	137	D	138	C	139	C	140	D
141	B	142	A	143	D	144	A	145	C
146	D	147	A	148	B	149	C	150	C
151	C	152	B	153	C	154	B	155	A
156	D	157	A	158	C	159	A	160	C
161	D	162	C	163	A	164	D	165	C
166	B	167	B	168	A	169	D	170	D
171	C	172	C	173	C	174	D	175	A
176	C	177	A	178	C	179	D	180	B
181	C	182	A	183	D	184	C	185	D
186	C	187	A	188	D	189	B	190	C
191	B	192	A	193	A	194	C	195	B
196	D	197	A	198	B	199	C	200	A

TEST 3

101	D	102	C	103	D	104	B	105	A
106	C	107	D	108	B	109	C	110	A
111	A	112	C	113	B	114	D	115	B
116	D	117	D	118	C	119	C	120	B
121	B	122	D	123	A	124	C	125	B
126	D	127	B	128	C	129	C	130	A
131	C	132	B	133	A	134	D	135	B
136	C	137	D	138	A	139	B	140	D
141	C	142	A	143	B	144	D	145	C
146	A	147	C	148	B	149	C	150	A
151	C	152	B	153	A	154	A	155	D
156	A	157	C	158	D	159	C	160	C
161	B	162	A	163	C	164	A	165	B
166	D	167	B	168	B	169	A	170	B
171	C	172	C	173	C	174	B	175	A
176	A	177	B	178	A	179	C	180	D
181	C	182	D	183	A	184	B	185	C
186	D	187	A	188	C	189	B	190	C
191	A	192	C	193	C	194	B	195	B
196	A	197	B	198	D	199	D	200	B

TEST 4

101	D	102	D	103	C	104	A	105	D
106	A	107	C	108	A	109	B	110	B
111	D	112	A	113	B	114	A	115	D
116	B	117	C	118	C	119	C	120	A
121	C	122	C	123	B	124	A	125	A
126	D	127	A	128	A	129	B	130	A
131	C	132	B	133	C	134	D	135	D
136	A	137	C	138	B	139	B	140	A
141	D	142	B	143	D	144	B	145	A
146	B	147	B	148	D	149	D	150	B
151	B	152	C	153	C	154	A	155	D
156	A	157	B	158	D	159	D	160	D
161	C	162	D	163	B	164	C	165	B
166	D	167	C	168	B	169	C	170	A
171	D	172	D	173	A	174	C	175	A
176	D	177	A	178	C	179	B	180	D
181	A	182	B	183	C	184	C	185	A
186	A	187	A	188	B	189	C	190	D
191	A	192	B	193	D	194	C	195	A
196	A	197	D	198	B	199	B	200	D

Test 5

101	B	102	D	103	A	104	D	105	D
106	A	107	C	108	A	109	D	110	C
111	D	112	C	113	D	114	D	115	C
116	A	117	B	118	A	119	D	120	B
121	A	122	A	123	B	124	A	125	C
126	B	127	D	128	B	129	C	130	C
131	D	132	A	133	B	134	C	135	B
136	C	137	A	138	B	139	C	140	D
141	A	142	C	143	D	144	B	145	D
146	A	147	D	148	B	149	D	150	A
151	C	152	D	153	C	154	D	155	B
156	A	157	D	158	B	159	B	160	D
161	D	162	A	163	D	164	B	165	C
166	D	167	D	168	B	169	B	170	C
171	C	172	B	173	B	174	A	175	B
176	C	177	D	178	A	179	B	180	B
181	C	182	D	183	B	184	B	185	A
186	C	187	B	188	C	189	B	190	B
191	D	192	B	193	A	194	C	195	D
196	D	197	C	198	A	199	B	200	D

Test 6

101	D	102	D	103	D	104	C	105	A
106	D	107	B	108	A	109	A	110	B
111	C	112	D	113	C	114	A	115	A
116	A	117	C	118	D	119	D	120	D
121	B	122	A	123	C	124	D	125	B
126	B	127	D	128	B	129	C	130	D
131	A	132	C	133	D	134	B	135	B
136	C	137	A	138	D	139	A	140	A
141	D	142	B	143	B	144	D	145	B
146	A	147	A	148	C	149	C	150	A
151	C	152	B	153	C	154	C	155	B
156	C	157	B	158	C	159	A	160	C
161	B	162	B	163	A	164	D	165	C
166	D	167	B	168	C	169	C	170	D
171	C	172	C	173	B	174	D	175	A
176	C	177	D	178	A	179	C	180	B
181	D	182	B	183	D	184	C	185	A
186	A	187	A	188	C	189	A	190	D
191	A	192	A	193	C	194	A	195	A
196	A	197	B	198	C	199	C	200	D

TEST 7

#	Ans	#	Ans	#	Ans	#	Ans	#	Ans
101	B	102	C	103	A	104	C	105	B
106	D	107	A	108	B	109	B	110	B
111	C	112	B	113	C	114	A	115	C
116	B	117	C	118	A	119	B	120	D
121	A	122	D	123	D	124	B	125	C
126	A	127	B	128	C	129	C	130	C
131	C	132	A	133	D	134	B	135	D
136	C	137	A	138	B	139	B	140	D
141	B	142	A	143	D	144	B	145	C
146	D	147	C	148	A	149	A	150	B
151	B	152	C	153	D	154	C	155	A
156	B	157	C	158	A	159	C	160	C
161	C	162	D	163	A	164	D	165	C
166	B	167	D	168	C	169	C	170	C
171	D	172	D	173	C	174	A	175	C
176	D	177	B	178	A	179	C	180	D
181	A	182	C	183	D	184	C	185	B
186	A	187	D	188	B	189	B	190	D
191	D	192	C	193	A	194	D	195	B
196	B	197	B	198	C	199	A	200	B

TEST 8

#	Ans	#	Ans	#	Ans	#	Ans	#	Ans
101	C	102	B	103	B	104	C	105	B
106	C	107	D	108	C	109	B	110	C
111	A	112	C	113	D	114	D	115	A
116	C	117	C	118	C	119	C	120	C
121	D	122	C	123	C	124	B	125	D
126	D	127	A	128	A	129	C	130	A
131	B	132	C	133	D	134	A	135	B
136	A	137	C	138	D	139	C	140	D
141	B	142	A	143	B	144	B	145	A
146	D	147	B	148	C	149	C	150	C
151	D	152	B	153	C	154	D	155	A
156	C	157	C	158	A	159	C	160	D
161	C	162	B	163	C	164	A	165	D
166	A	167	B	168	C	169	B	170	C
171	B	172	B	173	D	174	D	175	A
176	D	177	C	178	B	179	A	180	B
181	B	182	B	183	A	184	D	185	C
186	D	187	C	188	B	189	A	190	C
191	B	192	C	193	A	194	C	195	A
196	A	197	B	198	A	199	A	200	B

Test 9

101	A	102	B	103	C	104	D	105	B
106	A	107	C	108	A	109	A	110	C
111	B	112	C	113	B	114	B	115	A
116	D	117	A	118	A	119	C	120	B
121	D	122	D	123	C	124	A	125	D
126	D	127	A	128	D	129	C	130	D
131	C	132	D	133	C	134	B	135	D
136	D	137	A	138	C	139	B	140	A
141	D	142	C	143	A	144	B	145	C
146	C	147	B	148	A	149	B	150	C
151	A	152	B	153	B	154	C	155	A
156	D	157	C	158	B	159	C	160	A
161	B	162	C	163	D	164	A	165	C
166	C	167	A	168	B	169	B	170	A
171	D	172	A	173	C	174	C	175	B
176	C	177	A	178	B	179	B	180	C
181	B	182	C	183	D	184	D	185	C
186	D	187	A	188	D	189	C	190	B
191	C	192	B	193	C	194	C	195	C
196	C	197	B	198	A	199	C	200	D

Test 10

101	A	102	B	103	A	104	D	105	B
106	B	107	C	108	A	109	C	110	B
111	C	112	C	113	B	114	C	115	D
116	C	117	D	118	B	119	A	120	A
121	A	122	D	123	D	124	A	125	B
126	B	127	B	128	B	129	C	130	D
131	C	132	A	133	C	134	D	135	D
136	A	137	B	138	D	139	B	140	A
141	B	142	C	143	C	144	B	145	D
146	A	147	C	148	A	149	D	150	B
151	A	152	C	153	D	154	B	155	B
156	C	157	A	158	A	159	B	160	C
161	A	162	B	163	D	164	C	165	D
166	B	167	B	168	B	169	C	170	A
171	C	172	A	173	C	174	A	175	D
176	D	177	D	178	D	179	A	180	C
181	A	182	C	183	D	184	C	185	A
186	C	187	B	188	B	189	A	190	C
191	A	192	C	193	B	194	D	195	D
196	D	197	D	198	A	199	B	200	D

Answer Sheet
TEST 02

TEST 01

Answer Sheet

TEST 09

READING (PART V~VII)

No.	ANSWER	No.	ANSWER	No.	ANSWER	No.	ANSWER	No.	ANSWER
	A B C D		A B C D		A B C D		A B C D		A B C D
101	Ⓐ Ⓑ Ⓒ Ⓓ	121	Ⓐ Ⓑ Ⓒ Ⓓ	141	Ⓐ Ⓑ Ⓒ Ⓓ	161	Ⓐ Ⓑ Ⓒ Ⓓ	181	Ⓐ Ⓑ Ⓒ Ⓓ
102	Ⓐ Ⓑ Ⓒ Ⓓ	122	Ⓐ Ⓑ Ⓒ Ⓓ	142	Ⓐ Ⓑ Ⓒ Ⓓ	162	Ⓐ Ⓑ Ⓒ Ⓓ	182	Ⓐ Ⓑ Ⓒ Ⓓ
103	Ⓐ Ⓑ Ⓒ Ⓓ	123	Ⓐ Ⓑ Ⓒ Ⓓ	143	Ⓐ Ⓑ Ⓒ Ⓓ	163	Ⓐ Ⓑ Ⓒ Ⓓ	183	Ⓐ Ⓑ Ⓒ Ⓓ
104	Ⓐ Ⓑ Ⓒ Ⓓ	124	Ⓐ Ⓑ Ⓒ Ⓓ	144	Ⓐ Ⓑ Ⓒ Ⓓ	164	Ⓐ Ⓑ Ⓒ Ⓓ	184	Ⓐ Ⓑ Ⓒ Ⓓ
105	Ⓐ Ⓑ Ⓒ Ⓓ	125	Ⓐ Ⓑ Ⓒ Ⓓ	145	Ⓐ Ⓑ Ⓒ Ⓓ	165	Ⓐ Ⓑ Ⓒ Ⓓ	185	Ⓐ Ⓑ Ⓒ Ⓓ
106	Ⓐ Ⓑ Ⓒ Ⓓ	126	Ⓐ Ⓑ Ⓒ Ⓓ	146	Ⓐ Ⓑ Ⓒ Ⓓ	166	Ⓐ Ⓑ Ⓒ Ⓓ	186	Ⓐ Ⓑ Ⓒ Ⓓ
107	Ⓐ Ⓑ Ⓒ Ⓓ	127	Ⓐ Ⓑ Ⓒ Ⓓ	147	Ⓐ Ⓑ Ⓒ Ⓓ	167	Ⓐ Ⓑ Ⓒ Ⓓ	187	Ⓐ Ⓑ Ⓒ Ⓓ
108	Ⓐ Ⓑ Ⓒ Ⓓ	128	Ⓐ Ⓑ Ⓒ Ⓓ	148	Ⓐ Ⓑ Ⓒ Ⓓ	168	Ⓐ Ⓑ Ⓒ Ⓓ	188	Ⓐ Ⓑ Ⓒ Ⓓ
109	Ⓐ Ⓑ Ⓒ Ⓓ	129	Ⓐ Ⓑ Ⓒ Ⓓ	149	Ⓐ Ⓑ Ⓒ Ⓓ	169	Ⓐ Ⓑ Ⓒ Ⓓ	189	Ⓐ Ⓑ Ⓒ Ⓓ
110	Ⓐ Ⓑ Ⓒ Ⓓ	130	Ⓐ Ⓑ Ⓒ Ⓓ	150	Ⓐ Ⓑ Ⓒ Ⓓ	170	Ⓐ Ⓑ Ⓒ Ⓓ	190	Ⓐ Ⓑ Ⓒ Ⓓ
111	Ⓐ Ⓑ Ⓒ Ⓓ	131	Ⓐ Ⓑ Ⓒ Ⓓ	151	Ⓐ Ⓑ Ⓒ Ⓓ	171	Ⓐ Ⓑ Ⓒ Ⓓ	191	Ⓐ Ⓑ Ⓒ Ⓓ
112	Ⓐ Ⓑ Ⓒ Ⓓ	132	Ⓐ Ⓑ Ⓒ Ⓓ	152	Ⓐ Ⓑ Ⓒ Ⓓ	172	Ⓐ Ⓑ Ⓒ Ⓓ	192	Ⓐ Ⓑ Ⓒ Ⓓ
113	Ⓐ Ⓑ Ⓒ Ⓓ	133	Ⓐ Ⓑ Ⓒ Ⓓ	153	Ⓐ Ⓑ Ⓒ Ⓓ	173	Ⓐ Ⓑ Ⓒ Ⓓ	193	Ⓐ Ⓑ Ⓒ Ⓓ
114	Ⓐ Ⓑ Ⓒ Ⓓ	134	Ⓐ Ⓑ Ⓒ Ⓓ	154	Ⓐ Ⓑ Ⓒ Ⓓ	174	Ⓐ Ⓑ Ⓒ Ⓓ	194	Ⓐ Ⓑ Ⓒ Ⓓ
115	Ⓐ Ⓑ Ⓒ Ⓓ	135	Ⓐ Ⓑ Ⓒ Ⓓ	155	Ⓐ Ⓑ Ⓒ Ⓓ	175	Ⓐ Ⓑ Ⓒ Ⓓ	195	Ⓐ Ⓑ Ⓒ Ⓓ
116	Ⓐ Ⓑ Ⓒ Ⓓ	136	Ⓐ Ⓑ Ⓒ Ⓓ	156	Ⓐ Ⓑ Ⓒ Ⓓ	176	Ⓐ Ⓑ Ⓒ Ⓓ	196	Ⓐ Ⓑ Ⓒ Ⓓ
117	Ⓐ Ⓑ Ⓒ Ⓓ	137	Ⓐ Ⓑ Ⓒ Ⓓ	157	Ⓐ Ⓑ Ⓒ Ⓓ	177	Ⓐ Ⓑ Ⓒ Ⓓ	197	Ⓐ Ⓑ Ⓒ Ⓓ
118	Ⓐ Ⓑ Ⓒ Ⓓ	138	Ⓐ Ⓑ Ⓒ Ⓓ	158	Ⓐ Ⓑ Ⓒ Ⓓ	178	Ⓐ Ⓑ Ⓒ Ⓓ	198	Ⓐ Ⓑ Ⓒ Ⓓ
119	Ⓐ Ⓑ Ⓒ Ⓓ	139	Ⓐ Ⓑ Ⓒ Ⓓ	159	Ⓐ Ⓑ Ⓒ Ⓓ	179	Ⓐ Ⓑ Ⓒ Ⓓ	199	Ⓐ Ⓑ Ⓒ Ⓓ
120	Ⓐ Ⓑ Ⓒ Ⓓ	140	Ⓐ Ⓑ Ⓒ Ⓓ	160	Ⓐ Ⓑ Ⓒ Ⓓ	180	Ⓐ Ⓑ Ⓒ Ⓓ	200	Ⓐ Ⓑ Ⓒ Ⓓ

Answer Sheet

TEST 10

READING (PART V~VII)

No.	ANSWER	No.	ANSWER	No.	ANSWER	No.	ANSWER	No.	ANSWER
	A B C D		A B C D		A B C D		A B C D		A B C D
101	Ⓐ Ⓑ Ⓒ Ⓓ	121	Ⓐ Ⓑ Ⓒ Ⓓ	141	Ⓐ Ⓑ Ⓒ Ⓓ	161	Ⓐ Ⓑ Ⓒ Ⓓ	181	Ⓐ Ⓑ Ⓒ Ⓓ
102	Ⓐ Ⓑ Ⓒ Ⓓ	122	Ⓐ Ⓑ Ⓒ Ⓓ	142	Ⓐ Ⓑ Ⓒ Ⓓ	162	Ⓐ Ⓑ Ⓒ Ⓓ	182	Ⓐ Ⓑ Ⓒ Ⓓ
103	Ⓐ Ⓑ Ⓒ Ⓓ	123	Ⓐ Ⓑ Ⓒ Ⓓ	143	Ⓐ Ⓑ Ⓒ Ⓓ	163	Ⓐ Ⓑ Ⓒ Ⓓ	183	Ⓐ Ⓑ Ⓒ Ⓓ
104	Ⓐ Ⓑ Ⓒ Ⓓ	124	Ⓐ Ⓑ Ⓒ Ⓓ	144	Ⓐ Ⓑ Ⓒ Ⓓ	164	Ⓐ Ⓑ Ⓒ Ⓓ	184	Ⓐ Ⓑ Ⓒ Ⓓ
105	Ⓐ Ⓑ Ⓒ Ⓓ	125	Ⓐ Ⓑ Ⓒ Ⓓ	145	Ⓐ Ⓑ Ⓒ Ⓓ	165	Ⓐ Ⓑ Ⓒ Ⓓ	185	Ⓐ Ⓑ Ⓒ Ⓓ
106	Ⓐ Ⓑ Ⓒ Ⓓ	126	Ⓐ Ⓑ Ⓒ Ⓓ	146	Ⓐ Ⓑ Ⓒ Ⓓ	166	Ⓐ Ⓑ Ⓒ Ⓓ	186	Ⓐ Ⓑ Ⓒ Ⓓ
107	Ⓐ Ⓑ Ⓒ Ⓓ	127	Ⓐ Ⓑ Ⓒ Ⓓ	147	Ⓐ Ⓑ Ⓒ Ⓓ	167	Ⓐ Ⓑ Ⓒ Ⓓ	187	Ⓐ Ⓑ Ⓒ Ⓓ
108	Ⓐ Ⓑ Ⓒ Ⓓ	128	Ⓐ Ⓑ Ⓒ Ⓓ	148	Ⓐ Ⓑ Ⓒ Ⓓ	168	Ⓐ Ⓑ Ⓒ Ⓓ	188	Ⓐ Ⓑ Ⓒ Ⓓ
109	Ⓐ Ⓑ Ⓒ Ⓓ	129	Ⓐ Ⓑ Ⓒ Ⓓ	149	Ⓐ Ⓑ Ⓒ Ⓓ	169	Ⓐ Ⓑ Ⓒ Ⓓ	189	Ⓐ Ⓑ Ⓒ Ⓓ
110	Ⓐ Ⓑ Ⓒ Ⓓ	130	Ⓐ Ⓑ Ⓒ Ⓓ	150	Ⓐ Ⓑ Ⓒ Ⓓ	170	Ⓐ Ⓑ Ⓒ Ⓓ	190	Ⓐ Ⓑ Ⓒ Ⓓ
111	Ⓐ Ⓑ Ⓒ Ⓓ	131	Ⓐ Ⓑ Ⓒ Ⓓ	151	Ⓐ Ⓑ Ⓒ Ⓓ	171	Ⓐ Ⓑ Ⓒ Ⓓ	191	Ⓐ Ⓑ Ⓒ Ⓓ
112	Ⓐ Ⓑ Ⓒ Ⓓ	132	Ⓐ Ⓑ Ⓒ Ⓓ	152	Ⓐ Ⓑ Ⓒ Ⓓ	172	Ⓐ Ⓑ Ⓒ Ⓓ	192	Ⓐ Ⓑ Ⓒ Ⓓ
113	Ⓐ Ⓑ Ⓒ Ⓓ	133	Ⓐ Ⓑ Ⓒ Ⓓ	153	Ⓐ Ⓑ Ⓒ Ⓓ	173	Ⓐ Ⓑ Ⓒ Ⓓ	193	Ⓐ Ⓑ Ⓒ Ⓓ
114	Ⓐ Ⓑ Ⓒ Ⓓ	134	Ⓐ Ⓑ Ⓒ Ⓓ	154	Ⓐ Ⓑ Ⓒ Ⓓ	174	Ⓐ Ⓑ Ⓒ Ⓓ	194	Ⓐ Ⓑ Ⓒ Ⓓ
115	Ⓐ Ⓑ Ⓒ Ⓓ	135	Ⓐ Ⓑ Ⓒ Ⓓ	155	Ⓐ Ⓑ Ⓒ Ⓓ	175	Ⓐ Ⓑ Ⓒ Ⓓ	195	Ⓐ Ⓑ Ⓒ Ⓓ
116	Ⓐ Ⓑ Ⓒ Ⓓ	136	Ⓐ Ⓑ Ⓒ Ⓓ	156	Ⓐ Ⓑ Ⓒ Ⓓ	176	Ⓐ Ⓑ Ⓒ Ⓓ	196	Ⓐ Ⓑ Ⓒ Ⓓ
117	Ⓐ Ⓑ Ⓒ Ⓓ	137	Ⓐ Ⓑ Ⓒ Ⓓ	157	Ⓐ Ⓑ Ⓒ Ⓓ	177	Ⓐ Ⓑ Ⓒ Ⓓ	197	Ⓐ Ⓑ Ⓒ Ⓓ
118	Ⓐ Ⓑ Ⓒ Ⓓ	138	Ⓐ Ⓑ Ⓒ Ⓓ	158	Ⓐ Ⓑ Ⓒ Ⓓ	178	Ⓐ Ⓑ Ⓒ Ⓓ	198	Ⓐ Ⓑ Ⓒ Ⓓ
119	Ⓐ Ⓑ Ⓒ Ⓓ	139	Ⓐ Ⓑ Ⓒ Ⓓ	159	Ⓐ Ⓑ Ⓒ Ⓓ	179	Ⓐ Ⓑ Ⓒ Ⓓ	199	Ⓐ Ⓑ Ⓒ Ⓓ
120	Ⓐ Ⓑ Ⓒ Ⓓ	140	Ⓐ Ⓑ Ⓒ Ⓓ	160	Ⓐ Ⓑ Ⓒ Ⓓ	180	Ⓐ Ⓑ Ⓒ Ⓓ	200	Ⓐ Ⓑ Ⓒ Ⓓ

[동시토익]